MASTERPLOTS II

JUVENILE
AND
YOUNG ADULT
LITERATURE
SERIES
SUPPLEMENT

MASTERPLOTS II

JUVENILE AND YOUNG ADULT LITERATURE SERIES SUPPLEMENT

1

A–Gho

Edited by
FRANK N. MAGILL

Project Editor
TRACY IRONS-GEORGES

SALEM PRESS

Pasadena, California　　　Englewood Cliffs, New Jersey

Editor in Chief: Dawn P. Dawson
Project Editor: Tracy Irons-Georges
Research Supervisor: Jeffry Jensen
Production Editor: Janet Long
Proofreading Supervisor: Yasmine A. Cordoba
Layout: William Zimmerman

Library of Congress Cataloging-in-Publication Data
Masterplots II. Juvenile and young adult literature series:
supplement / edited by Frank N. Magill; project editor, Tracy
Irons-Georges.
    p.   cm.
Supplements the Juvenile and young adult fiction series
(1991) and the Juvenile and young adult biography series
(1993); includes for the first time poetry collections, plays,
short-story collections, and books on art, history, sociology, and
science for young readers; the cumulative indexes cover the
contents of the earlier series as well as those covered in the
Supplement.
Includes bibliographical references and indexes.
    1. Children's literature—Stories, plots, etc. I. Magill, Frank
Northen, 1907-　. II. Irons-Georges, Tracy. III. Masterplots
II. Juvenile and young adult fiction series. IV. Masterplots II.
Juvenile and young adult biography series.
Z1037.A1M377　1991 Supplement
011.62—dc21　　　　　　　　　　　　　　　　　96-39759
ISBN 0-89356-916-X (set)　　　　　　　　　　　CIP
ISBN 0-89356-917-8 (volume 1)

First Printing

PUBLISHER'S NOTE

Books for children and young adults, although sometimes overlooked or undervalued in intellectual circles, have an essential place in the literary canon. Many authors have made distinguished careers out of addressing the thoughts and emotions of children, and many more writing for an adult audience have found their works embraced by readers of all ages. The impact of juvenile and young adult literature can be tremendous. Children and teenagers searching for vicarious adventure, journeys into the imagination, role models, and an understanding of how the world works can turn to books and be rewarded with rousing tales, inspiring biographies, and valuable knowledge. *Masterplots II: Juvenile and Young Adult Literature Series, Supplement* continues the vital study of such books and their influence on generations of children and adults alike.

The *Supplement* expands in significant ways the coverage of children's and young adult literature found in the four-volume *Masterplots II: Juvenile and Young Adult Fiction Series* (1991), which analyzes 480 novels, and the four-volume *Masterplots II: Juvenile and Young Adult Biography Series* (1993), which examines 521 autobiographies and biographies. The *Supplement* not only offers articles on more novels and biographical works but also examines other important literary forms in fiction and nonfiction. For the first time, poetry collections, plays, short-story collections, and books on art, history, sociology, and science, both those designed for young readers and those popular among them, are reviewed.

With articles on 377 titles, the *Supplement* focuses on literature written for, taught to, or appreciated by readers between the ages of 10 and 18. As with the first two sets, efforts were made to provide a broad range of titles by genre, time period, culture, country of origin, and subject matter and to discuss influential and celebrated works. Included are 11 Newbery Medal-winning titles, such as Jerry Spinelli's *Maniac Magee* (1990), Phyllis Reynolds Naylor's *Shiloh* (1991), Cynthia Rylant's *Missing May* (1992), and Sharon Creech's *Walk Two Moons* (1994); 42 Newbery Honor Books are also represented. The coverage of novels is widened from the *Fiction* series by 207 titles to include further classic tales by Roald Dahl, Charles Dickens, Madeleine L'Engle, Marguerite Henry, Jack London, E. Nesbit, Robert Louis Stevenson, Mark Twain, Jules Verne, and E. B. White, as well as additional works by acclaimed contemporary writers Avi, Judy Blume, Beverly Cleary, Robert Cormier, S. E. Hinton, M. E. Kerr, Walter Dean Myers, Scott O'Dell, Gary Paulsen, and Cynthia Voight. In addition to the books covered in the *Biography* series, another 21 autobiographies and biographies are discussed in the *Supplement*; they profile such heroic figures as test pilot Chuck Yeager, undersea explorer Jacques-Yves Cousteau, and Israeli prime minister Golda Meir.

Short stories have always been at the heart of the literary canon for young readers. Often arising from an oral tradition and written down in the form of myths, legends, fables, fairy tales, and folktales, these stories explain natural phenomena, impart religious values, teach lessons about proper behavior, or pass on cultural information to the next generation of listeners and readers. The *Supplement* examines 41 short-story collections that range from antiquity to the 1990's and address tales from all over the world. Such classic works of short fiction as *Aesop's Fables* (4th century B.C.), *The Arabian Nights' Entertainments* (15th century), *Grimm's Fairy Tales* (1812, 1815), Peter Christen Asbjørnsen and Jørgen Moe's *East o' the Sun and West o' the Moon* (1841-1844), Carl Sandburg's *Rootabaga Stories* (1922), and Dylan Thomas' *A Child's Christmas in Wales* (1954) are included along with more recent collections, which often seek to redefine traditional tales, such as Ethel Johnston Phelps's *The Maid of the North: Feminist Folk Tales from Around the World* (1981) and Virginia Hamilton's *The People Could Fly: American Black Folktales* (1985).

The *Supplement* traces the illustrious history of children's poetry in 23 articles. Collections by renowned poets who usually wrote for adult audiences, such as Gwendolyn Brooks, T. S. Eliot, Robert Frost, Langston Hughes, June Jordan, and Henry Wadsworth Longfellow, are represented, as are poets who gained fame for their children's verse, such as John Ciardi, Edward Lear, Eve Merriam, Ogden Nash, and Shel Silverstein. While relatively few plays have been written for young people, many dramatic productions are both of interest to and appropriate for this audience, especially high school students. The *Supplement* covers 25 plays, including such perennial favorites as William Shakespeare's *Romeo and Juliet* (1595-1596), Thornton Wilder's *Our Town* (1938), Tennessee Williams' *The Glass Menagerie* (1944), and Arthur Miller's *The Crucible* (1953). It should be noted that the books discussed in all three sets are viewed from the perspective of juvenile and young adult literature, and the articles about works originally intended for adult readers analyze what they offer young people.

The remaining articles in the *Supplement* analyze works of nonfiction: history (30 titles), science (22), sociology (4), and the arts (4). Through these books, young people can learn about chemistry, the Olympic Games, mummies, African American soldiers in the Civil War, castles, the Holocaust, pyramids, frontier life, the framing of the U.S. Constitution, American Indian ceremonies, volcanos, computers, and many more fascinating subjects. Noted nonfiction authors Russell Freedman, Jim Haskins, Patricia Lauber, and Milton Meltzer are represented.

The *Juvenile and Young Adult Literature, Supplement* is arranged alphabetically by the title of the work under discussion. Each essay begins with ready-reference front matter: the author's name and years of birth and death; the date of first publication, including information about alternate titles and whether the book was illustrated in its original edition; type of work (art, autobiography, biography, drama, history, novel, poetry, short fiction, science, or social science); and, if applicable, type of plot (such as adventure tale, folktale, science fiction, or social realism), time of work, and locale. Also provided for each article is a list of categories of the book's subject matter, ranging from coming-of-age, family, friendship, love and romance, nature, race and ethnicity, and the supernatural to more serious topics such as death, gender roles, poverty, sexual issues, social issues, and war. The front matter concludes with a recommendation of the age range for which the book would be most appropriate, standardized and limited to the groupings of 10-13, 13-15, 15-18, or a combination such as 13-18. A one-sentence summary describes the work—its principal subject, importance, and relevance to juvenile and young adult literature—and, if applicable, a list of the principal characters (for novels and plays) or principal personages (for historical and biographical works), including brief descriptive phrases, is provided.

The text of each article contains three subsections. The "Form and Content" section summarizes the contents of the work for those who may or may not already be familiar with it, provides a general discussion of the story or the information being presented to young readers, and discusses the work's format, including its structure (such as chapters, acts, or sketches), type of narration (such as first-person or third-person), and other features (such as illustrations, appendices, or notes). The "Analysis" section provides a more in-depth discussion of the book, elaborates on several of its themes, describes the author's approach, and examines the way in which the book addresses young people. The "Critical Context" section evaluates the book in terms of the author's career, the critical reception of the work and any awards that it won, and the status of the title in the canon of juvenile and young adult literature, both past and present.

At the end of volume 3, a general Bibliography provides annotated entries for works about children's literature, information about sources for finding additional titles that are appropriate for young readers, and lists of further sources to consult regarding some of the most important authors of literature for children and young adults. In addition to the above-mentioned writers, individual bibliographies are devoted to Hans Christian Andersen, Ray Bradbury, Vera and Bill Cleaver, Elizabeth Coatsworth, Meindert De Jong, Elizabeth Enright, Paula Fox, Kenneth Grahame, Hadley Irwin, Randall Jarrell, Rudyard Kipling, E. L. Konigsburg, Lois Lowry, David Macaulay, Robin McKinley, Margaret Mahy, Mary Norton, Katherine Paterson, Richard Peck, Isaac Bashevis Singer, Ivan Southall, William Steig, Laurence Yep, and Paul Zindel, among many others. An important feature of the *Supplement* that allows the full scope of the *Masterplots II: Juvenile and Young Adult* series to be seen are the four cumulative indexes that follow the Bibliography. The Title Index and Author Index list the entire contents of the *Fiction* and *Biography* sets in addition to those books covered in the *Supplement*. The Biographical Index organizes the autobiographies and biographies found in the *Biography* series and the *Supplement* according to the individuals who are profiled. The helpful Subject Index, compiled from the subject categories in the front matter of all articles in the three sets, allows the user to seek out titles about a specific topic, type of work, group of people, or genre. Codes are used to indicate the set, volume number, and page number of each entry in these indexes.

Salem Press wishes to express gratitude to the many academicians, librarians, and scholars who contributed articles to the *Supplement*; their dedication to and belief in the value of literature for children and young adults has made the publication of this set possible. A list of their names and academic affiliations can be found in the front of volume 1.

CONTRIBUTING REVIEWERS

Richard Adler
University of Michigan, Dearborn

Julie Nell Aipperspach
Independent Scholar

Amy Allison
Independent Scholar

Stanley Archer
Texas A&M University

Frank Ardolino
University of Hawaii

Gerald S. Argetsinger
Rochester Institute of Technology

James Barbour
Arizona State University

Henry J. Baron
Calvin College

David Barratt
Independent Scholar

Ronald Barron
Richfield Senior High School

Kathleen M. Bartlett
University of Central Florida

Paulina Bazin
Loyola University, New Orleans

John D. Beach
State University of New York, Cortland

Cynthia S. Becerra
Humphreys College

Gaymon L. Bennett
Northwest Nazarene College

Mark Bernheim
Miami University

Cynthia A. Bily
Adrian College

Robert G. Blake
Elon College

Shelley Blanton-Stroud
Sacramento City College

Kevin J. Bochynski
Salem State College

Samantha Bonar
Independent Scholar

Sandra F. Bone
Arkansas State University

Bernadette Lynn Bosky
Independent Scholar

Wesley Britton
Grayson County College

Esther Broughton
Mesa State College

Paul Buchanan
Biola University

Katherine T. Bucher
Old Dominion University

Paul James Buczkowski
University of Detroit, Mercy

Jeffrey L. Buller
Georgia Southern University

Susan Butterworth
Independent Scholar

Mingshui Cai
University of Northern Iowa

Ann Cameron
Indiana University, Kokomo

Edmund J. Campion
University of Tennessee

Gena Dagel Caponi
University of Texas, San Antonio

Sonya H. Cashdan
East Tennessee State University

Christine R. Catron
St. Mary's University

Cida S. Chase
Oklahoma State University

Joel D. Chaston
Southwest Missouri State University

Eric Chilton
Arizona State University

Winnie Ching
*St. Joseph's College
State University of New York, Stony Brook*

C. L. Chua
California State University, Fresno

Jane Claes
Independent Scholar

Daniel A. Clark
Independent Scholar

David W. Cole
University of Wisconsin Center, Baraboo/Sauk

Helen O'Hara Connell
Barry University

Emma Cox-Harris
East Tennessee State University

Virginia Crane
California State University, Los Angeles

Anita Davis
Converse College

Delmer Davis
Andrews University

Mary Virginia Davis
Independent Scholar

Laura Davis-Clapper
Kent State University

Frank Day
Clemson University

William Ryland Drennan
University of Wisconsin Center, Baraboo/Sauk

Stefan Dziemianowicz
Independent Scholar

Harry Edwin Eiss
Eastern Michigan University

Catherine L. Elick
Bridgewater College

Don Evans
Trenton State College

Sarah W. Favors
South Carolina State University

James Feast
Baruch College

Tom Feller
Independent Scholar

Edward Fiorelli
St. John's University

Thomas B. Frazier
Cumberland College

Janet Fujimoto
California State University, Fresno

Robert L. Gale
University of Pittsburgh

Ann Davison Garbett
Averett College

Janet E. Gardner
University of Massachusetts,
Dartmouth

Ellen Garfinkel
Hood College

Patricia Gately
Truman State University

Eleanor Parks Gaunder
University of North Alabama

Victoria Gaydosik
East Central University

Joshua Alden Gaylord
New York University

Carol Ann Gearhart
Kutztown University

Susan Y. Geye
Crowley Independent School
District

Craig Gilbert
Portland State University

Daniel Glynn
Highland College, Kansas

Lucy Golsan
Independent Scholar

Karen Gould
Independent Scholar

Charles A. Gramlich
Xavier University of Louisiana

James Green
Arizona State University

John L. Grigsby
Tennessee Technological
University

Dana Anthony Grove
Indian Hills Community College

Morris Allen Grubbs
University of Kentucky

Barbara J. Hampton
Independent Scholar

Katherine Hanley
St. Bernard's Institute

Tina L. Hanlon
Ferrum College

Luther Hanson
San Diego State University

June Harris
East Texas State University

Maverick Marvin Harris
East Texas Baptist University

Kathleen M. Hays
Morningside College

David M. Heaton
Ohio University

Peter B. Heller
Manhattan College

Michael Hennessy
Southwest Texas State
University

Joyce E. Henry
Ursinus College

Barbara Hershberger
Maranatha Baptist Bible
College

Katharine D. Herzog
Morehead State University

Donald R. Hettinga
Calvin College

June Hetzel
Biola University

Michael R. Hill
University of Nebraska, Lincoln

Arthur D. Hlavaty
Independent Scholar

James L. Hodge
Bowdoin College

John R. Holmes
Franciscan University of
Steubenville

Gregory D. Horn
Southwest Virginia Community
College

Pierre L. Horn
Wright State University

George F. Horneker
Arkansas State University

Kenneth L. Houghton
Independent Scholar

Steven R. Huff
Oberlin College

Caroline C. Hunt
College of Charleston

E. D. Huntley
Appalachian State University

Mary Hurd
East Tennessee State University

Niels Ingwersen
University of Wisconsin,
Madison

Duane Inman
Northwestern State University

John Jacob
Northwestern University

David Johansson
Brevard Community College

Frances Agnes Johnson
University of Texas of the
Permian Basin

Douglas A. Jones
Andrews University

Michelle L. Jones
Muskingum College

Leela Kapai
University of the District of
Columbia

Daven M. Kari
California Baptist College

Cherrie L. Kassem
Piedmont College

Hugh T. Keenan
Georgia State University

Fiona Kelleghan
University of Miami, Florida

Margot Ann Keller
Lima Technical College

Cassandra Kircher
Elon College

Paula Kiska
University of Texas at El Paso

Susan S. Kissel
Northern Kentucky University

Laura L. Klure
Independent Scholar

Grove Koger
Boise Public Library

Helene W. Lang
University of Vermont

Douglas Edward LaPrade
University of Texas, Pan
American

Eugene Larson
Los Angeles Pierce College

CONTRIBUTING REVIEWERS

William Laskowski
Jamestown College

Carol Lauritzen
Eastern Oregon State College

William T. Lawlor
*University of Wisconsin,
Stevens Point*

Elisabeth Anne Leonard
Kent State University

Shwu-yi Leu
*University of Illinois,
Urbana-Champaign*

Leon Lewis
Appalachian State University

Thomas Lisk
North Carolina State University

Bernadette Flynn Low
Dundalk Community College

Lynda R. Ludy
Alma College

Susan Lytle
Claremont Graduate School

Janet McCann
Texas A&M University

Gina Macdonald
Loyola University, New Orleans

Joan S. McMath
Ohio University

Michele McNichols
Clark Atlanta University

Mary H. McNulty
Francis Marion University

David W. Madden
*California State University,
Sacramento*

Mary Mahony
*Wayne County Community
College*

Ramona Madson Mahood
University of Memphis

Florence H. Maltby
*Southwest Missouri State
University*

Denise Marchionda
*Notre Dame College,
Manchester*

Leslie Marlow
Northwestern State University

Gyde Christine Martin
University of Texas, Arlington

Rob Marus
Independent Scholar

Karen Cleveland Marwick
Independent Scholar

Charles May
*California State University,
Long Beach*

Laurence W. Mazzeno
Ursuline College

Constance A. Mellon
East Carolina University

Julia M. Meyers
North Carolina State University

Michael R. Meyers
Shaw University

B. Diane Miller
Independent Scholar

P. Andrew Miller
Independent Scholar

Christian H. Moe
*Southern Illinois University,
Carbondale*

Kay Moore
*California State University,
Sacramento*

Trevor J. Morgan
Howard Payne University

Gordon R. Mork
Purdue University

Bernard E. Morris
Independent Scholar

JaNae Jenkins Mundy
Texas Woman's University

C. Lynn Munro
Independent Scholar

Russell Elliott Murphy
*University of Arkansas, Little
Rock*

Mary M. Navarre
Aquinas College

Claudia Nelson
*Southwest Texas State
University*

Jane Laurenson Neuburger
Cazenovia College

Terry L. Norton
Winthrop University

Anita Obermeier
Arizona State University

Stephen C. Olbrys
Independent Scholar

James Norman O'Neill
Bryant College

Lisa Paddock
Independent Scholar

Linda M. Pavonetti
University of Houston

Matthew J. Perini
Independent Scholar

Michele Perret
University of Michigan

Earleen De La Perriere
*State University of New York
College at Brockport*

Dennis R. Perry
University of Missouri, Rolla

Marion Boyle Petrillo
Bloomsburg University

Allene Phy-Olsen
Austin Peay State University

H. Alan Pickrell
Emory & Henry College

Marcia Brown Popp
*Southern Illinois University,
Edwardsville*

Clifton W. Potter, Jr.
Lynchburg College

Verbie Lovorn Prevost
*University of Tennessee,
Chattanooga*

Ellen Puccinelli
*Northeast Louisiana
University*

Christian L. Pyle
University of Kentucky

Josephine Raburn
Cameron University

Kevin Railey
Buffalo State College

Inez Ramsey
James Madison University

R. Kent Rasmussen
Independent Scholar

Sandra Ray
Independent Scholar

Alan I. Rea, Jr.
Bowling Green State University

Rosemary M. Canfield
  Reisman
Independent Scholar

Carole S. Rhodes
Pace University

Marilyn M. Robitaille
Tarleton State University

Carl Rollyson
*Baruch College of the City
  University of New York*

Joseph Rosenblum
*University of North Carolina at
  Greensboro*

Linda Runyon
Independent Scholar

Margaret Theresa Sacco
Miami University of Ohio

Lynn Sager
Independent Scholar

Angela M. Salas
Adrian College

Alexa L. Sandmann
University of Toledo

Gary D. Schmidt
Calvin College

Kathleen Schongar
The May School, Albany, NY

John Sekora
*North Carolina Central
  University*

Chenliang Sheng
Northern Kentucky University

Agnes A. Shields
Chestnut Hill College

Amy Shollenberger
Independent Scholar

Sanford S. Singer
University of Dayton

Amy Sisson
Independent Scholar

Jean M. Snook
*Memorial University of
  Newfoundland*

Brian Stableford
Independent Scholar

Barbara C. Stanley
Independent Scholar

August W. Staub
University of Georgia

Joshua Stein
*University of California,
  Riverside*

Susan Steinfirst
*University of North Carolina at
  Chapel Hill*

Judith L. Steininger
*Milwaukee School of
  Engineering*

Eric Sterling
*Auburn University at
  Montgomery*

Geralyn Strecker
Ball State University

Trey Strecker
Ball State University

Michael Stuprich
Ithaca College

Roy Arthur Swanson
*University of Wisconsin,
  Milwaukee*

James Tackach
Roger Williams University

Konny Thompson
Gonzaga University

Joni Thornburg
East Tennessee State University

Christine D. Tomei
*Harriman Institute, Columbia
  University*

Anne Trotter
Rosemont College

J. Don Vann
University of North Texas

Constance Vidor
*Cathedral School, St. John the
  Divine*

G. A. M. Vissers
Independent Scholar

Mark Vogel
Appalachian State University

Pat Waits
University of Central Oklahoma

Charlotte Zoë Walker
*State University of New York
  College at Oneonta*

Steven C. Walker
Brigham Young University

Qun Wang
*California State University,
  Monterey Bay*

Betty-Lou Waters
*West Virginia Institute of
  Technology*

Earl Wells
Independent Scholar

Phyllis West
El Camino College

Gary Westfahl
*University of California,
  Riverside*

Lana White
West Texas A&M University

Barbara Wiedemann
*Auburn University at
  Montgomery*

Jeffrey D. Wilhelm
University of Maine

Thomas Willard
University of Arizona

Bettye J. Williams
*University of Arkansas, Pine
  Bluff*

Sidney Glover Williams
Independent Scholar

Michael Witkoski
Independent Scholar

Qingyun Wu
*California State University, Los
  Angeles*

Beverly B. Youree
*Middle Tennessee State
  University*

Stanley J. Zehm
University of Nevada, Las Vegas

LIST OF TITLES IN VOLUME 1

ABBY, MY LOVE

Author: Hadley Irwin (Lee Hadley, 1934-   ; and Annabelle Bowen Irwin, 1915-1995)
First published: 1985
Type of work: Novel
Type of plot: Psychological realism
Time of work: The 1980's
Locale: A fictional suburban town
Subjects: Family, friendship, love and romance, and sexual issues
Recommended ages: 13-18

Chip Martin learns about love, family, and friendship when Abby Morris reveals to him that she is being sexually abused by her father.

> *Principal characters:*
> CHIP MARTIN, a teenager who is trying to understand the nature of love
> JEAN MARTIN, Chip's mother, who is also falling in love
> ABIGAIL (ABBY) MORRIS, Chip's friend, whose father has been sexually abusing her for years
> PETE MORRIS, Abby's younger, tomboy sister
> DR. MORRIS, Abby's father, a dentist who wants to keep Abby for himself
> PEG MORRIS, Abby's inadequate, self-denying mother
> JAKE, a former judge involved with Jean Martin
> MR. HANSEN, an influential high school English teacher

Form and Content

Abby, My Love trusts its first-person narrator, Chip Martin, to describe everything as truthfully as possible, a difficult job for a young man growing and changing as the book progresses. The novel is a quick read, perhaps because chapters are relatively short, as is the book itself. The presentation is interesting, starting with Abby's high school graduation and class valedictory address, then flashing back as far as the eighth grade for Chip and the seventh grade for Abby. Time is generally presented in a linear manner after that until near the end of the novel, when flashbacks occur again.

The reader knows from the start that this is a book about families. Chip Martin's father was a jet pilot shot down over Vietnam and never recovered. Chip has only his mother, who is remarkably self-sufficient. Chip meets Pete Morris in a local park, and slightly afterward her sister, Abby. This is the beginning of a friendship with both sisters that lasts throughout the novel, up to Chip's return home after his first year in college.

Chip must deal with growing up, with Abby's "coldness," with his sudden interest in poetry and plays, with his mother's romantic interest in Jake (whom he thinks is "almost" old enough to be his grandfather), and finally with Abby's confession to him about her father's sexual abuse and her protectiveness of Pete all these years.

Chip's reactions to events in his life are realistic: He is often confused and angry, and he does not know what to do with what he discovers. Chip placidly accepts his mother's plans to marry Jake but is often frustrated by Abby's changing moods. They do not actually date, but they do spend enough time together for Dr. Morris to suggest to Mrs. Martin that Chip should turn his attention elsewhere, which greatly angers Chip. Eventually, the incest becomes unbearable, and Abby confronts her mother. Because Chip is the narrator, however, readers are not privy to that scene. It is only known that while Mrs. Morris does not deny the abuse, she thinks that the family must stay intact and that her husband's dentistry practice will suffer if the secret is discovered. In other words, she either is in denial or does not care about what happens to Abby.

When Chip visits Abby at home, he notes how odd and unsettling it feels in their house: Pete, who is usually running around, is quiet; Abby has a blank stare on her face; Dr. Morris only reads the newspaper; and Mrs. Morris seems nervous and agitated. Chip sees this again when he visits with his mother, a travel agent who has prepared vacation plans for them.

Even outside her house, Abby can be thrown into a cold, vacant place by the wrong words ("abuse") or by Chip or anyone else coming too close to her. She only truly acts alive when fantasizing, when she and Chip create president Millard Fillmore's first wife, "Mildred." It becomes a standing joke, a place of reprieve for both Chip and Abby that they allow no one else to enter.

Chip learns about love on multiple levels, both within families and without, and in the last two or three pages, Abby confesses that she loves Chip. She has moved beyond Pete and the rest of her family. She also faces the physical breakup of her family: Her father is teaching at a dental college in Georgia, and the other members of her family are in therapy in Collinsville.

The ending is not happy in a predictable sense. Abby needs time to deal with her trauma, and Chip is willing to give it to her, but no one knows what will happen to either of them in college. Part of the message is that Dr. Morris' evil has been done. One cannot predict if it will be erased.

Analysis

Opening this novel, one assumes that it will be a love story, possibly a predictable love story. Even the opening scene, that of Abby's graduation and valedictory address, shows an attendant Chip in the audience. When one learns that Chip is going to review the events leading up to this moment, there is still nothing to reveal how shocking and serious things will become before the novel reaches its conclusion.

Chip's life is relatively normal for a young man without a father. He does the laundry, cooks, cleans the kitchen, and pays his share of the phone bill. He and some young friends briefly go through a rebellious stage—growing their hair, not taking showers, letting their grades lapse. That changes for Chip in English class with the study of poetry, and possibly because both Pete and Abby can identify Chip blind from his smell alone.

Before Abby, there was Karen, whom Chip got to know through acting in plays. Abby is also a good actress, although not on stage; she has to act in order to survive. Chip is surprised when Abby enters high school and becomes involved in student activities before school, after school, and on weekends. Eventually, he figures out why she stays away from home.

Although Chip is comfortable in his own home, he knows that it is not a "normal" home, especially when he and his mother go on vacation to Colorado and she spends a night dining and dancing with Jake and Chip stays up until she returns at three in the morning. The character of Jake could have been more fully fleshed out. He flies in from Colorado when Abby confesses to the incest. Does he offer advice as a judge or as a friend of the Martin family? Because the narration is limited to what Chip sees and learns, readers never know what he says to Abby.

In fact, the reader is not given enough details about what happens to Abby's family. The message is clear, as Mrs. Morris returns to school and opens up her own accounting office, that a family need not have a man at its helm. At various turns in the story, neither family includes a father although just as Chip leaves, Jake enters. From the book, one can learn much about love—for one's parents, for those taking the place of parents, for those of the opposite gender. One should also learn something about what Abby feels, in the end, for her father. Unfortunately, readers do not learn this. It is revealed that Chip wants to kill Dr. Morris, that Abby loses a part of herself when she is reminded of her own father, and that he claimed to have been protecting her all these years, a common statement by incestuous fathers.

The novel shows that love is unpredictable and that one must be patient. Chip's mother is patient: She carries the burden of wondering whether her husband might still be alive, since his body was never found. Can she be happy with another man? Can Chip deal with personality changes in Abby? Many young men would not; they would move on to someone easier to predict and to handle. Will Abby ever truly be able to have a normal romantic relationship? She tells Chip that she wants to, that she wants his hands on her, but not now. More important, Abby learns to say "I love you."

Abby, My Love shows that even the typical happy family—with a mother at home, an athletic younger daughter, a smart older daughter, and a dentist making a lot of money, enough to give Abby a Rolex that she says feels "like a handcuff"—may not be happy at all, while the fatherless family across town might be wonderful. Among other things, the novel points out that things are not always what they seem.

Critical Context

Most readers and teachers know that there is no one called "Hadley Irwin." Two writers, Lee Hadley and Ann Irwin, joined to share their names and talents. Irwin died in 1995, and readers assume that Hadley will continue writing on her own.

In some ways, this novel was an anomaly for the authors. Most of their books are for younger readers, and many do not utilize psychological realism. *Abby, My Love* came out in the middle of a trend in young adult literature toward examining incest and other forms of sexual abuse. Other topics of serious concern only started to appear in the 1970's, titles dealing with suicide, anorexia, scarification, madness, and rape. A similar title on which Hadley and Irwin collaborated is *What About Grandma*, a story about how old people are often seen as disposable in the United States.

Chris Crutcher, Norma Fox Mazer, and Francesca Lia Block have all written young adult novels about incest. It is telling that none of them, and not *Abby, My Love*, seem sufficient to deal with the incest theme alone. There are always major subjects or plot twists added to this main theme. Perhaps the novel should have been more grim in order to make its point.

John Jacob

ABEL'S ISLAND

Author: William Steig (1907-   )
First published: 1976; illustrated
Type of work: Novel
Type of plot: Adventure tale and fantasy
Time of work: From August, 1907, to August, 1908
Locale: An uninhabited island
Subjects: Arts, friendship, love and romance, and nature
Recommended ages: 10-13

Marooned on an island, a rich, pampered mouse discovers within himself both survival skills and artistic ability before making his way home to his wife.

> *Principal characters:*
> ABEL (ABELARD HASSAM DI CHIRICO FLINT), a wealthy Edwardian
>   mouse who, stranded by flood waters, is left to survive alone on a
>   small island for a year
> AMANDA, his newlywed wife, who waits for him at home
> GOWER GLACKENS, an elderly frog who becomes Abel's companion
>   when he, too, is trapped on the island for a few months

Form and Content

Like Daniel Defoe's *Robinson Crusoe* (1719) and Scott O'Dell's *Island of the Blue Dolphins* (1960), William Steig's *Abel's Island* takes on the challenges of the survival story. The protagonist's isolation throughout most of the novel prevents reliance on the standard narrative building blocks of dialogue and character interaction. Instead, Steig makes his mouse hero's solitary musings and his conflicts both with nature and himself the central focus.

One afternoon in August, 1907, newlyweds Abel and Amanda leave their comfortable home in Mossville for a picnic outing. When a violent storm arises, they find shelter in a cave until Abel recklessly pursues Amanda's windblown scarf. Buffeted by torrential rains, Abel clutches desperately at a rusty nail in a board until this makeshift raft comes to rest in the branches of a birch tree on a small river island.

At first, Abel believes his family will mount a search party to rescue him. When he realizes that he must save himself, he makes many ingenious but unsuccessful attempts at escape: adapting a rudder to his nail-and-board boat, engineering another boat of driftwood and bark, lashing together twigs to make a catamaran, flinging a woven grass rope across the river with his suspenders as a slingshot, and building a bridge of stepping stones.

By September, Abel accepts that he is an inhabitant of the island and takes pride in providing for his needs. He experiments with different natural foods and outfits a hollow log as a snug shelter. As autumn deepens, he diligently stores nuts and seeds, weaves a winter cloak of grass stuffed with milkweed fluff, and insulates his log home. The energy of nature as it prepares for winter spurs him to even greater creativity, and he tries his hand at sculpting clay statues of Amanda and his family. In further exploration of the island, he discovers a human-sized pocket watch and a novel, giving him the rhythmic ticking of the watch and daily-rationed reading of chapters.

The winter months Abel spends miserably in the darkness of his log, waking only long enough to munch a little in his food stores. The depression of this dark time is made worse by the freezing cold and by a predatory owl who returns several times to threaten Abel.

The return of spring is marked not only by a resurgence of energy and joyfulness in Abel but also, amazingly, by the arrival of a visitor, an elderly frog named Gower Glackens who is washed ashore by the rain-choked river. Mouse and frog become fast friends, sharing stories of their families and artistic interests. Abel honors his friend by adding a sculpted likeness of Gower to his collection, and Gower assures Abel that sculpting is surely his vocation.

When Gower leaves the island in mid-June, Abel is more lonely than before. In August, a full year after landing on the island, the drought-diminished river convinces Abel that he now has a chance of crossing it safely. Saying a loving farewell to his statues and to the island that nurtured him, he begins to swim across the stream. Once on shore, an encounter with a cat gives him another chance to prove the survival skills and self-confidence that he has lately acquired. Making his way through Mossville, he spots Amanda sitting alone in a park but decides to continue on and surprise her alone at home. She enters, spots first her restored scarf and then her husband, then melts tearfully into his arms. Steig's own ink-and-wash illustrations, which have enriched the narrative throughout, are used here instead of words to recount the final touching moments of this tale.

Analysis

As in any good survival story, the protagonist must learn to accept the forces of nature and accommodate himself to them. At first, Abel resents nature when it conflicts with his will. He imagines the rain as inconsiderate when it interrupts his picnic, and he resents the power of the flood-swollen river, resolving to beat it. Gradually, he becomes attuned rather than resistant to the rhythm of the seasons: He passes the winter months in a mostly somnolent state, then revives with the spring, dancing and yodeling for the sheer joy of living. He loses his city-bred taste for mushroom omelettes and caviar and enjoys the fresh taste of strawberries and cherry birch bark, which he is somewhat shocked to learn that his own teeth are ideally adapted to gnawing. Perhaps the most significant example of Abel's growing acceptance of the natural order of things is the attitude that he demonstrates toward the two predators he faces in the course of the novel. He sees the owl as a personal enemy. His deep hatred for the owl motivates him to fight back not only with weapons—his pocketknife tied to a stick to make a spear—but also with bloodcurdling curses chanted over the owl's feathers, kept for their talisman-like power. Months later, Abel's reliance on instinct rather than anger to elude a hunting cat and his matter-of-fact acceptance of its predatory behavior as simply part of its makeup suggest a mouse who has become wise in the ways of the natural world.

Psychological survival and maturation are just as important to Abel's success as physical survival. Although Abel is an adult when circumstances take him from his home, inherited wealth and a pampered lifestyle have allowed him to remain immature. Discovering that he can provide his own food and shelter gives him a warm sense of accomplishment. Never having worked before, he now finds in himself artistic ability, which he takes pains to develop. Also, he lessens his loneliness by developing a warm friendship with Gower, a creature whom he would formerly have felt to be beneath his acquaintance. Finally, he strengthens his will to continue his solitary existence by speaking aloud to himself, his sculptures, his birch tree, and his special evening star.

When Abel speaks aloud to his star or the statue of Amanda, he often does so to commune with his beloved absent wife. One important theme of *Abel's Island*, unusual for a children's novel, is the power of conjugal love. Paradoxically, Abel's yearlong exile is both more painful because of his separation from Amanda and easier to endure because of his certainty of a continued link with her through his dreams and spoken thoughts.

It is primarily Steig's style, which has been described as remarkably literate, even courtly, that allows him to handle such mature themes as married love and the growth of the artist. Few authors of children's literature can broach such challenging themes naturally while still making them accessible to young readers. One example of this thematic depth occurs when Abel grapples with God's motives for creating owls, snakes, and other predators, thereby becoming a mouse-sized Job in quest of metaphysical meaning.

Critical Context

His sophisticated style and thoughtful subject matter have prompted several critics to compare William Steig to E. B. White and Steig's Abel to White's Stuart Little. Like White, Steig is famous for a long association with the urbane magazine *The New Yorker* and for his work for adults, in Steig's case sardonic line drawings and cartoons. In both cases, the authors have managed to impart the wit and wisdom of their adult work to their children's writing as well.

Steig is also a brilliant illustrator of his own fiction. He has written many picture books, winning a Caldecott Medal for *Sylvester and the Magic Pebble* (1969) and the American Book Award for *Doctor De Soto* (1982). Thoughtful characterization, strong adventure plots, and an ear for the absolutely apt word mark all of Steig's narratives, short and long. Although magic is frequently the transformative element in picture books such as *Sylvester and the Magic Pebble*, character transformations occur more naturally and gradually in longer works such as *Abel's Island*.

In addition to the motif of transformation, a romance or quest element exists in several of Steig's creations. Molding his animal characters on such legendary beings as Odysseus or Aeneas, Steig has Abel and the dog protagonist of *Dominic* (1972) face a series of trials in a hostile world before achieving peace at home; they emerge as both active heroes and contemplative artists.

Finally, Steig underscores the classic quality of his work by adapting traditional narrative forms to his own purposes. Many of his picture books employ folktale motifs, *Dominic* has been called a picaresque novel, and *Abel's Island* is in the tradition of the Robinsonnade or survival story.

Catherine L. Elick

AESOP'S FABLES

Author: Aesop (c. 620-c. 560 B.C.)
First published: Aesopea, fourth century B.C. (English translation, 1484); illustrated
Type of work: Short fiction
Subjects: Animals, education, and the supernatural
Recommended ages: 10-15

This collection of entertaining, polished short stories, in which the principal characters are usually animals, offer either a moral or practical advice to gain advantage over life's circumstances.

Form and Content

Several hundred fables have been associated with the ancient Greek storyteller Aesop. It is difficult to determine with certainty the number of fables composed by him (the estimate stands at about 231), because little is known of the legendary fabulist himself. The fifth century B.C. historian Herodotus writes that Aesop was a slave who belonged to Iadmon, a man who lived on the Greek island of Samos. Impressed by Aesop's stories, Iadmon apparently freed him. Herodotus also notes that Aesop lived during the reign of the Egyptian pharoah Amasis; that is, during the mid-sixth century B.C. Tradition holds that Aesop was murdered at the Greek city of Delphi in a dispute with the inhabitants. Still later, colorful tales were added about his life; most notable was the rumor that he was disfigured, ugly, and mute.

The absence of an established text presents another difficulty in determining which fables were originally composed by Aesop. It is not likely that he wrote down his stories himself. The task of recording the fables was undertaken by later writers, notably the first century A.D. Latin writer Phaedrus and the second century A.D. Greek writer Babrius. This act of preservation provided ample opportunity to add new stories, a practice that continued throughout the centuries and that further increased the difficulty of identifying Aesop's own work.

Generally, the fables are short stories that offer a moral or some worldly advice. The meaning of the tale is understood within the story itself, but later commentators on the fables thought it necessary to add a short statement or proverb for further explanation. This custom may have been especially common for the Christian writers who inherited the fables from the Greco-Roman world. The protagonists of these stories are usually animals, and often two or more of them are engaged in some contest. The animals represent human behavior in a most candid way.

Most of the stories occur in natural settings or open places, often in the ancient world or in a timeless locale. Certain fables concern the heroes and gods from Greek and Roman mythology; Zeus, Hermes, and Hercules are particular favorites who often whimsically involve themselves in the creation and affairs of humankind.

Other stories (attributed to Aesop but certainly not his own) involve the Roman imperial world and its relation with everyday folk. Perhaps the best example is the fable of "The Lion and the Shepherd," in which a shepherd who shows generosity to a lion suffering with a thorn in its paw is rewarded a thousandfold. This fable formed the basis of the later story of Androcles, the good Christian thrown to the lions for the emperor's amusement. Still other stories represent people whose livelihood depends on nature (such as farmers, fishermen, and hunters) or who are craftsmen and the experience that they gain from their mistakes and struggles throughout life.

Analysis

Although the fables themselves did not originate from folk tradition but rather from a particular, skilled storyteller, they nevertheless reflect a wisdom important for understanding certain lessons in everyday living. These lessons do not prescribe ethical actions by which one may improve one's character and be judged a good person. Rather, more often they offer advice to help the reader secure a safe future—a future marked by fewer mistakes in judgment. In this way, the animal protagonists may represent the worst of human nature and suggest the ramifications of such behavior on one's personal fortune. In the popular fable of "The Fox and the Grapes," for example, a hungry fox who fails to jump high enough and reach the tantalizing fruit above snidely concludes in his frustration that the grapes must be sour. The fable thus satirizes the less industrious who would rather find fault in challenging tasks rather than work harder for a worthy profit.

Often, the fables describe a contest between two animals of different species and character. The famous fable of "The Hare and the Tortoise," for example, illustrates and recommends the benefit of being steady in one's attitude toward life and success. Often in the fables, scores are evened between two protagonists. In these cases, the motive may be turnabout or revenge: The fable of "The Fox and the Crane" provides an excellent example of this simple aspect of human nature. In other cases, the motive may be repayment for a previous act of kindness. Perhaps the best-known example of this lesson is the fable of "The Lion and the Mouse," in which the former spares the life of his little suppliant and later finds the act repaid in full when the mouse gnaws through a net that holds the lion captive. In this way, the fables of Aesop do not merely illustrate or poke fun at certain human behavior; they also suggest a practical magnanimity that may eventually be profitable.

The fables are not, however, always proponents of such good-spiritedness. They often suggest ways in which one may gain from another's mistake. In so doing, they also recommend against imprudent acts and poor judgment. In the fable of "The Fox and the Raven," the fox outwits the bird into dropping a savory and coveted morsel of cheese. The trickery of the wily fox is to be admired and perhaps emulated as much as the foolishness and vanity of the raven is to be avoided. In a similar fashion, Aesop's fables strongly warn against the acceptance of things on their face value, for appearances may deceive the unwary: A wolf may easily hide in sheep's clothing.

Aesop's fables often provide a mild if not humorous account of improper social behavior. For example, the fable of "The Wolf and the Crane," while it depicts with the highest wit a wolf who repays a crane's favor—the bird removed a bone from the wolf's throat—with a trick, it also illustrates the dangers of greed. Similarly, the fables regularly recommend that one both adhere to one's position in life and avoid impulsive desires. In this way, the stories reinforce the practical wisdom that one cannot ask for too much without running the risk of serious trouble. The best-known—and most mild—version of this wisdom is the fable of "The Country Mouse and the City Mouse," in which the influence of one's upbringing is charmingly emphasized.

Above all, the fables direct the reader to activity that brings a profit or, conversely, admonish those actions that would threaten one's security. The fable of "The Ant and the Grasshopper," for example, illustrates the importance of taking the opportunity to prepare in prosperous times for harder days to come. As the story suggests, one must never expect security and must always be responsible for one's own welfare.

Aesop's fables were not originally intended for a young audience, and their introduction to children came when they found favor among the folk and then were incorporated into a young man's education in rhetoric. Their simple wisdom has been so attractive and persuasive, however, that they have repeatedly been welcomed into the education of the young.

Critical Context

The fables of Aesop are not difficult for a young reader to understand and are certainly entertaining to the imagination, but certain stories do represent life circumstances with a frank brutality that may unsettle some children. A notable example is the fable of "The Dying Lion," who is beaten severely by his old enemies, the boar and the bull, and then by the cowardly donkey, who takes advantage of the lion's weakness.

Nevertheless, the fascinating possibilities of the fables have attracted many artists and writers throughout the ages, such that Aesop's name now suggests the genre itself. Since the nineteenth century, English-speaking audiences have found delight in the many translations and adaptations available. More important, the fables have long been welcomed as a way to teach children the pleasures of reading and other intellectual skills, as well as the wisdom or advice of the stories themselves, such as personal responsibility and prudence. The simple story lines and captivating antics of the animal protagonists have made the fables true classics, and they offer new insights with each reading and for each age group. In this way, they are excellent mediators between the young and their parents or teachers.

Every major writer of allegory owes some debt to Aesop's fables. Although the precise number of fables that were composed by Aesop himself may never be established and the various collections that are available often offer stories from later writers, it is without question that the fables shall remain poignant and charming examples of practical wisdom and good wit.

Stephen C. Olbrys

AFTER THE RAIN

Author: Norma Fox Mazer (1931-   )
First published: 1987
Type of work: Novel
Type of plot: Domestic realism
Time of work: The late 1980's
Locale: A city in the Eastern United States
Subjects: Coming-of-age, death, and family
Recommended ages: 13-18

When the family learns of Grandfather Izzy's impending death, Rachel undertakes his daily care and discovers that she deeply loves Izzy's gentle side, which he has carefully hidden from the family.

> *Principal characters:*
> RACHEL COOPER, a fifteen-year-old who is trying to balance her coming-of-age with her grandfather's death
> IZZY SHAPIRO, Rachel's eighty-three-year-old grandfather
> SHIRLEY, Rachel's sixty-one-year-old mother
> MANNY, Rachel's father
> JEREMY, Rachel's thirty-five-year-old brother, a Vietnam veteran
> LEWIS, Rachel's first boyfriend
> HELENA, Rachel's best friend

Form and Content

In *After the Rain*, Rachel Cooper's emotions and feelings are revealed through her letters to her absent brother, Jeremy. As the story progresses and Rachel gains inner strength, the letters change to journal entries. Rachel and Izzy resembling parrying fencers, and the extensive dialogue between them enhances the novel's readability. Short chapters introduce new action and conclude with thoughts that sum up the experience. The subplot of Rachel's first romance prevents the major plot of Izzy's death from becoming sentimental or melodramatic.

Rachel's maternal grandfather, Izzy, is diagnosed with terminal cancer associated with exposure to asbestos. Because of his age and the nature of the disease, nothing can be done for him. With only a few weeks to live, he will quickly weaken. The doctor suggests that the family not inform Izzy of the diagnosis but make him as comfortable as possible.

Rachel dutifully calls Izzy weekly, but their distant relationship is void of affection. To her, he is a cranky old man who always gets his way. Izzy, a stonemason by trade, has always been physically strong and independent. When he falls during one of his daily four-mile walks, family members try to persuade him to move in with them, but he refuses. To appease her mother, Rachel agrees to accompany him on his walks, but she does not intend for them to become a daily ritual. After all, she has her own life to live, and she wants to spend time with Lewis, her first boyfriend. When she does not show up one day, Izzy calls and wants to know why she did not come; he had been waiting for her. Rachel realizes that he has begun to expect her companionship. When she tries to tell her parents that she does not want this responsibility, her mother thanks her for her help.

Although Izzy has been an ever-present force in her life, this is the first time Rachel remembers being alone with him. The realization sinks in that Izzy is enjoying her company. Rachel turns the walks into a project of trying to learn family history. Izzy withholds information and resents her inquisitiveness until the day he guides her to the bridges that he helped build over Clearbook Creek. Together they search for, but do not find, his handprint left on one of the bridges.

As Izzy weakens, Rachel's care for him expands. Hesitantly, he reveals some of his inner thoughts, and she senses the strong love he had for his wife. She realizes that Izzy only tells what he wants others to know. She begins to see through the rough façade that he has created.

Knowing that their time together is brief, Rachel becomes devoted to Izzy. When his death occurs, she is beside him. The gap between them has narrowed into an affectionate relationship. Rachel is resentful because it took his death to bring them together but thankful that they made peace before it was too late. After his death, she enlists the help of Lewis, and together they search the bridges until she finds his handprint, the symbol that his life had value.

Analysis

The strongest theme of *After the Rain* is that even though individuals may be separated by a generation gap, they still share common worries, emotions, and internal conflicts. Sixty-eight years separate geriatric Izzy and teenage Rachel, but many parallels exist between them. Their emotions mirror each other and vacillate between anger, fear, sorrow, hope, and love. They try to balance between the extremes of being independent and being needed.

Both feel betrayed. Izzy feels betrayed by his age, his failing health, and his imminent death. He experiences humility, an emotion foreign to someone of his former strength. He can no longer be independent and needs someone to care for him. Rachel feels betrayed because her mother was forty-six when Rachel was born. Her parents are old, sensitive, and too easily pleased. She missed a family closeness that was never there for her. She is offended when her niece talks about her close relationship with Grandmother Shirley, because Rachel never had this type of relationship with Izzy. She never even liked him, and now she wonders if she is using his death to make herself important with her family and friends. Is she merely using the situation to obtain attention? Is she betraying herself by concealing her own emotions? She uses self-restraint to avoid crying and grieving until after his death. Rain symbolizes her pent-up emotions. Once the rain has passed, she can release the grief and anger that she suppressed and move on with her life.

Fear of what the future holds is another common emotion shared by Izzy and Rachel. Izzy knows that his death is unavoidable, and he even accepts it to some degree, but death frightens him. He uses his irritability and stubbornness to hide his fears. Rachel writes to her absent and unresponsive brother, Jeremy, because he is a nonjudgmental, outside audience. He serves as a confessor to whom she can relay her true thoughts and emotions. Because she needs immediate responsiveness, she begins to rely less on her letters and leans more toward Izzy for his wisdom. They both know that Izzy's death is beyond their control, but they draw strength from each other in order to cope.

Both are undergoing rites of passage. Izzy's death is analogous to Rachel's coming-of-age. Both are completing cycles of life that, once gone by, can never be reclaimed. Izzy's death will complete the circle of his life, while Rachel will enter a new phase of her life.

Both have anger. Izzy is angry because he has lost control. Rachel is angry because in the past, Izzy made no move to be close to her. She feels cheated that she was "locked out of the world of feeling" with him for all those wasted years. She hates being his caretaker, begrudges the time that it takes away from her life, and resents that she is the only one who has the time to tend to Izzy.

As Izzy's barriers dissolve and Rachel pulls toward him, another main theme develops. When people expand their boundaries, they can discover that they truly care for one another. Rachel and Izzy learn from each other, accept each other's weaknesses and strengths, and love each other unconditionally. Rachel begins to understand why her grandfather behaved as he did. As Izzy becomes weaker, Rachel becomes stronger. Their juxtaposition forms a bond between them that would never have developed without having taken the time. They discover that people are not always what one thinks they are, that one must give others a genuine chance and make an effort to understand them. Rachel is able to come to terms with her anxieties and learns that death and grief are a part of life.

Critical Context

Loss and the healing process are the main topics in many of Norma Fox Mazer's books. In *Out of Control* (1993), the protagonist must deal with the loss of innocence when her view of the world through rose-colored glasses is shattered by a sexual harassment incident. In this story, forgiveness is the instrument that allows healing to occur. Loss of security is the subject in *Downtown* (1984) and the near loss of virginity is portrayed in *Up in Seth's Room* (1979). Newly discovered love is the vehicle that Rachel uses to deal with and heal from the loss of her grandfather in *After the Rain*. All of Mazer's books address natural coming-of-age experiences that teenagers undergo. A budding romance is used as a subtheme in *After the Rain* to soften the impact of death. The ending allows the reader to realize that loss is part of life.

This theme can be seen in other young adult titles. Cynthia Rylant's *Missing May* (1992) uses flashbacks to relate how the protagonist deals with the death of her aunt. Similarly, fond memories are used to describe a child's grief for her deceased mother in *Walk Two Moons* (1994). Jan Hudson's *Sweetgrass* (1991) looks at death through what might have been had a young person not died. Unlike these titles, *After the Rain* does not use the past to portray the grief caused by death, instead using present relationships subtly to relay the sorrow felt when death occurs. *After the Rain* stresses the importance of putting things right while there is still time.

Pat Waits

AFTERNOON OF THE ELVES

Author: Janet Taylor Lisle (1974-   )
First published: 1989
Type of work: Novel
Type of plot: Psychological realism
Time of work: The 1980's
Locale: An American suburb
Subjects: Emotions and friendship
Recommended ages: 10-13

Hilary never finds out whether elves really built the tiny village in Sara-Kate's backyard, but she learns much about friendship as she gets to know the troubled, imaginative, and mysterious older girl.

Principal characters:
>   HILARY LENOX, a warm-hearted, trusting fourth-grader whose safe yet boring family life has left her with a yearning for mystery and magic
>   SARA-KATE CONNOLLY, a fascinating and enigmatic fifth-grader who lives next door to Hilary
>   MR. and MRS. LENOX, Hilary's kind, dull parents
>   MRS. CONNOLLY, Sara-Kate's mother, who is mentally and physically ill
>   JANE WEBSTER and ALISON MANCINI, Hilary's closest fourth-grade friends, staunch upholders of a feminine camaraderie maintained through conformity

Form and Content

Afternoon of the Elves is that rarity in children's literature—a delicate and complex psychological study of characters and relationships presented in a swift-moving, lively, and intriguing plot. The story focuses on the friendship between the sweet but unremarkable Hilary and Sara-Kate, whose unkempt appearance, temperamental personality, and mysterious family background have made her a social outcast at the suburban school that they both attend. Through her stories of elves and elfin ways, Sara-Kate introduces Hilary to the world of fantasy and magic; through her mercurial moods and secretive ways, she gives Hilary a glimpse of the ambiguities of human nature. When Sara-Kate's tragic family circumstances are revealed, she opens Hilary's eyes to the world beyond Hilary's own carefully controlled and circumscribed family life.

Sara-Kate initiates the friendship by inviting Hilary, her next-door neighbor, to look at an "elf village"—a collection of tiny houses made from sticks and leaves in a corner of her backyard. Hilary is immediately intrigued and listens eagerly to Sara-Kate's explanations of how the elves live. Hilary's two best friends, Jane and Alison, frown on this new friendship. They mock Sara-Kate's shabby clothes and scoff at the talk of elves. Hilary's highly conventional parents also express uneasiness at their daughter spending time in her new friend's junk-strewn, poison ivy-infested backyard.

Despite the warnings of her friends and family, Hilary is insistently drawn to Sara-Kate and the elf-village. "Put yourself in the position of the elves!" urges Sara-Kate, and Hilary gradually finds her perceptions of both nature and people sharpening. She exists in a state of perpetual expectation that the elves will appear and even speculates about Sara-Kate, whose odd ways and deep knowledge of elf lore suggest that she might be an elf herself. The mysterious delight of the elf village is mixed with growing bewilderment as Hilary learns about her friend's sad home life. She eventually discovers that inside the dilapidated house, away from the magic of the backyard and the elf village, Sara-Kate lives in destitution, caring as best she can for an incapacitated and reclusive mother. When Hilary accidentally glimpses Sara-Kate holding her frail mother on her lap as she sits in a rocking chair, she is so astonished by this scene, which is so foreign to her own life experience, that she at first assumes it is an elf-induced vision. Soon, however, Hilary realizes that the rocking chair scene is real. Hilary sympathizes deeply with her friend's plight, so much that she accompanies her on a thieving raid of a local grocery store.

Having gained Sara-Kate's trust, Hilary is now welcome to visit inside the older girl's house. One afternoon, Hilary's mother comes looking inside the dilapidated house for her daughter and discovers Sara-Kate's plight. This discovery brings the novel to an end, as Sara-Kate's mother is hospitalized, Sara-Kate is sent to live with relatives in another state, and the house is repaired and sold to a more conventional family. Hilary consoles herself over the loss of her friend by transporting the elf village to a quiet spot behind her own garage, her hope in the possibility of elfin magic undimmed.

Analysis

Afternoon of the Elves has significant ties to the genre of enchanted realism. Typically, a novel written in this genre portrays a magical person or object that enters the life of a contemporary child in an otherwise realistic and ordinary setting. By presenting magical experiences in this way, authors can make magic seem immediate and credible to young readers. Janet Taylor Lisle, however, chooses to emphasize the uncertain, unprovable, and elusive qualities of magic. Hilary longs to see the elves in person and to have her faith in magic confirmed by observation, but her most careful and persistent attention is constantly frustrated: "She was never sure what she had seen. It was maddening."

Only once in the novel does the author describe an event that Hilary unequivocally accepts as having a magical provenance. In this scene, a bicycle wheel that serves as an elfin Ferris wheel seems to turn around of its own accord, as if by magic. Readers are aware, however, that Hilary is deeply susceptible to Sara-Kate's hypnotic personality, that this perception may have been induced by her friend's powers of suggestion.

Although the elves remain hidden and unproven throughout the story, the powerful allure of magical possibilities is reinforced. The reader sees how Hilary's interest in the elves leads her to a more reflective, curious, and analytical pattern of thought, how it motivates a keener observation of the natural world, and how it adds a more empathic and compassionate dimension to her relationships with other people. The author's goal is not to convince the reader of the existence of a magical world but to provoke and stimulate readers to become more perceptive and imaginative observers of their own worlds.

Afternoon of the Elves also fits within the tradition of miniaturism in children's literature. Beginning with the tiny race of Lilliputians in Jonathan Swift's *Gulliver's Travels* (1726), writers of juvenile literature have exploited the device of small beings to present life from novel perspectives. Seen through the eyes of a very small personage, both comic and tragic aspects of the normal-sized world are magnified. In *Afternoon of the Elves*, the tiny village, with its Ferris wheel made of a bicycle wheel and its rooftops made of leaves, has a purely physical charm that engages the reader's interest. More important, the intriguing details of the elf village help the reader follow Sara-Kate's injunction to consider the elves' point of view, to try to see beyond immediate appearances.

The elements of both miniaturism and enchanted realism support the central concern of the novel, which is the evolving psychological relationship between Hilary and Sara-Kate. The games that they play in the elf village mediate the friendship, as Sara-Kate uses the elf stories she relates to Hilary as a way of revealing her own feelings about the world. Hilary realizes at the end of the story that "every single thing Sara-Kate had taught her about elves had turned out to be true about the thin girl herself." When Sara-Kate exhorts Hilary to "look deep" when looking for elves, the reader understands that Hilary must also look very deeply to see her friend truly, clearly, and completely. Like the elves, however, Sara-Kate ultimately remains elusive, her motivations and intentions never fully explained. Like Hilary, the reader leaves the story without any final answers but with a sense that the search for human connection, like the search for magic, can be an experience of wonder and fulfillment.

Critical Context

Although many books for young readers address the theme of friendship, few explore its ambiguous psychological nuances as intently as *Afternoon of the Elves*. In this regard, it is also unique within Janet Taylor Lisle's oeuvre, although her earlier novel *Sirens and Spies* (1985) also emphasizes friendship and the importance of probing beyond surface appearances. Her novels *The Great Dimpole Oak* (1987), *The Lampfish of Twill* (1991), and *Forest* (1993) are whimsical fantasies that emphasize action over reflection and incorporate large casts of extraordinary characters. With such books as *The Gold Dust Letters* (1994) and *Looking for Juliette* (1994) in the series Investigators of the Unknown, Lisle returned to realistic settings with hints of magic but kept her narratives focused on action rather than on her characters' interior lives.

Afternoon of the Elves won high critical esteem in the year of its publication, when it was named both a Newbery Honor Book and an American Library Association Notable Book. Steady paperback sales since then suggest that children as well as adults find this story of friendship and imagination highly readable. With its evocative yet economical style and its emphasis on themes that have timeless appeal to young readers, *Afternoon of the Elves* is likely to become a minor classic in the canon of children's literature.

Constance Vidor

AH! WILDERNESS

Author: Eugene O'Neill (1888-1953)
First presented: 1933
First published: 1933
Type of work: Drama
Type of plot: Domestic realism
Time of work: July 4 and 5, 1906
Locale: A small seaport town in Connecticut
Subjects: Coming-of-age, family, love and romance, and sexual issues
Recommended ages: 15-18

Richard Miller and his parents recognize that adolescent rebellion is best handled in an atmosphere of love, patience, and gentle reproof.

> *Principal characters:*
> RICHARD MILLER, a nearly seventeen, idealistic teenager who is
>   iconoclastic in his choice of books, politics, and values
> NAT MILLER, Richard's father, a newspaper editor who patiently deals
>   with Richard's behavior
> ESSIE MILLER, Richard's somewhat indulgent mother
> MURIEL McCOMBER, Richard's naïve sweetheart
> SID DAVIS, Essie Miller's alcoholic brother
> LILY MILLER, Nat Miller's "spinster" sister
> BELLE, a prostitute who fails in her attempt to have sex with Richard

Form and Content

Ah! Wilderness is a domestic comedy in four acts, centering on Eugene O'Neill's nostalgic memories of turn-of-the-century family life in New England. The play is structured around the growing-up experiences of Richard Miller as he rebels against small-town morality in his reading, politics, and idealistic romance. Strong family ties and patient parental attention help Richard to resist temptation and accept the positive qualities of his domestic situation.

The action takes place over a two-day period, beginning on the Fourth of July, 1906. In act 1, as family members prepare to celebrate the holiday, Richard is at odds with the others as he lashes out, idealistically, against capitalism and quotes passages from authors considered to be "racy" and avant-garde. His reading is the springboard for the play's development. When some quotations that Richard has shared with his sweetheart, Muriel McComber, are discovered by her father, Mr. McComber not only tries to prevent Muriel from further contact and communication with Richard but also demands that Mr. Miller discipline Richard harshly.

Richard's reaction to his father's reprimand and the break-up with Muriel constitute idealistic martyrdom. In act 2, during the family meal—with comic relief from the interactions of the old suitors, Sid Davis and Lily Miller—Richard maintains his pose of disdain and pessimism about life. He rebelliously looks forward to a forbidden night out with one of his brother's friends and the chance to be with a "fast" woman.

In act 3, at a saloon with a prostitute, however, Richard only succeeds in making himself foolishly drunk. Although he kisses Belle, he resists the temptation of going upstairs to a room together. Richard's drunken return to his house is met with parental severity, but Uncle Sid, recognizing that Richard is really ill from the side effects and himself used to the impact of too much drink, escorts Richard to bed.

Although discipline is threatened the next day, in act 4, Essie, Richard's mother, begins to feel sorry for her son. Richard, moreover, receives word that Muriel still loves him and was forced to write the break-up letter. Ever the romantic, Richard ignores his parents' wishes once more, sneaking out the next night for a secret meeting on the beach with Muriel. In this contrasting scene to the saloon meeting with the prostitute, Richard and Muriel commit themselves to an undying love and innocently exchange a kiss. When Richard returns home, his regret about his night at the saloon and his commitment never to drink again or get involved with "fast" women are so sincerely convincing that his father settles the issues with advice about how to live a good middle-class life. The play ends with Richard's acceptance of his need to attend college before he and Muriel can marry.

Analysis

A major American dramatist, Eugene O'Neill is best known for his unrelentingly tragic dramas and concentration on adult themes and contexts. *Ah! Wilderness* is the major exception in the O'Neill canon in its comic approach to family problems. Although certainly not originally intended for the young adult audience, the play evocatively captures bittersweet memories of growing up in the early twentieth century. Indeed, the play is perhaps most meaningfully understood as an American nostalgic family comedy, a subgenre of romantic comedy, in which a past time, often the childhood context of the author, provides the setting, with details projected realistically and evocatively. The characters are likeable and well meaning, if comical, and characterization dominates action, with children playing an important role. The playgoer or reader experiencing the nostalgic family comedy often feels that the past presented in the play is somehow better than the present and mourns the loss of values and the passing of a simpler way of life.

O'Neill's attention to evoking exact details from his childhood is masterful. Whether it be lyrics to popular songs of the time, the use of slang, attention to details about Fourth of July celebrations, room furnishings and clothes, or the proverbial double-standard morality in relation to gender issues, the play is rich in its creation of the past. The major characters are likable but not without flaws. Richard is presented as an intelligent and enthusiastic, if rebellious and impetuous, teenager whose commitment to ideal goals and high romantic standards save him from temptations that might ruin his future. Essie and Nat are wise but sometimes overindulgent parents, puzzled by their children's and especially by Richard's actions. Yet their love for each other and their family, their patience and understanding, allow them to guide Richard through his struggles toward maturity without undue family tension.

In many ways, the most remarkable characters in the play are Sid Davis and Lily Miller, ill-fated lovers whose proposed marriage has been put on hold because of Sid's drinking problems and continued association with loose women. O'Neill sets these comic realizations up as contrasts to Richard and his sweetheart, Muriel McComber. All of Sid's drunken actions, however humorously regarded by the family and by the audience, cannot hide the serious nature of his problem, which has frustrated his career and his love affair. It is not only Richard's adverse reaction to his own first drunkenness but also his understanding of what drink has done to his uncle that leads him to reject a similar way of life for himself.

Although this play is set in the era of the playwright's own adolescence, O'Neill's growing-up years were considerably different from those of the Miller children. O'Neill traces some of the difficulties of the tragic relationships in his own family in such plays as *Long Day's Journey into Night* (1956) and *A Moon for the Misbegotten* (1947). In *Ah! Wilderness*, however, O'Neill intentionally chose a different tone and approach to the past. His own comments about the play put it definitively in the category of American nostalgic family comedy. In *Contour in Time: The Plays of Eugene O'Neill* (1988), Travis Bogard quotes O'Neill as saying that *Ah! Wilderness* was "the way I would have *liked* my boyhood to have been" and "a nostalgia for a youth I never had." Yet, O'Neill's statements ignore the play's many autobiographical details. The house in which the play is set is clearly based on the O'Neill summer cottage, with the same rooms as those used for the setting of *Long Day's Journey into Night*. Richard, moreover, seems closely patterned on the playwright himself both in description ("sensitiveness . . . restless, apprehensive, defiant, shy, dreamy, self-conscious intelligence) and in his forbidden reading choices. Indeed, O'Neill's own adolescent devotion to Edward FitzGerald's somewhat racy version of *The Rubaiyat of Omar Khayyam* led him to the title of the play, based on a slightly modified version of the following familiar lines:

A Book of Verses underneath the Bough,
A Jug of Wine, a Loaf of Bread—and Thou
Beside me singing in the Wilderness—
Oh, Wilderness were Paradise enow!

O'Neill's change of "Oh" to "Ah" underscores the play's emphasis on nostalgic longing. The title reveals the playwright's devotion to picturing the "wilderness" of adolescence with a sigh of longing and love for Richard and his parents as they help him in his journey toward productive maturity.

Critical Context

Although not primarily intended for young adults, *Ah! Wilderness* can be enjoyed by this age group because of its sensitive depiction of adolescent and parental interactions. Perhaps for young readers the most accessible of O'Neill's plays, the drama effectively reveals the positive qualities of American nostalgic family comedy and provides an interesting comparison to other works in the genre, including such plays as Clarence Day's *Life with Father* (1920) and John Van Druten's *I Remember Mama* (1944) and such television shows as *Happy Days* or *The Waltons*. What sets *Ah! Wilderness* apart from many other American nostalgic family comedies, however, is O'Neill's refusal to allow the work to become overly sentimental. By including Sid's unrelenting alcoholism and its codependency effect on the other family members, O'Neill keeps the tragic elements that are so pervasive in his other plays close to the surface of this comedy and keeps the drama from becoming hopelessly maudlin. O'Neill's tragedy *Long Day's Journey into Night* can be profitably read as a contrasting but parallel play about a family (O'Neill's own) whose members fail to come to grips with relationships in the constructive manner portrayed by the Millers.

Delmer Davis

AKU-AKU
The Secret of Easter Island

Author: Thor Heyerdahl (1914-   )
First published: Aku-aku: påskeøyas hemmelighet, 1957 (English translation, 1958); illustrated
Type of work: History
Time of work: 1956
Locale: Easter Island, in the Pacific Ocean
Subjects: Arts, race and ethnicity, and science
Recommended ages: 15-18

Curious about the colossal stone heads on Easter Island, Heyerdahl set out on a year-long expedition and found his strangest adventure.

Principal personages:
>THOR HEYERDAHL, a man with a scientific curiosity about the stone heads, who made them, how they were constructed, and the secrets that they hold
>
>GONZALO, the mayor, who appears foolish but who actually knows all the secrets of Easter Island
>
>FATHER SEBASTIAN, a missionary
>
>LAZARUS, the guide who taught Heyerdahl how to enter a cave

Form and Content

Thor Heyerdahl's *Aku-aku: The Secret of Easter Island* offers a vicarious adventure for young adult readers. The most striking human accomplishment on Easter Island is the construction of what appeared to be colossal heads that turned out to be statues with the torso mostly buried. The adventure begins with a mystery: How did the ancient people of Easter Island make and move these huge, numerous stone figures? Early in the book, it seems that no living soul knows how these colossal stone heads were carved out of rock or how they were lifted to an upright position. The ancient people who lived there buried their dead at the foot of the giant heads, until silence came to the island: There were no more people, no more sculpting, and no more signs of life. Such mysteries prompted Heyerdahl's voyage, which required a year of planning.

The exploring team soon located the place where the sculpting work took place. Heyerdahl explains how the topography assisted in the sculpting of the gigantic heads. The ancient remains of volcanoes had become like small mountains with carved out tops that held water in natural pools. One of these water-filled volcanoes is called Rano Raraku, and it is here that the ancient sculptors seemed to have been most busily at work. The whole mountain was reshaped as hundreds of thousands of cubic feet of rock were cut out and tens of thousands of tons of stone were carried away. In the midst of the mountain's gaping top lie more than a hundred and fifty gigantic stone men in all stages of completion, from those just begun to those just finished. At the foot of the mountain stand finished stone men, side by side like an army.

Heyerdahl describes the team's examination of the site and its findings. They first studied the numerous figures in various stages of production on the ledges in the quarry itself. It was clear that the work had been broken off suddenly. Thousands of primitive, unpolished stone picks still lay in the open-air workshop. Since different groups of sculptors had worked simultaneously on many different statues, all stages of carving production were represented. The stonecutters first attacked the bare rock itself to carve the face and the front part of the statue. Then, they cut channels along the sides and made giant ears and arms; they always carved extremely long and slender fingers over the belly. Next, they cut their way underneath the whole figure from both sides, so that the back part took the shape of a boat with a narrow keel.

When the figure was completed in every minute detail, it was rubbed with a sort of pumice and thoroughly polished. The only thing that the sculptors did not do was to mark the eye itself under the overhanging brows; at that point, the giant was to remain blind. Then, the keel was hacked away under the back while the colossus was wedged up with stones to prevent it from sliding down into the abyss. It seemed that the sculptors were indifferent as to whether they carved the figure out of a perpendicular wall or a horizontal slab, with head upward or downward, since half-finished giants lay bent in every direction. The only consistent thing about them was that the back was the last part to remain attached to the rock.

The solution to the mystery about how the colossi were moved is described. When the back was cut loose, transportation down the cliff to the foot of the volcano began. In some cases, colossi weighing many tons had been swung down a perpendicular wall and maneuvered over lower ledges, where there were statues on which work was still proceeding. Many figures were broken in transport, but the overwhelming majority had come down complete—that is to say, complete without legs, for every single statue ended where the abdomen ends and the legs begin, making them lengthened busts with complete torsos. The giant stone men were raised into a standing position at the bottom of the hill, where the sculptors worked on the unfinished back. Heyerdahl notes that the only articles of clothing carved onto the statue were belts decorated with rings and symbols. With only one exception, the colossi were all male figures.

Analysis

Much of Heyerdahl's evidence concerning the statues and the history of the island comes from native legends. The natives tell legends of ancestors who would rather eat members of their own species than fish or fowl. They have also persistent legends of a still-earlier time of greatness when another people, the long-ears, had lived at peace with their ancestors, the short-ears. The long-ears demanded too much labor of the short-ears, however, and in the end there was a war in which nearly all the long-ears were burned in a ditch. From that day, no more statues were made, and many of those standing were pulled down with ropes. Civil war, family feuds, and cannibalism marked the years that followed, right up to the time when a missionary named Father Eugenio landed two generations before and collected the inhabitants peacefully around him in the village of Hangaroa.

When Heyerdahl asked the local residents if they could tell him how these stone giants could have been carried about in old times, one answer was that they went by themselves. Another reply was a legend about a witch and a lobster. An old witch lived at Rano Raraku at the time when the sculptors made the great figures. It was her magic that breathed life into the stone giants and made them move. One day, the sculptors ate a big lobster. When the witch found the empty shell and realized that none of the lobster had been given to her, she was so angry that she made all the walking statues fall flat on their noses, and they have never moved since. When Heyerdahl discovered a people from a land with generations of experience in maneuvering monoliths, he believed that he had solved the mystery presented by the movement of the colossal statues. His more practical solution involves speculation about seafaring men using rigs.

Heyerdahl reports that the history of Easter Island had three distinct epochs. First came a highly specialized culture with a South American type of masonry employed on Easter Island. Buildings had no parallel in the later history of the island. Gigantic blocks of hard basalt were cut like cheese and fitted carefully to one another without a crack or a hole. These constructions, with their elegant, steep walls, stood for a long time, resembling altar-shaped and partly stepped fortresses all round the island.

In the second stage, most of the classical structures had been partially pulled down and altered, a paved slope had been built up against the inland wall, and giant figures in human form had been brought from Rano Raraku and erected with their backs to the sea on top of these rebuilt edifices, which now often contained burial chambers. It was while this gigantic task was at its height in the second epoch that everything came to an unexpected standstill. Little more than a century before the Europeans came in 1722, a wave of war and cannibalism swept over the island.

With the arrival of the Polynesians, all cultural life came to an abrupt end and the tragic third phase of Easter Island's history began. No one chiseled great stones, and the statues were pulled down without reverence. Boulders and shapeless blocks were flung together to make funeral mounds along the walls, and great fallen statues were often used as improvised roofs for new burial vaults. The work was makeshift and utterly lacking in technical ability.

Dutch explorers landed in 1722 on Easter Day, giving the island its name and spending only a day before leaving. Next, the Spaniards arrived in 1770; after a ceremony declaring ownership of the island, they promptly left. The next visitor was Captain James Cook in 1774. Twelve years later, in 1786, the next European visitor was the Frenchman Comte de La Pérouse, who brought pigs, goats, and sheep and sowed a quantity of seed. All the animals and seeds were eaten by the hungry natives before they had time to propagate, however, and the island remained unchanged.

For Heyerdahl, the history of Easter Island was for the first time beginning to have depth. He knew that the specialized South American technique of mural construction was brought to Easter Island in a fully developed form; it was used by the people who had first landed on the island. This discovery took the expedition a step closer to solving the riddle of who constructed the colossi but failed fully to answer the question of the first sculptors. The mystery surrounding the identity of the long-ears who carved the gigantic statues was resolved when the local mayor, a descendent of the long-ears, demonstrated his ability to reproduce and move the statues.

Critical Context

Although *Aku-aku* is a scholarly work, it has qualities that appeal to young adult readers. The reasons for creating art may seem strange and mysterious to those looking at artifacts from an unknown culture. These artifacts may include knowledge, beliefs, styles, and several other characteristics of the originating culture. This 384-page book offers many illustrations to provide the vicarious experience of visiting Easter Island. The landscape, the residents, and Thor Heyerdahl and his team are shown in color photographs, and maps, drawings, and an index are also included.

Some young adult readers are looking for adventure—for travel across the high seas or for a visit to a remote tropical island. All these elements can be found in *Aku-aku*, which describes a heroic quest. Heyerdahl's expert use of description allows the reader to imagine every setting. He creates suspense and engages his reader's intellect with questions, supplying an answer to each one. Reviewers referred to the book as absorbing or as being a vigorous adventure story, with the lure of mysteries to be solved.

The context of the book places a seemingly heavy emphasis on race and ethnicity. Special value is accorded to European influences, while the native people, such as the mayor, seem to be less important in their own land. By the end of the expedition, however, this relationship is shown to be reversed. Heyerdahl reveals the apparently ignoble mayor to be the one who holds the keys to all the mysteries that Heyerdahl and his fine team of experts were at a loss to discover on their own. Heyerdahl likes to provide his book with some intriguing turns. He asks challenging questions before he offers answers; he sets up mysteries that he later solves. It could be that the racial and ethnic emphasis in *Aku-aku* was another technique to lead readers to make certain superficial judgments, only to be caught by surprise when these presumptions are overturned.

Heyerdahl is also the author of *Kon-Tiki ekspedisjonen* (1950; *Kon-Tiki: Across the Pacific by Raft*, 1950), which chronicles his voyage on a craft made of balsa.

Earleen De La Perriere

ALL THE COLORS OF THE RACE

Author: Arnold Adoff (1935-   )
First published: 1982; illustrated
Type of work: Poetry
Subjects: Emotions, family, race and ethnicity, and social issues
Recommended ages: 10-13

These brief, original poems reflect the inner thoughts and feelings of a girl whose identity comes from her black mother and white father.

Form and Content

Arnold Adoff's *All the Colors of the Race* contains thirty-six short free-verse poems celebrating heritage, identity, and a sense of self. The poetry can be read as individual works or as one narrative work. The poems are told in the first person from the point of view of a daughter who is a member of a biracial family. They are vehicles to express the girl's thoughts and feelings about her ancestors, about her place in the world, and especially about the place that she feels most welcome—the satisfying home created by her Jewish father and her African American mother.

The themes of pride in a diverse family background, of appreciation of one's ancestry, the cultural bias prevalent in the world, family love, and hope for the future transcend the daughter's immediate situation and become a mirror for both races and sexes. The language is simple, and the recognition of the positive aspects of both her black and her Jewish heritage on the girl's personality is evident throughout the poems. The works are sometimes thoughtful, sometimes reminiscent, sometimes observant, and sometimes questioning, but they always reveal a pride in diversity and hope that people will become more tolerant of others.

The poems fall into rough groupings. The first two deal with the colors that all human beings share, and the next four examine the past, such as ancestors and heritage. The largest section of poems treats the search for self-identity and the recognition and appreciation of the girl's racial background, as well as her Protestant and Jewish faiths. These poems are followed by more general reflections about race relations in the United States and the prejudice that often arises. The last poems offers a celebration of family and hope for the future.

The entire book is only fifty-six pages long and can easily be read in less than an hour; some poems are as short as two lines, and much white space appears on the pages. Yet, the poems are meant to be read slowly and thoughtfully. Words fall across the page, and often one word becomes an entire line. Adoff communicates not only through his choice of words but also through the placement of words on the page, as is evident in "Sum People":

> The   black   man
> said

                    I was a   half
                                   breed,
                    but I told
                                   him
                    to
                    check   out   his
                                   math:
                    like
                          one
                                   plus
                    one.

Titles do not always use capital letters, which is reflective of one of Adoff's literary influences, E. E. Cummings.

Illustrations by noted African American artist John Steptoe accompany the text. These framed portraits of the girl and/or her family and her ancestors reflect the pride and joy that are evident in the poetry. The illustrations are in shades of brown and white, as are the cover and the endpapers.

Analysis

Although *All the Colors of the Race* is aimed primarily at children aged ten through thirteen, the poetry and art can be read, examined, discussed, and appreciated by children and young people of all ages. African American children gain strength in their knowledge of themselves and their heritage, while children of other races gain knowledge of another culture, from which can come respect and understanding.

Rhythm and music are found in the language of the poetry. Adoff believes that poetry requires the active participation of the reader and that every poem should be read at least twice: first for meaning and then for rhythm. His poetry in this collection is best appreciated when read aloud and shared.

The verbal and visual images of *All the Colors of the Race* are dedicated to Adoff's own children and to "their brothers and sisters of every race and every wonderful blend of races." Adoff views faith in young people as the key to a hopeful future. This message is set forth in the book: It is "a presentation of power and love. Celebrate the meaning and music of your lives. Stand free and take control." The first poem in the collection is the title poem, and it expresses the intention of the book.

            All the colors of the race
            are
                  in my face, and just behind my face:
                                    behind my eyes:
                  inside my head.

            And inside my head, I give my self a place
                  at the end of a long
                              line   forming

it self into a
circle.

And I am holding out my hands.

The poem is accompanied by an illustration of the daughter's face looking outward with a hopeful expression and with hands flung upward.

The impact of and respect for heritage are expressed in three poems about the daughter's Jewish great-grandmother Ida, who came from a village in Poland to America. Ida's ancestry is traced in one poem, and her life in the United States is recounted in the second. "I Know We Can Go Back So Far" draws a parallel between the death of some of Ida's family members in the Nazi death camps of World War II with the deaths of the daughter's black great-grandmother's family members in the Civil War and in the slave trade.

The emotions and moods expressed vary from poem to poem, ranging from thoughtfulness to fear and from dreaming to playfulness. Throughout, hope and optimism transcend all else. Introspection is the prevailing mood in "I Am Making a Circle for Myself." Into this circle, the daughter is placing white and Jewish and black and Protestant because not to include all of these would mean that either her mother or her father remain outside the circle. She also is including Golda Meir, David Ben-Gurion, and Moses along with her Grandpa Jack. Fear is the dominant emotion in "Bad Guys," which recalls Sundays in Ohio when the family walks in the park and eats Sunday dinner out. The daughter notes that while most people smile at the family, an eye must always be kept out for any bad guys that might cross the family's path in their Sunday pleasures. The mood becomes playful in "A Song," as the daughter muses that she has the black forehead of black farmers but also has the Russian Jewish nose that bumps and jumps. Hope and optimism are summed up in a later poem: "Stop looking./ Start loving."

Adoff, who is white and Jewish, is married to acclaimed children's author Virginia Hamilton, who is black and Protestant. His poetry is a reflection of his own family's life and his sense of affiliation with all the colors and cultures that culminate in a unique self for each person.

Critical Context

Arnold Adoff was a pioneer in bringing the poetry of African American authors to young people, and he continued this tradition with his original poems for children and adolescents. His book of original poems *Flamboyan*, published in 1988, describes the life and dreams of a young girl who is of mixed racial heritage. In the mid-1990's, he was working on an anthology of women's poetry and an anthology of American Indian poetry, areas that Adoff believes have been neglected as much as African American poetry.

Adoff recognized early in his career that there was insufficient representation of black poetry in literature and in school textbooks. He set out to remedy this situation by organizing two anthologies that he hoped would represent the finest authors in content, racial vision, and message. *I Am the Darker Brother: An Anthology of Modern Poems by Negro Americans* was published in 1968 and was followed by *The Poetry of Black Americans*, an American Library Association (ALA) Notable Book for 1973.

Pivotal factors in Adoff's life were his early years as a member of a family to whom both music and reading were important and his experience of growing up in a mixed, working-class New York neighborhood. He discovered the literary works of Langston Hughes and Gwendolyn Brooks. Later, living in Greenwich Village and teaching in the Brownsville section of Brooklyn, he came into contact with black jazz musicians of his day. One musician, Charlie Mingus, became a role model for Adoff in communicating thoughts and feelings via rhythm and language.

The work of Arnold Adoff is recognized and appreciated by students, peers, and critics. His poems and poetry collections are used in classrooms to read both for pleasure and for analysis. They also serve as vehicles for discussion. His works have been honored by the ALA, the Child Study Association of America, the National Council for Social Studies, the International Reading Association, and the Children's Book Council.

All the Colors of the Race was an ALA Notable Book in 1982 and was cited for special recognition by the Jane Addams Peace Association in 1983. Adoff himself is the recipient of the poetry award bestowed by the National Council of Teachers of English.

Lynn Sager

ALONG CAME A DOG

Author: Meindert De Jong (1906-1991)
First published: 1958; illustrated
Type of work: Novel
Type of plot: Adventure tale
Time of work: Spring
Locale: A barnyard and a swamp
Subjects: Animals, emotions, and friendship
Recommended ages: 10-13

A determined dog proves his loyalty to a man and a toeless hen and, in so doing, finds a home.

> *Principal characters:*
> JOE, a poultry farmer who talks to animals
> LITTLE RED HEN, Joe's favorite animal because she alone survived a slaughter by wild dogs the previous year
> THE DOG, a black stray in search of a home

Form and Content

Along Came a Dog, by Meindert De Jong, is a Newbery Honor Book that tells the story of a lonely stray dog who is determined to have a home. He devotes himself to protecting a hen who is the farmer's favorite and who has recently lost her toes because of the frost. The man, Joe, repeatedly tries to "lose" the dog by driving him away from the farm, but the dog persists in his quest and quietly guards the hen throughout the long nights and while she broods under a willow tree. De Jong portrays the farm as a small community of one man and some animals who finally manage to trust one another.

The story is simple and at times exciting. The hen is often in danger because of her lack of toes, and the dog must be careful not to be seen by Joe. The illustrations by Maurice Sendak add to the text and help young readers visualize the story. The desperate wish of the dog to find a home is easy to relate to, whether the reader enjoys a stable family environment or struggles with a broken home, and the hen's need to fit into the flock is universal as well.

The Little Red Hen is Joe's favorite animal because she was the only chicken to survive an attack by wild dogs the year before. The new flock is white, but Joe holds the red hen dear. Unfortunately, when her toes freeze off, Joe is not able to protect her from the frenzied attacks of the flock that come because of her strange appearance and gait. She must fend for herself until the dog comes along and adopts her.

Joe initially distrusts the dog because of the tempting presence of the chickens, and so he drives the dog far away. The dog returns, however, and, unknown to Joe, becomes the Little Red Hen's guardian. The dog protects the hen, even though Joe believes that the dog has killed the hen and drives him even farther away. Each time that he is driven away, the dog comes back because of his belief that Joe will eventually accept him. When Joe realizes that the dog has been loyal and saved the hen's chicks from hungry hawks, he welcomes the dog into his home and assures the dog's place by promising to give him a name.

Analysis

The main theme of *Along Came a Dog* involves the need to be accepted. This theme is developed both through the dog's desperate attempts to find a home and through the hen's repeated returns to the flock even though she is attacked for being toeless.

Although Joe drives the dog away each time that he comes to the farm, the dog persistently returns because he knows that Joe is kind and good. He also knows that he needs a home, and he makes the farm his home even before Joe accepts him. The dog adopts the Little Red Hen and learns from her and the other chickens how to behave on the farm. For example, he learns that whole eggs are not for him, but broken eggs can be eaten without remorse or punishment. He also seems to know intuitively that the chickens are not for him to eat, although he would obviously enjoy them as a meal. Instead, he survives on the grain that Joe tosses on the ground for the flock, broken eggs, and some parsnips that he finds in last year's garden.

Although the hen does not seem to be explicitly aware of an emotional need to be accepted, it is necessary for her to be accepted by the flock in order to survive physically. Because of her lack of toes, she is lowered to the last position in the pecking order and, as a result, is often attacked by the easily enraged chickens. Consequently, she is often unable to eat without the dog's protection. Furthermore, because of her toeless feet, she is unable to grip the chicken ladder and therefore cannot sleep in the coop with the other chickens. She is forced to spend the long dark nights in the barnyard. If the dog did not accept her and decide to protect her, she probably would not have survived the dangers of the night. De Jong is careful to point out that all chickens are helpless in the dark, since they are unable to see anything without the assistance of light. As a result, whenever the hen is in danger during the night, she simply freezes in place and huddles wherever she is, making herself an easy target.

For children who are approaching their teenage years, the need to be accepted is a familiar one. Most children will be able to relate to the dog's desire and determination to prove to the man that he is loyal and deserving of Joe's trust and affection. Children will also be able to relate to the hen's confusion when she is attacked by the flock simply because of a slight defect that is beyond her control. Many children are teased for wearing glasses, for having freckles, or for having a handicap and are frustrated because they cannot change their situation. These children also feel confused because it is difficult to understand why someone would reject a person for a physical quality that cannot be altered.

A subtheme of the book involves prejudice. De Jong is careful to portray Joe as an animal lover. Joe refuses to kill the Little Red Hen when she loses her toes because of his affection for her, and he even tries to make her rubber toes. He is also the man to whom the boss comes when a prized mare cannot be quieted during a difficult labor. Joe assumes, however, that the dog will cause trouble simply because a group of dogs had killed the flock of red hens. Even though the dog is obedient and meek, Joe believes that he is a threat. He even accuses the dog of killing the Little Red Hen at the very time when the dog is faithfully protecting the hen and her eggs. The hen also experiences a kind of prejudice. Even though the white chickens know her, they fear and attack her because of her difference.

In both cases, the prejudices are shown to be irrational fears that are proven to be unfounded. The dog protects the hen, and the hen produces four chicks, which will enlarge the flock. In the end, Joe admits his mistake, lamenting that he almost killed the dog with his own hands before he knew the dog's loyalty and other admirable qualities. He promises to give the dog a name, which reinforces his acceptance of the dog as a member of the family.

Written at a time when issues of prejudice and friendship across societal boundaries were moving to the forefront of American life, *Along Came a Dog* confronts these issues in a nonthreatening way, and it quietly shows that friendship and loyalty can overcome the initial difficulties that differences may cause.

Critical Context

Animal stories have been a popular form of children's literature throughout history. From Aesop's fables to Jack London's dog stories, there is a long tradition of addressing important issues through the use of animals as characters. Meindert De Jong participated in this tradition, not only with *Along Came a Dog* but also with many of his other works, including *The Last Little Cat* (1961), *Puppy Summer* (1966), and *A Horse Came Running* (1970). Most of De Jong's works focus on the themes of loneliness and prejudice.

Although De Jong was seen as an old-fashioned writer toward the end of his career, in his prime he was well known and highly honored. He was awarded several Newbery honors, as well as the Hans Christian Andersen Award for the complete body of his work. His style may be dated, but his themes are universal and his characters—both human and animal—are well developed. He both acknowledges that prejudice exists in the world and offers hope that it can be overcome.

Amy Shollenberger

AMERICAN MODERN DANCERS
The Pioneers

Author: Olga Maynard (1902-   )
First published: 1965; illustrated
Type of work: Biography
Time of work: 1840-1960
Locale: New York; Los Angeles; San Francisco; Chicago; Bennington, Vermont; Germany; France; and England
Subjects: Dancers and educators
Recommended ages: 15-18

Maynard explains the origins and development of modern dance in the United States and situates this movement within a context of contemporary cultural and social events.

Principal personages:
FRANÇOIS DELSARTE, a French theoretician of movement and expression in the arts
MARY WIGMAN, a German dancer and teacher, a chief exponent of German modern dance
ISADORA DUNCAN, the originator and inspiration of modern dance in the United States
RUTH ST. DENIS, a dancer and founder with Ted Shawn of the Denishawn Dance Company
TED SHAWN, a dancer, dance educator, and founder of the Denishawn Dance Company and Jacob's Pillow
MARTHA GRAHAM, a dancer, choreographer, and founder of the Martha Graham Dance Company
DORIS HUMPHREY, a dancer, choreographer, and dance teacher
CHARLES WEIDMAN, a dancer and collaborator with Doris Humphrey
HANYA HOLM, a German modern dancer who taught dance in the United States
HELEN TAMIRIS, a dancer and choreographer

Form and Content

American Modern Dancers: The Pioneers follows the genesis of modern dance in the United States from its origins around 1900 through its development into an established art form by the middle of the twentieth century. Following an introduction, Olga Maynard divides her book into four chronological sections: "The Beginnings," "Denishawn," "The Burgeoning," and "A Summation." The book also contains an appendix with a diagram of the "family tree" of modern dance and endnotes that add further explanation to some of the topics mentioned in the text.

The first section, entitled "The Beginnings," examines the formative influences on American modern dance. This background reaches back to the mid-nineteenth century in Europe and encompasses the work of theorists and dancers in France, Switzerland, and Germany, including François Delsarte, who formulated laws of expression in the arts, and Émile Jacques-Dalcroze, who espoused the use of rhythm to connect music with body movement. A number of dancers in Germany created a modern dance movement. Among these figures, the ideas and dance style of Mary Wigman were most influential in the United States. In the United States, Isadora Duncan was the first modern dancer. Her approach to dancing was personal and unique. Her work was not fully appreciated in the United States, however, and she found greater acceptance in Europe.

The collaboration of two dancers, Ruth St. Denis and Ted Shawn, provided the real foundation of modern dance in the United States. St. Denis developed a personal vision of dance inspired by Oriental culture. Shawn began dancing as a form of physical therapy after a serious bout with diphtheria and then danced professionally in Los Angeles. He met St. Denis in New York. They married and established a dance company known as Denishawn. Their dance troop and school provided the training for many American modern dancers in the 1920's. Shawn later founded a male dance group and set up a dance center at Jacob's Pillow in New England.

By the 1930's, Martha Graham, who studied and danced with Denishawn, became the most recognized modern dancer in the United States. Her style was based on the fundamental elements of natural movement, and her dances were often introspective expressions of human emotions. Like Graham, Doris Humphrey also began her dance career with Denishawn; she broke away to develop her own approach to dance based on the idea of movement as fall and recovery. She teamed with Charles Weidman in many of her dances. Weidman also received his initial training with the Denishawn company. His particular contribution was to bring the elements of comedy, irony, and satire to dance.

Two other dancers made important and original contributions to American modern dance in these crucial formative years. Hanya Holm was a German dancer who studied with Wigman in Germany. In the early 1930's, Holm came to the United States and established a school that was significant for introducing the German modern dance approach, especially as practiced by Wigman. Holm trained a number of teachers who brought her system of dance into the curriculum of higher education in colleges throughout America. Helen Tamiris was more individual in her dance style. Her grace and spontaneous movement were reminiscent of Duncan. She also choreographed Broadway musicals.

By the middle of the twentieth century, modern dance was well established in America. There were many opportunities for aspiring dancers to participate in modern dance, from college campuses to a variety of schools and dance companies headed by important dancers such as Graham, Shawn, Humphrey and Weidman, and Holm. Audiences could view many different types of modern dance in performance by the companies and groups headed by these leaders of dance. They could also experience the influence of modern dance in the choreography for the musical theater. In many ways, modern dance had become an essential expression of American culture.

Analysis

The primary organizational principle of *American Modern Dancers* is biographical. Maynard presents, in basically chronological order, the successive figures who pioneered the development of modern dance in the United States. She concentrates on several key individuals: Isadora Duncan, Ruth St. Denis, Ted Shawn, Martha Graham, Doris Humphrey, and Charles Weidman. She presents an overview of their lives from childhood through a survey of the major steps in their careers. In each case, Maynard emphasizes formative influences and the basic and distinctive style or technique that characterizes their dance, and she explains their influential contributions to American modern dance.

Maynard introduces others who had an impact on modern dance in the United States. Many of these individuals were from Europe, and the author demonstrates the interrelationships between the theories and practice of modern dance in Europe and the United States. Examples include the nineteenth century theorists Delsarte and Dalcroze and the German school of modern dance. Maynard does not provide extensive biographical information about these individuals; rather, she integrates key aspects of their life and work into the context of their contributions, both direct and indirect, to American modern dance.

Another facet of American modern dance that emerges in conjunction with the author's essentially biographical approach is the role of dance in American education, especially higher education. Modern dance as a science of movement became a significant feature of the curriculum of physical education throughout the United States by 1950. Shawn developed a dance course in the physical education department at Springfield College in Massachusetts that drew many men into the field of modern dance. Holm's teaching system was especially influential in training teachers who went on to head dance programs at major colleges. This aspect of modern dance in the United States, although often overlooked, was ultimately more responsible than individual dancers for spreading the practice of modern dance and building support and appreciation of this dance form in the United States.

Maynard weaves together the biographies of major figures in American modern dance by placing them within their historical context. In particular, she connects aspects of modern dance with other developments in modern culture. Because dance is integrated with music, theater, and the visual arts, Maynard shows the points of contact among all these art forms. Dancers choreographed pieces to the music of contemporary composers, such as the famous piece *Appalachian Spring* that Graham created to accompany the music of Aaron Copeland. Likewise, modern artists contributed stage settings and provided inspiration for dance costumes.

Another aspect of the historical place of American modern dance is its relationship to social movements and political ideas. While some modern dance pioneers (such as Duncan) regarded dance as a pure art form, others (such as Graham and Humphrey) created dances that commented on social injustice or represented a reaction to the conservative trends of mainstream American culture. *Inquest*, one of Humphrey's most memorable dances, was based on the social indignities that the working class suffered in Victorian Britain. Graham refused to perform in Nazi Germany. Although many of these dancers were sympathetic to social causes, they refrained from using their dances for the purposes of political propaganda. Maynard's integration of the historical backgrounds of these dancers and their compositions shows that American modern dance in the first half of the twentieth century was not isolated but rather participated fully in the ongoing changes that characterized American culture and society.

Critical Context

Olga Maynard is a distinguished writer on the theatrical arts, particularly dance. She has written a number of books for adults, as well as several other books on the appreciation of ballet and opera for younger readers. Her works have been praised by critics for the enthusiasm that they display toward their subjects and the clarity with which Maynard presents complex developments in dance and opera.

American Modern Dancers remains the only book for a juvenile audience on the subject of modern dance as a whole. According to the author, the book is intended not only to relate the history of the foundations of modern dance in the United States but also to be used by teachers in conjunction with dance classes. From this perspective, the discussions of the techniques used by the dancers are particularly helpful. Because Maynard covers modern dance only up to the early 1960's, teachers using this book would need to find supplemental material that continues the story of American modern dance.

Karen Gould

AMERIGO VESPUCCI

Author: Nina Brown Baker (1888-1957)
First published: 1956; illustrated
Type of work: Biography
Time of work: 1463-1512
Locale: Peretola, Florence, and San Marco, Italy; Seville, Spain; Venezuela; Haiti; Lisbon, Portugal; and Brazil
Subjects: Educators and explorers
Recommended ages: 10-15

Amerigo Vespucci, like Christopher Columbus, explored the New World, but throughout his life Vespucci sought knowledge, not material wealth.

> *Principal personages:*
> AMERIGO VESPUCCI, an explorer whose life is followed from age twelve to his death
> UNCLE GIORGIO, a scholar and priest who guides young Amerigo into true learning at a monastery in San Marco
> DR. TOSCANELLI, in Amerigo's youth the world's greatest geographer and one of Amerigo's teachers at San Marco
> UNCLE GUIDO, a representative for the Medicis who brings Amerigo into the Medici business
> CHRISTOPHER COLUMBUS, an explorer who comes to Vespucci's company to obtain ships and supplies for his second voyage to the New World
> JUAN DE LA COSA, a ship's pilot who teaches Vespucci the practical side of navigation
> GIOVANNI VESPUCCI, Amerigo's nephew, who is taught by Amerigo and who accompanies him on his voyages
> ALONSO DE HOJEDA, a Spanish nobleman who investigates charges against Columbus

Form and Content

In twelve chapters, Nina Brown Baker sketches Amerigo Vespucci's life from age twelve in Peretola, Italy, to his death forty-nine years later in Seville, Spain. Through third-person narration, Baker puts in chronological sequence the major events that led Vespucci to be the man with the knowledge to perceive what Christopher Columbus and others did not know—that, in sailing west, they had come to a vast, unknown continent.

The first chapter of *Amerigo Vespucci* establishes the young boy's interest in charting the constellations. An incident also establishes his natural ability in business. In the second and third chapters, two of Amerigo's uncles help him become both scholar and businessman. By the fourth chapter, the adult Vespucci is a Medici representative in the import-export trade in Seville. In this position, Vespucci, in chapter 5, meets Columbus, who comes to Vespucci's company to outfit seventeen ships for his second voyage to the land that he believes is India. As Columbus leaves Spain for Hispaniola (now called Haiti), Vespucci is urged to come along but refuses.

In the sixth chapter, Vespucci is asked to investigate rumors of Columbus' cruelty as royal governor of Haiti. Vespucci sets forth on his first voyage to the land believed to be the Asian continent in 1499. The next three chapters recount Vespucci's explorations along the coast of what would become known as South America. Vespucci studies the changing positions of the known constellations as his ship moves south of the equator. After months of exploring, Vespucci arrives in Haiti to find that Columbus is to be returned in manacles to Spain. In chapter 10, Vespucci makes a second voyage to explore the land that he reached on his first voyage, sailing under the Portuguese flag. As master pilot, Vespucci plots the course of the fleet. On his second voyage, he concludes that the earth must be much larger than any mapmakers have ever calculated. Vespucci is the first to know that Columbus had not reached Asia but had landed on an unknown continent. In the eleventh chapter, Vespucci returns to Lisbon with much knowledge for the Portuguese king and the European world. Vespucci writes of the new continent to Lorenzo di Pier Francesco de' Medici. After the death of Medici, Vespucci's letters are published in Vienna. Cartographers agree with his new view of the world as it is expressed in the letters, and, when cartographers revise their maps, they name the new continent "America." The closing chapter reveals that although Vespucci had hoped to make other voyages, he was not destined to do so. He died in 1512, his health undermined by the malaria that he had contracted while in the New World.

Paul Valentino's illustrations show Toscanelli's map as it misled Columbus and others, as well as the route traveled along the South American coast by Vespucci on his second voyage. Valentino's pen-and-ink drawings also depict the sailing ships and the instruments used by mariners of Vespucci's time.

Analysis

A central theme—that the purpose of an individual's life is to add to the world's store of knowledge—unites the events that Baker selects to tell in *Amerigo Vespucci*. Vespucci becomes Baker's heroic embodiment of this theme.

Amerigo's preparation for adding to the store of knowledge began when Uncle Giorgio took him into the monastery for intensive schooling. During the fifteen years Amerigo studied, he copied maps for Dr. Toscanelli, then considered to be the world's greatest geographer. One copy of this map showing a globe-shaped world without the American continents was sent to an unknown sailor who wanted to sail west to reach India.

After Vespucci left the monastery, he went to Paris with another uncle who traveled as a representative of the Medici business. From this uncle, he learned business practices and social skills. Within two years, Vespucci himself worked for the Medici family. In 1491, he was the Medici representative in Seville, where he first met

Christopher Columbus, the sailor for whom he had copied the Toscanelli map and for whom he now equipped ships. These ships for Columbus' second voyage west would carry the men and supplies to colonize the Indies. Alonso de Hojeda, Columbus' second-in-command, teased Vespucci about coming along on the voyage, but, at forty-one, Vespucci saw himself as a businessman, not an explorer.

Hojeda returned to Spain after leaving the colonists with Columbus as the royal governor. After six years, rumors of Columbus' harsh rule reached Spain, and King Ferdinand ordered Hojeda to sail to the colony to observe Columbus' behavior. Again Hojeda asked Vespucci to accompany him. Although he refused to take part in the observation of Columbus, Vespucci agreed to serve as pilot. His lifelong study of the stars and sailing charts was put to practical use at last.

They sailed in May of 1499. Hojeda's two ships stayed with Vespucci's two until they reached the Cape Verde Islands; then Hojeda sailed due west while Vespucci headed southwest. Not wishing to be present when Hojeda investigated the charges against Columbus and wishing to explore, Vespucci crossed the equator and sailed along a coast believed to be a part of Asia. During the time that Vespucci completed his explorations and sailed to the Indies, the dispute about Columbus' cruelty had not been settled. Wanting to remain uninvolved, Vespucci left the Indies and sailed to the Bahamas for timber to repair his ships. When Vespucci returned to Spain in June of 1500, Columbus had been brought back and relieved of his position as governor of the Indies.

Vespucci's first voyage only whetted his desire to add to the store of geographic and astronomic knowledge. On his second voyage, begun in May, 1501, Vespucci suspected that the land mass known today as South America was not the continent of Asia. When the approach of winter drove Vespucci back to Europe, he carried with him new knowledge about navigation and about a new land. He believed that the world was bigger than the old cartographer Toscanelli had envisioned it.

Vespucci wrote of his newfound knowledge to Lorenzo de' Medici in Florence. When Medici died in 1503, Vespucci's letters were published as *Mundus Novus*; the book created a sensation. By 1507, cartographers meeting at a French university agreed that the land in the western Atlantic was a new continent. These cartographers named the continent "America" after the man who was the first to know that a New World had been discovered.

Although Amerigo Vespucci yearned to continue his explorations, he never sailed again. Nevertheless, his expertise was to be of use: King Ferdinand requested that Vespucci conduct a school of navigation for Spanish pilots. As pilot major, Vespucci continued to add to humankind's quest for knowledge until his death.

Critical Context

Amerigo Vespucci carries a clear message: Vespucci contributed to knowledge. Nina Brown Baker contrasts Columbus, who sought riches and power, with Vespucci, who practiced tolerance and sought the truth. Columbus lost all, while Vespucci kept his wealth and gained honor.

American writer Baker acknowledged that she wrote with a purpose and that she liked writing biographies. Out of the twenty biographies that Baker wrote, twelve feature heroes from nations other than the United States because, through their lives, she could promote an understanding of other cultures. Her first biography, *He Wouldn't Be King* (1941), celebrates Simón Bolívar. It won the Intra-American Award of the Society for the Americas. Her other biographies of foreign heroes include *Juarez: Hero of Mexico* (1942) and *Bruce: King of Scots* (1948). Baker's biographies of Americans include *Nickels and Dimes: The Story of F. W. Woolworth* (1954) and *Nellie Bly* (1956), which was reissued in 1972.

Baker's sixteenth biography, *Amerigo Vespucci*, exemplifies her method of writing. After reading from a number of authoritative sources, she made an outline of dates of significant events. In *Amerigo Vespucci*, the first event portrayed is Amerigo's being alone at night so that he can study the constellations. Other events that show his eagerness to learn make up much of the biography. In old age, he reaps the benefits of his learning: Continents are named for him and the king appoints him pilot major. Through this position, he passes on his knowledge to people who continue to explore and to contribute to knowledge.

Lana White

ANASTASIA KRUPNIK

Author: Lois Lowry (1937-   )
First published: 1979
Type of work: Novel
Type of plot: Domestic realism
Time of work: The late 1970's
Locale: Boston
Subjects: Arts, education, and family
Recommended ages: 10-13

Anastasia Krupnik comes to understand much about her family and her acquaintances during the event-filled year when she is ten.

> *Principal characters:*
> ANASTASIA KRUPNIK, a ten-year-old who is confronted with the
> impending arrival of a sibling
> MYRON KRUPNIK, Anastasia's father, who is a college professor and
> poet
> KATHERINE KRUPNIK, Anastasia's mother, who is an artist
> GRANDMOTHER KRUPNIK, Myron Krupnik's mother and Anastasia's
> grandmother
> MRS. WESTVESSEL, Anastasia's teacher

Form and Content

Anastasia Krupnik is a short novel about her tenth year, during which she learns about herself and others. Anastasia is the only child of a professor-poet father and an artist mother, and her life is a relatively happy one until a series of events causes her to consider her situation. First, she gets an F on a poem that she wrote for Mrs. Westvessel's class. Anastasia has written the poem in a style she learned from her father, but that style does not meet with Mrs. Westvessel's approval. Anastasia is humiliated and hurt until her father assures her that she is not a bad poet.

Soon the F seems a minor issue when she learns that her parents are expecting another child. Anastasia is unhappy with this turn of events: She considers the impending birth of her baby brother to be a humiliating and completely unnecessary occurrence. She thinks that her parents are much too old to be having a baby. "Thirty five is too old?" her mother asks. "You don't need a baby," Anastasia argues, "You have me." She decides that she will move out of the apartment to make room for the baby. Her father convinces her that she need not make that decision immediately.

Anastasia keeps a green notebook in which she lists the most important things that happen to her during her tenth year, and she has a page divided between "THINGS I LOVE" and "THINGS I HATE." During the course of the novel, several items jump back and forth between the lists as Anastasia revises her opinions.

During this year, Anastasia experiences a variety of revelations. She considers becoming a Catholic but ultimately changes her mind. She falls in love but again changes her mind. She dreads visits with her senile grandmother but comes to understand her.

Anastasia's grandmother is ninety-two years old and is losing touch with reality. Grandmother Krupnik cannot remember Anastasia's name or who her granddaughter is. Anastasia has a difficult time coping with her grandmother's wandering memory.

One of the hardest things to understand, she decides, is love. In her search for understanding of love, Anastasia listens to her grandmother talk about Sam, Anastasia's late grandfather, and learns something about her grandmother's younger life. She quizzes her parents about the love interests that they may have had before they met each other. She also spends some time considering her own feelings for Washburn Cummings, the boy she loves. He is also one of the items that jumps back and forth between her "THINGS I LOVE" and "THINGS I HATE" lists.

Ultimately, Anastasia experiences both loss and renewal. She is sad when her grandmother dies, but the cycle of life becomes clearer to her. When the birth of her brother occurs, she is faced with a choice that forces a degree of maturity. Anastasia has been given the responsibility of naming her new brother, and she does so in her own inimitable way.

Analysis

Anastasia Krupnik is a novel which seems so light that it is can be dismissed as merely another amusing children's or young adult's novel. That light appearance, however, hides the fact that the book covers some territory of considerable interest and significance to young readers. In the hands of a less-skilled writer than Lois Lowry, the book could easily have degenerated into the merely silly. As it is, this book is comic, enormously touching, and remarkably insightful.

The novel is primarily concerned with family—the way in which family members relate, the accommodations that they make to the demands of the family situation, and the insights that they acquire. The Krupniks are an example of one of the happier and more functional and loving families in children's and young adult literature. Even so, the adjustments that Anastasia must make in order to understand and flourish in her family are carefully and splendidly delineated by Lowry.

Anastasia is angry and unhappy at the discovery that she is no longer to be an only child, but she realizes the selfishness and egocentric nature of her attitude even as she experiences it. She is saddened and somewhat repelled by her senile grandmother, but she also realizes the sadness that both she and her parents feel at the clear deterioration of her grandmother's mental faculties.

Lowry's skill in character depiction is evident, and both the adults and the younger characters ring very true. Anastasia seems a credible, if very bright, ten-year-old girl. Her father and mother also seem to be believable, realistic parents of a ten-year-old girl. The writer resists the temptation to make any of the characters flat. Anastasia has definite negative impressions of her teacher, the man at the drugstore, and other people. She is forced to revise those opinions, however, upon further encounters. That people are more complex than any initial encounter might indicate is one of the themes of the novel.

Another theme is that Anastasia herself (and, by extension, the reader) is capable of change and growth in the light of developing events. She comes to understand her grandmother, to love her baby brother, and to see that her teacher and others are really not the people she has believed them to be. Indeed, one of the insights Anastasia acquires is the knowledge that teachers can make mistakes, that Anastasia herself is more than the mark she receives on a paper. Students are often conditioned by their school systems to accept their teachers' evaluations of them, believing that grades are equated with their self-worth. Lowry creates a rebuttal to that commonly held belief.

The sweetness and humor in the novel do not detract from its serious underlying themes, which is probably one of the reasons for the book's continuing popularity. Anastasia, her parents, and the supporting characters in the novel seem to be genuine, believable, and likable. The bibliotherapeutic uses of this novel are clear, and as an example of the functional family at work, the book may be difficult to surpass.

Critical Context

That Lois Lowry is a splendid writer for children and young adults is attested by the Newbery Medals that her books have earned. The first of these awards was for *Number the Stars* (1989), a book dealing with the efforts of Danish citizens to save their Jewish friends and neighbors from the Nazis during World War II. A second was for *The Giver* (1993), a fantasy/science-fiction book dealing with an oppressive cult. *Anastasia Krupnik* garnered no such awards, but it did engender numerous sequels; indeed, the Anastasia books have become like a series.

Series books are generally held in low regard by children's literature critics, although there are exceptions. Beverly Cleary's Ramona books are almost universally beloved, although whether these books could truly be classified as series in the same way as the Babysitter's Club books is debatable. Whether the term "series" could apply to the Anastasia books is also questionable, but the novels have been so popular that Lowry had written a total of nine books in the group by 1996.

Unfortunately, books as smoothly written, as light, and as humorous as the Anastasia books seldom reach the consideration of Newbery Medal committees. Nevertheless, these novels are high in quality and have significance. Teachers and students might become aware of them for the pleasures and the values they impart. Anastasia herself is an interesting, rounded, realistic character, and she seems to have found a place in the hearts of many young readers.

June Harris

AND QUIET FLOWS THE DON

Author: Mikhail Sholokhov (1905-1984)
First published: Volumes 1 and 2 of *Tikhii Don*, 1928 (English translation, 1934)
Type of work: Novel
Type of plot: Historical fiction and psychological realism
Time of work: 1913-1918
Locale: The Cossack village Tatarsk in the Don region, Russia
Subjects: Family, love and romance, nature, and war
Recommended ages: 15-18

    This novel depicts the harsh life and the dramatic fate of the prewar Don Cossacks, the changes imposed on them by World War I, and their political dilemma during the Bolshevik Revolution and the Russian Civil War.

    Principal characters:
        GREGOR MELEKHOV, a Don Cossack
        NATALIA, Gregor's wife
        AKSINIA ASTAKHOVA, Gregor's mistress
        STEPAN ASTAKHOV, Aksinia's husband
        PIOTRA MELEKHOV, Gregor's brother
        DARIA, Piotra's wife
        PANTELEIMON PROKOFFIEVICH MELEKHOV, Gregor's father
        ILINICHNA, Gregor's mother
        EUGENE LISTNITSKY, Aksinia's aristocratic second lover
        OSIP STOCKMAN, a Bolshevik
        ILIA BUNCHUK, a Bolshevik

Form and Content
    And Quiet Flows the Don depicts four periods in the life of a Cossack family: the harsh but simple, everyday realities of the rural, prewar Don region; the disruptive demands of war commitments, which separate families, take men away from the land, and bring sacrifice and loss; the confusing period of revolution, with competing political groups seizing and losing power; and the civil war that results from world war and revolution. The story begins with the Melekhov family, Cossacks with Turkish blood, who are neither aristocrats nor peasants, but independent, spirited warriors committed to land, horses, battle, and the czar. The oldest son of the family, Gregor, seduces his neighbor's wife, Aksinia, while her husband, Stepan, is away in the army. To end this affair, Gregor's father forces him to marry Natalia, a nice girl from a rich family, who is beautiful, hardworking, and in love with him. After the wedding, however, her sexual inexperience drives him back into the arms of the lascivious Aksinia, and their scandalous, open affair ultimately forces Gregor to leave his wife and family for the Listnitsky estate, where he and Aksinia live and work

together. After a confrontation with Aksinia, who bears Gregor's daughter, Natalia tries to commit suicide by falling on a scythe but recovers slowly, her neck permanently twisted. Although she comes back in shame to her father's house, she eventually returns to the arms of the Melekhovs, who feel deep affection for her and treat her like their own daughter. While Gregor fulfills his military service, his daughter dies, and Aksinia accepts the sexual advances of Eugene Listnitsky, becoming his mistress. Upon his return, Gregor learns the truth; disillusioned and jealous, he savagely beats Eugene, slashes at Aksinia, and returns to his wife's bed. Natalia bears twins, a son and a daughter, while Gregor serves at the front of World War I.

Gregor overcomes his aversion to killing and distinguishes himself in battle. Aksinia's husband tries to kill him on several occasions, but Gregor eventually saves Stepan's life. As winner of the Cross of St. George for bravely saving a wounded officer, Gregor becomes the pride of his village and of his father. At one point, he is reported dead and the family mourns, but he recovers to be wounded and cured several more times.

Gregor's first encounter with Bolshevik ideas was with Osip Stockman, who raised questions that made locals rethink their politics, but while in the hospital, Gregor falls under the influence of the Bolsheviks and is confused about which political direction to take. A subplot with machine-gunner Ilia Bunchuk explores the motives that led some Cossacks to fight on the side of the Bolsheviks. Gregor does so, briefly, and receives officer status. As the counterrevolutionary forces move forward and the Bolsheviks retreat, however, Gregor, disturbed by his choice, returns home to resume his civil life. When the Red Army gains strength again and approaches Tatarsk, the majority of Cossacks unite their forces to fight the Bolshevik army. The members of the Tatarsk regiment nominate his brother Piotra to be their leader and insist that Gregor join them to prove his allegiance. When the regiment joins the rest of the Cossacks, they find out that the Red Army has been defeated; however, they capture and execute a group of Cossacks who fought with the Reds, among them a former friend of Gregor, whose accusations of betrayal make Gregor verbalize the contradictions that sway his loyalties. The revolutionists die predicting the future success of their cause as Gregor turns away and returns home to the rich black soil of the Cossack land that calls to him from afar. The river Don flows ever onward, its beauty and its nature changing with the seasons, a natural life force that gives strength to the people touched by it despite changes of government and political confrontations.

Analysis

Mikhail Sholokhov's style in *And Quiet Flows the Don* is personal and inventive, with neologisms and other created words and images in Russian that are lost in translation, folk songs, prayers, and sayings, and a variety of dialects, including Cossack words related to unique objects and concepts of Cossack life. Metaphor dominates, even more than in the English translation, with recurring imagery that focuses on the natural, the animalistic, and the simple, commonplace farm and village experience. Characters and landscapes are like wolves, caterpillars, ants, and serpents.

One man chews his lip like a horse; another crows like a cock as he repeats the same old story. The czar is a horseradish, and the mist crawls "into the cliff like a grey, headless serpent." Aksinia is "like rain in autumn—one continual drizzle," and her thoughts drive away sleep "as wind does a haycock." The Don yawns, swallows, and lashes into fury. The personification of the Don and the recurring descriptions of its moods and seasons indicate that river's symbolic significance in the novel. The title sums up the essential argument that humans come and go but nature endures. It also captures the irony of the times, for the "quiet Don" is as far from quiet as the civil turbulence that envelopes the inhabitants along its banks.

The absence of authorial interruptions editorializing and lecturing readers on how to interpret characters and events requires a close textual analysis of the type accorded drama in order to determine value and meaning. No one of the competing voices and perceptions can be called representative of Sholokhov's views, except perhaps the central character, Gregor, whose perspective, interpretation, and loyalty constantly shift with changing times, situations, information, and influences. The clues to Sholokhov's personal values lie in the nature of the novel's descriptions, which eulogize the land and capture the violence and senseless destruction of war with brutal realism; the changed style of passages designed to denote unrealizable and perhaps foolish dreams of the future; and the recurring imagery that makes clear humanity's close ties to the land and to nature.

Despite critical claims that Sholokhov's novel is a brilliant example of socialist realism, it neither makes concessions to politics nor tries to beautify reality. It is stark and grim, carefully researched and historically accurate. For example, Sholokhov accurately describes the sore bottoms and poor horsemanship of the Red Brigade, whose machinists and city boys were unaccustomed to the seat of a horse. This portrait is in contrast to the opposing Cossacks, who were so at home astride a horse that they could stand in the stirrups and charge with saber swinging with deadly force. *And Quiet Flows the Don* captures the confusions and tragedy of the time, the regional loyalties, and the difficulty that participants had seeing an overview of those controversial years.

Critical Context

Sholokhov's novel is a classic text used mainly in classrooms for book reports or for drawing parallels with the American nineteenth century antiwar novel *The Red Badge of Courage* (1895), by Stephen Crane. Like Crane, Sholokhov relies on realistic details and verifiable facts to capture the violence, brutality, and horror of civil war. Like Crane too, he uses a detached and distant narrative voice to give the reader a sense of looking in on events as they happen rather than of being told what someone else has seen. Like Vicente Blasco Ibáñez in *Los cuatro jinetes del Apocalipsis* (1916; *The Four Horsemen of the Apocalypse*, 1918), he deplores the nightmare of trench warfare and the impersonality of machine guns and airplanes compared to brave Cossacks with raised sabers atop fiery steeds. Like Leo Tolstoy in *Voyna i mir* (1865-1869; *War and Peace*, 1886), he provides sweeping panoramas and detailed descriptions of battles, intermingling them with peaceful scenes of prerevolutionary Russian life. Where Tolstoy focuses on the Russian nobility, however, Sholokhov spans classes and shows Cossack life at all levels for the first time.

This novel should be particularly appealing to young people because it was written when the author was barely twenty years old, and his perceptions of age and love are youthful. For example, the love of the twenty-year-old Aksinia for Gregor is described as a "late love," and Natalia's sixty-nine-year-old grandfather is depicted as being as old as time. Nevertheless, the author's deep knowledge of history, his accurate depiction of historical events, and his realistic, credible characters confirm his maturity. Sholokhov lived most of his life among the Don Cossacks and grew up with eyewitnesses to the times and events that he describes; in a way, the people and families of his novel were a part of his personal life.

The full-length Russian original consists of four volumes, which were first translated into English as two separate novels: *And Quiet Flows the Don* and *The Don Flows Home to the Sea* (1940). Complete English translations were published as *The Silent Don* in 1942 and *And Quiet Flows the Don* in 1967.

Paulina Bazin and Gina Macdonald

ANDERSEN'S FAIRY TALES

Author: Hans Christian Andersen (1805-1875)
First published: Eventyr, 1835-1872 (as *The Complete Andersen,* 1949; as *Fairy Tales,*
  1950-1958; as *The Complete Fairy Tales and Stories,* 1974)
Type of work: Short fiction
Subjects: Arts, coming-of-age, gender roles, religion, and social issues
Recommended ages: 10-18

*Andersen wrote 157 tales, many based upon folklore, that deal with the complexities
of life and that often have wrongly been considered innocent stories for children only.*

Form and Content

Hans Christian Andersen's tales appeared nearly yearly in small collections from
1835 to 1872; the first complete edition was gathered during Andersen's lifetime as
Eventyr og Historier (1863-1874; fairy tales and stories); the English translation used
here is *The Complete Fairy Tales and Stories* (1974), by Erik Haugaard.

Andersen often imitated the magic tale—ancient, oral stories that begin with the
tantalizing "once upon a time" and, after many tribulations for hero or heroine, end
with the deeply satisfying "and then they lived happily ever after," as shown in "The
Traveling Companion" (1835), "The Tinderbox" (1835), and "The Wild Swans"
(1838). The same structure is used, if more freely, in "The Ugly Duckling" (1837),
"The Snow Queen" (1845), and in "The Little Mermaid" (1837). The protagonists are
striving for a goal, meet opposition, must pass tests, and finally are rewarded with
their dreams being realized: In "The Snow Queen," the powers of cold reason are
defeated, and heroine and hero are reunited; "The Little Mermaid" seems to fail the
tests that will grant her the prince's love, but she is nevertheless rewarded by being
the recipient of that which she desired most of all, not mortal love but an immortal
soul. These tales tend to be optimistic, but, more explicitly than the folktales, they
confront existential issues—such as growing up, dreaming oneself away from this
world, and even death. Andersen, however, always added touches of humor and could
even poke fun of these quest stories, as in "The Princess on the Pea" (1835) and "The
Talisman" (1857).

In other tales, among them those in which Andersen allows inanimate objects (for
example, a collar, a candle, a broken bottle, or a tin soldier) or animals (a butterfly, a
mole, a snail, or a sparrow) to have human voices, the effect is, as a rule, humorous,
but Andersen frequently views society satirically. "The Shepherdess and the Chimney
Sweep" (1845) reveals that women can be so brainwashed by patriarchal opinions that
they have no real chance of breaking away from the gender roles assigned to them. In
"The Emperor's New Clothes" (1837) and "Little Claus and Big Claus" (1835), the
plots of which stem from traditional trickster stories, humanity is depicted as medio-
cre, foolish, if not immoral. Although the humor of these comedies is rollicking, they
are, on the whole, dark and subversive.

Many of Andersen's tales rely on folk beliefs found in legends. These tales tend to voice Andersen's darkest insights into existence. In "The Shadow" (1847), the evil character marries the princess, and she proposes that they do away with the hero; the magic tale has been turned topsy-turvy. In "The Evil Prince" (1868), a ghastly dictator conquers the world in ghoulish ways, and, in "The Story of a Mother" (1848), a woman whose child has been abducted by Death refuses to give up on her baby and chases Death to his home, but in vain.

Andersen also wrote a number of realistic short stories: In "She Was No Good" (1855) and "The Little Match Girl" (1848), the reader encounters a class hierarchy that persecutes the poor. In some less realistic tales, however, Andersen gives an idyllic view of poverty, as in "The Nightingale" (1844) and "The Candles" (1872).

One essential aspect of Andersen's technique was his sense of detail, which gave his texts a rich texture. For example, the Snow Queen promises the young boy she abducts "the whole world and a new pair of skates," and when Andersen, in the same tale, wants the child to grasp the concept of the devil, he makes that evil entity concrete by calling him "the most evil troll of them all."

While the standard plots of the folktale genre are quite predictable, Andersen plays with those plots. He may imitate them fairly closely, but he may also add so much of his own or subvert the folkloric plot that the reader hardly knows what to expect.

Analysis

For readers who take Andersen seriously, as an author who probes into social, psychological, and religious issues, the impossibility of designating a single world-view as Andersen's may seem baffling. His views of life seem to fluctuate, and one text may easily contradict the next—for example, the harmonious tale "The Snow Queen" is placed next to "The Pine Tree" (1845), which ends with the unfulfilled protagonist dwindling into nothingness. A contrast can be detected by juxtaposing "The Ugly Duckling" with "In the Duck Yard" (1861). In the former, the ugly duckling goes through many hardships, but in the end all turns out well, for he is in reality a swan and has now found his true home. In the latter, a little songbird finds himself among philistines and eventually is destroyed. Both stories are strongly autobiographical: In one, a perfect future life is envisioned, and in the other a destiny that could have been Andersen's is imagined. Andersen wrote often about artists and art, but, once again, one should not expect consistency: In "The Nightingale," the artist is the vehicle for truth and beauty, and art is seen as a life-giving force; but in "The Flying Trunk" (1839), the artist is not only a parasite but also a subversive prophet of social change. In "The Professor and the Flea" (1868), the artist is a self-serving con man, and, in the late "Auntie Toothache" (1872), the artist belittles and rejects his own talent. Both the agony and the ecstacy of Romanticism speak through Andersen's tales: "The Nightingale" is a textbook example of harmonious Romanticism, in which the natural and the artificial in life are juxtaposed, and the natural emerges victorious; but in "The Shadow," the person inspired by romantic ideas is proven to be a fool and is destroyed.

One reason for the inconsistencies in the body of the tales may be found in Andersen's position as an artist. He had risen from poverty to the high bourgeoisie of Denmark, but to be accepted by such a culture meant to adapt to that society's values: His works had to please his audience. Consequently, some lesser stories are sentimental, overly pious, superficial, and filled with artistic compromises, but many others are exactly the opposite and in many of them one encounters a scathing view of Andersen's audience. For example, in "In the Duck Yard," the audience is, for all practical purposes, homicidal. In "The Professor and the Flea," the audience is compared to cannibals, and even in the optimistic tale "The Nightingale," the audience lacks any comprehension of the beauty of the bird's song. Darkness can be found in many supposedly happy tales.

This is especially the case whenever Andersen deals with sexuality. Even if many stories have happy endings, others show that sexuality can become a destructive obsession, as in "Under the Willow Tree" (1853) and "The Steadfast Tin Soldier" (1838), and that sexual attraction can be demonic in nature, as in "The Snow Queen" and "The Ice Maiden" (1862). Once again, Andersen sends an ambivalent message: In some texts, he seems to advocate spiritual love, as in "The Little Mermaid" and "The Bog King's Daughter" (1858), whereas in others the physical aspects of sexuality are deemed to be an essential part of humanity, as in "The Garden of Eden" (1839) and "The Butterfly" (1862).

A preoccupation with the spiritual-physical dichotomy also marks those tales in which Andersen deals with religious matters; some texts seem to be filled with piety, for it is demanded that human beings admit to their sinfulness and humble themselves in the dust before they can gain salvation, as in "The Red Shoes" (1845) and "The Girl Who Stepped on Bread" (1859); others are pantheistic, as in "The Bell" (1850). In some tales, Andersen leaves absolutely no doubt as to the existence of an eternal life, as in "The Dead Child" (1860) and "On the Last Day" (1852), whereas in "The Story of a Mother" Andersen has Death call afterlife "the unknown land." In "Auntie Toothache," Andersen finally admits that human beings can know little about "God, death and immortality." The tales, taken together, create a puzzling, fascinating, and unsettling ambiguity.

Critical Context

Hans Christian Andersen's tales made him world famous; his tales are translated into numerous languages, and the anthologies that continue to be published suggest that he is very much alive today. His other works—novels, plays, and poetry—have fared less well, but his lively travel chronicles—for example, *En Digters Bazar* (1842; *A Poet's Bazaar*, 1988)—have kept their charm. He has also had an impact on other writers of tales, who have often tried to interpret his complex texts by rewriting them; a notable example is the Dutch author Cees Nooteboom's *In Nederland* (1984; *In the Dutch Mountains*, 1987), in which "The Snow Queen" is playfully redone. The film industry has, naturally, taken to Andersen's fairy tales, for example with versions of *The Red Shoes* (1948) and *The Little Mermaid* (1989). These films tend to demonstrate how difficult it is to transfer the complexity of Andersen's tales to the big screen.

By using the ancient form of the tale in experimental ways, Andersen incorporates the entire gamut of human emotions, from rollicking comedy to bleakest tragedy, and in that span of emotions—as in his truly innovative narrative technique—lies his greatness.

Niels Ingwersen

THE ANIMAL FAMILY

Author: Randall Jarrell (1914-1965)
First published: 1965; illustrated
Type of work: Novel
Type of plot: Fantasy, folktale, and moral tale
Time of work: A pretechnological age
Locale: A forest next to an ocean
Subjects: Animals, coming-of-age, family, and love and romance
Recommended ages: 13-15

A lonely hunter, a recluse in a forest, creates a ideal substitute family by taking in a mermaid, a bear cub, a lynx, and an orphaned boy.

> *Principal characters:*
> THE HUNTER, a skilled and sensitive outdoorsman
> THE MERMAID, a seal-like creature with silvery blue-green hair who lives with the hunter
> THE BEAR CUB, an animal adopted as their first attempt to have a child from among the forest creatures
> THE LYNX, the second animal that they adopt
> THE BOY, an orphan found by the lynx and bear cub

Form and Content

The seven lyrically written chapters of *The Animal Family*, told by an omniscient narrator, give a simple yet psychologically complex revision of the old Scottish folktale of the seal-like selkie who is tricked into becoming the wife of a human being. In the original story, the selkie sheds its skin on the shore, revealing its lovely human form to a fisherman. He hides the skin and then takes the woman home and marries her. Long after becoming a devoted wife and mother, she discovers her original seal skin and escapes to the ocean, abandoning both husband and children.

Randall Jarrell's unnamed, orphaned hunter has built and furnished a one-room log cabin near the ocean, its floor covered with seashells and the skins of seals and deer. His sensitive, artistic nature is shown by the "fireplace of pink and gray and green boulders" brought from the shore and by the animals carved on some of the interior logs and the planks of the chairs.

Despite his comfortable and self-sufficient life, the hunter is troubled by dreams of his dead mother and father and by the lack of anyone to share his life. One night, the voice of a mermaid singing on the beach reminds him of his mother's singing. Seeing him, the mermaid promptly dives under the water, but each night they draw closer together as he attempts to repeat her songs. Finally, they learn each other's language.

Becoming quite adept at human speech, the mermaid learns how "new" and "different" the land is from the sea and chooses to live with the hunter, sleeping chastely on top of the bearskin comforter. He introduces her to fire; to the curiously human domestic comforts of furniture, dishes, and clothes; and to nursery rhymes and simple children's games. She tells him sea stories and brings him treasures from the sea, including a necklace of "gold and green and blue stones" and a ship's figurehead. At the end of their adjustment period, they are still very different, but to each other they seem "exactly alike" and they live happily.

A dream of his parents and their shadows disturbs the hunter. The mermaid interprets this bad dream as his need for a boy to fill that empty place inside him. They cannot have children, however, and are too remote from other humans to "beg or borrow or steal a child." When the hunter kills an attacking mother bear, he brings home the small cub to raise. Soon tamed, it is at first an attractive substitute child— inquisitive and playful. Yet, in less than a year, he becomes grown and wants only to eat and sleep. When the bear hibernates, the couple loses his company.

In the spring before the bear wakes up, the hunter steals a lynx cub from its mother as a surprise for the mermaid. This "spotted kitten big as a cat" soon becomes tame and proves much more playful, active, and intelligent than the bear. At three years, however, he is grown.

When the lynx discovers a dead woman and her live baby in a wrecked lifeboat, he and the bear herd the boy into the hunter's house, where he falls asleep. Both animals then lure the hunter and mermaid to the baby. At once, the mermaid recognizes how the boy is a fulfillment of their wish for a child. The hunter buries the dead mother, and together they care for the child.

The book concludes with the boy having become an inseparable part of their family. They teach him the ways of the sea and the land, so the boy is adept in both. After many days and years pass, the hunter, mermaid, and boy play a game, telling variant stories of how he came to live with them.

Analysis

The Animal Family is a autobiographical fantasy, a twist on a familiar folktale, and a sensitive, subtle psychological story of human maturation based on Jarrell's study of psychology.

Many of the story's details are drawn from Jarrell's own life. The setting is the California coast of his wife, Mary, whom he called his mermaid. According to a letter to her in 1951, the story began as ideas for a poem to be called "The Poet-Cook." The furnishings of the log cabin are from the couple's North Carolina home. The astute descriptions of the bear and the lynx are a result of the couple's frequent visits to the Washington Zoo while Jarrell was a poetry consultant at the Library of Congress. The story also reflects deep psychological details of the author's life, such as the trauma of his parents' early divorce. Jarrell's compensation for this separation anxiety is a child-centered world in which the child is the fusion of both parents and all living things around him.

As a fairy tale, the story gives a positive, comic twist to the familiar tragic Scottish love story of the selkie and the fisherman. Unlike that tricked but dutiful mermaid, the seal wife in Jarrell's fairy tale retains her shape and freedom while choosing to remain on land. The story never spoils the fantasy by having the mermaid give birth or even describing how she is able to move about on land given her seal shape. In moments of crisis, the hunter picks her up and carries her. Like a true sea creature, she proves an inept cook and housewife on land, but the hunter cheerfully takes over most of these chores.

The psychological dimensions of the story make it superior to Jarrell's other three children's books: *The Gingerbread Rabbit* (1964), *The Bat-Poet* (1964), and the posthumous *Fly by Night* (1976). Change and metamorphosis operate throughout the story. From the beginning, the hunter is identified both with animals and with the mythical hunter Orion. Just as he recalls the songs of his mother in the singing of the mermaid, other details and bits of dialogue are recycled throughout the story.

The hunter's Freudian/Jungian dreams for a family are fulfilled by the mermaid and the boy. Together, the mermaid, bear, lynx, and boy come to enrich the artistic, spiritual, and emotional life of the hunter. To the bear and lynx, he is a tamer and an indulgent observer. For the mermaid, he is an instructor and a companion. For the boy, he becomes a role model.

The bear and the lynx represent the familiar stages of baby and infant by their actions and their ages of maturity. When the boy first appears, he calls the lynx "Kitty, kitty," representing the third critical stage of human development, familiar from developmental psychology: the acquisition of speech. The remainder of the story deals with how speech and stories are used by the boy and his parents to organize, explain, and manipulate human experience.

Critical Context

The Animal Family belongs to the second "golden" age of children's literature in the 1960's when editors encouraged successful adult writers to write books for children. In 1961, Michael di Capua, then a young junior editor at Macmillan, invited Jarrell to translate a few fairy tales by the Brothers Grimm and to write his own children's books. Published after two translations of fairy tales and two original books, *The Animal Family* received rave reviews from such writers as P. L. Travers and John Updike. It was a Newbery Honor Book in 1966 and received the Lewis Carroll Shelf Award in 1970. The visual images conjured by the words were so compelling that Maurice Sendak restricted his work to "decorations" for the book, landscape settings with no figures present. The result is an exceptionally harmonious blend of text and illustrations.

A few critics mistakenly connect Jarrell's story to Hans Christian Andersen's lachrymose mermaid tale. For most readers and critics, however, *The Animal Family* is not only Jarrell's best children's book but also a modern classic still read in both hard-cover and paperback editions. It is often compared to Antoine de Saint-Exupéry's *Le Petit Prince* (1943; *The Little Prince*, 1943), another book for both children and adults. Jarrell's transformation of a stern folktale into a psychological fairy tale realizes the promise of the book's prefatory quotation from Rainer Maria Rilke: "Say what you like, but such things do happen—not often, but they do happen." Jarrell made such things possible.

Hugh T. Keenan

ANNIE JOHN

Author: Jamaica Kincaid (1949-   )
First published: 1985
Type of work: Novel
Type of plot: Psychological realism
Time of work: The 1950's and 1960's
Locale: The Caribbean island of Antigua
Subjects: Coming-of-age, emotions, friendship, and gender roles
Recommended ages: 13-18

Annie John, reared on a tiny Caribbean island, experiences an Edenic childhood until puberty, when the natural growing-up process leads to a traumatic separation from her mother and culminates with Annie's traveling to England at age seventeen.

> *Principal characters:*
> ANNIE JOHN, a young girl, who must create her own identity apart
>   from her mother's as she matures
> HER MOTHER, also named Annie, a homemaker who instills in Annie
>   the traditional lore and culture of the island
> GWEN, a girlfriend of Annie John
> THE RED GIRL, another girlfriend, who appeals to the rebellious side of
>   Annie John

Form and Content

Annie John, a slim novel—the chapters of which originally appeared as short stories in *The New Yorker*—is a first-person account of the childhood and adolescence of Annie John, a girl reared on the small Caribbean island of Antigua.

Annie experiences a childhood paradise. Her island home explodes with bright colors: the brilliant, flamboyant flowers, white sand, and blue sky and sea. The close community nurtures her. Mr. Earl and Mr. Nigel catch the fish that Annie and her parents eat. Mr. Kenneth, the butcher, offers Annie a piece of raw liver, one of the few foods that she enjoys, and Miss Dewberry bakes the buns that Annie's parents serve at tea. Annie is also part of an affectionate and supportive family. Together, she and her father, a carpenter, select the lumber that he will fashion into her bedroom furniture. Most important, however, Annie loves and is loved by her mother. Her mother teaches Annie about washing (white clothes are to be bleached by the sun on a stone) and about cooking traditional dishes (such as pumpkin soup, banana fritters, and stewed salt fish)—skills that Annie will need when, it is assumed, she establishes her own household on the island. Annie enjoys the days spent with her mother, days filled with walking to the grocer's; arranging her mother's trunk that holds memorabilia such as Annie's wool booties, certificates of merit, and dresses worn on special occasions; bathing together in water seasoned with bark, bay leaves, and flowers; and wearing dresses patterned after her mother's. Yet, the closeness with her mother cannot last, since Annie will need to create her own existence separate from her mother's, as her mother realizes. Thus, one day her mother purchases different fabrics for their dresses, shocking Annie. From then on, Annie's world has changed.

Annie spends her adolescence in a love-hate relationship with her mother: "I missed my mother more than I had ever imagined possible and wanted only to live some-where quiet and beautiful with her alone, but also at that moment I wanted only to see her lying dead, all withered and in a coffin at my feet." Annie longs for the love and the closeness that once was even though she often incurs her mother's displeasure by playing marbles or dawdling on the way home from school and then lying about her actions. Her rebelliousness leads her to steal books from the public library and to befriend the Red Girl, who climbs a tree to pick guavas like a boy, not throwing stones to dislodge the fruit as a girl should.

The conflicts of adolescence lead Annie to sail to England at the age of seventeen to study nursing, not a career that she desires but one that offers an escape from the island. As she walks between her parents to the jetty, her departure is edged with conflicting emotions. She, "on the verge of feeling that it had all been a mistake," almost regrets her decision: "I don't know what stopped me from falling in a heap at my parents' feet." On the other hand, she wants to escape the "unbearable burden" that her life has become and escape to "a place where nobody knew a thing about me."

Analysis

Annie John is about the complex process of maturation, a child's transition from the world as circumscribed by parents to a larger one in which parents are no longer central. The process involves recognizing one's mortality. Annie, intrigued by death, first watches mourners in a cemetery, then, unknown to her mother, attends funerals of acquaintances as well as of strangers. When her mother prepares a child for burial, Annie is fascinated and repelled by her mother's hands. Even though her island world is limited, Annie's coming-of-age experiences are universal: her hesitation and excite-ment at going to a new school, her boredom with the slow pace of the classes, her concern about making friends, and her devotion to a best friend.

The maturation process also involves coming to terms with the strangeness of one's own changing body. Meeting secretively among the tombstones, Annie and her friends rub their breasts: They have heard that breasts will grow if a boy massages them and, since they have no contact with boys, they must do the task themselves. Familiar to all young women will be Annie's surprise at the "small tufts of hair" under her arms and her confused response when she starts menstruating.

The physical changes are small, however, compared to the psychological ones. Annie must travel from a oneness with her mother to a separation from her, from an Edenic childhood to an adolescence fraught with deception, anger, and isolation. She visualizes her profound unhappiness as taking "the shape of a small black ball, all wrapped up in cobwebs" and believes that "everything . . . had turned sour," even her friendship with the beloved Gwen with whom she could not share her sadness: "How to explain to her about the thimble that weighed worlds, and the dark cloud that was like an envelope in which my mother and I were sealed?" The emotional trauma becomes so great that Annie succumbs to a physical illness, replete with high fevers and hallucinations. Her illness mystifies the doctors but is treated with an herb-filled sachet and vials of fluids by Annie's grandmother and a local obeah woman, both versed in folk remedies. After three months, Annie recovers but feels constricted by the island and her mother. For Annie, the closeness that sustained her in childhood is suffocating her as she matures.

The maturation process involves being aware of one's culture, but it also means being able to see beyond one's community to the larger world. The novel paints a vivid picture of the island culture: the daily activities and occupations of the residents; the variety of food ranging from dasheen, figs, and breadfruit to the many edible fish such as angelfish, kanya fish, and lady doctorfish; and the folklore, including the prevalent belief in the spirit world and in the ability of herbs and elixirs to combat evil.

Part of the island's history is its legacy of racism and colonialism. Annie, in her schoolgirl way, defaces a textbook page with a negative comment about Christopher Columbus, who represents for her exploitation and colonialism. She looks with sadness at a young English classmate, knowing that the girl had to bear the burden of "the terrible things her ancestors had done." Annie's understanding of the political world is unusual for one so young.

Critical Context

Annie John is one of the first novels to examine the complex relationship between mother and daughter, a bond that although nurturing in the child's early years, turns oppressive in the teenage ones. It chronicles the need for a separation between a parent and child in order for the child to establish autonomy. Although the break in Annie's case is traumatic, it need not be so. The themes of *Annie John*, Jamaica Kincaid's first novel, are continued in *Lucy* (1990), a novel about a young woman's experiences after leaving her Caribbean island home. Although the protagonist is named Lucy, the novel could easily be the continuation of Annie's story. An earlier work, *At the Bottom of the River* (1983), a collection of short stories, also explores, in a prose filled with surreal images, the mother-daughter relationship.

Jamaica Kincaid is familiar with her subject matter. She herself grew up on Antigua and left, like her protagonists, at seventeen, not to return for nineteen years. For her, the rupture with her mother was occasioned by the birth of a brother when Kincaid was nine, to be followed by two more; the brothers occupied her mother's time and also were considered for opportunities that she was not. Although her fiction is autobiographical, it goes beyond simply a recounting of events and moves into literature characterized by an accomplished prose with lyrical repetitions and rhythms. Kincaid's fiction is not specifically aimed at a young adult audience, but these readers will benefit from the insight evident in Kincaid's description of coming-of-age.

Barbara Wiedemann

ANPAO
An American Indian Odyssey

Author: Jamake Highwater (1942-   )
First published: 1977; illustrated
Type of work: Novel
Type of plot: Allegory and folktale
Time of work: The beginning of time to the arrival of Europeans in North America
Locale: North America
Subjects: Nature, race and ethnicity, and social issues
Recommended ages: 13-18

In this award-winning epic saga, which combines American Indian legends from many tribes, Anpao journeys to the Lodge of the Sun and takes an allegorical trip from the beginning of time to the coming of white people to North America.

> *Principal characters:*
> ANPAO (AHN-PAY-OH), a young man who journeys to the Sun
> KO-KO-MIK-E-IS, the maiden who sends Anpao on his journey
> MOON, the wife of the Sun
> OAPNA, the opposite or contrary twin brother of Anpao
> SUN, a powerful being and the father of Anpao
> WASICONG, a holy man and the narrator of the story

Form and Content

Anpao: An American Indian Odyssey is written as a series of stories within a story. In his "Notes on Sources" and bibliography, Jamake Highwater briefly discusses these tales and legends, often noting their tribal origins and indicating where other versions can be found. Highwater also includes a section called "The Storyteller's Farewell." In it, he explains his reasons for writing the book and outlines the meanings that he hopes readers will find.

According to the story told by Wasicong, Anpao and his "contrary" twin brother, Oapna, know nothing about their past. While they are traveling the world, Anpao falls in love with the beautiful Ko-ko-mik-e-is, whose name means "moon" ("night-red-light"). Although she has refused all other men, she tells Anpao that she will marry him if he will journey to the Lodge of the Sun to have the scars removed from his face. Knowing that no one has made such a journey, Anpao nevertheless accepts and Oapna agrees to accompany him.

After the journey begins, Oapna is kidnapped by the Moon. With the help of an old swan-woman, Anpao makes a daring rescue. The swan-woman then tells the twins the story of how Old Man created the world and how a foolish woman created death. This woman later went to the World-Above-the-World, became the mistress of the Sun, and had a child named Anpao. When the woman tried secretly to return to the earth with her child, the Sun killed her. Although Anpao survived the fall to the earth, his mother's blood became the scars on his face and he could remember nothing about his past. Reared by Grandmother Spider, Anpao was playing with his hoop and cut himself in half, becoming Anpao and Oapna. Grandmother Spider then sent the boys out into the world. When Anpao learns about his past, the two opposite parts of his personality (Anpao and Oapna) reunite, and Anpao continues his journey. In his travels, he meets Snake Boy, Deer Woman, Turtle, and Farting Boy, and he learns about corn, deer, and buffalo. Finally reaching the Lodge of the Sun, Anpao saves Morning Star, the son of the Sun and Moon, from the terrible birds.

After the Sun removes his scars, Anpao returns to the earth. Unfortunately, destruction is everywhere. Believing the end of the world has come, Anpao hurries to reach Ko-ko-mik-e-is. He meets Smallpox, who is bringing death to the people and who tells Anpao about the Big Knives that have come from the East, across the great water.

Tricking Smallpox, Anpao hastens to the village of Ko-ko-mik-e-is. The people will not listen, however, when he tries to tell them about the terrible things that are coming. Finally, Anpao takes Ko-ko-mik-e-is and flees to the safety of a village below the surface of a great water. It is here, according to Wasicong, that they reside today.

Analysis

The prose saga of *Anpao* is a blending of history and myth, for within the novel are two distinct journeys. First is the trip through American Indian legends that the boy undertakes on his quest to find the Lodge of the Sun. The story of this journey, written with the cadence of the storyteller, incorporates many techniques found in the oral tradition. The voice of Wasicong, the storyteller, is formal as in Western European epics. The settings are intentionally vague, with many flat, one-dimensional characters and many stereotypes and symbols. Each adventure represents at least one of the four main types of American Indian myths: family drama, trickster tale, transition story (from life to death), and passage through the animal world. As he makes his journey, Anpao learns about many things that became important in American Indian culture, such as corn and buffalo, and about the respect that people should have for nature, animals, and their elders. The final uniting of Anpao and Ko-ko-mik-e-is can be seen as the unification of the Sun and Earth (Anpao) with the Moon (Ko-ko-mik-e-is).

This first journey of Anpao has been compared to parts of Homer's Greek epic *The Odyssey*. Just as *The Odyssey* blends stories from various parts of the ancient Aegean world into the adventures of a young boy on a quest to become a man, *Anpao* draws its tales from a variety of American Indian tribes. Among the tribes represented are the Blackfeet, Kiowa, Cheyenne, Papago, Zuni, and Sahaptian.

The other journey is a trip through the history of American Indians from the beginning of time to the coming of white people in an attempt to explain American Indian culture and values and to show what can happen when two different cultures interact. In the first part of the book, Anpao sees the world that American Indians have grown to love and understand. When he returns from the Lodge of the Sun, however, he sees the effects of the coming of the Big Knives. The Big Knives, and their ally Smallpox, seem intent on destroying the traditional American Indian world. Although

Anpao sees this fate, he is not successful in preventing it.

Some critics see Anpao's final descent below the waters as an attempt to save the traditional values from certain destruction. After his quest, Anpao has returned to save his people. Although not all will follow him, a few go with him to the village beneath the water, where they are waiting to return and lead their people again. At the end of the book, Highwater uses words from a song of the Ghost Dance movement of the late nineteenth century to predict that the traditions kept alive by Anpao and Ko-ko-mik-e-is will return to earth.

Other critics, however, see a much darker message. To them, rather than the person who saves American Indian traditions, Anpao is a failed leader who abandons his people. Although he is given several gifts by the Sun and the Moon, including a horse and magical raven feathers, and is told to construct a medicine lodge that resembles the Lodge of the Sun, Anpao uses none of his gifts except the horse. He takes the secret of the Sun's medicine lodge with him to the underwater village, where it cannot be used by people on the earth. Just as in the stories of Old Man (the creator), Snake Boy, and Turtle, water becomes a symbol of death.

The theme of death is found throughout the book, not only in the stories of Deer Woman and Smallpox but also in the illustrations. An owl, the Navajo bird of death, precedes part 1 of the book, foreshadowing the events to follow. Introducing the last section is a drawing of a skeleton, a universal image of death.

Critical Context

Anpao was published at a time when people were beginning to realize that American Indians had a "literary" heritage that was well established when the first explorers came to the North American continent. The novel was named a 1978 Newbery Honor Book and received a *Boston Globe*/Horn Book Honor Award. In addition, it was named a Best Book for Young Adults in 1978 by the American Library Association. With *Anpao*, Jamake Highwater became the first author to unite tales and legends from a variety of American Indian tribes into a single story.

Highwater continued to explore the history of American Indians and the decline and fall of their world in many of his other books for young adults, including his Ghost House Cycle: *Legend Days* (1984), *The Ceremony of Innocence* (1985), *I Wear the Morning Star* (1986), and *Kill Hole* (1992). Beginning shortly before the arrival of white people in North America, these partially autobiographical novels follow the story of Amana Bonneville, her daughter, and her grandsons. Like Anpao, Amana, a member of the Blackfeet tribe, sees her people destroyed by disease and the traditions of the past replaced by alcohol and the values of the Europeans.

Along with N. Scott Momaday, Leslie Marmon Silko, James Welch, and Simon J. Ortiz, Highwater is given credit for beginning the writing of serious American Indian fiction. He sees his works as forming a bridge between the private, traditional world of American Indians and the public, often-destructive world of Western Europeans.

Katherine T. Bucher

THE ARABIAN NIGHTS' ENTERTAINMENTS

Author: Unknown
First published: Alf layla wa-layla, fifteenth century (English translation, 1706-1708)
Type of work: Short fiction
Subjects: Love and romance, social issues, and the supernatural
Recommended ages: 13-18

This marvelous collection of Middle Eastern folktales has influenced Western literature since the early eighteenth century and continues to influence popular culture.

Form and Content
The Arabian Nights' Entertainments, sometimes referred to popularly as *A Thousand and One Arabian Nights*, consists of interwoven folktales told by a new bride to her misogynistic husband. After executing his adulterous wife, King Shahriyar of Persia persuades himself that women are naturally unfaithful and resolves to marry a new bride each night and execute her the next morning, before she has a chance to betray him. After three years, wise Shahrazad, the eldest daughter of the grand vizier, volunteers to marry the king. That night, she starts to tell a fascinating story about a merchant's dealings with Jinni (genies), supernatural spirits who, according to Muslim belief, occasionally interact with human beings. As the night passes, Shahrazad leaves her story unfinished, connecting it to a further story. The king is enchanted by the ever-growing series, and she is granted reprieve after reprieve as the marvelous tales continue. Finally, after a thousand and one nights and many more interwoven stories, the king repents of his evil ways and accepts his clever bride.

Most of the stories in the collection feature the dovetailing of the marvelous and the mundane; merchants, sailors, and explorers struggle against magicians, monsters, and villainous Jinni. Not all stories concern supernatural events; some are simply clever tales about human error. For example, in "The Story of the Humpback," four cowardly characters—a tailor, a physician, a sultan's steward, and a broker—are on trial for the death of a hunchback. In the first part of the tale, a hunchback apparently suffocates while he is being entertained by a tailor and his wife. Afraid of being tried for murder, the tailor carries the corpse to a physician's house and leaves him in the lobby. The doctor, accidentally kicking the corpse in the dark, concludes that it is he who has killed the man. Like the tailor, the doctor fears that he will be accused of murder and sneaks the corpse into the house of a local sultan. The sultan's steward also mistakenly "kills" the man and is also afraid of punishment; the steward carries him to the marketplace, placing him against a post. In the marketplace, the drunken broker bumps into the corpse and, thinking that the hunchback is mocking him, strikes him several times. When the hunchback falls over, the broker is convinced that he has committed murder and finds himself arrested by the city guard. Soon, all four men stand accused before the sultan. After each man tells of his own background, a barber revives the hunchback, who had passed out after choking on a fishbone.

Set against such satiric tales, other stories applaud human achievement, especially the tales of Aladdin, Sindbad, and Ali Baba. Still other, less well known tales are more ambiguous about human abilities. In "The City of Brass," for example, a caliph hears about Solomon's authority over Jinni and how he sealed spirits who would not accept God in lead bottles. Intrigued, the caliph orders Musa, his general, to find a bottle, rumored to be in a fabulous metallic city far away on the plains of Africa. When he reaches the deserted city, Musa is struck by its magnificence but realizes that for all its glory, it is little more than a sepulchre for a dead race. Thus chastened, Musa returns to Baghdad with bottles in tow, regretting the years of his life lost serving the whim of a caliph.

Analysis

Although English-speaking audiences have been familiar with this collection since the early eighteenth century, much about it, such as the place and date of composition, remain unknown. Some scholars believe that the earliest tales were composed in the eighth century, with additions until the sixteenth. Others are certain that the work was more or less set by the thirteenth century. Almost all scholars are convinced that no single author created the more than one thousand stories in the collection. Like other works composed orally before they were printed, existing manuscripts vary widely, with different versions containing different stories and arrangements. It is likely that the original collection consisted of a new framework imposed on preexisting folktales from Arabia, Iran, India, and perhaps other countries. There is some evidence to support this theory in the amassing of stories about heroic characters in the collection. There are seven voyages of Sindbad, for example, which probably represents the addition of several later stories to a few original tales about the intrepid merchant.

The stories provide some insight into Middle Eastern culture during the tenth through the thirteenth centuries. Although care must be taken in extrapolating too far, these stories suggest a worldview in which each human action reveals a divine plan, in which taking a wrong turn might actually fulfill one's destiny. For example, after a disastrous voyage, in which he falls off his ship and faces a variety of magical dangers, Sindbad finds himself at the exact port in which his ship has landed; his former shipmates eventually recognize him, and his goods are restored. Economically, he is none the worse for the experience; personally, he is much enriched.

The Arabian Nights' Entertainments contains recognizable motifs and themes for young adult readers, although they are dressed in the trappings of different cultures: triumphing over danger, turning hatred into love, and confronting the mysterious in the universe and inside oneself. Shahrazad implicitly demonstrates to young readers that cleverness and kindness will win out over evil. Other readers might learn about themselves in stories such as "Aladdin and the Wonderful Lamp," which suggests that even a poor youth can succeed.

It is probably as a result of themes such as these that *The Arabian Nights' Enter- tainments* has become a staple of young adult literature. The stories that Shahrazad tells are about young people confronting cunning, seemingly more powerful elders. Young people have always had to grow into an understanding of the mysterious, sometimes bewildering culture that surrounds them. Reading about others confronting the same fundamental conflicts allows young readers to examine their problems from a fresh perspective. While young people today are not likely to encounter Jinni in magical rings or lamps, to argue that fact is missing the point: The tales are object lessons about the often-painful lessons of growing up.

Critical Context

The popularity of *The Arabian Nights' Entertainments* has only increased since it was first translated into English between 1706 and 1708. That is an ambitious statement, since the collection set off a wave of enthusiasm for things Middle Eastern during the eighteenth and nineteenth centuries. Samuel Johnson's novel *Rasselas* (1759), the story of an Ethiopian prince, was heavily influenced by *The Arabian Nights' Entertainments*. The novel replicates the style of the collection, particularly in the names of characters and in their manner of speaking to one another, but the resemblance between the two works is only skin deep. The eighteenth century novel was a vehicle for moral instruction above all, and Johnson's purpose was to mimic the grandeur and mystery of *The Arabian Nights' Entertainments* without making use of supernatural elements, which were thought improbable at best and superstitious at worst.

Another late eighteenth century novel indebted to this collection was William Beckford's *Vathek* (1786), which purports to be the story of Haroun al'Raschid's grandson, another caliph of Baghdad. Unlike Johnson, however, Beckford charged his work with the occasional supernatural atmosphere of the Arabian collection; where Aladdin or Sindbad the sailor might persuade a genie to rescue them from desperate danger, however, Beckford steeps his character in unholy magic. To win the secret of eternal life, for example, Vathek goes to excessively evil lengths, such as murdering children and making a pact with an infernal spirit. Vathek's callous disregard for any human life but his own essentially turns the reader's sense of wonder into a sense of disgust.

To a certain extent, the collection was given to an English-speaking audience at the right time, since Great Britain was beginning to extend its empire. In this sense, geographical imperialism was mirrored by literary imperialism. For example, Sir Richard Burton, a nineteenth century explorer who traveled through Africa and the Middle East, also translated *The Arabian Nights' Entertainments*. Since the nineteenth century many Western writers have been influenced by the collection: a partial list includes Henry Rider Haggard, Robert Louis Stevenson, and John Barthes. Further, such figures as Aladdin, Ali Baba, and Sindbad have featured in several films directed for young audiences, none of which are close in either content or atmosphere to the stories in this collection. Be that as it may, these various folktales anthologized by Arab writers during the Middle Ages have certainly become a part of Western culture.

Michael R. Meyers

THE ART OF ANCIENT GREECE

Author: Shirley Glubok (1933-   )
First published: 1963; illustrated
Type of work: Art
Subjects: Arts and religion
Recommended ages: 10-13

This informative and introductory survey of all forms of art in ancient Greek society also explores the relationship between art and such aspects of culture as religion, politics, and everyday experience.

Form and Content

Shirley Glubok's *The Art of Ancient Greece* provides a plethora of information on both the techniques and the content of ancient Greek art. Her book, written with the interests of the younger reader in mind, serves as a solid—if not primary—introduction to the subject. Glubok's admiration for ancient Greek art guides her discussion throughout the book. The work is not lengthy, but it contains a wealth of important information for the novice to the world of art and archaeology.

The layout, designed by Oscar Krauss, provides copious illustrations on every page, with contributions from many significant art collections. In total, twenty major museums are represented, from the Museum of Fine Arts, Boston, to the Delphi Museum in Greece. Furthermore, *The Art of Ancient Greece* includes many of the most important and famous examples of certain styles, techniques, or works themselves; the Venus de Milo and Myron's *Discobolus* (discus thrower) are notable examples. Consequently, some illustrations contain nudity, but its appearance is neither extensive nor gratuitous, as it is an important component for understanding ancient Greek culture and art.

Glubok's work provides a highly serviceable examination of pottery painting, sculpture, architecture (including the Parthenon), jewelry, and coins; the illustrations represent all these art forms. In addition, Glubok provides brief definitions of concepts important to art, such as shape, line, and balance; offers introductory explanations of vase types and terms such as "frieze," "relief," and "pediments"; and furnishes notes on the development of artistic styles in the ancient Greek world, particularly black-figure and red-figure painting. Subsequently, the work introduces some Greek words, especially those for the various types of vases, such as the *skyphos* and *kylix* (types of drinking cups) and the *lekythos* and *amphora* (containers for oil or perfumes), or objects from everyday life, such as the *chiton* (a type of dress) and the lyre. Glubok fully explains the purpose of these objects, and the illustrations aptly complement the commentary.

The work further explores, in addition to the art and artistic techniques prominent in ancient Greece, the ways in which the art reflects ancient Greek culture. Therefore, the young reader finds an encompassing introduction to mythology and religion, politics, entertainment, some history, and many people important to ancient Greek society. *The Art of Ancient Greece* covers all artistic periods, from the Minoan-Mycenaean terra cotta figurines of about 2500 B.C. to the imperial Roman copies of earlier Greek statues, and offers an interesting survey on the development of decoration.

Analysis

The Art of Ancient Greece systematically and comprehensively addresses the major issues of art in the ancient Greek world and provides ample illustrations of these issues for a younger audience. Glubok is always careful to present the information on an introductory level, but her discussions are never pedantic; rather, the tone is welcoming and explorative so as to arouse curiosity for the material. In this way, she convincingly introduces the young reader to a foreign and ancient culture through its surviving art.

Glubok's work includes many references to the heroes and fantastical creatures from ancient Greek mythology. The adventures of Herakles (whom the Romans called Hercules), Bellerophon, Achilles, and Odysseus all occupy prominent discussions. In this manner, the author introduces the *Iliad* and the *Odyssey*, two extremely important epics by the poet Homer. Glubok briefly identifies the nearly invincible Achilles as the central hero of the Trojan War and explains a red-figure vase painting of Odysseus outwitting the sirens, bird-women who lure sailors to their destruction. A terra cotta statuette from the National Museum in Athens of Bellerophon, the hero who rides the winged horse Pegasus and conquers the many-headed Chimera, and two statues of Herakles, from the Metropolitan Museum of Art and the Glyptothek Museum, provide discussion on both the development of artistic techniques and the popularity of such heroic stories. The reader also encounters the Amazons, female warriors who lived outside the realm of men and who regularly appeared in ancient Greek art. Another central heroic myth, Theseus' conquest of the Minotaur (a man-bull creature), bears illustration without commentary.

Glubok describes the pantheon of Greek divinities and their importance in both art and culture. The illustrations include representations in every art form of these gods and goddesses. She discusses both the major divinities, who live on Mount Olympus, and relatively minor figures. Of the major Olympians, Glubok briefly identifies Zeus, Poseidon, Aphrodite, Athena, Apollo, Artemis, Hermes, and Dionysus. Gods and goddesses of lesser significance include Eros, the mischievous Pan, Nike, Triton, and the nymphs who tend to the goddess Persephone. In nearly all cases, Glubok explains the importance of each divine being and the elemental forces that she or he oversees, an important feature for readers who may be embracing for the first time the sometimes confusing world of Greek mythology.

Not all the images in *The Art of Ancient Greece*, however, represent the grandiose and extreme actions of heroes and divinities; Glubok eagerly explores the artistic representations of everyday experience. She illustrates the importance in ancient Greek society of olive harvests, daily business at the market, washing (with oil and a *strigil*), foreign trade, feasting and drinking, and education. In this manner, she explains the connection between culture and art to younger readers. For example, in her discussion of a vase painting from the State Museum in Berlin, in which students surround their teachers and await instructions in poetry and music, Glubok clearly draws a parallel to her own readers. Subsequently, she examines the importance of the military (providing an explanation of armor) and of sports (including chariot racing, boxing, discus throwing, and hunting) in ancient Greek culture. She also introduces the Greek innovations in both drama and philosophy.

In correlation to these issues, Glubok offers informative remarks on many important people and events from ancient Greece. She provides solid details about the Greek political leader Pericles, who ruled Athens during the "Golden Age of Greece," and Alexander the Great, who created an empire that extended from Greece eastward into northern India and southward into Egypt. Glubok also introduces the famous philosophers Socrates, Plato, and Aristotle as men of tremendous understanding. Her intention is not to linger on potentially confusing philosophical material; it suffices for her to explain philosophy as the "love of wisdom" and explain the ways that images of wise, older men differ from the sleek bodies of athletes and soldiers. Through this method, Glubok both stresses developments in artistic representation and the different contributions made by the Greeks.

The Art of Ancient Greece appropriately provides some information on ancient Greek artists. Glubok mentions Praxiteles, in relation to his marble statue of Hermes at the Olympia Museum in Greece, and Myron, with the bronze Roman copy of his famous *Discobolus* at the Terme Museum in Rome. She also describes the artist Polykleitos, who wrote an art manual called the *Canon*, and Pheidias, the famous Athenian sculptor.

Important places from Greece, Italy, Africa, Asia, and India are mentioned in Glubok's work. In an explanation of the evolution of Greek figurines, for example, she introduces Mycenae, one of the earliest settlements in mainland Greece. Further discussions encompass Olympia, where the great Temple to Zeus was located and where the Olympic Games began in 776 B.C., and Delphi, with its Temple to Apollo. Special attention is paid to the Parthenon, the temple to Athena on the Acropolis, the hill that stands above the city of Athens. Glubok explains the architecture, the decoration on the pediments of the temple, and the yearly procession to robe the image of Athena, which inspired the frieze of divinities on the cella of the temple. To explain the ancient Greek inclination for perfection, she even discusses the way in which the temple was carefully engineered to appear absolutely symmetrical and straight. This thoughtful explanation provides advanced ideas for the young reader to consider.

Critical Context

Since its initial publication in 1963, *The Art of Ancient Greece* has been firmly established as an important and comprehensive introduction to the subject matter for young readers. Shirley Glubok's book successfully makes difficult concepts accessible, provides a solid overview of the issues, and balances the concerns of both art and culture. It thereby provides a means for a young reader to approach ancient Greece within its cultural context. The book also explores the surviving influence of ancient Greek culture.

Glubok's other works include a series of introductory art books for young readers. Other topics include the art of ancient Egypt, the lands of the Bible, ancient Rome, Africa, Inuits, and North and Central American Indians. Glubok's books stem from her own training in archaeology and her experience as a teacher of children.

Although there is some necessary nudity in *The Art of Ancient Greece*, the minor amount should not discourage a younger audience. For an attentive reader, Glubok's work suggests discussion on many subjects, including polytheistic religion, slavery, military service, and rituals of death and burial. These issues, as well as the sheer prominence and influence of ancient Greek art, introduce a beautiful and sometimes mysterious world that young readers would no doubt find rewarding to explore.

Stephen C. Olbrys

ARTHUR, FOR THE VERY FIRST TIME

Author: Patricia MacLachlan (1938-   )
First published: 1980; illustrated
Type of work: Novel
Type of plot: Domestic realism
Time of work: The late twentieth century
Locale: Northern farm country of the United States
Subjects: Coming-of-age, family, and friendship
Recommended ages: 10-13

When ten-year-old Arthur Rasby grows dissatisfied with his life at home, he visits the farm of his aunt and uncle, where he meets several unconventional characters who teach him about love, life, and himself.

> *Principal characters:*
> ARTHUR RASBY, a young boy who is unhappy about his mother's pregnancy
> AUNT ELDA, his eccentric great-aunt
> UNCLE WRISBY, his equally unusual great-uncle
> MOIRA MACAVIN, an independent young girl who has been abandoned by her parents
> MOREOVER, Moira's grandfather, the local veterinarian

Form and Content

Arthur, for the Very First Time is the humorous story of a ten-year-old boy who learns to accept himself, his family, and his life. It is filled with charming and eccentric people and animals, such as an aunt who climbs out on a tree limb to leave a hank of her hair for a mockingbird to use in its nest and a chicken who sleeps in a crib and responds best when addressed in French. Patricia MacLachlan skillfully blends her unusual characters in a world that verges on fantasy but retains a unique and charming reality.

Arthur Rasby is miserable as summer begins. His parents are fighting, his friends are away, and his mother is pregnant. After Arthur deliberately makes his mother sick by asking for a pet rat, his parents take him to stay with Aunt Elda and Uncle Wrisby on their farm. Arthur is delighted there. The atmosphere is different from his home: He is able to choose whatever room he wants and is even able to pick the vegetables that he will eat.

The difference becomes even more obvious on his first morning there when Pauline, the chicken, awakens him. Shortly thereafter, Aunt Elda shows him a mockingbird outside his window, filling him with a sense of excitement about the interesting things that will happen during his visit. The adventures begin when he meets a young neighbor, Moira MacAvin, the granddaughter of Moreover, the veterinarian.

Moira gives Arthur the nickname "Mouse" and fascinates him with her independence and imagination. The two children become close, discussing their likes and fears: Arthur's journal and his love of writing, his mother's pregnancy, Moira's abandonment by her parents, and her fear that Moreover does not really love her. Moira encourages Arthur to develop his own imagination.

Although Arthur has received several letters from his parents, he refuses to read any of them. Instead, he reads a book about pigs that Moira gave him, soon deciding to build a birthing pen for Bernadette, Uncle Wrisby's pregnant pig. When the pen is finished, Bernadette refuses to go in it. Arthur is disappointed, but Aunt Elda makes him think about his reasons for building the pen by telling him the story of her Aunt Mag, a mail-order bride from Maine who brought a prism with her when she traveled west. A prism sends colors all over, reminding people of how they touch one another's lives.

Arthur decides that Pauline looks ill, so the two children dose the hen—and themselves—with Uncle Wrisby's "tonic." Both chicken and children get drunk. When Moreover discovers what they have done, he spanks Moira. She is happy because she realizes that he punished her because he feared losing her. She is finally convinced that he loves her.

At last, Arthur writes to his parents and reads their letters. Later, while Moira and Arthur are alone during a storm, they realize that Bernadette is in labor in the new pen. Fearing that the piglets will drown in the mud, they hold a tarpaulin over her and rescue the piglets. After Arthur saves the smallest piglet, Moira praises her friend by finally calling him by his real name.

Analysis

Arthur, for the Very First Time deals with the important issues of communication and perception. In the first chapter, MacLachlan introduces several examples of the inability to communicate effectively. As the story opens, Arthur is unhappy because his parents argue and whisper. When Arthur questions his father, it angers him so much that he throws a shovel against the garage. Later, his father suggests that the two of them fix supper, which Arthur realizes is his father's way of apologizing. Arthur knows—and resents—that his mother is pregnant; he also resents that neither of his parents have told him about it. In retaliation, he asks for a pet rat, knowing that his request will send his mother running to the bathroom. Arthur's family is loving and caring, but they do not always speak clearly, directly, or honestly with one another. The chapter ends with Arthur's surprise when he discovers that Uncle Wrisby wants to talk with him.

The novel is filled with many other illustrations of the failure to be honest or to communicate, such as Arthur's refusal to read his parents' letters. More serious examples occur in Moira's life. Her father abandoned her, saying that he would return soon but never coming back. When Moira's mother left, she vowed that she would never return. She does come back; unfortunately, it is only to borrow money, not to visit Moira. Because Moreover has never told her that he loves her, Moira thinks that he does not care any more for her than for the animals that he treats. He once said that one should not care too much: The hurt is too great when the object of that love is gone. When Arthur, certain that Moreover truly does love Moira, asks Uncle Wrisby for confirmation of this, Wrisby replies, "How many people tell those they care about just how much they care?" After Arthur meets Moira, he becomes more honest. When she asks if he wants to see her pet snake, he tells her "no," trying out the truth.

The different ways in which individuals perceive themselves and the world is another important element in the novel. Arthur has kept a journal ever since he was able to write; it is his way of organizing his world. Neither Uncle Wrisby nor Moira understand this need. Wrisby says that he only believes in the things that he sees. Moira warns Arthur that he spends so much time writing about things that he does not have time to experience them; she compares him to the social worker who visits her, writing down endless notes but doing nothing. Soon, Arthur begins to see things in more than one way. Although he could not understand at first why his uncle likes to look through binoculars the wrong way, he eventually discovers a reason: He is afraid to climb trees, but if he just imagined them through the wrong end of the binoculars, they could be climbed easily. Arthur begins to understand himself, and others, a little better.

MacLachlan describes Arthur's growth in wisdom and self-confidence by stressing the phrase "for the very first time" throughout the story. When he first comes to stay at the farm and realizes how different his relatives are, Arthur feels a new and powerful sense of excitement. He learns to use his imagination when Moira helps him to make braces. He cleverly outwits Yoyo, a peddler. When he builds the pen for Bernadette, he learns how to plan things and carry out those plans; in the past, he accepted that things either went his way or did not, believing that there was nothing he could do to change his situation. At the end of the story, he has accepted his parents and saved the piglets. Moira congratulates him by calling him "Arthur, for the very first time."

Critical Context

Patricia MacLachlan is an award-winning author particularly identifiable by the warm, eccentric families that populate her novels. Born in Wyoming and reared in Minnesota, she bases many stories on her life and on tales about her ancestors. Aunt Mag was based on a distant relative, a mail-order bride from the East Coast. The character was more fully developed in *Sarah, Plain and Tall* (1985), which won the Newbery Medal. MacLachlan frequently redevelops characters; for example Moira's background is used in *Journey* (1991).

Arthur, for the Very First Time won the Gold Kite Award from the Society of Children's Book Writers in 1980. MacLachlan describes it as one of her favorite stories. It is typical of her books, filled with articulate and thoughtful young people and adults who defy the established norms. She clearly shows that it may be difficult to be different. Characters such as Arthur, children who must learn to live with eccentric people, frequently grow themselves as they learn to experience the world in a new way. MacLachlan's characters are warm and loving. Although many of her details verge on the fantastic, such as animals that seem almost human, she never strays too far from realism. Instead, she leaves the reader with a picture of a world where both adults and children learn to follow their dreams.

Mary Mahony

ARTIFICIAL INTELLIGENCE

Author: Margaret Hyde (1917-   )
First published: As *Computers That Think?: The Search for Artificial Intelligence,*
    1982; revised in 1986; illustrated
Type of work: Science
Subjects: Science and social issues
Recommended ages: 13-18

Hyde discusses the concept of intelligence before she traces the evolution of computers—from the first gigantic, relatively slow models to those that are imitating human intelligence in limited ways.

Form and Content

In *Artificial Intelligence*, Margaret Hyde explains from the third-person objective point of view that early computers—the data processors that merely receive, store, and display information—are evolving into artificial brains that can learn, reason, and form conclusions. As scientists work to create these "fifth-generation" computers, they are realizing the complexity of the brain-driven activities of humans. Through a network of billions of neurons, the brain gives a human powers that scientists find amazingly intricate when they try to duplicate them in the sequence and parallelism necessary for programming a computer. The human intellect can store much information and then find relations among seemingly disparate bits of information in order to arrive at conclusions that fit ever-changing circumstances. Computer scientists face the challenge of creating artificial intelligence that is adaptable to such variance. The first three chapters of the book establish the human brain as a pattern for advanced computers.

In the seven chapters that make up *Artificial Intelligence*, Hyde includes many photographs. Some show the changes in size and shape as computers have evolved. The reduction of computers from the five-ton Mark I of 1944 to much smaller computers occurred chiefly because of the move from vacuum tubes to transistors in silicon chips to operate the off-and-on circuits that are the bases of computer operation. As more transistors were squeezed on a silicon chip, size continued to decrease while speed and efficiency increased. One photograph shows a silicon chip fitting into the eye of a needle.

Beginning with chapter 4 and continuing through chapter 7, the closing section, Hyde discusses computerized robots. After a brief review of robots in fiction, she enumerates industries that use these machines. She stresses the advantages of having robots relieve humans from monotonous, strenuous, and dangerous work. Drawings and photographs from such sources as International Business Machines (IBM), General Motors, and the National Aeronautics and Space Administration (NASA) illustrate how and where robots work. Computer-driven robots do not suffer from physical, mental, or emotional stress and thus are more reliable than humans in jobs that include welding on assembly lines, spray painting in excessive heat, and inspecting work with a mechanical vision.

Scientists have equipped advanced computers with senses such as sight and touch. Diagrams in chapter 5 establish the complexity of human sight, which depends on what the brain knows as well as on what the eye sees. Other diagrams show how scientists enable advanced computers to see in a limited manner. Chapter 6 explains and illustrates the value of computers that speak, listen, read, and understand languages. In order for computers to use language, they must be programmed with general and specific knowledge; otherwise, inferences that lead to meaning cannot be drawn.

In the concluding chapter, Hyde discusses the most advanced computers, those that can reason, make judgments, and draw conclusions. Some of these fifth-generation computers go where humans cannot—into the core of nuclear reactors or the depths of the oceans—to reason and then to perform the work that they deem necessary. Others, the expert systems, serve as consultants to remind humans of the multiple possibilities in complicated circumstances. At the end of *Artificial Intelligence*, Hyde includes a list of suggested readings related to intelligence and computers.

Analysis

The major theme of *Artificial Intelligence* is the rapid evolution of computers. The computer originated in mathematical theory, chiefly the binary system of algebra worked out by George Boole during the mid-nineteenth century. Another mathematician, Charles Babbage, constructed an "analytical engine" considered to be the forerunner of the computer. Impetus in the development of computers occurred during World War II. Mark I, completed in 1944 after five years of work by Harvard University and IBM, is considered the world's first electromechanical computer. The Colossus, a British computer, broke German codes and helped the Allies win World War II. All these early computers used vacuum tubes through which electrons moved to create the circuits that enable computers to calculate.

In 1947, Bell Telephone Laboratories revolutionized the computer industry by inventing the transistor to replace the vacuum tube. Electrons move through solid crystal instead of evacuated space in transistors. Gradually, the size of transistors was reduced. In 1960, one transistor fit on one silicon chip; by 1980, a hundred thousand fit on one silicon chip. Simultaneous with this reduction in size came an increase in speed. Circuits within computers can switch off and on in trillionths of a second because of integrated circuits or microprocessors.

Along with the evolution of the physical properties of computers came the evolution of their capabilities. Since the original systems that simply processed information, scientists have begun to create artificial intelligence patterned after human intelligence. Research into enabling computers to see, touch, listen, speak, read, and reason is ongoing. One such program is BACON, an expert system that can rediscover scientific laws, such as Boyle's law of gases, when it is supplied with the data from scientific experiments that led scientists to form the law originally. The hope is that eventually BACON can discover new scientific laws.

A related theme in *Artificial Intelligence* establishes the marvels of human intelligence, marvels often taken for granted until scientists have tried to reproduce them for computer programs. For example, the brain allows a human to recognize scissors from different perspectives, while a computer must be systematically "taught" the way in which scissors appear from different perspectives. In order to teach a computer to recognize letters, the programmer must include the varying shapes of letters in different typefaces. In order to teach a computer to read a story, the scientist must provide the computer with multiple definitions of each word and with general knowledge about a society, such as the relation between father and daughter. If a computer designed to help a doctor diagnose infectious diseases does not know the difference between animate and inanimate nouns, the computer will try to find the best antibiotic to fix a flat tire on a bicycle. When computer scientists attempt to explicate human thought processes in order to create artificial intelligence, scientists specializing in human thought gain insight into the reasoning processes that are codified and mimicked in computer programs. These mutually enriching studies doubly benefit humankind.

A third theme sustained throughout *Artificial Intelligence* is the benefit gained by humans through the creation of machines that think. Anticipating negative reactions to computers, Hyde recounts the negative reactions to machines during the Industrial Revolution. She then emphasizes that computers in the forms of robots can do jobs that are too dangerous for humans. Even though a robot may replace about a dozen workers at a plant that makes thermometers, that the robot is doing the work protects human workers from the possibility of mercury poisoning. Computers can compensate for handicaps; the Kurzwell Reading Machine enables the blind to read and the dyslexic to read faster. Computers help in the military and in space probes.

Hyde not only provides interesting examples in her book but also expresses information so that it is readily understandable. To show the speed at which computers operate, Hyde asks the reader to imagine the half second that it takes coffee spilled from a pot on a table to reach the floor. During this half second, a computer can debit 4,200 checks to 630 bank accounts, examine the electrocardiograms of 210 patients, score 315,000 answers on 6,300 examinations, and figure the payroll for a company with more than two thousand employees.

Critical Context

Artificial Intelligence is a revision of *Computers That Think?: The Search for Artificial Intelligence* (1982). To gather information for the book, Margaret Hyde consulted experts in various pertinent fields, ranging from C. D. Siegchrist, the IBM technical director who provided some calculations for the book, to Dr. Patrick H. Winston of the Massachusetts Institute of Technology, who was programming a computer to see. By contacting people who were engaged in research, Hyde had the double advantage of getting the most recent information and having experts who could check her material for accuracy.

Hyde's first book was published in 1941. In 1992, she wrote *Peace and Friendship: Russian and American Teens Meet*. Through these fifty-one years of writing, she published sixty-four books. All except the first, which was fiction, explore subjects from the sciences or social sciences. Often, the two areas are mixed. *Animal Clocks and Compasses* (1960) won the Thomas Alva Edison Foundation National Mass Media Award in 1961 for the best children's book. In 1964, Hyde published *Your Brain, Your Computer*. Other related books include *Brainwashing and Other Forms of Mind Control* (1977) and *The Violent Mind* (1991). Many of Hyde's social sciences books examine problems that beset young people during a particular era, as shown by *Cancer in the Young: A Sense of Hope* (1985) and *AIDS: What Does It Mean to You?* (1986; rev. ed., 1990).

Lana White

ASH ROAD

Author: Ivan Southall (1921-   )
First published: 1966
Type of work: Novel
Type of plot: Psychological realism
Time of work: The 1960's
Locale: Australia's bush country
Subjects: Coming-of-age, death, emotions, and nature
Recommended ages: 10-15

The children of Ash Road face a horrendous brushfire with only the aid of two old men and the three teenage boys who accidentally started the fire.

> *Principal characters:*
> GRAHAM, a fifteen-year-old with a gentle, sensitive disposition who accidentally sets a bush fire
> HARRY, a clever boy on the camping holiday with Graham
> WALLACE, a big strong boy also on the camping holiday
> LORNA GEORGE, a fourteen-year-old responsible for keeping house for her father and older brother John because her mother is in an invalid's hospital
> PIPPA BUCKINGHAM, a twelve-year-old girl living on Ash Road
> STEVIE, Pippa's younger brother
> JULIE, Pippa's younger sister
> PETER, a thirteen-year-old visiting his grandparents on Ash Road
> GRAMPS FAIRHALL, Peter's grandfather, a retired farmer living well on an inheritance with his wife
> GRANDPA TANNER, an old retired farmer living alone who befriends the Buckingham children, especially the youngest, Julie

Form and Content

Ash Road is a novel with a plot that resembles the wild fire that devours the Australian bush. It moves rapidly and alights in various places. An omniscient narrator introduces and keeps track of a multitude of characters with a point of view that shifts rapidly, often moving several times within a single chapter. In the first chapter, Ivan Southall places three city teenagers in the bush country, a setting created in such minute detail that one can almost feel the hot, arid wind, smell the parched earth, and hear the crackle of the dry brush. Several times, the boys are warned about the danger of fire, but the predictable happens: In the night, a fire is accidentally started and nearly engulfs the boys as they flee for their lives. Realizing their guilt, they head for the home of a school acquaintance on Ash Road to hide out.

In the second chapter, the rest of the characters who live on Ash Road, both young and old, are revealed as they begin the morning of the thirteenth of January. Each family is engaged in the affairs of the day—the Georges are desperately picking berries that are turning to mush in the heat, the Buckinghams are cleaning up from an overflowing bathtub so that they can begin their holiday at the beach, the Fairhalls are punctually eating their six o'clock breakfast, and Grandpa Tanner, who has risen early with a sense of foreboding, comforts little Julie, who has accidentally caused the bathtub to overflow.

The fire siren starts a chain reaction of events. Sometimes, the characters seem to be in control of their actions; at other times, the events seem to control them. John deserts Lorna to continue picking the rotting raspberries with their father, who is too stubborn to admit defeat. Pippa, sent to find Julie, encounters Peter instead. Their petty argument sends Pippa to the George house, where old man George has collapsed from a heat-induced stroke. At that point, the three teenage boys appear on Ash Road in their flight. Harry and Wallace agree to help Lorna move her father. Graham goes into hiding and is tracked by Peter, who draws the intuitive conclusion that these boys have caused the fire. Meanwhile, all the adults except Gramps and Grandpa Tanner leave to fight the fire or to provide aid to the refugees. As Gramps, Wallace, and Harry try to take old man George to the hospital, they make a desperate run through the fire, but George dies before they can get help. The children are left to their own devices to survive the natural disaster. As the fire approaches, each realizes the imminent danger and seeks safety. Grandpa Tanner has lowered Julie into his well and is prepared for his own life to end. Lorna forces Graham out of his hiding place to seek refuge under the irrigation sprinklers. Pippa tries to get Stevie to the fallow potato paddock, but she must follow as he runs the other way. Peter runs toward the fire in search of his grandmother. All seem doomed, but they are saved by a miraculous rainstorm that emerges out of the fire's cloud of destruction.

Analysis

Readers of *Ash Road* gain the utmost respect for the power of fire. Yet, the most important lessons to be learned from the novel come not from the natural disaster itself but from the characters' responses to it. In *Ash Road*, Southall provides a painfully realistic view of how individuals cope with an extraordinary event. The reader vicariously experiences the frenzied emotions and panic of both children and adults and witnesses how in the fight for survival humans can exhibit both their worst and their best traits. The general portrayal is bleak, but Southall does allow some room for the characters to demonstrate growth, especially the young. Unlike the adults, the children mature as a result of their ordeal. As Peter ran to seek his grandmother, he knew "that he was running into manhood and leaving childhood behind." He accepted Gran's hug as a man. As Graham and Lorna faced the fire in the carrot paddock, they knew "that they would continue to know each other for the rest of their lives." The bond that they have formed during the crisis will give Graham the strength to admit his mistake and Lorna the pride and dignity to meet whatever life would give her. Gran, on the other hand, is merely "confused and revived," and Grandpa Tanner feels disappointment that he is still alive.

The story has the structure of a live-action television report as it moves from views of the fire to focus on one character after another as they respond to the events of the day. The speed of the fire seems to control the pacing of the plot, forcing the characters into action. Since Southall has introduced a wide cast of characters, he must keep returning to each of them as they respond to the fire and the other events of the day. As the action moves forward, it does so on many fronts at once. The roving point of view both adds to and fits into the frenzy of the events. Southall's storytelling skills keep the suspense building until the end, and one is left wondering what will happen to these people in the aftermath of the fire.

When Southall wants the reader to consider significant themes, he slows the action with reflections from or about the characters. One message about human weakness that the book examines is the lack of preparedness and organization that allows the damage from the fire to be far more extensive than necessary. Grandpa Tanner's reflection about the world's distorted values in the chapter "Men Stand Up and Fight" allows the reader time to ponder the need for having dignity, making the ultimate effort, and even sacrificing oneself for the benefit of others. The arguments between Pippa and Peter, Stevie's quiet stroking of the cat and his thoughts about the meaning of nothing, and Peter's realization that his grandparents have first names are other little pools of relief from the fast action of the plot. The conclusion of the book also offers these moments of reflection.

Part of Southall's success in this story is his ability to incorporate his own experiences into his writing. In *Ash Road*, it is evident that he has lived in the Australian foothills. His descriptions of the enormous brushfire are accurate and full of ominous detail: "Trees and plants were bowing and bending . . . as if suffocating, as if throwing themselves about in search of cool, fresh air." The sky is described as "threatening" and "ugly." The day is "savage in itself, actively angry against every living thing." The fire is "an insane creature of immense greed consuming everything around it." Through this personification the setting, the weather and the fire function as characters in the story and have a strong impact on the reader.

Critical Context

During a writing career spanning more than fifty years, Southall became a well-known, popular, and award-winning writer for children and young adults. His desire to surround the great moments of life with words and protect them for young readers has been appreciated by both children and critics. *Ash Road* is one of the novels for which Southall received the Australian Children's Book of the Year Award. It displays many of the elements found in his other works: *Hills End* (1962), *To the Wild Sky* (1967), *Finn's Folly* (1969), and *Chinaman's Reef Is Ours* (1970) are all fast-moving survival tales. In each, young people face adversity with little or no adult support. This formula appears to be successful: Although *Ash Road* was first published in 1966, it has a contemporary feel and retains its appeal as a compelling survival story.

Carol Lauritzen

ATLANTIS
The Biography of a Legend

Author: Marjorie Braymer (1911-   )
First published: 1983; illustrated
Type of work: History
Time of work: The legendary past, ancient Greece, and the sixteenth through twentieth centuries
Locale: Primarily Central America and Santorini Island (Thera) near Crete
Subject: Science
Recommended ages: 13-18

Braymer summarizes the legends surrounding Plato's account of the legendary city of Atlantis and describes the excavation of ancient Thera, now the Greek island of Santorini.

> *Principal personages:*
> PLATO, the ancient Greek philosopher who tells the legend of Atlantis in two of his dialogues, the *Timaeus* and the *Critias*
> JOHN LLOYD STEPHENS, an American diplomat whose book *Incidents of Travel in Central America, Chiapas, and Yucatán* (1841) destroyed any claim to a Mayan Atlantis
> FERDINAND FOUQUÉ, a French geologist who began the excavation of Thera in 1866
> SIR ARTHUR EVANS, a British archaeologist who began excavating Knossos on Crete in 1899
> SPYRIDON MARINATOS, a Greek archaeologist who directed the excavation of the stunning discoveries at Thera

Form and Content

In *Atlantis: The Biography of a Legend*, Marjorie Braymer divides her story into twenty-seven short chapters, each having its own neatly defined subject. Numerous black-and-white illustrations clarify the narrative. Plato's description of Atlantis, for example, benefits from three diagrams that help readers visualize a layout that otherwise might be difficult to fix in the mind. The puzzling writing system of the ancient Maya is illuminated by seven illustrations, and two illustrations from the modern edition of John Lloyd Stephens' work *Incidents of Travel in Yucatán* (1962) enliven the account found in *Atlantis*.

By far the most important illustrations, however, are the sixteen photographs and several drawings that show the excavations done at ancient Thera, now the Greek island of Santorini. The complex of buildings found there was dug up very carefully, and the black-and-white photographs of the delicately preserved wall murals can still thrill the viewer who realizes that they date back to about 1500 B.C.

Braymer begins her story with a fifty-page summary of the account of Atlantis that Plato (427-347 B.C.) gives in the *Timaeus* and the *Critias*. Plato identified as his source the Greek statesman Solon (seventh and sixth centuries B.C.), who had heard the story in Egypt. The legend of Atlantis ends, in a sense, with Braymer's four introductory chapters on Plato, and she then goes on to eight chapters that summarize the centuries of sometimes fantastic speculation that culminated with Stephens' convincing refutation of claims that Atlantis had been discovered in the Americas.

The second half of the book recounts in some detail what becomes the main interest of Braymer's narrative: The story of Thera, a tiny island (and its encompassing ring of islands) sixty miles north of Crete in the Aegean Sea. Thera became prominent when the French engineers building the Suez Canal needed a source of cement, which was discovered on this small island. Thera remains an active volcano, and many centuries ago it erupted with such force that its central volcanic mountain exploded and left only its outer shell. The steaming sea poured in to fill in the crater, which became what is called a caldera (or "cauldron"). Oregon's Crater Lake is an example of such a phenomenon in North America. Braymer's account of the excavations at Thera examines real history and creates a genuine scholarly hero in Greek archaeologist Spyridon Marinatos.

Analysis

As Plato tells it, Atlantis was a huge island west of the Pillars of Hercules in the Atlantic Ocean. When invaders from Atlantis threatened the eastern Mediterranean, the Athenian army defeated the attackers. Later, Athens was devastated by earthquakes and floods, and Atlantis was destroyed by earthquakes so powerful that the island was completely swallowed up in a day. Whether Plato's Atlantis really existed—and if so, where it existed—have been disputed for centuries by believers in the legend. Places as far apart as Spain, Mongolia, Nigeria, Brazil, Greenland, and Yucatán have had their supporters.

The notes that Plato summarized from Solon told how Poseidon, the god who ruled the sea and stirred up earthquakes, built for his wife, Cleito, a hilltop palace surrounded by three rings of water and two of land. Plato describes in detail the resulting Metropolis and its environs, abundant in everything (including herds of elephants) needed to develop a great civilization. The government was just and the domestic life was peaceful until the spark of divinity that the island inherited from Poseidon died out. At this time, the citizens became undisciplined and their rulers grew overreaching in ambition. Beholding these conditions, Zeus assembled the Olympian gods to pronounce his punishment for Atlantis, but Plato never reveals Zeus's judgment. His story breaks off abruptly with the words "and when he had gathered them together, he said . . . ." This is all that is known from Plato.

Over the years, self-designated "Atlantologists" propagated much nonsense about the legendary city. One of the most interesting figures who turn up in the story is a young missionary friar, Diego de Landa, who arrived in Yucatán in 1550 and by 1562 was that region's bishop. Although Bishop Landa did not link the ancient Maya of

Yucatán to Atlantis, he became obsessed with his conviction that Mayan civilization was declining from a brilliant past and that its mysterious painted books were of diabolical origin. These inscrutable books frustrated him, and he heaped them up and burned them in the town, where they were kept by priests. The books that survive are mostly religious and astronomical. Mistakenly thinking that he had deciphered their writing system, Bishop Landa compiled an account of Yucatán that included the remark that "Some of the old people say that they have heard from their ancestors that this land was occupied by a race of people who came from the East and whom God had delivered by opening twelve paths through the sea."

Although these "twelve paths" suggested "descendants of the Jews" to Landa, when Charles Étienne Brasseur, a French church historian, discovered the bishop's long-neglected book in 1865, he began translating the remaining Mayan books with the bishop's meaningless "key." Brasseur's efforts led him into delusion and scholarly disgrace, as he wrote doggedly on about a land of "Mu" that he derived from two Mayan hieroglyphs and insisted was the legendary Atlantis.

Brasseur's fantasies inspired a pseudo-scholar named Augustus Le Plongeon to meld refugees from Mu and Atlantis into the founders of the Maya civilization. Beginning in 1875, Le Plongeon and his wife spent thirty years studying such ruins as those at Uxmal and Chichén Itzá, squabbling over antiquities with the Mexican government, and publishing an absurd tome about Atlantean refugees entitled *Queen Moo and the Egyptian Sphinx* (1896). These colorful characters are among those who have been enticed almost into madness by Plato's narrative.

Convincing scholarly theories about Atlantis begin to emerge with the excavations at Knossos on Crete that played such an important role in unraveling the history of Thera. The Minoan culture on Crete was very powerful by 1600 B.C., but Sir Arthur Evans' excavations at Knossos in 1899 convinced him that the Minoan civilization's rapid decline culminated in a disastrous fire around 1450 B.C. Some scholars, especially the classicist K. T. Frost, concluded that Crete could easily have been Atlantis. Frost's conjecture must have sounded reasonable at the time, but the Greek archaeologist Spyridon Marinatos, working near Knossos in 1932, began to think about Thera and what its volcanic eruptions might have meant to Crete. Once Marinatos began his excavations at Thera, the whole picture of where Atlantis may have been located and what happened to it took on the clearest shape yet. Although Marinatos tired of the question and absolute proof is impossible, locating Atlantis on Thera becomes entirely plausible in the absorbing account that dominates Braymer's book.

Critical Context

Marjorie Braymer's master's degree from Columbia University Teachers College led to twenty years of teaching at Sequoia High School in Redwood, California, a career that well complements the success of the two books she has written for young adults. Her first book, *The Walls of Windy Troy* (1960), was a biography of Heinrich Schliemann, the archaeologist who discovered ancient Troy. It was named both *The New York Herald Tribune*'s Spring Book Festival Honor Book and an American

Library Association Notable Book. Given Braymer's interest in Mediterranean archaeology that she showed in her first book, an account of the Atlantis legend seemed an inevitable subject for a second book.

The bibliography in *Atlantis* includes all the pertinent works that Braymer mentions and more, but the serious student will want to look at the dozen entries by Spyridon Marinatos, especially the series of annual reports for the Archaeological Society of Athens that he published between 1968 and 1976. The Maya script was still a puzzle to scholars when Braymer wrote about the efforts of Bishop Landa and Charles Étienne Brasseur, but the puzzle has now been solved, as explained in Michael D. Coe's engrossing *Breaking the Maya Code* (1992).

Frank Day

AWAY GOES SALLY

Author: Elizabeth Coatsworth (1893-1986)
First published: 1934; illustrated
Type of work: Novel
Type of plot: Historical fiction
Time of work: 1790, just after the American Revolution
Locale: The move from Massachusetts to Maine
Subjects: Family and travel
Recommended ages: 10-13

In 1790, Sally Smith and her loving family of three aunts and two uncles experience a winter move from Massachusetts to settle in Maine, making the trip in a little house on runners.

> *Principal characters:*
> SALLY SMITH, the central character of the story, a young orphan girl who is loved by and lives with her three aunts and two uncles
> AUNT NANNIE, the oldest aunt, an energetic decision maker
> AUNT DEBORAH, the "middle" aunt, who is cautious
> AUNT ESTHER, the youngest of the three aunts, who is twenty years old, pretty, and curious
> UNCLE JOSEPH, the head of the household and the brother of Aunt Nannie, Aunt Deborah, and Aunt Esther
> UNCLE EBEN, another brother, who seems to have a good sense of humor and loves to eat

Form and Content

Away Goes Sally contains thirteen relatively short chapters with a poem written by the author, Elizabeth Coatsworth, at the end of each chapter. The poems generally concern nature and describe the season of the chapter. They appeal to the senses, conjuring up feelings of warmth. The book is written in the third person and contains much dialogue. Eleven full-page, black-and-white illustrations by Helen Sewell, adapting the technique of old woodcuts, can be found as decoration within the text. Many of them have a delicate, thin line decorative border. In addition, some pages of text contain illustrations pertinent to the story.

Sally Smith's parents are dead, and she lives on a farm in Massachusetts with her mother's three sisters—Aunt Nannie, Aunt Deborah, and Aunt Esther—and two brothers—Uncle Joseph and Uncle Eben—in a close-knit family. Aunt Nannie is the oldest of the sisters and is the most decisive, while Aunt Deborah cannot readily make a decision. Aunt Esther, the youngest, is pretty and curious. Aunt Nannie is the head of everything that goes on in the house, while Uncle Joseph is the head of everything outside the house, such as the farm.

Uncle Joseph receives a letter from Cousin Ephraim Hallet, who has moved to Maine. Ephraim invites them to settle there, where land is cheap and more opportunities exist for them than in Massachusetts. Uncle Joseph is in favor of going, and all the other family members eventually approve of the move—except for Aunt Nannie, who declares that she will never leave her own house or her own fire nor sleep in any bed but her own. Joseph is firm about going, but Nannie is just as firm about staying. She would like to relent, but she has taken her stand.

One winter day, Joseph arranges to have Sally and the sisters visit a great-aunt. When they come home, they see a strange sight. Unbeknown to them, Joseph has built a little house on runners, to be pulled by oxen, for Nannie. In this way, she can travel to Maine and never leave her own fire. Aunt Nannie is surprised and replies that she will go willingly. The rest of the book concerns what happens on their journey to Maine.

Analysis

Away Goes Sally is a calm, quiet work of historical fiction describing the life of one family in 1790. Coatsworth evokes both a nostalgic warmth and a feeling of anticipation about what will happen next. Her choice of words in the poems at the end of the chapters appeals to the senses: In one of the poems, the reader can almost feel the coziness as "the cat sleeps warm beneath the stove" in the middle of winter, and Dinah, Sally's cat, "folded her paws before the fire and purred herself to sleep." Coatsworth helps the young reader identify with the story through the character of Sally Smith. Sally performs chores, sews, and makes tea and serves it to the family, roles befitting a young girl of the late eighteenth century. She also notices and shows appreciation for what is around her.

The letter from Cousin Ephraim Hallet asking the family to come to Maine to live is the focal point of the book because it requires a decision to be made. Another message is delivered in the letter: As Ephraim writes of his wife, "Jennie says that she prefers being the head of the poor to being the tail of the rich."

The most important theme in this book is the love and respect that the family members show one another. Aunt Nannie is adamant about not wanting to leave the farm in Massachusetts. She also believes that Sally should not go, despite the young girl's enthusiasm for the idea. Uncle Joseph, who has been instrumental in persuading the others to move to Maine, is as firm in his convictions as Nannie is, but he works out a plan that allows Nannie to save face and acquiesce to the move. The house pulled by oxen is quite a sight to all the onlookers as the family makes its way to Maine. Sally refers to the little house as a doll's house on runners. She pretends that she is a doll and waves stiffly to people as the little house passes by. The house is also referred to as a "go-abroad" house.

The rest of the story concerns the actual journey from Massachusetts to Maine and the events that occur along the way. A painter paints a portrait of Sally, and Sally discovers that it is not simply moving that counts, that meeting people is the nicest part of the adventure. Uncle Eben buys a bear cub named Hannibal to keep him warm in the sleigh. The family encounters a bad snowstorm, and Hannibal finds a man almost buried in the snow, who must be treated for frostbite. Sally does not understand the treatment at first and is afraid that the man will die. The other members of the family are not sure he will live, but he responds to their treatment. Upon tending to him, "There was an air of relief and satisfaction in the room that one could feel as truly as the heat of the fire." The man is a peddler who gives Sally a beautiful wooden doll, whom she names Eunice. The family finally reaches the destination, Pleasant Valley, and is welcomed by Cousin Ephraim and his family.

This novel provides an excellent example of historical fiction that examines love among family members and care for others. Coatsworth describes tasks common to home and farm life in the late eighteenth century and depicts a unique mode of travel in the little house on runners.

Critical Context

In *Away Goes Sally*, Elizabeth Coatsworth's first period story, she uses terms appropriate for 1790 and for the setting. In setting her work in Massachusetts and Maine, she was writing about places that she knew well and loved. While Coatsworth does not delve into the psychological depths of her characters, they are believable nevertheless. She believes in using an economy of words and is precise, writing exactly what she means. Coatsworth displays considerable warmth in her storytelling, and *Away Goes Sally* moves along as leisurely as the little house on runners. Sally and her family reappeared in *Five Bushel Farm* (1939), in which the family is established on the new farm in Maine, and in *The Fair American* (1940). In the latter story, Pierre, a French boy of the aristocracy, boards an American ship in an attempt to escape the aftermath of the French Revolution. Sally helps to save his life when a French officer comes aboard to look for refugees.

Many of Coatsworth's books of historical fiction deal with problems that are universal, not caught in time: moving to what is hoped to be a better place to live in *Away Goes Sally*, building and getting settled in a new home in *Five Bushel Farm*, and suddenly becoming a refugee and finding a place to belong in *The Fair American*.

Florence H. Maltby

BABE
The Gallant Pig

Author: Dick King-Smith (1922-   )
First published: 1983; illustrated
Type of work: Novel
Type of plot: Fantasy and moral tale
Time of work: Undefined
Locale: The English countryside
Subjects: Animals, friendship, and nature
Recommended ages: 10-13

A young pig demonstrates a remarkable talent not only for sheep herding but also for promoting tolerance and understanding on Hogget's sheep farm.

>   *Principal characters:*
>   BABE, a pig who dreams of becoming the greatest sheep dog in the country
>   FARMER HOGGET, Babe's taciturn but kind-hearted owner
>   MRS. HOGGET, Farmer Hogget's loquacious wife
>   FLY, a sheep dog who adopts Babe and teaches him to herd sheep
>   MA, an old sheep who befriends Babe and divulges the secrets of her species

Form and Content

Babe: The Gallant Pig is the tale of a pig who follows an unusual dream and teaches tolerance and understanding to his fellow farm animals along the way. A short novel, arranged in twelve chapters illustrated by Mary Raynor, *Babe* employs an omniscient, third-person narrator and blends straightforward prose with dialect. The reader soon becomes comfortable with the notion that the animals speak to and understand one another, and this device becomes an integral part of the narrative. A deceptively simple story, *Babe* can be enjoyed both as a delightful fantasy and as a moral tale.

When Farmer Hogget wins a piglet at the local fair by correctly guessing its weight, he has nothing more in mind for its future than a prominent spot on his Christmas dinner table. When Hogget lodges the pig in the stable with his sheep dog Fly and her puppies, however, Fly's maternal instincts overcome her prejudice against pigs, and she becomes quite fond of young Babe. Although she has always believed pigs to be stupid, she soon realizes that Babe does not conform to her preconceived notions of his species. After her own pups are sold, Fly turns all of her maternal attentions to the pig and at Babe's request begins to teach him how to herd sheep.

When Babe uses his newly acquired herding skills to save Farmer Hogget's sheep from rustlers, Mrs. Hogget vows never to make a meal of him, and Farmer Hogget begins to entertain ideas of training Babe for the Grand Challenge Sheep Dog Trials.

Although Babe practices and works hard at his exercise and diet regime, he also owes much of his success to his friendship with Ma, an old sheep with whom he occasionally shares the stable. Although Fly attempts to instill a prejudice against sheep in her young protégé, Babe learns from Ma that sheep are not stupid creatures and that they want only to be treated with dignity and respect by the "wolves," as they refer to sheep dogs. This understanding, along with hard work, helps Babe develop into the finest "sheep-pig" in the country.

The sheep believe in Babe so completely that they entrust him with their secret password, which assures him a perfect score at the sheep dog trials—a feat never before accomplished by a dog, let alone a pig. As a result of Babe's influence, Fly changes her opinion of sheep, the sheep learn that the terms "sheep dog" and "wolf" are not synonymous, and Farmer Hogget realizes his dream of winning the Grand Challenge Sheep Dog Trials.

Analysis

Babe weaves its themes of tolerance and individuality so seamlessly throughout the narrative that the young reader will almost effortlessly absorb the novel's lessons of tolerance and individuality. Dick King-Smith manages to convey several layers of meaning without resorting to preaching or didacticism, making this novel valuable for teaching to and discussing with young readers.

Babe deftly dramatizes the dangers of stereotyping to both its victims and its perpetrators, illustrating how readily prejudice can be born of ignorance when its characters make unwarranted assumptions about one another. Fly's puppies ask their mother if pigs are stupid: "Fly hesitated. On the one hand, having been born and brought up in sheep country, she had in fact never been personally acquainted with a pig. On the other, like most mothers, she did not wish to appear ignorant before her children. 'Yes,' she said. 'They're stupid.'" After only brief acquaintance with Babe, however, she realizes that he does not conform to her preconceived ideas of pigs.

Fly also believes that sheep are stupid, that their bleating is meaningless, and that she can only control them through coercion. The sheep, in turn, are culpable of thoughtless prejudice by making no distinction between sheep dogs and wolves, lumping herders with predators. Through Babe's efforts to know and understand both the sheep and the sheep dog, stereotypes are broken and knowledge leads to greater tolerance and cooperation between the species.

Although following one's dream is a familiar theme in juvenile literature, it is given a refreshing variation in *Babe*. While both Babe and Farmer Hogget pursue dreams, these dreams are, to say the least, very personal and eccentric. Each character values his own individuality by following visions that to others appear absurd. Although none of the farm animals takes Babe's determination to be a "sheep-pig" seriously, he remains undeterred, listening carefully to his teacher, training hard, and dieting. By remaining true to himself, he eventually makes believers out of the entire country. Farmer Hogget has enough experience of the world to keep his dream to enter a pig in the sheep dog trials under wraps (not even his wife is aware of his intentions), but he pursues his own individual course to its successful conclusion, despite the fact that he receives some ridicule along the way.

By remaining open to possibilities and following unusual paths, Babe, Farmer Hogget, and Fly achieve personal fulfillment. Hogget had almost given up having a sheep dog good enough to enter in the Grand Challenge trials until Babe came along, but, by keeping an open mind, he recognizes the pig's potential. Fly, in turn, is able to give full expression to her maternal instincts by accepting a pig into her family, despite her initial prejudice against the species. Babe, by keeping his mind open to possibilities, finds a mother in Fly, a friend in Ma, and fame and fulfillment in an unexpected "career."

The key to the message of *Babe*, however, can be found in the sheep's password, which is also the key to Babe's success at the trials: "I may be ewe, I may be ram,/ I may be mutton, may be lamb,/ But on the hoof or on the hook,/ I bain't so stupid as I look." The novel's crucial messages of tolerance, understanding, and suspicion of stereotypes are contained in that simple phrase. Although Babe professes not to understand "all that stuff about 'I may be you,'" he has lived, and thrived, by the golden rule of treating others as he wished to be treated himself.

Critical Context

Dick King-Smith's background as a farmer is evident in his books, which often feature rural settings and animals who possess magical or extraordinary attributes and who have the power to transform the lives of those around them. *Babe* fits squarely into this body of work, which includes another novel about an extraordinary pig, *Ace: The Very Important Pig* (1990). Ace, who claims to be a distant relation of the famous sheep-pig Babe, has the amazing ability to understand human language and makes a name for himself as the pig who watches television and enjoys a bowl of beer at the local pub on occasion. King-Smith's works about extraordinary animals also include *Pretty Polly* (1993), featuring a chicken whose ability to speak English propels her to worldwide fame; *The Invisible Dog* (1993), about Henry, an imaginary dog who comes to life; and *Harriet's Hare* (1995), revolving around a space alien disguised as a hare who finds a new wife for Harriet's widowed father.

Ironically, while the pig in literature often symbolizes humanity's worst traits, it is also used, particularly in children's literature, to illustrate what is best in people. The pig as a figure of innocence, dignity, and innate wisdom appears frequently in juvenile literature, calling to mind the purity of childhood before it becomes tainted by contact with society. Babe clearly falls within this tradition, along with other great literary pigs, including Piglet in A. A. Milne's *Winnie-the-Pooh* (1926) and Wilbur in E. B. White's *Charlotte's Web* (1952). Particularly since the 1995 release of the motion picture *Babe*, based on the novel, *Babe: The Gallant Pig* should be assured of a place in the pantheon of worthy literary pigs.

Mary Virginia Davis

BARON MÜNCHAUSEN'S NARRATIVE OF HIS MARVELLOUS TRAVELS AND CAMPAIGNS IN RUSSIA

Author: Rudolf Eric Raspe (1737-1794)
First published: 1785
Type of work: Novel
Type of plot: Adventure tale and fantasy
Time of work: The mid-eighteenth century
Locale: Lithuania, Russia, Marseilles, the East Indies, Egypt, England, North America, and the moon
Subjects: Social issues, the supernatural, and travel
Recommended ages: 13-18

The great raconteur Baron Münchausen relates his hilariously improbable, extraordinary, and absurd military, hunting, and travel exploits.

Principal character:
BARON MÜNCHAUSEN, a North German nobleman who has served as an officer in two Russian campaigns against the Turks in 1740 and 1741 and traveled widely

Form and Content

In *Baron Münchausen's Narrative*, a series of tall tales purportedly document the adventures and exploits—both on land and at sea—of the infamous Baron Münchausen. (In English-language editions, the name is commonly spelled "Munchausen" or "Münchausen"; the real figure on which the character is based was Baron Münchhausen.) Told in the form of first-person memoirs as if to a circle of intimate friends, these short narratives derive their charm in large measure from the tension between the constant and overstated reassurances of their veracity and the patently impossible situations that they describe. In this spirit, several of the editions are prefaced by a sworn attestation that the adventures are true to fact, and the alleged document is signed authoritatively "in the absence of the Lord Mayor of London" by such reliable witnesses as Gulliver, Sinbad, and Aladdin.

The humorous vignettes depicted in this collection present the Baron as an extraordinarily fortunate fellow. Wherever his travels take him, he manages to find himself in the most miraculous of circumstances. On his way to St. Petersburg, Russia, for example, a blizzard prevents him from locating a certain Lithuanian town in which he had intended to seek lodgings. At the point of exhaustion, he hitches his horse to a lone post jutting out of the snowy ground and lies down in the open to rest. At daybreak, he awakens in a village square without his horse. Soon he hears neighing and looks upward to see the horse hanging from the top of a church. He surmises that previously the village had been covered with snow, but that a weather change during the night caused the snow to melt. As a result, the Baron had been gradually lowered to the ground, while his horse was hitched to what turned out to be a church steeple. A skilled marksman, the Baron shoots the bridle in two, which brings the horse down and allows him to proceed on his journey to St. Petersburg.

The waggish storyteller always manages to underscore his own irrepressible ingenuity. In another preposterous episode, he recounts a hunting expedition during which he runs out of ammunition just as a stately stag happens upon the scene. Ever the master of his predicament, Münchausen quickly loads his rifle with a handful of cherry stones left over from a recent snack. He is able to hit the animal between its antlers, but this action only stuns it and the beast staggers off relatively unscathed. A year later, on another hunting party in the same forest, Münchausen spies the same stag. In the meanwhile, the cherry stone has taken root and a full-grown cherry tree extends from between its antlers. The Baron takes aim and is this time more successful: A single shot results in a meal of savory venison accompanied by a delicious cherry sauce.

The adventure to end all adventures is without question Münchausen's successful, if not entirely intentional, journey to the moon. While on an ocean expedition to the South Seas, a fortuitous combination of meteorological events carries the Baron's ship to the moon. The diverse lunar population, the reader is informed, includes natives of the dog-star, whose faces are like those of large mastiffs but without eyelids. Their long tongues cover their eyes at night during sleep. The indigenous inhabitants, by contrast, are no less than thirty-six-feet tall and have only one finger to a hand; their heads are generally located under their right arms but can be conveniently removed if necessary, for example when exercising. Readers are never told how Münchausen accomplishes his return to the earth, but that feat—one can be certain—would have been hardly a challenge for the celebrated Baron.

Analysis

It is difficult to see in the Münchausen stories much more than their obvious entertainment value. They are inspired by the memoirs of the real-life Baron Karl Friedrich Hieronymus von Münchhausen (1720-1797), who indeed served in the Russian army in two campaigns against the Turks and is said to have had a penchant for gross exaggeration in the retelling of his adventures. Rudolf Eric Raspe was a court librarian at Cassel when he became acquainted with the stories, but it was only after he fled to England to escape a criminal charge that he first compiled and published in English a version of the narratives. The collection enjoyed immediate and enormous popularity among English readers and quickly saw a second edition. The German *Sturm und Drang* poet Gottfried August Bürger (1747-1794), adding additional anecdotes, translated Raspe's work into German, and it was Bürger's version in 1786 that secured for the mendacious Baron lasting popularity with the German reading public. The figure of Münchausen has attained to the status of folk hero in German-speaking countries, where he is often referred to as "der Lügenbaron" (the baron of lies).

These sometimes grotesquely absurd tales—one describes a horse that was cut in half by a town gate, drank ravenously from a fountain, and then was sewn back together—fit neatly into a long and distinguished tradition of literary prevarication that stretches far back into classical antiquity and includes the prose satires of the Greek writer Lucian, certain Talmudic stories, and *The Arabian Nights' Entertainments*. In the same vein, though of more recent provenance, belong the German Till Eulenspiegel stories, Jonathan Swift's *Gulliver's Travels* (1726), as well as the American Paul Bunyan and Johnny Appleseed tall tales.

What perhaps accounts for the success of the Münchausen tales, beyond their sheer hilarity, is the positive representation of what even in the eighteenth century were already becoming old-fashioned values: the pleasures of eating, drinking, riding, hunting, fishing, and warring. With the help of Baron Münchausen's down-to-earth inventiveness, these essentially feudal pastimes are set in direct opposition to those values associated negatively with Enlightenment intellectualism and the rise of a society forced to rely increasingly on dehumanizing technology. While these themes and motifs found a distinct resonance in particular during the historically momentous period immediately preceding and following the French Revolution, it may be that the triumph of human wit and imperturbability against overwhelming odds are themes that retain universal applicability. One may suspect, however, that it is most likely the humor in these tales, not their meager social content, to which their long-lived success must be attributed.

Critical Context

Although *Baron Münchausen's Narrative* was clearly not conceived in the first place as juvenile or young adult literature, it has over the past centuries become a perennial favorite, more so perhaps in Europe than in North America. Young readers will no doubt appreciate the tales primarily for their humor and their ability to amuse. They exhibit little, if any, psychological complexity, and there is no character development. The world portrayed in the stories—both in its absurdity and its sociohistorical remoteness—has little to do with modern times, and no attempt whatsoever is made to inculcate in any form, not even surreptitiously, a moral lesson. In short, while a modern audience is unlikely to discern in the stories the fairly well concealed social commentary that was surely more perceptible to Raspe's contemporaries, *Baron Münchausen's Narrative* can nevertheless be recommended as a genuinely comic and entertaining book. The humor found here is laughable, ridiculous, and often delightfully sophomoric, but it is never salacious or malicious.

A wide variety of editions and versions of the Münchausen tales exists under various titles, including some of more recent publication. In addition, the original collection by Raspe has inspired numerous sequels and as been translated into many languages. Most versions are furnished liberally with comical illustrations. Because the stories are now considered public domain (some, in fact, no longer credit Raspe at all), editors have felt free to adapt them to the needs and sensibilities of specific audiences. One version by Brian Robb in 1978, for example, makes the narrative quite accessible to readers well before their teenage years. Given the immense and enduring popularity of the stories, it is not surprising that other media have been drawn to Baron Münchausen's exploits as well. Several animated cartoons, sound recordings, and a Hollywood feature motion picture, *The Adventures of Baron Munchausen* (1989), prove the continuing viability of the tales.

Steven R. Huff

BASEBALL IN APRIL AND OTHER STORIES

Author: Gary Soto (1952-   )
First published: 1990
Type of work: Short fiction
Subjects: Coming-of-age, emotions, family, love and romance, and sports
Recommended ages: 10-13

This collection of eleven short stories explores the theme of growing up Hispanic in Fresno, California.

Form and Content

Baseball in April and Other Stories provides a reassuring look at growing up. Written for a middle-school audience, this collection of short stories offers a window into how circumstances in the lives of students in this age group are often perceived and how problems are resolved.

"Broken Chain" centers on first love and troublesome brothers. In preparing his bike for his first date with Sandra, Alfonso breaks the chain. Although his brother Ernie will not change his plans to help Alfonso, he does come through in time so that Alfonso can use Ernie's bike for his date. At least Alfonso can "ride" Sandra on his handlebars. The story ends with her hands on his, and "it felt like love."

"Baseball in April" also focuses on two brothers, Jesse and Michael, nine and ten years old, respectively, who hope to play Little League Baseball. Not making the cut, they join the Hobos, the leftovers, but only Jesse stays with the team. Despite their best efforts, the Hobos lose all their games. One day, only four boys show up for practice. Jesse fails to show up the following day and feels guilty, worried that a sole teammate will find himself on the bench, waiting.

In "Two Dreamers," a boy and his grandfather think about speculating in real estate. Hector's grandfather Luis is inspired by his son-in-law's ability to buy and sell a house with enough profit to buy a brand-new car and to build a brick fence around his house. Unsupported by his wife, Luis and nine-year-old Hector inspect a house, and his grandfather persuades Hector to call the agent to learn the price. When it is far more money than anticipated, and because Hector's grandmother almost catches them, Luis and Hector gratefully escape to mow the yard—two "hardworking guys" who still have dreams.

In "Barbie," owning a real Barbie is Veronica's dream. A Christmas ago, she received an imitation Barbie, and this Christmas there was no doll at all until Uncle Rudy surprises her with a real Barbie. Ecstatic, she takes her doll to play with her friend Martha, but when Martha tries to switch Barbies, Veronica leaves. On the way home, Veronica realizes that Barbie's head is missing and spends hours searching for it. Heartbroken, she goes to bed, cradling both of her "Barbies."

"The No-Guitar Blues" features Fausto, a boy with a dream to start his own band by playing the guitar. When he pretends to find a lost dog and receives twenty dollars as a reward for returning it, Fausto feels guilty. He redeems himself by going to Mass and placing the bill into the offering basket. That night at dinner, his mother offers him a bass guitarron that had belonged to his grandfather. Goodness appears to prompt rewards and nurture dreams.

In "Seventh Grade," Victor experiences the complications of love. Trying to impress Teresa, he pretends that he can speak French, which he cannot. An understanding teacher keeps his secret, and Teresa is suitably impressed, enough to ask him to help her with her French assignments.

The story "Mother and Daughter" honors this special relationship. Because there is no money for a new dress for the dance, Mrs. Moreno dyes Yollie's summer dress to go with her new black shoes. Feeling stylish, Yollie goes to the dance, but a rainstorm causes her dress to run. Yollie runs home, embarrassed and angry. When Ernie calls the next day to find out why she ran away and to see if she would like to go to the movies, her mother reveals her secret stash of money, money she had put aside for Yollie. Mrs. Moreno wonders why they did not use it earlier, and the pair go shopping for clothes guaranteed not to bleed.

To be "The Karate Kid" is a dream of virtually all young boys at one time or another, and fifth-grader Gilbert is no exception. Convinced that learning karate will help him defeat the playground bully, Gilbert persuades his mother that he needs lessons. The lessons are taught by an uninspired and uninspiring instructor, and Gilbert soon wants to quit. He finally gets his wish when the studio closes. Looking for other solutions to handle the school bully, Gilbert begins reading Superman comic books.

"La Bamba" is the humorous story of Manuel, who yearns for the spotlight and so volunteers to lip-synch the song "La Bamba" for the school talent show. On stage, Manuel is doing fine until the record gets stuck on the line, "*para bailar la bamba*." Nearly crying by the time he gets off stage, he is amazed when classmates congratulate him on his comic act. When he receives a burst of applause during the curtain call, he cares little about why he is receiving so much attention; he simply enjoys the fact that he is.

"The Marble Champ" refers to Lupe, a girl who is frequently in the limelight for academic achievements but never for athletic ones. Finally, she tries marbles and assiduously practices for weeks before the marble championship. Using the same powers of concentration and commitment that have caused her to do well academically, she learns the game and indeed becomes the champion.

"Growing Up" describes the dilemma of all adolescents as they try to differentiate themselves from their families. Based on the disappointments of previous vacations, tenth-grader Maria decides that she is not going this year. When she hears that a family is hurt in a freeway accident, Maria spends the following days worrying about her family's safety. When they return and describe the best vacation ever, she is upset with them for leaving her behind. Hugging her dolls, Maria realizes that she is growing up—and she even enjoys her brothers' antics at dinner.

Analysis

The strength of Gary Soto's work is that these stories could be written about young people of any culture. Equally so, another strength of these stories is that they are written with names and characteristics of Hispanic youth and culture. All young people must have literary heroes if they are to believe that literature can speak to them. These stories are particularly important for Hispanic youth because there are so few pieces of literature for them and because the tales are so well written. Fresh imagery abounds in the text; comparisons are made that are easily accessible to and enjoyable for younger readers. Soto deftly weaves Spanish words, phrases, and expressions into the text (and provides a list of these with their translations in the back of the book) so that both language and culture come through in an authentic, realistic way.

The themes of first love, sports, dreams, coming-of-age, and family are central to these stories and to adolescence itself. Consequently, middle-school readers will find their thoughts and feelings validated on these pages. "Broken Chain," "Seventh Grade," and "Mother and Daughter" all address the complexities and confusion of first love. "Baseball in April," "The Karate Kid," and "The Marble Champ" address willed prowess in various athletic endeavors and how success nurtures self-esteem. The power of dreams is central to "Two Dreamers" and "The No-Guitar Blues," while "Barbie," "La Bamba," and "Growing Up" reveal the difficulties of coming-of-age. Sometimes strained but important relationships among family members are featured in these stories as well, evidence of the realities of maturation.

Critical Context

Gary Soto is of critical importance to children's and young adult literature because, with *Baseball in April and Other Stories* in 1990, he became the first Mexican American author to have a children's book released by a mainstream publishing company. *A Fire in My Hands*, Soto's book of poetry for children, was also published that year, and two more poetry collections soon followed: *Neighborhood Odes* (1992) and *Canto Familiar* (1995). It is not surprising that poetry would be included in his introductory year to children's literature, since most of Soto's earlier works consisted of poetry for adults.

Another collection of short fiction by Soto that is appropriate for this age group is *Local News* (1993). Some of his novels that middle-school students might enjoy are *Taking Sides* (1991), a story of loyalties both on and off the basketball court; *Pacific Crossing* (1992), a story of martial arts and a summer in Japan; *The Pool Party* (1993), a young boy's reconciliation with his identity as a Mexican American in Southern California; *Crazy Weekend* (1994), a hilarious "cops and robbers" kind of adventure; and *Jesse* (1994), a realistic look at the potential of Mexican American youth. Soto's collections of autobiographical essays include *Living up the Street* (1985), *Small Faces* (1986), and *A Summer Life* (1990).

Soto's strength as a writer is exhibited in the variety of genres and audiences that he has addressed. Younger students might enjoy his short novel *The Skirt* (1992), the tale of a girl named Miata who loses the special skirt that she needs for the *folklorico*, or his picture books *Too Many Tamales* (1993), a Christmas Eve story involving a missing wedding ring and "too many tamales," and *Chato's Kitchen* (1995), in which a cat attempts to rid his barrio of little mice and ends up having them for dinner as guests instead of as the main course.

Alexa L. Sandmann

THE BAT-POET

Author: Randall Jarrell (1914-1965)
First published: 1964; illustrated
Type of work: Novel
Type of plot: Fantasy and moral tale
Time of work: Undefined
Locale: The area around a house
Subjects: Animals, arts, and nature
Recommended ages: 10-13

. In this classic children's story, which can also be enjoyed by adults, a little brown bat becomes a poet and searches for an audience.

Form and Content

Randall Jarrell's story is presented in the form of a folktale in which animals are given human characteristics. It is also an allegory about poetry. Illustrated by Maurice Sendak, whose black-and-white drawings correspond to the narrative, the story is told by a first-person narrator. The narrator refers to himself only once, at the beginning, when he focuses attention on the bats hanging upside down from the roof of his porch. The narrator then effaces himself, drawing the reader into the world of a little brown bat.

The little bat is different from the other bats. He wakes up during the day, when bats normally sleep, and looks out into the sunlight. He has never seen the birds and the other animals before. He has heard the mockingbird, however, because the bird sings half the night, imitating the other creatures with his songs. This gives the little bat the idea to make up his own songs, or poems, to tell the other bats about the daytime. Yet, when he recites his first poem to the bats, they refuse to believe in the reality that it shows them.

The little bat is disappointed, but he continues to compose poems. He wonders if the mockingbird would listen to them. The mockingbird has bad days, when he chases everything out of the yard. On good days, he simply sings to himself, not paying attention to anything. The little bat approaches the bird with anxiety and asks if he would listen to the poem that he has made up about the owl. When the mockingbird praises the poem's technique but says nothing about the owl—which almost killed the little bat—the bat-poet realizes that the problem is not creating poems but persuading someone to listen to them.

The little bat wonders if the chipmunk would listen to a poem about chipmunks. To show the chipmunk what a poem is, the bat-poet recites his poem about the owl. The chipmunk likes the poem, but it terrifies him. He decides to go to bed earlier from now on, before the owl is out, and to dig more holes. The bat-poet is glad that the chipmunk did not comment on technique and instead was scared by the poem. The chipmunk also likes the poem that the bat-poet writes about him. It goes in and out, like a chipmunk going in and out of his holes.

His success with the chipmunk encourages the bat-poet to try the mockingbird again. The little bat thinks it strange that the mockingbird drives away the birds and animals that he imitates in his songs. The bat-poet makes up a poem about this fact and recites it to the mockingbird. Instead of learning something from the poem, the mockingbird becomes defensive and accuses the little bat of thinking that there is something wrong with driving things away. The bat-poet gives up on the mockingbird and decides to try again to communicate with the other bats.

He begins a poem about a mother bat and her baby. When it is finished, he tries it out on the chipmunk, who is amazed by all the things that bats can do. Winter is coming, and the bat and the chipmunk feel sleepy all the time. The little bat flies home; the other bats will be waking up. In preparation for reciting his poem to them, the bat-poet begins to say it over to himself. After a few lines, he forgets what comes next. He wishes he had said that bats sleep all winter. He starts over. After two lines, his eyes close, he yawns, and he snuggles closer to the others.

Analysis

The most apparent theme of *The Bat-Poet* is the value of looking at life from a different point of view. This theme is developed through contrasts between the bat-poet and the mockingbird, who represent different kinds of poets, and between the chipmunk and the other bats, who represent different kinds of audiences. Although the story is about poetry, *The Bat-Poet* is ultimately concerned with the nature of life and how one should live it. The attitudes toward poetry of the animals in the story represent various ways of relating to life and to others.

The mockingbird substitutes poetry for life. An egotist, he feels superior to the other creatures, whom he either drives out of *his* territory or ignores completely. All that he wants is to listen to the sound of his own voice singing his own songs. Although he enjoys being praised, he is not interested in knowing and communicating with others. The bat-poet, on the other hand, is curious about life. He wants to know what happens in the daytime. He wants to know the other animals and to communicate with them. He writes poems not for himself but to please others, to warn them against danger, and to show them things that they do not know, even about themselves.

The difference between the mockingbird and the bat-poet is reflected in their attitudes about form and content. The mockingbird imposes form on content; this parallels his domination of the other birds and animals. For the bat-poet, on the other hand, form is a result of content. In its form, his poem about the chipmunk goes in and out because it reflects the activity of chipmunks going in and out of their holes. The last line of his owl poem is minus two poetic feet because the little bat was holding his breath when the owl was out, not because he was thinking about metrical structure when he composed the poem.

The chipmunk represents the ideal audience for the poet. He is willing to listen and to learn. He is open to the poem's content and to its meaning. Most important, he is willing to change his life because of the poem, deciding to go to bed earlier and to dig more holes for escape in case he does encounter the owl. In contrast, the mockingbird is not interested in the owl and responds to the content of a poem only when it is about him. He then becomes defensive when he thinks that he is being criticized. Unwilling to admit his faults and unable to empathize with others, the mockingbird, ironically, never really knows the world that he imitates in his songs.

The other bats, as an audience, are not much different from the mockingbird. The bat-poet wants them to stay awake during the day so they can experience the world that they never see. They consent to listen to his poem about the daytime only to be polite, then interrupt him to argue about its accuracy. Their minds are closed to any reality other than their own. As a result, their lives are impoverished; they are asleep to the possibilities of life. This is ultimately what *The Bat-Poet* is about.

To be truly alive, human beings must be curious about the world, willing to learn about themselves and about others. The ability to do so depends on giving up egocentric views and developing the capacity for empathy. This need is exemplified by the narrator's self-effacement at the beginning of the story. The conclusion of *The Bat-Poet* shows that there is hope for the bats—and for human beings as well. Perhaps they will respond positively to the little bat's poem when they wake up from their hibernation in the spring.

Critical Context

Randall Jarrell was not primarily a writer of children's stories. Although his reputation as a literary critic overshadowed his importance as a poet during his lifetime, Jarrell's most important work was his poetry. He had a lifelong interest in fairy tales, however, and in 1962 was commissioned to translate some of the stories of the Brothers Grimm. Jarrell's editor was pleased by the result and suggested that he write a children's story. That summer, Jarrell wrote *The Gingerbread Rabbit* (1964) and began *The Bat-Poet*. He completed this book and wrote two more children's stories, *The Animal Family* (1965) and *Fly by Night* (1976), as well as one of his finest books of poetry, *The Lost World* (1965), before his death in 1965. The lost world of this title is, among other things, the lost world of childhood. Jarrell included three poems from *The Bat-Poet* in this book.

Although *The Bat-Poet* is Jarrell's most popular children's story, it is difficult to narrow its audience to a specific age group. A two-year-old would enjoy listening to it, and students and teachers of literature have reason to study it for what it reveals about Jarrell's poetic theory and for its treatment of themes that are characteristic of Jarrell's work. Not least among its readers are poets and creative writers of all ages. *The Bat-Poet* truly is one of those stories that can be read and enjoyed by anyone. With its combination of children's story and allegory about poetry, it is especially suited for introducing elementary students to literature, as well as interesting them in writing their own stories and poems.

James Green

THE BEACON AT ALEXANDRIA

Author: Gillian Bradshaw (1956-   )
First published: 1986
Type of work: Novel
Type of plot: Historical fiction
Time of work: 371-378 A.D.
Locale: Ephesus, Alexandria, and Thrace, far-flung regions in the Roman Empire's
    eastern Mediterranean area
Subjects: Gender roles, health and illness, and religion
Recommended ages: 15-18

> *Disguising herself as a eunuch, Charis flees from Ephesus to study medicine in Alexandria, where she is sucked into the religious and political turmoil of the dying Roman Empire and then thrust out to its threatened northern borders as a military doctor, only to discover there her true calling.*

Principal characters:
    CHARIS/CHARITON, the daughter of Theodoros of Ephesus, a brilliant
        medical student, physician to an archbishop, and head of a Roman
        military hospital
    PHILON, the Jewish doctor who takes Chariton as an assistant
    ARCHBISHOP ATHANASIOS, a figure at the center of the Arian/Nicene
        controversy in Alexandria
    ATHANARIC OF SARDICA, a Gothic agent of Rome who saves Chariton's
        life and career because of a blood debt
    FRITIGERN, a Gothic nobleman, the husband of Lady Amalberga
    FESTINUS, the governor of Asia, who is betrothed to Charis

Form and Content

    In order to explore the far frontiers and violent intrigues of the second century, most authors would probably not choose a female protagonist. The Roman Empire was a man's world where women were generally property or playthings. Yet Gillian Bradshaw does just that in *The Beacon at Alexandria*. Charis, however, is an unlikely heroine whose story is told in three settings: Ephesus, where she grew up; Alexandria, where she learned medicine; and Thrace, where she practiced it. Whether Charis can experience life fully as a woman, as a doctor, and as a Roman citizen is the novel's primary question.

    More interested in nursing sick animals than in dreaming of marriage prospects, fifteen-year-old Charis feels that the "girl in the mirror, the demurely proper, over-dressed doll" is not herself. Even though Festinus, the new governor of Asia, threatens her father's wealth and reputation and physically assaults her, Charis is forced to become engaged to him. Rather than submit to a life of hollow pretense with such a cruel man, she runs away, disguised as a eunuch, to study medicine in Alexandria.

In this Egyptian city, the academic capital of the Roman world and the center of the Nicene/Arian power struggle in the Christian church, Charis, now called Chariton, finds it difficult to enter the closed medical community. Only a kindly Jewish doctor, Philon, will take her on as an assistant. He is a practitioner of the Hippocratic method of medicine, which has always attracted her. She learns to live as a man, soaks up the lectures, and gains valuable experience with Philon's patients, finding herself eventually called to treat the Nicene archbishop, Athanasios. If he dies, Egypt will erupt in violence and Rome will impose an Arian archbishop. She saves his life but at the cost of her secret. Despite the knowledge that Charis is a woman, he makes her his doctor, but his power cannot protect her after his death. Only Athanaric, a Gothic agent of Rome whose life she has also saved, is able rescue her from the prospect of imprisonment and death by signing her on as an army doctor in his homeland of Thrace.

Charis runs the hospital competently and, through Athanaric, helps the family of Gothic nobleman Fritigern. Nevertheless, she is keenly aware that to maintain her much-loved art of healing, she has given up any chance of normal family life. This dilemma becomes secondary as conditions deteriorate along the frontier. She is kidnapped by the Goths and forced to meet their desperate medical needs. Fritigern's wife, who had realized Charis' gender at their first meeting, now exposes it to prevent her escape. She may be both a woman and doctor, but now she cannot be a Roman, an identity that she has come to value. It seems that all three roles are incompatible. When she is rescued by Athanaric, whom she has loved for years and who is fully aware of her true identity, Charis is given the chance for wholeness even as the Empire stumbles toward its inevitable death.

Analysis

Each of the strands that make up Charis' life—her gender, her calling, and her citizenship—becomes Bradshaw's avenue to explore the quality of life in the late Roman Empire. In an atmosphere of hostility toward women, it seems impossible for these identities to be woven into a pleasing pattern of psychological wholeness.

Charis realizes that her Ephesian life, split between social expectations and hidden study, is a pretense, and she fears that she will become the false plaything that she has pretended to be. Even though this realization gives her the courage to run away, she must continue to pretend—this time that she is a "man," for only men could study medicine. Charis thrives in her study, outshining all fellow students, but she must balance what she has gained with what she realizes that she has lost. She laments, "Never to be loved by some tall young man. . . . Not if I wanted to practice my art. Not if I stayed myself. And if I stayed myself, I was simply my own grave, with no free outlet to the world til death came to claim me." This dilemma only deepens when she falls in love with Athanaric.

Alexandria is the center of the book as well as the beacon of the title. There Charis could learn medical truths both in the city's classrooms and famous libraries and as practiced in its crowded streets and dirty homes. Her learning is always tested against the touchstone of Hippocrates—Charis is nothing if not a passionate follower of Hippocrates. Others in Alexandria are following a beacon as well, although caught up in her own passion, Charis never understands their passion for theology. She respects such devotion, however, especially in the ascetic Archbishop Athanasios. He longs for heaven, yet he knows that his death will consign many of his followers to a hell on earth. He will not bow to Rome's wishes because, as he tells Charis, "at the bottom of everything [is] what one believes about God." When Charis is forced to leave the city, she realizes that "Alexandria's freedom is like Christ's peace: 'not as the world's' . . . a liberty to search for truth and to define your own law . . . [it] casts its light a long way through the wastes of darkness."

Even though Charis has little interest in the Empire's politics while managing her hospital on its threatened northern edge, she slowly begins to realize that for all its injustices toward women and those it has subjugated—symbolized by Festinus' treatment of the Goths—the Empire itself is also a beacon of light. Alexandria is part of the Empire, representing its truest impulses. Athanaric, himself a Goth, serves the Empire as devotedly as Charis serves medicine. When she is dragged outside its boundaries, when she realizes that Rome might fall to the invaders, she embraces her citizenship, for she is "entirely a creature of the empire, formed by it through [her] education, fed by its learning, nourished by its peace."

Bradshaw brilliantly weaves the three strands of Charis' life, three strands of life in the second century, into a pattern both profound and disturbing but ultimately satisfying when, with Athanaric, the heroine is finally able to embrace her identity as a woman, practice medicine, and remain a Roman citizen. Before Athanasios appears to her in a dream, Charis had wondered if such wholeness could only be possible in heaven. He assures her, however, as a Nicene would, that the earth is God's realm as well. None of her identities is eternal—her gender, her profession, her citizenship—but all are valuable. His prophecy, complete with its intimation of the death of the Empire, is fulfilled with Charis' marriage to Athanaric.

Critical Context

Gillian Bradshaw established her reputation as a novelist while still in college, receiving the Jule and Avery Hopwood Award for Fiction from the University of Michigan for *Hawk of May* (1980), the first volume in what would become an Arthurian trilogy. After completing a master's degree in classics from Cambridge University, she continued to explore and re-create the latter days of the Roman Empire and the early Middle Ages. So seamlessly does she weave in the historical facts that give believability to her stories that the reader does not even notice these lessons. In *The Beacon at Alexandria*, for example, many fascinating snippets describe how medicine was learned and practiced at that time in history and what a primitive military hospital might have been like. These facts heighten the sense of loss that Bradshaw obviously projects at the death of the Roman Empire, even though she does not romanticize second century life. Two other books, while not constituting a formal trilogy with *The Beacon at Alexandria*, continue her exploration of life during the collapse of the Roman Empire: *The Bearkeeper's Daughter* (1987) and *Imperial Purple* (1988).

Bradshaw did not write her books for a young adult audience, but they have been embraced by teenagers who although realizing the chasm between these civilizations and their own, recognize a commonality between their situations and those of Bradshaw's characters. Any young woman who has been hindered from pursuing her dreams (although with far fewer obstacles) will see in her own circumstances a reflection of Charis' story. *The Beacon at Alexandria* received the American Library Association's Notable Book award.

Barbara J. Hampton

BEAUTY
A Retelling of the Story of Beauty and the Beast

Author: Robin McKinley (1952-   )
First published: 1978
Type of work: Novel
Type of plot: Fantasy and folktale
Time of work: The eighteenth century
Locale: A city, a little house in the country, and a castle in an enchanted forest
Subjects: Family, friendship, and love and romance
Recommended ages: 13-18

Plain, studious, and hardworking Beauty goes to live with the Beast in order to fulfill a promise made by her father, becomes beautiful, and learns to love the Beast.

> *Principal characters:*
> BEAUTY, the youngest of three daughters, known as "the clever one"
> GRACE, the oldest daughter, who has beautiful blond hair and blue eyes
> HOPE, the middle daughter, who has beautiful chestnut-brown hair and smoky green eyes
> MR. HUSTON, the father of the girls
> GERVAIN WOODHOUSE, a blacksmith who is in love with Hope
> THE BEAST, who is about seven feet tall, has human eyes, and walks upright

Form and Content

Robin McKinley's *Beauty: A Retelling of the Story of Beauty and the Beast* is effectively written in the first person, allowing the reader to share readily in Beauty's feelings. The novel is an adaptation or retelling of the 1757 story "Beauty and the Beast" by Madame Le Prince de Beaumont.

Beauty's given name at her baptism was Honour. At the age of five, however, not understanding the word "honour," she told her father that she would rather be Beauty. Thus, Beauty is the name by which she is called throughout the story. Her oldest sister, Grace, is beautiful, tall, and blond and has blue eyes. Hope, her other sister, is beautiful, tall, and slender with chestnut-brown hair and large green eyes. Both sisters are kind-hearted and have small, delicate hands and feet. At twelve, Beauty has mousy hair, muddy hazel eyes, is small of stature with big hands and huge feet, and has a skin problem. Beauty is known as "the clever one" and likes to read and study.

Their father, Mr. Huston, is one of the wealthiest merchants in the city. At nineteen, Grace becomes engaged to Robert Tucker, Father's most promising young sea captain, while Gervain Woodhouse, an iron worker in Father's shipyard, is in love with Hope. Father's ships meet with disasters, however, and there is no word about the fate of Robert Tucker. Father soon loses his fortune.

The family is aided by Gervain, who asks for Hope's hand. He does not like the city and has found a small house with a forge and a shop near his home village, where he will work as a blacksmith. Gervain proposes that the family move with them and that they all live in the house, a plan that Father accepts. The city house and most of the family's goods are sold at auction. Beauty is given Greatheart, a beautiful, huge horse, because she fed and took care of him when he was young and he misses her when she stays away. Eventually, they reach their new home. Gervain makes the sisters promise never to walk in the woods behind the house without either himself or Father for company. He tells Beauty that the forest may be enchanted and that it is said that a monster who had the form of a man lives in a castle there.

Father receives word that one of his ships is returning to port. He leaves for the city to meet it, telling the family not to look for him until springtime, when traveling will be easier. Father returns in late March after a blizzard. He holds in his hand a large scarlet rose, which he gives to Beauty. She had asked for some rose seeds, if they were not too expensive, when Father asked if they wanted anything from the city. Father tells his story: He became lost in a blizzard and stayed at a castle. When he was ready to leave, he picked the bud of a beautiful rose. A beast who walked upright like a man roared that since Father stole the rose, he had to die. Father pleaded with the Beast, who agreed to spare his life if he would give him one of his daughters. The Beast promised not to harm her but demands that she come of her own free will, loving her father enough to want to save his life. The Beast would give him a month to decide.

Beauty is obstinate in her insistence that she be the one to go. Father travels with her until Beauty asks him to return home. With fear and trepidation, Beauty enters the castle and meets the Beast. She is given beautiful clothes and has everything done for her. Every night, the Beast asks, "Beauty, will you marry me?" and every night she says "no." Eventually, while she is visiting her family, Beauty realizes that she is in love with the Beast and will agree to marry him.

Analysis

In her version of "Beauty and the Beast," McKinley seeks to create complex, genuine personalities out of one-dimensional fairy-tale characters. Much love is reflected in the feelings of the family members for one another. The father is past sixty and, when he loses his fortune, begins to look his age. He becomes a broken man. The sisters are loving and considerate of one another and of their father. Grace and Hope are beautiful, while Beauty, who is twelve at the beginning of the novel, considers herself to be plain and avoids mirrors. An awkward and shy girl, she shuns other people, preferring the company of books. Many young girls reading this story can identify with Beauty's feelings. When the family moves to the country, Grace and Hope divide the housework and Beauty does the remaining chores: She splits, chops, and stacks wood. Beauty believes that it would have been more convenient if she had been a boy and that she looks like one. Beauty takes pride in her intelligence, however, and has hopes of studying at a university. Although such ambition was unheard of for a woman at that time, Beauty's father does not discourage her.

In Beauty, McKinley creates a young woman who is both ordinary and heroic. At first, Beauty is afraid of the Beast, but she tries not to let her voice or actions show it. She finds it difficult to look at the Beast's face because he has human eyes. He is full of contradictions: His voice is gruff and harsh, yet he wears beautiful velvet clothes. Beauty thinks that he may be intending to eat her, but the Beast promises that no harm will come to her. Throughout the story, Greatheart, her horse, is of much comfort to her, and she even succeeds in calming the horse in the Beast's presence. Animals do not like the Beast, although some birds do come to Beauty's window. McKinley's portrait of life at the castle is strange and exciting. Beauty hears the voices of invisible beings who dress her and serve her breakfast. The library in the castle contains both classic books and those that have not been written. There are no mirrors or quiet waters to reflect one's image.

During the course of the novel, Beauty's perceptions—and those of the reader—change, reflecting her growing maturity and self-confidence. Beauty begins to enjoy the companionship of the Beast. The only flaws in her enjoyment of this new life are a longing to see her family and having to refuse the Beast's marriage proposal each night. When the Beast finally allows her to go home for a week, Beauty, now eighteen, finds that she has grown taller than Hope. She also realizes that she really does not belong there and that she truly loves the Beast and wishes to marry him. Upon Beauty's declaration of love, the enchantment is broken and the Beast becomes a handsome man. To convince her that she is beautiful, he escorts her to a mirror that has reappeared. Beauty finally realizes that the copper-haired woman with amber eyes holding hands with the man in golden velvet is herself. The reader is left feeling that both names—Beauty and Honour—are appropriate for this young woman.

Critical Context

Beauty was Robin McKinley's first novel. Her descriptions are so vivid that one can immediately conjure up visions of Beauty, the Beast, the castle, and the enchanted forest. McKinley also develops complex characters with genuine strengths and weaknesses. For example, her depiction of the journey from the city to the country examines the difficulties encountered by formerly wealthy people who have been accustomed to having servants and who now must adjust to doing everything themselves.

Love and romance, the young adult's struggle for identity and self-esteem, and strong-willed female protagonists can also be found in McKinley's first two original novels. *The Blue Sword* (1982), set in the mythical desert kingdom of Damar, features Harry Crewe, a courageous woman trained to be a warrior who will save the kingdom. *The Hero and the Crown* (1984) is a "prequel" to *The Blue Sword*. Aerin, an ancestor of Harry, is shy and clumsy, but courageous, independent, and stubborn. She is invested with the Blue Sword by a wizard, who has trained her to be a warrior to lead the Damarians in battle. *The Blue Sword* was a Newbery Honor Book in 1983, and *The Hero and the Crown* received the Newbery Medal in 1985.

Florence H. Maltby

BED-KNOB AND BROOMSTICK

Author: Mary Norton (1903-1992)
First published: The Magic Bed-Knob, 1943; *Bonfires and Broomsticks*, 1947; combined edition, 1957; illustrated
Type of work: Novel
Type of plot: Adventure tale and fantasy
Time of work: Two summers after World War I and August, 1666
Locale: England and an island in the South Seas
Subjects: The supernatural and travel
Recommended ages: 10-13

Three English siblings discover that the pleasant lady living nearby is a witch; together, they have surprising adventures by traveling to interesting places and to the past on a magic bed.

Principal characters:
> MISS PRICE, a respectable and ladylike woman in her middle years who teaches piano, visits the sick, tends her gardens, and practices witchcraft with varying successes
> CAREY WILSON, a proper English girl who keeps her head under unexpected circumstances
> CHARLES WILSON, her brother, a young man who shows courage and resourcefulness when these are required
> PAUL WILSON, their brother, a six-year-old who is the recipient of the magic bedknob that starts their adventures
> EMELIUS JONES, a necromancer scraping together a living from the tricks that he learned during an expensive apprenticeship to a charlatan

Form and Content

The parts of *Bed-Knob and Broomstick* work effectively together as a unified novel. Each section has ten chapters and begins with a connection between the Wilson children and Miss Price, then proceeds through some obstacle to an adventure that leads to more ambitious goals, resulting in a close brush with disaster. The first section closes with the magic connection temporarily broken, while the closing of the second section permanently severs it. The children and Miss Price learn valuable lessons about solving real-world problems.

The Wilson children are spending the summer with their aunt when the first section opens. The carefree days offer no excitement until their neighbor, Miss Price, hurts her ankle. Carey and Charles suspect nothing extraordinary until Paul explains that she has fallen off her broomstick. For several nights, whenever he happens to be awake at the right time, he has seen Miss Price mastering the art of flying a broomstick, and he has even seen her fall once before.

Miss Price is aghast that the children know her secret, especially since she is extremely deficient in the wickedness required to silence them. Carey suggests that, instead of threats or intimidation, Miss Price should give them a magic gift that would cease to function if they reveal her secret. With a powerful spell, Miss Price charms Paul's bedknob to make the bed fly anywhere that he wishes. A twist in one direction will make it fly through the air to a new place; the other direction will take it through time.

Eventually, the children persuade Miss Price to join them in an excursion to a reportedly uninhabited island in the South Seas. The island, however, turns out to be peopled by cannibals and their witch doctor. Only a magic confrontation can save them, but it cannot save the bed from a rising tide. When the children's fantastic explanation fails to satisfy Aunt Beatrice upon their wet return, she orders them home. The children learn that Miss Price has decided to give up magic.

Two years later, Aunt Beatrice has died, and the children have no summer retreat. Then Carey notices an advertisement that seizes their attention: Miss Price is seeking boarders for the summer. Soon, they are with her, and they discover that the bed for which Paul still has the magic bedknob is now owned by Miss Price. Since she has kept her promise to give up magic, the children must persuade her to allow them to travel again, this time to the past.

In 1666, the children meet Emelius Jones, a professional sorcerer, and invite him to return with them to meet Miss Price. The two share many interests, but eventually Emelius must return to his own time. Unfortunately, he finds himself accused of using witchcraft to cause the Great Fire of London. On the day that he is to be burned at the stake, the children and Miss Price effect a daring rescue. Miss Price decides to accept Emelius' subsequent proposal, and she returns with him to his era, taking the bed and its magic knob with her.

Analysis

Bed-Knob and Broomstick is an excellent investigation of the human urge to explore and take risks. Carey, Charles, and Paul are curious, active children seeking to know more about the world. Having discovered one amazing fact—that Miss Price is a witch—they immediately apply that knowledge to the task of discovering more about the world. The magic bedknob is their opportunity to explore in person rather than merely through geography or history books. Their adventures begin with challenges that they are able to manage, such as the explanation to a London policeman as to why their bed is in the middle of the street outside the locked door of their own home in the middle of the night and their subsequent escape from the police station. Their explorations take them into difficulties from which they are able to extricate themselves by their own efforts; consequently, they seek more challenging adventures until they reach the limits of their abilities and Miss Price rescues them. Such adventures have their cost: Once the children exceed their own capacities and are rescued, events transpire that restrict their opportunities for further similar adventures.

Small adventures lead to larger and more reckless ones until adult judgment intervenes to protect the children from harming themselves. Once their options are restricted, the children have time to reflect on their choices and how they managed them, to think about the significance of what they learned from their adventures.

Magic is an important theme throughout the novel. Miss Price has come to the study of witchcraft too late in life ever to become truly proficient in its darkest secrets. This recognition of her deficiency in wickedness lends moral integrity to her character. Paul, as the most innocent of the children, is still touched by childhood's magic, and so he and Miss Price form a special bond: It is for him that Miss Price casts a spell on the bedknob so that only Paul can operate it. Yet, even Paul understands that magic used wrongly is a kind of cheating, and his casual comment about fair play causes Miss Price to repudiate her studies and her quest to grow the largest rose at the point when she has already magically created one the size of a cabbage.

The children inadvertently steer Miss Price into the path of virtuous fair play, but that act in turn presents them with difficulties that they must overcome when they next spend time with her, since their curiosity to explore the world is not yet satisfied. Having turned Miss Price away from magic, they must persuade her to make one more foray into it so that they may explore time as well as space. In their time travel, they discover the perfect match for Miss Price. After nearly losing Emelius to the frenzy of a superstitious inquisition, another challenge that exceeds the ability of the children, the two lonely adults are united in a bond stronger than magic. Their departure to a quiet corner of the seventeenth century once again restricts the children's opportunities for further adventures, since Miss Price and Emelius can only return from the past on the magic bed and only Paul has the power to set it in motion.

Critical Context

Although Mary Norton originally began to write books for young adult readers out of financial motivations, her work demonstrates that her imagination was adequate to the task. She went on to write a series of award-winning classic adventure novels, *The Borrowers* (1952) and its sequels. Her flair for plotting adventure stories, however, is already apparent in her first novel, *The Magic Bed-Knob* (1943). This story and *Bonfires and Broomsticks* (1947) show her ability to mix realistic and admirable characters with fantastic plot elements in which readers would like to believe. The Wilson children in particular are interesting representations of the ways in which real children between the ages of six and twelve might behave, speak, and think in a variety of challenging situations. Carey is particularly skillful in speaking and represents the interests of all of them in their dealings with Miss Price. Charles is unobtrusive and observant, showing his courage at decisive moments. Paul is still under the spell of a carefree and secure childhood. The minor flaws of Miss Price make her a fully rounded character: her insufficient wickedness, her forgetfulness, and her passion to win the rose competition. Only Emelius Jones suffers somewhat as a rather pale and flat character, and his historical era is delineated with only the broadest strokes.

In 1971, *Bed-Knob and Broomstick* was made by Disney Studios into a musical film employing both live action and animation, but the characters, settings, and plot developments were broadly reinterpreted in the transition from the page to the screen.

Victoria Gaydosik

THE BELL JAR

Author: Sylvia Plath (1932-1963)
First published: 1963
Type of work: Novel
Type of plot: Psychological realism
Time of work: 1953
Locale: New York City and a suburb of Boston
Subjects: Coming-of-age, gender roles, health and illness, sexual issues, and suicide
Recommended ages: 15-18

College student Esther Greenwood narrates her emotional crisis and suicide attempt, followed by a period of healing

Principal characters:
ESTHER GREENWOOD, a young woman who has been awarded a trip to
    New York because of her talent as a writer
MRS. GREENWOOD, Esther's mother
DOREEN, a wild young woman whom Esther meets in New York
BUDDY WILLARD, Esther's former boyfriend
DR. NOLAN, the doctor who helps Esther recover

Form and Content

The Bell Jar traces college student Esther Greenwood's trip to New York City, awarded to her for her literary skills, and her subsequent breakdown. Esther narrates how, unsuccessful both professionally and socially in New York, she falls into a depression that leads to an obsession with suicide and finally to a serious suicide attempt. She feels, she says, like a person in a bell jar, breathing her own sour air and looking out at a world distorted by the curved glass. The tale reflects in its form Esther's psychological deterioration, as the chapters become shorter and the transitions blur as she moves toward her major breakdown. The narrative then becomes coherent again as Esther, through hospitalization and the concern of a sympathetic female psychiatrist, Dr. Nolan, gradually works her way back toward mental health.

The story begins in New York, where Esther is one of a group of young women who have been awarded guest editorships at a fashion magazine in New York. Esther has always been a top student and a scholarship winner, but she finds herself unprepared for the challenges of the city. She cannot bond with her fellow award winners, not the wild Doreen nor the innocent Betsy nor any of the others. Moreover, she finds herself unable to accomplish anything. Her editor is critical of her work, and she does not succeed in losing her virginity, one of her goals. Flashbacks describe her relationship with her former boyfriend, Buddy Willard, who had betrayed her by having an affair—now she wants to get even. After a few sad attempts at adventures and after becoming ill with food poisoning, Esther returns home to the Boston area in a depressed state.

Upon her return, Esther finds that she has not been admitted to a writing course for which she had applied; that disappointment proves to be the last straw. She slips deeper and deeper into depression, focusing on obsessive thoughts: the death of her father when she was a child, Buddy's treachery, and suicide. Rough, misguided attempts to cheer her up or to cure her only make her worse. Ultimately, only suicide can hold her interest, and she makes some halfhearted attempts to kill herself before hiding behind boards in an unfrequented part of her house and taking a great quantity of sleeping pills.

Fortunately, Esther is found in time and hospitalized. Now treated as an object in the hospital, she feels the contempt of her caretakers. Through the help of writer Philomena Guinea, however, she is transferred to Dr. Nolan's private hospital, where she is given the best of care and Dr. Nolan's personal attention. Shock therapy and psychoanalysis help her toward restored mental health. Esther works her way up through the levels of the hospital, which rewards good behavior by moving the patient to wards with more privileges. Dr. Nolan helps Esther further by showing that she too disagrees with the double standard of sexual behavior. She writes Esther a prescription for a birth control device, and when Esther has both lost her virginity and earned the right to leave the mental institution, she feels finally free. She is ready to meet a man with whom she can make a commitment and have a child. Esther begins her reminiscences with an indication that she has a child, implying that she has been able to reconstruct her life.

Analysis

Any analysis of *The Bell Jar* is complicated by the fact that its story is a thinly disguised version of Sylvia Plath's own breakdown and suicide attempt, which took place when she was twenty. The novel has a positive ending: Freed from her obsessions and her virginity as well, Esther Greenwood is ready to return to the world, play an adult's part, marry, and bear the responsibilities of parenthood. Plath, however, committed suicide not long after the novel was first published in England. It is therefore tempting to graft Plath's later story onto Esther's, to see Esther Greenwood as someone who does not really understand the roots of her illness and is deluded as to the success of her healing. Plath saw her novel as the story of a survivor and intended to write a sequel that would show "that same world as seen through the eyes of health."

The arguable issue of the novel's outcome set aside, *The Bell Jar* leaves plenty to discuss. At least part of Esther's discomfort comes from the limitations of her society, which had only a few areas women could comfortably enter, nearly all of which required submissiveness to men. Everywhere Esther looks, she sees women in supporting roles, never as lead players. She sees Buddy Willard's mother, college educated, spending her life cleaning. She sees Dodo Conway, who seems ecstatic about bringing child after child into the world. She sees her own widowed mother, eking out a living by teaching service courses at a college and wanting her daughter to marry well. Even Esther's recognized literary talent has allowed her to write only for a fashion magazine. The conformity and self-righteousness of the 1950's—the opening paragraph locates the time as 1953, "the summer they electrocuted the Rosenbergs"—were especially confining when applied to women. None of the roles Esther sees as satisfying for other women feels comfortable to her. Her inability to accept the goals of her generation contributes to her breakdown.

The novel's portrayal of the sexual double standard provides another interesting sidelight on the era. Esther is bothered by the fact that women are supposed to be "pure" (that is, virginal), while different standards are expected of men. Esther's mother sends her clippings about chastity, while Buddy's mother apparently knows about her son's affair with a waitress and is untroubled by it. Esther is occupied with Buddy's treachery and with the double standard itself to the point of obsession. When she succeeds in losing her virginity, she feels freed from the double standard, although the reader may think otherwise.

An element of *The Bell Jar* that sometimes goes by unremarked is its humor. Plath's sharp eye catches the comic elements of coming-of-age in the early 1950's—the extremes of style, the oddities of dating behavior, the naïveté of the conversation among Esther's friends. There is a self-deprecating irony in Esther's descriptions of herself during the period of mental illness. The first attempts to commit suicide are narrated humorously—at one point, for example, she has decided to hang herself with the belt of her mother's bathrobe and tells of "a discouraging time of walking about with the silk cord dangling from my neck like a yellow cat's tail and finding no place to fasten it." Describing her despair with humor, however, does not lessen its intensity.

Critical Context

The Bell Jar was not originally intended as a book for young readers, and in fact the sexual content and the emphasis on suicide may still make it disturbing to some adolescent readers. Yet at the time of its American publication in 1971, the tendency for young adult literature to be all innocence and optimism was beginning to diminish. J. D. Salinger's *The Catcher in the Rye* (1951) had been on the shelves for two decades, its popularity increasing. While *The Catcher in the Rye* was not always welcome in the classroom, many teachers were willing to brave possible opposition to include it on their reading lists. The first reviewers of *The Bell Jar* were quick to compare it with Salinger's work. The quest of the two protagonists is similar—they want to find a world that will accept and celebrate them as they are, and they are equally unsuccessful in achieving their goals. Their flight into madness is similar.

The Bell Jar raises the additional question of the special limitations placed on women. Esther Greenwood's ambitions do not lend themselves to early 1950's opportunities. The detailed description of how women functioned in their strictly defined sphere during the era shows modern adolescent readers some of the reasons behind the women's movement. Plath's precise observations and keen awareness of social ironies help to re-create the world of the 1950's with a vividness no history book could approach.

Janet McCann

BEN AND ME

Author: Robert Lawson (1892-1957)
First published: 1939; illustrated
Type of work: Novel
Type of plot: Adventure tale, fantasy, and historical fiction
Time of work: 1744-1787
Locale: Philadelphia and Paris
Subjects: Animals, friendship, politics and law, travel, and war
Recommended ages: 10-13

The story of the adventures of Amos, a churchmouse, with Benjamin Franklin, his friend and colleague, before and during the American Revolution.

> *Principal characters:*
> AMOS, a churchmouse in Philadelphia
> BENJAMIN FRANKLIN, a printer, inventor, and statesman
> SOPHIA, a beautiful white mouse at the French court
> RED JEFFERSON, Thomas Jefferson's mouse colleague
> GEORGE WASHINGTON, a revolutionary war hero and the first president
> of the United States

Form and Content

Ben and Me is the story of the friendship between Amos, a mouse, the oldest of twenty-six siblings of a poor mouse family living in a Philadelphia church, and Benjamin Franklin, one of America's most famous and beloved historical figures. In the introduction, author Robert Lawson claims that he is only an editor relating Amos' story, which was written on a manuscript the size of a postage stamp and discovered during the alteration of an old Philadelphia house. What follows are fifteen short chapters, told in the first person and illustrated by Lawson.

Because of their poverty—they were poor as church mice—Amos left home in 1745, hoping to assist his struggling family. Exhausted, he finds himself in the rooms of the already-famous Benjamin Franklin and falls asleep in Franklin's fur cap. When he awakens the next morning in a cold room, Amos tells Franklin that the fireplace is inefficient because too much heat goes up the chimney. He suggests placing a heat source in the middle of the room, similar to the hot chestnut around which he and his family sometimes gathered to keep warm. The result is the so-called Franklin stove. Afterward, a bargain is struck between man and mouse: Twice each week, Franklin provides Amos' family with cheese, rye bread, and kernels of wheat, and in return Amos assists Franklin. By inhabiting the latter's fur cap, Amos frequently offers advice to Ben, being thus the cause of Franklin's success and fame.

A series of episodic events follows. Franklin experiments with lightning and electricity, although Amos is not convinced that these discoveries are of any value.

Another episode relates how Amos reedits, somewhat disastrously, Franklin's *Poor Richard's Almanack*, with resulting confusion among the people of Philadelphia. Of the American Revolution, Amos claims that the origins of the Declaration of Independence lay in a previous manifesto, written by Red Jefferson, a mouse who had come to Philadelphia in the saddlebags of Thomas Jefferson. Red had drafted a statement of mouse complaints against humans, but after Amos shows it to Franklin, Ben transforms it into a declaration of inalienable rights by which the American colonists justify their rebellion against Great Britain.

George Washington asks Franklin to represent America abroad, but it is Amos who convinces Ben to choose France after Amos points out to the less perceptive Franklin the advantages of French pastry, French wine, and beautiful French women. There, wearing his ever-present fur cap inhabited by Amos, Franklin creates a sensation and successfully raises considerable funds for the colonists' cause. Amos is also involved in revolutionary activity through his attempt to free the young mice children of Sophia, a beautiful white mouse from Versailles who lives in the high headdress, or wig, of Madame Brillon. Moved by gallantry and opposed to the dastardly actions of the aristocratic white mice who have persecuted Sophia, Amos recruits Red Jefferson, who is in Paris with Thomas Jefferson, as well as the rats from the ships of John Paul Jones, who is also in France. In the subsequent Battle of Versailles, the American mice win the day, the effete aristocratic French mice are defeated, and Sophia's children are saved. Unfortunately, Amos admits, the victory is at the cost of Franklin's reputation: The French court is not amused by the mouse war.

Franklin and Amos soon return home to Philadelphia. Both by now are old, and on the occasion of Franklin's eighty-first birthday (which occurred in 1787), Amos presents Ben with a new French-style hat, with Amos to continue to reside in the old fur cap. At this point, Amos' narrative ends.

Analysis

Using animals as surrogate humans—by anthropomorphizing them—has a long tradition in literature, starting with Aesop's fables. This tradition is perhaps even more evident in children's literature in the late nineteenth and twentieth centuries, with animals regularly been portrayed with human traits. Amos is thus only one in a long line of both predecessors and successors. What is unique in Lawson's *Ben and Me* is his pairing of an animal—Amos, a mouse—with such a prominent historical figure as Benjamin Franklin. When the book first appeared in 1939, the author could assume that most of his readers would know something about Franklin, the "inventor" of electricity, the printer of *Poor Richard's Almanack* (1733-1758), and the revolutionary war hero, and Lawson could thus build on that knowledge in his novel. *Ben and Me* is both highly readable entertainment and an attractive method of inculcating or reenforcing historical information in a humorous fashion.

The novel is picaresque in its approach, beginning with the first contact between Amos and Franklin shortly after the former leaves his church home to seek his fortune. The reader is led through the predictable litany of well-known Franklin accomplishments as inventor, printer, scientist, politician, statesman, and diplomat. What makes the novel more than merely narrative history is the author's—or Amos'—claim that it is the mouse, not the man, who is the inspiration for most of Franklin's contributions. Through Amos' first-person narration, this conceit is accomplished with much humor and in no manner diminishes Franklin. Already one of the more humanly accessible and memorable of the Founding Fathers, Franklin is made more so by *Ben and Me*, even if all of the events are not truly historical.

The book is most successful when Amos and Franklin occupy the stage together; it is their relationship that charms the reader. The culminating event, however, is the mouse war at Versailles, but here Franklin plays only a walk-on part, unknowingly carrying many of the protagonists in his pockets. The preparations and the battle itself are interesting enough, but something is lost to the reader when Franklin becomes only a secondary figure in this section of the novel.

Ultimately, *Ben and Me* has remained popular because it describes a deep friendship between an animal and a human, a relationship that most children cannot resist. To the mouse, Franklin the man is often less than heroic: In the first scene in Franklin's room, Amos describes Ben not as great and famous but as cold—they had not yet invented the Franklin stove—"and a bit silly." On another occasion, Amos reports that Franklin, after going for a swim, is discovered by the people of Philadelphia "muddied, bruised and scratched, his bathing trunks torn, his glasses missing." Amos' Franklin is anything but the larger-than-life figure featured too often in children's history books. Moreover, the reader is never left with any doubt about the deep feelings each holds for the other, and those feelings are portrayed though good-natured humor. If Franklin becomes something of a figure of fun in Amos' narrative, it is good fun, and Ben retains the reader's admiration, if only because he has had to put up with an extremely opinionated and domineering mouse.

Lawson's drawings demand special comment. The author was a successful illustrator before he became a storyteller, and the reader can only wish that he had included even more illustrations in Amos' autobiographical saga of "Ben and me."

Critical Context

Ben and Me remained in print well into its second half-century, testifying to its enduring popularity. It has continued to find a place in schools as secondary reading and has been translated into the medium of animation as a successful feature film. An illustrator since the 1910's, Robert Lawson achieved wide recognition in 1936 when he illustrated the famous story of Ferdinand the bull in the version told by Munro Leaf.

In 1940, Lawson portrayed the history of his own family in *They Were Strong and Good*, a work that was primarily illustration, with only a few words of narrative; it was awarded the Caldecott Medal. *Rabbit Hill* (1944), his book for younger readers, is the story of Little Georgie, a young rabbit, and his adventures with the "new folks"; it won the Newbery Medal in 1945. After *Ben and Me*, Lawson wrote other animal-narrated historical biographies, including *I Discover Columbus* (1941) and *Mr. Revere and I* (1953), which have, respectively, a parrot and a horse as the animal characters.

A prolific author of children's stories and a brilliant illustrator, Lawson was one of the major figures in children's literature for many decades. *Ben and Me* continues to be one of his most popular and most endearing works.

Eugene Larson

THE BEST CHRISTMAS PAGEANT EVER

Author: Barbara Robinson (1932-   )
First published: 1972; illustrated
Type of work: Novel
Type of plot: Domestic realism and social realism
Time of work: The 1970's
Locale: An American town
Subjects: Family, friendship, poverty, and religion
Recommended ages: 10-13

The six Herdmans, impoverished children who steal, smoke cigars (even the girls), and lie, come to church one Sunday for the refreshments, become involved in the community Christmas pageant, and learn that the Christmas story is about people like themselves.

Principal characters:
> THE NARRATOR, a twelve-year-old girl whose mother is in charge of the Christmas pageant
> RALPH HERDMAN, the oldest brother in the Herdman family, who decides to be Joseph since Imogene wants to be Mary
> IMOGENE HERDMAN, the oldest sister, who decides to play Mary when she hears the Christmas story and who threatens to beat up anyone else who might want the part
> LEROY, CLAUDE, and OLLIE HERDMAN, brothers who play the Wise Men because no one else will volunteer
> GLADYS HERDMAN, the youngest and meanest Herdman of all, who plays the angel

Form and Content

The Best Christmas Pageant Ever is the story of the year that the Herdmans took part in the town's Christmas pageant. The book consists of seven short chapters, each smoothly written and easy to read. Although the illustrations are limited to a small number of black-and-white sketches, Barbara Robinson provides descriptions that create images in the reader's mind. Most of the book is presented as a narrative, written in the first person by an anonymous twelve-year-old girl who relates conversationally the humorous stories and situations in which the Herdmans and their classmates become involved. Adults play a minor part in the story, being limited to teachers and the narrator's parents. The viewpoint of the narrator is that of an observer who, in her words, is a medium kid who keeps her mouth shut. In this capacity, she is able to observe and report on the actions of the Herdmans and others without actually being a part of the story. While some bias from the narrator is obvious at the beginning of the story, as the Christmas pageant unfolds the narrator begins to examine some of her perceptions and to report with less bias. The story itself focuses on the actions and emotions of the characters, particularly the Herdmans, and does not attempt to teach the Christmas story.

This short, humorous piece of fiction is fast-paced and believable. From the first page, readers are drawn into the lives of the Herdmans as they set the toolhouse on fire, steal a chemistry set, bring an untamed cat to show-and-tell and let it run free in the classroom, start rumors about classmates in order to blackmail them, and take dessert from other people's lunch boxes. These situations are typical of adolescents, things that many teenagers do and that others wish they were brave enough to do.

For most of the kids in the town where the story takes place, Sunday is the best day of the week because the Herdmans do not attend Sunday school: It is a day of rest from the antics of the Herdmans. Then the Herdmans learn from the brother of the narrator that people who attend Sunday school can get all the free desserts they want. This begins the Herdmans' interaction with Sunday school, because they want to see if there really is such a thing as free food. On the first Sunday that the Herdmans attend, the yearly Christmas pageant is discussed, and Imogene is immediately attracted to the plight of Mary in the Christmas story. From that point on, her main objective is for the Herdmans—herself, Ralph, Ollie, Leroy, Claude, and Gladys—to have the major parts in the Christmas pageant, and they threaten their classmates with innumerable problems if anyone else volunteers for the parts. Each day, and particularly on the weekends, new ideas brought about by Imogene's research and interpretation of the Christmas story instigate different and entertaining situations. Since the Herdmans had never heard of the Christmas story, they interpret it as if it came right out of an adventure novel, with the Wise Men being referred to as a bunch of spies. Hilarious situations ensue throughout rehearsals and up to the main performance, at which time something rather interesting happens, and not only to the Herdmans.

Analysis

Barbara Robinson has produced a wonderful, humorous book for children that, as all realistic fiction must do, tells a good story while at the same time addressing issues of concern to young people. The Herdmans are referred to as "the worst kids in the history of the world," and yet, even when they are at their worst, there is nothing malicious or vindictive about them. They are real children with problems similar to those still encountered by many adolescents. Because of their circumstances— coming from a poor family, living in less-than-excellent surroundings, and being visited consistently by a social worker who reports on them but never attempts to improve their conditions—the Herdmans are acting out inappropriate behaviors in their attempt to show the world that they do not mind being different from everyone else and in fact go out of their way to do so.

As the story unfolds, a number of issues pertinent to adolescents are addressed: living in a family, finding peer acceptance, making friends, growing toward maturity, defining one's identity, and living in a diverse world. The author carefully blends these issues into the actions and conversations of the principal characters, showing the evolution of both middle-class and impoverished characters. Because of the differences in the ages of the children, readers of various ages can identify with multiple characters and their situations. These associations help readers discover that their problems are not unique, that they are not alone in experiencing certain situations involving themselves, their friends, or their families. Readers can draw personal conclusions from the actions of the characters and will probably be left with questions at the end of the story. As in real life, there is no simple ending or conclusion to a problem; the author does not account for all the loose ends.

One issue addressed in the story is the existence of nontraditional families. Nevertheless, a strong theme of family unity is apparent. Although the Herdmans have no strong parental influence, the children stick together and look out for one another. As the narrator states, "the Herdmans pretty much looked after themselves. Ralph looked after Imogene, and Imogene looked after Leroy, and Leroy looked after Claude and so on down the line." This description provides contrast between the Herdmans and the other families within the story, most of which have two parents to whom the children are accountable. Although the adult parental figures do not play a prominent part in the story, the underlying knowledge of the difference between the Herdman family and the others is referred to by the narrator at various times, sometimes with envy and sometimes with curiosity. The similarities between the children in these families are more prominent than their differences, however, and readers will leave the book with a positive feeling and the knowledge that support between friends and siblings can create positive results.

Critical Context

Realistic fiction such as *The Best Christmas Pageant Ever* did not exist prior to the 1970's, when much of the fiction written for adolescents began to focus on children's discovery of self and the development of maturity in relation to siblings and peers. Robinson's book effectively addressed these issues in the 1970's and continues to do so. The novel was made into a film for television and, in some places, is played on commercial television each December. The film closely follows the book and, instead of replacing it, appears to encourage adolescents to read Robinson's story. In many schools around the country, *The Best Christmas Pageant Ever* is one of the most popular books to be checked out during the holiday season. It provides students who are not familiar with the tradition of the Christmas pageant with information on its history, while at the same time focusing on family and peer relationships in a modern society. It was also cited on a list of top ten books of realistic fiction for younger adolescents.

Robinson continues to write books for readers in this age range. *My Brother Louis Measures Worms and Other Louis Stories* (1988) also humorously depicts family situations while at the same time focusing on the very real concerns of adolescents.

Leslie Marlow

BEYOND THE CHOCOLATE WAR

Author: Robert Cormier (1925-   )
First published: 1985
Type of work: Novel
Type of plot: Psychological realism and social realism
Time of work: The early 1970's
Locale: A Catholic boys' school in a New England mill town
Subjects: Coming-of-age, sexual issues, and suicide
Recommended ages: 13-18

As Obie and Carter try to escape Archie's control, Jerry Renault returns to Monument to learn that individuals can endure despite the evil around them.

> *Principal characters:*
> ARCHIE COSTELLO, the cruel leader of The Vigils, whose members orchestrate happenings at Trinity
> OBIE, the former passive ally of Archie, who undergoes a change
> JERRY RENAULT, the protagonist of *The Chocolate War*, who returns to Monument to redeem himself
> ROLAND "GOOBER" GOUBERT, Jerry's best friend, who is guilt-ridden over the events of *The Chocolate War*
> RAY BANNISTER, a newcomer to Trinity who is an amateur magician
> BUNTING, the sophomore being groomed as next year's assigner of tasks by The Vigils
> EMILE JANZA, the sadistic henchman of The Vigils, who tries to victimize Jerry again
> LAURIE GUNDARSON, the love of Obie's life
> BROTHER LEON, a sinister priest and the headmaster at Trinity
> DAVID CARONI, a sensitive straight-A student who is given an F by Brother Leon

Form and Content

Beyond the Chocolate War continues the somber tale of the abuses of power begun in *The Chocolate War* (1974). Several characters introduced in the first novel struggle against the cruel Archie and the unethical Brother Leon. Using an omniscient point of view, Robert Cormier divides his novel into four parts, with the first two focusing on specific individuals and their particular problems. The third section brings the characters and their subplots together in a fast-moving climax. The fourth section indicates that corruption will continue at Trinity.

Each of the characters in Cormier's sequel has been affected by the events in *The Chocolate War*. Jerry Renault has spent a year in Canada recuperating from the physical and emotional havoc wreaked by Archie Costello and Brother Leon. Jerry's return to Monument forces his friend Goober to admit his guilt for not trying to stop the brutal fight that ends the first novel. Goober warns Jerry that Emile Janza is stalking him, and the two follow Janza for a confrontation in an alley.

In the meantime, Archie, the manipulative leader of the secret group called The Vigils, continues making humiliating "assignments" to other students during his senior year. For example, Archie's plan for only one student to be in school during the day of the bishop's visit is canceled when a student named Carter informs Brother Leon by letter. Archie tricks Carter into revealing that he is the "traitor" and intimidates him by replacing the boxing trophies in the trophy case with a toilet-shaped ashtray.

Archie also feels the growing separation between himself and Obie, who has fallen in love with Laurie Gundarson. Bunting, who is being groomed to take Archie's place, finds out about Obie and Laurie and stages an assault on them where they often park to make out. After this scene, Laurie feels violated and breaks up with Obie. When Obie learns who has staged this terrible event, he plots revenge, enlisting the aid of the newly arrived Ray Bannister, an amateur magician. Obie switches marbles in The Vigils' black box so that Archie himself has to play the Fool on Fair Day. Although students are afraid to kick Archie or dunk him, he must put his head in Bannister's guillotine.

David Caroni, too, has been devastated by the intrigues of the previous year, when Brother Leon gave him an F. Caroni's growing obsession with revenge leads to his attempt to kill Brother Leon. When this plot fails, the desperate Caroni turns the violence upon himself.

Analysis

Beyond the Chocolate War deals with the complex issue of how to define power and with the psychological problems of fear, intimidation, and control. Jerry Renault has traded T. S. Eliot's "Do I dare/ Disturb the universe?" for A. E. Housman's "I, a stranger and afraid/ In a world I never made." Housman's despairing words signal a kind of realization on the part of Jerry that although there exist multiple attacks on integrity, individuals must depend on themselves for physical and intellectual survival. Jerry's scene with Janza illustrates the power of passive resistance to irrational and obsessive brute violence. Despite Janza's violent punches, Jerry refuses to fight back, and his inner strength allows him to withstand the blows. He tells Goober that the confrontation was something that had to be won alone. Janza, on the other hand, feels like he "has lost something" in this battle, and what he has lost is power. Here Cormier also touches on the close kinship of brutal power and sexual power when he writes that Janza's attack on Jerry is "nothing sexual."

The issues pertaining to sexuality are further illustrated in Obie's and Laurie's experiments with sex. Although their physical exchanges are called love, the two actually time their fondling and caresses to keep themselves under control. Bunting, on the other hand, does lose control during his assault on them, and what was originally planned only as a scare tactic almost turns into rape. Laurie feels abused when her unknown assailant (Bunting) squeezes her breast; the same act by Obie had been viewed another way. Now Laurie sees Obie and their sexual foreplay from an entirely different perspective. Cormier thus illustrates the fine line between romantic sexuality and ruthless sexuality.

The role of illusion in the attainment of power is another theme that runs through *Beyond the Chocolate War*. Ray Bannister's guillotine and card tricks show that there are real steps to what appears to be magic. Archie's talent of selecting the white marble from the black box so that he does not have to carry out assignments is likewise a nonmagical sleight-of-hand trick. "Tubs" Casper's illusions of becoming thin are too difficult to act upon, so he is victimized into accepting an assignment to gain twenty more pounds.

Finally, Cormier shows the reader that evil may thrive because of institutions. Evil may be hiding behind innocence and benevolence. More important, there may be evil in everyone—a dark side that the individual shuns or tries to repress. Archie tells Jill Morton that all people have secret imperfections that they try to conceal. In the final scene with Obie, in a line similar to the lyrics of the Rolling Stones song "Sympathy for the Devil," Archie sums up one of Cormier's themes: "Because I'm you. I'm all the things you hide inside you. That's me—"

The Chocolate War and *Beyond the Chocolate War* are often used in conjunction with William Golding's *Lord of the Flies* (1954) and other literature that deals with individuals in conflict with group obligations. *Beyond the Chocolate War*, like Golding's work, graphically portrays how games can escalate into real violence. The killing game in *Lord of the Flies* begins with Ralph pretending to machine-gun Piggy, continues with pretending to kill Maurice as a pig, proceeds with the boys hurting Robert as a pig, and climaxes with the killing of a sow and, soon after, Simon. Obie's use of magic and Bunting's staged attack are examples of games or play evolving into real violence; David Caroni's fantasies of revenge intensify into obsession and ultimately turn on Caroni himself.

Often taught with *The Chocolate War*, Cormier's sequel presents the ambiguities of right and wrong confronting the adolescent. The multiple plot lines in the sequel provide an introduction to reading more complex novels about adolescents. Despite its grim depiction of the exploitation of power, *Beyond the Chocolate War* deals realistically with making choices for what is socially appropriate and individually responsible behavior.

Critical Context

Beyond the Chocolate War, as well as Robert Cormier's other novels, are outstanding examples of social and psychological realism for young adults. Cormier received the ALAN Award given annually by the Assembly on Literature for Adolescents of the National Council of Teachers of English to honor those individuals who have made important contributions to adolescent literature. He also received the Margaret A. Edwards award, presented each year by the Young Adult Services Division of the American Library Association. This award is given to authors who write about authentic adolescent experiences and emotions.

Cormier's novel *Fade* (1988) continues the themes of secrets, illusions, and power depicted in *Beyond the Chocolate War*. The protagonist Paul Moreaux finds that his genetic ability to become invisible allows him to learn the secrets of others. He realizes that actions and individuals are interconnected and that it is necessary to act responsibly toward other people. In addition to novels, Cormier has written short stories, brought together in the collection *Eight Plus One* (1980). He prefaces each story with details about the sources of the characters and plot, as well as any problems he had in writing the story. Some of the stories take place in the 1930's, when Cormier was growing up, while others are set in the 1970's. Despite the difference in setting, all the selections deal with the problems of growing up.

Helen O'Hara Connell

BIG RED

Author: Jim Kjelgaard (1910-1959)
First published: 1945; illustrated
Type of work: Novel
Type of plot: Adventure tale
Time of work: Probably the 1930's
Locale: A wilderness area known as the Wintapi, probably in northwestern Pennsylvania
Subjects: Animals, coming-of-age, and nature
Recommended ages: 10-13

Danny Pickett finds his place in the world when he and his Irish setter, Red, meet the challenges posed by their wilderness home, as well as those of the world outside.

> *Principal characters:*
> DANNY PICKETT, a seventeen-year-old trapper, hunter, and woodsman
> ROSS PICKETT, Danny's father
> RED, an Irish setter
> DICK HAGGIN, a wealthy industrialist and landowner
> OLD MAJESTY, a black bear

Form and Content

Big Red is told in the third person almost entirely from the point of view of Danny Pickett, a young man intimately familiar with and deeply fond of the Wintapi, a wilderness area on the border of thinly settled farm and ranchland. Danny is introduced to a tantalizing new world when he first sees a splendid Irish setter being groomed as a show dog by Dick Haggin, who owns the estate on which Danny and his father, Ross, live in a squatter's cabin. Danny is following in his father's footsteps, helping him make their living off the land as trappers and hunters. Danny has a chance to explore a new way of life, however, when Mr. Haggin, recognizing the camaraderie between the dog and the young man as well as Danny's innate dog-handling skills, asks Danny to take care of Red and learn how to train and breed show dogs while training Red as a bird-hunting dog. Danny and Red grow significantly through the course of the novel, both as individuals and closer together as comrades. By the end, they are well prepared to face their greatest challenge—the threat of Old Majesty, a powerful, dangerous black bear who seems to prey at will on livestock and who eventually badly hurts Ross when he tries to track down the wily old marauder.

The novel is divided into twelve titled chapters, each recounting a key experience in the lives of Danny and Red. In "Irish Setter," Red picks up the trail of Old Majesty and tracks the big bear to a standstill, "the only dog with the heart to do it and the brain to handle the bear after he did," in Danny's admiring words. Yet, Danny is worried that Red might get injured and be ruined as a show dog; he does not take a shot and brings Red home safely. In "The Journey" and "The Dog Show," Mr. Haggin takes Danny to New York City, where Red competes in a dog show. In "Danny's Humiliation" and "Red's Education," Danny has to struggle with Red's undisciplined energy and his sensitive, proud nature in order to train the dog in the ways of the woods and to harness his hunting instincts without resorting to the traditional, harsh training methods that his father suggests. In "The Leaves Rustle" and "Partridge Dog," Red protects Danny from a lynx and finds Ross in a snowstorm. Danny discovers, just when he was beginning to doubt Red's abilities, that Red is everything that he hoped the dog would be.

In "Read the Sign" and "Trap-Line Pirate," Danny and Red's relationship solidifies. Working together as a close-knit, mutually supportive team, they capture an escaped convict. They also kill a wolverine that had been threatening their livelihood by stealing animals from their traps and that turned the tables on Danny and Red by stalking them. By the chapter entitled "Sheilah MacGuire," Danny and Red have become as close as brothers, and Red has a difficult time accepting the new mate that Mr. Haggin sent for him. Finally, in "Old Majesty" and "Trophy for Red," Danny and Red come into their own as they hunt down Old Majesty and Danny and Ross embark on a new life as dog breeders, beginning with the pups of Red and Sheilah.

Analysis

Jim Kjelgaard employs a clear and direct style to tell his story. He brings the many scenes of nature to life through the use of precise and apt nouns and modifiers. His language appeals to the senses: "Crisp, frost-curled leaves crackled underfoot when they entered the beech woods." Kjelgaard saves more elaborate figures of speech to lend color to the often-idiomatic dialogue, especially the lines spoken by Ross, and to emphasize the key thoughts and feelings of the characters. For example, he writes at one point that, to Danny, Mr. Haggin's estate—and by implication Danny's dream of owning a dog like Red—was "like a mirage . . . unattainable as the moon."

The basic theme of the book is Danny's coming-of-age, which Kjelgaard explores in three ways: Danny's relationship with his father, Danny's ability to survive in the world of the Wintapi, and his ability to move beyond that world and prosper in the new world offered by Mr. Haggin.

Danny has a close, interdependent relationship with his father at the beginning of the book; they work as a team. When necessary, they consult on what jobs have to be done and who should do them, but often each simply sees what has to be done and does it—whether it is cooking breakfast or felling trees for firewood. In addition to the great love that they feel for each other, Danny respects his father's judgment in general and his knowledge of the woods in particular. In turn, Ross respects Danny, who under his tutelage has turned into an able woodsman in his own right. Ross does not try to impose his will on the young man; even when he disagrees with Danny, Ross lets him make his own choices.

When Danny meets Red, this relationship is tested. Danny sees in Red something more than he has ever seen in the hounds that his father has raised, and he instinctively knows that Red should not be trained the way in which the hounds were. Danny rejects his father's suggestion to "give him a lickin'" and resists his idea that Red will make a great dog for chasing assorted "varmints." This causes a rift between the two proud, stubborn men, even though Ross always believed that Danny, who takes after his late mother in many ways, had it in him to find contentment in a life other than that of a trapper. Danny does not want to hurt his father's feelings, but he cannot let himself stray from the new path that he has found. His friendship with Red is deep and rewarding, and Mr. Haggin's spirited description of the deeper meaning of the seemingly trivial dog show gives Danny a glimpse of a future in which he can apply his natural abilities to something creative and enduring, that future generations might look to and build upon: the breeding of fine Irish setters.

Danny's rite of passage involves using the skills that his father has taught him, his own intelligence and courage, and the qualities that he has been able to nurture in Red to do what even Ross was unable to accomplish, and what nearly costs Ross his life: bring Old Majesty to bay. In the final encounter, something that Danny always feared happens: Red is injured badly enough to ruin him forever as a show dog. Yet, having mastered the world of the wilderness, Danny now feels ready to try his way in another world. He accepts full responsibility for the damage to Red and vows to pay Mr. Haggin every cent of the $7,000 that the dog is worth. Before, the amount "was an unheard-of sum to one who knew triumph when he captured a seventy-five cent skunk or weasel pelt." Now, he has "cast off the old shackles" and feels that "if others could do big things, so could he."

Another significant aspect of the novel is the substantial amount of lore that Kjelgaard presents about hunting, tracking, fishing, and trapping. He also depicts both the beauty of nature and its role as an adversary that can test a person's mettle. A strong sense of community is portrayed in the novel, both in the sense of neighbor helping neighbor and in the sense of citizens obeying laws, such as game laws, intended for the common good. The novel has a male-dominated atmosphere; the only human female character is a flighty friend of Mr. Haggin's who has the men so cowed that she almost takes Red away as her plaything until Red runs afoul of a skunk, which is too much for her "delicate" nature.

Critical Context

Big Red, Jim Kjelgaard's third novel, was published in April, 1945, by Holiday House, with illustrations by Bob Kuhn. In writing the book, Kjelgaard made use of his own experiences as a woodsman and a lover of Irish setters. The book has been enduringly popular, with a paperback edition published by Scholastic Book Services that was widely available to schoolchildren in the 1960's. By the 1990's, the hardcover was still in print and Bantam's trade paperback edition had more than twenty-five printings. *Big Red* earned for Kjelgaard an award from the Boys Club of America. Among his many other books about dogs, other animals, young men, and the outdoors are two more about Irish setters, both featuring sons of Red. In *Irish Red* (1951), the future of Danny, Ross, and the dogs depends on the least promising of Red and

Sheilah's pups. In *Outlaw Red* (1953), a troubled young man forms a close bond with another of Red and Sheilah's offspring, but these two find themselves on the wrong side of the law.

In 1962, the Disney Studios released a film version of *Big Red*, directed by Norman Tokar from a script by Louis Pelletier. Although entertaining, the film has a different plot from the book. In the film, the story takes place in Quebec and is cast in the form of Red's escape from being sold and his quest to return to the young boy he loves.

Earl Wells

THE BLACK ARROW

Author: Robert Louis Stevenson (1850-1894)
First published: 1888
Type of work: Novel
Type of plot: Historical fiction
Time of work: The mid-1460's
Locale: Southern England
Subjects: Coming-of-age, love and romance, and war
Recommended ages: 13-18

> *Dick Shelton, a young nobleman, learns about being true to himself and his loved ones during the Wars of the Roses.*

Principal characters:
DICK SHELTON, the young heir to the estate of Tunstall
JOANNA SEDLEY, a young woman who escapes from captivity
    disguised as a boy named "John Matcham"
SIR DANIEL BRACKLEY, the traitorous knight who rules Tunstall Manor
ELLIS DUCKWORTH, a disgruntled peasant who disguises himself as
    "John Amend-all" and takes revenge on Brackley and his associates
RICHARD CROOKBACK, the young duke of Gloucester, whose energy
    and ruthlessness make him destined for greatness

Form and Content

Robert Louis Stevenson's *The Black Arrow* is the story of a young man's maturation during the mid-fifteenth century, when England was torn by thirty years of civil war, known as the Wars of the Roses. As such, the novel combines several important conventions of historical fiction, as well as those of the coming-of-age novel: The hero learns about himself and his place in a world fraught with danger and violence. The internal narrative of events in the life of the young hero and the external events concerning warfare between two English royal houses are mixed in this complex novel. Ultimately, the two skeins are inextricably tangled, as national events give Dick Shelton the means to discover who he really is and who he wants to be.

The intermingling of personal and national concerns dominates this fascinating novel. Shelton, the son of the former lord of Tunstall Manor, has been reared by Sir Daniel Brackley, to all appearances a virtuous, although stern, nobleman. He begins to learn the truth about Brackley, however, when an outlaw, John Amend-all, vows revenge against Brackley and his followers. Shelton finds a threatening message in which Amend-all pledges to kill the murderer of Sir Harry Shelton, the young hero's father. After Shelton learns that Brackley may have been responsible for the murder, he is profoundly shaken, having realized that things are not always as they seem.

Shelton begins to look into his father's murder but finds his investigation thrust aside by larger events that demand an ever-increasing amount of his attention. Shortly after Amend-all begins his campaign of vengeance, Shelton meets another young person, John Matcham, and helps him escape from Brackley. Shelton is put in the position of reconciling his friendship with Matcham with his loyalty to his foster father.

Eventually, Shelton and Matcham are persuaded to return to Tunstall Manor, partly because Brackley lies to Shelton and partly because he invokes Shelton's sense of duty: Even Tunstall Manor has become embroiled in the Wars of the Roses, and Shelton believes that he must put personal concerns aside. Although their escape is finally unsuccessful, the two young people become friends; and when he learns that Matcham is actually a young noblewoman, Joanna Sedley, Shelton realizes that he has fallen in love.

Shortly thereafter, Shelton tries to rescue Joanna several times, each time more certain that he loves her. Meanwhile, he meets and befriends another, more ruthless young man, Richard Crookback, the duke of Gloucester, who compensates for his physical disabilities with an arrogant demeanor and a determination to win the civil war. Joining Duke Richard's forces, Shelton lays siege to the town of Shoreby, where Brackley's forces are concentrated. Even though their army is outnumbered, Shelton and Duke Richard win the battle, forcing Brackley to flee with Joanna back to Tunstall Manor. Just as Shelton catches up with them and rescues Joanna, Amend-all's last black arrow kills Brackley.

Analysis

Although the literary style of *The Black Arrow* might make it difficult for younger adolescents, the story's quality rewards the effort. As a young adult, the hero must shape his existence in a world of conflicting loyalties. He confronts a series of interconnected choices, all of which can be subsumed into the choice between love and violence. Southern England, the novel's setting, is fraught by war and local unrest. All the people Shelton respects and loves are threatened by John Amend-all: his foster father, his spiritual adviser, and even Shelton's best friend, a soldier in Brackley's service. Curiously, Shelton himself is excepted from the grievance list; vengeance is claimed in his name.

Caught on the horns of a dilemma between friendship and suspicion, Shelton vacillates between the two extremes. Another young man, "John Matcham," begs Shelton to help "him" escape from Brackley and forces Shelton into action. As the two steal away, they become friends, although Shelton frequently complains about Matcham's physical weakness and sensitivity. Kindness to others is not weakness, however, which the novel points out. Matcham, really a pampered young noblewoman in disguise, is easily the equal of Shelton. First of all, she is just as brave, vowing to stay by him in spite of all danger. Further, she is more compassionate; he is frequently ruthless, as for example, when Shelton surprises and kills one of Amend-all's followers with a hunting knife.

As the reader might expect, Shelton is little more than a boy when he first helps Matcham escape; he learns about caring from Matcham and matures as a result. When the two are angry at each other, they come to blows and decide to go their own ways; afterward, ashamed of himself, Shelton agonizes about his friend's safety. At first, Shelton offers to leave his crossbow; when Matcham refuses to use it, Shelton decides to swallow his anger and continue along with his friend. This loyalty to his friend is the first stage in Shelton's growth, clearly intended for the novel's young adult audience.

Shelton's choices are difficult, particularly when they are compounded by a secondary theme in *The Black Arrow*, that of disguised intentions. In a very real sense, Brackley's true motives and character are always hidden behind a disguise. For example, although he murdered Shelton's father and usurped his domains, Brackley rears young Shelton. He does so, however, out of an evil desire to have his potential rival within easy reach. Further, although he commands military forces, Brackley is reluctant to commit himself to either side in the civil war; he waits until the battles are decided before he sends in his troops on the side of the victors.

Unlike thousands of other noblemen, Shelton follows his heart; in fact, he tries to stay out of the war, wanting only to set Sedley free. It is significant that when Shelton does engage in combat, he learns to temper his valor with mercy. For example, Brackley moves Sedley to a manor house near the ocean, and Shelton attacks a group of soldiers, assuming that they are her guards. After defeating them, Shelton learns that the group was led by Sedley's father; Shelton's truculence has weakened both a potential ally and himself. Later, during the battle of Shoreby, Shelton has the opportunity to practice this lesson: He takes a defensive posture during combat and avoids unnecessary bloodshed. His mercy makes Shelton a target for the mockery of his erstwhile friend, Duke Richard Crookback, who mistakes sensitivity for weakness. Crookback revels in bloodshed; Shelton's rejection of him indicates how much he has matured, and how valuable a role model he is for the young adult reader.

Critical Context

Like most other historical novels, *The Black Arrow* shows the influence of both history and literature, particularly in the characterization of Duke Richard. The Wars of the Roses (1455-1485) was a sporadic conflict between the House of Lancaster (whose heraldic symbol was a red rose) and the House of York (a white rose). Essentially, it was a family quarrel blown out of proportion. All the claimants to the English throne were related to one another, as descendents of King Edward III (1327-1377); both sides had periods of victory and defeat. The cultural chaos in the novel shows Brackley's traitorous nature and provides both a cause and a context for Shelton's maturation.

Robert Louis Stevenson was also influenced by the traditional representation of the historical figure of Richard Crookback as a violent brute. One of the first such treatments was in William Shakespeare's play *Richard III* (1592), which purports to show Richard's career as a murderous and grasping political intriguer who is eventually defeated in battle by the rightful king, Henry Tudor. Shakespeare's play was written during the reign of Queen Elizabeth I, Henry's granddaughter, and thus was more a politically inspired fiction than an accurate portrayal. *The Black Arrow* makes use of some aspects of this portrait, representing the younger Duke Richard as energetic and ambitious, with an incipient mean streak. Young adults, reading the work, probably will not recognize the character, nor the irony of his involvement in the plot; Shelton's success is made possible by this literary incarnation of ruthless violence. What the young adult reader should recognize more easily is that Shelton and Richard are parallel characters. Shelton's rejection of violence makes him ultimately a sympathetic character; Richard's cruelty leads to his downfall.

Michael R. Meyers

THE BLACK PEARL

Author: Scott O'Dell (1898-1989)
First published: 1967
Type of work: Novel
Type of plot: Adventure tale
Time of work: The 1960's
Locale: La Paz, Baja California, Mexico
Subjects: Coming-of-age, family, jobs and work, and religion
Recommended ages: 13-18

Finding a black pearl, an astounding treasure, leads sixteen-year-old Ramon Salazar to adulthood as he learns the nature of evil and the redemptive power of love.

Principal characters:
    RAMON SALAZAR, a young man who begins training in his family
        business in the summer of his sixteenth year but soon learns more
        about himself and about life than he learns about pearl diving
    MANTA DIABLO, a legendary kite-shaped sea monster reputed to have
        seven eyes and seven rows of teeth and capable of easily destroying
        a ship
    BLAS SALAZAR, Ramon's father and, of the five pearl dealers in La Paz,
        the most renowned and respected for the honesty of his dealings and
        the quality of his pearls
    GASPAR RUIZ, a physically and emotionally intimidating young man
        claiming to be from Spain, a boastful, bullying liar and a rival to
        Ramon for possession of the black pearl

Form and Content

The Black Pearl is Ramon Salazar's first-person account of the events of the summer of his sixteenth year. He tells his tale in retrospect from the vantage point of his newfound wisdom and his newly acquired adulthood. Since his sixteenth birthday in July, he has been a partner in his family's business. In a short time, he has learned to dive for pearls, has discovered an astounding treasure, and has emerged as a local celebrity. In only four months, however, he has also suffered the bullying of Gaspar Ruiz, the attacks of the Manta Diablo, the death of his father in a great storm, the theft of his treasure, threats to his life, and the challenge of becoming the breadwinner of his family. Ramon's narrative recounts his education into the myths and repressions of his culture, his training in his profession, and his first efforts to construct his own identity and values.

Once a child who smiled at his mother's tales of the monster Manta Diablo, Ramon now gives an eyewitness account of both the terror and the beauty of the giant sea creature. The symbolism of the Manta Diablo—the largest of the devilfish, the manta ray—is made clear by an old priest's tale of how the ancient manta was a land animal long ago cast into exile in the sea just as Lucifer, the enemy of humans and God, was cast out of heaven by the Archangel Michael. In his excursions into the realms of the tropical waters that provide his livelihood, Ramon symbolically delves into the mysterious realms of his unconscious being. Indeed, the ocean and its Manta Diablo offer travelers terror and death, but Ramon testifies to his discovery that the ocean and its awesome winged demon are also keepers of inestimable wealth and absolute beauty. The manta's amber eye and silver back gleaming in the moonlight of the Vermillion Sea show Ramon the sacred in the universal cycles of death and life, evil and good.

There are eighteen chapters in the novel, depicting three cycles of growth. Ramon is first on land, challenged with new responsibilities in the business office of Salazar and Son, pearl dealers. He then actively seeks the danger of the sea and the challenge of learning to dive for pearls. The hero's quest for a great black pearl and the material success and ego satisfaction that it represents alternates between sea and shore, at first with the fleet and then totally alone in strange, dark waters. The final and most critical choice in Ramon's journey is to determine whether the pearl should remain in the lagoon where he found it or should be brought inside the church in the center of his community. That he returns the pearl to the church signifies his decision to ally his powers with the human community.

Like most tales of the initiation of a young person into adulthood, *The Black Pearl* features a young protagonist who is obedient and responsible, with a strong work ethic. He also has egoistic dreams of success and nagging feelings of inadequacy because of his small stature and sheltered lifestyle. In the classic mythic pattern, Ramon's journey of initiation requires that he move outside his own society, conquer the monster of his own fears, and then find, seize, and return home with the great treasure—a magnificent, flawless, sixty-two-carat black pearl. This pearl becomes a gleaming symbol of his newly discovered adult identity. The final dilemma in Ramon's journey is deciding the destiny of the pearl and the destiny of his adult identity. Gaspar Ruiz operates as a foil illuminating his choices. Gaspar chooses false ego, boundless greed, and murderous violence at sea. At last, adrift but alive, Ramon wills the pearl of his life not be dedicated to fear, superstition, and evil. It will remain in the outstretched hand of the statue of the Madonna at the center of the church in the center of his hometown, a perpetual emblem of love, faith, and goodness.

Analysis

Ramon Salazar's timeless journey of the soul introduces young readers to that seemingly universal dialogue of cultures, the dialogue between fear and love, authority and personal autonomy, superstition and faith. Early in his tale, Ramon's choices are adaptations to traditional values of fear, competitiveness, acquisitiveness, ego, and wishful thinking. Feeling weak, he seeks empowerment by becoming a diver. Feeling inferior to Gaspar, he dreams of the most extraordinary accomplishment, finding treasure. Once a doubter and now an eyewitness to the evil Manta Diablo, Ramon discovers its greater reality; like all the powers of the physical universe, the Manta Diablo's power is both horrifying and awesomely beautiful. This greater awareness allows Ramon to mature and move toward choices that affirm his love of his father, with all his imperfections. Without peer pressure or an exemplary model, Ramon actively constructs his own identity and values and returns to his home and his mother and sisters with a dawning sense of his own self-worth. His final choice, to return the stolen pearl to its sanctuary in the open hand of the Madonna, symbolizes a triumph of human love and faith over all those fearful powers of nature, humankind, and demons.

Although triumphant, Ramon is far from perfect. He spins a yarn of good and evil very like the standard gothic tale designed to thrill, with glowering monsters and dark and stormy nights. As a narrator, he appears to have no sense of humor and little awareness of the racism and sexism informing his world and his own words and deeds. As an autobiographer, he seems bland and self-absorbed. Perhaps his lack of critical faculties emphasizes how his transformation is not powered by the exercise of reason. His transformation is accomplished by a series of affective, value-laden choices between self and other, good and evil, fear and love.

Critical Context

The Black Pearl is among more than two dozen works by one of the most highly respected American writers of fiction for children and young adults. *Island of the Blue Dolphins* (1960), certainly Scott O'Dell's best-known work, won the Newbery Medal in 1961. The Hans Christian Andersen Author's Medal, the highest international recognition for an entire body of work written for young readers, was given to O'Dell in 1972, a first for an American writer. Born in Southern California, O'Dell was particularly drawn to subjects involving the histories of its native peoples. His works have remained popular in classrooms not only because of his trustworthy research on events, culture, and customs but also because the experiences of the protagonists show readers both conflicts of social values and individual desires common to all. Other powerful and universal concerns, such as the relationship between humans and their physical universe and the enigma of humankind's seemingly boundless inhumanity, are dramatically and vividly explored.

Because *The Black Pearl* represents and affirms aspects of comfortable family life in a Mexican city, it offers an attractive classroom alternative to more common tales of poverty, struggle, and desperate attempts at escape. It is nevertheless far less popular among teachers and students than *Island of the Blue Dolphins*, perhaps because of the protagonist's culturally induced male myopia. Women are inconsequential in the novel; their only role in the provincial and patriarchal world represented by the protagonist is to submit to men's will and look to a man, even a sixteen-year-old, for leadership and the determination of the future. There is also an unquestioned and unexamined hint of racism in Ramon's participation in the disdain with which local Indian cultural views are regarded. Even the novel's dominant characters, Ramon and the macho Gaspar, seem one-dimensional as foils for each other, and their fates seem more didactic than satisfying. Yet, the metaphor of a jewel of personal self-esteem discovered by a young man and shared with his world glows in a reader's memory.

Virginia Crane

THE BLUE BIRD

Author: Maurice Maeterlinck (1862-1949)
First performed: L'Oiseau bleu, 1908
First published: 1909 (English translation, 1909)
Type of work: Drama
Type of plot: Fantasy
Time of work: "Once upon a time"
Locale: A woodcutter's cottage and various fantasy locales
Subjects: Coming-of-age, death, family, friendship, nature, and the supernatural
Recommended ages: 13-18

Two children of a poor woodcutter set out to find the Blue Bird of Happiness and,
after many adventures, return home only to find the bird in their own cottage.

> *Principal characters:*
> TYLTYL and MYTYL, a brother and sister, the children of a poor
>   woodcutter
> BERYLUNE, a fairy who helps them
> BERLINGOT, their neighbor
> TYLO, the dog
> TYLETTE, the cat
> LIGHT, BREAD, SUGAR, FIRE, and WATER, some of the substances that
>   come to life

Form and Content

The Blue Bird, a fantasy in six acts, is intentionally cast in fairy-tale form. The play opens in the cottage of Tyl, the woodcutter. While their parents sleep, the children, Mytyl and Tyltyl, see through their window the house of their rich overlords, where an extravagant party is taking place. The children are saddened because they have been told that there is no money for Christmas at their house. Suddenly, a thin, hunchbacked woman appears. The children think that it is their poor neighbor, Berlingot, but the woman claims to be a fairy named Berylune. As proof, the fairy produces a magic diamond that allows the children to see the internal selves of objects and animals. With one magic turn, the dog and the cat assume human shape, although they each retain the facial features of their species. With another turn, the cottage begins to transform: Bread, Fire, Water, Sugar, and Light begin to speak and take on human characteristics. Each creature and object has its own inherent personality. Tylo, the dog, is filled with exuberant love and kind words for the children; Tylette, the cat, begins immediately to seek allies in a revolt against human dominance. Sugar tries to settle this conflict with sweet words. As the children are astounded by the transformations, Berylune advances her request: that Mytyl and Tyltyl undertake to find the Blue

Bird of Happiness, which will aid her in making Neighbor Berlingot's little daughter well. The children and their transformed friends set off to search for the Blue Bird.

The search occupies acts 2 through 5, with each act divided into two or more scenes. Each scene takes the children, under the guidance of Light, to different exotic locales, including the fairy's house, the Land of Memory, the Palace of Night, the Palace of Happiness, the Graveyard, and the Kingdom of the Future. In each locale, the children seem to find the Blue Bird, but something always occurs to bring failure. In one place, a blackbird appears to turn blue, only to revert to black when it is taken from its natural habitat. In the Palace of Happiness, Tyltyl and Mytyl discover literally dozens of blue birds, but they all die as quickly as they are caught.

Other events occur at each of the locales which make for puzzling, frightening, or uplifting experiences. In the Palace of the Night, the children encounter ghosts and terrors; in the Land of Memory, they are reunited with their dead grandparents and even with their brothers and sisters who died. In the Kingdom of the Future, they meet children yet to be born.

In act 6, the children return home empty-handed on Christmas Day, only to discover that their pet turtledove has a decidedly bluish tint and that when Neighbor Berlingot's daughter sees the turtledove, she is cured and becomes happy.

Analysis

It is under the guise of naïveté that *The Blue Bird* makes its sophisticated points. Indeed, the play's value for young audiences may well be that Maurice Maeterlinck presents some of life's hardest questions in a form usually reserved for escapist literature. When Mytyl and Tyltyl begin their search for the Blue Bird of Happiness, there is never any doubt that they will find the creature right in their own backyard. It is the search, not the discovery, that is Maeterlinck's point. Specifically, the playwright wishes the young audience, in the midst of an incredible adventure, to come upon the fundamental problems of growing up, problems that cannot be blinked away even in fairy tales.

In the Land of Memory, for example, the children must deal immediately with the first, and most inescapable, fact of life: death. While there is nothing gruesome about the presentation, the children do meet their dead grandparents and, sadly, a good number of dead brothers and sisters. Young people expect that adults might die, especially older adults such as grandparents, but brothers and sisters are another matter. Young audiences are thus brought without compromise to a confrontation with death. Death is humankind's fate and constant companion, promising an end to the future just as it fills the past with memories. Maeterlinck starts his emotional journey through life by bringing his audience to the contemplation of death. Until one accepts death, there can be no happiness in the present.

Facing unnamed fears is also a burden of every human, and thus the next stop for Mytyl and Tyltyl is the Palace of Night, where ghosts, diseases, and nameless terror are waiting behind every door opened in the search for the Blue Bird. Luckily, the children have the strong vision of their friend Light to guide them. In the Palace of

Night, they find a blackbird that seems to turn blue but when taken into the light reverts to its midnight hue. Dreams are not to be trusted, but then again—since the children exit the Palace without harm—nightmares, once faced, are not to be feared.

It is with more complex but ordinary problems that the seekers must spend the most time. In places such as the Palace of Happiness, the children are permitted to see the internal essences of animals and trees, only to discover that most of these entities resent humanity's blithe misuses of nature. Even the creatures closest to humans, Tylo the dog and Tylette the cat, have been misused. Tylette, the more intelligent of the two, resents her enslavement deeply and attempts to manipulate the children and gain control. Tylo is the more cruelly misused because he has been so dominated that he cannot conceive of any state other than abject enslavement.

Perhaps the most significant experience in the Palace of Happiness is the encounter with the Joys. Not surprisingly, the Palace of Happiness is filled with enticing and joyous blue birds, and the children gather many of them, only to find that they die as soon as they are caught. As Light remarks, "Generally the Joys are very good, but there are some of them that are more dangerous and treacherous than the great miseries."

The last two stops are the Graveyard and the Kingdom of the Future. The Graveyard reintroduces the ultimate question with which the living, even the younger of those alive, must deal. Before the Graveyard, there is the Kingdom of the Future. Here, the seekers meet the souls of children yet to be born, many of whom will never be born because there are more wishing life than there are available lives. These unrealized babies are the profound answer to Tyltyl's complaint about the elusive birds: "Is it my fault they change color, or die or escape?" As Light points out, "There are many more happinesses on earth than people think." In *The Blue Bird*, Maeterlinck asks young people to face squarely the issues of maturity and to rejoice in the gift of life.

Critical Context

The Blue Bird belongs in the long tradition of fairy tales, placed there deliberately by Maurice Maeterlinck, who believed that children and the literature created by and for them had a closer touch with inner reality than did adults and their literature. This play and his earlier work, *Pelleas and Melisande* (1892), are responsible for his international reputation and his being awarded the 1911 Nobel Prize in Literature. As the leader of a group of writers and artists known as the Symbolists, Maeterlinck offered *The Blue Bird* as a counterpoint to the Naturalists' emphasis on surface realism. He was convinced that deeper realities remained shrouded in mystery and could only be approached obliquely as in fairy tales, not through realistic illusion. So persuasive was his work that an early twentieth century master of Naturalism, Constantine Stanislavski, premiered *The Blue Bird* at the Moscow Art Theatre in 1908. The work has been produced worldwide and has inspired several film versions. While James M. Barrie's *Peter Pan* (1904) is perhaps generally better known, *The Blue Bird* has been influential in the serious use of the fairy tale as drama in such works as Karel Capek's *R.U.R.* (1920) and *The Insect Comedy* (1921), George

Bernard Shaw's *Androcles and the Lion* (1913), and Stephen Sondheim's musical *Into the Woods* (1987), as well as countless films both in animated and in conventional form, such as *The Wizard of Oz* (1939) and the Broadway musical *The Wiz* (1975).

August W. Staub

BLUE WILLOW

Author: Doris Gates (1901-1987)
First published: 1940; illustrated
Type of work: Novel
Type of plot: Historical fiction
Time of work: The late 1930's
Locale: San Joaquin Valley, California
Subjects: Family, poverty, and social issues
Recommended ages: 10-13

Driven from a Texas ranch by the Great Depression, the Larkin family works hard to survive and Janey Larkin looks forward to having a real home again.

Principal characters:
JANEY LARKIN, a ten-year-old girl whose blue willow plate is her
    prized possession
LUPE ROMERO, a ten-year-old Mexican girl who lives across the road
CLARA LARKIN, Janey's stepmother
JIM LARKIN, Janey's father
BOUNCE REYBURN, the foreman of the Anderson Ranch
NILS ANDERSON, the owner of the ranch

Form and Content

The Great Depression has driven the once prosperous Larkin family out of northern Texas. For the last five years, its members have traveled constantly, "wanderers in search of a livelihood." Through the ten chapters of *Blue Willow* and the accompanying black-and-white drawings, the story of this stalwart family unfolds.

It begins on a sweltering summer day with the Larkins moving into an abandoned shack. Jim Larkin goes immediately to his job digging up irrigation ditches, while Clara and Janey Larkin settle in. Soon, another girl about Janey's age appears, carrying a baby—Lupe Romero and her sister Betty. Janey is envious that the Romeros have lived in their house for more than a year. Her father always says that they can only stay in a spot "as long as we can." Searching for something to impress Lupe, Janey shows her a blue willow plate and tells her the legend of the Chinese lovers who miraculously change into doves and escape from the girl's angry father. Lupe does not share Janey's enthusiasm for the plate, but this day starts a close friendship between the girls and their families.

The Larkins' tenuous peace is overshadowed by the presence of Bounce Reyburn, who demands five dollars rent for the shack in the name of Nils Anderson, the owner of the ranch. This is money the family can ill afford to spend, but Mr. Larkin pays, demanding a receipt. When work dwindles, the family decides to relax at the nearby river.

With its willow trees and catfish to catch and eat, the river is an idyllic location. While her parents nap, Janey explores the area and ends up at the Anderson Ranch, which reminds her of the scene on the blue willow plate. Reyburn sees Janey and accuses her of being there to steal. Janey hits him but is stopped by Mr. Anderson, who appears on the scene. Janey leaves with a dozen fresh eggs and a warm feeling for the ranch owner.

The warm weather finally fades into foggy mornings and cool days. This change makes Mrs. Larkin ill, but she refuses to see a doctor because there is no money for his fee. Janey persuades the doctor to come and offers the blue willow plate as payment, but the doctor refuses. Mrs. Larkin regains her health, but her illness has delayed the family's move to find more work. Mr. Larkin refuses to pay more rent, and Janey offers Reyburn the plate in order to avoid a fight. When the moving day finally arrives, Janey journeys to the Anderson Ranch to see her beloved plate one last time. Mr. Anderson knows nothing about what has been happening with the Larkins, and Janey explains their situation. Mr. Anderson acts quickly: He fires Reyburn and offers the job of foreman to Mr. Larkin.

The good life has returned to the Larkins. The family lives in an adobe house built by Lupe's father, and Janey attends regular school. The blue willow plate has a permanent home, and Mr. Larkin can finally say to Janey that they will stay "as long as we want to!"

Analysis

On the literal level, *Blue Willow* is the satisfying story of a young girl obtaining her heart's desire. If the novel is reviewed with a probing eye and a literary background, however, shades of T. S. Eliot, Ernest Hemingway, and F. Scott Fitzgerald appear. *Blue Willow* is John Steinbeck's *The Grapes of Wrath* (1939) written for children. Doris Gates has set her characters in a modern wasteland, but unlike the other authors, who were writing for adults, the Larkin family is allowed to escape.

Gates carefully uses four main settings to move the family symbolically from security to despair and back to hope. While their Texas home is only sketchily portrayed, in Janey's memories it represents stability and all that is good. As seen at the county fair and camp school, Janey loves books and reading, which she attributes to her experiences with books on the Texas ranch. The second setting, the dust bowl locale of their shack in California where the story starts, reflects their poverty. A reprieve from this precarious state is offered by the third location, the river, which Mrs. Larkin describes as the biblical phrase "rivers of water in a dry place." During their day at the river, Janey wanders into the final setting, the Anderson Ranch, which parallels the dream world of the willow plate. This setting foreshadows the possibility of a change for the family. Yet, as in the stories of King Arthur and the fairy tales that Janey loves, they must overcome an evil opponent in the guise of Bounce Reyburn. The blue willow plate is the catalyst that brings Janey to the Anderson Ranch, where she tells Mr. Anderson what has occurred. This act ultimately leads the family back to a secure life living on a ranch and completes the circular plot line.

A strength of this novel is its depiction of close family relationships and the courage of each individual member. Janey is told by her father that "it takes just about as much courage to live like that [their transient lifestyle] without losing your grip on things as ever it took to buckle on armor and go out to fight some fellow who had a grudge against you." Mr. Larkin's knowledge as a rancher has little value as he picks cotton in California, but no matter the circumstances, he looks for positive in the situation. Mrs. Larkin attempts to make their meager living quarters homelike and cares for another woman's child. Janey is told by the doctor that it is Mrs. Larkin's courage that pulls her through pneumonia. Janey realizes that her stepmother's constant washing and scrubbing was a means of coping. Janey's courage is seen through her changing attitude toward the blue willow plate. At first, the plate is a vehicle for escaping her life; she would never think of parting with it. In the end, she willingly gives it up in order to help her family.

A negative aspect of the novel's character development is its stereotypical gender roles. Mrs. Larkin does not work outside the home and is the main child care provider. Even at her young age, Janey knows that "there are times when only men are important, when even grown-up women don't matter at all." Initially, she can perceive her father as being brave, but not her mother and herself. Like a knight in olden days, Mr. Larkin will defend them whenever necessary. This stereotyping caused some unfavorable comments when *Blue Willow* was first published and is still a viable concern.

Although Gates sought to paint an accurate picture of life during the Depression era, she also created a memorable story. The novel exemplifies the resilience of the human spirit in the face of adversity—a power that has taken *Blue Willow* through many editions and that will take it through many more in the future.

Critical Context

Based on visits to migrant schools while Doris Gates was director of the children's department at the Fresno County Public Library, *Blue Willow* is often cited as one of the first books to bring contemporary social issues into children's literature. It was named an American Library Association Notable Book in 1940 and a Newbery Honor Book in 1941.

Gates is best known for *Blue Willow*, but she wrote other pieces of realistic fiction drawing upon events in her own life. Her first book, *Sarah's Idea* (1938), features Jinny, the burro that she rode to school as a child. Her love of horses is exemplified in *Little Vic* (1951). Notable for its African American main character in the era before the Civil Rights movement, this rags-to-riches story was the basis of a television film in 1977. *Elderberry Bush* (1967) is an autobiographical novel of her childhood. Gates published more than twenty books for children, including six volumes of Greek myths. Some of her stories were written especially for basal reading textbooks. As a result of this literary legacy, Gates is often labeled a notable author in textbooks on children's literature.

Many of Gates's books are out of print, and her content and style may seem simplistic when compared to more recent, realistic fiction. Her attitude toward feminine roles in society may prompt criticism, but there is a lasting quality in her very traditionalism. Like all good storytellers, Gates had a desire to delight children with a well-told tale. In that goal, she amply succeeded with *Blue Willow*, which is still read in some classrooms and is available in most school and public libraries.

Kay Moore

BLUES PEOPLE
Negro Music in White America

Author: Amiri Baraka (Everett LeRoi Jones, 1934-   )
First published: 1963
Type of work: History
Time of work: 1619-1963
Locale: The American continent
Subjects: Arts and race and ethnicity
Recommended ages: 13-18

Baraka presents a history of African American culture as reflected by its music.

Form and Content

In his introduction, Amiri Baraka states that *Blues People: Negro Music in White America* is a theoretical book exploring the movement of black Americans from African slaves to American citizens using the analogy of black music. One can learn, Baraka believes, much about American society by looking at how slaves saw music as compared to how modern African Americans see themselves as expressed through jazz.

In the first of his fifteen essays, Baraka begins tracing how Africans became Americans by combining studies of anthropology, sociology, history, linguistics, and musicology. He discusses the changes in slavery from the first generations through the nineteenth century, showing how Africanism became less distinct in slave life as old customs lost meaning and the introduction of Christianity changed religious values. Baraka then maps how the black church became the center of life for both slaves and freed people; Christianity became the social and religious center, creating a social hierarchy for Americanized blacks. Work songs became spirituals and eventually secular forms that dominated American popular music. The leader/response form, in particular, became the church shout, combining song and dance that developed into musical forms in vaudeville, the musical stage, and modern recorded music.

Throughout this history, Baraka traces general social movements, including the effects of emancipation, which decentralized black life as a result of secularization and more formal education. The growth of "separate but equal" segregation and Jim Crow laws gave rise to a consciousness resulting in the blues, which reflected a desire for self-determination and a place in the post-Civil War economic system. The early blues were unique, as the form was the first black music sung by individuals rather than choirs or work gangs.

Baraka's discussion of music becomes more detailed in his essays dealing with the period after the Civil War. Instruments such as guitars and harmonicas gave way to European instruments in jazz settings, but black musical forms still followed call-and-response patterns. Baraka then shows how modern performance culture reflected society's view of black life, especially in white minstrel shows and swing dance bands, where white performers acted out what they perceived African American culture to be. As musical forms became more standardized, performers such as Ma Rainey, Ida Cox, and Bessie Smith popularized black music, and consequently it gained more prestige throughout American culture. Jazz and blues developed into more universal forms bringing white musicians such as Paul Whiteman into jazz, transforming it into a more urban form as blacks migrated from the rural South into the industrialized North.

Baraka then traces the growth of race records and dance bands beginning in the 1920's, which influenced a new generation of young black people, particularly those who participated in the two world wars and now showed dissatisfaction with existing social conditions. In this section, Baraka begins to analyze critically both African American culture and its changing self-awareness and the music of the 1930's and afterward. His history becomes more interpretative—comparing, for example, jazz soloists "Bix" Beiderbecke and Louis Armstrong and the varying, regional schools of music that developed.

Blues People concludes with a lengthy evaluation of the music of the 1940's through the early 1960's after the massive social changes of post-World War II America. Baraka discusses the "cool" school attitudes of young black people creating a new racial identity, and he predicts that black music will come full circle by abandoning Western approaches that had become integral to jazz by 1963.

Analysis

This study of African American history remains notable for both its straightforward, objective style and its detailed, informative content, which is clearly written and logically organized. Until the third section of *Blues People*, Baraka's personal opinion is less important than those of the scholars and contemporary authors whom he cites throughout the book to develop and illustrate his points, demonstrating Baraka's wide range of reading and research. His study is credible and authoritative because of the care and intelligence devoted to the project, and young readers can rely on *Blues People* to be a useful, imaginative, and readily understandable overview of black life in America up to 1963.

Readers should be aware, however, that Baraka keeps to his thesis of using music as his focal theme and that much of African American culture is not touched on in *Blues People*. For example, he has little to say about the Harlem Renaissance of the 1920's, and there are only passing references to African American literature, political leaders, or spokespeople outside of the musical milieu. Early critics of the book decried these omissions. As Baraka himself remains a noted dramatist, poet, essayist, and important civil activist on black issues, such omissions may seem surprising in the context of his prolific and productive writing career. Yet, on its own, *Blues People* amply serves the author's stated purpose and is an important cultural study of its intended subject.

The book can be divided into three parts—the first (chapters 1 through 5) being a historical background of black culture and music, the second (chapters 6 through 10) being a detailed history of black music, and the third (chapters 11 and 12) being an interpretative survey of important black musicians after 1930. During the first third of *Blues People*, Baraka's scope is broad and inclusive, but it narrows when he begins his discussion of music in the twentieth century. In the middle chapters, he presents a detailed chronicle of African American music that, while discussed in a wider social context, is primarily useful as a cursory overview for those readers interested in black musicology.

The third section, being more subjective and analytical, is also more personal. Baraka integrates recollections from his youth with an encyclopedic knowledge of the music of his own generation to describe the musicians and developments as both musical and cultural criticism. For example, he praises the "hard" blues that honestly reflect a culture and decries the watered-down commercialism of swing and rhythm-and-blues artists sculpted by record companies into popular trends geared for radio airplay.

These observations are not distracting but are rather integral to the book, making the author a participant in the history that he is recording and lending *Blues People* an authority beyond the research that provides the bulk of the information. While contemporary critics complained that *Blues People* viewed music on a functional, ideological level without delving into the aesthetics and poetry of the music itself, the final chapters reveal Baraka's knowledge of the musicians' art, describing the styles and innovations of "bebop" jazz musicians such as Earl Hines and Charlie Parker. Yet, as some reviewers noted, Baraka's attempt to keep his music/culture analogy consistent occasionally results in straining and an uneasy fitting of musical forms into American class structure. His own involvement with the bebop scene allows him vividly to describe the setting of the music discussed in his final chapters. Because he writes these passages in the present tense, however, new readers may feel some confusion about his pronouncements regarding the future of black culture.

The latter chapters are both deeper in content and more judgmental regarding the assimilation of black people into mainstream American life, giving *Blues People* its individual voice beyond its introduction and overview of Baraka's themes.

Critical Context

As Nat Hentoff, a noted critic for *The New York Times*, observed in 1963, *Blues People* was a pioneering book, the first to explore music in the continuum of African American history. Hentoff pointed to minor historical inaccuracies in the book and questioned Amiri Baraka's musical judgments, but he hailed the book as a significant contribution in the study of African American culture. Yet, fellow black writer Ralph Ellison, with whom Baraka is often compared, complained that *Blues People* did not show how black Americans transcended and overcame the oppression reflected in the music of blues and jazz. Other unfavorable criticisms continue to center on what the book does not contain, while some historians note that the book appeared before Baraka became interested in Black Nationalism. In this context, *Blues People* stands as one of the author's least controversial works, written before his angrier, more polemic efforts of the late 1960's when he became interested in separation from white America, not the assimilation that was a key aspect of *Blues People*.

Other critics, however, have been more enthusiastic, calling the book an innovative "jazz masterpiece." As Bob Bernotas noted in *Amiri Baraka* (1991), a biography written for young readers, *Blues People* was written during a fruitful period for then-youthful LeRoi Jones, and many critics saw the book as but one manifestation of a promising career for an energetic, talented black writer.

Since its first publication, *Blues People* has, on many levels, been superseded and updated by a wealth of studies on jazz, the blues, and black history; what keeps the book alive is Baraka's continuing reputation as an important black writer and the individuality of his perspectives expressed in *Blues People* and elsewhere. It remains a solid, easily understood history of African Americans before the Civil Rights movement of the 1960's.

Wesley Britton

A BOOK OF NONSENSE

Author: Edward Lear (1812-1888)
First published: 1846; illustrated
Type of work: Poetry
Subjects: Animals, education, and emotions
Recommended ages: 10-18

Lear combines 112 delightfully nonsensical limericks with his own whimsical pen-and-ink illustrations to create the Victorian genre of nonsense verse.

Form and Content

A Book of Nonsense was not only the first book in English to indulge in verbal nonsense for its own sake but also the book that popularized the limerick form. Indeed, many standard reference books attribute the invention of the form to Edward Lear, although earlier published examples have been recorded. The nature of the limerick lends itself to light verse; its meter being anapestic—two unstressed syllables followed by a stress (da-da-DUM)—gives it a playful jingle. The first two lines and the last all have the same rhyme sound; these lines each have three stresses. The third and fourth lines are shorter, with only two stressed syllables, and these have their own rhyme sound. The first verse in A Book of Nonsense demonstrates the form:

> There was an Old Man with a beard,
> Who said, It is just as I feared!—
> Two Owls and a Hen,
> F our Larks and a Wren,
> Have all built their nests in my beard!

The drawing that accompanies this verse is as silly as the limerick: A man with a huge black beard longer than his body rocks back on his heels, arms flailing, and scowls at the birds mentioned, which all appear rather contented in his beard.

The sort of nonsense represented by this first poem—a sort of a bewildering pointlessness—is only one type of Lear nonsense. Another comic effect found in the limericks of A Book of Nonsense is multisyllabic rhyme, often involving a feigned mispronunciation or dialect spelling, as in the case of the "Old Man of Moldavia" and his "curious behavior" or the "Old Man of Columbia" who "called out for some beer." Slightly more than half of the limericks in A Book of Nonsense (57 out of 112) have at least one multisyllable or "feminine" rhyme of this type. A third type of nonsense is Lear's neologisms, or coined words, which he disguises with logical Latinate forms so that they appear to be real words. Although in his later books this would be Lear's most common type of nonsense word, there are only three examples in his first nonsense book: "ombliferous," "scroobious," and "borascible."

Each limerick follows the same pattern: "There was" a "Lady," "Man," or "Person," either "Old" or "Young," usually "of [Someplace]" (88 of the 112 limericks have a place name in the opening line). The closing line often repeats part of the first, adding an adjective that is either inappropriate or nonsensical in context: For example, there seems to be no meaning in calling an Old Woman "incongruous" or an Old Man "intrinsic." Sometimes, the adjective has a surprising appropriateness, as when the man about to fall from a casement is described as "incipient." Whether appropriate or not, the adjectives provide a tool for expanding the vocabularies of the children who enjoy the poems.

Analysis

The appeal of *A Book of Nonsense* is nearly universal. Children can enjoy its verbal playfulness virtually as soon as they are verbal themselves, and adults appreciate the limericks on several levels. Although generations of children have read Lear's works, they are by no means exclusively children's literature. Nevertheless, like many children's books, especially of the Victorian era, *A Book of Nonsense* originally began as trifles invented to amuse other people's children—in Lear's case, the grandchildren of his patron, the Earl of Derby. Lear, who had built a reputation as a painter of animals, was commissioned by the earl to capture his menagerie collection on canvas. During his stay at the Derby estate in Knowsley, Lear entertained the children with his nonsense rhymes, which he later published under the pseudonym "Derry Down Derry."

Critics of Lear's verses, building on the observations of novelists Aldous Huxley and George Orwell, see the world of the limericks as one of confrontation between Victorian conformity, represented by the eccentric subjects (the "Old Man" or "Young Person" or "Young Lady" in the first line of each poem) and an intolerant society (almost invariably called "they"). Yet, this point of view was developed largely as a reaction against Victorianism: The eccentric person in the poems is not always harmless. The "Old Man with a poker," for example, "knocked them all down" with it, his only provocation being their calling him a "Guy." Conversely, "they" often show kindness to the eccentric subject, such as keeping the "Old Person of Rheims" awake in order to protect him from his "horrible dreams."

Regardless of how one characterizes the subject or "them," however, most of the limericks in *A Book of Nonsense* present a tension between the two. This tension is essential to the nonsense itself and may be a key to children's delight in them. Children's understanding is challenged whether they identify with the eccentric subject or with the conventional "they." If identifying with convention, the child can enjoy a sense of self-esteem in rising above the silliness of the Young Lady of Norway who sat in a doorway, or the Old Man of Dundee who sat in a tree, or the man of Whitehaven who danced with a raven. If identifying with the eccentric, the child can validate feelings of alienation from the adult world which, particularly in the nineteenth century, stigmatized the imaginative peculiarities of children.

Another reason that *A Book of Nonsense* is popular with children is that the illustrations are as whimsical and crude as the rhymes. This is odd, because Lear, recognized as one of the foremost landscape and wildlife painters in England, could certainly draw better than the rough sketches illustrating *A Book of Nonsense*. Their childish simplicity, however, appeals to both juvenile and adult readers, and the situations in the limericks are so far-fetched that a more realistic style of illustration would be inappropriate. In Lear's illustrations, perspective and proportion are virtually nonexistent; characters torture themselves into impossible positions, often floating above the horizon line that separates the illustration from the text below it.

A third source of appeal to children in the limericks is the large number that refer to animals. Some 40 of the 112 limericks mention animals, and others show animals in the accompanying illustration. If the animal is presented in the limerick as threatening the subject, it is drawn to resemble the human it annoys. The bee boring the Old Man in a tree looks just like him, down to the pipe that he smokes. The Old Man of Quebec resembles the beetle on his back, the Old Man of Whitehaven lifts his coattails to imitate the wings of a raven, and the Old Man who said "Hush" has a beak and circular eyes like the bird in a bush. One Old Man not only looks like his cow but also holds his arms over his head in an awkward position mirroring the cow's horns.

Lear's limericks have delighted generations of readers, and they fascinate literary critics and psychologists as well as children, who can be adept at both criticism and psychology. Later generations accused Lear's of valuing sense and conformity, but the fact that these poems revelling in nonsense and nonconformity were immediately popular show him to be in touch with his times and with children of all eras.

Critical Context

No children's literature known as "nonsense," or resembling Lear's form of it, existed before *A Book of Nonsense* appeared in 1846. Only Lewis Carroll came close to Lear in spirit, and his first "nonsense" book was not published until nearly two decades later, in 1865. Before that time, Lear had published an expanded edition of *A Book of Nonsense* (1861). More nonsense (although not in limerick form) followed in *Nonsense Songs, Stories, Botany, and Alphabets* (1871); *More Nonsense* (1872), including one hundred new limericks with drawings; and *Laughable Lyrics* (1877). The posthumously published *Nonsense Songs and Stories* (1895) concluded Lear's output of nonsense.

Lear's non-limerick poems, the most famous being "The Owl and the Pussycat" (1871), continue some of the themes of alienation and nonconformity established in *A Book of Nonsense*. Another 1871 nonsense song, "The Jumblies," presents the familiar "they," the voice of conformity telling the Jumblies that their adventure is foolish. Yet the Jumblies succeed, and the scoffers praise the Jumblies and want to be like them. As in the limericks of *A Book of Nonsense*, the childlike eccentrics in Lear's nonsense poems sometimes triumph; their childlike nature itself, which values the nonsense, makes that triumph possible. All of Lear's nonsense books feature a lavish sampling of his delightful drawings, which often provide a complementary (and sometimes contradictory) reading of the situations in the poems; *Laughable Lyrics* even includes Lear's own musical settings of two of his poems.

John R. Holmes

BORN FREE
A Lioness of Two Worlds

Author: Joy Adamson (1910-1980)
First published: 1960; illustrated
Type of work: Autobiography and science
Time of work: The 1950's
Locale: Kenya, East Africa
Subjects: Animals, nature, and science
Recommended ages: 10-18

> *Joy and her husband George, a wildlife warden in Kenya in the late colonial era, establish a rare personal bond with three orphaned lion cubs, one of which they retain as a personal pet and later reintroduce into the wild.*

Principal personages:
JOY ADAMSON, a childless, middle-aged woman whose boundless love for animals encompasses three orphaned lion cubs
GEORGE ADAMSON, her husband, a dedicated senior game warden who helps care for the orphaned cubs and reintroduce Elsa to the wild
ELSA, the weakest of the pride of lion cubs, who is adopted by the Adamsons
PATI, a rock hyrax, a pet of the Adamsons who comes to accept and enjoy the presence of the lioness Elsa

Form and Content
At the beginning of the narrative, Joy Adamson introduces herself as the English wife of a game warden responsible for a huge territory of untamed African wilderness. Joy recounts how George kills a dangerous lioness, unaware that she has three small cubs. Since abandoning them would mean their certain death, George brings the cubs home to raise them. The couple ultimately devises a bottle formula that the cubs can tolerate, and they grow normally.

The author introduces Pati, a rare African catlike creature called a rock hyrax, to which she is very attached. Pati develops an unexpectedly close relationship with the lion cubs, who soon greatly exceed her in size. Throughout these early months, Joy feels herself becoming most fond of the smallest and most tame of the cubs, which she names Elsa.

After six months of living in and around their home, the cubs have clearly grown too large to continue as house pets and arrangements are made for flying two of them to a European zoo; the third, Elsa, will be retained. In the absence of her siblings, Elsa seems to deepen her bond with the Adamsons and to fear separation from them. They take her with them on safari, recognizing that they have become, in her eyes, "her pride." They give the young lioness every opportunity to make exploratory forays into the wild, by herself or accompanied by their Somali servant, Nuru. Elsa displays a remarkable sense of fun in her interactions with smaller animals and yet is clearly developing some of the instinctive skills of a predator. She seems entirely fearless and ignores the size and anger of even elephants, rhinoceroses, and buffaloes, natural enemies of lions. Chapter 3 depicts Elsa as a one-year-old, "luminous, iridescent" creature who, on safari to the Indian Ocean, loves to walk the beach, chase coconuts, and dig in the sand. George's bout with malaria on this trip foreshadows the imminent death of Pati, an event that deeply grieves Joy.

The narrative recounts hereafter a variety of George's official expeditions for inspection, the prevention of illegal poaching, and the hunting of dangerous lions, on which he is accompanied by Joy and Elsa. The writer's accounts of these trips center constantly on the activities of the developing lioness. By the age of eighteen months, Elsa has progressively honed her tracking and hunting skills, although she has still failed to display any instinct to kill food for herself. The difficulties of some of these extended and exhausting safaris seem only to strengthen the bonds between Elsa and her human adoptive parents.

By age two, the lioness is fully mature and, in one of her not infrequent absences from home, makes contact with a pride of lions, mating with one of them. The Adamsons observe that Elsa is increasingly expressing a desire to be with her own kind, and they determine to facilitate her break with themselves by transporting her to an area many miles from their home. They successfully encourage her to learn to kill for herself and then leave her, with government permission, in a highland game preserve. When they later return to assure themselves of Elsa's well-being, however, they find her in poor health, her immune system apparently unable to adapt to a climate so different from that of her birth. Permission is obtained to relocate Elsa closer to her own birthplace and, having conducted her there and seen proof of her ability to kill to survive, the Adamsons quietly break camp and leave her. They are sure that Elsa, now in heat, will integrate with a pride in the wild.

Analysis

Born Free is the personal account of a remarkable bond between Elsa and Joy and of the woman's determination to return the lioness fully to the environment of her birth. The text is illustrated with numerous black-and-white photographs taken by the author and her husband. It details the circumstances of their association and Joy's dedication to the hitherto never accomplished feat of returning a domesticated lion to the wild. The author renders the couple's affection for the lioness believable by endowing her with credible, quasi-human personality traits. As well as fearless, Elsa is at times affectionate, protective, loyal, playful, and even childishly willful—those characteristics that cat lovers commonly attribute to their pets.

The preface by Lord William Percy and the foreword by C. R. S. Pitman, the former game warden for Uganda Protectorate, support the veracity of Adamson's account, its setting, and the extraordinary magnitude of her accomplishment. As is clear through-out the work from their discussions with one another and with others, the Adamsons were fully aware that by adopting Elsa they were taking on a great responsibility and had to ensure her best interests. They devoted themselves tirelessly to their objective of enabling Elsa to rejoin the world into which she had been born. The book records the steps that they took to achieve this goal.

In a series of postscripts and a later publisher's note, readers learn of friendly contacts in the intervening months between Elsa and George and eventually between Elsa and Joy, following her return from her London publisher, and that cubs have been born to the lioness. In a final message, Joy expresses both her grief at having parted with Elsa and her pride that she has fulfilled her conviction that an animal "born free" should be allowed to remain in freedom.

Critical Context

Born Free is a truly extraordinary account of an apparently unique interaction between human beings and a lioness born in the wild. The work gives innumerable examples of the strength of the mutual bond between Elsa and the Adamsons. It centers on the maternal instincts of Joy that find expression in her concern for the animals under her care. The understatement and at times humor with which she narrates the strains and difficulties of their life emphasizes the authenticity of the work and the dedication of herself and her husband to the Africa that they so clearly love. The work's simple style and direct, chronological narration emphasize rather than detract from the depth of the bond between the Adamsons and the lioness. Joy Adamson displays throughout the book a deep-rooted respect for animal life in all its African variations. The unemotional detachment with which she describes their activities and observations of wildlife also endow the work with a scientific objectivity. Its close and intimate portrayal of Elsa and many other animals grants the reader a sense of personal observation and participation in life in the African wild.

The author makes no effort to idealize the role played by those like herself and her husband. The scene is one of constant struggle for existence, with danger lurking not only in the climate and the wildlife but also in the ever-present native poachers seeking to pursue their own livelihood in ways traditional to the area before the arrival of the game wardens and conservationists.

This best-selling work, and the film made from it, were highly influential in the 1960's. Its publication no doubt gave impetus to the movements for animal rights and the protection of wildlife and the environment that have developed. The work, therefore, has the cachet of a classic, and it has been widely translated and frequently republished. *Born Free* was followed by a sequel, *Living Free* (1961), also made into a film, which describes the relationship that the Adamsons reestablished with Elsa, who lived independent of humans with her three cubs in the African bush. The experiment was so clearly successful that the work's final notation of the premature death of Elsa, from a blood parasite, does not suggest that she should have been retained in captivity, as was the case with her siblings.

Michele Perret

BRIGHT APRIL

Author: Marguerite de Angeli (1889-1987)
First published: 1946
Type of work: Novel
Type of plot: Psychological realism and social realism
Time of work: The late 1940's
Locale: Germantown, Pennsylvania
Subjects: Family, friendship, race and ethnicity, and social issues
Recommended ages: 10-13

> *Nine-year-old April Bright learns much about herself, her family, and others as she attends public school, participates in Brownie activities, and experiences for the first time the racial discrimination often encountered by African Americans in the 1940's.*

> *Principal characters:*
> APRIL BRIGHT, a nine-year-old African American girl who is striving to excel and to deal with discrimination
> CHRIS and KEN BRIGHT, April's older siblings, who do not live at home since Chris is a seventeen-year-old student nurse and Ken is in service
> TOM BRIGHT, April's brother who lives at home, loves to use his drumsticks on whatever is near, and encounters the police when he is out with some dishonest boys
> PAPA BRIGHT, April's father, who is a postal worker and who encourages Chris to remain pleasant toward those who wrong her so as to shame them into better behavior
> MAMA BRIGHT, April's mother, who is a homemaker and who charges April to be clean, respect herself, do her best, and be pleasant to others so that those who discriminate against her will come to love her
> MISS BELL, April's public school teacher
> SOPHIE, April's best friend
> MISS COLE, April's Brownie leader, who says solemnly that color may limit April
> FLICKER, the Brownie guest lecturer
> PHYLLIS, who at first dislikes April because of her color and who, after getting to know her better, becomes a good friend

Form and Content

Bright April is an account of a six-month period in the life of April Bright, a nine-year-old African American girl. Although the book takes place in Germantown, Pennsylvania, the setting is only a backdrop since the events could occur in almost any American locale in the 1940's. The social realism of the novel is evident from page 1, when a white child looks at April and exclaims, "You're brown!"

April is a typical nine-year-old who does the things that a girl of any color might do: interact with her family, attend a public school, participate in Brownie meetings, go to a social, and mingle with adults and peers—sometimes with unsatisfactory results. The events of the novel are easy to understand. The book does contain some vague references larger social events such as systemic discrimination, sit-ins, and sanitation strikes, but overall the plot is clear and to the point.

The story begins as April and her mother return on the bus from the dentist's office. A young white passenger makes a comment about April's color, and April experiences racial prejudice for the first time. April's mother reminds her that all people are alike inside and that April is the beautiful color of coffee with cream. Subsequent themes include interactions and achievements within the Bright family, the pleasures of friendship, and the pain of discrimination when peers whisper about April, when Phyllis will not sit with her at a social outing because of April's color, and when Mrs. Cole warns that color may limit her.

April has a dedicated teacher, Brownie leaders who challenge her to achieve, and parents who encourage her and advise her on how to contend with discrimination. For example, Mrs. Bright advises April to deal with discrimination by doing whatever she does well and by always being pleasant. Mama explains that when she is feeling "edgewise" toward someone, she does something positive for that person. Similarly, Mr. Bright advises April's brother Chris to treat everyone kindly. He explains that others will become ashamed and return the good treatment.

As her mother has instructed her, April is pleasant at the overnight social on her tenth birthday. Even though Phyllis does not want to sit beside April, April treats her well. During a storm, the two find that they have much in common and become fast friends. April returns home to share her experiences with her mother. She tells Mama that as in a verse from the New Testament, "The truth shall make you free": Phyllis found out about their similarities and this truth made her free to accept April as a new friend.

Analysis

The basic message of *Bright April* is clear: All people are the same within, although they may vary on the outside. This didactic book presents both those who are "pink" and those who are "coffee-colored" as similar, equally important people. Marguerite de Angeli also depicts the likenesses—not the differences—between Sophie's Judaism and April's Christianity. This concentration on similarities and the presentation of minorities as positive, main characters were important breakthroughs in children's literature.

A second prominent theme also emerges: doing one's best. In social encounters, at Brownie activities, and in school, this second lesson is quite explicit in *Bright April*.

Bright April is moralistic. Through example, mottoes, and long, verbal discourses, the adults (Mama Bright, Papa Bright, Miss Cole, Miss Bell, and Flicker) seek to instill in April certain values: cleanliness, thriftiness, pleasantness, quality of perform-ance, education, and respect of self and others. April is a model child who listens, accepts, and tries to emulate these behaviors. The results for April are the love of others, promotion, and achievement. These explicit admonitions and how they help April are quite apparent to young readers.

Throughout the book, the author also presents readers with much information about the world. For example, the reader finds data about the American postal service as April prepares a school report. Flicker gives the Brownies details about nature as she takes them on walks and talks about birds and the environment.

In *Bright April*, de Angeli uses primarily denotation: She says what she means without many stylistic devices. In a few instances, however, she employs similes and metaphors. For example, de Angeli uses similes when she describes Tom's arms as being like pipe stems, when she says that the blossoms fell like snowflakes, and when she refers to the hills as being like great breasts. De Angeli uses metaphors when she calls the buds on the trees "knobs" and the falling blossoms "cherry rain."

Despite her usual directness, however, de Angeli does avoid the use of certain terms. For example, she does not use "Jewish" or "Judaism" when referring to Sophie and Sophie's beliefs; likewise, she avoids the terms "Christian" or "Christianity" when referring to April and April's religion. Similarly, de Angeli never mentions in the written text that Mrs. Cole, the Brownie leader, is African American. It is only through de Angeli's illustrations that the reader becomes aware of Mrs. Cole's color and why she may know of the limitations that color may place upon April.

Critical Context

Bright April was an important novel in the 1940's, a decade that featured few multicultural children's books, because it has an African American both as a main character and as a positive role model. Until that time, few children's books even included minorities among their characters. *Bright April* is, therefore, a landmark book.

Although de Angeli had more than twenty self-illustrated books to her credit, only *Bright April* features an African American as a main character. Historians of children's literature recognized this book as her breakthrough novel. Because of *Bright April*, de Angeli is considered a pioneering author and illustrator.

The "likeness" among people in *Bright April* was an important idea to present in a society that often concentrated on differences and inequalities. De Angeli stressed similarities and equality among all people in both the text and illustrations of *Bright April*. For example, the only real difference in the sweet, pretty faces of the "pinks" and of those "the color of coffee" is the shading. Neither the text nor the illustrations in *Bright April* accentuate physical differences or cultural diversity, but, given the time period, this omission seems appropriate. *Bright April*, however, is not without flaws. On occasion, it seems to lack realism: That a minority child in the 1940's could be almost ten years old before encountering racial prejudice is highly unlikely. The novel abounds with propaganda about morals and values and imposes many facts and much information upon the reader. The closing references to Bible verses may be offensive to some groups. As a result, *Bright April* may be too preachy for some youngsters.

Nevertheless, *Bright April* was an important milestone in children's literature and was by no means a commonplace achievement. De Angeli's introduction of important, positive minority characters who possess common qualities helped to ready the public for later books that portrayed minorities even more realistically.

Anita Davis

BRIGHTON BEACH MEMOIRS

Author: Neil Simon (1927-   )
First presented: 1982
First published: 1984
Type of work: Drama
Type of plot: Domestic realism
Time of work: September, 1937
Locale: Brighton Beach, Brooklyn, New York
Subjects: Coming-of-age, family, sexual issues, and war
Recommended ages: 13-18

Eugene Jerome learns that despite jealousies and differences of opinion, a strong, loving family provides its members with the only real security in a chaotic world.

Principal characters:
EUGENE JEROME, the protagonist and narrator, a fifteen-year-old boy
STANLEY "STAN" JEROME, his eighteen-year-old brother
JACOB "JACK" JEROME, their father
KATE JEROME, their mother
BLANCHE MORTON, Kate's widowed younger sister
NORA MORTON, Blanche's sixteen-year-old daughter
LAURIE MORTON, Nora's younger sister

Form and Content

Brighton Beach Memoirs is a comedy about a Jewish working-class family living in Brooklyn during the Great Depression. The first act begins at 6:30 P.M. in September, 1937, the second at 6:30 P.M. a week later. There is a single setting, the home of the Jerome family in Brighton Beach. The action moves from room to room, however, and even just outside the front door.

In the first act, Neil Simon establishes the problems that his characters are facing, as shown not only in dialogue and action but also in Eugene Jerome's asides. Eugene's function in the play is twofold. He is the protagonist, a teenager preoccupied with his own problems, and he is also an observer, making notes from which he will eventually write this play. One of the story lines deals with the Jerome family as an entity, about to break apart because of financial pressure and personal differences; the other focuses on Eugene, who sees himself as the family scapegoat but is even more disturbed about the onset of puberty.

The tension in the Jerome household is evident from the moment that the curtain rises. The small home is overcrowded, containing not only Jack and Kate Jerome and their sons, Stanley and Eugene, but also Kate's widowed sister, Blanche Morton, and her two children, Nora and Laurie. Blanche earns some money through sewing, and

Stanley turns over his wages to his parents, but it is Jack who provides most of the support for the family.

Hoping to acquire a husband so that she can move out, Blanche makes a date with a neighbor. Kate is appalled, both because the man drinks and because he is Irish. Nora also has a scheme, but it, too, meets with objections: None of the adults feels that she should quit school in order to try her luck on Broadway. The financial pressures are mounting. Jack has lost his extra job, and Stanley is on the verge of being fired.

When the second act begins, matters have worsened. Jack has had a mild heart attack. Stanley has lost his salary in a poker game. Nora is furious with her mother for blocking her way to stardom. Finally, the Irishman has indeed turned out to be an alcoholic. It is all too much for Kate. She tells Blanche how much she has always resented her and concludes by blaming her sister for Jack's heart attack. Despite Jack's intervention in the quarrel, Blanche begins to pack her bags. Meanwhile, Stanley goes off to join the Army.

Late that night, however, the breaches are healed. Nora and Blanche come to a new understanding, as do Blanche and Kate. Stanley returns, bringing money that he has earned at an extra job. He also presents Eugene with his heart's desire, a picture of a naked woman. When Jack informs Kate that his cousins have escaped from Poland and will soon be in New York, she immediately begins making plans to take them in. The play ends with a triumphant announcement from Eugene: Now that he has seen a woman's body, his puberty is over.

Analysis

Although *Brighton Beach Memoirs* was written for a general audience of theatergoers, it has a special appeal for young adult readers. Four of the seven characters are in their teens, and, although each of them has a unique set of problems, there is nothing that Nora, Laurie, Stanley, and Eugene face that young people of their age group cannot recognize.

One source of tension in the household is sibling rivalry. Because Blanche is so obviously partial to Laurie, using her supposed health problems as an excuse for spoiling her, Nora feels the loss of her father even more acutely. One positive result of Kate's outburst is that Blanche is finally able to understand the feelings of her older daughter. Kate never realizes, however, that she is always catering to Laurie at Eugene's expense. Fortunately, Eugene has a superb sense of irony; moreover, he views his mother as a character in the play that he will write someday.

The two older young people in the household are also impatient to be independent. Although she knows that her uncle has her best interests at heart, Nora finds it difficult to take Jack's advice and turn down a producer's offer. She would like to be on her own, or at least head of the Morton household, rather than a dependent of the Jeromes. Stanley, too, wants to get away. As long as he lives at home, he must account for every penny that he makes. He leaves to join the Army not only so that he can avoid telling his father about his gambling losses but also because he wants his freedom. He returns because he knows that he cannot leave with his father ill and Blanche not yet established in her own home. In time, he will leave, probably to fight in the impending war, and Nora, too, will eventually attain the independence that she craves.

Another reason that Stanley is needed at home is to act as Eugene's mentor while he struggles toward adulthood. During this one eventful week, Stanley has taught Eugene much about his sexuality. With his information about first cousins, Stanley has even persuaded Eugene to turn his attention away from Nora. Despite Eugene's final declaration, it seems likely that in the weeks to come there will be other questions plaguing him. It is fortunate that Stanley will be there to answer them with his usual patience and understanding.

Although *Brighton Beach Memoirs* is a comedy, full of wonderful one-liners and hilarious scenes, Simon's primary theme is a serious one: that while at times one family member may feel an overwhelming desire to see the last of another or of the whole lot, in the final analysis only family ties can provide individuals with a real sense of security. Even unwelcome advice, such as Kate's warnings about the Irishman, is prompted by real concern, and sometimes, as when Nora contemplates leaving school, the intervention of the family can prevent a terrible mistake. Moreover, however poor the Jeromes are, they will always find room in their house and in their hearts for family members who are even poorer. The real message of *Brighton Beach Memoirs* is that among all the uncertainties of life, poverty and unemployment, poor health and death, even such convulsions as the Great Depression and the Holocaust, a strong family can endure.

Critical Context

Neil Simon's twentieth play, *Brighton Beach Memoirs* was the first in a semiautobiographical trilogy including *Biloxi Blues* (1986) and *Broadway Bound* (1987). Throughout the plays, Eugene is almost synonymous with Simon himself, except for a five-year difference in age, and Stanley represents the playwright's older brother Danny. In *Broadway Bound*, Stanley is shown as the father-substitute that Danny evidently was for Simon. Like Danny, he encourages Eugene to write and even becomes his collaborator. In *Broadway Bound*, however, the marriage of the Jeromes is a disaster, ending in divorce, as was the case with Simon's parents. The Pulitzer-Prize-winning *Lost in Yonkers* (1991) also draws on the playwright's memories of his childhood: Unlike the dependable Jack Jerome of *Brighton Beach Memoirs*, Simon's father used to disappear for months at a time, often forcing his wife and children to be taken in by relatives. *Brighton Beach Memoirs*, then, can be seen as presenting Simon's ideal of what a family should be, rather than as an accurate portrait of his own experience.

Although these autobiographical details are of interest, any literary work must stand on its own merits. *Brighton Beach Memoirs* confused the critics. Some of them insisted that it was just another Simon play, notable for the gags, while others complained that the wisecracking weakened a serious realistic drama. Other critics labeled it sentimental, pointing to the facile ending. The public, however, was enthusiastic. The play became a hit, had a three-year run on Broadway, was made into a film, and continues to be a staple among local and regional theatrical companies. *Brighton Beach Memoirs* is often studied in high school and college classes as a comic but perceptive dramatization of what it is like to be a young adult.

Rosemary M. Canfield Reisman

BRONZEVILLE BOYS AND GIRLS

Author: Gwendolyn Brooks (1917-   )
First published: 1956; illustrated
Type of work: Poetry
Subjects: Animals, coming-of-age, emotions, family, and friendship
Recommended ages: 10-13

Brooks's children present their views of important events and emotions in their lives, as the titles of such poems as "Cynthia in the Snow," "Rudolph Is Tired of the City," and "John, Who Is Poor" suggest.

Form and Content

The forty poems included in African American poet Gwendolyn Brooks's first collection for children, *Bronzeville Boys and Girls*, depict society from the children's perspective. Many of the poems are brief, rhythmic, and childlike, while a few are told from an omniscient, third-person point of view, such as "Maurice" and "Eppie." The characters include Robert, who is a stranger to himself; Gertrude, who is touched when she hears Marian Anderson sing; and Marie Lucille, whose process of maturation is like a ticking clock.

The settings, like the characters, are uncomplicated and are presented realistically. The city is confining because the buildings are too close. It is so unlike the country, where one is free to go "A-SPREADING out-of-doors." The narratives in the poems are easy to follow, especially when the persona describes his or her situation in the first person, as in "Rudolph Is Tired of the City." As Rudolph says, "These buildings are too close to me./ I'd like to push away./ I'd like to live in the country,/ and spread my arms all day."

Ideas that children can easily comprehend are depicted in these poems. Some of the verses present clear themes such as that uprooting can be painful, as one learns from "Lyle":

> Tree won't pack his bag and go.
> Tree won't go away.
> In his first and favorite home,
> Tree shall stay and stay.
> Once I liked a little home.
> Then I liked another.
> I've waved Good-bye to seven homes
> And so have Pops and Mother.

In "Narcissa," readers learn that some children enjoy their individuality. Some dare to be different from other children, who enjoy playing jacks or ball. Little Narcissa prefers sitting in her backyard gazing at tiger lilies while daydreaming about being an ancient queen dressed in finery; she imagines being a singing wind or a nightingale.

Her imagination allows her to be anything that she wants to be.

An inviting rhythm is created because of the rhymes in these poems, as in "Skipper":

> I looked in the fish-glass,
> And what did I see.
> A pale little gold fish
> Looked sadly at me.
> At the base of the bowl,
> So still, he was lying.
> "Are you dead, little fish?"
> "Oh, no! But I'm dying."

The rhyme scheme of *abcbdece* is not perfect, but for children it makes the poem easier to read.

Figurative language is another element of Brooks's poems. Lightning, thunder, and rain are personified in "Michael Is Afraid of the Storm": "Lightning is angry in the night./ Thunder spanks our house./ Rain is hating our old elm—/ It punishes the boughs." Metaphors abound in "Narcissa": "First she is an ancient queen./ Soon she is a singing wind./ And, next, a nightingale." A simile and hyperbole can be found in "Cynthia in the Snow" as the color of the snow is "Still white as milk or shirts./ So beautiful it hurts."

These poems appeal to young readers because of their themes, characters, and poetic elements. They also appeal to more mature readers because of their no-nonsense way of looking at life from a child's point of view.

Analysis

Bronzeville Boys and Girls is not as critical as Brooks's other volumes of poetry for children because there is no moral preaching. The children in these poems respond simply to their environment in a natural manner. Life does not seem too cruel to them, even though poverty and sickness exist. Although most of the children are African American, in all but a few of these poems these boys and girls could be of any race or nationality. In "Jim," the helpful little boy is caring for his mother because she is ill and needs medicine, broth, and cocoa. Like any little boy, he misses being able to play baseball, but he is sensitive to his mother's needs and therefore puts her first.

Bronzeville boys and girls are real, honest, and inquisitive. One is struggling with being trapped in an urban environment in "Rudolph Is Tired of the City." Another deals with having to do without, as the title "John, Who Is Poor" suggests. John is lonely because his father is dead, and his mother has to work all day. The speaker asks the children to share their treats and not ask questions about why John is hungry and when his hunger will end. The persona in "Michael Is Afraid of Storms" is typical of any child who wants the security of an adult when the thunder roars or the lightning pops. Brooks also captures reality in "Robert, Who Is Often a Stranger to Himself." The child looks at his reflection in the mirror and wonders who he is. Just as adults often place restrictions on children, the persona in "Paulette" wants to run and play and chase the flying squirrel and bustling ants, but she cannot because her mother says that at age eight she needs to start acting like a lady.

Some of the children of Bronzeville are creative and manage to escape some of the restrictions of their environment. By using their imaginations, these children recognize the differences between grownups and children. In "The Admiration of Willie," the young boy acknowledges the qualities and responsibilities of adults. They are wise; they tie ties, bake cakes, ease pain, build walls, find balls, make planes, cars, and trains, and kiss children after they have said their prayers. A few of the Bronzeville boys and girls enter into a fantasy apart from the real world. For example, in "Mexie and Bridie," two adolescent girls, one black and the other one white, play together oblivious to race. They enjoy a congenial tea party beneath the clouds and among the ants and birds. Like these girls, two adolescent boys in "Luther and Breck" escape the confinement of their enclosed space to the imaginary world of historical England. After they visualize the castles in England with brave knights, these boys care nothing for the wooden walls of "HERE."

Critical Context

Gwendolyn Brooks writes poetry for and about children. The boys and girls in Bronzeville are more imaginative than the children in her later works *Aloneness* (1971) and *The Tiger Who Wore White Gloves* (1974). Even though some of the children in the poems are poor, other children are advised to share what they have with them. Still other children survive their limited environment by using their minds to escape. Brooks believes in her children; her Bronzeville boys and girls are survivors. Like the adults in her poetry, these children are not sheltered from the socioeconomic and human rights problems that confront adults. These children survive because they use their imaginations to cope with stark reality.

Bronzeville Boys and Girls captures the natural wonder of childhood while offering a hint of social protest. Even though the protest or comment is not too biting, Brooks may have written this collection of poetry as a social statement. There are many poems, however, that seem to originate from within the child who is looking out at the world—such as Tommy, whose seed popped out without "consulting" him. While the title *Bronzeville Boys and Girls* implies that these poems are only about the experiences and fantasies of Bronzeville youngsters, these poems are true portraits of young people from everywhere interpreting life as they see it.

Sarah W. Favors

BROWN GIRL, BROWNSTONES

Author: Paule Marshall (1929-   )
First published: 1959
Type of work: Novel
Type of plot: Psychological realism and social realism
Time of work: 1939-1947
Locale: Brooklyn, New York
Subjects: Coming-of-age, family, and race and ethnicity
Recommended ages: 15-18

Selina Boyce, a first-generation American of West Indian heritage, learns to reconcile the conflicting values of her mother's pragmatism and her father's idealism as she struggles to establish her own identity.

Principal characters:
SELINA BOYCE, a young girl trying to understand the world around her
SILLA BOYCE, Selina's mother, a hardworking woman whose aim is to own property and succeed in life
DEIGHTON BOYCE, Selina's fun-loving father, who lives in the nostalgic memories of his homeland
INA BOYCE, Selina's older sister
BERYL CHALLENOR, Selina's close friend
SUGGIE SKEETE, a tenant in Silla's brownstone
MISS THOMPSON, an African American hairdresser who is Selina's mentor and confidante
CLIVE SPRINGER, Selina's lover

Form and Content

Brown Girl, Brownstones depicts the coming-of-age of Selina Boyce. Narrated in the third person, the novel is divided into four books that cover the growth and maturation of Selina from the age of ten to eighteen. The first two books bring out the basic conflict in the novel. The Boyce family lives in a leased brownstone in Brooklyn. As young as she is, Selina is aware of the tension between her parents. She is devoted to her father, Deighton, an impractical dreamer who lacks the ambition and energy of other immigrants from the West Indies. He likes to bask in the sun and flit from one plan to another, without applying himself enough to achieve any goal. Silla, Selina's mother, offers a stark contrast; she works two jobs and is determined to succeed in attaining the American Dream. Selina's inability to reconcile the two conflicting forces in her life is further complicated by her own emerging sexuality and consciousness of race. Beryl, Suggie, and Miss Thompson are her confidantes during this period.

The underlying conflict deepens when Deighton Boyce inherits two acres of land in Barbados. Silla wants him to sell the land and use the cash as a down payment on their brownstone. Deighton refuses to consider the option and dreams of building a beautiful house on the land. As the United States enters World War II, Silla and her fellow countrymen find better-paying jobs and begin to acquire properties at a faster pace. Envious of her friends, Silla takes drastic measures to own her house. She forges her husband's signatures and manages to sell the land in Barbados; Deighton, in turn, pays her back by squandering the fraudulently obtained money on frivolous gifts for himself and his family.

Selina hates her mother for destroying her father's dreams. On Selina's fifteenth birthday, Deighton's right arm is mangled in an accident at his workplace. The resulting forced retirement, along with the rejection by his wife and by the Barbadian community, gradually causes Deighton to seek solace in a cult. He distances himself from the family—even from Selina, his favorite daughter—and moves out. Silla, defeated in every way, takes revenge by reporting him to the immigration authorities. Deported because of his illegal status, Deighton commits suicide as his ship approaches Barbados.

The last section of the novel deals with the aftermath of this tragedy. Mourning her father, Selina refuses to forgive her mother for her betrayal. Her isolation is increased as Beryl moves away and Suggie is evicted by her mother. She goes to college on her mother's insistence but refuses to study for a respectable profession. Selina finds more joy and fulfillment in ballet and modern dance, which are considered useless by her mother. During this period, she has an affair with Clive Springer, a jobless war veteran who is a failure by the community's standards.

Selina has a rude awakening when she confronts racism on a personal level. She realizes that to the white people around her, she is no more than another member of the black race. When Clive refuses to break out of his mother's manipulative control, Selina decides to make it on her own. She recognizes how similar she is to Silla in her determination and her will to succeed. She decides to follow her own interests and finally makes peace with her mother.

Analysis

Brown Girl, Brownstones is a novel of Selina's growth from an immature ten-year-old to a self-confident young woman on the threshold of adulthood. Adolescence, in general, is a difficult time, and in Selina's case the problems are compounded by the fact that her parents are immigrants trying to make a place for themselves in a new country. The West Indian community depicted in the novel prides itself in its members' ability to work hard, save money, and acquire property in order to achieve the American Dream of success. People such as Deighton Boyce and Clive Springer who do not follow the norm are looked down on by the community.

Selina's life is further complicated by her inability to understand the love-hate relationship between her parents. Silla wants Deighton to be like other West Indian men and be a financial success. Selina feels closer to her father, who dwells in the nostalgic memories of his homeland and lacks the tenacity to stick to a goal and achieve it. She is turned off by her mother's single-minded devotion to making money. She is baffled and irritated by her sister Ina's complacent attitude, not realizing that Ina's turn to religion and desire for an unruffled life is her way of coping with the discord at home. Yet, even as Selina openly derides her mother's ways, she cannot help admiring her strength, determination, and ability to express herself.

Like most adolescents, Selina is unsure of her own identity. Initially, she desires to be like her father; she admires his easygoing ways, his love for life, and his ability to keep dreaming despite constant setbacks. She shares with him his disdain for his fellow Barbadians who become workhorses in pursuit of wealth. Later, as she sees her father collapse before her eyes when his empty dreams disappear and his failures confront him, she grudgingly admits that it is the strength of her mother that keeps the family going. Nevertheless, Selina finds it hard to declare a truce with her mother because of her betrayal that eventually leads to her father's suicide. Her refusal to pursue a profession that her mother desires and her clandestine affair with Clive are expressions of her rebellion. In college, however, Selina finds her own niche in dance, which gives her an avenue for self-fulfillment and a direction in life. She also recognizes the futility of counting on Clive and thus takes the decisive step to break with him and move on with her life.

Although *Brown Girl, Brownstones* is not primarily a novel about race relations, Selina's dawning awareness of how she is viewed by mainstream society is a part of her maturation process. A firsthand experience of hearing the carelessly spoken words of her classmate's mother denigrating the black race makes Selina realize the hardships endured by women such as her mother and by her fellow Barbadians who take back-breaking menial jobs and save incessantly for the education of their children in the hope that they will be spared such pain. She cannot condone her mother's actions, but at least she begins to comprehend the motivation behind them. As a child, Selina used to imagine belonging to the gracious world of the white family that had owned their house previously. Now grown up, she knows her place is with her community, flawed although it may be. At the end, when she decides to go to the West Indies to claim her past and make it a part of her American life, she is admitting the necessity of combining the understanding of heritage with the need to act—a synthesis of the conflicting views held by her parents.

Critical Context

Brown Girl, Brownstones, Paule Marshall's first novel, was published in 1959. Although the novel received good reviews, it did not enjoy commercial success and went out of print. It was given a new life when the Feminist Press reprinted it in 1982. Since then, the novel has been widely read and used in classrooms. It belongs to the tradition of *Bildungsroman*, a novel dealing with the theme of coming-of-age. It is one of the few novels that portray the inner life of a young, first-generation American woman of West Indian origin.

Like many first novels, *Brown Girl, Brownstones* draws heavily on the author's own life. Marshall's parents also came from Barbados, and, like Selina, Marshall also had a father who failed his family. Selina's introspective nature and her desire to understand the world around her is also based on Marshall's adolescence. In several interviews, she has commented that when she was growing up, she could find no books that depicted people like her; she wrote *Brown Girl, Brownstones* to fill that vacuum. Marshall has expressed her debt to Thomas Mann and Gwendolyn Brooks in the writing of her first novel. Following Mann in *Buddenbrooks* (1901), she attempts to trace the development of her main character in the context of her family. Emulating Brooks in *Maud Martha* (1953), Marshall focuses on the mind of a young African American woman. The novel succeeds in re-creating the world of a female protagonist in much the way that James Baldwin did for a young male protagonist in *Go Tell It on the Mountain* (1953).

Leela Kapai

BUILDING BLOCKS OF THE UNIVERSE

Author: Isaac Asimov (1920-1992)
First published: 1957
Type of work: Science
Subject: Science
Recommended ages: 13-15

Asimov presents the story of the chemical elements—their properties, discovery, and importance to life on Earth.

Form and Content

Isaac Asimov's *Building Blocks of the Universe* is a compendium of facts suited to introducing the subject of chemistry to young readers. The book is divided into twenty-three chapters, each dealing at length with one element and in most cases more briefly with related elements. The first element covered is oxygen, because of its commonness on earth and its critical importance to life. The last chapter is devoted to uranium and the other unstable elements. The intermediate chapters are ordered based on such considerations as the element's familiarity, commonness, significance to life, relation to elements already covered, and position on the periodic table.

The periodic table is used as a tool to organize what could otherwise appear to be disparate information. It is described in the introduction, and a version containing atomic numbers but not the names of the elements is reproduced at the beginning of the book. Another version, containing only the names of the elements, is printed at the end. The two versions serve to highlight the structure of the table and emphasize how the elements fit. Each chapter heading contains a simplified periodic table that includes only the atomic numbers relevant to that chapter. For several elements, Asimov describes the historic usefulness of the periodic table as a means of predicting the existence of unknown elements that were later discovered.

Each chapter is an account of interesting characteristics of an element or group of elements. Asimov generally describes the element in its natural state, notes the temperatures at which the element changes its state, lists other elements with which the element commonly reacts, and describes the nature of those reactions. He often deals with the way in which atoms or molecules combine—the nature and strength of the formation and the consequences of these characteristics. For example, in the chapter on carbon, Asimov briefly explains why the carbon atom is so important to life. He also describes each element's discovery (if it has not been known since antiquity) and its use by and effect on human beings.

Asimov expands the vocabulary of the reader by introducing and defining many terms necessary to an understanding of chemistry. The first time that he uses a new term, he presents it in italics and immediately defines it. He allows the reader to absorb the new information by not providing background material unless and until it is needed. In this manner, Asimov presents an extensive set of scientific words in this introductory text, including "element," "molecule," "compound," "allotrope," "electrolysis," "acid," "base," and "amalgam."

The style of the book is clear, simple, and informal. Asimov often writes in the first person and addresses the reader directly. To bring a point home, he occasionally offers personal anecdotes and calls upon readers to consider likely experiences from their lives that are germane. The book offers many cross-references, as well as a detailed index.

Analysis

In the introduction, Asimov states that his goal is to "tell a little about every element." He achieves this simple goal, but, in doing so, he also achieves a more difficult goal: to tell much about chemistry in particular and science in general, especially as it relates to human society.

Asimov employs a variety of techniques to make potentially difficult material understandable and potentially dry material interesting. For example, to help readers understand how atoms group together to form different kinds of molecules, he uses the analogy of men and women grouping to form different kinds of families. To affix a new idea in the reader's mind, he attaches the new idea to something already familiar to the readers. An example is his explanation of how lungs take oxygen from the air, in which he mentions the time that President Dwight Eisenhower had to be put in an oxygen tent so he could breathe easier, a fact that was known well by most young readers when the book was first published. Asimov also makes use of personification, such as his explanation of nitrogen's lack of reaction with most other elements by describing the element as "standoffish."

To describe the similarities of liquid ammonia to water in an interesting way, Asimov briefly mentions the intriguing speculation that on other planets, there may be a system of chemistry and even a form of life based on ammonia. Asimov uses humor to enliven his account of how bismuth can be mixed with other elements to form substances that melt at low temperatures by noting a practical joke that can be played with it. In addition, Asimov makes some of his points more vivid by citing facts that are unusual or colorful. To emphasize the importance of copper as a trace element in living tissue, Asimov reveals that some animals, such as squids, have a copper-containing compound in their blood to carry oxygen, making their blood blue.

Three implicit themes in this book are of value to young readers. The first is that science is multifaceted, both in the way in which it is carried out and in its effects. Asimov shows that the classic image of science as the confirmation of a hypothesis by means of an experiment—exemplified by Mendelev's successful prediction that three new elements would be discovered to fill the holes in his table of elements— is only one part of the picture. Another part is that science sometimes advances by happenstance, as when Charles Goodyear accidentally discovered the vulcanization process for making rubber by spilling a mixture of rubber and sulfur on a hot stove. Asimov also shows that the results of science are as varied as its processes; an example is that sulfur atoms are found both in mustard gas, a lethal weapon used during World War I, and in life-saving penicillin.

The second valuable theme explored indirectly in *Building Blocks of the Universe* is that science is an ever-evolving body of knowledge, not a static collection of facts. Asimov makes this point by taking a historical approach, recounting how humankind's understanding and/or use of a given element changes over time; such is the case with aluminum, which was once so hard to obtain and therefore so valuable that only the most wealthy could afford to use aluminum tableware. Asimov also takes a future-oriented approach, depicting areas of science in which discoveries have yet to be made. His statement that "we haven't the glimmer of a notion yet" how to use liquid fluorine in rocket fuel might have inspired young readers of the day to think about careers in chemistry.

The third important theme is that science is not an isolated endeavor pursued for other than typically human reasons; it is an integral part of human culture, and scientists are as human as everyone else. Asimov shows the interrelatedness of science and culture by describing the influence of science on language, as in the adoption of the term "bromide," sometimes used as a sedative, to apply to dull people or statements. He also describes the influence of mythology on science, as in the naming, by a chemist with "a streak of poetry" in him, of the element selenium after Selene, the Greek goddess of the moon, because of its similarity to tellurium, recently named after Tellus, the Roman goddess of the earth. Asimov shows scientists as human by mentioning all of their characteristics—their intelligence and their good works, as well as their frailties, exemplified by the scientist who may have surrendered to his ego and found a tricky way to name the element gallium after himself.

Critical Context

Building Blocks of the Universe was one of a series of books on science for young adults that Isaac Asimov wrote for Abelard-Schuman. The series had a significant effect on Asimov's writing career. When publisher Henry Schuman approached Asimov in 1953 about writing science books for teenagers, Asimov was a successful science-fiction writer, as well as a professor of biochemistry at the Boston University School of Medicine. In both endeavors, he believed that he had gone as far as he could go. He was looking for something that would take him further, and he found Schuman's suggestion very attractive. In retrospect, Asimov considered the first book that he wrote for Abelard-Schuman, *The Chemicals of Life* (1954), as the initial step toward the greater success that he eventually achieved as a prolific writer of nonfiction books for the nonspecialist. The success of these and other books allowed Asimov to become a full-time writer in 1958.

The book is now dated, both by the discovery of new elements since the 102 mentioned in the book and because of the occasional expressions of old-fashioned gender stereotypes. Asimov went on to write many more up-to-date books on science for the layperson—a dozen more in the fields of chemistry and biochemistry alone. In its time, however, *Building Blocks of the Universe* was widely read. Abelard-Schuman published a revised edition in 1961, and Cadmus Books published a special hardcover edition in 1965. The book was available in mass-market paperback editions from Lancer through the 1970's. In 1958, the book earned an award from the Thomas Alva Edison Foundation.

Earl Wells

BURY MY HEART AT WOUNDED KNEE
An Indian History of the American West

Author: Dee Brown (1908-   )
First published: 1970; illustrated
Type of work: History
Type of plot: Adventure tale and moral tale
Time of work: The latter half of the nineteenth century
Locale: The western United States
Subjects: Politics and law, race and ethnicity, and war
Recommended ages: 13-18

Brown explains how, using the motive of Manifest Destiny, white settlers encroached upon and confiscated western land inhabited by numerous tribes of American Indians, ultimately decimating the native populations.

> *Principal personages:*
> GEORGE ARMSTRONG CUSTER, the best known of U.S. military leaders in the West, who was killed at the Battle of the Little Bighorn
> CRAZY HORSE, the chief of the Oglala Sioux and one of leaders at the Battle of the Little Bighorn
> SITTING BULL, also known as Hunkesni, a medicine man and the leader of Hunkpapa Sioux
> RED CLOUD, a warrior and the chief of the Oglala Sioux, the only American Indian considered to have won a war against white people
> WILLIAM TECUMSEH SHERMAN, a U.S. general and the head of the peace commission that ended the war with Red Cloud
> PHILIP SHERIDAN, a U.S. general and the foremost leader in post-Civil War fighting against American Indians
> BIG FOOT, the chief of the Minneconjous, among the bands massacred at Wounded Knee Creek

Form and Content

A prevailing force within the United States in the nineteenth century was the concept of Manifest Destiny, the belief that the entire continent was destined to be settled and ruled by (white) settlers from the East. In search of wealth or land, tens of thousands of settlers began moving west in the decades before the Civil War, quickly coming into conflict with the indigenous population: American Indian tribes that had long been settled on the land.

Bury My Heart at Wounded Knee is a historical account of this movement, and its effects on the American Indian peoples, as seen through their eyes. The period between 1860 and 1890 is the major focus of the book. This period represented the peak years of conflict between the white settlers, the military sent to protect them, and the American Indian tribes already present on much of the land. The period was bounded in the beginning with the start of the Civil War and ended with the massacre at Wounded Knee Creek, the last major incident between native tribes and the U.S. cavalry.

Dee Brown follows a sequential series of events, basing much of his work on American Indian accounts, including records of treaty councils held during formal negotiations between U.S. representatives and tribal chiefs. Even councils held in remote areas generally included interpreters and recorders. Chiefs or older members of the tribes were free to present their thoughts, even those recounting past events. The result was a rich history available to someone willing to search them out, as Brown did, in government archives. Many first-person accounts by the American Indians involved in these events can be found throughout the book.

Brown's narratives of the tragedies that unfolded during these years are gripping in their pathos. It was said that the only promise the white people unfailingly kept was that they would take the land. Treaties would be made, promising that the land would remain within the hands of the native tribes in perpetuity. As Brown continuously documents, such treaties remained valid only until white settlers and the U.S. government desired the land. Members of the tribes would then be either moved again or killed. To many of the soldiers, it made little difference as to which occurred. General Philip Sheridan summed up this attitude with his statement "The only good Indians I ever saw were dead."

Brown completes his account of these years with the description of events at Wounded Knee Creek in 1890. Leaderless after the assassination of Sitting Bull on the Sioux reservation, hundreds of the Hunkpapa Sioux sought refuge with Big Foot and his people near Pine Ridge, in present-day South Dakota. Sighting a cavalry detachment, Big Foot placed his people under their protection in the vicinity of Chankpe Opi Wakpala, known as the creek at Wounded Knee. He ordered them to surrender any weapons to the soldiers. A gun discharged, probably accidentally, and soldiers began to fire indiscriminately. Before the firing ended, some three hundred American Indian men, women, and children were dead.

Analysis

Brown attempts to explain the plight of modern-day American Indians, too often the victims of poverty and hopelessness and often presented as caricatures, by showing what these proud people once were. If they appeared naïve in their dealings with white people, it was only because they were left with little choice. Their land would be taken anyway.

Conflict between native tribes and Europeans began almost immediately upon the arrival of Christopher Columbus in 1492. As Brown notes, word of European barbarism was quickly outpaced by the spread of conquest. Within three centuries, white settlers had reached the Mississippi River, pushing native tribes before them.

Brown has used the period between 1860 and 1890 to illustrate the conflict between native peoples and the U.S. military. Each chapter presents events that occurred during specific years within that era, as viewed by individual tribes or tribal leaders. The result is a long series of descriptions, often depressing, of cruelties inflicted on innocent people.

The Sand Creek affair was typical of the dealings between American Indians and the U.S. military. Motavato (Black Kettle), as chief of the Southern Cheyenne, recognized the futility in fighting the white people and was willing to make every effort to promote peace. Just prior to the start of the Civil War, Black Kettle agreed to settle his people in a small region near Sand Creek, in present-day Colorado. In return, they would be allowed freedom of movement to hunt buffalo. For some years, peace was kept. Although distrustful of the Cheyenne, Major Edward Wynkoop, the commanding officer at nearby Fort Lyon, was at least willing to deal honestly with them; over time, he developed a strong respect for the tribe. Yet, the author uses Wynkoop to illustrate the duplicity inherent in the white people's dealings. Because Wynkoop had become "too friendly," he was removed as commander. Colonel John Chivington had no such compunction. Leading a black regiment of cavalry, Chivington attacked the native settlement along Sand Creek in November, 1864. Black Kettle's tepee was in the center of the camp, an American flag flying above it. Before Chivington ended the rampage, more than three hundred men, women, and children, including Black Kettle's wife, had been killed. Even Kit Carson, no friend of American Indians, was sickened by what he called a massacre. Black Kettle himself escaped, only to be killed several years later in a similar attack led by George Armstrong Custer.

Brown moves his story from event to event in similar fashion. Outnumbered, with little recourse, the American Indians rarely triumphed. Only Red Cloud, the chief of the Oglala Sioux in areas of Montana and South Dakota, could be said to have won a peace. The U.S. Army had built several forts in the region soon after the Civil War to protect settlers moving through the area, a trail that passed through Sioux hunting grounds. In what was called Red Cloud's War, the Sioux besieged the forts until, in 1868, the U.S. government agreed to abandon them. Ironically, the peace with Red Cloud would endure.

Yet, as Brown continually notes, such a peace was an exception. More typical was the unrelenting pressure of western movement, pushing the native tribes until there was no longer anywhere to go.

Critical Context

Bury My Heart at Wounded Knee was among the first critical accounts dealing with the opening of the American West from the viewpoint of the original inhabitants, the American Indians. Numerous accounts have been written on the movement of the white settlers through this portion of the United States in the years after the Civil War; nearly all conferring the view of the settlers themselves or the history, both real and mythic, that arose from this period. Dee Brown provides an alternate viewpoint: that of the persons displaced, and all too often murdered, as a result of such movement. This book was not his first on the subject; *Fighting Indians of the West* (1948), coauthored with Martin Schmitt, was an earlier account of the same topic. Although profuse in use of early photographs, the discussion in the earlier book is much more condensed and contains little in the way of first-person description.

Bury My Heart at Wounded Knee was written during the 1960's, a turbulent period in the United States that represented a questioning of the country's values. The concept of Manifest Destiny would find no exception to such analysis. Brown provided straightforward accounts of the inhumanity often exhibited by soldiers and settlers, of treaties broken nearly as quickly as they were signed, and of soldiers whose claims to fame were based on how many deaths they had inflicted. The book quickly served as an alternate version of history and as source for a more realistic analysis of the western United States between 1860 and 1890. As such, it was also among the first written from the viewpoint of the victims. Quickly becoming a best-seller, *Bury My Heart at Wounded Knee* has undergone numerous printings in subsequent years, reflecting the book's importance in the subject.

Brown followed this work with an extensive analysis of American Indian folklore in *Folktales of American Indians* (1993) and a more general work on the history of the Southwest in *American West* (1994).

Richard Adler

CARRIE

Author: Stephen King (1947-   )
First published: 1974
Type of work: Novel
Type of plot: Moral tale, psychological realism, and thriller
Time of work: 1970
Locale: Chamberlain, Maine
Subjects: Coming-of-age, family, friendship, and the supernatural
Recommended ages: 13-18

Carrie White, a social outcast with telekinetic powers, is pushed over the edge by a prank by her classmates, leading to the destruction of her entire world.

> *Principal characters:*
> CARRIE WHITE, a sixteen-year-old high school student trying to fit into her school's social scene
> MARGARET WHITE, Carrie's domineering, unstable mother
> SUSAN SNELL, the one high school girl who regrets having played cruel jokes on Carrie and tries to become her friend
> TOMMY ROSS, Susan Snell's boyfriend, who agrees to be Carrie's date for the prom
> MISS DESJARDIN, Carrie's gym teacher, who attempts to make Carrie's classmates stop persecuting her
> CHRIS HARGENSON, the leader of the girls who constantly torment Carrie
> BILLY NOLAN, Chris's roughneck boyfriend and the leader of the gang that plays the last prank on Carrie at the prom

Form and Content

Carrie is a clear, often harsh account of a young girl's attempt to fit into the social life of her high school. In spite of the constant pranks played upon her by her classmates, Carrie White holds some hope that she will be accepted. *Carrie* is a retelling of the Cinderella story, allowing readers to witness the transformation of "ugly" Carrie White into the queen of the prom, escorted by the most handsome boy in school. Like Cinderella, Carrie is forced back into her real world at the end of the ball. Unlike Cinderella, however, Carrie is not rescued by the handsome prince at the conclusion of her story, and the tale ends tragically.

The history of Carrie White and the eventual destruction of Chamberlain, Maine, is told through the manuscript invention technique. Stephen King creates newspaper articles, scientific studies, and even a long autobiographical work called *My Name Is Susan Snell* in order to tell the events presented in *Carrie*. This technique, one often used by horror writers, lends credibility to the supernatural events that occur in the story.

All that Carrie White wants is to no longer be a social outcast or ugly duckling. Because of her physical appearance and her mother's strange behavior, however, Carrie has little chance of seeing her dream become a reality. Margaret White is a mentally unstable woman and an extreme fundamentalist who sees sin everywhere. She attempts to keep Carrie locked away from all contamination; she does not even explain the meaning of Carrie's menstrual periods to her.

When Carrie experiences her first menstrual period and thinks that she is dying, the girls in her gym class have even more ammunition with which to barrage the already fragile Carrie. Because of the cruel joke that they play on Carrie in gym class, the girls are punished by having their prom privileges taken from them. Believing this punishment overly harsh, they plot the ultimate revenge against Carrie. One girl, Susan Snell, thinks that the gang has gone too far and tries to make things better for Carrie. She persuades her own boyfriend, Tommy Ross, to escort Carrie to the prom.

Carrie's preparation for and anticipation of the prom are further darkened by her mother, who fears that Carrie will fall into a situation that will lead to her destruction. Mrs. White, trying to convince Carrie that going to the prom is unwise, uses harsh punishment on her daughter. Carrie's determination is not lessened, however, and her supernatural powers gain strength as a defense mechanism.

Carrie White and Tommy Ross are chosen queen and king of the prom, the first step in Carrie's final humiliation at the hands of her angry classmates. As they sit in their place of honor, Carrie and Tommy are drenched with blood from a bucket placed above their heads; the bucket falls and strikes Tommy, fatally injuring him. At this point, Carrie is unable to control her emotions and uses her supernatural powers to retaliate against everything that has made her life unbearable: her classmates, her town, and her mother. With her powers, Carrie traps the prom goers in the gym and sets it on fire, walks through town destroying all that reminds her of her torment, and goes home to kill her mother. Carrie eventually dies from a stab wound suffered during this final fight with her mother. The only survivor is Susan Snell, the one girl who tried to be a friend to Carrie; she records many of the events told in the novel.

Analysis

Supernatural elements aside, *Carrie* is a story to which anyone who has felt estranged from a group can relate. This seemingly simple story contains several parallel themes that create its underlying complexity and conflict: the difficulty encountered when trying to become a member of a group, the problems associated with standing up to negative peer pressure, and the results of extreme emotional strain for a young person. *Carrie* is a good, contemporary example of initiation literature, in which the reader witnesses a character's growth out of the innocence of childhood into the more complex world of adulthood.

Carrie White is representative of the many young people who are denied entry into the peer group socialization required for satisfactory completion of the maturation process. In order to develop into a well-adjusted adult, a young person must be included into the group dynamic. Carrie makes every attempt to fit in, but her appearance and her backwardness resulting from the bizarre actions of her mother will not permit her to fit in. Carrie has been taught that life is sinful, and she approaches each event in her life with great trepidation and tries to make her mother proud of her bravery and strength.

As she begins to mature and develop the human need for peer acceptance, however, Carrie starts to question her mother and her mother's values. This clash of values places Carrie at odds with her mother, but she is still not accepted by her peers. Even as she actively attempts to free herself from her mother's emotional apron strings, the majority of her peers continue to distance themselves from her. With each failed attempt at gaining acceptance, Carrie becomes more emotionally fragile.

Another aspect of the peer acceptance dynamic operating in *Carrie* is demonstrated by Susan Snell's fall from grace when she decides that perhaps she and her cohorts have gone too far in their mistreatment of Carrie. Even more disturbing to Susan's friends is the extent to which she is willing to go in putting the situation right: She persuades Tommy Ross to escort Carrie to the prom, where the couple are elected king and queen. Because of her defense of Carrie White and her condemnation of the way in which the other students have treated her, Susan is ostracized, shunned by those who had been her friends.

Because of the excessive amount of emotional and psychological pressure that she is put under by her mother and her peers, Carrie eventually loses control and lashes out with the only weapon that she has at her disposal, her telekinetic powers. Many beginning readers may become caught up in the excitement of Chamberlin's destruction, but the more experienced reader will recognize that the center of the story is the destruction of Carrie White by her environment. As media coverage has disclosed, young people such as Carrie often react with extreme violence when they reach their emotional breaking point. *Carrie* is an important work of literature because it attempts to probe the psychology of young people who are on the threshold of adulthood.

Critical Context

Carrie places Stephen King in good company with other authors who have attempted to depict the psychological and emotional traumas of growing up. As in such novels as Sylvia Plath's *The Bell Jar* (1963) and J. D. Salinger's *The Catcher in the Rye* (1945), *Carrie* deglamorizes the maturation process. In addition, *Carrie*, King's first published novel, paved the way for such later works as *The Shining* (1977), "The Body" (1982), *The Dead Zone* (1979), and *Dolores Claiborne* (1993), all of which investigate the psychology of those individuals who are kept outside the traditional socialization process. Like many of King's later works, *Carrie* couches its psychological foundations in supernatural events to give the narrative added suspense and excitement.

Carrie brought King to the forefront of popular horror fiction. Like other writers in the genre, King attempts to show the extent to which people may go to confront or escape their fears and concerns. The horror that King depicts is not necessarily the horror of monsters confronting one from without; rather, he shows that the monsters that confront one from within create the most lasting results in the individual's psychological growth.

Thomas B. Frazier

CASTLE

Author: David Macaulay (1946-   )
First published: 1977; illustrated
Type of work: History
Time of work: 1283-1295
Locale: Aberwyvern, an imaginary town in Wales, Great Britain
Subjects: Jobs and work and war
Recommended ages: 10-18

> *The new English settlement at Aberwyvern is protected by a town wall and a mighty castle, but the fortifications become unnecessary when the English and Welsh learn to accept one another.*

Principal characters:
KEVIN LE STRANGE, the lord of Aberwyvern
LADY KATHERINE, his wife
JAMES OF BABBINGTON, an architect and builder
PRINCE DAFFYD OF GWYNEDD, the leader of the Welsh rebels

Form and Content

Castle gives a step-by-step account of the construction of a medieval castle. Author and illustrator David Macaulay explains in the preface that Aberwyvern is an imaginary setting. The lord of Aberwyvern, his lady, his architect, and his enemy are imaginary characters. The only historical personage is Edward I of England (1239-1307). Aberwyvern is very similar, however, to real places in the northwest of Wales, especially Colwyn Bay. The castle and town at Aberwyvern are composites; their history and architecture are based on places that Macaulay visited and sketched.

King Edward was an aggressive ruler who tried to expand the influence of England in the British Isles. In Scotland, he fought against William Wallace (the "Braveheart" of modern cinema) and Robert Bruce. In Wales, he established settlements in strategic locations and rewarded his loyal followers by making them lords in the area. When King Edward rewards Kevin le Strange by making him lord of Aberwyvern, he recommends a master engineer, James of Babbington, as the architect for Lord Kevin's castle.

The story begins as Lord Kevin and Master James sail to Aberwyvern with their workers, guards, and supplies. Macaulay's architectural illustrations dominate the book; they are made with a drawing pen in black and white. They show the workers and the life of the castle at every stage of development. The story line explains the drawings.

Master James helps to select the final site, a limestone outcropping that overlooks the Wyvern River near the seacoast. Guarded by soldiers, he and his staff build their barracks where the castle will eventually stand. They then dig a deep trench where the town wall will go. When the town is fortified, they bring laborers from England:

quarrymen to dig rocks and masons to lay them, carpenters to build shops and houses, and a blacksmith to make tools and fittings. Meanwhile, Lord Kevin begins to collect taxes from his new subjects.

Work on the castle can be measured by the winters, for construction must stop when the mortar begins to freeze. Sections of the castle's outer wall go up before the first winter sets in. Several towers are erected before the second winter. The outer wall is finished, except for the gatehouses, before the third winter, and the inner wall is under way. The town wall is almost complete before the fourth winter. Welshmen come to work in the town: shoemakers, tailors, and others to service the people working on the castle. The gatehouses are complete before the fifth winter, and before the sixth winter the castle's great hall is ready. Lady Katherine and her children arrive the next spring.

King Edward visits the castle in 1594, eleven years after Lord Kevin first came to Aberwyvern. The town is now thriving. Rebel forces are afoot, however, and Prince Daffyd of Gwynedd attacks the castle in 1595. The castle withstands attempts to bombard it and undermine its walls. Yet, the real success story is the town itself, which begins to grow beyond the town walls. When the English and the Welsh live together peacefully, there is no more need for a castle.

Analysis

Castle is, strictly speaking, a book of architectural history—not a history of castle life or a historical novel. The challenges that Lord Kevin faces with his English workers, his Welsh subjects, and the rebel forces are all based on historical conditions, but they are simply typical. They are not developed in any detail and do not hold the reader's attention. One does not learn when Lord Kevin and his family leave the castle, only that it is abandoned as the town thrives. The lords and ladies are always in the background, mere shadows in the picture of a feast to celebrate King Edward's visit, while the workers and their work are shown in loving detail. One may wonder about the life of a stone mason or shopkeeper, just as one may wonder about the lives of people in a town one visits, but the emphasis is on the construction.

Master James's story is quite straightforward. He is an experienced builder and a good planner. Construction proceeds smoothly, interrupted only by the cold winters. The real complexity lies in the building itself. Macaulay anticipates all the questions that readers might have. Where was the dungeon? What did they do for windows or for bathrooms? How would enemies storm a castle? How could people who were inside escape? Macaulay lets readers look at the construction from different perspectives. He provides aerial views, cross-sections, exteriors, interiors, and closeups. He devotes whole pages to illustrations of the tools and weapons that people used.

All the tools are hand tools. Readers sense the monumental effort expended during the six years of construction. They can share the workers' sense of progress and their pride in a job well done. They can also share Macaulay's sense of excitement at figuring out how anyone managed to pile the stones on top of one another to form such an imposing structure at the edge of a cliff. Seeing the job of castle-building broken down into its many separate activities gives one a much better grasp of the overall building process. Because Macaulay illustrates tools and techniques from the Middle Ages, he instructs older readers as much as younger ones. Some of the same architectural features show up in modern buildings—the corbels and finials, for example. So do the principles of a strong foundation and good town planning.

Macaulay does not preach about the values of hard work, cooperation, and good craftsmanship. He simply shows the people at work. His own draftsmanship is of a high standard. The book itself required much hard work to sketch each building in the growing town, each stone on a wall. Small details such as a mouse in the corner or a sword falling from a siege tower set the monumental labor in perspective.

There is a saying—based on a remark by Jesus in the Gospel of Luke—that stones would cry out if an important story had to be told. Macaulay's challenge, in making this book, has been to look at the stones of castles in Wales and to let them tell their story. Readers watch the stones rise up into walls and towers, inner and outer curtains, according to the master plan. They watch the stones take the forms of gatehouses and garderobes, and they learn the technical names used in architecture. Each architectural or military term is explained at its first mention but is also listed with a definition in the glossary at the end of the book. In all, there are three dozen terms.

Critical Context

Castle was received enthusiastically. It was named Caldecott Honor Book in 1977 and was named an honor book by the *Boston Globe* in 1978. In was adapted for public television, with narration by Macaulay on location in Wales, and broadcast in October, 1983.

Castle followed the same format as Macaulay's earlier guides to architectural history—*Cathedral: The Story of Its Construction* (1973), *City: A Story of Roman Planning and Construction* (1974), and *Pyramid* (1975). All four books combine simple story lines and intricate pen-and-ink drawings. They have a similar look and feel, partly because they had the same publisher, Houghton Mifflin, and the same editor, Walter Lorraine. Macaulay's other books include *Underground* (1976), which takes readers into the infrastructure of a modern city; *Unbuilding* (1980), which shows how the Empire State Building might be demolished; and *The Way Things Work* (1988), a colorful and often humorous guide to inventions throughout the ages.

In interviews, Macaulay explains that he was trained in architectural design and, therefore, starts with what he knows. He often builds models of the structures that he draws in order to see how the light will fall on them. Yet he always wants to know how the structures were connected with the people who designed and built and used them. When he imagines what their lives would have been like, he comes up with stories. *Castle* makes it possible for readers to envision life working on or in a castle. It could help them design their own model castles or write their own stories about castle life. Above all, it shows how a building can have a life of its own. The castle might even be called the book's main character.

Thomas Willard

CATCH-22

Author: Joseph Heller (1923-   )
First published: 1961
Type of work: Novel
Type of plot: Psychological realism
Time of work: 1944
Locale: Italy and the island of Pianosa
Subject: War
Recommended ages: 13-18

This antiwar novel with satirical, tragicomic sensibilities describes a world hostile to individuals and ambivalent to morality.

> *Principal characters:*
> YOSSARIAN, a World War II bombardier who, fearing for his life, searches for a way out of bombing missions
> COLONEL CATHCART, the officer in charge of Yossarian's unit on Pianosa, who heartlessly raises the number of missions required
> MILO MINDERBINDER, a soldier-turned-businessman who trades anything with anyone, including the Germans
> NATELY, a friend of Yossarian
> ORR, a seemingly dim-witted pilot who crashes his plane every time that he flies
> AARFY, a relentlessly cheery, essentially amoral navigator who always gets lost
> A. T. TAPPMAN, the group chaplain with a shakable faith

Form and Content

In forty-two dizzying chapters, *Catch-22* tells the story of Yossarian's increasingly desperate attempts to avoid flying any more bombing missions during World War II. His superior officer, Colonel Cathcart, progressively increases the number of required missions, starting at thirty-five and going up to eighty, when Yossarian finally takes an effective stand. During that time, readers are witness to an absurd series of mishaps developing from (or in spite of) an incompetent U.S. military, which is somehow winning the war against Germany.

The chronology of events signaled by the number of missions that Yossarian has flown at any particular point, is deliberately obscured. Among chapters, and even in individual chapters, scenes occur out of order. Colonel Cathcart raises the required missions to fifty near the beginning of the book, but later readers learn about earlier missions; a soldier's death, recounted at the end of the book, in fact precedes most of the other action. Yet, the subversion of a standard chronological sequence does not necessarily make the novel less accessible. Taken in the light of the novel's subject—the insanity of war—Joseph Heller's decision to depart from a conventional plot structure seems perfectly natural. Indeed, the unconventional storyline captures something of the turmoil inherent in his protagonist, Yossarian.

A psychiatrist diagnoses Yossarian at one point with a "morbid aversion to dying." There is little doubt about Yossarian's unwillingness to fight. He feigns sickness, shows up naked for inspection, fakes equipment failure, and puts soap in the squadron's mashed potatoes—all attempts to avoid one mission or another. He also entreats Major Major (who earned his rank through a computer with a sense of humor), Milo Minderbinder, and the chaplain to speak to Colonel Cathcart about his cruel habit of increasing the required missions just when Yossarian is about to finish. Cathcart is unshakable, however, and Yossarian ends up flying nearly eighty missions. As a bombardier, he has numbed himself to the destruction that he causes, although he is acutely aware of the threat to his own life. "They're trying to kill me," Yossarian complains early in the novel, unconsoled by the knowledge that the Germans are also trying to kill everyone else. Yet, something keeps Yossarian from simply leaving, or refusing to fly, until the end of the novel. It is true that he fears personal retribution, but he also acts with some unaccountable faith in others. He feels genuine compassion for dead and dying soldiers, expects (even in the end) that a murderer will be held accountable, and chooses to desert rather than to accept a deal that would allow Cathcart to continue exploiting the other men in the squadron. Yossarian retains a vestige of moral sense in a world that has shirked it.

Intertwined with Yossarian's story are those of the people around him—generals concerned more with fighting one another than the Germans; a doctor who thinks that his own situation is incomparably worse than that of his patients; a hospitalized soldier who may or may not exist underneath a full-body cast; and Milo Minderbinder, who will sell military plans as readily as Egyptian cotton. These characters and their stories are not truly secondary, because they prove relevant to Yossarian. For example, the pilot Orr, whose habits of stuffing his cheeks with crab apples and crashing his plane appear absurd and random, is actually planning for his own escape, which in turn inspires Yossarian.

Analysis

Few would argue that *Catch-22* realistically depicts World War II or the time since then, but few would disagree that Heller has illustratively captured an aspect of American society—in wartime or peacetime—that haunts and resonates within all people. By placing exaggerated characters in absurd situations, Heller creates an analogy, rather than a literal representation, of the world. In so doing, he reveals a society so inured with systems and bureaucracy that individuals seem irrelevant and morality nearly absent.

The novel's title refers to a rule invoked whenever Yossarian has a chance to avoid flying. Hoping to be declared insane and sent home, Yossarian learns about the catch: To fly missions in the face of death is insane, to refuse to fly is sane, and sane people cannot be exempted from duty and so must continue to fly missions. Such perverse nonlogic is the essence of the so-called Catch-22, later reduced to "Catch-22 says they have a right to do whatever we can't stop them from doing." "They" is something much bigger than the U.S. military. At issue is the structure and use of power in society. The Catch-22 is a bureaucratic invention: absurd, illogical, but not benign, since it ends so often in death.

If the system against which Yossarian attempts to rebel were discreet, or even identifiable, he might have better luck. Colonel Cathcart raises the number of missions, but his motives are not openly sinister; his greatest aspiration is to be mentioned in *The Saturday Evening Post*. Entrepreneurial Milo Minderbinder buys and sells, sometimes to the harm of "his side" as when he sells Germans information about a planned attack, but his intention is only to make a profit. Indeed, the system that oppresses Yossarian is so effective because it is a system, not dependent on individual whims. Individuals appear helpless even to affect a system grown perilously out of control.

Like real villains, real heroes are also lacking in the novel. Yossarian is hardly exemplary; the best that he can do is look out for himself. His escape at the end is exactly that. Powerless to confront the system that he despises, he runs away. No other character stands out as heroic. Religion, even to the chaplain, seems untenable or, worse, inconsequential. The "war effort" is a distant abstraction rather than an inspiration. Moral purpose seems to have disappeared along with consequential individuals. Yossarian's escape at the end of the novel suggests a glimmer of hope, but, in the face of all that has come before, his success seems compromised at best. Yossarian's "moral" decisions are often indistinguishable from desperate self-preservation in a dark and hostile universe.

What makes *Catch-22* palatable, however, is the comedy that coexists with tragedy. Heller's broad cast of characters gives him ample tools for satire. Often, the sources of humor are simultaneously tragic. For example, Heller uses Yossarian to satirize the pomp of the military when he shows up naked to receive a medal. Yossarian's humorous act has a serious motive, however, since he stopped wearing clothes after bloodying them on a soldier whom he failed to revive. Far from minimizing the novel's impact, the satirical and comedic moments punctuate Heller's message.

Catch-22 is of interest to young adult readers for the same reason that it interests all other readers: It examines humanity with both gravity and whimsy. The novel is challenging, but not out of accordance with the rewards that it offers. Its unconventional plot may be read on a number of levels: under critical scrutiny, which reveals a careful strategy, or with faith in the eclectic, frenetic narrative, which overwhelms and convinces.

Critical Context

Catch-22 has proven to be a popular as well as a critical success. During the Vietnam War, its biting satire of the military found resonance with many readers, and the book has become a staple of college-level literature courses. Although authors such as Nathanael West, Samuel Beckett, and William S. Burroughs preceded Heller in the use of black humor, Heller's novel attracted centerstage attention in both popular and academic circles. Likewise, many novels before *Catch-22* had protagonists with ambivalent or unsavory motives, including "antiheroes," but, in Yossarian, Heller created a character with lasting relevance. What ensures *Catch-22*'s continued prominence in American literature is its exploration of the brutal and absurd potential of humanity in the twentieth century. Heller's later novels, including *Something Happened* (1974), *Good as Gold* (1979), and *Closing Time* (1995), a sequel to *Catch-22*, have not approached the considerable success of his first book, but Heller still stands as one of the most important novelists of his time because of his influential experiments with plot and his concern with the moral implications of a technocratic society.

Eric Chilton

CATHEDRAL
The Story of Its Construction

Author: David Macaulay (1946-   )
First published: 1973; illustrated
Type of work: History
Time of work: 1252-1338
Locale: France
Subjects: Arts and jobs and work
Recommended ages: 13-18

Detailed drawings clarify the construction of an eleventh century cathedral in France.

Principal characters:
> SAINT GERMAIN, a knight of the First Crusade whose skull and forefinger were sent back from Constantinople by Louis IX
> THE BISHOP, the head of the church in Chutreaux
> WILLIAM OF PLANZ, a Flemish architect
> ROBERT OF CORMONT, the architect who replaced William of Planz when he became too old to supervise the construction
> ROLAND OF CLERMONT, the cleric who replaced the Bishop, who died in 1281
> ETIENNE OF GASTON, the architect who replaced Robert of Cormont, who died in 1329 after falling from the scaffolding of the cathedral

Form and Content

David Macaulay's *Cathedral* explains and shows the construction of a Gothic cathedral during the thirteenth and fourteenth centuries. The time span is idealized, since most cathedrals took two hundred years to be constructed instead of the eighty-six years in the book. The only other imaginary aspects are the name of the community and its inhabitants; they did not exist. In all other parts, faithful adherence to cathedral construction is followed.

The reasons for construction include people's desire to give thanks for God's kindness or to ask for God's mercy. In the thirteenth century, there were no wars to fight and the plague was gone. Crops flourished and business was good, so the city of Chutreaux planned to build God a new cathedral. The relics of Saint Germain, a knight of the First Crusade, included his skull and forefinger; these relics were sent from Constantinople by Louis IX and needed a worthy resting place. The people of Amiens, Beauvais, and Rouen were building new cathedrals, and Chutreaux did not wish to be outdone. All these factors led to the construction, but the final factor was when their existing cathedral was damaged by lightning. Thus, work began on the longest, widest, highest, and most beautiful cathedral in all of France.

Clergymen hired William of Planz, a Flemish architect, to design and supervise the construction of the new cathedral. William hired master craftsmen to quarry, cut stone, sculpt, make mortar, do masonry and carpentry, and serve as blacksmiths, roofers, and glass makers. Each craftsman had his own workshop where apprentices worked to learn the trade while laborers did the heavy work. The tools were made of metal or wood, and each task performed is illustrated in the book. Forests were cleared, and stones were quarried as soon as the Bishop approved the designs submitted by William. Location was cleared accommodating the old crypt and allowing space for the aspe and choir.

The Bishop blessed the foundation on April 14, 1253. Each foundation stone had to be perfectly level before accepting the walls and columns. Tracery, cut from templates, formed the stone framework of the windows. The buttresses were then built to relieve the pressure that the vaults put on the piers. As height was achieved, scaffolding became necessary.

The detail of this construction progresses in an informative text that describes the parts of the cathedral, from the clerestory to gargoyles. By 1280, when the choir was to be constructed, the aging William was replaced by Robert of Cormont. A brief delay in 1281 was caused by the death of the Bishop of Chutreaux; he was replaced by Roland of Clermont.

Ribs, called voussoirs, were installed, along with lagging and webbing stones to complete the vaulting. Following May Day, 1302, the cathedral began to receive its windows of blown glass. In 1306, work stopped because of a lack of funds. Money was raised from the display of Saint Germain's relics. The bells, the spire, and sculptures placed in the niches were done by midsummer of 1338. Many generations had worked to see the beautiful cathedral completed, and the final display of banners, candlelight, song, and music filled the hearts of the people of Chutreaux with great joy.

Analysis

Macaulay's talent as artist, architect, draftsman, and interpreter of the built environment is well presented in *Cathedral: The Story of Its Construction*. The significance of this first book did not go unrecognized; the Caldecott Committee named it an Honor Book. The same honor was bestowed on Macaulay's *Castle* (1977). These works and others by the author provide understanding about important construction facts, including terms related to architecture, tools, and building techniques. Of greater importance is the fact that Macaulay is able to create social history through his text and illustrations. With clear statements in a minimum of words, he conveys a clear understanding of the times, the people, and their feelings. The book works on many levels: as art and architecture, as history, as travelogue, as social commentary, and as a pleasant reading experience.

Macaulay chose not to overwhelm the reader with too many complex ideas or too much detail. Yet, he never talks down to the reader. Accurate terminology is used in a meaningful context. Triforium, clerestory, tracery, and vaulting are explained in text and clearly illustrated in diagrams. Locations within the cathedral—such as the apse, transept, choir, and nave—are visually clear when readers are given a bird's-eye view of the cathedral. Buttresses and flying buttresses, along with keystone, voussoirs, and trusses, are illustrated and explained as to their purpose and function in building construction. These terms are listed in a glossary in the back of the book.

The lives of the people and the customs in the countryside are conveyed in a thoughtful and caring manner. *Cathedral* enables the reader to see and feel what life was like in France during the years between 1252 and 1338. Knowing the difficulties involved in cathedral construction and feeling the strain of hard work offers the reader a vicarious experience that is both absorbing and informative.

It is difficult to place *Cathedral* in an age-specific category because its audience extends beyond students to adult and general audiences. Religious architecture exists worldwide, and interest in its construction has engaged people for many centuries. This curiosity and the resulting quest for knowledge have been answered in *Cathedral*, in a book of only eighty pages of simple text and magnificent black-and-white drawings.

Macaulay's pen drawings relate information clearly and create the mood. The use of cross-hatching creates depth of field and an appropriate rendering for the time period. Full-page, partial-page, and double-page spreads provide variety and are used effectively to convey space and distance. The detailed and delicate drawings invite studied responses and call to be revisited time and again. Cross-sections, aerial views, and a drawing's placement on the page challenge the viewer to change viewpoints for study and observation. There is so much to see, so much to absorb, but Macaulay is constantly at the viewer's side advising, guiding, and prodding one to see more, know more, and feel more.

Macaulay's voluminous knowledge speaks to the reader yet never overpowers; instead, the author benevolently informs. Like the generations of quarrymen, carpenters, stone cutters, sculptors, masons, roofers, and glass makers, the author brings the reader to the tremendous awe and great joy felt by the townspeople of Chutreaux, who constructed the longest, widest, highest, and most beautiful cathedral. *Cathedral* is a celebratory book.

Critical Context

David Macaulay has chosen to share his extensive art background in books for young readers and has expanded his audience to include general readers. After *Cathedral*, which won national and international acclaim, similar titles followed: *Pyramid* (1975) and *Castle* also enthralled readers. No one before Macaulay had made knowledge about buildings, especially monumental buildings, intelligible to a younger audience. These books reach beyond an encyclopedia to convey information in an interesting format. His large pen-and-ink sketches, rendered in black and white, are detailed in design and pleasing in arrangement.

Cathedral received the distinguished German Jugendbuchpreis and *The New York Times* Best Illustrated Book of the Year and was named an American Library Association Notable Book. Macaulay's books have been translated into many languages, and he has received many other awards, including a medal from the American Institute of Architects that reads "an outstanding illustrator and recorder of architectural accomplishments."

In addition to the triad of books on the construction of internationally known edifices, Macaulay has created related books, including *Mill* (1983), about nineteenth century mills in New England, and *Ship* (1993), which describes the recovery of artifacts from a ship that sank more than five hundred years ago. *The Way Things Work* (1988) offers detailed drawings, this time in color, with humorous analogies. This offbeat sense of humor is also evident in *Why the Chicken Crossed the Road* (1987), *Black and White* (1990), and *Shortcut* (1995). These three books are more appropriate for a younger audience, although they are intended for all ages. It is with humor, extensive knowledge, and masterful artistic talent that David Macaulay enriches his readers.

Helene W. Lang

THE CHANGEOVER
A Supernatural Romance

Author: Margaret Mahy (1936-   )
First published: 1984
Type of work: Novel
Type of plot: Fantasy
Time of work: The 1980's
Locale: Gardendale, a city subdivision in New Zealand
Subjects: Coming-of-age, love and romance, and the supernatural
Recommended ages: 13-15

In this romantic quest, a modern girl, by changing herself into a witch to save her little brother from an evil lemur, finds both love and maturity for herself.

> *Principal characters:*
> LAURA CHANT, a fourteen-year-old from a broken home
> JACKO, Laura's three-year-old brother
> CARMODY BRAQUE, an antique shop owner
> KATE, Laura's attractive mother
> CHRIS HOLLY, Kate's male friend
> SORENSEN (SORRY) CARLISLE, a male witch who is Laura's love interest
> MIRYAM, Sorry's mother, an affluent witch
> WINTER, Sorry's grandmother
> STEPHEN CHANT, Laura's father

Form and Content

In this British fantasy, a third-person narrative divided into thirteen chapters, Margaret Mahy has taken the Arthurian myth of male development and reworked it for a female protagonist. Instead of the passivity expected of female characters in the standard formula for romance, *The Changeover* shows an innocent girl who confronts evil, defeats it by her own actions, and moves independently toward maturity.

Laura Chant and her brother Jacko live with their divorced mother, who works in a bookstore. One evening, while waiting for their mother to get home from work, the children go to the library and Jacko checks out three books. Jacko is upset that the librarian is too busy to stamp both of his hands, and, when the peppermint-smelling man in a little miniature shop down the street offers to stamp his left one, he eagerly holds it out. The man's own face is indelibly placed there, and Jacko becomes dangerously ill. Laura is sure that the shopkeeper, Carmody Braque, is an evil lemur, a dead soul from Hell who survives by stealing life from children. Jacko smells like peppermint, and he is racked by convulsions.

Laura's mother is frantic. Her new admirer, Chris Holly, consoles her while Laura slips away to engage the help of a male witch who attends her school. His name is

Sorensen Carlisle, or Sorry, and he has been in foster care most of his life. Abused and afraid of his feelings, he now lives with his newly discovered mother, Miryam, and grandmother, Winter. The next day, Sorry visits Laura at her home and agrees with the diagnosis of Jacko's illness. The only cure is for a witch to gain power over the lemur and command him to release his victim. Since he would recognize a witch and protect himself from her, they decide to ask Sorry's grandmother what to do. She tells them that Laura is a sensitive who could easily become a witch and thus fool the lemur, who now thinks her a harmless girl.

When Jacko worsens and must go to the hospital, Laura stays with Sorry's family, and they help her transform herself. The three of them: Miryam, the enabler; Sorry, the gatekeeper; and Winter, the concluder, guide her on a journey that takes her back through all of her past experiences. When Laura is reborn as a witch, Winter hands her a wooden stamp with her own image reversed on it. She and Sorry take this tool to Carmody Braque's house, and Laura gains control of him by stamping his hand with her own image. Jacko improves immediately when the lemur is banished from his body, but Laura is vindictive and wants to punish the evil man. She makes him suffer until Sorry shames her for her cruelty. Finally, she lets Carmody Braque dissolve into a pile of dry leaves in the park.

At the end, Chris and Kate plan to marry, Laura forgives her father for leaving, and Sorry is in touch with his feelings again. The young witches, Sorry and Laura, decide to wait until they are older for a relationship, but they will continue to communicate by telepathy over distance.

Analysis

In *The Changeover*, the symbolism of moon mythology is combined with romantic conventions, quantum theory, the black holes of astronomy, and Jungian psychology to construct a concept of being in which fantasy and reality exist together. Mahy's metaphor for life is a hologram: Since each piece of a hologram is exactly like the rest of it, inner or subconscious experience and outer reality cannot be separated.

This romance, like a folktale, uses psychological truths in opposition. Good is almost overcome by evil but triumphs in the end. Mahy sets the stage for her supernatural plot with the generous use of personifications. By endowing inanimate objects with human characteristics, the author creates a world where magic is possible.

The traditional symbols of romance are present, and feminine motifs and imagery are used lavishly. Although Laura uses the male symbols of the sword and the wand, she also has a womb symbol for herself, an opal cup. Pink, a feminine color, is evident in the pink crocodiles, pigs, and rosebuds of the novel. Laura's father wears a pink shirt when he comes to the hospital. The number three, which is also considered feminine, abounds in the story. There are three people in the Chant and Carlisle families. Jacko is three years old. Three adults "mother" Laura: Kate, her natural mother, and Sorry's mother and grandmother, who personify moon goddesses. Laura's father left his family for another woman three years ago. Three older men cause Laura pain: her father; Chris Holly, who is a potential stepfather; and Carmody Braque, an ancient demon. Her boyfriend, Sorry, is three years older than she. Three people help Laura become a witch.

A mirror is used as a symbol of Laura's self-absorption as she approaches womanhood. It predicts a change, especially a sexual one. The mirror is also a literary device used to show transfer into a fantasy world. Mist symbolizes Laura's change and water her sexuality.

A tiger accompanies Laura on her inner journey. It is the Jungian animus, or masculine part of her subconscious, which comes from her father and which can give her power to work magic. Sorry provides the relationship that must exist before the animus can be realized. At the lowest point of Laura's descent, Sorry has the stripes of the tiger across his face, showing that Laura has projected some of her feelings for her father onto him.

Trees symbolize libido, and one of the trees in Laura's inner landscape has rosy apples that, on a closer look, become bleeding hearts. To Laura, her parents' divorce was like having her heart torn out. The fiend who is consuming Jacko is a symbol of the resentment that Laura feels toward her father. When she destroys Braque, she comes to terms with this festering wound within herself.

Silver chains that can change from brightness to dark like the moon ward off evil. Candles for spiritual protection have flames which signify prayers offered in the dark of the moon. These symbols are connected to moon mythology, as are the herbs used in the novel. Laura's name comes from the laurel, the sacred herb of Artemis, goddess of the moon. It is a love charm that cures madness and epilepsy. Artemis is a healer, as are witches. Carmody Braque smells of peppermint, the sacred herb of Hades, the god of the underworld. Named after a beautiful woman, it was used in early times to mask the smell of death. Hecate, the old woman who controls birth and death, keeps the keys of Hades where peppermint grows. She carries a snake in one hand and a tool in the other. Winter, Sorry's grandmother, personifies this goddess, who is associated with the waning of the moon. The snake spirals Laura up into rebirth, and the tool endows her with the power to control her destiny.

Critical Context

First published in Britain in 1983, *The Changeover* established a new formula for female initiation stories. Laura is a true heroine who "slays the dragon" by her own brave actions in a modern city—with all of its problems, such as divorce, child abuse, and crime. She does not need a male figure to rescue her, although one does help her. She falls in love but does not have sexual relations with or marry him, as most female characters do in romances. She pulls together the skeins of her ancestry, her cultural heritage, her literary experience, and her psychological self to fashion herself as a loving, nurturing young woman. This feat is accomplished through the feminine characteristics of imagination and intuition. To tell Laura's story, Margaret Mahy uses allusions to familiar folktales and to children's fantasies such as Lewis Carroll's *Alice's Adventures in Wonderland* (1865) and L. Frank Baum's *The Wizard of Oz* (1900). "The Tyger," a poem from William Blake's *Songs of Innocence and of*

Experience (1794), is the source of the book's most powerful symbol, the significance of which is pulled from the psychological theories of Carl Jung. In 1984, *The Changeover* was awarded a Carnegie Medal, the United Kingdom's annual award for the most outstanding children's book of the previous year. It was Mahy's second Carnegie Medal, the first coming in 1982 for *The Haunting*.

Josephine Raburn

THE CHANGES TRILOGY

Author: Peter Dickinson (1927-   )
First published: Heartsease, 1969; *The Weathermonger,* 1969; *The Devil's Children,*
   1970; as *The Changes Trilogy,* 1985
Type of work: Novels
Type of plot: Science fiction
Time of work: The near future
Locale: Southern England
Subjects: Social issues and the supernatural
Recommended ages: 13-15

   A supernatural hatred of machinery is unleashed on the population of Great Britain,
causing fundamental social changes and a reversion to medieval lifestyles.

>   *Principal characters:*
>   NICOLA (NICKY) GORE, a young girl from London who is separated
>   from her parents in a mass flight to France
>   AJEET, a quiet Sikh girl of Nicky's age, with a gift for storytelling
>   THE GRANDMOTHER, the matriarch of the Sikh group that shelters Nicky
>   KEWAL SINGH, one of the Sikh leaders who allows Nicky into their
>   group
>   THE MASTER, a giant of a man who rules the village of Felpham after
>   the Changes
>   MARGARET, a young girl living on her uncle's farm, a good
>   horsewoman
>   UNCLE PETER, a farmer in the Cotswolds
>   AUNT ANNE, his repressed wife, who is on the edge of nervous
>   breakdown
>   JONATHAN, the son of Peter and Anne, a clever and ingenious teenager
>   LUCY, a serving girl, apparently an orphan
>   TIMOTHY, her mentally retarded brother
>   MR. GORDON, the village sexton and local witchfinder
>   OTTO, an American spy who is captured and stoned as a witch
>   GEOFFREY, an adolescent, a former weathermonger of Weymouth who
>   is put out to drown as a witch
>   SALLY, his sister, whose drawings bring on her the accusation of
>   witchcraft
>   MR. FURBELOW, an apothecary who is responsible for finding Merlin
>   and keeping him drugged

Form and Content

   The Changes Trilogy consists of three separate novels depicting a seven-year span
of time during which a hatred of machinery destroys modern Western civilization in

Great Britain. In the chaos that ensues, various social structures emerge, all in some ways reminiscent of the Dark Ages or early medievalism. The source of the antimachine hatred is finally traced to Merlin, King Arthur's wizard, who has been disturbed in his long underground sleep and who has been seeking to return Britain to his Arthurian age. He is sent to sleep again, and modernity reemerges.

The first novel of the trilogy, *The Devil's Children*, is placed near the commencement of "the Changes," as the antimachine hatred is called. London is abandoned, since it is full of machines, even though most of them lie smashed. Nicola Gore's parents have fled to France with millions of others, but she has been separated from them in the panic. As previously instructed, she returns to London to await a rescue that never comes. Driven by loneliness, she joins a group of Sikhs who seem unaffected by the psychological disturbances. They use her as their "canary," to warn them of danger from the remaining populace if the group does anything that might inflame their anger.

The group locates an abandoned farm in Hampshire. The nearby village of Felpham regards them with suspicion, calling them "The Devil's Children." Nicky acts as intermediary between the Sikhs and the "Master," a huge former farmhand who has assumed feudal control of the village. A barter trade is established. The delicate balance is broken when a marauding band of robbers kills the Master and takes the village children hostage. The Sikhs rescue the children and kill or drive off the robbers. Out of this incident, a more integrated and democratic system of government for the village emerges, and its prospers.

The second novel, *Heartsease*, named after the wild pansies that are Aunt Anne's favorite flower, is set a few years into the Changes, when contact between Britain and the rest of the world has ceased. An American spy, Otto, is sent to discover what is happening; he is caught and stoned as a witch—witchcraft now being defined as anything to do with machinery.

Jonathan and Margaret hear Otto still groaning under a pile of stones and decide to rescue him, as they have not been as affected by the changes as the adults. Aided by the serving girl, Lucy, and her strong but mentally retarded brother, Tim, they hide Otto on their farm and make plans to get him out of the country. They realize that their best chance is to transport him to the nearest city, Gloucester, since it is connected by canal to the Severn estuary, and to find a seaworthy boat, such as a tug. When they overhear Mr. Gordon, the local witchfinder, lining up Tim as the next witch, they realize that Lucy and Tim must leave as well.

Although still badly injured, Otto is able to direct Jonathan in restoring the engine of a suitable tugboat that they have reconnoitered. Otto, Tim, and Lucy are placed on board, but, just as Jonathan and Margaret are about to leave, their plans are discovered. In the confusion, they escape, helped by Aunt Anne, and manage to start the tug's engines and open the canal bridges and lockgates. Their pursuers are routed by a bull that has previously chased Margaret and given her nightmares.

At the end, Margaret, with her horse Scrub, believes that she must return to her aunt and uncle, leaving the others to sail to Ireland. When she arrives at the farm, she finds that Mr. Gordon, the instigator of much trouble in the village, has been killed and that a new harmony is achieved.

The third novel of the trilogy, *The Weathermonger*, tells of the end of the Changes. One of the other manifestations of the supernatural has been the ability of certain individuals to control the weather. This power has brought about perfect growing conditions, helping to compensate for the primitive farming methods now employed. Geoffrey is such a "weathermonger," although he is still a teenager. He has grown rich but also overconfident. Geoffrey has never developed antimachine hatred and he has been caught fixing his dead uncle's boat. He and his sister, Sally, are put out to drown by the incoming tides, but Geoffrey conjures up a fog and they escape. He manages to start the boat, and, despite being pursued, they reach France.

The authorities there ask them to return to Britain, however, to investigate rumors of the "Necromancer," who is somewhere in the Welsh hills. They agree, landing near a Motor Museum, from which they take an antique Rolls Royce. Geoffrey and Sally have numerous adventures in motoring over backroads until their automobile is destroyed by a sudden bolt of lightning as they approach the Welsh border.

They escape and take to horses, eventually tracing the source of the Necromancer. Again pursued and almost captured, they discover a mysterious forest and tower. In the tower, food magically appears for them. The only human there is Mr. Furbelow, who talks of having found Merlin, King Arthur's wizard, and having wakened him. He is now seeking to control Merlin through morphine addiction. He has no idea of the devastation caused by the power that Merlin has released through the country.

Geoffrey and Sally finally confront Merlin for themselves and persuade him to refuse morphine, but return to sleep. As soon as this is done, the antimachine rage ceases and the country reawakens to modernity.

Analysis

Peter Dickinson's success comes from taking a radical idea, keeping it simple, and applying it to very specific situations and plots. By doing so, he is able to draw on the strengths of the traditional quest or flight story, with youthful heroes and heroines showing typical virtues of courage, resourcefulness, perseverance, and sympathy without sidetracking interest too far down a science-fiction bypath.

The main themes of the trilogy fall into psychological and sociological categories. Dickinson shows the effects at general and familial levels of fear, as well as the ways in which individuals and society deal with it: scapegoating (of witches, outsiders, and the mentally retarded); authoritarianism (reversions to patriarchal norms and feudal hierarchy); and ritual (the reemergence of a highly liturgical form of Christianity). Children are shown to have greater resilience than adults and to be much more flexible in their thinking.

At a sociological level, Dickinson depicts a society in chaos and how attempts to restore order are made. By showing how quickly a highly developed civilization disintegrates, he poses searching questions about the depth of Western norms and institutions, both morally and structurally. In his treatment, the hatred of machinery, while basically shown to be harmful, has about it a certain ambivalence. The rustic lifestyle and lack of rush are portrayed almost nostalgically at times.

Of the trilogy, *Heartsease* is the most carefully written and seems to have a depth that the other two books lack. The final denouement of *The Weathermonger* reveals the thinness of the supernatural motif in its bathos.

Critical Context

Peter Dickinson wrote for both adults and children. His children's fiction is entirely fantasy, but the supernatural is rarely taken seriously for itself. Rather, it is a peg on which to hang an often fascinating and complex scenario, as in *The Gift* (1973), *Annerton Pit* (1977), and *Tulku* (1979). This is certainly true of *The Changes Trilogy*. A number of other children's fantasies were published just after the trilogy, all concerning the collapse of Western civilization—reflecting, it would seem, a general pessimism about the future of the West. In the United States, one example would be Robert C. O'Brien's *Z for Zachariah* (1975), which concerns survivors of a nuclear holocaust. In the United Kingdom, John Christopher's *The Guardians* (1970) and *The Sword of the Spirits* trilogy (1972) cover similar ground. Both Christopher and Dickinson use science fiction as a fantasy mode, but Dickinson moves more toward the "uncanny" in his use of supernaturalism.

David Barratt

CHEYENNE AUTUMN

Author: Mari Sandoz (1896-1966)
First published: 1953
Type of work: History
Time of work: 1877-1879
Locale: The Great Plains
Subjects: Gender roles, race and ethnicity, social issues, and war
Recommended ages: 15-18

*Little Wolf, Dull Knife, and their Cheyenne followers exhibit courage, resourceful-
ness, and honor in the face of deprivation, death, government duplicity, and aggressive
pursuit by the U.S. Army.*

> *Principal personages:*
> LITTLE WOLF, the leader of a resolute party of Cheyennes from
>   Ft. Reno, Oklahoma, to Fort Keogh, Montana, against great odds
> DULL KNIFE, the leader of a splinter group of Cheyennes into virtual
>   annihilation
> LITTLE FINGER NAIL, a young warrior and a follower of Dull Knife
> LIEUTENANT WHITE HAT CLARK, a U.S. Army officer
> THIN ELK, a member of Little Wolf's band
> CAPTAIN WESSELS, a U.S. Army officer
> SINGING CLOUD, a young woman in Little Wolf's band
> BUFFALO CALF ROAD, a warrior woman, veteran of the Battle of the
>   Little Big Horn
> BLACK COYOTE, a keeper of old Cheyenne ways

Form and Content

Cheyenne Autumn is an unflinching historical portrait of a people confronting
physical extermination and cultural annihilation at the hands of duplicitous government forces. This work is a chronicle of a Cheyenne outbreak starting in Oklahoma
and ending in the surrender of Little Wolf and his followers hundreds of miles and six
months later in Montana. The northern Cheyennes of the Yellowstone region are
promised land, food, and protection in treaties signed by the U.S. government. These
agreements, however, are repeatedly and brutally broken by the government.

Hundreds of northern Cheyennes agree, under government coercion, to removal to
Oklahoma on condition that they can later return north if they choose. Finding the
Indian Territory in what is now Oklahoma unacceptable, Little Wolf leads his people
back to the Yellowstone region. In returning north, the Little Wolf Cheyennes face
massive resistance and retaliation by the U.S. Army. The Cheyennes' struggle to return
home is a study in human contrasts: of loyalty and betrayal, resolve and hesitation,
mutual cooperation and unthinkable brutality. Mari Sandoz describes a native culture

placed under extreme and unpardonable duress by a dominant white society motivated by greed, fear, and the changing winds of popular opinion.

The central narrative details the difficult challenges encountered by Little Wolf: first, the need to elude U.S. troops while simultaneously securing horses, food, and temporary shelter for his followers during the bitter winter of 1878-1879; and, second, the need to control members of his band who oppose his decisions and who threaten to further endanger the little group of Cheyennes by taking revenge against white settlers. Ultimately, a schism between Little Wolf and Dull Knife deepens into the fateful division of the northward-moving Cheyennes into two groups.

The Dull Knife contingent is captured and incarcerated at Fort Robinson, in western Nebraska. Learning that they are scheduled for involuntary restoration to Oklahoma, the Dull Knife Cheyennes launch a desperate escape during January, 1879. Only a few Cheyennes survive the Army's relentless onslaught under Captain Wessels.

Meanwhile, the Little Wolf Cheyennes winter among the Nebraska sandhills and then resume their flight toward Yellowstone. Rather than witness the unavoidable slaughter of his people, however, Little Wolf eventually surrenders to Lieutenant White Hat Clark in March, 1879. By this time, however, adverse publicity has reversed the government's removal policy, and the surviving Little Wolf Cheyennes are allowed to stay in the north in what is now Montana.

Drawing on archival records, historical documents, and interviews with Cheyenne informants, including a survivor from Little Wolf's band, Sandoz crafts an epic tragedy that reads more like a novel than the sociologically astute historical account that it actually is. This effect is created by Sandoz's poetic and sonorous prose, evocative descriptions, and liberal use of imagined dialogues. Her authoritative narrative voice—together with documentary notes, maps, photographs of several participants, and an index—frames the dialogues and soberly reminds readers that the unfolding story is not at root a work of fiction.

The interconnected sagas of the Little Wolf and Dull Knife bands are embedded in past conflicts with white people, and these events are woven into the story as flashbacks. Sandoz employs the Cheyenne convention by which significant historical events "become as today" when one nears or stands on the place where the events originally took place. Thus, as the Cheyennes move northward, they also travel back in time to earlier pivotal struggles of the nineteenth century, including the Washita fight, in which General George Armstrong Custer smashed a Cheyenne village in 1868, and the Battle of the Little Big Horn, in which the Sioux destroyed Custer and his troops in 1876. The temporal organization of the work as a whole is progressive, however, and opens with an historical forward that sets the stage for Little Wolf's northward march. The book ends with an afterword describing Little Wolf's sub-sequent fall from leadership and his death in 1904.

Analysis

Mari Sandoz adopts an empathetic approach to her subjects and their situations. Her work is fortified by numerous interviews and extensive documentary research in libraries and archives. This vital event in Cheyenne history is told primarily through the personal stories and experiences of the principal American Indian participants.

Cheyenne Autumn articulates several social and personal issues that confront many young adults, including questions about ethnic identity and trusting people from other races and cultures; the reciprocity and interchangeability of male and female roles; the personal capacity for leadership, honor, hardship, and adaptive change; and attitudes toward violence, retribution, and forgiveness.

Sandoz portrays people with moral flaws as well as a potential for rectitude and generosity. Although her word choices are highly circumspect, Sandoz does not sidestep acts of brutality, including rape, mutilation, murder, and infanticide. Her references to bodily elimination, sexual awakening, and married love are candid and appropriate without being gratuitous or inflammatory. Compassion and treachery are evidenced by Cheyennes as well as by white people, with no race having a monopoly on either virtue or corruption. The fundamental villains in *Cheyenne Autumn* are institutionalized social patterns: deceitful government policies, economic opportunism, and barbaric racism. Empathetic readers are challenged to weigh how they might respond if subjected to similar social situations and interpersonal circumstances.

Little Wolf is challenged throughout the northward flight by questions of personal morality and responsibility. For example, Thin Elk persistently pursues Little Wolf's wives and daughter, but Little Wolf—as an Old Man Chief and keeper of the Sacred Bundle—must think first of the safety of his little band. Thus, he suffers insults to his manhood that he could have answered easily when he was only a young warrior with few responsibilities. So, too, many of the Cheyenne men, such as Little Finger Nail, must think through their obligations to one another, to the Cheyennes as a whole, to themselves, and to the Powers, in a new and troubled era where traditional ways and wisdom appear less certain and less reliable. Some, such as Black Coyote, become mentally unbalanced and unable to make thoughtful choices.

The Cheyenne women also confront difficult alternatives. Some, such as Buffalo Calf Road, become warriors who fight alongside the men. Others, such as Singing Cloud, learn the healing ways, realizing that the traditional knowledge that could help save their little band is being lost. Still other women, facing ruthless assaults by U.S. Army troops, make the awful choice between killing themselves and their children, on the one hand, and surrendering to a life of captivity, on the other.

Critical Context

Cheyenne Autumn is one of several of Sandoz's books recommended by the Mari Sandoz Heritage Society for study and discussion by high school readers. Her works are less well known than those of another Nebraska author, Willa Cather. Whereas Cather's novels are fiction, Sandoz's works—including such novels as *Slogum House* (1937), *Capital City* (1939), *The Tom-Walker* (1947), *Miss Morissa, Doctor of the Gold Trail* (1955), and *Son of the Gamblin' Man* (1960)—are products of exhaustive historical research. As gateways to human experiences in accurately described historical settings, her writings are perhaps superior to those of Cather.

Chronologically, *Cheyenne Autumn* stands midway in a progression of sociohistorical studies that Sandoz called her Great Plains series, specifically *Old Jules* (1935), *Crazy Horse* (1942), *Cheyenne Autumn*, *The Buffalo Hunters* (1954), *The Cattlemen from the Rio Grande Across the Far Marias* (1958), and *The Beaver Men* (1964). Sandoz was an accomplished historian who, as a young writer, worked for the Nebraska State Historical Society and coedited its scholarly journal, *Nebraska History*. Meticulous concern for historical accuracy is a hallmark of her work.

A useful companion reading is Karl Llewellyn and E. Adamson Hoebel's *The Cheyenne Way* (1941), a classic interdisciplinary study of law and anthropology on which Sandoz drew when writing *Cheyenne Autumn*. In addition, a short novel by Sandoz, *The Horsecatcher* (1957), depicts the exploits of a young Cheyenne brave. This fictional coming-of-age story is more accessible than *Cheyenne Autumn*, portrays the Cheyenne people in much happier times, and is suitable for younger readers.

The film version of *Cheyenne Autumn*, directed by John Ford in 1964, radically distorts the mood, intent, and historical basis of Sandoz's study. Many inaccuracies and inside jokes portrayed on the screen are raucously ridiculed in Tony Hillerman's enjoyable Navaho mystery novel *Sacred Clowns* (1993). Sandoz considered the film a disaster.

Michael R. Hill

CHILDREN OF A LESSER GOD

Author: Mark Howard Medoff (1940-   )
First presented: 1979
First published: 1980
Type of work: Drama
Type of plot: Social realism
Time of work: The early 1980's
Locale: A state-run school for the deaf
Subjects: Emotions, love and romance, and social issues
Recommended ages: 15-18

Speech teacher James Leeds, working at a state school for the deaf, falls in love with and marries one of his students, Sarah Norman, but their marriage is torn apart by his pity for her because she does not speak and by her struggle for independence.

> *Principal characters:*
> JAMES LEEDS, a speech teacher at a school for the deaf
> SARAH NORMAN, a student at the school who is totally deaf
> ORIN DENNIS, a student at the school who has residual hearing and reads lips
> MRS. NORMAN, Sarah's mother
> MR. FRANKLIN, the supervising teacher at the school
> LYDIA, a student at the school who has residual hearing and reads lips

Form and Content

James Leeds, a teacher in his thirties, is new to the state school for the deaf and he is assigned to teach Sarah Norman, a student in her mid-twenties who has been deaf since birth. Because of her profound deafness, learning speech is difficult if not impossible for Sarah and she resists James's teaching methods, arguing that she does not need speech in order to communicate. At the same time, James is also teaching Lydia and Orin, both of whom have residual hearing and some proficiency at speech. Lydia, only in her late teens, has a crush on James and is jealous of the time and attention that he pays to Sarah. Orin is motivated to learn speech so that he will not be pitied and so that he can be an effective social advocate for deaf people.

Even though their teacher-student relationship is combative, James and Sarah are intrigued by each other, and they begin dating. James visits Sarah's mother in an attempt to find out more about her; Mrs. Norman tells him about Sarah's difficult childhood. At first, Sarah was labeled retarded. When her profound deafness was understood, she was sent to the school, where she has lived since she was five. On visits home, Sarah dated her sisters' friends; Mrs. Norman says they treated her like she was a lady, like she was "normal." Sarah later reveals, however, that the boys never bothered to learn sign language—they were just interested in Sarah because she would have sex with them.

When Sarah tries to avoid James, he sneaks into her dormitory to see her. She admits her fear that she would never see him again, and they make love. Orin and Lydia have heard about and seen James sneaking into the girls' dormitory, and both try to interfere with the relationship. Mr. Franklin, James's supervisor, warns James about his behavior. Sarah confides in James that she wants to get married and have a middle-class life, that she wants to go to school to become a teacher. James encourages her, despite warnings from Orin and Franklin that their relationship will not work. Feeling pressured on all these fronts, Sarah and James decide to marry, and they visit Sarah's mother, whom she has not seen in eight years.

After Sarah has moved in with James, they entertain Franklin and Mrs. Norman with dinner and bridge. Franklin praises James for teaching her so well, and James confides he has not given up trying to get her to speak.

Meanwhile, Orin recruits Sarah to help him in suing the school for discriminating in hiring practices against the deaf. She finally feels a sense of purpose, and when James tries to discourage her, she becomes even more determined to speak for herself in the hearings. When James tries to help, she accuses him of pitying her, and he accuses her of using her deafness to manipulate people, of controlling others by refusing to speak. She finally uses her voice, screaming unintelligibly at James. She goes home to her mother, and James realizes that his efforts to force her to enter the hearing world were wrong. Lydia tries to seduce James, and Orin's suit wins some minor concessions from the school, but James is focused on trying to repair his relationship with Sarah. In the end, they realize that they come from two very different worlds, but they reconcile and decide to renew their efforts to meet in "another place; not in silence or in sound but somewhere else."

Analysis

Children of a Lesser God was not originally written for a young adult audience, but the 1987 film version starring Marlee Matlin and William Hurt was popular and had a wide appeal. It should be noted that there are significant differences between the play and the film.

The play deals not only with the relationship between James and Sarah but also with the cultural conflicts that take place within the deaf and hearing-impaired communities and with the larger hearing world. Young adults may not be fully aware of the difference between being profoundly deaf and hearing impaired, the considerable training and practice required for lip-reading and speech, or the difference between American Sign Language (ASL) and various forms of signed English. It is also important for them to understand that much of deaf culture revolves around residential deaf schools such as the one in the play and that the community is often very insular.

According to the author, the play "takes place in the mind of James Leeds," so his impressions control the way in which the action is seen. Through him, the audience sees Orin as annoying, Lydia as childish, Franklin as cynical, and Sarah as compelling. This point-of-view approach may make it difficult for the audience to judge James objectively—naturally, he seems sympathetic. His own failure to realize how much his prejudices affect his relationship with Sarah make it that much harder for the audience to see them.

Because virtually all of Sarah's dialogue takes place in ASL, James's character is responsible for translating for the audience. This factor is dictated by the performance of the piece before nonsigning audiences, but it illustrates one aspect of the political struggle going on in the play. James's job is to instruct the students to speak correctly, a standard upheld by the hearing world, but the students are unable to hear or feel the accuracy of their pronunciation. In an early scene, Orin cannot tell James whether an utterance felt right until James tells him that it sounded right. Speech is the ticket into the hearing world, where success in conventional terms is achievable. Orin wants to use his speech in order to effect change in the deaf community, specifically in the school's prejudice in hiring deaf instructors. Once he achieves proficiency in speech, however, his status in the deaf community is marginalized. He needs Sarah, as "the pure deaf person," to join him in order to legitimize his objective.

While Sarah finds meaning in her participation, she discovers that it means she will again have to let someone else speak for her. The lawyer from the Equal Employment Opportunity Commission that takes up Orin's cause is ignorant of the issues that face the deaf, and she is patronizing to both Orin and Sarah. James worries that Sarah will embarrass herself if she tries to present her own case. The address Sarah practices for James eloquently explains that her inability to speak in no way diminishes her as a person. James's insistence that she could speak if she wanted to and his pity for her make it impossible for him to understand her. Orin is willing to exploit pity to achieve his goals, but Sarah will have none of it.

The title of the play ironically suggests the prejudice inflicted on deaf people: They are to be pitied because, through no fault of their own, they have been deprived of sound and speech; they were made in the image of some lesser divinity than the one that made the hearing world. Sarah and, eventually, James reject this prejudice and try to see each other as they really are, without imposing their own expectations.

Critical Context

Children of a Lesser God is one of two plays by Mark Howard Medoff that deal with deaf characters. *In the Hands of Its Enemies* (1987) features a major character who is profoundly hearing impaired, but the play is less political than *Children of a Lesser God* and far less didactic. The play focuses on a playwright who is writing a play about a woman's sexual abuse. The character's deafness functions as a metaphor for the difficulty that the main characters have in communicating with characters from their past.

Critic Otis L. Guernsey, Jr., called the Tony-award winning *Children of a Lesser God* "an outcry for a group which, it insists, speaks more eloquently for itself in signs than hearing people are able to manage with mere words." The success of the play led to the film version, which in turn led to some interest in popular culture in the 1980's and 1990's in deafness and the issues facing deaf people. Yet there are few literary works that feature deaf people in main roles. Carson McCullers' novel *The Heart Is a*

Lonely Hunter (1940) and *Children of a Lesser God* are the most notable of those that have achieved any popularity, and Medoff's works are almost unique in the realism of their portrayal of deaf people.

Daniel A. Clark

CHILDREN OF THE WOLF

Author: Jane Yolen (1939-   )
First published: 1984
Type of work: Novel
Type of plot: Historical fiction, psychological realism, and social realism
Time of work: 1920
Locale: An orphanage in India near Midnapore and the Morbhanj jungle
Subjects: Coming-of-age, emotions, friendship, and social issues
Recommended ages: 13-15

*In being kind to the jungle wolf-girl whom he befriends and introduces to civiliza-
tion, Mohandas Jinnah discovers the power of words and the importance of action in
facing the cruelty of others and the indifference of the world.*

> *Principal characters:*
> MOHANDAS JINNAH, a sensitive, intelligent, and introverted
>   fourteen-year-old male orphan
> RAMA, slightly older, Mohandas' charismatic and dashing best friend
> KAMALA, the older of the two wolf-girls
> AMALA, the younger wolf-girl
> THE REVEREND MR. WELLES, the director of the orphanage
> MRS. WELLES, his gentle, softspoken wife
> INDIRA, a spiteful and mean boarder at the orphanage
> VEDA, KRITHI, and PREETI, other orphans at the school

Form and Content

In *Children of the Wolf*, Jane Yolen spins a tale of friendship and betrayal adapted
from the diary of a missionary who rescued two feral children from the Indian jungle
in 1920. She tells the story through the eyes of an older Mohandas Jinnah as he looks
back on events that shaped his life as a fourteen-year-old boy at the orphanage.

Mohandas, the second oldest boy at the orphanage and a writer at heart, begins with
the night that "unraveled all our lives"; the night before he, Rama, and the Reverend
Mr. Welles leave to hunt the reported *manush-bagha* (ghost) of a neighboring village.
Life is peaceful, the moon is full, and Mohandas envies the daring Rama, who has
snuck out to enjoy a night on the town. All this swiftly changes. Mohandas will
discover the need to speak up and take decisive action, but he will be too late.

Mohandas, Rama, Mr. Welles, and several villagers track and capture the *manush-
bagha*, which is actually two wild girls, one about ten and the other three, who have
been living with a mother wolf and her pups in an abandoned termite mound. The
girls, dubbed Kamala and Amala, are brought to the orphanage, and Mohandas is
charged with teaching them to speak and to walk upright. He works diligently to be
worthy of the responsibilities that Mr. Welles has entrusted to him. The assignment is

difficult; the wolf-girls roll in the dust on their arms and legs, eat raw meat, capture lizards, soil themselves, and howl at the moon. In addition, everyone else appears to have an ulterior motive in their desire to civilize them; Mohandas alone is altruistic. Amala, the younger girl, soon falls sick and dies of dysentery and worms. Mohandas resolves to prove himself with Kamala, even as he begins to question the rightness of the world around him.

When Kamala utters Mohandas' name, he swells with pride over his accomplishment and trains her to walk upright. Mr. Welles comments that he is much like her brother, but in truth Mohandas does not take the initiative that an older brother might. Mr. Welles is sure that words are the magic to free Kamala from her animal nature, and for a while it appears that he is right. As Kamala increases her rudimentary language, she joins in activities at the orphanage, acquires a rag doll—her only possession—and engages Rama's interest. Mohandas is no longer her central focus; he is crestfallen and withdraws into himself again. This is unfortunate, for the mean-spirited boarder Indira, chagrined at losing Rama's attentions, abuses Kamala. Mohandas does not intervene until too late; Indira drives Kamala back into the darkened jungle. Mohandas finds her and brings her back, but things are never the same and Kamala does not speak again.

Analysis

Yolen's postscript at the novel's end gives credit to her research on feral children, Indian folklore, and jungle life after her discovery of the diary of a Mr. Singh. Her genius lies, however, in the well-turned tale, excellent characterization, and exceptional themes. Readers readily empathize with Mohandas' efforts to create a social and ideological identity. He must reconcile his Bengali past with his British present, his Hindu beliefs with Christianity and his admiration for the Reverend Welles, and his social inferiority with his intellectual and imaginative superiority. Many young people have also encountered a Rama, the always-better-at-everything charmer with a winning smile; a Mr. Welles, the patient taskmaster whose aloof idealism does not fit life's reality; or an Indira, the fathomless and furious bully.

What Mohandas must acknowledge is the power of language and action, a major theme of the novel. He has, after all, the soul of a writer, the imagination to see possibilities and to spot the inconsistencies and ironies of life. Yet, until he has the courage to act, he cannot capture the power inherent in words. As he watches, Kamala learns to speak, only to be subjected to the other children's cruelty; she is different and therefore rejected by the orphanage society. He feels a kinship with this abandoned orphan and her wildness, seeing "my other self, different, full of unspoken words, and alone" mirrored in her. Until he can accept and name this side of himself, he cannot be transformed. When he does, the story reaches its climax: He goes alone into the dark jungle to search for Kamala, realizing at last that he is both beast and human, belonging to this world and yet living beyond it.

Another quiet theme in this book is the necessity of creating one's own self. Mohandas scorns his countrymen when they torment the captured wolf-girls and is disappointed in Rama's lack of courage on the jungle trek. Yet, he cannot totally identify with British culture either. Caught between two cultures, he can neither escape his Indian terror of the *manush-bagha* nor dismiss the ghosts as impossible through Christianity. (The ghosts in Charles Dickens' *A Christmas Carol* confuse him.) Since he is empathetic to the girls—who, like him, inhabit "an alien world"—he agrees to serve as their *gillie*, or animal-tamer, for Mr. Welles. Mohandas is seeking acceptance from his Indian culture, from Rama, and from Mr. Welles. He remains powerless to act except on Mr. Welles's suggestions and yet questions his wisdom; "Perhaps . . . we should never have taken them from the jungle." When they bring Kamala out of the jungle the second time, it is finally Mr. Welles who seeks advice from Mohandas, and it is Mohandas alone who carries her back, with Rama and Mr. Welles holding back the thorns and bushes in the path. Mohandas' quest for identity is over: He is complete, and the others recognize his transformation.

Mohandas' journey of self-discovery is symbolically a writer's journey. Early in the novel, he senses that power over another can come from owning that person's words, and he is frightened when Rama reads his journal. He creates his own private cipher to keep his journal private and will share only translated pieces with Mr. Welles. Rama is more at ease speaking Bengali; Mr. Welles, English. To survive, Mohandas combines the two languages, thus defining his own culture and inventing his own stories to dream from and remember back to; he fashions his own past and his own mythology. This is Yolen as folklorist and fantasy writer; this is the creed of the storyteller and the power of the word. If the story is well and rightly told, its magic will touch others through the ages. This story explores the importance of language to memory, culture, and humanness itself. The feral child deprived of language and human contact—whether living in the jungles of India or modern-day suburbia—cannot become enculturated or experience full humanness without words or memories of a cumulative past. Yolen's ultimate message is that Mohandas learns, grows, and survives only because he "had the words to tell of it."

Critical Context

Children of the Wolf is a special touchstone in Jane Yolen's prolific career. Already an acknowledged leader in picture books, fantasy, and literary folktale with more than seventy books published before 1984, Yolen made her serious debut into historical fiction with this book.

Its forerunner and Yolen's first young adult novel, *The Gift of Sarah Barker* (1981), is a fictionalized story set in the nineteenth century about two Shakers who fall in love. Sarah and Abel must choose between their own love and banishment from their society. Yolen followed *Children of the Wolf* with *The Devil's Arithmetic* (1988), a historically correct time-warp story of the Holocaust that concentrates on the importance of Hannah's remembering. *All Those Secrets of the World* (1991) is an autobiographical picture story book about a summer on the Chesapeake when Michael, Steve, and Janie's dad goes off to war. *Letting Swift River Go* (1992) shows how Sally lets go of the past and welcomes the changes brought to her rural Massachusetts town brought on by the new Quablin Reservoir. *Encounter* (1992) is the story of a young Taino boy's premonition about Christopher Columbus that warns of the consequences of not respecting other's rights in any encounter. In these novels, Yolen addresses serious, real issues in the collective past, interweaving in them motifs and themes from folklore and mythology.

Jane Laurenson Neuburger

A CHILD'S CHRISTMAS IN WALES

Author: Dylan Thomas (1914-1953)
First published: 1954
Type of work: Short fiction
Subjects: Family and friendship
Recommended ages: 10-13

In a series of episodes, an adult narrator nostalgically recounts, in vivid and humorous detail, typical Christmas experiences in Wales when he was young and shared the holiday with his peculiar aunts and uncles at his parent's home.

Form and Content

A Child's Christmas in Wales begins with a mesmerizing reference to snow that seems to symbolize the illusive passage of time. The narrator describes how snow grows from the trees as well as falling from the sky, reminding the reader that the season described by the narrator is not the ordinary one experienced by most people, but a magical one brought to life by the imagination of a child.

The first episode involves the narrator and his friend Jim Prothero throwing snowballs at cats. This escapade of mock heroism is broken off by a faint cry for help from neighbor Mrs. Prothero, whose home is spewing forth smoke, and the narrator and Jim dutifully call the fire department. The firemen promptly arrive and douse the interior of the house with water, thereby ruining the nicely decorated home. Mr. Prothero, who seems not to know how to deal with the crisis, discovers that he has dropped his smoldering pipe in his chair, thereby causing the smoke. The elderly Miss Prothero adds more wry humor to the occasion when she asks the firemen if they would like something to read. The whole situation strikes the little boys as being wonderfully absurd.

The next story focuses on the postman and all the presents that are given at Christmas time. For the narrator, presents can be divided into two categories—the useless and the useful. Useless presents include such items as zebra scarfs and oversized hats, things that are intended to be useful but that are absurdly ill-suited to the comfort and needs of a little boy. Useful presents include items such as a conductor's cap and ticket machine, a painting book, and Easy Hobbi-Games for Little Engineers, which is like the American Erector Set. Numerous candies are also placed in this category, including candy cigarettes the young narrator uses in an attempt to fool older people into thinking that he is smoking.

Another episode describes the peculiar aunts and uncles who people the narrator's home during the Christmas season. The common activities of taste-testing new cigars, sampling various drinks, and stuffing oneself with turkey and blazing pudding eventually resolve into nap time for the corpulent uncles, who unbutton their vests and attempt to sleep as the young narrator pops balloons and tries to disturb their heavy snoring. Of special note is Auntie Hannah, whose love for port and singing have led her into the yard. She sings like a big-bosomed thrush, much to the embarrassment of the other ladies in the house.

The last story reviews a variety of activities, such as playing in the snow and singing Christmas carols to the neighbors. The evening concludes with a time for playing the piano and the violin and singing an odd variety of popular songs. Then, the young narrator recounts how he would finally go to his bedroom, listen to the music drifting from other houses, and fall asleep in the "close and holy darkness."

Analysis

The idea for creating *A Child's Christmas in Wales* probably began with Dylan Thomas' talk "Reminiscences of Childhood," which aired on the Welsh BBC in 1942. By 1945, the poet had developed this material into a talk called "Memories of Christmas," which appeared on the Children's Hour of BBC. It then became an essay entitled "Conversations about Christmas" in 1947, which Thomas sold to *Picture Post*, and later "A Child's Memories of Christmas in Wales," which he sold to *Harper's Bazaar* in 1952. The book with the present title appeared in 1954 shortly after the author's death.

A Child's Christmas in Wales is a nostalgic review of life for a little boy in Wales during the 1920's. The stories are not so much about the festivities of Christmas as about the peculiar habits of people as revealed in this season of feasting and merriment. The book moves quickly from episode to episode, with the primary focus resting on how unusual the world appears through the eyes of a little boy who is still discovering life. The author has a young boy prompt the adult narrator from time to time to focus on matters important and interesting to little children.

While Thomas makes no direct claims to be writing autobiographical pieces, the nature of the story as set in Wales is clearly connected to his childhood experiences at his parent's home on Cwmdonkin Drive in Swansea. Like so many poems by Thomas, these stories represent his collective experiences in West Wales. The opening of the book alerts the reader to the author's intentional confusion as to whether he was twelve or six years old when these events took place. The answer to this supposed puzzle is "both and neither." Thomas is choosing freely those events that illustrate his view of the humorous and sometimes absurd qualities of life.

Many of the passages in this book vibrate with humor. For example, Mr. Prothero proves himself to be a bumbler, using his shoe to swat vainly the smoke created by the smoldering pipe that he has dropped into his easy chair. The absurdity of his efforts to brush away the smoke without first discovering the source of it is exceeded only by his spinster sister's query as to whether the firemen would like something to read after putting out the fire. One can find more humor in the actions of the aunts and uncles in the narrator's home, for these older folks are in many ways overgrown children indulging themselves in pranks, port, and cigars.

Themes in this collection are less important than the role of imagination in making a commonplace world entrancing. Nevertheless, several themes emerge, such as the importance of play and role-playing for people of all ages. The stories also quietly reveal a lonely little boy who tries numerous tricks in order to gain attention. Most of all, the collection treats the beauty of life when seen imaginatively through the eyes of a child.

Critical Context

A Child's Christmas in Wales belongs to a long tradition of children's literature written by prominent poets. For example, Christina Rossetti wrote a delightful collection of poems entitled *Sing Song* (1872), along with a wide variety of other poems for children. T. S. Eliot published *Old Possum's Book of Practical Cats* in 1939, a collection that was transformed into the popular Broadway musical *Cats*. Theodore Roethke wrote several fine selections of poems for children, including "Lighter Pieces and Poems for Children" in *Words for the Wind* (1958), and "Nonsense Poems" in *I Am! Says the Lamb* (1961). Thomas' short-story collection is not as fine a piece as these selections of poetry, but *A Child's Christmas in Wales* does feature a highly poetic style that sings with the same beauty as many of his lyrical poems and plays, such as *Under Milkwood* (1954).

Thomas evidences the Welsh love for language. For example, the opening paragraph of the first episode contains this sparkling sentence: "All the Christmases roll down toward the two-tongued sea, like a cold and headlong moon bundling down the sky that was our street; and they stop at the rim of the ice-edged, fish-freezing waves, and I plunge my hands in the snow and bring out whatever I can find." This is fine writing reminiscent of Old English poetry, with its use of kennings, or compound nouns, such as "whale-road" and "swan's-path" to rename common things such as the sea. The mesmerizing language of *A Child's Christmas in Wales* makes even the most trivial of childish escapades worth hearing again and again. This book continues to be very popular for its portrayal of childhood as well as for its musical language.

Daven M. Kari

CHINESE MYTHS AND FANTASIES

Author: Cyril Birch (1925-   )
First published: 1961; illustrated
Type of work: Short fiction
Type of plot: Fantasy and folktale
Time of work: Ancient times
Locale: China
Subjects: Religion and the supernatural
Recommended ages: 13-18

Birch retells Chinese creation myths, ghost stories, and witchcraft fantasies in a most vivid and comprehensible manner.

Form and Content

Chinese Myths and Fantasies has three parts. The first part contains three creation myths. In "Heaven and Earth and Man," the god P'an Ku, after sleeping eighteen thousand years in the midst of chaos, hacked chaos with an axe into heaven and earth. Over the next eighteen thousand years, he grew into a giant, separating the earth from the sky with his body. After the earth and the sky became fixed in their places, P'an Ku died, giving his breath to form the winds and clouds, his body for the mountains, his hands and feet for the two poles of the east and west, his blood for the rivers, his flesh for the soil, and the hairs of his body for flowers and trees. Then, the goddess Nü-kua created humans with mud. She also paired them by male and female and taught them the ways of marriage. Many years later, Kung-kung, the spirit of water, and Chu-jung, the spirit of fire, battled against each other. In his defeat, Kung-kung struck his head against Mount Pu-chou-shan, the pillar holding up the sky in the western corner. The sky cracked and the earth tilted up. To free humans from the catastrophe, Nü-kua patched the sky with molten colorful stones and propped the sky firmly with giant turtle legs.

In "The Greatest Archer," Yi, the greatest of all archers during the reign of the sage Emperor Yao, shot down nine of the ten suns and slew a monstrous serpent on the Tung-t'ing Lake. In "The Quellers of the Flood," Kun was punished with death by his grandfather, the Yellow Emperor, the Ruler of Heaven, for stealing the Magic Mould to stop an all-consuming flood in order to save the suffering world. After three years, however, Yü was born from Kun's corpse to complete Kun's duty to save humankind. Through his humility, Yü won forgiveness from the Yellow Emperor and was given as much of the Magic Mould as his black tortoise could carry. After thirty years of hard work harnessing the flood, Yü married Nü-chiao. When his wife saw him in the form of a huge bear tunneling through a mountain to channel the floods, however, she was so frightened that she transformed herself into a boulder. Yü got his son, Ch'i, from the boulder. He also moved Mount Kun-lun from the Heaven to the earth as a ladder between them. For his achievements, Yü the Great was made the ruler of the Hsia Dynasty by his people.

The second part of the book contains nine stories: three marriage fantasies, two ghost tales, and four about magic and witchcraft. The third part is a Buddhist tale. It tells the adventures of Eggborn, a boy born from an egg. After his two guardians, the Abbot and Old Dog Liu, died, Eggborn left the monastery. After repeated efforts, he copied the Text of Heaven from a cave guarded by the White Monkey. Then, he learned magic from the text with the help of Aunt Piety. Because Aunt Piety had abused the magic art to help the rebel Captain Wang Tse in battles against the imperial army, the White Monkey used the celestial mirror of exorcism to render her into a powerless hag and her brood into their true form—red foxes. In the end, Eggborn became the holy abbot, while Aunt Piety was shut in the cave of the Text of Heaven.

Analysis

The Chinese myths are the most valuable part of Cyril Birch's book. The images of P'an Ku as a superman and of Nü-kua as the overmother are associated with the human power of creation. They also share the same spirit of sacrifice. P'an Ku gave up everything, including his breath, to create the universe. Nü-kua died of exhaustion from mending the sky. The other two myths develop around the conflicts between sons and fathers. When the ten sons (suns) ignored an order from their Supreme Father and came out to play all at once, the world suffered disaster. Yi, under the order of Emperor Yao, shot nine sons. The killing signifies the ultimate triumph of the father over the son. Similarly, Kun was punished with death by his grandfather, the Yellow Emperor, for stealing the Magic Mould to stop the flood. His own son, Yü, could harness the flood only by abandoning Kun's rebellious spirit and observing the codes of obedience to the Yellow Emperor. Comparing this outcome with the Western myth of Prometheus, who was punished for stealing fire for humankind, it seems that Chinese myths, as told in this collection, are much influenced by Confucian ideology. The heroic deeds of Yi and Yü are dimmed by their obedience to authority.

The fairy tales, ghost stories, and magic adventures reflect universal moral concerns: The good and the kind will be rewarded, and the bad and the evil will be punished. These stories, like the myths, are also pervaded by patriarchal Confucianism. "The Dinner That Cooked Itself" is a male fantasy about a perfect wife whose diminutiveness is well contained in a snail shell but whose diligence runs his house and results in delicious meals. The demands for obedience to patriarchal authority reach their culmination in the longest story of the collection, "The Revolt of the Demons." The only female emperor, Wu Tse-t'ien, has been vilified as "a fox with nine tails" in history. In this story, Wu Tse-t'ien is reborn as the male rebel Captain Wang Tse. Aunt Piety, a fox spirit, married her daughter to Wang Tse. Although Wang became the rebel king with the assistance of the fox spirits, he was defeated by the imperial army with the help of Eggborn and the White Monkey. The Chinese emperor is traditionally called the Son of the Heaven. Thus, patriarchy rules Earth from Heaven. The female emperor Wu had to be defeated in the next life for her transgression.

Apart from this dominant patriarchal ideology, the book is indeed an excellent selection of Chinese myths, ghost stories, and fantasies. Because most of these tales were fragmented, Birch did not merely adapt them but re-created them with vivid imaginative details. He provides the reader with ideas for comparison between the Western biblical myths and the Chinese myths whenever he can. Birch also tries to capture the Chinese supernatural imagination from different angles. He strings several mini-tales into "A Shiver of Ghosts" to show how ancient Chinese people acted differently in the presence of ghosts. Sung Ting-po, a stalwart young man, even cleverly discovered what a ghost feared most and sold the ghost that he was traveling with as a sheep in the market.

This fine collection is a good sample of the Chinese fantastic imagination. It is culturally informative as well as intriguing and entertaining.

Critical Context

Published in 1961, this collection was one of the earliest introductions to Chinese myths and fantasies for juvenile readers in the West. Cyril Birch is a well-known scholar of Chinese literature. *The Peony Pavilion* (1980), Birch's translation of T'ang Hsien-tsu's *Mao-tan t'ing*, is among the best lyrical translations in English of a Chinese play. It is not surprising that *Chinese Myths and Fantasies* benefited from his erudite knowledge and lyrical talent. It has contributed to understanding of the Chinese fantastic imagination.

Because of this collection's early publishing date, however, further readings in this field are highly recommended. Since the 1980's, Chinese scholars have shown great interest in the origins of myths. They have discovered many versions of creation myths in different regions. It has been recognized that China was matriarchal in its first historical stage, and consequently the myth of Nü-kua appeared much earlier than the myth of P'an Ku. There are two modern trends in the study of Chinese myths: First, some poets and writers rewrite the myths in new historical contexts, as Lu Hsun did in the early twentieth century; second, some critics use feminist, Freudian, and other approaches to reinterpret old myths. The Western interest in Chinese myths and fantastic tales has been maintained by English translations of P'u Sung-ling's *Liao-chai chih-i* (1766; *Strange Stories from a Chinese Studio*, 1880) and by Yuan Ke's *Dragons and Dynasties: An Introduction to Chinese Mythology*. The former is a masterpiece of supernatural tales, and the latter is the best version of Chinese myths from the extant text *Shan hai ching*. Nevertheless, Birch's collection, with its superb storytelling, remains the best introduction for young readers.

Qingyun Wu

CHITTY-CHITTY-BANG-BANG
The Magical Car

Author: Ian Fleming (1908-1964)
First published: 1964; illustrated
Type of work: Novel
Type of plot: Adventure tale
Time of work: The early 1960's
Locale: Near Canterbury and Dover, England; and Calais, France
Subjects: Crime, family, the supernatural, and travel
Recommended ages: 10-15

A magical car transports a family into adventures involving a gang of criminals.

> *Principal characters:*
> COMMANDER CARACTACUS POTT, an eccentric inventor known as "Crackpot Pott"
> MIMSIE POTT, his wife
> JEREMY and JEMIMA POTT, their children, eight-year-old twins
> JOE THE MONSTER, a famous criminal

Form and Content

Framed in the voice of a narrator retelling a story that he has overheard, *Chitty-Chitty-Bang-Bang* is a three-part, primarily third-person adventure narrative built around an eccentric family and their magical car. The warmth and color of the text is supported by illustrator John Birmingham's drawings and paintings, both small and full-page, which enliven the reading experience. Much of the book's tone is built on Ian Fleming's use of onomatopoeia and his chatty, rambling, and informal style. His lively, descriptive language prevents any details of scientific solemnity from distracting from his primary purpose—to entertain children.

In the first part of *Chitty-Chitty-Bang-Bang*, the Pott family is introduced. Having a lineage going back to the Romans, the Potts live beside a lake near a turnpike outside Canterbury, England. Jeremy and Jemima are eight-year-old twins living with their mother, Mimsie, and their father, Commander Caractacus Pott, a humorous, dreamy, unsuccessful explorer and inventor known in the neighborhood as "Crackpot Pott." They are poor, without money to buy a car, but happy.

The unconventional Commander invents "Crackpot's Whistling Sweets," a combination toy and candy that he sells to a candy maker, Lord Scrumptious, for one thousand pounds. This money allows the family to buy an extraordinary automobile. They discover an old wreck on its way to the junkyard, a car that was clearly once so special that the entire family falls in love with it. Its magical properties are first indicated by the license plate, "GENI." The Commander repairs the automobile and hears its characteristic startup noises of "chitty chitty bang bang," which becomes the car's name. The special car can go up to one hundred miles an hour, but the Commander worries when he finds that the car has made improvements on its own at night; it now has rows of knobs that he cannot explain. On the way to a picnic, they get bogged down in slow traffic. The car shows irritation and gives the Commander instructions on the mysterious knobs. The Commander does as the car asks, and Chitty-Chitty-Bang-Bang suddenly grows wings and flies over the other cars.

In part 2, the adventures begin as the Potts land on a sandbar in the English Channel. After picnicking, all five family members—now including the car—doze off and nearly drown until Chitty-Chitty-Bang-Bang warns the others. The car becomes a hovercraft, skimming over the water to France, where they seek shelter in a cave.

The Potts explore the long cave, which reveals many traps designed to scare visitors away. Finally, they find a secret underground warehouse full of boxes containing guns, bombs, and weapons. They also find a paper revealing the vault belongs to a famous criminal named Joe the Monster. The Potts light a fuse to a bomb and drive out of the cave, leaving the explosives to blow up behind them. Joe the Monster and three of his gangsters are waiting for them, but Chitty-Chitty-Bang-Bang sprouts its wings and flies away to a hotel in Calais, France.

Part 3 is entirely set in France, where the gangsters track down the Potts and kidnap Jeremy and Jemima. The children are forced to participate in a robbery of a candy store. They are alert, however, and trick the gang while their parents and Chitty-Chitty-Bang-Bang capture Joe's gang. The family earns a reward for their heroics, and they fly off in their magical car in search of new adventures.

Analysis

Chitty-Chitty-Bang-Bang is more than an imaginative adventure story for children with a warm tone that is both appealing and encouraging for young readers. Its themes include the need for family cooperation and an enthusiasm for exploration and ingenuity. In addition, the story promotes the advantages of being different. Throughout the adventures, all the family members are portrayed as individuals with intelligence, compassion, and an interconnectedness and a reliance on one another that make them an engaging group. While the magical car becomes the means to experience adventures, it too depends on the skills and care of its owners; its abilities are only a part of the family's successes. The togetherness and love of the Potts family give the book an educational slant and moral dimension useful for teaching values in the home and the classroom.

As with Fleming's twelve James Bond novels and short-story collections, *Chitty-Chitty-Bang-Bang* relies on the author's interest in mechanical gadgets, an element that made the book readily filmable and gave it lasting appeal for readers in a technological age. In his introduction to *Chitty-Chitty-Bang-Bang*, Fleming claims that his book is based on the original Chitty-Chitty-Bang-Bang, a car built by a Count Zborowski in 1920 on his estate near Canterbury, England. Fleming described the unusual car as having a pre-1914 chain drive engine and a Mercedes chassis installed with a six-cylinder, seventy-five-horsepower military engine used in German zeppelins. It had a gray steel body with a eight-foot-long hood and weighed four tons. The car won several racing awards in 1921 and 1922 until it was wrecked in an accident.

Fleming's use of such detailed accuracy in all his imaginative books lends them an air of believability and credibility despite their obviously fantastical elements. In this, his only book written for a juvenile audience, he merges his trademark eye for meticulous detail with a lighthearted humor. That combination makes *Chitty-Chitty-Bang-Bang* far different from his other, darker novels and stories, which are often described as works centering on sex, sadism, and snobbery—notably *Casino Royale* (1953), *From Russia with Love* (1957), *Doctor No* (1958), and *Goldfinger* (1959).

The initial popularity of *Chitty-Chitty-Bang-Bang* was augmented by the then-intense media interest in the author, which led to wide-scale merchandising of the book and its spinoff projects. The book was published in 1964, just before Fleming's death, at a time when popular books and films featuring his super spy character, James Bond, agent 007, were the center of an international phenomenon. These works served as an inspiration for a number of television shows and films about Cold War espionage, as well as interest in other authors writing about that subject. A few years later, this attention widened to include Fleming's book for children: United Artists and Albert Broccoli, the producer of the James Bond films, decided to issue a musical film loosely adapted from *Chitty-Chitty-Bang-Bang* and based on the formula that had made Walt Disney's 1964 film version of P. L. Travers' classic Mary Poppins books (1934-1952) such as a financial and critical success.

The 1968 film starred popular entertainers Dick Van Dyke and Sally Ann Howes as Commander Pott and Truly Scrumptious, a romantic interest created for Commander Pott, who was now portrayed as a widower. A massive promotional effort by the studio included a popular theme song and soundtrack record album. Random House also issued a print tie-in version of the story called *The Adventures of Chitty-Chitty-Bang-Bang*, illustrated with photographs from the film. Writer Albert G. Miller's book version of the screenplay kept the Fleming tone and flavor but added new characters and adventures, including the parts of Grandpa Pott and Truly Scrumptious. Also in 1968, Random House issued *Meet Chitty Chitty Bang Bang: The Wonderful Magic Car*, by Al Perkins; this version of the tale was specifically written for readers under the age of ten. The motion picture was universally panned by critics, many of whom believed that the film version lost much of the magic and humanity of the original book. Nevertheless, interest in Fleming's version was renewed in 1993 with the issue of the musical film as a video for children. In 1996, it was reported that one scene in the motion picture, in which Jemima Pott refuses candy from a dangerous stranger, helped teach children the dangers of accepting gifts from people they do not know.

Critical Context

In 1964, mystery writer Rex Stout claimed that four out of five children would love *Chitty-Chitty-Bang-Bang*, most preferring to trade in their parents for Commander Pott. Library journals universally praised the book, as well as John Birmingham's illustrations, as a story for all ages, notable for its use of descriptive language. Some reviewers believed that the story was more appropriate for boys. This attraction has largely remained intact in the decades since the book's initial popularity, and the story in its various incarnations remains widely available in school and public libraries.

Wesley Britton

CHOU EN-LAI

Author: Jules Archer (1915-   )
First published: 1973
Type of work: Biography
Time of work: 1898 to the 1970's
Locale: China, France, Germany, the Soviet Union, and various countries in Asia and
    Africa
Subjects: Politicians and revolutionary leaders
Recommended readers: 15-18

*Chou En-lai played an important leadership role in bringing the twentieth century
Chinese Revolution to victory and making modern China one of the influential powers
in the world.*

Principal personages:
    CHOU EN-LAI, a leader of the Chinese Revolution and the premier of
        the People's Republic of China from 1949 to 1976
    TENG YING-CHAO, his wife, a revolutionary
    MAO TSE-TUNG, the chairman of the Chinese Communist Party and the
        People's Republic of China
    CHU TE, an army officer who led the Chinese Revolution
    SUN YAT-SEN, a leader of the Chinese democratic revolution
    CHIANG KAI-SHEK, the head of the Nationalist People's Party (KMT)
        and the Republic of China
    JOSEPH STALIN, the general secretary of the Soviet Communist Party
        from 1929 to 1953
    NIKITA KHRUSHCHEV, the general secretary of the Soviet Communist
        Party from 1958 to 1964
    JOHN FOSTER DULLES, the U.S. secretary of state from 1953 to 1959
    RICHARD M. NIXON, the president of the United States from 1969 to
        1974
    HO CHI MINH, the president of North Vietnam from 1945 to 1969

Form and Content
    Chou En-lai is a giant in modern Chinese and world history—a great revolutionary,
military strategist, diplomat, and statesman who was well loved by the people and
highly respected by his friends and foes alike.
    In *Chou En-lai,* Jules Archer portrays his subject's accomplishments and personal-
ity against the panoramic history of Chinese revolution and socialist reconstruction.
He traces Chou's life journey from his birth in 1898, when China was shaken by a
democratic revolution led by Sun Yat-sen against the decadent Manchu Dynasty, to
his survival of the Cultural Revolution from 1966 to 1976, which brought China to
the verge of self-destruction.

Despite his family background as a well-to-do mandarin, Chou started his revolutionary career when he was a high school student; he was put in jail for leading a student demonstration against the warlord government. After being released, Chou sailed for France, where he pursued the study of Marxism and organized a Chinese Communist Youth Corps. Returning to China a seasoned revolutionary in 1925, he was to shape the major historical events in modern Chinese history. Chou held a leading position in Sun Yat-sen's united front of Communists and Nationalists against warlords; organized a large-scale uprising of workers in Shanghai, gaining control of the biggest city in China; together with Chu Te, founded the Chinese Red Army; shared with Mao Tse-tung the command of the unprecedented Long March to North China to fight Japan; forced Chiang Kai-shek in the Sian Incident to form a new alliance of Communists and Nationalists against Japan; assumed the office of the first premier and foreign minister of the People's Republic of China; organized a Third World united front against the Superpowers through diplomatic manoeuvering in Asia and Africa; orchestrated the normalization of Sino-American relations through so-called ping-pong diplomacy; and moderated the Cultural Revolution to protect thousands of communist leaders from being purged and to keep China from total political chaos and economic bankruptcy.

Archer recounts Chou's monumental accomplishments in chronological order. Altogether, there are sixteen chapters in the book, the last presenting an overview on his success as one of the most powerful figures in China. Chou was often described as indestructible: He survived many political upheavals. He was also indispensable to China because he was able to deal with impossible situations when no one else could. He was trusted not only by Mao and other communist leaders but also by the people. The important role that Chou played in China is best summed up in this quote from *Chou En-lai*: "If Mao Tse-tung was the theoretician of Red China, Chou En-lai was the man of action who breathed life into Mao's theories." Chou and Mao are like the two wheels of the cart that drove the Chinese Revolution forward.

Sources for the biography are documented in an appended bibliography. In the body of the text, however, no citations are given for quotes or biographical information. Some books listed in the bibliography are marked as recommended readings. There is also an index for cross-reference.

Analysis

Archer's *Chou En-lai* is not a mere chronicle of this leader's historical accomplishments. It is a remarkable portrait of Chou as a man of brilliant wit, stern integrity, radiant exuberance, charming grace, extraordinary courage, and composure. With clarity, sensitivity, and momentum, Archer delineates these qualities, which made Chou a charismatic leader. To create a three-dimensional character, he portrays Chou's personality not only in his political life but in his personal life as well, especially his love for and marriage with Teng Ying-chao. Archer not only directly narrates Chou's actions and reactions at critical moments but also includes dramatic scenes that reveal his character, such as his meeting during the Sian Incident with

Chiang Kai-shek, who put an $80,000 bounty on his head, or his encounter at a Geneva conference with U.S. secretary of state John Foster Dulles, who said that he expected to meet Chou privately only if their automobiles collided. Observations of Chou by his admirers, detractors, and adversaries are also incorporated into the narrative in order to shed light on his character from different angles. Thanks to Archer's skillful characterization, the reader can visualize Chou's image even without the aid of photographs or other illustrations.

Archer employs a dispassionate tone, but he is not apathetic. In writing the biography, he entered into a certain relationship with his subject and, according to noted children's literature author Jean Fritz, "put his stamp on the material." His attitude toward Chou is explicitly expressed in valuative comments, as shown in his description of the controversy over Chou's political flexibility and resilience. Chou was derisively dubbed as "the elastic Bolshevik" and "the Confucian Communist." Archer does not refrain from defending him: Chou's gift to get out of tight spots, he writes, "was less that of an opportunist than of an amiable man who mixes well with others and is personally popular at all levels." Apart from direct authorial comments, the reader can also detect between the lines the author's respect for his subject. This does not mean that Chou is always shown in his best colors. Archer does not hesitate to mention Chou's weaknesses, failures, and even occasional cruelties. The result is a realistic, balanced, and, at the same time, affectionate portrait.

While recounting Chou En-lai's historical accomplishments, Archer smoothly integrates sufficient contemporary information into the narrative to establish the political scene for Chou's activities. A description of China being decimated by corruption, poverty, and wars under warlord rule in the 1920's provides a backdrop for the rise of student movements in which Chou stood at the forefront; the account of Nikita Khrushchev's attack on Joseph Stalin in the Soviet Union, the split within the communist world that followed, and the subtle give-and-take relationship between the Chinese and Soviet communist parties put in clear focus the magnitude of Chou's firm yet tactful struggle with the Kremlin. This concise background information creates a context especially helpful to readers less knowledgeable about the modern history of China.

Overall, this biography is true to historical facts, but a few minor inaccuracies should be noted. For example, in the chapter dealing with the Cultural Revolution, the author writes that "confessions of errors" permitted Liu Shao-chi and Teng Hsiao-ping to keep their positions in the all-powerful Politburo. In reality, they were both deposed and jailed. Liu later died in limbo, while Teng survived. Despite such blemishes, Archer's *Chou En-lai* remains a fascinating authentic biography for young adults and adults as well.

Critical Context

Jules Archer is a prolific author of nonfiction. He has written more than sixty books, many of which are biographies. His subjects range from U.S. presidents to civil rights advocates to such communist leaders as Mao Tse-tung, Ho Chi Minh, Tito, and Joseph

Stalin, as well as Italian fascist Benito Mussolini. Archer broke away from the tradition of presenting to young people only famous American figures with accomplishments and personalities worthy of emulation. Whoever his subject is, he does serious research to arrive at the whole truth and tells it honestly, the good and the bad alike. *Chou En-lai* is a typical example of Archer's biographies and one of the best juvenile biographies that present an important worldview to young people.

Among biographies of Chou En-lai accessible to young people, Archer's *Chou En-lai* stands out strikingly. Dorothy and Thomas Hoobler's *Chou En-lai* (1986), with many illustrations and a brief text, is intended for younger readers and does not have a narrative as rich and lively as Archer's. Ed Hammond's *Coming of Grace* (1980), also liberally adorned with photographs, does not have a poignant style or a well-wrought characterization comparable to Archer's biography. John Roots's *Chou: An Informal Biography of China's Legendary Chou En-lai* (1977) benefits from the author's personal knowledge of Chou but to some extent also suffers from his closeness to the subject: His portrayal of Chou is not as balanced as Archer's.

Mingshui Cai

A CHRISTMAS CAROL

Author: Charles Dickens (1812-1870)
First published: 1843
Type of work: Novel
Type of plot: Moral tale
Time of work: The 1840's
Locale: London
Subjects: Death, friendship, religion, social issues, and the supernatural
Recommended ages: 13-18

> *Ebenezer Scrooge learns that selfishness leads only to an empty life and that love of humanity brings fulfillment.*

Principal characters:
EBENEZER SCROOGE, a selfish, uncaring miser
JACOB MARLEY, his former business partner, who has been dead for seven years
FRED, Scrooge's nephew
BOB CRATCHIT, Scrooge's desperately poor clerk, the father of a large family
TINY TIM, Bob Cratchit's crippled, dying child
THE GHOST OF CHRISTMAS PAST
THE GHOST OF CHRISTMAS PRESENT
THE GHOST OF CHRISTMAS YET TO COME

Form and Content

In *A Christmas Carol*, three spirits take Ebenezer Scrooge on tours of his past to show him where he went wrong, of the present to introduce him to the joy of the holiday season, and of the future to warn him of what may happen unless he changes. Scrooge learns his lesson well and is transformed into a man with a conscience.

On Christmas Eve, Scrooge terrorizes his clerk, Bob Cratchit, and reluctantly grants the poor man a day off. Impatient with those who waste their time on any pursuit other than making money, Scrooge angrily dismisses two gentlemen collecting for the poor and repulses his nephew, Fred, who invites him to Christmas dinner. At home that evening, Scrooge is confronted by the ghost of his dead partner, Jacob Marley, who warns him against purely materialistic pursuits and tells him that he will be visited in the night by three spirits.

The first spirit, the Ghost of Christmas Past, gives Scrooge a series of visions of his childhood and early manhood. Scrooge sees himself as a neglected child at school, then as an apprentice of Mr. Fezziwig, enjoying warm festivities on Christmas Eve, and finally as a prospering entrepreneur whose fiancée breaks their engagement because Scrooge loves money more than he loves her. He must suffer the agony of the vision of her with another husband and their children.

The second spirit, the Ghost of Christmas Present, takes Scrooge out onto the streets on Christmas morning to see many happy families and, in particular, the love and warmth of Bob Cratchit's home. Although they have barely enough to live on, the members of the Cratchit family share a devotion to one another that the old man recognizes as absent in his own life. The mild-mannered Cratchit is adored by his wife and children. Scrooge is concerned about their crippled child, Tiny Tim, and is informed that Tim will not live to see another Christmas unless circumstances change. Finally, the spirit deposits Scrooge into Fred's home, where a jolly evening of games is taking place. Scrooge sees good friends enjoying one another's company and is reluctant to depart when the ghost tells him it is time to move on.

The final spirit, the Ghost of Christmas Yet to Come, is shrouded in black, with only a hand showing. It first takes Scrooge to the stock exchange, where he hears his business associates speaking of a recent death, but Scrooge does not know whose. He then witnesses a scene in a junk shop as two women and a man bring in objects plundered from the dead man's house, even from the death bed, while his body was still there. The spirit then shows Scrooge his stripped bed, with his own body upon it, in his empty house. Upon asking whether anyone will feel emotion at his death, he sees a couple who owe him money; they are relieved and hope that their debt will be transferred to a less relentless creditor. Scrooge has another glimpse of the future: It is the Cratchit home, with Bob Cratchit as a broken man because of the death of Tiny Tim.

As Scrooge has one final glimpse of the future—that of his own grave—he pleads with the ghost to assure him that the visions are of what may be, not what will be. He desperately grasps the hand of the spirit and sees it turn into his bedpost: He is in his own bed, alive, and is a new man delighted with the opportunity to change his life. He begins his transformation immediately by sending an enormous turkey to the Cratchits and then goes through the streets wishing all a Merry Christmas. In the afternoon, he astounds Fred by showing up for Christmas dinner. The next morning at the office, when Bob Cratchit comes in late, Scrooge makes the clerk think that he is about to be fired, then announces that he will receive a raise. Scrooge provides the help needed so that Tiny Tim will not die. The new Scrooge becomes as good a man, as good a friend, as good a master as London ever knew, because he has learned how to keep Christmas.

Analysis

In *A Christmas Carol*, an allegory of spiritual values versus material ones, Charles Dickens shows Scrooge having to learn the lesson of the spirit of Christmas, facing the reality of his own callous attitude to others, and reforming himself as a compassionate human being. The reader is shown his harshness in the office, where he will not allow Bob Cratchit enough coal to warm his work cubicle and begrudges his employee a day off for Christmas, even claiming that his clerk is exploiting him. In the scene from the past at Fezziwig's warehouse, Scrooge becomes aware of the actions of a conscientious, caring employer and feels his first twinge of conscience. The author suggests an origin for Scrooge's indifference to others as Scrooge is portrayed as a neglected child, the victim of a harsh father intent on denying him a trip home for the holidays and only reluctantly relenting.

The ghost of Marley teaches his former partner the lesson of materialism, as Marley is condemned to drag an enormous chain attached to cash boxes: "I wear the chain I forged in life," the ghost explains. "I made it link by link." Marley warns Scrooge that he is crafting a similar fate for himself and that the three spirits are coming to give him a chance to change. Marley is filled with regret for good deeds not done. This theme is repeated when the first spirit exposes Scrooge to phantoms wailing in agony, many of whom Scrooge recognizes. The phantoms suffer because they now see humans who need their help, but they are unable to do anything: It is too late; they have missed their opportunity.

The novel contains important social commentary. As the two gentlemen are collecting for the poor on Christmas Eve, Scrooge contemptuously asks, "Are there no prisons?" One of the gentlemen says that many of the poor, rather than go to the detested workhouses, cruel and inadequate residences for the destitute, would prefer to die. Scrooge replies that "they had better do it, and decrease the surplus population," a reference to Thomas Robert Malthus' *An Essay on the Principle of Population* (1798), a treatise predicting that population would soon outstrip food production and result in a "surplus population" for which society could not provide. Later, in response to Scrooge's plea to allow Tiny Tim to live, the Ghost of Christmas Present throws Scrooge's words back at him: "What then? If he be like to die, he had better do it, and decrease the surplus population."

Observing two ragged children clinging to the skirts of the Ghost of Christmas Present, Scrooge asks about them and is told, "They are Man's. . . . This boy is Ignorance. This girl is Want." The spirit has a warning: "Beware them both, and all their degree, but most of all beware this boy, for on his brow I see that written which is Doom, unless the writing be erased." This warning suggests that those who do not share in the prosperity may in time prove dangerous to society. The revolution in France half a century earlier may have been on Dickens' mind. An important idea that the author stresses is that humans are responsible for their own destiny, both as individuals and as a group. He is writing in the tradition of a religion that teaches that people will one day have to answer for their failure to fulfill their responsibility.

Critical Context

A best-seller at the time of its initial publication, *A Christmas Carol* has become the most famous secular Christmas story in English. Although the novel is full of flaws— it is a trite story of an unfeeling miser becoming a sensitive person that employs stereotypes, such as the crippled dying child—Dickens makes readers suspend their disbelief because he speaks to them on an emotional rather than an intellectual level. Critics agree that Dickens added an important element of human warmth and love to the holiday season with this work.

J. Don Vann

CHRISTY

Author: (Sarah) Catherine Marshall (1914-1983)
First published: 1967
Type of work: Novel
Type of plot: Social realism
Time of work: 1912
Locale: Cutter Gap, or "the Cove," in the Great Smoky Mountains of Tennessee
Subjects: Coming-of-age, education, friendship, health and illness, and poverty
Recommended ages: 13-18

Nineteen-year-old Christy Huddleston leaves her sheltered home environment for the first time in order to teach unschooled children in the one-room school of a remote mountain community virtually unchanged from the early nineteenth century.

Principal characters:
CHRISTY HUDDLESTON, a young woman from a comfortable home in a
large Southern city
ALICE HENDERSON, a Quaker missionary-teacher and Christy's mentor
DAVID GRANTLAND, a young, idealistic minister
DR. NEIL MACNEILL, the Cove's agnostic doctor
FAIRLIGHT SPENCER, an uneducated, highly intelligent mountain
woman, who becomes Christy's dearest friend
OPAL MCHONE, the focus of Christy's first experience with practical
Christianity

Form and Content

Christy, in a prologue and forty-six chapters, recounts eleven months in the life of naïve, untried nineteen-year-old Christy Huddleston. Through a first-person narrator, Catherine Marshall has set out a young woman's coming-of-age, the struggles and triumphs of her first year on her own.

In the novel's prologue, Marshall explains that her purpose is to describe a pivotal year in her mother's life. The facts are true; the characters are drawn from real people, and the locale is identical to that of her mother's youth—only names are altered. Without its prologue, *Christy* is fiction—with it, *Christy* takes on the reality of a biographical account. The straightforward narrative unfolds through the eyes of the nineteen-year-old protagonist. With her parents' reluctant consent, Christy responds to a call for volunteers to teach school in the remote mountains of Tennessee. Although no one greets Christy at the railroad station when she arrives, she finds her own way to her destination of Cutter Gap. When she finally reaches the Cove, she discovers that the man sent to meet her train has been seriously injured on his way there and she witnesses a crude surgical operation under primitive conditions that saves his life.

Christy moves into the mission house under the watchful eye of Alice Henderson, the Quaker missionary-teacher in charge of Cutter Gap school, where Christy discovers that she is expected to teach sixty-seven children, ranging in age from three to seventeen, in a one-room church building with no running water and heated only by a pot-bellied stove. After her first few days, Christy falls prey to discouragement and finds herself unsure of her ability to live and teach in the harsh conditions of Cutter Gap, where the students are unwashed, foul-smelling, and unkempt—some with their underclothing sewed on for the winter. With few textbooks, no blackboards, and no writing materials, Christy has only her native ability and intuition upon which to draw.

Alice Henderson, in her quiet Quaker manner, explains that Christy must find within herself the strength that God will provide to meet her challenges. As Christy overcomes her initial fears, she wins over her students. With the school year well advanced, and at their request, she also begins to teach some of the mothers to read. In doing so, she makes fast friends with Fairlight Spencer and Opal McHone, each of whom are important in different ways to Christy's passage into adulthood. Opal McHone's husband, Tom, is murdered in a senseless blockade feud, and the beautiful Fairlight falls victim to a typhoid epidemic and dies. After weeks of nursing typhoid patients, Christy contracts the dreaded fever herself and recovers after a near-death experience.

Threaded through the narrative are the stories of two very different men, the preacher and the doctor, both of whom love Christy. Their competing loves, along with various events, births, and deaths among the people she has come to love deeply, place her faith in a fiery cauldron from which it emerges strong and whole.

Analysis

Catherine Marshall's *Christy* is a well-researched, in-depth portrayal of the highlanders of southern Appalachia and their Scottish forebears. The Appalachian mountain dialect, descriptions of music and musical instruments, superstitions and folkways—all bear the stamp of authenticity. The novel's audience is not confined to juveniles and young adults, but the book appeals to this age group, especially since the protagonist is a young woman in her first solitary confrontation with adult issues. The issues treated are a timeless series of "firsts": living away from home for the first time, facing the challenges of a first job, developing a personal identity, testing inherited beliefs, enduring the first close encounter with illness and death, and falling in love. Christy's rites of passage are the major theme of the novel.

In telling her mother's story, Marshall describes a classic coming-of-age pattern for young Christian women: An idealistic young woman of Christian beliefs answers a lofty call to serve humanity; she emerges at the end of the experience with idealism intact but well-tempered by a large dose of reality. After nearly a year of trial by various ordeals, she has tested her inherited beliefs, sorted them out, and claimed them as her own. This process, the discovery of the self, forms part of the passage into adulthood for every young person; Marshall portrays it with acute insight and sensitivity.

Christianity gleams as a bright thread throughout this novel, which is permeated by the author's deeply held religious beliefs. The invitation to examine those beliefs is presented to the reader with grace and without pressure through the actions and reactions of the novel's young protagonist. In addition, Marshall has used another of the novel's major characters to present her beliefs by setting out the Christian lifestyle in the words and actions of Alice Henderson, whose quiet strength steadies Christy throughout her tumultuous year in the Cove.

Friendship forms a second bright thread in *Christy*. With Fairlight Spencer, Christy experiences her first adult friendship—not dependent on similar backgrounds or similar intellect, but upon a calling together of similar souls. Christy's love for Fairlight, a far different relationship from those of her childhood, makes earlier friendships seem shallow in comparison. Fairlight's sudden and untimely death from typhoid forces Christy into her first confrontation with handling the loss of a beloved peer, causing her to question even God's love.

The importance of education is a third bright thread in the tapestry of Christy's experience. Apart from the role that education plays in the plot structure, Marshall makes a real attempt to describe the role of education in bettering the lives and circumstances of individuals in the poverty-stricken pockets of southern Appalachia. The novel describes the impact of learning to read, especially by adults, in enthusiastic detail; the liberating effect of literacy stands side by side with the sobering portrait of the tremendous hold of superstition and folkways over the unschooled mountain people.

Marshall uses illness and death as a bleak fourth thread to bring *Christy* to its gripping climax. A typhoid epidemic erupts in the Cove, spread by ordinary house-flies, outdoor privies, and the resulting impure water from springs used for drinking and cooking. The epidemic decimates the population of the Cove, turns the mission house into a makeshift hospital, claims Fairlight and several adults and students, and nearly kills Christy. The searing description of mountain homes with no inside plumbing, no means of sterilizing water, food, and utensils; of the proud mountaineers in their reluctance to ask for help until desperation sets in; and of the unnecessary deaths caused by ignorance and lack of resources sets the scene in which Christy contracts typhoid and almost dies.

Critical Context

While the collection of works by Catherine Marshall over her lifetime is extensive, *Christy* is the one work that can be singled out as appealing specifically to juveniles and young adults.

Although an excellent coming-of-age vehicle, *Christy* is perhaps inappropriate for general use in the public school system because of its heavily religious overtones. Nevertheless, this novel's carefully researched and finely drawn portraits of the proud mountain men and women of the Tennessee Great Smoky Mountains make it of particular interest to colleges and universities with an Appalachian studies concentration. It is also of interest and great encouragement to young persons in the Appalachian region of the United States who must contend with the "hillbilly" stereotype associated with their birthplace, and it provides realistic depictions of Appalachian life for those unfamiliar with the region. In the early 1990's, a television series based on *Christy* became popular for several seasons before its syndication in early 1995.

Christy is Marshall's only novel among her series of biographical and Christian devotional works. In 1951, she published *A Man Called Peter: The Story of Peter Marshall*, a biography of the life of her first husband, a well-known minister and chaplain of the Senate from 1947 until his death in 1949. Her devotional books include discussions of prayer and of the Holy Spirit; the better-known works are *God Loves You* (1953), *To Live Again* (1957), *Beyond Our Selves* (1961), and *Something More* (1974). A second novel, set in Pennsylvania in the 1930's, was never completed. In addition to her fiction and devotional works, Marshall edited several volumes of her late husband's sermons, collectively entitled *Mr. Jones, Meet the Master* (1949; rev. ed., 1950).

Because the major themes of *Christy* are universal, the novel itself is timeless; Marshall has produced a vivid and enduring contribution to the field of young adult literature.

Barbara C. Stanley

CITY
A Story of Roman Planning and Construction

Author: David Macaulay (1946-   )
First published: 1974; illustrated
Type of work: History
Time of work: 26 B.C.-A.D. 100
Locale: The Po Valley of Northern Italy
Subjects: Arts and jobs and work
Recommended ages: 10-18

Macaulay describes the planning and building of Verbonia, an imaginary Roman city typifying hundreds of such cities founded all over the Roman Empire between 300 B.C. and A.D. 150.

> *Principal characters:*
> APPIUS FLUVIUS, the chief water engineer of Verbonia
> MARCUS LICINIUS, the city's affluent baker
> QUINTUS AURELIUS, a barber whose shop provides a meeting place for the people of Verbonia

Form and Content

The informative nature of David Macaulay's *City: A Story of Roman Planning and Construction* rests as much on the illustrations as on the text. The narrative, broken up into short paragraphs, is clarified and enhanced on every page by Macaulay's architectural drawings: plan views, elevations, cross-sections, and full-page perspectives—all done freehand, in pen and ink, the traditional tools of architects and engineers. A glossary of architectural and engineering terms is included at the end of the book.

The story of Verbonia's construction began in 26 B.C. when Emperor Augustus ordered the founding of a new city in the Po Valley to replace several villages swept away by spring floods. The fertile river valley had long needed an efficient trading center from which the area's produce could be dispersed to other cities, and the presence of a fortified city promised greater security for this region so close to the unconquered Alps.

Without delay, Augustus dispatched a corps of military engineers to select a site, survey the area, draw plans, and establish a military camp in the center of the future city. Like other Roman cities, Verbonia was to be laid out like a chessboard and surrounded by a wall to prevent both enemy invasion and uncontrolled urban sprawl. The workforce consisted of two thousand soldiers, retired by Augustus and ordered to settle in Verbonia; farmers from the area; and slaves, some of whom were skilled stonecutters, masons, and carpenters. Since the materials—limestone, timber, marble, and clay for bricks and tiles—had to be brought in from other regions, new roads and a permanent bridge across the Po were the first priorities. Only then could work begin on the massive crenelated city wall, its watchtowers and vaulted gates. Simultaneously, water engineers built an aqueduct to supply Verbonia with fresh water from mountain lakes many miles away. The same engineers laid water and sewer lines underneath the city streets to service public fountains and some individual houses.

As in other Roman cities, the two most important public buildings were erected in the center: the market and the forum. The latter contained a platform for public announcements and a temple to the gods Jupiter, Juno, and Minerva. Since a Roman city was intended not only as a center of commerce, government, and religion but also as a pleasant place to live, Verbonia was given a theater for dramatic performances, an amphitheater for gladiator fights, and heated public baths, replete with gymnasium. Verbonia's inhabitants, depending on their station in life, lived in private homes, in apartment houses, or above the shops lining the city streets. Strict building codes, however, regulated the height of all buildings so as not to deprive any dwelling of sunlight.

As Verbonia, in the course of 125 years, slowly grew toward its surrounding wall, subsequent generations of builders continued to work from the original plans, building additional markets and baths on dedicated sites. When the city, which was designed for maximum population of fifty thousand, reached its capacity, a new one was founded in another advantageous location. Roman planners were well aware of the dangers of random urban growth and overpopulation.

Analysis

By telling the story of an imaginary city rather than chronicling the history of a real one, Macaulay has freed himself from the constraints of historical truth. This freedom has two advantages. First, it enables him to make Verbonia more typical than any particular Roman city and thereby to make his story of the construction more comprehensive. Second, it allows him to ignore the historical details of "who," "where," "when," and "why" and concentrate on what truly interests him, namely, how these cities were built. In telling the story of Verbonia's construction, Macaulay does not limit himself to the phases of construction but presents each individual step in detail. When he writes, for example, that Verbonia was laid out like a chessboard, he explains the use of a groma, a forerunner of modern surveying instruments, with which the builders made sure that the streets met at right angles and walls were raised perpendicular to the ground. When he relates the building of the permanent bridge, he shows in several cross-sections how the builders were able to anchor the bridge piers underwater. When he describes the vaulting of the city gates, he demonstrates in a series of diagrams how wedge-shaped stones were cut with such precision as to form an arch and how this arch was kept aloft until the keystone could be inserted.

While Macaulay's thorough research of these construction processes is impressive in its own right, his real achievement lies in making this highly technical information interesting and enjoyable to the reader. Knowing that interest in a subject depends first of all on comprehension, Macaulay has kept the text to a minimum and left the burden of communication to the drawings. The text, in fact, seldom occupies more than one-fifth of the page. The black ink drawings on white background also leave ample blank space so that the page never appears crowded and the amount of information is never overwhelming. With comprehension of each step in the process comes appreciation for each elegant solution and for the accomplishment as a whole.

In addition to making the various construction processes comprehensible, Macaulay also brings Verbonia to life. Along with the many technical drawings—the diagrams, plan views, and cross-sections designed to clarify aspects of construction—*City* contains just as many full-page, or even double-page, perspective drawings, showing street scenes busy with vendors and artisans, customers in a snack bar, or a child at play in the column-lined atrium of his home. The presence of human figures and everyday objects transforms these architectural drawings into scenes of Roman life. Macaulay's narrative achieves the same effect with the introduction of fictitious personages, such as Appius Fluvius, the chief water engineer; the well-to-do baker, Marcus Licinius; or the barber Quintus Aurelius, whose shop is the city's clearinghouse for news and gossip.

These side glances at Roman life, together with the prodigious effort of planning and building cities such as Verbonia, give the reader an impression of Roman culture as a whole and an idea of the formidable political power that gave rise to hundreds of such cities from Spain to the Near East. It is important to note, however, that these peripheral views and insights contain no subjective commentary on the culture. From start to finish, Macaulay maintains an objective focus on his subject: the planning and construction of a Roman city.

Critical Context

City is the second book in Macaulay's architectural series that began with *Cathedral: The Story of Its Construction* (1973) and includes, among others, *Pyramid* (1975) and *Castle* (1977). Almost all the books in this series have won prestigious awards in the United States and elsewhere, and several have been animated and adapted for television. Although Macaulay has written and illustrated a number of storybooks as well, most notably the Caldecott winner *Black and White* (1990), it is his architectural series that first established him in children's book publishing worldwide.

Moreover, the series marks a turning point in the history of children's picture books. The immediate success of *Cathedral* and *City* showed children's book publishers that black-and-white illustrations in picture books were not the risk that they had generally been deemed, an insight soon reinforced by the award-winning and commercially successful picture books by Chris Van Allsburg. More important, however, the success of the entire series helped prepare the way for a new generation of visually appealing information books on subjects previously believed to be too sophisticated for young readers. Examples of this new type of nonfiction book, which emerged in the 1980's and 1990's, are the many *Eyewitness* publications, distinguished for their close-up photography; Stephen Biesty's *Incredible Cross-Sections*, showing buildings and vehicles; and Macaulay's *The Way Things Work* (1988), subtitled *A Visual Guide to the World of Machines.*

In an interview for *Contemporary Authors* (1991), Macaulay explained the origin of his fascination with construction and technology: "I grew up in a time when it was still possible to see cause and effect, see how things worked. . . . It's not just pressing a button somewhere and magically something else occurs." In the age of microtechnology, in which visible effects have invisible causes, a book such as *City* not only enables its readers to comprehend these particular architectural feats but also gives them confidence in their ability to comprehend other forms of technology, for nothing built by humans is beyond human comprehension.

Gyde Christine Martin

THE CLAN OF THE CAVE BEAR

Author: Jean M. Auel (1936-   )
First published: 1980
Type of work: Novel
Type of plot: Historical fiction
Time of work: The Middle Paleolithic epoch (approximately 35,000 years B.C.)
Locale: The Crimean Peninsula near the shores of the Black Sea
Subjects: Coming-of-age, friendship, gender roles, and race and ethnicity
Recommended ages: 15-18

Ayla, a young Cro-Magnon girl adopted by Neanderthals, tries to conform to the rigid and gender-specific rules of the Clan, but her innate individuality and otherness keep asserting her separate identity.

> *Principal characters:*
> AYLA, a young Cro-Magnon girl growing up with a Clan of
> Neanderthals who struggles with ancient Clan rules as she matures
> into an independent young woman
> BRUN, the leader of the Clan, in whose hands the fate of Ayla often rests
> IZA, the chief medicine woman of the Clan, who first finds and rescues
> Ayla and becomes her adoptive mother
> CREB, the magician, or Mo-gur, of the Clan, who accepts her into the
> Clan and becomes her adoptive father
> BROUD, the arrogant and brutal son of Brun, who hates Ayla
> DURC, Ayla's mixed-race son, born of a violent rape

Form and Content

The Clan of the Cave Bear is a story set in prehistoric Europe during the last ice age; it has sometimes been categorized as "caveman" fiction. The novel's exact setting on the Crimean Peninsula is detailed in a map preceding the text. The heroine of the captivating story is Ayla, a Cro-Magnon girl who, at age five, loses her family in an earthquake and survives a number of terrifying events, including the attack of a cave lion, before she is found half-dead by Iza, the medicine woman of a Neanderthal clan uprooted by the same earthquake and in search of a new cave. Iza empathizes with the barely alive child and convinces her brother Brun, the leader of the Clan of the Cave Bear, to let her bring the child along. When the girl recuperates from her wounds, it is obvious that two separate worlds have met: The Neanderthal Clan members are described as short, stocky, bowlegged, dark-haired, with large heads, and communicating mostly with hand gestures; Ayla, on the other hand, is thinner, taller, blond, blue-eyed, and talking freely in a language that the Clan does not understand.

Initially, everyone is suspicious of the orphan, who is so different from them and who belongs to what the Clan terms the Others. Ayla's biggest supporter is Creb, the

Mo-gur, the mighty magician of the entire Clan of the Cave Bear. Creb, brother to Iza and Brun, is a misshapen, one-eyed cripple, who, as a child, had survived the attack of a cave bear. Ayla shows him the affection that he never received from anyone else, and a deep bond develops between the disparate pair. Creb officially accepts Ayla, who accidentally discovered the new cave, into the Clan at a special ceremony, scandalizing the Clan by assigning her the powerful cave lion totem and laying the groundwork for the hatred of the arrogant and brutal Broud, whose own manhood ceremony is eclipsed by Ayla's discovery of the cave and her totem ceremony.

From that time on, Ayla must learn how to be a Clan woman, whose tasks and rules are very different from those of the men. Ayla is especially adept at assimilating Iza's medicinal knowledge and is groomed for the prestigious role of medicine woman. Ayla's real trouble starts when she secretly learns to hunt with a sling, an enormous taboo for the women of the Clan and punishable by a form of exile. Because of her analytical skills, intuitive thinking, and tenacity, Ayla survives the exile and returns to the Clan. Broud, however, is pushing Ayla to the extreme, abusing her verbally and physically, eventually brutally raping her. The result of the rape is Durc, Ayla's son, whom the Clan wants to reject and who is eventually accepted because of Creb's influence. The novel ends as it began—with an earthquake, in which Creb is killed. Ayla is exiled by Broud, who has finally become the Clan leader.

Analysis

The Clan of the Cave Bear is an interesting novel for juvenile and young adult readers as it chronicles the coming-of-age of its young heroine, Ayla. In this initiation story, however, the main character grapples with being initiated not only into the strange world of adulthood but also into a world of an entirely different culture. Her initiation is accompanied by loss, violence, denigration, and self-effacement, yet also by grit, determination, tenacity, and triumph. Novelist Jean Auel presents the quintessential scenario of an outsider entering a homogenous group. Ayla is successfully and painfully ushered into the adult world, but her acceptance into the Clan of the Cave Bear ultimately fails.

Ayla is an outsider because she is different, both physically and mentally. Her slender, tall, blond, and blue-eyed appearance provides a stark physical contrast to the short, stocky, dark-haired Neanderthals, who consider her ugly and unmarriageable. Her analytical abilities, intuitive thinking, and inventive spirit advance her mentally over the Clan's people, whose knowledge comes from memory and who communicate telepathically during their ritual ceremonies. While they have reached the end of their evolutionary line, Ayla is the future of humankind. The Clan members are half-aware of that fact, although none of them as much as Broud, Ayla's nemesis.

As an outsider, Ayla is expected to conform to the ways of the Clan. Initially, she must unlearn her spoken language and adopt the sign language of the Clan. Because of the brain structure of the Clan's people, tasks are divided along gender lines. No one person could hold all the survival information necessary to do both the chores of men and women. Since Ayla learns by imitation and invention, she ventures into the forbidden realm of the men: hunting. Women cannot even touch hunting weapons; if they do, the tool is considered worthless. Therefore, Ayla's ultimate offense is to learn the sling hunting method and improve on it by firing two pebbles in succession.

The evil of that Paleolithic community is personified by Broud, who has no qualms condemning Ayla to death for saving his own son from the attack of a hyena by using a slingshot. Broud is a symbol for pettiness, jealousy, machismo, and rigid, unwavering commitment to ancient tradition, and therefore a force against which maturing young people often rebel. It is ironic that Broud himself is only a few years older than Ayla, that the rejection of Ayla comes from a young person, not an old one. The more Ayla rebels, however, the more Broud oppresses her. Her determined and individualistic spirit is almost broken by the beatings and the brutal rape. It is the love of Creb and Iza that supports her in those tough times. When Creb and Iza are both near death, Ayla loses her protection against Broud, who is next in line for Clan leader. Broud's exile of Ayla represents both her failed initiation into the Clan and her triumph over Broud, whom she humiliates before the entire Clan before she goes.

Readers of all ages can benefit from the message of *The Clan of the Cave Bear*, a message about tolerance toward and acceptance of outsiders and about the destructiveness of hatred. The novel also speaks more specifically to young people about the struggles of growing up, as well as the price that one pays both for conformity and for individuality. If the novel gives young people these messages in general, it does so specifically for girls and young women, as there is a definite feminist bent to Auel's work. Among the many things in which Ayla is a pioneer, she can also be called the first feminist, since it is exclusively male dominance and brutality that she defies.

Critical Context

The Clan of the Cave Bear is the first novel in Jean Auel's six-volume, prehistoric saga called Earth's Children, pioneering the genre of "caveman" fiction. The novel was a huge commercial and critical success, winning the Pacific Northwest Booksellers Association Award for excellence in writing (1980) and the Friends of Literature's Vicki Penzinger Matson Award (1981) and being nominated for the American Book Award for best first novel in 1981. The sequel to *The Clan of the Cave Bear*, *The Valley of Horses* (1982) depicts Ayla's struggle for survival after she had been cast out of the Clan. She eventually meets Jondolar, another Cro-Magnon man, and becomes his mate. Additional installments, such as *The Mammoth Hunters* (1985) and *The Plains of Passage* (1990), have been published. The sequels to *The Clan of the Cave Bear* have not been as critically acclaimed because of the many gratuitous sex scenes that they contain.

Anita Obermeier

CLEVER GRETCHEN AND OTHER FORGOTTEN FOLKTALES

Author: Alison Lurie (1926-   )
First published: 1980; illustrated
Type of work: Short fiction
Subjects: Emotions, family, gender roles, love and romance, and the supernatural
Recommended ages: 10-15

> *This collection of fifteen folktales from various ethnic traditions is united by an emphasis on the overlooked powers of the female protagonists to remedy problems and emerge as heroes.*

Form and Content

   Clever Gretchen and Other Forgotten Folktales is a collection of fifteen folktales from various cultural and ethnic traditions rewritten by Alison Lurie. She selected these tales because each narrates an adventure in which a female protagonist shows her bravery and intelligence. Lurie prefaces the collection with a brief introduction in which she explains her foremost aim: to restore the active nature of girls and women to folktales and to combat the stereotype of passivity and helplessness in most stories, in which the female characters are totally dependent on male heroism to rescue them from situations in which the male characters have placed them. The fifteen stories vary in length and complexity, and each is accompanied by a black-and-white illustration by Margot Tomes done in a simple style.

   The title story introduces the theme of ingenuity with the tale of Gretchen, a lord's daughter whose father will not marry her to anyone he does not judge to be the best horseman in the world. A poor widow's son attempts to win Gretchen in marriage, but she must intervene and help him in his quest when he makes a pact with the Devil, who is disguised as a wandering stranger. Gretchen recognizes the trick and devises a question for her suitor to ask the Devil that he will not be able to answer after he has helped Hans prove his skills; the Devil must accept his defeat and leave Gretchen and Hans to marry happily.

   The second story, "Manka and the Judge," presents a clever young poor woman who wins the favor of a young judge by solving all the riddles that he likes to pose. They marry, and she evens helps him resolve difficult cases by showing him that feelings and emotions are more valuable than material goods, a lesson that he accepts from her.

   "The Black Geese," the third story, combines Russian folklore of the evil witch Baba Yaga with the virtues of being kind to animals, who help a brave little girl rescue her brother and return home safely. The fourth story, "Mizilca," is the only one in which a female character actually disguises herself as male in order to overcome animal menaces and outwit all her foes, in ways that her lazier sisters cannot.

   Of the remaining stories, "The Mastermaid" and "Molly Whuppie" both show young female characters who accomplish Herculean tasks by outsmarting ogres and beasts to win marriage with young nobles. "The Hand of Glory" is a macabre story of a brave young servant girl who defeats robbers in an inn by overcoming their gruesome black magic. "The Sleeping Prince" is a close relative to "Sleeping Beauty," with a male sleeper who must be rescued by the bravery and devotion of a young woman. "Gone Is Gone" is a familiar cross-cultural tale in which a peasant couple reverses their household tasks at the wife's suggestion in order to teach the husband the lesson on how much more difficult her responsibilities are than he cavalierly assumes.

"Tomlin" is a traditional Scottish folktale of an enchanted forest where a brave young woman, who has taken as her lover and the father of her child an elf, helps him break a magic spell that is imprisoning him out of his human form. Virtues are taught in "Mother Holle" in which contrasting stepsisters meet an old woman in what is taken to be Heaven. The good sister returns to life rewarded, while the wicked one is suitably punished and disgraced. Similarly, in "The Baker's Daughter," two girls—in this case, twin sisters—reveal contrasting traits of goodness and selfishness. A spirit disguised as a beggar arranges for each to be rewarded or disgraced.

Three of the stories are more complex. "Cap O'Rushes" parallels William Shake-speare's *King Lear* closely, with three daughters interrogated by a father as to their measure of love and devotion. The youngest replies in a riddlelike fashion, which is eventually solved when her love is recognized.

"Kate Crackernuts" includes elements of the animal-to-human metamorphosis in the story of royal stepsisters who overcome the jealousy of the queen, who wishes to divide them and favor her own daughter. The girls' mutual devotion and courage save them both and enable them to marry princes, including one who suffers from a spell very similar to the story of the "Twelve Dancing Princesses."

"Maid Maleen" is the most complex tale in the volume. A clever young princess overcomes her father's cruel plans for her marriage by finding a way to marry the prince whom she has always loved. She escapes entombment and defeats an ugly and lazy rival for the prince by her wits and faithfulness.

Analysis

Lurie has achieved wide recognition not only as a writer for children but also as a social critic and adult novelist and essayist. Her overriding concern when she approaches children's literature is the degree to which all readers can understand the issues that connect literature for young readers with that for adults. She perceives a real danger in the separation of the two and prizes especially the degree to which children's fiction stands as a challenge to social conventions. As in her successful adult fiction, including Pulitzer Prize-winning *Foreign Affairs* (1985), Lurie presents characters who upset traditional values. She includes children as important protagonists in the struggle for a wiser and more just life, and she has been a leading feminist whose interests have taken in the ways in which stereotyped images of female weakness and passivity have been passed down through the ages through folktales and fairy tales, as well as through other means.

Clever Gretchen and Other Forgotten Folktales is part of Lurie's longtime interest in redirecting popular understanding of gender roles toward more socially responsible and realistic aims. She explains in her introduction to the collection that these tales reflect a different reality from the stereotypical one of a passive and completely dependent female character who awaits a male rescuer. She insists that women have always played a major role in the affairs of society and that most stories do not reflect this fact because of the historical dominance of men in selecting what was deemed appropriate to be preserved and recorded. Lurie proposes an honesty that would praise the "subversive" nature of children's literature as a force that has the potential for reforming abuses in society. Ten years after this collection, she published her essays on children's literature and social reform as *Don't Tell the Grown-ups* (1990); these writings are anticipated by the selection of tales in *Clever Gretchen and Other Forgotten Folktales*, in which each story shows the accomplishments of wise, brave, and adept female characters.

Critical Context

Clever Gretchen and Other Forgotten Folktales was praised in some reviews and criticized in others. Some critics pointed out that while Alison Lurie challenged the passivity of female characters and tried to show them as actively heroic (unless they were the evil contrasts to the other, good girls and women), she did not go far enough to portray their possible rejection of other stereotypes, such as marriage. Their fulfillment was still dependent on the choice and whim of the male characters, usually princes or other nobles. These critics wondered why Lurie was content with reforming the perceptions and portrayals of the female characters but letting the old images of noble and warlike male characters go unchallenged. In addition, they expressed the desire for a less dogmatic feminist view that did not ignore the possibilities for wise behavior from a male character as well.

Other critics noted that Lurie did not succeed in bridging the gap between important writing for juvenile and adult readers but rather privileged the former and mistakenly assumed that adult writing might not have the same important "subversive" potentials. Moreover, while some critics paid much attention to Lurie's obvious feminism, others noted that many of the tales were not "forgotten" at all and that many of them had long been accessible and available in other sources. The *Horn Book* magazine of April, 1980, in particular, documented in detail the common sources of many stories in Lurie's book, including *Womenfolk and Fairy Tales* (1975), edited by Rosemary Minard, a third of which are the same tales.

The growing importance of feminist literary criticism in the years since Lurie's book appeared would indicate that she was among the first to work toward a reevaluation of the portrayal of both children and female characters in some of the most lasting and influential stories that continue to be passed on from generation to generation.

Mark Bernheim

COLONIAL LIVING

Author: Edwin Tunis (1897-1973)
First published: 1957; illustrated
Type of work: History
Time of work: 1564-1770
Locale: Maine, New Hampshire, Massachusetts, Connecticut, New York, Pennsylvania, New Jersey, Maryland, Delaware, Virginia, North Carolina, South Carolina, Georgia, and Florida
Subjects: Arts, education, family, jobs and work, and travel
Recommended ages: 10-18

This readable text, augmented by more than two hundred drawings, portrays the details of everyday life in North America during the seventeenth and eighteenth centuries.

Form and Content

In *Colonial Living*, author-illustrator Edwin Tunis describes the "small, common things of Colonial existence" in America: food, cookery, crafts, clothing, furniture, houses, travel, education, and the tools and technology that supported everyday life. The book is divided into three chapters. The first, "Sixteenth and Seventeenth Centuries: The Beachheads," describes in a few brief paragraphs the living conditions in each of the earliest settlements at St. Augustine, Roanoke, Jamestown, Plymouth, New Amsterdam, Massachusetts Bay, Maryland, and New Sweden. The second chapter, "The Seventeenth Century," describes aspects of life in that century as settlements multiplied in New England, New Netherland, and the Southern colonies. The third chapter, "The Eighteenth Century," briefly considers Pennsylvania as a separate entity and then moves on to a lengthy discussion of life in the coastal colonies, essentially the rest of the country. The structure of the book is thus loosely chronological, progressing from the first settlements through the eighteenth century, although it is also geographical insofar as it expands outward from the beachheads with each chronological leap. Tunis' illustrations are an important part of the book, and every page contains one or more fine black-and-white drawings, more than two hundred of them in total, captioned and closely keyed to the text.

Within the larger chronological and geographic framework, Tunis meanders gracefully from topic to topic. His underlying pattern is movement from the general to the specific as he presents material from the perspective of the average Colonial citizen, particularly in the section on seventeenth century New England, and builds upon that basic information in later sections. For example, he devotes the first four pages in the New England section to house building, beginning with a settler surveying his empty lot and ending with the expansion of the standard one-room or one-story structure into the more elaborate saltbox dwelling. The sections that follow include such topics as houses, cottages, plantations, and inns and note geographic, ethnic, and other differences. In spite of the fact that much of the material in the New England section applies to the seventeenth century in general, there is minimal repetition.

Having covered some of the basics of everyday life, Tunis moves on to consider elements that were distinctive about each period and geographic area. In the New Netherland section, for example, he describes hat making and windmills; under the Southern colonies, he discusses the raising and processing of tobacco; and, when he gets to Pennsylvania, he describes the peculiarities of the Germans and the Scotch-Irish. In the lengthy last section, on the coastal colonies in the eighteenth century, he draws together many threads and presents a more unified picture consistent with the colonies' expanding populations and improved communications.

Tunis gives careful attention to some of the less well known aspects of early American technology. He has a thorough appreciation for Yankee ingenuity and describes a variety of mechanical devices, from the ladies' farthingale to an adjustable hanging candleholder, in loving detail. He obviously delights in the interesting and unusual. The inquiring reader may be surprised to learn that an ox was supported by a sling during shoeing because it could not support its tremendous weight on three tiny feet. Readers will surely be amused at Tunis' explanation of bundling, the custom of allowing engaged couples to lie in bed together while fully clothed, as "nothing more than a practical way to provide warmth and chaperoned privacy for a courting couple under difficult conditions," claiming that they did "their whispering in full view of parental eyes."

Analysis

Tunis' tone resembles that of the learned but conversational museum curator presenting a guided tour. The text is liberally sprinkled with names of archaic objects and processes that will be unfamiliar to the general reader, such as a trammel (an adjustable pot hook). Most of these terms are defined in context or clarified by an accompanying illustration. Although the tone is informal, Tunis' sentences tend to be long and complex in structure. The combination of long sentences, unfamiliar words, abstract descriptions of technical procedures, and small print may render the text difficult for readers at the lower end of the recommended age group. The difficulty is countered somewhat by a skillful use of fictional techniques and humor, which bring otherwise dry passages to life: "The appearance of the slightest glow on the rags was a signal to commence a blowing operation that might succeed in nursing the spark into a small flame. Charles Dickens, who had made a fire that way, said that with luck it could be done in half an hour. That would be a long half-hour on a January morning, with the fire out." Tunis' humor most often points out the quirks of human nature, which one suspects he finds not much different from those of his own era. In spite of the fact that *Colonial Living* includes one long section on the Southern colonies, however, Tunis pays relatively little attention to the lives of slaves in the South and almost totally neglects African Americans as freemen.

Readers both young and old will be able to appreciate Tunis' marvelous illustrations. Beginning with a map on the endpapers identifying early settlements of North

America, painstakingly rendered pen-and-ink drawings present many of the most fascinating details unearthed by the author in his extensive research. Clean precise lines enable the reader to visualize artifacts and mechanical processes, bringing a bit of description to life or making an abstract description comprehensible. All illustrations are located adjacent to the text to which they refer and are accompanied by a helpful, often humorous caption.

Tunis has been careful to define his objective in writing *Colonial Living* in the preface: "This isn't history; it is rather a description of the stage set for history, and of the costumes and properties of the actors, spear carriers as well as the leads." It is well to remember his objective when evaluating the work, for it is likely to be more satisfactory for browsing and recreational reading than as a reference tool. In spite of the wealth of information that the book includes, the lack of an index presents a serious limitation. Someone looking for an explanation of the custom of bundling, for example, will be forced to leaf through the pages in hopes of serendipitously encountering the relevant term. Although the book includes a table of contents and a list of illustrations as prefatory matter, its loose organization and the repetition of some of the topics common to every geographic area are equally problematic for its utility as a reference aid. Another difficulty is the author's use of the generalized headings "New England," "New Netherland," "Southern Colonies," and "Coastal Colonies" without an explanation of which colonies or modern states fall under each. Finally, the book lacks a bibliography to give interested readers a start on tracking down further information on topics of interest.

Critical Context

Colonial Living, Tunis' fourth book, received the Thomas A. Edison Foundation Award. It was favorably reviewed at the time of publication by *The New York Times Book Review*, as well as by the standard children's book review journals such as *Booklist* and *Horn Book*. Tunis' *Frontier Living* was published as a companion volume to *Colonial Living* in 1961.

Although still held by many libraries and cited in the sixteenth edition of *Children's Catalog* (1991), the core list of books for children from preschool through sixth grade, *Colonial Living* is not mentioned in major textbooks on children's literature. This omission is probably attributable to the fact that most of these textbooks are limited to children's literature at the elementary level. Tunis' prose may be difficult for the average elementary school reader in an era in which the trend in nonfiction for children is the photo essay.

Another notable trend in children's nonfiction is the emphasis on careful documentation and provision of reference aids such as a glossary, a list of sources, and an index. *Colonial Living* includes none of the above. Although the depth of research suggested by the author's remarks in the preface and acknowledgments is impressive, most teachers and librarians would prefer to see a bibliography of the sources used.

Also important in quality nonfiction are the illustrations. A more recent book on the same topic would be more likely to include a variety of media, particularly photographs or contemporary illustrations, but Tunis' drawings should not be underestimated. In many cases, a good drawing is far superior to a photograph, and Tunis' skill with pen and ink, as well as his fascination with the technology of an earlier era, is strongly reminiscent of David Macaulay's works, such as the Caldecott Honor Book *Cathedral* (1974).

Kathleen M. Hays

COMMODORE PERRY IN THE LAND OF THE SHOGUN

Author: Rhoda Blumberg (1917-   )
First published: 1985; illustrated
Type of work: Biography and history
Time of work: 1853-1858
Locale: Shimoda and Hakodate, Japan
Subjects: Explorers, politics and law, and rulers
Recommended ages: 10-13

> *Arriving on the shores of a feudal and isolated Japan, Commodore Perry attempts to open that country to foreign trade and to force its entrance into the world community of nations.*

Principal personages:
> COMMODORE MATTHEW PERRY, a clever and aggressive naval officer determined to break the isolation of Japan
> KAYAMA, the principal Japanese conduit of negotiations between Commodore Perry and the ruling shogun
> OLIVER PERRY, the principal American conduit of negotiations
> THE SHOGUN, the real authority in Japan during the Tokugawa Period
> MANJIRO, a Japanese fisherman rescued from a desert island by Americans
> EMPEROR MEIJI, the ruler who brought Japan from a feudal past into the modern industrial world

Form and Content

Rhoda Blumberg's *Commodore Perry in the Land of the Shogun* follows the strategies, bluffs, and bullying of Commodore Matthew C. Perry as he arrived off the shores of Shimoda, Japan. He followed in the wake of several unsuccessful European and American attempts to open the feudal society to the outside world, and he was determined to succeed where others had failed; he never imagined that Japan had any right to remain as isolated as it wished. His first intent was to deliver a letter to the emperor from President Millard Fillmore, a letter that asked for ports to be opened to American ships so that they might obtain coal and provisions and for proper and humane treatment of any American sailors shipwrecked off the Japanese coast. After delivering the letter, Perry intended to sail away and return the next spring for his answer.

The arrival of Perry's ship caused an uproar of fear and confusion in Japan. Mired in a feudal system that existed by maintaining things as they had been for a thousand years, the Japanese people saw the entrance of these foreigners as a potential disaster; by law, they were not allowed to speak with foreigners, and anyone who lived abroad and then returned to Japan was subject to execution. Perry, however, isolating himself so that he might appear as mysterious and remote as the emperor, threatened not only to land but also to march to Edo (modern Tokyo) in order to deliver the letter to the emperor personally. To indicate his adamant position, Perry began to send out survey crews to map the coast. Eager to avoid contact, the Japanese negotiator Kayama brought a letter from the emperor to Perry indicating that the letter from President Fillmore might be delivered to Japanese officials. On July 14, 1853, Americans landed on the sacred soil of Japan for the first time. Three days later, Perry sailed away.

At first, the Japanese people sought simply to refuse all contact, but when Perry arrived the next February with an even larger force, a Treaty House was established and negotiations began. On the one side, there was a solid reluctance to change what had been in place for a millennium; on the other side, there was a blustery, aggressive intent to force the contact. At first, one port was offered, but it would not be opened for five years; this condition Perry would not accept. Thus began a series of elaborate rituals between the Americans and Japanese. The Americans gave fascinating gifts: a miniature railroad, Samuel Morse's new telegraph system, farm tools, a hose and folding ladder, and books. American clothing caused a special fascination. The Japanese gave rich gifts as well: scrolls, lacquer boxes and trays, silks, swords, and unusual seashells. The commodore, an amateur naturalist, was thrilled with the shells, but he did not perceive the fine quality of the Japanese gifts and was disappointed. Nevertheless, negotiations continued and delegations visited both the shore and the ships, culminating in a grand banquet on board the commodore's ship.

The Treaty of Kanagawa was finished at the end of March, 1854, and it provided for more than Perry had hoped; it essentially opened up Japan to American trade, opened two ports, and provided for a residence in Shimoda for an American consul. Visits to the two port cities soon showed that cultural differences between them were vast. Although Perry had never entered the capital city, he believed that he had succeeded. It was diplomacy, and not cannons, that brought the two countries into close contact.

Told in a narrative style, Blumberg's work is structured as a history. It follows closely the negotiations between the two cultures but stresses the narrative line until the end of the work, where Blumberg sets the notes that follow the peripheral stories of several of the minor personages and a series of appendices that translate the principal documents that were exchanged. Her afterword suggests the implications of Perry's contact, as quite soon after the conclusion of the treaty Americans began to visit Japan and affect its once-isolated world.

This intermixture of cultures is effectively shown by the illustrations that Blumberg gathered. All of these are contemporary, some drawn by American witnesses; these illustrations tend to emphasize the stateliness and order of the American regiments and delegations, as well as the seeming oddity of Japanese ways. Most of the illustrations, however, are Japanese portraits of the American visitors, their Caucasian features exaggerated, their stances and eyes an uneasy mixture of Japanese and American features, their odd customs and behavior prominent. In trying to render this new culture, the Japanese have depicted it as "other," yet alike as well—a metaphor for the first attempt at two cultures to understand each other.

Analysis

Blumberg crafts this story of Japan's opening and Perry's bravado as a narrative, using setting, character development, foreshadowing and suspense, and an episodic structure as a novelist might. The book begins, for example, in a moment of panic as four black ships enter the harbor and barbarians seem poised to invade Japan, setting temple bells ringing and messengers racing inland and families locking their doors. Such a gripping opening is the stuff of a novel. This technique gives Blumberg several advantages, the most important of which is the avoidance of the encyclopedic tone and the submergence of the reader into the perspectives and mindsets of opposing personages and cultures. This method also allows the author to hold information in abeyance, to generate suspense and to hold interest. Her narrative voice suggests the enormous importance of the opening of Japan, but it also maintains an impartial stance: Both sides maneuver and bluff, both sides deceive, both sides threaten force, and both sides experience gains and losses.

Yet, *Commodore Perry in the Land of the Shogun* is not a novel, and Blumberg wishes to show more than an isolated episode; she wants to depict an entire culture and its stern reluctance to change. She does this by interspersing the episodic narrative with historical explanations for why personages responded as they did. For example, she interrupts the narrative between the July and February visits by Perry to explore the various castes in Japan and how they might be affected by changes in the culture. These explanations are interwoven into the narrative as well to explain the intricate hierarchy of authority that Perry had to understand before he could approach the true governmental power structure.

Blumberg's principal success in this work is to explore the tension generated in Japan by contact with another, alien world and, by implication, to suggest what might happen when any two cultures collide. Perry forces the contact out of perceived American needs; his cannons ensure the contact. For Japan, however, there are gains and losses as it deals with a world that it had sought to avoid. The contact brings about a breakdown in the unjust and harsh feudalism of the country and a lessening of the autocratic rules of the Shogun. Yet, the contact also means harm for the purity and integrity of the culture; when the emperor adopts Western clothing, something has been lost. The history, then, takes on longer dimensions in exploring the complicated costs of intercultural communication.

Critical Context

Rhoda Blumberg's work lies in the forefront of nonfiction writing in children's literature. *Commodore Perry in the Land of the Shogun* was one of the first books to do effectively for historical studies what historical fiction had done for much of the twentieth century: use the novelist's form, although without the novelist's license, to describe and interpret a historical event. It began a series of such books for Blumberg, including *The Incredible Journey of Lewis and Clark* (1987), *The Great American Gold Rush* (1989), and *The Remarkable Voyage of Captain Cook* (1991). Each book is itself remarkable for its narrative handling of historical material and its sensitive and perceptive examination of the large cultural issues that lie behind a single historic moment. A work that combines text with contemporary illustration to produce both an aesthetically pleasing and informative book, *Commodore Perry in the Land of the Shogun* stands as one of the field's best attempts to speak to young readers about complex cultural historic events.

Gary D. Schmidt

A CONNECTICUT YANKEE IN KING ARTHUR'S COURT

Author: Mark Twain (Samuel Langhorne Clemens, 1835-1910)
First published: 1889; illustrated
Type of work: Novel
Type of plot: Adventure tale, fantasy, and science fiction
Time of work: The sixth century
Locale: England
Subjects: Education, religion, science, and social issues
Recommended ages: 13-18

Transported to Arthurian England by a blow to the head, a nineteenth century American tries to reform medieval Britain through modern technology and democratic principles.

> Principal characters:
> HANK MORGAN, a Colt arms factory foreman
> KING ARTHUR, the mythic king
> CLARENCE (AMYAS LE POULET), a page and Hank's righthand man
> SANDY (ALISANDE LA CARTELOISE), a damsel who accompanies Hank
>   on a mission and later becomes his wife
> MERLIN, a magician and Hank's chief rival

Form and Content

Combining elements of science fiction, adventure tales, broad burlesque, and social satire, *A Connecticut Yankee in King Arthur's Court* is a scathing commentary on injustice and oppression in all ages.

In England in 1889, a frame narrator meets an American at Warwick Castle. The curious stranger visits the narrator's room, introduces himself as a "Yankee of the Yankees," and tells how a blow to the head transported him to sixth century England. The visitor, later identified as Hank Morgan, becomes sleepy and leaves a yellowed manuscript detailing his story. With the exception of two postscripts, one by Clarence in the sixth century and another by the narrator, the remaining forty-three chapters are Hank's first-person account of his ten years in the sixth century.

Hank Morgan awakens in a strange place and is captured by Sir Kay, a knight in armor, who Hank thinks is from either an insane asylum or a circus. Forced to march to Camelot, Hank learns that he is at King Arthur's court in 528 A.D.

Condemned to death by Sir Kay, Hank uses his knowledge of an imminent eclipse to dupe his captors into believing that he has blotted out the sun. Terrified by Hank's sorcery, King Arthur makes Hank the kingdom's "second personage." Hank demotes Merlin to performing mundane tasks.

With the help of page Amyas le Poulet, whom he calls "Clarence," Hank reorganizes the kingdom. He secretly builds factories, schools, and military academies. He introduces many nineteenth century wonders, including the telephone, the telegraph, electrical generators, and firearms. He controls Merlin and others by performing additional "miracles" but remains wary of the ominous Established Church.

After devoting several years to creating his "civilization," Hank must prove his mettle in tournaments and by traveling among the people. While touring the kingdom incognito with King Arthur, Hank becomes acutely aware of injustice and oppression. His mission now changes to social, economic, and political reform.

Hank no longer works in secret after he defeats the massed chivalry of England. Tricked by the Church into leaving England, Hank returns to find the country divided by war and the Interdict. Only a few young men remain loyal to Hank. With Arthur dead, Hank declares a republic and challenges all of the knighthood. He and fifty-three young men retreat to a cave defended by electrified fences, explosives, and machine guns. In a battle between the forces of superstition and technological progress, Hank Morgan destroys not only the age of chivalry but the "civilization" that he painstakingly built as well. An enchantment by the previously ineffectual Merlin returns the Yankee to his own time, where he dies soon after the narrator finishes reading the manuscript.

Mark Twain's stinging social criticism was intensified by 220 drawings by Daniel Carter Beard. Often suggesting themes not found in the text, the pictures portray several notables as characters, including Alfred, Lord Tennyson, as Merlin and ruthless financier Jay Gould as a slave driver. Twain heartily approved of the added dimension that Beard's illustrations gave the novel.

Analysis

The themes in *A Connecticut Yankee in King Arthur's Court* are complex and often contradictory. Originally conceived as a comic contrast of the manners, social customs, and institutions of medieval England with those of the Machine Age, the novel evolves into a bitter attack against all forces of oppression throughout history. Initially, Hank Morgan makes wry comments about knight errantry, ignorance, and superstition, but he soon focuses on the harsh feudal system sustained by severe laws, a callous aristocracy, and an omnipotent church. These forces subjugate and exploit the common people, who have long been conditioned to accept their lot.

Part of the complexity of the novel derives from Hank Morgan's ambivalence and inconsistent philosophy. While Hank champions progress through technology, he is not above using scientific ingenuity to create showy effects in order to tighten his control over the kingdom. Although he calls Merlin a "cheap old humbug," he also gains power by sham and trickery in the form of modern "miracles." Hank dismisses Merlin as "a magician who believed in his own magic," but Hank is undone by his belief in his technological "magic."

The effect of training and conditioning is a constant theme and the target of Hank's contempt. He is ashamed of Sandy, who has been conditioned to believe that pigs can be enchanted princesses. He is horrified when Morgan le Fay casually kills a clumsy servant because law and custom permit it. King Arthur's training makes him an unfit judge because he always favors the aristocracy in disputes. Likewise, the freeman has been trained to accept injustice and abuse from the nobility and in turn persecutes his inferior, the slave. While Hank boasts of rapid industrial progress, he never succeeds in altering ingrained attitudes and superstitions. His system of technical schools and colleges cannot withstand the Church's disapproval. When the Interdict is proclaimed, only a few boys too young to fear the Church remain loyal to Hank.

While Hank Morgan is not strictly Twain's alter ego, both share similar social, political, and philosophical views. Like Twain, Hank sees human nature as contradictory—at times both admirable and contemptible. Hank regards King Arthur as an example of all that is wrong with monarchy. The king rules callously, often meting out injustice by enforcing laws favoring the privileged classes. When Arthur risks exposure to smallpox to help a dying peasant woman, however, Hank considers the king heroic for his compassion. Encountering a freeman who rejoices at the death of a despotic lord, Hank thinks that he has finally met a man who has not been crushed by oppression. Later, when the same freeman shows disdain for a passing slave, Hank remarks with disgust "there are times when one would like to hang the whole human race and finish the farce." Hank Morgan and Mark Twain share the same pessimism about human nature.

Hank's failure to reform the sixth century has more to do with the weaknesses of human nature than the clash between technology and the status quo. Twain shows that individuals often act courageously and humanely but are also capable of heartless cruelty as members of a group or community. Ironically, Hank Morgan embodies the contradictions of the human race as much as anyone whom he criticizes. While he shows compassion for the suffering of the weak and oppressed, he also indifferently hangs a teller of stale jokes and a band of bad musicians. The final battle between chivalry and technology is horrifying, but Hank derives satisfaction from the destruction—nearly thirty thousand knights are killed by machine gun fire, electrocution, or drowning. The violent confrontation between medieval and modern society raises such questions as "Can industrial progress bring enlightenment without similar growth in human compassion?" and "Is Hank's vision of a technological utopia impossible given the weaknesses of human nature?"

Despite its bleak ending, *A Connecticut Yankee in King Arthur's Court* remains popular with young adults because it ingeniously combines adventure, science fiction, comedy, and chivalric romance while challenging readers to consider serious issues.

Critical Context

The publication of *A Connecticut Yankee in King Arthur's Court* in 1889 was part of a progression in Mark Twain's writings to more serious themes. Twain's major popular works dealing with his travel experiences and his Mississippi River boyhood were already published and invariably ended positively. While his first historical novel, *The Prince and the Pauper* (1881), dealt realistically with similar social issues, it is lighter in tone and also ends happily.

In 1884, inspired by his reading of Sir Thomas Malory's *Le Morte d'Arthur* (1485),

Twain began sketching out a story line and worked on the novel sporadically until its completion in the spring of 1889. The author was also influenced by a resurgence in interest in Arthurian legend attributable in part to the popularity of Tennyson's *Idylls of the King* (1859-1885). Twain's novel is curiously similar to Charles Heber Clark's *The Fortunate Island* (1882), in which a modern American encounters Arthurian England, but Twain claimed never to have read Clark's book.

Although *A Connecticut Yankee in King Arthur's Court* is commonly regarded as a failure by literary critics, it has remained popular with readers since its initial publication. Hank Morgan's story has been adapted to the stage, film, and television, but Twain's bitter satire, social commentary, and violent finale are often omitted in order to make it suitable for young audiences. Young readers familiar with the story from popular culture will find the novel complex, challenging, and rewarding.

Kevin J. Bochynski

COSMOS

Author: Carl Sagan (1934-1996)
First published: 1980; illustrated
Type of work: Science
Subjects: Nature and science
Recommended ages: 13-18

Sagan explores the history of science, demonstrating the complex relationships between human evolution and culture and the physical universe.

Form and Content

Carl Sagan's *Cosmos* is one of the best-selling science books ever published in the English language, and there are myriad reasons for its popularity. Sagan reveals an extraordinary passion for science and an unsurpassed talent for disseminating the intricacies of science, without distortion, to any audience. His dedication to rationalism permeates every part of the book. Humans have evolved rationality, he claims, and the species has a natural inclination to interpret the cosmos scientifically. Sagan gives many examples of human scientific explorations throughout history, and he guides readers through the process of discovery, highlighting the frustrating setbacks along with the exhilarating moments of insight. The discovery of new truths is inevitably followed by a reluctance to accept these new ways of perceiving the universe, and Sagan provides dramatic portraits of human ignorance, fear, and hatred and the destructive conclusions to which these most primitive instincts can lead. Rationalism is ultimately optimistic, however, because it asserts that humanity can overcome any problem with which it is confronted; humans have the ability to reason, and *Cosmos* asserts that reason in science is most beneficial.

Cosmos discusses topics from the subatomic microcosm to the galactic macrocosm and beyond, always clearly making the necessary connections among the scientific disciplines of chemistry, physics, and astronomy. What takes Sagan's work beyond being simply a good textbook is his consistent focus on humanity, both its triumphs and its limiting inclinations. *Cosmos* consists of thirteen chapters roughly organized into four topical groupings, with cross-references between and allusions to other chapters. Chapters 1 and 2, "Shores of the Cosmic Ocean" and "One Voice in the Cosmic Fugue," address the physical proportions of the universe and human evolution and development within it. Chapters 3 through 6—"The Harmony of the Worlds," "Heaven and Hell," "Blues for a Red Planet," and "Travelers' Tales"—view the past and present of astronomy and speculate on its future. The fine line between physics and metaphysics is delineated in the next four chapters—"The Backbone of Night," "Travels in Time and Space," "The Lives of Stars," and "The Edge of Forever"— while the last three chapters—"The Persistence of Memory," "Encyclopaedia Galactica," and "Who Speaks for Earth?"—analyze humankind's place in the cosmos and its potential for both destruction and survival.

The book includes hundreds of outstanding illustrations that enhance the engaging text. Most noticeable are the stunning photographs of stars, interstellar phenomena, and galaxies taken at the world's best-equipped observatories. In addition, many artists' renderings of cosmic vistas are so realistically drawn as to appear to be photographs. Included, too, are reproductions of mosaics, tapestries, hieroglyphs, woodcuts, sand paintings, sculptures, and other historic artifacts from many world cultures, attesting humanity's obsession with and dedication to the physical universe. To keep the material understandable to the reader, Sagan also graciously provides many relevant maps, time lines, and charts in appropriate places. Models—for example, a model of the ancient library at Alexandria and a model of Martian volcanoes—aid in imagining sights no human can currently see. At the end of the book are two brief appendices and a list of suggested readings categorized by chapter.

Analysis

Sagan never had a reputation as one who shies from a controversial issue. Much of the strength of *Cosmos* rests in his ability to approach a number of social, political, religious, and philosophical issues and think them through critically to a conclusion counter to many populist beliefs. For example, his exposé of the gruesome murder of Hypatia, the last scientist at the library at Alexandria, in 415 A.D. by parishioners of Cyril, the bishop of the city, carries with it an unmistakable warning against religious fanatics: This scientist, dedicated to discovery and truth, had her flesh flayed from her bones, while Cyril was later made a saint by the Catholic church. Sagan is not adverse to tradition, per se; he only expresses his reactions when tradition is contrary to the conclusions of the scientific method. "Evolution is a fact," he states early in *Cosmos*, "not a theory," and, throughout the book, he logically demonstrates his position in a variety of ways.

Perhaps it is in his discussions of humankind's military proclivities that Sagan becomes most bold and direct. The wars of the ancients impeded the direction of human scientific exploration as much as did the Thirty Years' War (1618-1648) for the scientists of the Enlightenment. In the last two chapters of the book, he ironically applies modern society's postnuclear condition to the many examples that he notes from the past: Today's political and military establishments have made the discoveries of science the potential destruction of the entire planet. In many important ways, *Cosmos* is a cautionary tale.

Yet, it is also a journal celebrating human vision and the will to endure and triumph. Ultimately, *Cosmos* is a book of heroes—not military, religious, or political heroes, but heroes whose acts survive because of their conviction that truth can be found in applying human logic to sensory data and observation, all the time somehow ignoring social convention. Such renowned figures as Albert Einstein, Leonardo da Vinci, and Sir Isaac Newton are covered in the book, but Sagan also has a delightful knack of elevating lesser-known individuals to the status of their famous colleagues, conscious always to retain their humanity. From the ancient world, readers meet Hypatia, Eratothenes, and Democritus (the true "discoverer" of atoms about 430 B.C.). They also encounter Christiaan Huygens, Jean François Champollian (the decoder of the Egyptian hieroglyphs), and Johannes Kepler from past centuries. From the twentieth century, readers are introduced to scientists such as Robert Goddard and Wolf Vishniak (a researcher working on the Viking Mars probe who died during the experiments). Humans are "star stuff," Sagan says in the book, entirely composed of elements emitted from the stellar masses of the universe. Humankind's connection to the cosmos and apparently unstoppable drive to reach out to the stars, both literally and figuratively, is its redeeming grace as a sentient species.

The encompassing vision of *Cosmos* could not be conveyed successfully without down-to-earth rhetoric. Sagan's ability to relate the complexities and importance of electromagnetic spectral analysis, for example, demonstrates his talents for good, old-fashioned, effective teaching. Like the stars in a galaxy, the chapters are related to the overall concept of the book, yet are self-contained and of circular design—the initial theme is examined and reexamined within the chapter, only to be reaffirmed in a new light at the end. Sagan's narration is accentuated by his frequent anecdotal excursions highlighting ironies and human interest asides about his subjects, often from a personal perspective. The quotations that he uses to introduce each chapter signal to readers the important themes that follow and should be reread after finishing the chapter. Sagan's unwavering commitment to the methods of science frequently prompts his prose to be inspirational. Sagan calls Euclid's "elegant" book on geometry "a great read . . . even today." One must conclude the same with *Cosmos*.

Critical Context

A Pulitzer Prize winner, Carl Sagan first became one of the world's leading scientists, science advocates, lecturers, and teachers in the 1950's. He worked with the Apollo astronauts and was an instrumental participant in the Mariner, Viking, Voyager, and Galileo missions to the planets. His awards include National Aeronautics and Space Administration (NASA) medals for Exceptional Scientific Achievement, the John F. Kennedy Astronautics Award, the Public Welfare Medal (the highest award given by the National Academy of Sciences), and the Joseph Priestley Award, along with many honorary degrees from U.S. colleges and universities. It is with his books, however, that Sagan achieved his most popular acclaim. His works include *The Cosmic Connection: An Extraterrestrial Perspective* (1973), *The Dragons of Eden: Speculations on the Evolution of Human Intelligence* (1977), *Broca's Brain: Reflections on the Romance of Science* (1979), *Pale Blue Dot: A Vision of the Human Future in Space* (1994), and *The Demon Haunted World: Science as a Candle in the Dark* (1995). He was also a writer and producer of the film *Contact* (1996), based on his 1985 novel of the same name.

Cosmos was conceived and developed simultaneously as both a book and a thirteen-part Public Broadcasting Service (PBS) series aired in 1980. The series won both Emmy and Peabody awards and, now on video, had been seen by an estimated 500 million people in sixty countries by the mid-1990's. Although they can be studied and enjoyed individually, the book and series can effectively complement each other. The success of such an ambitious project is a testament to Carl Sagan and his *Cosmos*.

Dana Anthony Grove

COWBOYS OF THE WILD WEST

Author: Russell Freedman (1929-   )
First published: 1985; illustrated
Type of work: History
Time of work: 1865-1895
Locale: The Great Plains, from Texas to Montana and the Dakota Territories
Subjects: Animals, jobs and work, and nature
Recommended ages: 10-13

Freedman describes the life and work of a cowboy on the ranch, out on the open range, and up the trail during the famous cattle drives.

   Principal personages:
      TEDDY BLUE ABBOT, a wiry cowboy, loyal to his outfit, who enjoyed
         the tough, wild life of the range
      JAMES COOK, a cowboy who had a special relationship with his horse
      HIRAM CRAIG, a cowboy during the 1880's who described the workings
         of a roundup
      J. M. GRIGSBY, a cowhand who described the entertainment and songs
         of the cattle trail
      JIM HERRON, a cowboy who discussed the perils of the stampede
      JIM CHRISTIAN, a line rider on a huge Texas ranch
      CHARLES SIRINGO, the author of the first of many cowboy memoirs

Form and Content

   Russell Freedman's *Cowboys of the Wild West* describes the experience of cowboys during the days of the great cattle drives. These drives brought longhorns from Texas to the ranches and railroads further north, where the cattle were sent on to Chicago and the eastern meat markets. The era of the cattle drive lasted from the end of the Civil War in 1865 to the mid-1890's, when barbed wire, farms, and a more extensive railway system made the western cattle trail obsolete.
   The book is divided into six chapters that explore various aspects of cowboy lore and life. Chapter 1 discusses the history of the cowboy trade from its origins in Mexico. There, in the sixteenth century, Spanish ranchers used skilled horsemen called vaqueros to look after their herds. The vaqueros (from the Spanish word *vaca*, or "cow") developed techniques and tools such as lassoing and the lariat.
   The next chapter features cowboy clothes and equipment, which emphasized function over style and were a far cry from today's version of western wear. For example, few cowboys carried loaded pistols when they worked, and vests with deep pockets were a must. Denim did not exist until after the cowboy era. Following these two introductory chapters are fascinating sections describing the roundup on the open range, life on the trail, life on the ranch, and a poignant reflection on the legacy of the

cowboy life. The book is rounded out by a useful bibliography for those interested in reading primary sources and an index that would be useful for those using the book as a reference.

Each chapter opens with a verse from a cowboy ballad that immediately illuminates and enlivens the topic to be covered. Freedman provides specific summaries of each topic, punctuated by quotes from cowboy diaries, memoirs, interviews, and references to dime novels. Not a page is turned in the book without graphic documentation in the form of a period photograph, a line drawing, or a map. A series of four photographs displays real cowboys in the process of roping a calf. Other illustrations feature cowboys around a chuck wagon, posing in their best "duds," showing off their spurs at a roundup camp, breaking a wild bronco, branding cattle, crossing rivers, loading stock cars, and engaging in other typical activities. Other pictures and photographs document the typical environment and living conditions of cowboys: various scenes of the ranch and range, rooms and line camps, and camps on the trail.

One strength of the book is Freedman's use of primary source material throughout. This documentation gives the book a sense of authenticity, and, despite the third-person narration, readers will feel the immediacy of hearing real cowboys reminisce and describe, with great fondness and feeling, their lives of high adventure and camaraderie.

Analysis

In Freedman's biographical note, the author says that he "became a cowboy at an early age" while he was growing up in California during the Great Depression. As a boy, he was a voracious reader of dime novels about the cowboy. As a result, he thought a cowboy was a "fellow who says 'yup' and 'nope,' who never complains, who shoots straight and whose horse comes when he whistles." A few decades later, when he began research for this book, he found that many of his romantic notions about the cowboy were contradicted by the facts.

Nevertheless, Freedman's love of cowboy lore has clearly survived the correction of his misconceptions. He clearly admires the real cowboy who can be found beneath the veneer of the dime store novel and Hollywood Western. He writes with great respect about the realities of life on the range.

As a distinguished, award-winning biographer and historian, Freedman shows a concern with historical accuracy throughout the text. The book is like a documentary, and Freedman tries to let primary materials such as photographs and etchings, diary entries and interview excerpts, do most of the work of describing cowboy life. Despite the book's factual tone, *Cowboys of the Wild West* makes history comes alive through personal stories and specific details that paint an engaging and complete picture of the cowboy's world. The author pays scrupulous attention to the realities of the ranch and the range. These realities serve to debunk many myths of the West, while at the same time inviting the reader to experience both the hardship and the allure of working sixteen hours a day in the saddle and sleeping with one's outfit under the stars after yet another supper of boiled beans, biscuits, and prunes.

The book thoroughly covers its proposed topics. For example, when Freedman intends to describe the design and contents of the typical chuck wagon, he does so down to the typical medicines the cook would carry and administer and the cowhide "caboose" that was slung underneath the wagon to carry kindling. When he outlines a typical day on the trail, he starts before daybreak with the lighting of the cooking fire and continues through the routine and potential crises of the day such as river crossings, dust, American Indians, and people demanding tolls. He does not stop until the following night, with lively scenarios of both a typical watch and one on which problems such as predators or a night stampede have to be overcome. This specificity forcefully drives home the reality of life for a line rider on a Texas ranch or for a wrangler on his first trip up the Chisholm trail.

Freedman achieves much in this slim volume: The book can be praised as both an interesting overview and a specific look at central topics regarding cowboy life.

Critical Context

Russell Freedman, a former journalist, has written dozens of books on topics ranging from animal behavior to the daily lives of various cultural groups and prominent Americans. He is considered one of the foremost contributors to children's and young adult nonfiction writing.

Cowboys of the Wild West is a solid contribution to historical nonfiction and fills an important niche that is of interest to young adults. Although it did not receive the critical acclaim of many of Freedman's previous and subsequent efforts, reviews of the book were strong, and it stills enjoys a wide readership and considerable play in school book clubs and other forums.

Freedman's book *Children of the Wild West* (1983) won the Western Heritage Award and was selected as an American Library Association (ALA) Notable Book for Children. *Cowboys of the Wild West* is a sequel that takes a look at a topic of more general interest. Freedman's subsequent writings continued to be highly distinguished, and he won a Newbery Medal for *Lincoln: A Photobiography* (1987). His book *An Indian Winter* (1992), which chronicles the Mandèan experience in the winter of 1833, was cited as an ALA Best Book for Young Adults, an ALA Notable Book for Children, an IRA Teachers Choice, and a notable trade book in the field of social studies. In 1993, *Eleanor Roosevelt: A Life of Discovery* won these same awards and was also a *Booklist* Editors' Choice and was listed among the *School Library Journal* Best Books. With *Kids at Work: Lewis Hine and the Crusade Against Child Labor* (1994), Freedman continued his use of photography and first-person excerpts to create a powerful depiction of the life of child laborers. *Cowboys of the Wild West*, like the body of Freedman's nonfiction work, demonstrates that rigorous historical documentaries can be written that are engaging and informative for young adults and that make a significant contribution to an understanding of past eras and ways of life.

Jeffrey D. Wilhelm

CRACKER JACKSON

Author: Betsy Byars (1928-   )
First published: 1985
Type of work: Novel
Type of plot: Social realism
Time of work: The 1980's
Locale: The Midwestern United States
Subjects: Coming-of-age, family, friendship, and social issues
Recommended ages: 10-13

> *Cracker Jackson Hunter, an eleven-year-old boy, faces an adult problem as he tries to protect his former babysitter and her infant daughter from her abusive husband.*

Principal characters:
"CRACKER" JACKSON HUNTER, a sensitive and serious boy who lives
    with his divorced mother
RALPH "GOAT" McMILLAN, Cracker's mischievous best friend
ALMA ALTON, Cracker's naïve and vulnerable former babysitter
BILLY RAY ALTON, Alma's abusive husband
KAY HUNTER, Cracker's overprotective mother
MR. HUNTER, Cracker's father, who is divorced from his mother

Form and Content

    Cracker Jackson provides an accurate portrayal of domestic violence and its effects not only on the victims themselves but also on all those who are exposed to it. Betsy Byars combines this grim subject with a compassionate and humorous portrayal of the simpler problems that Cracker and his trouble-making friend, Goat, face in their everyday lives. This mixture of humor and grim reality allows young readers to gain an insight into a serious social issue. The setting is deliberately vague, since the story could, and does, occur throughout the United States.
    As the story opens, Cracker's pleasure at receiving a letter in the mail quickly vanishes when he reads the anonymous message, "Keep away, Cracker, or he'll kill you." He immediately realizes that the letter is from his former babysitter, Alma, the only person who ever called him Cracker. Worried about Alma, he visits her while her husband, Billy Ray, is out. When Cracker mentions her bruises, Alma covers up with many excuses, denying that Billy Ray has ever hurt her. Her excessive fear when Billy Ray suddenly returns and her comment that he has inherited his father's bad temper contradict this claim.
    Realizing that Alma's situation is very serious, Cracker tries to convince his parents that Billy Ray is abusing Alma, but they warn him not to interfere. Unable to find adult assistance, he enlists the aid of Goat to keep an eye on Alma. Goat visits Alma's house pretending to collect for UNICEF and reports that she looks terrible, with bruises and

marks on her face. Cracker's mother, however, who sees Alma a while later, continues to insist that everything is fine. In fact, she reports that Alma is glowing.

One morning, Alma calls Cracker in tears, admitting that Billy Ray often hits her. She has been driven to seek help this time, however, because he also hit their baby, Nicole. She is afraid to turn to anyone except Cracker. Cracker concocts a plan to borrow his mother's car so that he can drive Alma to Avondale, a town twenty-six miles away that has a shelter for battered women. With much difficulty and the help of some pillows, he and Goat manage to pick up Alma and find the road to Avondale. Unfortunately, when they are about halfway there, Alma reconsiders, deciding that she should go back to Billy Ray. Both Goat and Cracker try to stop her, but she insists. Cracker manages to make it home without damaging the car. The incident affects him deeply: He believes that this aborted heroic act has turned him into a failure.

At Cracker's insistence, his mother makes an appointment for Alma to visit her, insisting that Cracker leave the house while they talk. Cracker, spying from a distance to see if Alma seems all right, becomes increasingly upset when she does not appear, since she has always been punctual. Suddenly, his mother rushes out of the house, driving away quickly. Convinced that something is wrong, Cracker races to Alma's house. When he gets there, the house is a shambles. A neighbor informs him that Alma and Nicole have been taken to the hospital.

Alma has broken ribs, while Nicole has a concussion. Alma finally makes the decision to go to the shelter in Avondale. When Cracker's father returns home for a weekend, the family drives Alma to Avondale. The story ends as it begins, with a letter from Alma. She tells him that she has a job and is feeling a little better. It closes, "I love you, Alma."

Analysis

Cracker Jackson discusses many themes that are important to a young reader. First, it provides an accurate description of domestic violence. The reader gains insight into the development and behavior patterns involved in spousal abuse. While it is obvious that Billy Ray, with his unstable and explosive personality, is dangerous, the story also describes the changes that took place in Billy Ray as he acquired adult pressures and responsibilities. Cracker sadly remembers him as once being fun-loving and laughing. The novel is even more compelling in its portrayal of the victim, Alma. She is a good, caring person, but she is totally dominated by Billy Ray's violence. Her excuses and justifications allow the situation to continue. She proves unable, and in fact unwilling, to defend herself—and even more important, her baby—until tragedy occurs. The cyclical pattern of domestic violence becomes apparent when Billy Ray's mother tells Alma that there is nothing wrong with a man hitting his wife. To prove this, she describes how Billy Ray's father used to hit her, until his arthritis got too bad.

Cracker Jackson also describes a boy's introduction to the serious problems that may come with adulthood. Cracker tries valiantly to cope with the adult responsibilities that Alma has forced upon him. Ironically, his efforts are hindered by the adults around him. Cracker and Goat try to do what is right, in spite of the rules of the adult world. They provide both the moral and the logical core of the novel. During the aborted drive to Avondale, when Alma pleads for advice, Goat insists that she must leave Billy Ray before he kills her. Unfortunately, she ignores him. Later, she wishes that someone would have warned her about what might happen.

Betsy Byars develops this coming-of-age theme by blending humor with tragedy. She contrasts the everyday problems that Cracker and Goat face in school and at home with the harsh reality of Alma's situation; Cracker notes that his parents' divorce has not affected him nearly as much as the situation with Alma. The boys' problems are amusing, which only magnifies the grim nature of Alma's predicament. The first chapter illustrates this combination, comparing the two anonymous letters that Cracker has received in his life. The first—which said, "You stink"—had been left on his desk in first grade. He dealt with this situation by uncovering his tormentor in an ingenious and humorous manner. The second anonymous letter, however, brings Cracker face to face with an adult problem that he cannot solve on his own with a clever strategy.

Another subtheme in *Cracker Jackson* is the fallible and imperfect nature of adults, who often create more problems than they solve. Many of Byars' books focus on children who either choose to or are forced to solve problems on their own, or with the aid of their peers rather than with adult help, usually because of adult indifference, neglect, or abandonment. Alma, the beloved babysitter, is immature and naïve. She collects Barbie dolls for her daughter, Nicole, hoping someday to provide her with every Barbie ever made, and clings to the idea that a fortune teller can guide her out of this problem. Eventually, she places Cracker in an impossible situation. Even Cracker's parents, the more responsible adults, are also flawed. Both prove unwilling, at first, to deal with the problem of abuse. Cracker notes that his mother spends her time worrying about all the wrong things: razor blades in Halloween candy, diseases in rest rooms. Her code of "proper" behavior seems frivolous now that he is faced with Billy Ray's violence. His father's inability to take anything seriously has caused the divorce and left Cracker unable to turn to him in a crisis. Cracker must struggle to find answers within himself.

Critical Context

Betsy Byars consistently writes popular, realistic novels for middle-school readers. Her books have won numerous awards, including the Newbery Medal for *The Summer of the Swans* (1971). Many of her novels deal realistically and uncompromisingly with problems caused by the fragmented modern family, disrupted because of death, neglect, divorce, or abandonment. Although her characters are forced at times to cope with a difficult, or even insoluble, situation, Byars does not resort to formulaic happy endings. In *The Night Swimmers* (1980), a young girl struggles to care for her two younger brothers after their mother's death. *The Pinballs* (1977) deals with child abuse. *The Summer of the Swans* describes coping with a retarded sibling. *The Not Just Anybody Family* (1986) is the first of a series of novels featuring the trials of a family living on the edge of poverty. Byars never compromises the integrity of her

story by making reality more pleasant; instead, she uses humor, sympathetic characters, and convincing dialogue to explore the changing roles of children in society.

Mary Mahony

THE CRAZY HORSE ELECTRIC GAME

Author: Chris Crutcher (1946-   )
First published: 1987
Type of work: Novel
Type of plot: Social realism
Time of work: The late 1980's
Locale: Coho, a small Montana town, and a private school in Oakland, California
Subjects: Death, family, friendship, health and illness, and sports
Recommended ages: 13-18

Willie Weaver loses his athletic prowess and his self-image in a boating accident, then learns that what makes life valuable is meeting a challenge head on and becoming a better person as a result of the struggle to survive.

Principal characters:
> WILLIE WEAVER, a seventeen-year-old golden boy athlete who tries to come to grips with a debilitating handicap
> JENNY BLACKBURN, a seventeen-year-old beautiful athlete who is Willie's best friend as well as his girlfriend
> JOHNNY RIVERS, a seventeen-year-old with a rapier-like wit who plays baseball with Willie and who is liked by everyone
> WILL WEAVER, SR., Willie's father, who has a stubborn streak and who attempts to live his life through Willie
> LACEY CASTEEL, a kind-hearted pimp in Oakland who gives Willie a place to live
> LISA, a dedicated physical education teacher who helps Willie overcome his handicap through visualization and hard work
> SAMMY, a martial arts teacher who shows Willie how to unify his mind and body in order to defend himself

Form and Content

Using a seventeen-year-old golden boy athlete, Chris Crutcher weaves a realistic story about how fate rules life in *The Crazy Horse Electric Game.* The novel follows Willie Weaver from the height of his popularity as a baseball hero, which ends in a tragic boating accident, through the rebuilding of his life in Oakland, California, at the One More Last Chance High School. Crutcher uses short chapters, an easy-to-follow plot, strong characterization, and foreshadowing to hook and maintain the reader's interest. The third-person narration allows the reader to see inside the minds of the characters, feeling their emotions and drawing the reader into the nightmare that has become reality for Willie.

The game is a watershed event in Willie Weaver's life. His controlled pitching and awesome final catch take the championship away from the three-time winning team,

Crazy Horse Electric. He becomes the star player for Sampson Floral and the town hero. In the blink of an eye, however, Willie's life and the lives of his friends and family change forever. A water skiing accident leaves the left side of Willie's body paralyzed, impairing his speech and movement.

Lost in a world that he no longer knows, in a body that he no longer controls, Willie struggles to overcome his confusion and frustration by trying to play racquetball, managing the girls' basketball team, talking to a psychologist, participating in speech therapy, and going out with friends. The decisions that he makes are based on his emotions and have disastrous consequences. He simply cannot find the strength to face what his life has become.

Arriving home from school one afternoon, Willie hears his parents arguing and comparing his accident to his baby sister's death six years earlier from sudden infant death syndrome (SIDS). When Willie hears his father say, "It would have been better if he would have drowned," he realizes that he will not be able to overcome his disability in Coho. Willie packs a few things, takes some money, and boards the first Greyhound bus headed west, disappearing from the life that he always knew.

After changing buses several times to avoid being found, Willie ends up on the seedy side of Oakland, California. He has been beaten, robbed, and left for dead when a bus driver, Lacey Casteel, picks him up and buys him something to eat. Willie tells Lacey of his trouble, and Lacey offers him a place to stay for the night. Willie, broke and beaten, knows that Lacey is his only hope for survival and offers to work for him in exchange for room and board. Lacey agrees, and Willie soon realizes that his new acquaintance is a pimp who drives a bus as a cover. When they become friends, Lacey tells Willie about the son that he almost beat to death, leaving him retarded and living in an institution. Together, Lacey and Willie make great strides to heal their past hurts and cope with the pain of loss.

Lacey insists that Willie go to One More Last Chance High School, an alternative school for students with problems, which proves to be what Willie needs to accept himself and overcome the effects of his tragic accident. The people whom Willie meets and the difficult situations that he encounters there help him change his life by channeling his fear and anger into his rehabilitation.

After graduation, Willie returns home a whole person, ready to deal with the demons of his past. His best friend Johnny welcomes him with open arms and invites Willie to stay with him. Willie finds his father living in a rented room drinking himself to death and his mother remarried. His father gives him the Harley Davidson motorcycle that they used to ride together, and Willie rides back to Oakland.

Analysis

The knowledge that Willie gains in *The Crazy Horse Electric Game* parallels real life. Even though the trials that Willie faces may be more severe than those most teenagers encounter, the way in which he handles them is realistic. This novel illustrates the difficult decisions and choices that young adults in today's society must make, as well as the consequences those choices may bring.

Both the cover and the title of the book allude to baseball, and the main character achieves the goal dreamed of by every athlete. After Willie loses his identity as the golden boy athlete who has everything, he struggles to find himself in a society of which he no longer feels a part. This situation parallels the plight of many teenagers who struggle with the need to understand how they fit into the world and prove to themselves and others that they are people of value. Like Willie, most teenagers who take drugs, run away, skip school, or act as if nothing matters to them are wearing a mask designed to cover up the lack of control that they have over their lives. They assume that it is easier to hide their true feelings than to take the risk of being themselves. Reading about Willie's life may help them understand this feeling. Young adults feel his pain and sense of confusion and uncertainty, allowing them to see a glimpse of themselves in someone else's life.

Overcoming the loss of a loved one is difficult, and each member of Willie's family deals with the death of his six-month-old sister, Missy, differently: His father refuses to talk about Missy, denying her existence; his mother becomes depressed, taking no interest in anyone or anything; and Willie tries to remember her and the love that he felt for her, which his guilt about her death does not often allow him to do. Crutcher uses Willie's family to illustrate the effect that death has on families, as well as the fact that people have diverse ways of dealing with their grief.

Another difficult lesson that young adults must learn is accepting the good that life has to offer as well as the bad, and making the most out of either. Willie accepted the fact that he was a good athlete, well liked, and with a family that loved him, but when life dealt him a bad hand, he folded. He blamed others for his accident, hid himself from the people who wanted to help him, and refused to accept the responsibility for his own recovery, becoming bitter and angry. Willie learned at One More Last Chance High School that life goes on, and that learning to live with his disability made his life worthy of honor. He realized that everything that happens in a person's life is a part of who they are and that his sister and his athletic ability will always remain a part of him in the form of treasured memories.

Critical Context

The Crazy Horse Electric Game was the third book that Chris Crutcher published in a four-year period. His novels for young adults are about troubled teenagers with heartbreaking problems, and Crutcher deals with them in a realistic fashion; therefore, his books do not have "happily ever after" endings. His novels satisfy a need in young adult literature for stories with strong male characters, and the fact that his characters are athletes is a draw to often-reluctant male readers.

Crutcher confronts serious, controversial problems head on in his novels about teenagers who are coming-of-age. *Running Loose* (1983) deals with racial prejudice and the strength that one must have to stand up for personal beliefs. *Stotan* (1986) confronts the issue of physical abuse and white supremacist groups. *Chinese Handcuffs* (1989) breaks the silence on sexual abuse and suicide. *Staying Fat for Sarah Byrnes* (1993) brings to the light the teenagers who are not welcomed by the society in which they live. *Ironman* (1994) allows the reader to see how anger and control can shape lives. Crutcher's characters deal with reality in a sensitive, honest manner, learning to make the best of a bad situation.

Susan Y. Geye

CRIMES OF THE HEART

Author: Beth Henley (1952-   )
First presented: 1979
First published: 1981
Type of work: Drama
Type of plot: Domestic realism
Time of work: Fall, 1974, five years after Hurricane Camille
Locale: The MaGrath kitchen, in Hazlehurst, Mississippi
Subjects: Emotions, family, sexual issues, and suicide
Recommended ages: 15-18

After a "real bad day," three sisters learn that they are not alone and that brief moments of happiness are enough to make life worth living.

   Principal characters:
   LENNY MAGRATH, the matronly oldest sister, whose birthday is
       forgotten
   MEG MAGRATH, the favored middle sister, who returns home after a
       failed attempt at becoming a singer in California
   BABE BOTRELLE, the youngest sister, who shoots her husband because
       she does not like his looks
   CHICK BOYLE, the sisters' cousin, who is overly concerned with
       keeping up appearances
   BARNETTE LLOYD, Babe's lawyer, who seeks a personal vendetta
       against Babe's husband

Form and Content

   Crimes of the Heart is a play in three acts about three sisters—Lenny MaGrath, Meg MaGrath, and Babe Botrelle—who find life to be too difficult sometimes but who discover the courage and strength to overcome the "real bad days." As a dysfunctional family living in a small Southern town, the MaGrath sisters unite to fight one another's battles against an abusive husband, a failing career, and a sick, domineering grandfather. The secret to handling the really tough days lies in an understanding of their mother's suicide. As they reminisce about their childhood, they discover that their friendship binds them together so that they are not alone.

   Nothing seems to be going well for these sisters. Lenny's birthday has been forgotten by everyone except her snobby cousin Chick, who gives her a box of candies from last Christmas. Claiming that she does not like her husband's looks, Babe shot her husband and has just been released on bail. Unfortunately, her husband has pictures of her and Willie Jay, a fifteen-year-old African American boy with whom she was having an affair. Although the most joyous moment seems to be Meg's first return to Hazlehurst in five years, she admits that her singing career in California was a failure that she has been working in a dog food factory.

The MaGrath sisters are consumed by their mother's suicide, in which she hanged both herself and her cat, for which they can find no reason. All of them believe that a connection exists between their current troubles and this tragic event. At first, insanity seems to be the cause of their problems: Meg accuses Lenny of being obsessed with having a shrunken ovary, Lenny accuses Babe of being sick in the head, and Meg admits to having spent time in a psychiatric ward. Even though they think that they are peculiar, the sisters realize that they have one thing in common with the rest of humanity: the need to talk about problems, which Meg describes as a human need at the end of act 1. The ability to communicate with others will serve as a foundation for understanding their struggles. The MaGrath sisters strengthen their bond as Babe explains her reasons for shooting her husband, a bond that will eventually lead them to a revelation concerning their mother's suicide.

The second act provides a closer look at Lenny, Meg, and Babe. Babe remains the incorrigible flirt even when discussing the details of her husband's shooting. Meg attempts to maintain her loose reputation by going out with a married man rather than spending the evening playing cards with her sisters. Lenny's motherly concern for her wayward sisters, as she offers unwanted advice to Meg, illustrates her loneliness and frustration about staying home to take care of their grandfather.

The first two acts provide solid background for the third one. Although it opens with sorrow, it ends with joy. The sisters' grandfather suffers another stroke while Meg is out all night with a now-married former boyfriend, Doc Porter. Babe's husband threatens to have her institutionalized. Then, Meg happily announces that nothing happened between her and Doc. Lawyer Barnette Lloyd tells Babe that he plans to cut a deal with her husband, so she will not be tried for attempted murder. Lenny decides to call her lost love for a date, and he gladly accepts. Among all this rejoicing, surprisingly, Babe unsuccessfully attempts to kill herself. Her failed suicide attempt becomes the key to explaining their mother's suicide. Babe realizes that her mother killed herself not because she suffered from a broken heart or family problems but because she was having a "real bad day" and that she hanged the cat too so she would not be alone. Babe's epiphany proves to be the tie that binds the MaGrath sisters at the end of the play as they finally celebrate Lenny's forgotten birthday one day late.

Analysis

Beth Henley does not easily disclose the meaning of her play's title. Instead, she requires that the audience search for the meaning in the characters. A paradox exists between the play's title, *Crimes of the Heart*, and its genre, comedy. The characters constant references to illness, insanity, and incompetence suggests that the crime might be found in some form of incompleteness. The restoration of the sisters' relationships with one another and Babe's understanding of her mother's suicide (a key event for all three sisters) emphasize that the work is indeed comedic, not tragic.

The MaGrath sisters would not be considered normal by most people, yet their ability to work out their problems demonstrates that they might be better than normal. Although these women lead challenging lives, they maintain uncomplicated attitudes toward life. Babe's crime does not seem to change her quality of innocence; she is still the flirtatious and pampered little sister. Meg discovers that even though she failed as a singer in California, she has learned to care about someone other than herself. When Lenny overcomes her fear of rejection because of a physical problem (a shrunken ovary), she glows with young love. The sisters learn these things because they have been brought together on a "real bad day," as Babe says. Each sister faces a seemingly insurmountable defeat at the beginning of the play but wins her battle because she has two sisters to support her.

Perhaps the crime that Henley speaks of is committed not by one of the MaGrath sisters but by their cousin, whose constant emphasis on the family's social standing surpasses her ability for, or interest in, compassion. Although accepted by society as the most normal member of the family, Chick shows an insensitivity to her cousins that provides a comical contrast to the condemnation society presents the sisters. The MaGrath sisters are all guilty of some crime, legal or emotional—Babe's shooting, Meg's leaving of Doc Porter in a hurricane to go to California, and Lenny's rejection of men because of a physical abnormality. Their initial reaction is to blame everything on their mother's suicide. When Babe determines the reason for the suicide, they find a moment of joyous laughter. Babe's epiphany seems to encourage them to take responsibility for their own lives, which is most clearly seen in Lenny's decision to find a beau.

Although the situations portrayed in the play seem a bit unusual, there is an enchanting quality of realism. When Meg returns from her evening with Doc Porter to find her two sisters laughing about their grandfather's stroke, the listener/reader also smiles. The sisters know that their grandfather is very ill, yet their laughter seems quite natural. They are weary from a long day of legal battles, a snobby cousin, and a night at the hospital. Lenny and Babe's hysterical fits of laughter are more believable than any amount of tears. Another example of the realism in the play is seen when Lenny argues with Meg for eating her birthday candy. Lenny is not upset by her partially eaten gift but by Meg's insensitivity. Like many people, Lenny relieves her frustration by becoming angry about an insignificant event. This realism not only captures the audience's attention but also creates a bond with the character —an essential link in order to understand the play.

The play encourages young adults to work through tough problems, even ones that seem insolvable. Codependency and divorce are personal experiences for many young adults, and the MaGrath sisters offer a glimmer of hope. The answer seems to be more than simple survival through the days when everything that can go wrong actually does. Henley might be offering an alternative to a crime of the heart: friendship. For the sisters, this friendship is a pleasant surprise. Both the audience and the characters know that the moment of happiness that the sisters share at the end of the play is fleeting. Nevertheless, the MaGrath sisters believe that they need these moments to live a life free of crime.

Critical Context

Crimes of the Heart is Beth Henley's most significant work, for which she won a Pulitzer Prize and the New York Drama Critics Circle Award for Best American Play in 1981. The success of this play has been compared with the works of other Southern writers, such as Tennessee Williams, Eudora Welty, and Flannery O'Connor. Although Henley's subsequent plays did not achieve this level of success, she produced several of them as screenplays, including *Crimes of the Heart* (1986), *Nobody's Fool* (1986), and *Miss Firecracker* (1989).

Julie Nell Aipperspach

THE CRUCIBLE

Author: Arthur Miller (1915-   )
First presented: 1953
First published: 1953
Type of work: Drama
Type of plot: Allegory
Time of work: 1692
Locale: Salem, Massachusetts
Subjects: Politics and law, religion, sexual issues, and the supernatural
Recommended ages: 13-18

A group of young women falsely accuse people of witchcraft, sparking trials that would lead to several executions.

> *Principal characters:*
> JOHN PROCTOR, a farmer who opposes the witch trials
> ABIGAIL WILLIAMS, a seventeen-year-old girl, the ringleader among the accusers and Proctor's former lover
> REVEREND SAMUEL PARRIS, the local minister, who pushes the trials forward to increase his power in the community
> REVEREND HALE, a respected authority on witchcraft who gradually realizes that the trials are wrong

Form and Content

The Crucible is based on actual persons and events. While some dialogue and characterizations are based on legal records of the Salem witch trials, other details crucial to the play are inventions or suppositions by the author. The published version of *The Crucible* includes occasional prose discussions of the characters and themes that are not part of the play in performance. The play as published begins with several pages describing the Puritan environment in which the events take place. Arthur Miller explains that the witch trials occurred because of a theocratic government that repressed individual freedom.

The play opens in the home of Reverend Samuel Parris, where his daughter Betty is suffering from a mysterious ailment. Parris had discovered Betty and his niece Abigail Williams dancing naked in the forest and fears that Betty's ailment is supernatural in origin. Other Salemites—including Ann Putnam, who has lost several children—believe that witchcraft has been responsible for local misfortunes. The girls have, in fact, been playing at witchcraft, a crime that carries a penalty of death. In order to protect themselves from punishment, the girls confess that they were under the spell of other witches within the community, and they provide Parris with the names of those witches. Parris is a vain man who seeks to be the central power within the community. His sermons have more often concerned his desires for increased pay and gold candlesticks than spiritual or moral lessons. Lately, his congregation has developed a faction opposed to his authority. Parris sees the girls' accusations as a chance to regain the power that he has lost.

One of Parris' most vocal critics has been John Proctor, a farmer. Abigail had been a servant for Proctor and his wife, Elizabeth, until Elizabeth discovered that Proctor was having an affair with Abigail. Abigail still harbors a hatred for Elizabeth, and, as the trials progress, Elizabeth becomes one of the accused. In a scene that Miller added after the play was first produced, Proctor confronts Abigail after the arrest of Elizabeth, only to discover that Abigail has become insane.

Before long, many of the most respected citizens of Salem—especially Rebecca Nurse and Giles Corey—have been condemned or executed. Proctor defends his wife before the tribunal and even confesses his adultery, a ploy that fails because Elizabeth, not aware of his confession, denies her husband's sin in order to protect him. The Proctors' current servant, Mary Warren, who is also one of the accusers, knows Elizabeth to be innocent but lacks the courage to reveal the trials as a sham. The trials have become a self-justifying institution; anyone who attempts to oppose them instantly faces the accusation of witchcraft, and to be accused is to be assumed guilty. Proctor's defense sways Reverend Hale, a minister from a neighboring community, but even Hale cannot save Proctor from being placed under a sentence of death.

Those condemned for witchcraft can save themselves by confessing their guilt and naming other witches (thereby validating the trials). As Proctor and others await their executions, Hale pleads with them to confess because he knows their condemnations to be unjust. After much prodding, Proctor agrees to confess but refuses to name others. In the end, he goes offstage to be hanged.

Analysis

A primary inspiration for *The Crucible* was the search by the U.S. Congress for "communist sympathizers" in the 1950's, the time when Miller was writing the play. Those hearings were often denounced as a "witch-hunt," and audiences in 1953 instantly recognized the implied analogy between the Salem witch trials and the current "red scare." In both cases, accused persons were assumed to be guilty but, ironically, were excused from punishment if they were willing to accuse others. Many critics attacked Miller's analogy with an argument that there are communists in America but no witches. Miller's counterargument was that, regardless of whether witchcraft actually works, there are people who practice witchcraft. (In the play, Abigail has put a hex on Elizabeth.) Although many details in *The Crucible* are invented for dramatic purposes, such as the affair between Proctor and Abigail, the play can serve for young people as a powerful illustration of how paranoia can affect history.

It would be a mistake, however, to limit the play's relevance to the Salem trials or to the congressional hearings. Miller wants the audience to respond to the play's themes on a more universal level. He is perhaps primarily concerned with the conflict of the needs of society with those of the individual. It is the repressive atmosphere in which Abigail lives that causes her to rebel—by having an affair, by dancing naked in the woods, by experimenting with witchcraft. The society's need for order places Abigail in jeopardy, and she exploits that need for order by offering Salem with scapegoats for its problems. In such an environment, the need for order becomes a force that is beyond the power of individuals to control. Once the accusations have been made and the trials set in motion, any attempt to question the validity of the process is met with punishment. Miller's basic theme is central to American literature. The United States has a society based on individualism. Americans place primary emphasis on individual liberty, but any society must have restrictions if it is to have order. Within that paradox lies a central problem of defining the place of the individual in society. The question is further complicated because the forces of society (the trials) may be corrupted by self-interest (Parris).

Teenage readers and playgoers, more than anything else, probably relate to the characters' sense of helplessness. Many believe that parents, teachers, ministers, and other authority figures are arbitrarily restricting their individuality and their freedom. In its treatment of rebellion and repression, *The Crucible* presents its audience with a complex puzzle. Proctor is certainly right to oppose the trials and even to oppose Reverend Parris' vain and self-centered rule. It is Proctor's affair with Abigail, however, that places Elizabeth in jeopardy, and it is the rebellion of Abigail, Betty, and their friends that sets the tragic events in motion. Thus, rebellion against the trials is good (if ineffective), but the trials may not have existed in the first place without rebellion.

Critical Context

The Crucible draws on a long tradition of American writing. When the Puritans settled in the New World, they imagined themselves bringing the light of religion and civilization into a dark land ruled by the devil. The woods quickly became a symbol of ever-present temptation. The devil was always lurking just outside of the community, waiting to prey on those who wandered away from the light. Miller picks up on that belief by having Abigail and her friends go into the woods to dance and play at being witches. Those interested in these themes should read William Bradford's *History of Plimmoth Plantation* (1630-1651), which discusses how and why the Pilgrims came to America, or Mary Rowlandson's 1682 account of being tested by the devil while she was held captive in the wilderness.

The Crucible owes perhaps its greatest debt to Nathaniel Hawthorne. Hawthorne also drew on Puritan culture as a setting for allegories that placed the individual in conflict with society. Young Goodman Brown (in the 1835 short story of that name) discovers in the woods that everyone in town, despite an outward purity, is a worshipper of the devil. In Hawthorne's novel *The Scarlet Letter* (1850), Hester Prynne stands alone against society (as Proctor does in *The Crucible*), while Arthur Dimmesdale (like Mary Warren) lacks the fortitude to confess his sins publicly.

The theme of individualism in conflict with society can be found in a variety of American literature. In James Fenimore Cooper's novel *The Pioneers* (1823), for example, the rugged individualist Natty Bumppo runs afoul of the westward march of civilization when he is arrested for hunting deer out of season. Bumppo appears in four subsequent novels with similar themes, collectively known as the Leatherstocking Tales, and he is among the first incarnations of the classic American hero, who is always an individual apart from (and often against) the larger society. For another important perspective, readers should seek out Henry David Thoreau's essay "Civil Disobedience" (1849), which is also known as "Resistance to Civil Government," in which Thoreau argues that the individual has not only a right but also a duty to oppose unjust actions of the government. Thoreau makes the individual conscience a higher moral authority than the law.

Christian L. Pyle

CUSTARD AND COMPANY

Author: Ogden Nash (1902-1971)
First published: 1980
Type of work: Poetry
Subjects: Animals and family
Recommended ages: 10-13

A collection of poems drawn from Nash's earlier books, this work deals mostly with the comic, almost nonsensical attributes of animals and the loving, frustrating relationship of parents with their children.

Form and Content

Of the eighty-four poems forming Ogden Nash's *Custard and Company*, only two concern the title character. Custard is a pet dragon belonging to Belinda, a little girl who lives in a little white house with a mouse, a kitten, and a puppy. The dragon is called Custard because the other pets think him a coward. In the first poem, "The Tale of Custard the Dragon," Custard simply longs for the safety of a "nice cage," while Ink the cat and Blink the mouse chase lions down the stairs and Mustard the dog brags of his own bravery. Yet, when a pirate—with a pistol in one hand and a cutlass in his teeth—comes through the window, Belinda and her pets cry for help. Custard, "snorting like an engine," defends his friends, quickly devouring the pirate. A celebration ensues, and although Custard is praised as a hero, the cat, dog, and mouse still insist on their own personal bravery. Custard agrees that they are truly braver than he and longs once again for a safe, comfortable place like a cage.

The second Custard poem, the longest in the book at about 125 lines, expands on the first. Since having eaten the pirate, Custard spends his days dozing comfortably on the floor, dreaming "dragon dreams" as Belinda goes about her housework. One morning as Belinda is drying the dishes, she breaks into a song about Sir Garagoyle, a wicked knight who lives in a mountain castle. Ink the cat, Blink the mouse, and Mustard the dog reassure their mistress that they are not cowardly like Custard and that should Sir Garagoyle ever threaten her, they would come to her rescue. Just then, Sir Garagoyle appears, "twice as big as a gorilla," and the three pets flee as the knight carries off Belinda to his castle. Belinda's screams rouse Custard. He calls to the others to help, but each finds an excuse to conceal its own cowardice: Mustard complains of a toothache that would prevent him from biting, Ink claims a case of mumps, and Blink cries about an ingrown whisker.

Angry, Custard takes off "like a rocket" and swoops down at Sir Garagoyle's gates. Despite the knight's threats, Custard blows down the gates and battles Sir Garagoyle, flattening him "like tin foil" with his tail. Rushing down to the cave, Custard frees the enchained Belinda and carries her back home. Ink, Blink, and Mustard happily greet the pair and then tell Custard that he has returned just in time to chase from the kitchen a rabbit who has been eating the carrots. Custard declines, reminding them that he has always been cowardly, especially of rabbits. Although his fellow pets jeer, Belinda insists that although truly a coward, Custard "makes the nicest pet."

Many of the other poems in the book, some forty or more, treat an array of animals and animal-like creatures, the "company" of the book's title. Zoo animals such as the ostrich, the turtle, the panther, the rhinoceros ("how prepoceros"), and the camel come playfully into focus one by one, followed even by an imaginary beast called the Wendigo, whose eyes are "ice and indigo."

Finally, a group of poems treats special family situations and relationships. "To the Small Boy Standing on My Shoes While I Am Wearing Them" is a typical example, showing an adult's good-humored frustration at a child's playful exuberance. Several "Uncle" poems punctuate the comedy of family life—from Uncle Ed, who has three heads, to Uncle Hannibal, who is becoming a cannibal.

Analysis

Although the book is a collection of humorous poems that seem random in arrangement, an overall unity is achieved by several strategies. Short, whimsical pieces on animals, for example, frame the Custard poems. It is as if the reader, like Belinda herself, is beginning a kind of imaginary journey through a zoo, a menagerie ranging from baby pandas to a porcupine that sat on a splinter. The first Custard poem is then followed by a series of delightful verses on domestic subjects, such as sniffles, uncles, and even clean platters. After the tale of "Custard and the Wicked Knight," the journey concludes with a few poems on humorous insects such as the praying mantis, the centipede, and the ant and comes to an end with the galloping Wapiti, which goes "hippity-hoppity" off the final page.

The book gains significance as well from the tone and content of the Custard poems. They stand at equal positions near the beginning and end of the book and sound like bedtime stories told by a parent. The most implausible events—a pirate coming nonchalantly through a window or a wicked knight at the door—occur naturally to Belinda, as to any child, in a tone devoid of surprise or improbability. These events suggest that in Belinda's world of imagination, a knight can enter while she is doing the dishes, just as lions are naturally chased downstairs by her pets. Even a "realio, trulio little pet dragon" is part of that world, without reservation or explanation.

Although the collection is primarily intended for children, many of the poems bear the unmistakable characteristics of Nash's best work. He once claimed that his true vein as a poet was to portray the petty foibles of humanity, the silly and often superficial annoyances that frustrate the average person. A few poems here directly treat the frustrations of a parent or relative dealing with children, as in "Tableau at Twilight," in which a child drops an ice cream cone into the speaker's lap. Another poem, "Can I Get You a Glass of Water? or, Please Close the Glottis After You," depicts the adult struggling with a cough, especially one that "never quite comes off."

The poet never condescends. His language is never childish. His vocabulary is richly allusive, often sophisticated, and the humor is achieved not so much by a reliance on nonsense words as on the technique of mangling a sophisticated word and fracturing the rhythm of the line. A typical example is in the poem "The Toucan," in which the bird's profile is called "prognathous," but the last line asserts that if the poet can identify a "toucan," he is reasonably sure that the reader also "can."

In all the poems, one hears Nash's characteristic voice—a wry, gentle whimsy that sees through the silliness of the everyday. Such a voice insists on the peculiar bending of a word: The ostrich of the Sahara has a neck that is long and "narra," and, in the Custard poems, the pirate comes after Belinda by climbing through the "winda."

Critical Context

As early as 1936, Ogden Nash was producing poems that centered either on children or on adults' relationship with them. In fact, "The Tale of Custard the Dragon" was originally published in that year and collected in *The Bad Parents' Garden of Verses*. Some of his most famous animal poems, such as "The Turtle," appeared even earlier, in *Hard Lines* (1931). Thus, *Custard and Company* is in effect an anthology of some of Nash's most representative work, containing as it does poems written at the beginning of his career in the early 1930's and spanning three decades to include verse published at the peak of his powers in the early 1960's.

Custard and Company shows a writer who, like James Thurber and Robert Benchley, to whom he has often been compared, holds a comic vision about life's more mundane experiences. As a humorist, Nash often scoffs at himself as a representative of the "average guy," a comic Everyman who invariably sees the incongruities in domestic relationships but never indicts the world at large or meanly satirizes it. Little in his wit suggests desperation or bitterness, only a wry awareness of life's inanities. His poetic voice is sane, tolerant, and gentle.

Edward Fiorelli

CYRANO DE BERGERAC

Author: Edmond Rostand (1868-1918)
First presented: 1897
First published: 1898 (English translation, 1898)
Type of work: Drama
Type of plot: Historical fiction
Time of work: The 1640's
Locale: Paris and a fort near Arras
Subjects: Emotions and love and romance
Recommended ages: 13-18

A famous swordsman and poet is frightened to tell the woman he loves about his feelings, so he woos her through another and then keeps his love a secret for fifteen years.

Principal characters:
CYRANO DE BERGERAC, a fiery Gascon poet, intellectual, philosopher, and swordsman who has a very large nose
ROXANE, Cyrano's beautiful cousin
CHRISTIAN DE NEUVILLETTE, a handsome but shallow new cadet in Cyrano's regiment
THE COMTE DE GUICHE, the nephew of Cardinal Richelieu
RAGEUNEAU, a baker and a patron of poets, as well as Cyrano's friend
MONTFLEURY, a fat actor who mangles the verses of playwrights

Form and Content

Cyrano de Bergerac is a five-act play written in verse. Cyrano, the main character, is a master of all the manly arts, except one—romance. He is frightened of love because he has an enormous nose, which he believes makes his appearance grotesque.

The first act begins in a theater, before the debut of a new play. Cyrano has forbidden the actor Montfleury to appear on stage for a month because he "mouths" his lines. Cyrano evicts Montfleury, shutting the play down, which offends a foppish nobleman who has come to watch. In a memorable scene, Cyrano composes a poem while fighting the young fop, ending each verse with the line "And then I hit!" At the conclusion of the duel, Cyrano receives a message from Roxane, his great love, arranging to meet her the next day at Rageuneau's bakery. Impassioned by the note, Cyrano fights a hundred assassins sent to attack him in the dark.

The second act takes place in Rageuneau's bakery. Cyrano meets Roxane and is crushed to discover that she loves Christian de Neuvillette, a new cadet in the Gascon Guards, Cyrano's regiment. She makes Cyrano promise to defend Christian from the baiting that a new cadet experiences upon joining the regiment. When they meet, Christian teases Cyrano about his nose in order to prove his bravery. Rather than fight,

Cyrano befriends Christian and tells him of Roxane's feelings. He agrees to help Christian woo Roxane by writing her love letters.

By act 3, Roxane and Christian are deeply in love, with Cyrano's ardent letters the cause of this great passion. At night, standing beneath the balcony of Roxane's home, Cyrano feeds Christian expressions of poetic love, while Roxane listens above. When Christian keeps flubbing his lines, Cyrano takes his place and stands in the shadows, actually speaking for himself, as Roxane listens and believes Cyrano to be Christian. Meanwhile, the Comte de Guiche, the nephew of Cardinal Richelieu, arrives on the scene; he also desires Roxane and has come to force her to marry him. In a scene of tremendous imagination and poetic fancy, Cyrano delays de Guiche by describing a fictitious series of trips to the moon while Christian and Roxane are married. The couple are wed, only to be parted immediately, as de Guiche announces the mobilization of their regiment. Roxane makes Christian promise to write; Cyrano ensures that he will.

The fourth act finds Cyrano and Christian fighting the Spanish army at the siege of Arras. The French are starving. A Spanish attack is expected, and the Gascon Guards do not believe that they will survive. Despite the encircling Spanish troops, Cyrano has slipped through the lines every day to post letters to Roxane. Suddenly, Roxane arrives with a wagonload of food. She confesses that the passionate letters made it impossible for her to stay away from Christian. Tired of the charade, Christian makes Cyrano promise to tell Roxane who actually wrote the letters. Just as Cyrano is about to speak, Christian is killed by a sniper. Cyrano keeps the secret of the letters to himself.

The fifth act takes place fifteen years after the battle of Arras. Roxane now lives in a nunnery. Cyrano, still her faithful friend, comes once a week to tell her gossip from the outside world. He is late to deliver his "gazette," ignoring a mortal wound that he has just suffered in a cowardly ambush. After delivering his news, Cyrano recites "Christian's" last letter from memory. Roxane realizes that Cyrano is the poetic genius whom she has loved these many years. Cyrano's wound is very grave, and he dies from it, but not before knowing that Roxane truly loves him. Roxane cries out to the heavens that she has twice lost the man she loves.

Analysis

Cyrano de Bergerac is one of the greatest plays about unrequited love in literature. It has found a resonance with audiences since it was first performed in 1897. The story of an artist and man-of-arms with a brilliant mind who is frightened of declaring his love because of his appearance has a natural appeal for many people.

The character of Cyrano is particularly attractive. His verbal skills, wit, and daring are at the same time amusing and heroic. The paradox that Cyrano presents to the viewers of the play is that of a consummate renaissance man, who, despite his abilities, is prevented from gaining the ideal love that he seeks because of a physical fault. This tension between ideal love and physical beauty is one of the driving forces of the play.

This play's development is quite unique, in that it was written in response to a request by Constant Coquelin, a famous actor of the 1890's. Coquelin begged for an opportunity to star in a role written by Edmond Rostand. The play that Rostand wrote reflects aspects of Coquelin's personality but draws heavily upon elements of the historical Cyrano. The work proved to be an immediate success, later serving as a vehicle not only for Coquelin but also for the famous actress Sarah Bernhardt, who played Roxane in a later production.

The style in which the play is written is interesting as well. It is a highly romantic piece, reminiscent of the novels written by Alexandre Dumas, *père*, thirty years before. Yet, the prevailing literary style at the time the play was written was a naturalistic, journalistic approach, drawing material from common working people. The play's style certainly is a reflection of Rostand's personality, if not Coquelin's. Rostand's approach to writing a historical work was to create a fictional world within a framework of real events, such as the Battle of Arras. He drew heavily upon what was known of the real Cyrano, then, having assessed his character, fictionalized the man in such a way that is true to the available facts and to the artistic needs of Coquelin, the actor in the play. The brilliant, brash, insufferable, inspired, idealistic Cyrano is the result. Rostand's other works all demonstrate his profoundly romantic view of life, full of passion and verve.

Cyrano de Bergerac tapped into a vein of bruised patriotism in the France of 1896. It is unashamedly Gallic and jingoistic. The fourth act, in which Roxane brings a wagon of food to the starving soldiers of the Gascon Guards, found a receptive audience in Paris, which had suffered through a horrifying siege and famine during the Franco-Prussian War of 1870-1871.

Critical Context

Edmond Rostand wrote five volumes of poetry, as well as ten other plays, but none achieved the status of *Cyrano de Bergerac*. Nevertheless, Rostand's fame has been assured by this play. It received an enthusiastic reception in the United States and has been continuously produced since its debut in 1921. The play has been made into several memorable films, in both English and French. José Ferrer won an Academy award for Best Actor for his version of *Cyrano de Bergerac* in 1950. The play has also been adapted to modern themes, in films such as *Roxanne* (1987), which very successfully translates the plot and style into a contemporary American setting.

While *Cyrano de Bergerac* has come to be considered a classic, it is infrequently taught. It retains its importance because it is a performed work, not a heavily studied but underacted play, as many of William Shakespeare's works have become.

As a play, *Cyrano de Bergerac* is a fascinating work to perform because of its characters—not only Cyrano but many of the other roles as well. The language of the play is exciting, lyrical, and frequently humorous. Rostand's melding of romantic themes, wit, and dazzling imagery goes a long way to explain its continued popularity. Yet, there is another compelling explanation: the romantic tension that the play portrays, between an unattainable woman and a man who is worthy of her favors but is physically unattractive to her, is a type of situation with which almost everyone can identify. The language of the play saves it from merely being a tale of a Frenchman with a strange nose; Rostand's (and Cyrano's) spirit elevates it to the level of a classic story of romantic, bittersweet love.

James Barbour

DARING THE UNKNOWN
A History of NASA

Author: Howard E. Smith (1927-   )
First published: 1987; illustrated
Type of work: History
Time of work: 1892-1986
Locale: Kennedy Space Center in Florida, the Soviet Union, and the moon
Subject: Science
Recommended ages: 10-18

From the earliest inventors of rocketry through the landing of an astronaut on the moon to the advent of the space shuttle, Smith chronicles humankind's first steps into space and provides insights into the main decision makers and how their decisions were made.

Principal personages:

DR. ROBERT GODDARD, an American scientist who made the first liquid fueled rockets and who is commonly called "the father of modern rocketry"

DR. WERNHER VON BRAUN, the brilliant German scientist who came to the United States following World War II and headed the U.S. rocketry program

ALAN B. SHEPARD, the first American in space, aboard the Mercury capsule *Freedom 7*

JOHN H. GLENN, JR., the first American astronaut to orbit the earth, aboard the Mercury capsule *Friendship 7*

NEIL A. ARMSTRONG, the first American astronaut to walk on the moon

SALLY RIDE, the first American woman in space, as a member of a space shuttle crew

VALENTINA TERESHKOVA, the Soviet cosmonaut who was the first woman to orbit the earth

CHRISTA MCAULIFFE, a civilian high school history teacher who was aboard the space shuttle *Challenger* when it exploded upon launch

YURI GAGARIN, the Soviet cosmonaut who was the first human to orbit the earth

GULON BLUFORD, the first African American astronaut in space, aboard the space shuttle

Form and Content

Daring the Unknown provides a historical account of the National Aeronautics and Space Administration (NASA), looking first to the early scientists, such as Robert Goddard and Wernher von Braun, who provided much of the early research and technology that culminated in the creation of the United States' space program. In thirteen chapters, Howard E. Smith presents the successes that nations and individuals have achieved in space exploration. The author also furnishes insights into the ramifications of the political decisions underlying many of NASA's accomplishments. These decisions are set against the background of the Cold War rivalry between the Soviet Union and the United States and the accomplishments made by the Soviet cosmonauts, which provided much of the incentive for the U.S. program. Complementing the narrative are sixteen color photographs and forty-two black-and-white photographs depicting the people, places, and events that constitute NASA's history.

Smith traces the history of rocketry leading up to the creation of NASA, starting with the earliest rockets invented by Chinese scientists, probably in the thirteenth century. Another early contributor to space travel discussed in the book is the Russian scientist Konstantin Tsiolkovsky, whose writings in 1895 described many of the major problems that would be faced by those traveling by rocket. The next major figure in the development of space travel was Robert Goddard. His first rocket flew from his Aunt Effie's farm near Auburn, Massachusetts, in 1926. Goddard's practical rocket research yielded the first guidance systems and fuel pumps, which are critical components of all rockets. Much of his work is still incorporated into the rockets used today. Wernher von Braun, more than any other individual, is credited with leading the world into the space age. From von Braun's earliest works in guiding the development of the V-2 rocket in Nazi Germany through his tenure as the director of NASA, his genius and vision eventually led the efforts that placed humans on the moon.

The men and women who became astronauts and cosmonauts are profiled, with brief glimpses into both their personal backgrounds and their professional lives. Thus, these larger-than-life historical figures are made into human beings with whom young readers can identify and in whose footsteps the next generation can aspire to walk. From NASA's victories with the missions of Alan Shepherd, John Glenn, and Neil Armstrong through its dark hours with the Apollo 1 fire, the Apollo 13 near-disaster, and the *Challenger* explosion, the reader is brought along with the astronaut team, learning why things occurred, who made the important decisions, and how these decisions have made a lasting impact on space exploration.

In addition to a historical account of space exploration, *Daring the Unknown* also offers considerable information about the scientific data that the various space missions have provided, including discoveries about the planets and moons in our solar system and about other, more distant, celestial bodies. Finally, NASA's plans for the space program are discussed, including such topics as "Will humans explore the neighboring planets?" "Will humans return to the moon?" and "What are the plans for the development of a space station?" Although these questions are not answered definitively, readers gain a better idea of the decision-making process that will chart NASA's course and can glimpse some of the possibilities for future space exploration.

Analysis

Many historical accounts of space exploration and rocketry has been published, a number of which concentrate on the American involvement in space. In *Daring the*

Unknown, Smith includes the classical points of rocketry history, but he also provides a number of facts not commonly discussed, such as the contributions of Tsiolkovsky. One of the more important aspects of Smith's presentation of the history of NASA is the way in which it explores some considerations not commonly found in histories of space exploration—those related to the political context within which space exploration ideas and projects form. For example, the pressures and alternatives that shaped President John F. Kennedy's decision to commit the resources of the United States "to send a man to the moon and return him safely to Earth" are explained. The Soviet Union's decision not to send cosmonauts to the moon is also described within a contemporary political framework. Most other authors disregard this perspective, choosing to focus only on the accomplishments, the "whats" of space exploration, while ignoring the "whys and hows."

Another way in which this work brings history to life is the inclusion of a number of interesting and little-known facts about important events in space exploration that many major works omit. These details include Robert Goddard's launch of his first rocket at his Aunt Effie's farm, John Glenn's descriptions of his views of Earth as he completed the first orbit ever attempted by an American astronaut, Edwin "Buzz" Aldren's taking of Holy Communion while on the moon's surface, and the description by history teacher Christa McAuliffe, the first civilian astronaut who was killed in the ill-fated launch of *Challenger* in 1986, of her training in zero gravity aboard an Air Force plane, which she jokingly referred to as "the vomit comet." Facts and accounts such as these bring a human quality to the book and to the people who were part of the history of space exploration.

In addition to its historical account, *Daring the Unknown* presents young readers with a considerable body of scientific data. The framework within which this information is presented—as the result of human endeavors and explorations—lends an air of credibility and excitement that is sometimes absent in other scientific books, which often become compendiums of unrelated facts presented out of context. Smith speculates about why certain things are as they are and how certain phenomena have come to be, furthering adding to the interest generated by this work.

Critical Context

Space exploration is a popular subject among authors of literature for young readers. Howard Smith has taken this topic and effectively expanded the context of exploration to include interesting traits of the people who were the main players in the events of space exploration. The author has also done a good job in leading the reader behind the scenes into the political considerations that drive scientific efforts.

Thus, while the events that Smith describes are those one would expect to find in a work of this type, his descriptions of the characters and occurrences that surround and shape these events offer a fresh look at that which can easily become the commonplace. Famous people are portrayed in terms that emphasize their human nature. Instead of appearing as unapproachable folk heroes, the astronauts become as real as the people next door.

Daring the Unknown is a valuable resource in several subject areas. It offers a fresh historical account of the history of NASA, and it presents scientific information in a clear, approachable fashion, successfully integrating history and science to create an interesting work for young people.

Duane Inman

THE DAWN PALACE
The Story of Medea

Author: Helen M. Hoover (1935-   )
First published: 1988
Type of work: Novel
Type of plot: Folktale, historical fiction, and moral tale
Time of work: 1300 B.C.
Locale: Ancient Greece and the Black Sea
Subjects: Gender roles, love and romance, and the supernatural
Recommended ages: 15-18

Medea falls in love with Jason and helps him achieve his goals, but he is a self-centered opportunist who exploits and betrays her love.

Principal characters:
MEDEA, the daughter of the king of Colchis who is betrayed by Jason and gains a reputation as a witch because of her superior knowledge of healing and science
JASON, the leader of the Argonauts, a self-serving adventurer, and the husband of Medea
AEETES, Medea's father and the king of Colchis
CIRCE, Aeetes' sister, reputed to be a witch, who takes over the education of Medea
HERCULES, the legendary strongman and Jason's rival, who tries to warn Medea about Jason's true nature

Form and Content
The Dawn Palace retells the classic Greek story of Medea and Jason from Medea's point of view, thus making her the heroine. The story also provides a commentary on the difficulties confronting a strong, intelligent woman trying to maintain her identity in a male-dominated world. Deserted by her mother when she is three, Medea is told by her father, King Aeetes of Colchis, that her mother died, a statement that she learns is a lie when she secretly removes the death mask from the corpse that is supposed to be her mother's. Trained by Circe to become a priestess, Medea also becomes a gifted healer by the time that she is ten years old. Circe instills in her the desire to become a lifelong learner, a role that she fulfills admirably but that gives her a range and depth of knowledge that makes some people suspect her of being a witch.

Largely ignored by her father and without her mother, Medea grows up lonely and longing for love. When Jason arrives in Colchis searching for the Golden Fleece, Medea instantly falls in love with him, helps him complete the seemingly impossible tasks that Aeetes requires him to accomplish before he can have the fleece, and runs away with Jason when he leaves Colchis with the fleece. Medea sincerely believes

Jason's oath that he will marry her and always love her, in spite of warnings from Atalanta and Hercules that Jason is a calculating adventurer concerned only with meeting his own goals by whatever means he deems necessary.

When a fleet from Colchis pursues them, Medea is shocked when Jason kills Apsystus, Aeetes' only son, under a flag of truce and throws his body to the sharks to create a diversion so that the *Argo* can escape capture, but she still continues to love Jason and aid him in his quest for power. Eventually, Jason and Medea become king and queen of Corinth, the original home of her father, Aeetes. Although Medea works hard to improve the economy and life of the people of Corinth, Jason is content to philander and take credit for Medea's accomplishments.

Medea finally realizes Jason's true character when he returns from Thebes with plans to divorce her and marry the daughter of King Creon. Jason admits that he never loved her, that he merely used to her to gain his ends. In retaliation for Jason's betrayal, Medea sets fire to Corinth and King Creon's daughter, but not before Jason kills their three youngest children. Jason eventually dies in exile, punished by the gods for his unfaithfulness. Medea, on the other hand, returns to Colchis after a period of wandering, helps return Aeetes to the throne that he has lost to her uncle Perses, and is reconciled with Aeetes. She is confident that some day her oldest son, Medeius, who survived Jason's killing spree because he was living with the centaur Chiron, will succeed Aeetes as king of Colchis. At the end of the story, in response to Aeetes' question about what was the purpose of the events that happened to them, Medea replies, "There is a pattern, a purpose, but we can't see it clearly."

Analysis

In her author's notes, Hoover contends Medea has been the victim of "bad press," which she attributes to Euripides' *Medea*, the standard source for her story. Hoover indicates that she was inspired to research the Medea story after she read a comment in Robert Graves's *The Greek Myths* stating that Euripides was paid fifteen talents by the citizens of Corinth to write a play that would absolve them of any guilt in the murder of Medea's children. Concerned that Euripides' *Medea*, which she calls "propaganda as art," has become the accepted version of the Medea story, Hoover has set out to present what she sees as a more accurate picture of Medea and Jason. Therein lies one of the problems with the novel. Unless readers are familiar with the Euripides' play or sources derived from it, they may not recognize the full extent of the revisionist nature of Hoover's account. In fact, if the book is used in classrooms, it probably should be taught in conjunction with Euripides' *Medea*.

Rather than the heroic leader of the Argonauts, Hoover's Jason is cruel, self-serving, and arrogant. He drives Hercules from the *Argo*'s crew because Hercules is a potential rival for leadership, kills Apsystus under a flag of truce, and leads Medea to believe that he loves her, although he marries her only when he sees political advantage in allying himself to someone with ties to the throne of Corinth. He also takes credit for the improvements that Medea makes in the economy of Corinth, divorces Medea to marry King Creon's daughter, and kills his own children so that they will not be rivals for his position on the throne of Corinth. In her effort to show Jason's villainous qualities, Hoover sometimes makes Medea seem naïve because of her inability to see Jason's true character.

For the most part, however, Hoover's Medea is intelligent, caring, and modest. According to Hoover, Medea's reputation as a witch grew out of her superior knowledge of medicinal herbs and science, rather than supernatural abilities. In fact, the supernatural elements of the story are minimal, a unique quality considering the role that the supernatural usually plays in Greek mythology. For example, the serpent guarding the fleece is really a rock formation, and the dragon's eyes are lamps placed inside openings in the rock formation by the priest guarding the fleece. Even the destruction of Corinth by fire is given a sound scientific basis. Medea uses potassium, which produces a flame when the beeswax protecting it from the air melts, and sodium, which bursts into flame when it comes in contact with the water in one of the palace's fountains.

Hoover builds a strong basis for her revisionist account of Medea and Jason. As Hoover mentions in her author's notes, to the classical Greek male-dominated society, Medea "would not have represented the Greek ideal of a properly ignorant and submissive female." Thus, this type of audience would have been willing to accept Euripides' account of Medea because it reinforced their preconceived views of women. By contrast, to a contemporary audience, Medea becomes a tragic figure, deprived of the throne of Colchis (even though leadership is supposed to be transmitted matriarchally), cast off by the husband whom she has always loyally served, and mourning the death of three of her children. If Medea got bad press from Euripides, she definitely gets good press from Hoover.

Hoover's author's notes provide an interesting examination of the development of the Jason and Medea story, as well as a discussion of the variations that exist in the different accounts of that Greek myth. She also provides a bibliography that would be a good starting point for readers who want to examine the story in greater detail.

Critical Context

The Dawn Palace, like many of Helen Hoover's other books, is soundly grounded in historical research, as Hoover makes clear in her author's notes. In a similar fashion, *The Lion's Cub* (1974), selected as a Children's Book of the Year by the Child Study Association of America, is based on Hoover's reading of old journals and diaries. The book presents the story of Jemal Edin Shamyl, a little boy used as a pawn by his father, the imam of Daghestan, and Nicholas I during the Wars of the Caucasus. Hoover's interest in history is also reflected in *Another Heaven, Another Earth* (1981), selected by the American Library Association as a Best Book for Young Adults; it is based on fragments of a diary and the letters of a Virginia colonist who died waiting for a ship from the Old World that never came. Readers can be assured that all of Hoover's historical fiction is grounded in research.

Ronald Barron

THE DAYS WHEN THE ANIMALS TALKED
Black American Folktales and How They Came to Be

Author: William J. Faulkner (1891-1987)
First published: 1977; illustrated
Type of work: Short fiction
Subjects: Animals, race and ethnicity, and the supernatural
Recommended ages: 13-18

Faulkner, having enjoyed listening as a child to stories about the time before he was born, recorded this collection of tales told by a former slave who was a gifted storyteller.

Form and Content

In *The Days When the Animals Talked: Black American Folktales and How They Came to Be*, William J. Faulkner retells some stories about African American life in the antebellum South, as related to him as a boy in South Carolina by his friend Simon Brown, a former slave. Part 1 of the book contains Brown's recollections of his experiences as a young slave in Virginia. His stories explore the themes of punishment, courtship, and narrow escapes. Brown also weaves yarns that teach methods for solving problems, showing slaves using their wits to gain their freedom. Some stories examine cultural history by reporting on how slaves worshiped. Others are entertaining and feature scary ghost and witch stories. Part 2 of the book is a collection of folktales with animal characters that Brown told to Faulkner.

Many themes and messages can be found in these tales, such as the danger of wishing for too much power, especially by taking on an evil form. In "The Ways of a Witch," a woman is granted her desire to become a witch. Witches can get out of their skins and fly about invisibly. One time that she did so, a nasty surprise awaited her when she got back into her skin: She found that salt and pepper had been shaken into it and were burning her raw flesh underneath. Such intense misery is frightening to young readers and serves as a moral lesson.

Another story features a traditional Christmas practice: On Christmas day when two people meet, the first one to say the greeting "Christmas gift" is entitled to receive a gift at the expense of the other person. The story "A Riddle for Freedom" examines this exchange between Jim, a slave, and his master. Jim is the first to say "Christmas gift" and declares that for his gift he wants his freedom, provided that he can come up with a riddle that his master cannot solve. The master agrees, and the riddle that the slave tells is so difficult that the master gives him his freedom, as well as the colt that Jim is riding.

The Days When the Animals Talked includes the classic story of the foot race between the rabbit and the turtle ("Brer Rabbit and Brer Cooter Race"). Brer Rabbit has a special talent in his ability to run extremely fast by comparison to the turtle. On the other hand, Brer Cooter (turtle) and Brer Snail each carries his house on his back.

Brer Rabbit offers sympathy to the turtle and the snail for being heavily loaded, while at the same time making fun of their natural condition. He laughs at the turtle for carrying his house on his back and for being so slow. Brer Rabbit then draws a comparison between the turtle and Brer Snail, who also carries his house on his back and who is the only animal that is slower, thus humiliating both animals. Brer Rabbit doubles up with laughter as he looks down at Brer Cooter, who is both hurt and angry. The turtle quotes traditional wisdom for his case: "Hold on there, Mister Smart-Aleck. . . . Don't talk too fast. The old folks say, 'An empty waggin makes a heap of fuss.' " "Waggin" is a pun: There is a play on the word "wagging" (like a wagging tongue) and "wagon" (only a sufficiently heavy load can steady a wagon over the bumpy places in a road, and an empty wagon rattles). The implication is that a mind that thinks constructively takes time to function and a full or busy mind can offer more weighty ideas than one that is empty or idle. In other words, the turtle's point can be restated as "Do not talk before thinking." The rest of the story—in which the turtle wins the foot race because of his persistence, while the rabbit loses because of his overconfidence—is familiar to many young readers.

Analysis

The stories from the slave's experience told in part 1 of *The Days When the Animals Talked* are sharply poignant. Their effect can be explained by the line in a Negro spiritual that says, "I'm so glad, trouble don't last always," offering advice about thinking a positive thought in a troubled situation. The stories in which an enslaved person is successful in his or her attempt to avoid some measure of pain are not only captivating but also instructive; they teach others in a comparable situation, facing a strong adversary, how to survive and even profit. One lesson is about giving a humane response to inhumane treatment. While it is human to react negatively to negative behavior—to show anger in response to anger, resentment in response to resentment—such reactions are excluded from the folktales. Instead, the reactions of the characters are logical and carefully worked out. There is a distinct and vibrant spirituality in the songs and Golden Rule behavior in the tales in this collection. The morning and evening prayer of Simon Brown is especially noteworthy. Various artistic qualities are found in these narratives, but many embody a constant testimony to faith in a Supreme Being and the reward of joy from acting on that faith.

One characteristic of the animal stories in part 2 is a set of unstated messages about relationships between animals, which signify relationships between people, usually between an owner and an enslaved person. Brer Rabbit is identified with a slave, which colors the interpretation of the stories in which he interacts with stronger, more secure animals. Other animals highlight specific flaws in some aspect of human character. Another message is that regardless of his shortcomings, every character is deserving of respect; each animal has the title "Brer," or brother.

These stories teach readers to see behind the surface reality, a lesson not usually taught in formal education. Instead, that skill develops as a person matures. The tales often suggest more cautious (and safer) patterns of behavior and offer a sense of community for those who feel left out. The authors of these traditional stories were slaves who were treated unfairly and often inhumanely and were without recourse when they were abused. They identified with the plight of the rabbit, who seemed to be in a comparable position. The rabbit, as food for larger and stronger animals, had to be quick-witted and fast. This allegory was extended to conclude that the rabbit was on the side of God and was virtuous, while his enemy was on the side of the Devil and was wicked.

The word choices are often interesting in these stories. While Faulkner tries to avoid diction that invites ridicule because of stereotypical regional dialects, some of the words used are unique and provide color and historical context. For example, in the place of "porch" or "veranda," Faulkner substitutes "piazza," an Italian term that reflects Southern culture and dialect. Other uncommon words flavor the reading with a rich sense of history, such as "joggling board" ("pretty girl sat down with him on the joggling board out on the piazza"). Other examples of unusual words or a regional manner of speech are "Sunday-go-to-meeting" clothes (those worn on special occasions), "sun about half-an-hour high" (a rough estimate of a point in time after dawn), and "bic-a-boom" (onomatopoeia, or a word that imitates a sound), as in "Brer Cooter was a-jumpin' in a hollow log, bic-a-boom."

Critical Context

This collection of stories can be a source of humor and thought-provoking entertainment for more mature readers who can read between the lines to see the messages, images, and meanings that underlie the surface.

Critics debated William J. Faulkner's decision regarding the use of dialect in *The Days When the Animals Talked*. Reviewers are often divided on the merits of including dialect for the sake of cultural integrity at the risk of bringing embarrassment on the users of such speech and on members of a particular culture. On the other hand is the view that one should always avoid dialect and the derision that can result. Faulkner took the middle ground between these two positions. He retained regional dialect but used synonyms for certain words that had been used for humor or derision. One reviewer accused the author of violating the integrity of the oral tradition by rejecting the heavy use of dialect and using only a sprinkling of such words and phrases. Another reviewer claimed that the author substituted some dialect in favor of standard words and patterns in order to avoid perpetuating the negative Uncle Remus stereotype.

This book was the only publication by Faulkner, an academician who should not be confused with the celebrated Southern novelist and short-story writer of the same name. The lasting impression that traditional stories had on the author is demonstrated by this collection, which was published when Faulkner was eighty-six years old and after his professional career as a minister and dean at Fisk University in Nashville, Tennessee.

Earleen De La Perriere

DEATH OF A SALESMAN

Author: Arthur Miller (1915-   )
First performed: 1949
First published: 1949
Type of work: Drama
Type of plot: Domestic realism
Time of work: The 1940's
Locale: New York City
Subjects: Death, family, jobs and work, and suicide
Recommended ages: 13-18

In dire financial and emotional straits, Willy Loman considers suicide while denying that he has been a failure as a salesman, husband, and father.

> *Principal characters:*
> WILLY LOMAN, a sixty-year-old salesman facing the end of his career and the breakup of his family
> LINDA, his wife, who tries to hold the family together
> BIFF, his older son, a former football star and aimless wanderer
> HAPPY, his younger son, a low-level businessman
> UNCLE BEN, Willy's successful older brother, a figment of Willy's imagination
> CHARLEY, Willy's prosperous brother-in-law
> BERNARD, Charley's son, an attorney
> THE WOMAN, Willy's mistress
> HOWARD WAGNER, Willy's boss

Form and Content

Death of a Salesman is a modern tragedy depicting the last days in the life of Willy Loman. When the action occurs in the present, the drama is realistic, both psychologically and emotionally. When the action is set in the past, however, the drama becomes dreamlike. Thus, in the scenes in which Willy's sons, Biff and Happy, are in high school, only Willy can see them. This flashback technique is also used to incorporate Willy's older brother Ben, the man to whom Willy turns for advice when circumstances produce a level of stress beyond which Willy can no longer function.

The story of *Death of a Salesman* is complex not only because it combines past and present but also because it grows out of a lifetime of lies and denials. Willy, unable to maintain a strenuous life on the road as a traveling salesman, seeks a steady job in New York, only to be fired by his boss, Howard Wagner, the son of the man who initially hired Willy. With unpaid bills piling up, Willy is further burdened by the return of his thirty-four-year-old son Biff, who has returned from working as a ranch hand in Texas in the hopes of finding a white-collar job in New York.

Biff and his younger brother, Happy, move back into their parents' house and lament both the loss of their innocence and their failure to realize their dreams. Only their cousin Bernard, now an attorney, has achieved success. Consequently, both brothers blame their father for misdirecting them, although their bitterness is nevertheless fraught with admiration and love.

During a family quarrel, Linda reveals to her sons that Willy has been attempting suicide, both with the car in a series of staged accidents and with a rubber pipe fastened to a gas line in the basement. Biff resolves to reform his life for the sake of his father, and act 1 closes with the familiar denial of old wounds and Biff's promise to make a business deal in New York.

In act 2, after Willy has been fired, he meets Biff and Happy at a restaurant, hoping to hear good news from Biff. Instead of the promised deal, Biff reveals that he stole the fountain pen of the man who interviewed him. Stunned, Willy retreats to the bathroom, where he relives a pivotal moment in both his and Biff's life: the time that Biff caught him in a Boston hotel room with his mistress. Crushed by his father's betrayal of his mother, Biff refused to take a course in summer school and failed to graduate, thus beginning the string of small disasters and petty thefts that have ruined his life.

Having abandoned Willy in the restaurant, the family members reunite at home, where they have a final, explosive confrontation. Biff accuses Willy of having blown him full of hot air, and Willy accuses Biff of ruining his life out of spite. Forever the peacemaker, Linda tries to quiet them and is shouted down, as is Happy. Biff throws the rubber pipe onto the table and demands to know if Willy thinks that his suicide will make a hero out of him. Willy breaks down, and he and Biff are reconciled, but, when the rest of the family trudges off to bed, Willy speeds off in his car to kill himself, hoping that the insurance money will provide Biff with the new start in life that he so desperately needs.

Analysis

Death of a Salesman raises many issues, not only of artistic form but also of thematic content. Dramatically speaking, the play represents Arthur Miller's desire to modernize the tragedy of Aristotle described in the *Poetics*. Aristotle held that tragedy portrayed the downfall of a king or noble, whose fall from grace was the result of a tragic flaw—generally held to be hubris, or an excessive amount of pride. Miller, on the other hand, believes that tragedy—or the individual's desire to realize his or her destiny—is not solely the province of royalty. It also belongs to the common man—in this case the "low man," as in Willy Loman.

Willy's tragic flaw stems from the fact that he has misinterpreted the American Dream, the belief that one can rise from rags to riches. For Willy, the success of that dream hinges on appearance rather than on substance, on wearing a white collar rather than a blue one. It is this snobbery, combined with a lack of practical knowledge, that leads to his downfall.

Indeed, much of the lasting popularity of *Death of a Salesman* both in the world of the theater and in the canon of English literature, lies in its treatment of multiple themes. Too didactic or moralistic for some modern readers, who see the author as heavy-handed, the play nevertheless raises many pertinent questions regarding American culture. Many younger readers have even credited it with preventing them from making the same mistakes committed by the characters.

Chief among these themes is an indictment of the capitalist nature of the American Dream—the belief that through the pioneer virtues of hard work, perseverance, ingenuity, and fortitude, one might find happiness through wealth. Implicit within this dream, however, is the assumption that money leads to fulfillment, regardless of the type of work that one does in order to attain it. While Willy himself was never successful as a salesman, he remains confident that his son Biff will be able to make it big in business because of his good looks and his past glory as a high school football star. Willy makes the error of celebrating popularity over know-how, style over substance. He taught Biff that being "well-liked" would carry the day, thus ignoring the damaging truth that Biff's habit of petty theft—whether it was lumber from a nearby construction site or a football from the locker room—would ultimately lead to the boy's downfall.

The way in which this theme informs the play is also the key to its form, since Willy constantly relives the past through a series of flashbacks. These scenes present Biff and Happy as they appeared in high school, providing the audience with a glimpse into the happy past that shaped the unhappy present. Another theme thus emerges: that the decisions made in youth have a direct impact on one's life in maturity. In addition, by seeing past events, the audience is forced to admit that Willy lives in a world of fantasy and denial, where he is unwilling to confront his own role in contributing to his son's unhappiness.

Indeed, the linchpin of the play surrounds an event in Willy's past, when Biff discovered his father committing an infidelity with another woman. Crushed by his newfound glimpse into the world of adults, the adolescent Biff learned that his larger-than-life father was all too human, that he was "flawed." Thrust abruptly from the world of innocence into the world of experience, Biff sabotaged his own life by refusing to attend summer school, thus preventing him from making something of himself at the university. Instead, he took a series of menial jobs and wandered aimlessly, only to return home at the age of thirty-four, unsure of both his identity and his purpose.

The play returns, then, to its examination of the American Dream, asking such fundamental questions as "What is the nature of success, and how does one attain it?" For Willy, it means wearing a suit and tie and making a lot of money—in short, it means having pride, or hubris. Yet, when Biff confronts his father in the final scene, he has an epiphany, a sudden burst of knowledge: Biff realizes that success entails working at an enjoyable job, which for him means working on a farm, outdoors, with his shirt off. The life of business and the city is not for him, and he sees his happiness in day-to-day living rather than in the goals foisted on him by society or by his father. Happy, meanwhile, lacks the courage of honesty and remains caught in the rat race, still under the impression that wealth and status are the keys to fulfillment. In a sense, *Death of a Salesman* ends on an optimistic note, in that Biff discovers a new sense of himself, stripped of illusion, as he finally becomes a man with self-respect—one who paradoxically has found pride through humility.

Willy, however, remains imprisoned by a set of false ideals. Having devoted his life to a belief in the honor of a career as a salesman, he possessed too much snobbery to admit that his own destiny was in a simple career as a carpenter. Instead, he listened to his brother Ben, that figment of his imagination who told him that money was the true path to happiness. Out of options, Willy decides that suicide is his only exit, since Biff will then collect the insurance settlement and be able to launch a career in business.

Yet, although he remains misguided, Willy achieves the stature of a tragic hero. Fighting a world pitted against him, he fulfills his destiny and sacrifices himself for his son by paying a debt in blood. The futility of his life and dreams are revealed, however, when only his immediate family attends what Willy has imagined would be a magnificent funeral, thus exposing a legacy of only disappointment and death.

Nevertheless, the end is not entirely bleak: Through his father's sacrifice Biff escapes a vicious circle of greed and self-delusion; he is freed. Accordingly, the audience experiences a catharsis—the cleansing or purgation associated with classical tragedy. The play's final lesson, then, is that destiny lies in discovering one's true identity, in following one's bliss, and in being true to one's inmost and honest self.

Critical Context

Death of a Salesman remains one of the most widely produced and widely anthologized plays in American literature, embodying many of the characteristics of classical tragedy while also updating the form through its concern with common people. Certain critics view the play as too traditional, both in its stagecraft and its moralism, ignoring as it does the more obscure techniques of absurdist or surrealist theater. Nevertheless, its enduring popularity suggests that Arthur Miller hit on themes that continue to enthrall Americans in their two-edged pursuit of happiness, finding it through money on the one hand and integrity on the other.

David Johansson

DEATHTRAP

Author: Ira Levin (1929-   )
First presented: 1978
First published: 1979
Type of work: Drama
Type of plot: Thriller
Time of work: The present
Locale: Sidney Bruhl's study in Westport, Connecticut
Subjects: Arts, crime, and sexual issues
Recommended ages: 15-18

The importance of this play lies primarily in its form, which helped to establish the "comedy thriller" and provides the reader with an example of the writing process and a handbook on how to write a commercial thriller.

Principal characters:
SIDNEY BRUHL, a middle-aged playwright who has not had a
    commercial hit in eighteen years
MYRA BRUHL, Sidney's wife
CLIFFORD ANDERSON, an attractive writing student in his mid-twenties
    who has written a highly commercial thriller
HELGA TEN DORP, an eccentric Dutch psychic
PORTER MILGRIM, Sidney's attorney

Form and Content

Deathtrap's importance stems from its success as an example of the playwright's craft of plot construction and gamesmanship. Ira Levin has succeeded in the challenge to create a new variation in a genre where all possible variations seemed to have been discovered and to discuss within the context of the play exactly what those elements are.

Act 1 begins with playwright Sidney Bruhl devastated. He is reading the manuscript for *Deathtrap*, the most commercial thriller that he has read in over a decade, and it is not his play. His wife, Myra, who has been supporting him since his last success almost twenty years ago, suggests that he collaborate with the student writer, polishing *Deathtrap* for a Broadway production. Sidney unnerves Myra by plotting to invite the student to their house, kill him, and steal *Deathtrap* for himself. When Myra reminds Sidney that the famous crime-solving psychic Helga ten Dorp is vacationing nearby, he dismisses this threat as an example of his ability to recognize the dramatic possibilities for murder.

Clifford Anderson arrives in scene 2, anxious to review his manuscript with "The Master." Clifford admires Sidney's collection of exotic weapons while Sidney asks leading questions, suggesting that he is trying to arrange a murder. Just as Myra believes that Clifford is safe, Sidney attacks, garrotting him to death. Myra looks on, horrified, while Sidney wraps the body in a rug and babbles on about how wonderful it will be to have another hit play.

As scene 3 begins, Sidney has just returned from burying the body when psychic Helga ten Dorp rushes in, warning them of the pain that she feels emanating from the house. She rushes around receiving psychic impressions, uncannily revealing some information but completely misinterpreting important details. When she leaves, Sidney delights that she was so inaccurate about the events of the actual murder. Feeling confident, he is turning off the lights when he is suddenly grabbed through the curtain by Clifford. The mud-covered student brutally attacks Sidney exactly as Helga had predicted. Suddenly, Myra clutches her chest and collapses. When Clifford determines that she is dead, he exclaims to Sidney that everything went exactly as planned: The second "staged murder" by lovers Sidney and Clifford has shocked Myra, the intended victim, to death. Act 1 ends as the two exult in the dramatic craft of their murder.

Two weeks have passed as act 2 begins, revealing Clifford working at a furious pace while Sidney sits, still unable to write. Sidney's attorney, Porter Milgrim, cautions Sidney not to trust Clifford because he noticed Clifford discretely locking away his manuscript. Later, Sidney sneaks into the drawer to see Clifford's manuscript and is aghast to discover that he is writing *Deathtrap*, describing exactly how they killed Myra. Clifford convinces Sidney that the murder was so clever that they can get away with it, and Sidney agrees to plot the action for act 2.

Scene 2 reveals Helga again confiding to Sidney about terrible psychic vibrations surrounding Clifford. When she leaves, Sidney summons Clifford, telling him that he is ready to demonstrate how act 2 will progress. Sidney cannot endure the possibility of public revelation of a male lover and has determined to kill Clifford and burn *Deathtrap*. In the confrontation, Sidney first seems to have the advantage, but then there is a reversal. Sidney finally grabs a crossbow and shoots Clifford. The struggle finally seems to be over, but, as Sidney telephones the police, Clifford raises up behind him, wrenches the crossbow bolt from his chest, and plunges it into Sidney. They both collapse, dead.

Scene 3 reveals Helga and Porter moving through the room as Helga describes exactly what happened. When she discerns the name *Deathtrap*, they both realize that this is the perfect construction for a commercial thriller. The play ends as they fight over who will make a killing in the theater with *Deathtrap*.

Analysis

Even though thrillers have enjoyed continued popularity on the high school stage, *Deathtrap* was not originally intended for young people because it uses a homosexual affair between a husband and his student as the motive for murder. Nevertheless, it has become popular among older teenagers. The topic of homosexuality is no longer taboo for high school audiences. As society has become more accepting of various sexual orientations and as the incidence of acquired immunodeficiency syndrome

(AIDS) among teenagers has increased, homosexuality has emerged as a legitimate topic in sexual education courses and teen literature. Furthermore, the sexual issues in *Deathtrap* are subtle. There is no physical intimacy on stage. Indeed, even though Sidney and Clifford laugh that they have attacked each other all over the house, they never so much as embrace in view of the audience.

Levin has devised one of the most clever plot constructions ever incorporated into a thriller. In this story, the fictional world of the characters becomes the real world of two playwrights discussing the fictional world of a play that is based upon their own lives. This ingenious circular construction presents a "real" murder mystery within the context of writing a "fictional" murder mystery. It provides laughter, suspense, and surprise, delivering five murders among only three characters. Levin manipulates the traditional form of the thriller, forcing the audience to question what is real. The audience is deliberately and delightfully deceived. At first, viewers believe that they are witnessing the plans for and murder of Clifford. Suddenly, Clifford is alive and murdering Sidney. The audience discovers the deception when Myra dies of a heart attack because neither the attacks on Clifford nor the one on Sidney were "real"; they were staged in order to kill Myra.

This deception continues as the characters discuss writing a play about the murder. The audience members now believe that they are watching the play that those characters will write. Sidney will not allow that play to be written, however, so the audience is again off balance. The deception is deepened when Helga ten Dorp seems to interpret her psychic vibrations incorrectly but is later revealed to have been correct in every detail. When the two writers are actually dead, viewers discover that they have been watching Helga's play. There is sheer joy in working through the plot reversals and realizing how often one is deceived and how fun it has been because Levin maintains a sense of fair play.

Deathtrap has become popular among teachers of literature because the discussions of the two playwrights in *Deathtrap* constitute one of the best texts available on the classic thriller as a literary genre. The play provides a literary context for the thriller as it discusses Patrick Hamilton's *Angel Street* (1939), Frederick Knott's *Dial "M" for Murder* (1952), Agatha Christie's *Witness for the Prosecution* (1953), and Anthony Shaffer's *Sleuth* (1970). The writing of thrillers is examined at length as Sidney and Clifford discuss why their constructed context for murder is dramatically sound and how they have added convincing details and provided the proper motivation for characters and justifications for alibis. *Deathtrap* is at once an excellent thriller and a working example of the process of writing a thriller.

Critical Context

The murder mystery or thriller proved to be a staple of the English-language theater throughout the twentieth century: The two most-often-produced plays for more than forty years were J. B. Priestley's thrillers *Dangerous Corner* (1932) and *An Inspector Calls* (1946), The longest running play was Christie's *The Mousetrap* (1952). The elements of the successful thriller—clever plotting, engaging characters, and a unique twist—have sustained their appeal with teenagers. In these, the audience competes with a clever detective in deciphering clues presented in a manner of fair play. Shaffer's *Sleuth*, however, changed the rules. It used the traditional elements of the thriller but simultaneously undermined them, breaking the rules of logic and forcing the audience to question what is "real" and what is "staged." *Deathtrap* joined *Sleuth* in establishing this new subgenre, called the comedy thriller, in which the playwright "double-codes" the events on stage in an attempt to subvert the standard conventions of the thriller and add a new facet—keeping the audience off-balance. *Deathtrap* is often taught because, as a part of manipulating the rules, it so clearly defines and explains the rules of creating thrillers. Many comedy thrillers have attempted to duplicate its success, including Nick Hall's *Dead Wrong* (1985), Gerald Moon's *Corpse!* (1985), John Pielmeier's *Sleight of Hand* (1987), and Rupert Holmes's *Accomplice* (1990).

Gerald S. Argetsinger

DEENIE

Author: Judy Blume (1938-   )
First published: 1973
Type of work: Novel
Type of plot: Domestic realism
Time of work: The early 1970's
Locale: Elizabeth, New Jersey
Subjects: Emotions, family, friendship, health and illness, and sexual issues
Recommended ages: 10-13

Blume explores Deenie Fenner's trauma as a result of idiopathic scoliosis and what it means to be considered handicapped.

Principal characters:
> WILMADEENIE "DEENIE" FENNER, almost thirteen, who is diagnosed with adolescent idiopathic scoliosis
> THELMA FENNER (MA), her mother, who wants Deenie to be a model
> FRANK FENNER (DADDY), her father, a gas station owner
> HELEN, her sixteen-year-old sister
> JANET, her friend
> MIDGE, her friend
> BUDDY BRADER, an eighth-grade boy Deenie thinks is nice, who plays drums at a seventh-grade mixer
> MISS RAPPOPORT, the gym teacher

Form and Content

Deenie is a first-person narrative told through the eyes of Wilmadeenie Fenner. It is a fast-paced novel about relationships between Deenie and her friends Midge, Janet, and Buddy Brader and her family, particularly Ma and Daddy. The novel could occur anywhere in the United States, but it is set in suburban New York City. Deenie's name comes from a motion picture that Ma saw just before she was born. When Ma first held Deenie, she knew that the baby would turn out as she wanted—"beautiful"—if Deenie were her name. Ma's favorite comment is that Helen has brains but Deenie has beauty. Ma wants Deenie to use her looks and be a model. Appointments with various agencies are arranged, but Mrs. Allison in New York City says that there is something about Deenie's posture that concerns her. Ma accuses Deenie of slouching and not really trying to stand up straight.

Deenie tries out for the one seventh-grade spot on the cheerleading squad. She is devastated when Janet wins the coveted position and, instead of going home on the bus, seeks solace from her father at his gas station. The next day, Mrs. Rappoport, the gym teacher, wants to see Deenie after school, and Deenie thinks it is about cheerleading. When Mrs. Rappoport asks Deenie to bend over and touch her toes and to walk slowly across the room, she realizes that this meeting is about her posture. The teacher calls Deenie's parents and suggests that Deenie see a doctor. Dr. Moravia believes that she has adolescent idiopathic scoliosis (curvature of the spine) and sends her to an orthopedist for X rays and other tests that confirm the diagnosis. When she is told about the different kinds of treatment, Deenie chooses surgery, without consulting the doctor, and tells her friends. Midge and Janet surprise her with dinner and a gown to wear in the hospital.

Deenie does not have surgery and instead will wear a brace from shoulder to hip for four years. Much information about scoliosis is explained in the novel as Deenie is fitted for the Milwaukee brace and is taught how to put it on and take it off. This procedure is stressful, and Deenie must put her hand in a special place in order to get to sleep.

At the office, when Deenie gets the brace, Ma becomes hysterical, and the doctor sends her back to the waiting room, but Daddy is able to provide the needed support. He also tells Deenie that she is not sick and must go back to school on Monday. Deenie begins to reassess her problem in comparison to those who are truly handicapped. When Buddy Brader kisses her at Janet's party, she knows that everything will be all right.

Analysis

Deenie is easy to read, but many readers will understand only the main storyline of Deenie's scoliosis and treatment. There are a number of subthemes: sibling rivalry, being handicapped, sexuality, and parent/child relationships.

Deenie takes place over several months as she comes to understand herself and her family better. Family relations are explored from different aspects. Ma wants Deenie to be a model even though she is more interested in cheerleading. When Aunt Rae reports that the modeling agency will see her when the brace is off, Deenie is upset that they see her only as a face and not as a person. Helen and Deenie have never understood each other. Deenie believes that Helen hates her because Ma always says that Helen has brains and Deenie has beauty. Deenie knows that she is not expected to get high grades, just no *D*'s or *F*'s. When their parents discover that Helen has not been studying in the evenings but has been at the gas station with Joe Roscow, Joe is fired. Ma says that there are too many medical bills to pay, and Joe has dirty fingernails. Deenie remarks that anyone working in a gas station gets dirty fingernails, even Daddy, and that Deenie is the one seeing the doctor. The sisters fall into each other's arms, crying, as Ma says "I wanted better for you. Better than what I had for myself. That's what I've always planned for my girls."

Daddy provides support for Deenie when she finally gets the brace. She feels as if she is in a cage and must relearn simple tasks since she cannot bend her neck or back. Her clothes must be larger to go over the brace, and finding what she needs is difficult; for the present, she is content to wear Helen's clothes. The night of Janet's party, Deenie wants to be like everyone else and not wear the brace. Ma says that it will not hurt to go without it for a while, but Daddy tells Deenie that, although it is hard on him to see her wear the brace, she must wear it if she wants to go to the party. She plans to take the brace off after she arrives, but, once she is there, she realizes Daddy trusts her and that she does not want to break the trust between them.

Sexuality is alluded to in several incidents. Deenie wants to borrow Helen's sex education book, but it has been loaned to a friend. In frustration, Deenie asks Helen how sexual intercourse feels. Helen responds that she does not know and, with Joe gone, she will never know. Deenie puts her question into Mrs. Rappoport's box for the next anonymous monthly discussion. Deenie's other question is answered when Mrs. Rappoport talks about stimulating the genitals and uses the word "masturbation." Buddy and Deenie do some experimental kissing at the seventh-grade mixer. Buddy takes her into the locker room and presses her back against the wall. All that she can think of is the brace as Buddy puts his hand on her chest and begins kissing her. He accuses her of not kissing him. At Janet's party, they are in the laundry room kissing, and this time Deenie concentrates on kissing him back.

Wearing the brace is an adjustment for Deenie. The assistant principal calls her to the office and gives her a form for her parents to sign so that she can ride the free bus for special students. Deenie looks at the handicapped students in her school for the first time. In the past, she avoided looking at them. She knows that she is not handicapped because her situation is only temporary.

Jealousy and ostracism are explored as Deenie relates to her friends. She is jealous when Janet is chosen as cheerleader; Deenie wanted the other finalist to be chosen, so that she and Janet could be miserable together. Another student, Barbara, is new at school, and everyone avoids her because she has eczema on her hands. Deenie is forced to be her partner in gym, and Barbara tells her about eczema and that it is not contagious. When Deenie develops a rash on her body, however, she is convinced it came from Barbara. The rash is actually an allergic reaction because Deenie refuses to wear a shirt under the brace. As the girls discuss their problems in gym class, they become friends, and Barbara is drawn into the group.

Critical Context

Judy Blume remembers exactly what it was like to be young and what she wanted to know at certain ages as she was growing up. She is able to project herself back to specific stages of her life and is thus able to write as young people speak. She has also written about sexuality and relationships in her other adolescent novels. These books are often identified with specific sexual topics: *Deenie* with masturbation; *Are You There God, It's Me Margaret* (1970) with menstruation; *Then Again, Maybe I Won't* (1971) with wet dreams; and *Forever* (1975) with intercourse. Her books that explore social relationships include *Blubber* (1974), about ostracism and cruelty; *It's Not the End of the World* (1972), about divorce; *Tiger Eyes* (1983), about death; and *Just as Long as We're Together* (1987) and *Here's to You, Rachel Robinson* (1993), about family and peer relations. Blume is a favorite author of adolescents because she writes interesting stories with credible characters.

Ramona Madson Mahood

THE DEVIL'S STORYBOOK

Author: Natalie Babbitt (1932-   )
First published: 1974
Type of work: Short fiction
Subjects: Emotions, religion, social issues, and the supernatural
Recommended ages: 13-15

The Devil's antics in ten distinctly different tales display his inability to overcome goodness in spite of his sly nature and his mean efforts to subdue right-minded people.

Form and Content

The Devil's Storybook collects ten literary folktales, each of which depicts the Devil as a bungling, humorous figure. Although the characters, plot, and context of each of the tales differ, the tension usually resides in the various situations that provoke the Devil to exercise his evil power and tempt innocent humans. Young audiences will appreciate the juxtaposition of the humorous, folktale format and the stories' thematic concerns, which explore the strength of goodness and humankind's struggle to overcome pure evil at its very source. A brief synopsis of each of the tales emphasizes their individual plot characteristics while placing them within the larger context of a unified whole.

In "Wishes," the Devil tempts a farm wife, an old man, and a vain young man with the promise of a wish, an event that he hopes will lead to their moral destruction. Both the old man and the wife possess an inner strength and refuse the Devil's offer. The Devil tricks the young man into wasting his wishes, however, and then returns to Hell, happily aware that humans are easy prey.

"The Very Pretty Lady" relates the story of a beautiful woman whom the Devil determines to have for himself. When she learns that there is no love in Hell, she refuses his offer. In a fit of anger, he takes her beauty and returns to Hell with its fragments. Years later, the Devil returns to find the now-ugly woman, her ugly husband, and their ugly baby in a house filled with love. He angrily throws away her beauty; it floats toward heaven to become a star.

In "The Harps of Heaven," the Devil sends accomplished thieves Jack and Basil to steal a heavenly harp. The brothers' incessant fighting leads to their breaking the harp, and the Devil never fully realizes his goal. As punishment, the Devil makes Jack and Basil take lessons from an unpleasant piano teacher, but they learn only scales.

"The Imp in the Basket" examines the sacrifices of a gentle clergyman who adopts a demon baby that has been left at his door. When the community becomes fearful of the imp's evil connections, they set fire to the cottage while the clergyman and baby are inside. When the flames clear, the demon has disappeared, but the clergyman is unharmed. Everyone pronounces the event as a miracle, but the clergyman remains uncertain if it was God that saved him, or the Devil.

Babbitt explores the Devil's inability to entice humans to his service in "Nuts." The

Devil devises a scheme to trick an unsuspecting woman into cracking all his walnuts for him. Certain that he can appeal to the woman's innate human greed, he places a perfect pearl in a walnut and asks her to crack it for him. He expects her to find the pearl, keep it for herself, and crack the rest of the nuts in search of more treasure. Much to his disappointment, she hides the pearl under her tongue, says nothing, and leaves.

"A Palindrome," as the title implies, focuses on the disharmony that results when the Devil inverts an artist's life and work. The kind artist paints such devilish scenes that the Devil steals all the man's artwork to hang in Hell. Baffled at the theft, the artist becomes the most morose man in his village. Delighted to have caused such mischief, the Devil soon encounters a major disappointment: The unpleasant artist begins to sculpt heavenly creations. Although his paintings hang in Hell, his statues are admired in Heaven, and the palindrome is complete.

"Ashes" depicts Mr. Beezle's confusion, which results when he arrives in Hell after his cremation to find that a pig has suddenly become his doting companion. He confronts the Devil, who suggests that he go back to Earth to solve the mystery. Beezle learns that a careless housemaid knocked his ashes into the hearth, where they became mixed with the ashes of a pork bone. He works diligently to separate his ashes from the pig's, and, as he continues the tedious process, the pig becomes less attentive. About this time, the housemaid arrives in Hell and tidies Beezle's messy ashes, mixing them again. The pig returns, and Beezle teaches him to play cards.

The Devil dislikes perfect people, and, in "Perfection," he encounters Angela, a perfect child. He determines to find her flaws. Nothing that he does works until he discovers the one thing that causes her to lose her temper frequently: Angela grows up to have a perfect husband, a perfect house, and a "fair-to-middling" child.

One minor demon in Hell tries to bring beauty into the dreariness there. "The Rose and the Minor Demon" demonstrates that even the Devil can be outsmarted if goodness exists. When a rose blooms in the garden, the minor demon tries unsuccessfully to protect it from the Devil's wrath. After its destruction, he finds happiness in a flower pictured on a vase. After the Devil orders the vase destroyed, the minor demon rescues a fragment and hides it. It provides him secret happiness in Hell's dismal setting.

In "Power of Speech," the Devil yearns for a wise old woman's prize goat, Walpurgis. When he gives Walpurgis the power of speech, the goat becomes so belligerent, cantankerous, and gregarious that the woman removes his protective bell and sends him to the Devil. The Devil turns him into a stuffed goat and returns him to the woman. She realizes that his fate comes from his refusal to stop talking.

Analysis

Readers will find the bungling version of Satan in Natalie Babbitt's *The Devil's Storybook* more reminiscent of William Shakespeare's humorous Falstaff than an embodiment of evil. The delineation of the Devil as a comic figure reduces his traditional, epic proportions and affords a look at a cosmic landscape with relatively small dimensions. The Devil tries diligently to maintain his reputation as the supreme trickster; however, he fails miserably. From humans who outdistance his intellect to minor demons who diminish his power by insubordination, this version of Satan wades through one confrontation after another slightly out of control.

Each tale of the ten exhibits the literary elements of traditional folktales. The time and places are vague. Locales are thinly identified as "Heaven," "Hell," and "the World." Introductory phrases such as "There was a little girl once" echo fairy-tale openings and create a universal time frame. Human characters are flat and static, elements that underscore their one-dimensional qualities and relegate them to symbolic depictions of all humanity. The plots plunge quickly into conflict, and resolutions provide tidy, satisfying endings. The universal themes qualify the explicit didacticism present. "Nuts," for example, ends with the dictum "We are not all of us greedy." The third-person, omniscient point of view enables readers to observe the internal motivations of all the characters as they clash over issues of good and evil.

Critical Context

The Devil's Storybook returns the literary folktale to its traditional arena of storytelling appropriate for older audiences. Even though the Devil portrayed in this work cannot be taken seriously, his capacity to create chaos arbitrarily in human activity and to drive innocent victims to the brink lies quietly in the framework of each of the tales. Couched in a humorous context and peopled with stock characters, the ten tales coalesce to form an intricate whole that articulates the fact that evil lurks in the most unexpected places. This excursion into the literary folktale affords Natalie Babbitt with the opportunity to continue her exploration of the supernatural. *The Devil's Storybook* demands more of its audience than do such light fantasy titles as Babbitt's *Tuck Everlasting* (1975) and *The Eyes of Amaryllis* (1977). *The Devil's Storybook* and its sequel, *The Devil's Other Storybook* (1987), rely on a nonthreatening version of the Devil and the simple folktale form to make readers ponder their own ability and endurance to withstand the guile of evil in its most primary forms.

Marilyn M. Robitaille

DIEGO RIVERA

Author: James D. Cockcroft (1917-   )
First published: 1991; illustrated
Type of work: Biography
Time of work: 1886-1957
Locale: Mexico, Europe, and the United States
Subjects: Artists and race and ethnicity
Recommended ages: 13-18

This portrayal of Diego Rivera as both an artist and a man describes his work, his involvement with communism, his support of the common people, and his turbulent love life.

> *Principal personages:*
> DIEGO MARÍA RIVERA, an artist and sociopolitically involved leftist
> DIEGO RIVERA, SR., his father, a minor bureaucrat in the Mexican Department of Health
> MARIA RIVERA, his mother, a homemaker
> ANGELINE BELOFF, a Russian artist and revolutionary, the mother of Rivera's first son
> GUADALUPE MARIN, Rivera's tempestuous first wife
> FRIDA KAHLO, Rivera's second wife, also an artist and leftist
> EMMA HURTADO, an art dealer who became Rivera's third wife
> JOSÉ GUADALUPE POSADA, an engraver, artist, and radical whom Rivera viewed as his most important teacher
> AMADEO MODIGLIANI, a great Italian painter and sculptor and one of Rivera's good friends

Form and Content

James D. Cockcroft's *Diego Rivera* is a delightful biography describing the life of the great Mexican artist Diego María Rivera. It is part of a series of books entitled Hispanics of Achievement that seeks to describe contributions of great Hispanics both to American society and worldwide. The biography is divided into nine chapters, each a well-illustrated vignette describing a portion of the life and work of the artist. All the chapters, except for chapter 1, are in chronological order.

This first chapter, "Only in America," takes place in the 1930's, when the already-famous Rivera was in the midst of painting a mural commissioned by John D. Rockefeller, Jr., in the RCA building of New York City's Rockefeller Center. The mural, Man at the Crossroads Looking with Uncertainty but with Hope and High Vision to the Choosing of a Course Leading to a New and Better Future, was meant to honor the strivings of the working class. It soon became quite unsatisfactory to the artist's patron, however, because of the prominent inclusion of the communist leader Vladimir Ilich Lenin.

In the eyes of his patron, Rivera went too far, beginning what the news media named "the battle of Rockefeller Center." In the end, Rivera was paid completely for the unfinished work and fired. The mural was covered over and later destroyed. Rivera fought this drastic artistic censorship quite vigorously. The chapter summarizes his talents, tenacity, and love for life, communism, and the common people.

The next four chapters describe Rivera's beginnings, starting with his childhood in Mexico, continuing with his art study abroad, and ending with his return to Mexico in 1921. Included in the early Mexican portion are Rivera's decision at the age of ten to become an artist and his study at Mexico City's Academy of San Carlos. Rivera's revolutionary tendencies are also shown to be stimulated by strong interaction with José Guadalupe Posada; Cockcroft tells readers that the artist viewed Posada as his most important teacher.

In Europe, Rivera is depicted as working hard, reading on sociopolitical issues profusely, and developing both a strong sympathy for communism and his great artistic talent. Rivera's long love affair with Angeline Beloff, a Russian artist and revolutionary and the mother of his first son, is depicted but showed in balance with his ever-growing leftist tendencies.

Chapters 6 through 8 describe the tempestuous career of the artist, interweaving descriptions of the development of Rivera's art, his works, his role in the art world, his varied love life, and his continued deep fascination with communism. Throughout the book, Diego Rivera is depicted as mercurial both in his political convictions and in his love life. These chapters reveal the latter in his stormy relationship with his second wife, Frida Kahlo, a leftist and a famous artist in her own right. Also included are Rivera's affairs with other women, including the art dealer Emma Hurtado, who became his third wife in 1955.

Chapter 9, "God Is Dead," covers Rivera's last years, beginning with the onset of World War II. The ever-growing communist sentiment of his work is noted, as is his lust for life. Cockcroft ends by eulogizing Rivera, stating quite enthusiastically that through his art, "wherever there is greed, exploitation, and oppression, Rivera's defiant spirit will be at work against those forces."

Analysis

While there is no foreword to *Diego Rivera* to identify the author's aims in writing the book, there is an afterword at the end of chapter 9 in which Cockcroft identifies Rivera as a man who "left behind not only a wealth of painting but the very idea of people's art, inspiring others to paint with a social conscience." In addition, the introduction to the book makes it clear that the series editors saw Rivera as a Hispanic of achievement who influenced American and world art profoundly but who is not as well known as he should be. Cockcroft seeks to correct this situation by exploring Rivera's life thoroughly, defining the man, his belief system, and his art. A portrait of Rivera emerges that depicts a great artist, an individual with strong ideals, and a free spirit.

Throughout Rivera's life, he was acknowledged as a pioneer in the painting of modern mural art, and his work is found all over Mexico and the United States, as well as in Europe. Nevertheless, he has always been a vague and controversial figure to the general public. To most, he is seen as a man having little reverence for religion and as an outspoken communist. Cockcroft is successful in defusing this feeling somewhat by depicting Rivera as a sociopolitical idealist who sought to celebrate the affairs of common people with dignity. Despite his communist sympathies, Rivera seemed to portray that sociopolitical system as one desirable way by which such individuals may gain the respect that they deserve. The series editors support this point of view by the inclusion of more than thirty striking examples of Rivera's works in this 111-page book. These examples enable the reader to see the artist's social consciousness and sympathies quite clearly.

Rivera's sociopolitical beliefs are identified as arising in the course of living through a period of Mexican and world history in which the common people were overlooked and in many cases downtrodden. His worldview is depicted as beginning with his deep interaction with a revolutionary leftist mentor, José Posada. Furthermore, two of Diego Rivera's greatest loves, Angeline Beloff and Frida Kahlo, were leftists, and their views undoubtedly influenced him. Amid the bohemian milieu of Parisian café society, he was also exposed to this worldview almost continually. Finally, Rivera's exposure to conscientious leftist officials, such as one governor of Yucatán, as well as moneyed and corrupt "capitalist dictators," must have played a role in his beliefs.

Cockcroft portrays Rivera as a free spirit, a bohemian artist who sought to live his personal life free of the many social restraints engendered by public opinion. This lifestyle is made clear from Rivera's numerous love affairs and several marriages. Yet, he is also shown to be a man who is quite capable of prolonged serious romantic interactions, including ten years with Beloff and nearly a quarter of a century with Kahlo. His relationship with Kahlo, his second marriage, ended only with her death in 1955. An evaluation of Rivera's actions, which are not so different from those of many other rich and famous individuals, is within the purview of readers.

Critical Context

Diego Rivera is an excellent place to begin an exploration of the life and many artistic contributions of this great muralist. It is most suitable for art appreciation courses or for courses that delve into the psyches and social consciousness of great Hispanic individuals or of modern artists.

James Cockcroft portrays Diego Rivera, who is most often viewed solely as a stubborn, irreverent, and fanatical communist, as a thinking individual who developed a leftist sociopolitical viewpoint as a result of the political conditions existing in Mexico during his formative years. In addition, it becomes evident that Rivera both analyzed his own political ideology and was not fanatically adherent to communism. Rather, it seems likely that he saw communism as a way for the common people, whom he portrays so poignantly, to seek human dignity.

Diego Rivera provides a good sampling of black-and-white and color plates of the artist's works, which makes clear his talent and his efforts to condemn social injustice and celebrate the inherent greatness of the common people. These aspects of the text make it quite useful for young people as a primer for social consciousness and a yardstick for great twentieth century art. Another aspect of the book that makes it useful for study by young readers is the view that it gives of Mexico's political climate during Rivera's lifetime; Cockcroft describes the actions of Mexican public officials, including several presidents, and important historical events in that country.

Diego Rivera also fleshes out the entire life of the artist, in contrast to the partial coverage in Florence Arquin's *Diego Rivera: Shaping of an Artist, 1889-1921* (1971). Moreover, it places all of his art in context in comparison to specialized texts such as *Diego Rivera: Science and Creativity in the Detroit Murals* (1986), by Dorothy McMeekin. These other books do provide more details about specific aspects of Rivera's life and work, as do the many references in Cockcroft's section on further readings.

Sanford S. Singer

DINKY HOCKER SHOOTS SMACK!

Author: M. E. Kerr (Marijane Meaker, 1927-   )
First published: 1972
Type of work: Novel
Type of plot: Psychological realism
Time of work: The late 1960's or early 1970's
Locale: Brooklyn, New York
Subjects: Coming-of-age, drugs and addiction, emotions, family, and friendship
Recommended ages: 13-15

Fifteen-year-old Tucker Woolf befriends Dinky Hocker, an overweight teenage girl who deals with her insecurities and the fact that her parents ignore her by overeating and responding to the world with a cynical sense of humor.

> *Principal characters:*
> TUCKER WOOLF, a fifteen-year-old boy who hopes to grow up to become a librarian
> CAL WOOLF, Tucker's father, an out-of-work professional fund-raiser
> MRS. WOOLF, Tucker's mother, who has a Ph.D. in English literature but is working as an editor for *Stirring Romances*
> SUSAN "DINKY" HOCKER, an overweight teenager who is ignored by her parents
> NADER, a nine-month-old calico cat that Tucker allows Dinky to adopt
> NATALIA LINE, Dinky's cousin, who has recently been released from a school for teenagers with psychological and emotional problems
> HELEN HOCKER, Dinky's mother, who runs an organization for recovering drug addicts
> HORACE HOCKER, Dinky's father, a lawyer
> P. JOHN KNIGHT, one of Tucker's classmates at Richter School, an obese sixteen-year-old with extremely conservative views
> PERRY KNIGHT, P. John's father, who writes politically radical books

Form and Content

While related by an omniscient narrator, *Dinky Hocker Shoots Smack!* is filtered through the consciousness of fifteen-year-old Tucker Woolf, whose family has just moved to Brooklyn, which his father advises him to refer to as "Brooklyn Heights." Tucker's father has lost his job as a professional fund-raiser, and his mother is temporarily forced to work as an editor and writer for *Stirring Romances*. When Mr. Woolf develops an allergy to Tucker's cat, Nader, Tucker must give it up for adoption. Nader is adopted by Susan "Dinky" Hocker, an overweight teenager who manages to transfer to the cat her own compulsion for overeating.

Concerned with Nader's health, Tucker begins spending time with Dinky, who is interested in unusual and bizarre examples of human nature. Tucker soon becomes infatuated with Dinky's cousin, Natalia Line, who has recently been released from Renaissance, a school for teenagers with psychological problems. In order to take Natalia to a dance, Tucker lines up Dinky with another obese teen, the ultraconservative P. John Knight. P. John's ideas clash with those of Dinky's liberal parents, especially her mother, who runs Drug Rehabilitation, Inc. (DRI), which helps recovering addicts. Spurred on by P. John's attention, Dinky tries to remake herself, attending Weight Watchers with him and trying to become better read.

During one of Mrs. Hocker's DRI meetings, P. John prompts a fight between Dinky and her mother by telling Dinky not to eat a piece of chocolate cake. As a result, Mrs. Hocker orders P. John never to see Dinky again. When Dinky sneaks over to P. John's apartment, the Hockers call the police, which results in the arrest of an illegal immigrant named Dewey, one of the friends of P. John's father, Perry Knight. Soon after, Tucker's mother tells him that she is worried that he and Natalia are becoming too serious, a concern that Helen Hocker reiterates when Tucker visits the Hockers for Christmas dinner. When Mrs. Hocker misinterprets Tucker's Christmas gift to Natalia—a bunch of balloons filled with unfinished sentences written on slips of paper—Natalia has an emotional breakdown and temporarily returns to Renaissance. Consequently, Tucker is forbidden to see her. While Mrs. Hocker soon realizes that she has been mistaken about Tucker and invites him to work with a group of "ghetto children," she is oblivious to Dinky's problems.

After spending the spring with his aunt in Maine, P. John returns to Brooklyn Heights with a new outlook on life and a slimmer physique. Dinky, who has not changed, refuses to talk to him. The following night, Helen Hocker receives the Heights Samaritan Award for her work in the community. After the awards banquet, everyone emerges to see "Dinky Hocker Shoots Smack!" painted on sidewalks, car doors, and the sides of buildings. When questioned by Mr. Hocker, who realizes that Dinky had done the painting, Tucker explains that people who do not "shoot smack" have problems too. Finally recognizing that they have been contributing to her problems, the Hockers take Dinky to Europe for a vacation. At the end of the book, Tucker tells his mother that "Susan" has gotten out from inside "Dinky" and that, as for his relationship with Natalia, he is waiting until the fall to see what happens.

Analysis

In many ways, *Dinky Hocker Shoots Smack!* is a deceptively simple book. While some parts of the novel are not entirely believable—Natalia's penchant for rhyming when she is nervous, Dinky's defacement of the streets and sidewalks, and Helen Hocker's treatment of virtually everyone—M. E. Kerr deftly mixes humor and pathos in a way that will keep the attention of the reader. A summary of the novel's somewhat melodramatic plot does not do justice to its many humorous moments or to its treatment of important themes, particularly the need of teenagers for strong adult relationships in their lives, the frequent hypocrisy of the adult world, and the difficulties of developing honest relationships.

To some extent, each of the four teenagers in the novel are ignored by the adults in their lives. Tucker's parents are concerned with getting new jobs or education, Natalia's mother has committed suicide and she has been sent to live with her aunt and uncle, and P. John's father and Dinky's parents are more concerned with social causes than with the welfare of their own children. As a result, their children are slowly becoming cynical, particularly in the light of what appears to be hypocritical adult behavior. Tucker is asked to create fictions about the world in which he lives, referring to Brooklyn as "Brooklyn Heights" and saying that his mother works at Arrow Publications instead of *Stirring Romances*. Dinky's mother conducts therapy groups for drug addicts and yet tries to hide the fact that her niece has mental and emotional problems, at the same time encouraging her daughter's addiction to food.

Without positive reinforcement or role models, Tucker, Natalia, Dinky, and P. John all have a difficult time developing relationships with their peers. Tucker and Natalia can only talk to each other by creating puzzles and games, while P. John and Dinky cover up their insecurities by deliberately offending others. It is only when parents and children are forced to confront their problems and recognize their true feelings for one another that they gain a degree of happiness.

Critical Content

Dinky Hocker Shoots Smack!, M. E. Kerr's first novel for young adults, was widely praised on its first publication and was named a "Best of the Best" Book for Young Adults by the American Library Association, a Best Children's Book by *The School Library Journal*, and a Library of Congress Children's Book of 1972. It also received a Maxi Award from *Media and Methods*. Critic Alleen Pace Nilsen has suggested that the book is one of Kerr's most popular and that it remains one of her best. *Dinky Hocker Shoots Smack!* is still in print and is read in some schools; it was popular enough to be adapted to television as part of the *ABC Afternoon Special* series. While some of the characters and events are exaggerated and unbelievable, the relationships between the protagonists and their parents continue to appeal to young adults.

The somewhat unusual romantic relationships between Tucker and Natalia and between Dinky and P. John look forward to similar romantic entanglements in Kerr's other works, especially *The Son of Someone Famous* (1974) and *Him She Loves?* (1984), in which teenagers' love lives are complicated by their parents. As in *Dinky Hocker Shoots Smack!*, the parents in Kerr's *Gentlehands* (1978) are oblivious to the problems that their children face and occasionally are prejudiced, despite an attempt to appear politically correct. Like Dinky and P. John, Kerr's protagonists frequently break off budding romances as they begin to look at the world in more mature ways.

The character of Dinky Hocker is one of several young adults in novels of the 1970's whose parents ignore them until they unconsciously make a plea for help through socially unacceptable behavior. Like Patty Bergen of Bette Greene's *Summer of My German Soldier* (1973), Marcy Lewis of Paula Danziger's *The Cat Ate My Gymsuit* (1974), and Jerry Renault of Robert Cormier's *The Chocolate War* (1974),

Dinky ultimately dares to "disturb the universe" and question the behavior of the adults in her life.

The mixture of humor and pathos in *Dinky Hocker Shoots Smack!* is characteristic of most of Kerr's work, while Dinky's problems with obesity parallel those of the protagonists of works such as Judy Blume's *Blubber* (1974) and Robert Lipsyte's *One Fat Summer* (1977). The specific details that Kerr employs, including her characters' dress and dialogue, along with her treatment of hypocrisy and parent-child alienation, help *Dinky Hocker Shoots Smack!* to rise above its weaknesses, suggesting that it will continue to be popular in the future.

Joel D. Chaston

DISCOVERING LIFE ON EARTH

Author: David Attenborough (1926-   )
First published: 1979; illustrated
Type of work: Science
Subjects: Animals, nature, and science
Recommended ages: 10-15

> *Attenborough offers an introduction to the variety and abundance of animal life and behaviors found from early geological time to today in all of the earth's varied habitats.*

Form and Content

Approaching the diversity of animal life on Earth from a natural history and natural selection approach, David Attenborough provides a compact overview of what his first chapter calls "The Endless Variety." *Discovering Life on Earth* is referred to as a "shorter, simplified text" version of the thirteen-part television series on which it is based. Through the thirteen chapters of this book, the reader follows the development of the animal kingdom as illustrated by stories about increasingly complex organisms and their interrelationships with the various facets of their environment.

Simple, one-celled organisms begin the story and lead the reader into the fossil record of the earliest lifeforms. From there, the text progresses through the first forests and the animals that constituted the planet's first inhabitants. Attenborough then moves on to "The Conquest of the Waters" by aquatic organisms both great and small. From there, the emergence of complex lifeforms onto the lands of the earth is described. Insects, birds, marsupials, then predators and prey—all major groups of animals are considered, along with some of the less well known representatives that occupy specialized niches in the earth's vastly complex communities.

The chronicle of life on Earth concludes with "The Arrival of Mankind." In this chapter, the author describes the emergence of humankind on the African plains more than five million years ago, the lifestyle that these individuals are thought to have had, and the animals found in the environment in which they lived. The manner of evolution from ape to modern *Homo sapiens* is hypothesized, and some of the artifacts of humankind's history on Earth are described and illustrated. In concluding this chapter, the lifestyles of modern aboriginal peoples, which may be similar to those of humankind's earlier ancestors, are described.

Generously supplied color photographs (more than five hundred in number) and illustrations are found throughout the book, often three or more per page. These graphics fulfill an important function, and each provides a caption relating the image to the content within the text. In addition, several time lines are provided. These charts help the reader develop an understanding of the appearance and disappearance of important animal groups throughout geologic ages, and they provide a relative means of comparing when various lifeforms lived on the earth. Artistic renderings of what life may have looked like in the ancient coal forests, under the ancient seas, and in the times of the dinosaurs are also included.

Analysis

The number of natural science books available to young readers is large and ever-increasing. *Discovering Life on Earth* offers a high-quality, straightforward, factual approach that presents documentation about the variety of life that has existed on Earth through geological eras and that continues to exist today. The organization that Attenborough employs is logical and easy to follow. The development of life-forms from the simple to the increasingly complex is treated in an interesting manner with the inclusion of representative examples that capture the imagination and attention of the younger reader. While natural selection is an underlying theme of the book, Attenborough does not overtly address organic evolution.

This is an ambitious work. The animal kingdom is composed of several million species in existence today, and a vast number more are a part of the geological record of life on Earth. Paring down this population to a comprehensible level without losing meaning is a formidable task. As an accomplished scientist and producer of television programming that concerns animals, Attenborough has skillfully picked and chosen among the possibilities and has delivered a finished product that retains coherence and valid content. While the arrangement of the chapters does not deliver complete faithfulness to phylogeny, it is a logical approach to the animal kingdom and should not cause any discernable conceptual errors.

Each chapter brings the reader into immediate involvement with the topic, losing no time to long-winded introductions. Attention-getting incidents and stories carry the reader into the content of the chapter, with many engrossing examples provided along the way. There is a captioned photograph for almost every animal described. Stories unfold as Attenborough presents puzzles and questions faced by scientists in attempting to understand fossil records of animals that existed on Earth millions of years ago. One such story concerns the fossilized remains of an ancient animal scientists called Archaeopteryx: When did it live? Was it a reptile or a bird? Why did it have wing feathers? What is the significance of Archaeopteryx to the modern world? Other stories focus on the questions that scientists have about the animals with which humans share the earth today. As Attenborough examines these questions, he illuminates the scientific method of investigation. The author emphasizes the attempts of scientists to achieve an understanding, thereby conveying the important concept that scientists do not have all the answers.

The puzzle of the duckbill platypus, a egg-laying mammal, illustrates how the emergence of new data can be difficult for the scientific community to accept. Reports of this Australian animal near the end of the nineteenth century forced scientists to rethink a number of ideas that they had considered to be "natural laws." Here was an animal that did not fit the rules. As a result, scientific knowledge had to be rearranged, emphasizing the changeable nature of "scientific fact."

Another specific example illustrating how Attenborough treats natural history much as a puzzle to be solved is provided in the chapter "The Hunters and the Hunted." The author presents problems faced both by predators and prey in ensuring their respective survival. This chapter underscores the interdependence of all organisms in the scheme of life on Earth, using examples from the African plains, the South American forest, and the North American grasslands.

An important feature of this book is the approachable manner in which the information is presented. The language that the author uses, while technical where necessary and desirable, is clear and unambiguous. The reader is treated with intellectual respect, not patronized. The pacing is fast as the narrative moves from example to example and topic to topic. While a truly in-depth treatment of the subject of animal diversity cannot be accomplished by a work of such relatively modest length, the text does provide sufficient interest and motivation for young readers. They could well be encouraged to seek out additional information about animals and topics of particular interest to them.

The most important aspect of this work, in Attenborough's view, is that "we can see that we are ourselves are part of that natural world and are dependant on it, and that natural world, since we have become the most powerful of all creatures, is now dependent upon us." This message, while explicit in the introduction, is not stated as boldly within the text itself. Rather, the book is a series of vignettes depicting varied organisms experiencing various life experiences on Earth with the scientist as an interested onlooker, more apart from the experience than a part of the experience.

Critical Context

Discovering Life on Earth demonstrates to the reader that zoology is a fascinating, diverse, and complex science. Attenborough has done a commendable job of condensing his thirteen-week television series into a book that can be comprehended by young readers. His approach to natural history—in which specific, isolated examples of behaviors within the animal kingdom are described and illustrated—can be criticized for being scattered. Yet, it can be argued that the amount of information available on this subject is too vast to present in its entirety in a way that would engage young readers.

Given Attenborough's intention, the flow of the subject matter and the coherence among the chapters are commendable. *Discovering Life on Earth* delivers a large number of interesting stories and examples that should inspire young readers to keep reading, to seek other sources in order to learn more about animal behaviors and relationships. The text is useful both as an entire volume and as a reference work on specific animals, animal behaviors, and the diversity within the animal kingdom.

Duane Inman

THE DISCOVERY OF THE TOMB OF TUTANKHAMEN

Authors: Howard Carter (1873-1939) and A. C. Mace (1874-1928)
First published: 1923; illustrated
Type of work: Science
Subjects: Death, religion, and science
Recommended ages: 15-18

Carter and Mace chronicle the most important archaeological discovery in twentieth century Egypt and report their initial findings at the site.

Form and Content

Although it represents a scientific report and a classic study of archaeology, *The Discovery of the Tomb of Tutankhamen* includes a varied array of prose genres. The book is dedicated to the earl of Carnarvon, who sponsored the excavations of Howard Carter; it opens with a biography of that nobleman written by his sister Winifred, Lady Burghclere. This account is followed by eleven chapters arranged chronologically but varying greatly in contents and level of generality. These chapters are divisible into two major sections. The first five narrate the history of the reign of Tutankhamen, describe his burial site in the Valley of the Kings, explain archaeological work in the valley, and report the discovery of Tutankhamen's tomb. The second part, consisting of six chapters, explains in detail the work of Carter and his team during the first season of excavating the tomb.

Primary credit for discovery of the tomb must be accorded to Carter, who, against all expert opinion, had the courage to pursue an improbable hypothesis. By the time that he began, he was thoroughly steeped in archaeology, having served an apprenticeship under the exacting archaeological pioneer Flanders Petrie. Before the idea of searching for Tutankhamen developed, Carter had explored widely in the Valley of the Kings near Thebes and had made significant discoveries.

Before Carter began his search, historians had already accounted for almost all dynastic rulers of Egypt. Their tombs had been identified, and the few objects overlooked by grave robbers from antiquity had been discovered. Yet, the boy king of the eighteenth dynasty, the successor of Akhenaten, remained a mystery. Before his death at the age of eighteen, Tutankhamen had ruled Egypt for nine years in the mid-fourteenth century B.C. Although his influence was not great, historical interest in him was high, for he served immediately following the turbulent reign of Akhenaten. After archaeologists had discovered occasional objects bearing Tutankhamen's seal near the tombs of Akhenaten and Ramses VI, Carter decided to concentrate his search in that area.

First, his team had to remove tons of earth and debris left by previous explorers in order to reach the original ground level. In November, 1922, a worker discovered the first of sixteen steps leading down to a sealed door. Beyond the door lay a twenty-five-foot-long passageway obstructed by shards and detritus. At its end, Carter found a second door bearing the seal of Tutankhamen. Having summoned his patron from England, Carter forced a small opening in the door and peered into an anteroom filled with objects that had lain undisturbed for three thousand years. When Carnarvon asked whether he could see anything, Carter replied, "Yes, wonderful things."

Carter had discovered the antechamber of Tutankhamen's four-room tomb. Although pilferers had entered the room a few years following Tutankhamen's death and stolen some small and easily portable items, they had abandoned the site and resealed its doors, leaving most of the contents undisturbed.

Instead of entering the antechamber to survey everything, Carter proceeded cautiously and methodically. Before moving anything, he hired a professional photographer to document the existence and location of every item. Chests, robes, couches, beds, chariots, jewelry, walking sticks, gloves—all were documented and cataloged. Carter took the necessary steps to safeguard the site from would-be collectors and curious tourists and notified all the proper officials. Then, in a nearby tomb, he set up a laboratory equipped to protect items that were in a state of decay and to preserve everything possible. Only after this preliminary cataloging and treatment would items from the tomb be transported to the museum in Cairo. As news of the find spread, Carter found himself deluged by members of the press eager to see any objects from the site, as well as by hoards of tourists who congregated nearby, hoping to observe something important.

After sufficiently clearing the antechamber of its wealth of objects, Carter opened another sealed door and found a large, gilded shrine surrounded by numerous other objects. He knew this to be the actual tomb and expected to discover the young pharaoh's mummy under layers of gold-covered boxes. The arrival of summer's intense heat, however, forced him to end his excavation for the year, leaving the burial chamber undisturbed for another season. He had processed one-fourth of the items in the tomb, but the entire project was to require ten additional years of work.

Analysis

Although his friend A. C. Mace is listed as coauthor in recognition of his contribution toward preparing the book, this archaeological work is Howard Carter's, and full credit for the discovery belongs to him. Through the book, Carter sought to describe his discovery to an excited public, to justify his own controversial career in archaeology, and to explain the careful, systematic treatment of the site.

Like many important explorers, Carter was a maverick of sorts—in his case, an abrasive one. Before his quest for Tutankhamen's tomb began, he had made minor discoveries in the Valley of the Kings, only to have his work halted through disagreements with superiors. His meeting with Lord Carnarvon was fortuitous, for the two formed a lasting bond of friendship and mutual respect. Carter was to try his patron's patience and draw heavily on his support as he worked fruitlessly for six years before his momentous discovery.

The book reveals his courage in the pursuit of an improbable hypothesis—that he could find a tomb that had eluded grave robbers and archaeologists for centuries. In addition, Carter himself understood that experts were almost totally united against the effort. Just when he began to think that he had been beaten, the discovery was made. Carter refers to his discovery in a personal sense as "The Freedom," meaning that his long quest was successfully concluded, thus freeing him from his obsessive determination. In a larger sense, however, the term suggests that his discovery was so momentous as to endow him with lasting fame, and he therefore no longer needed to struggle in order to justify his existence.

The tomb itself was not large by Egyptian standards, nor were its walls elaborately painted like those of better-known pharaohs. Its significance lay in the fact that its treasures had been left largely undisturbed while the other tombs in the Valley had been thoroughly plundered. Tutankhamen's tomb was a treasure trove of precious items from antiquity that also provided a wealth of information about life under the pharaohs.

The book's second half (chapters 6 through 11) represents a justification of Carter's archaeological methods. In a revealing sentence, the book explains, "It had been our privilege to find the most important collection of Egyptian antiquities that had ever seen the light, and it was for us to show that we were worthy of the trust." Showing himself worthy meant that he must treat all objects in accordance with the best scientific principles.

Often drawing attention to some of the seventy-nine photographic plates depicting scores of artifacts, Carter explains his proceedings in identifying each object in place and removing it to the nearby laboratory in preparation for transport to the Cairo museum. His task was formidable, since the antechamber alone contained more than six hundred objects, and it became even more difficult because many of the items required careful handling and even preservation through chemicals or stabilization through wax. He had to deal with objects of various kinds, including wood, linen, papyrus, stone, metals, and clay. The final section of the book provides a clear impression of the mundane, everyday work of the archaeologist, as opposed to the excitement of discovery. Carter returns to the heightened sense of discovery in the final chapter when he describes the opening of the door leading into the burial chamber.

Critical Context

Carter and Mace offer an unusual combination in their description of an exciting discovery and their explanation of the science of archaeology. The text allows readers to share in the exhilaration associated with great quests like those of Sir Richard Burton and John Hanning Speke for the source of the Nile, or of Robert Scott and Roald Amundsen's polar expeditions. In archaeology, the closest important analogy would be the excavations of Heinrich Schliemann at Hissarlik and Mycenae, but, while Schliemann made spectacular discoveries, he was no scientist; his amateurish methods and haste destroyed much evidence of the cultures that he attempted to understand.

By contrast, descriptions of Carter's attempts to protect and preserve objects from

Tutankhamen's tomb introduce the reader to what were then the most advanced practices of field archaeology. His zeal for protecting the thousands of individual items in the tomb was motivated in part by the awareness that many would be of interest to future students of the culture and art of Tutankhamen's era. His careful work ensured that the civilization of Tutankhamen's time would be better understood, and items that he preserved from the tomb have brought aesthetic pleasure to millions.

Stanley Archer

DOCTOR DE SOTO

Author: William Steig (1907-   )
First published: 1982; illustrated
Type of work: Novel
Type of plot: Fantasy
Subjects: Animals, health and illness, and jobs and work
Recommended ages: 10-13

> *Dr. De Soto, a mouse dentist, faces a moral dilemma when he discovers that the ailing fox he is treating plans to eat him at the conclusion of his services.*

Principal characters:
DR. DE SOTO, a mouse dentist who treats all animals, except the dangerous
MRS. DE SOTO, his wife and assistant
THE FOX, who is rescued from his pain by the De Sotos

Form and Content

Doctor De Soto tells the story of a mouse dentist who takes pity on a fox with a toothache. Told in third-person narration, the lively story presents several moral dilemmas. It is Dr. De Soto's established rule, posted by sign, that he does not treat animals that are potentially dangerous to him. Out of compassion for a fox who is in great pain, however, he sets aside this rule and provides treatment. Under anesthesia, the fox reveals his fondness for mice as food, and the dentist must decide whether to continue treatment the following day. The fox, on the other hand, wonders only briefly if it would be "shabby" to devour his benefactors; by the next day, he has overcome his thin moral resolve with plans to eat Dr. and Mrs. De Soto as soon as his new tooth is in place.

The compassion of the mice is matched by their courage and cleverness. After a night of debating whether to continue treating the fox, Dr. De Soto decides to follow his father's principle of always finishing what he starts. When the fox arrives the next morning, the De Sotos have a plan in place. After the new tooth is installed, the dentist offers to coat the fox's teeth with a substance that will prevent any further tooth decay, and the fox eagerly consents. After all, if he eats the dentist, he will have eliminated the very person who might treat him for future dental distress. The mixture seals the fox's teeth together temporarily, and the outwitted fox must leave without devouring the De Sotos.

This bright, lively story is easy to read and provides a satisfactory conclusion. The De Sotos struggle with their natural tendency to protect themselves against a predator in order to perform an act of compassion for the agonized fox. While the fox is unable to overcome his natural tendency to the consume mice as an act of appreciation for their kindness, he still receives the treatment that he needs and wanders out of the story somewhat stunned but out of pain.

William Steig uses an economy of line to create the settings for the narrative and to convey the emotions and intentions of his characters. The illustrations on each page provide the reader with interesting and humorous details and help make the story entirely believable, within the boundaries of the fantasy created. While mice are not dentists with large animals for patients, Steig shows how this would be possible if they were. Dr. De Soto uses a miniature form of standard dental equipment but reaches his patients by ladder and works directly inside their mouths, using boots to keep his feet dry. Indeed, the kindly dentist is quite popular with larger animals because of his delicate touch and dainty drills. For work that calls for additional strength, such as pulling teeth, Dr. De Soto is assisted by his wife, who skillfully operates a system of ropes, cranks, and pulleys.

Analysis

As fantasy, *Doctor De Soto* involves a plot that requires that the main characters not only act and respond in terms of their animal identities but also dress and act like humans and face dilemmas unique to the human situation. In this sense, the story is similar to a fable, although there are no didactic overtones. Young readers can relate to the De Sotos as successful problem solvers and can evaluate their actions in terms of moral criteria. Because the story examines the moral deliberations of both the mice and the fox, readers have the opportunity to evaluate the moral principles of each character and raise questions about their processes of decision making. Is the fox evil, as Dr. De Soto pronounces him, or is he simply following his basic instincts? The mice overcome their instinctual fear of the fox in order to treat his pain; should not the fox similarly overcome his desire to eat the mice out of gratitude for their compassion? It is interesting to note that in the De Sotos' case, moral principles are followed not rigidly, but reflectively. Exceptions are considered, and the higher principle of compassion for a fellow being is followed. Their decisions are principle-led, rather than rule-based. They soon discover, however, that they must proceed with additional caution and use their wits in order to complete safely the procedure that they have begun.

The conflict presented in the story is relevant to young adult readers, who are in the process of finding out what kind of persons they are and what kind of persons they want to become. They are dealing with questions similar to those of the protagonists: How should one respond to a potentially dangerous situation? How can an individual get out of dangerous predicaments safely? What kinds of precautions does one need to take? How can someone be a friend in a situation where he or she might get hurt? The De Sotos exhibit the reflective use of intelligence in their dilemma, creating a viable plan and using all necessary caution to treat the fox without being devoured.

Steig's writing style is witty and urbane, reflecting his years of experience as a cartoonist for *The New Yorker* magazine. Although *Doctor De Soto* is frequently found in preschool and primary libraries, it is also included in collections for older children, who can appreciate the philosophical issues involved and the practical concerns addressed. The illustrations are full of interesting details, and readers are often intrigued by the characters' subtlety of expression. Illustrations for the book are drawn in ink and brought to life with a bright watercolor wash, which draws the reader into the pages and renders the settings and characters more credible. Steig once declared that he preferred drawing to illustrating, and this feeling is evident in the sketched and spontaneous appearance of his pictures. One critic called him a "sublime doodler," which he considered a high compliment.

Steig claimed that his stories always evolve from a character, and this development is evident in most of his books. His stories are compelling, but it is the characters that one remembers years later: Amos, the courageous little mouse who saves a whale in *Amos and Boris* (1971); the reflective Abel in *Abel's Island* (1976), who survives and matures after being marooned on a desert island; and the resourceful De Sotos, who continue their adventures in *Doctor De Soto Goes to Africa* (1993).

Because much of the literature produced for young adults is bleak and depressing, Steig's work deserves a place in this age group for its unfailing optimism. His stories, although fanciful in content or illustration, present dilemmas and encourage discussion without the accompanying pessimistic tone of much realistic fiction. His characters model hope, problem-solving, courage, and a sense of humor as tools for addressing and overcoming life's challenges. The author was quoted as saying that if children "are going to change the world, they have to start off optimistically." The upbeat tone of his works confirms his claim that he "would not consider writing a depressing book for children."

Critical Context

As a young man, William Steig proclaimed his ambition to be a writer, but he turned his talents to cartooning as a way to make a living. At the suggestion of Robert Kraus, a children's writer and colleague at *The New Yorker*, Steig began writing books for children. *Doctor De Soto* was named a Newbery Honor Book in 1982, the second of his books to receive that honor. Steig's *The Amazing Bone* (1976) was named a Caldecott Honor Book and *Abel's Island* was named a Newbery Honor Book. Before that, he won the Caldecott Medal in 1969 for *Sylvester and the Magic Pebble*, a fantasy featuring a stone that grants wishes.

Seemingly defenseless animals who survive by their own wits or magic are featured in other books by Steig. He created Amanda the pig, who uses a talking bone to escape capture in *The Amazing Bone*, and Solomon the rabbit, who turns himself into a nail in order to avoid a cat in *Solomon the Rusty Nail* (1985). In folktale fashion, Steig's protagonists are transformed in some way for the better by their experiences, developing patience, insight, courage, or a sense of humor out of the ordeals that they face.

Doctor De Soto Goes to Africa, the sequel to *Doctor De Soto*, features Mrs. De Soto in a more prominent role and provides her name (Deborah) for the first time. Both books portray the De Sotos in the classic tradition of husband-and-wife teams: warm and loving, quick-thinking and courageous. They encounter serious problems but retain their sense of adventure with unfailing humor.

Marcia Brown Popp

DOCTOR ZHIVAGO

Author: Boris Pasternak (1890-1960)
First published: Doktor Zhivago, 1957 (English translation, 1958)
Type of work: Novel
Type of plot: Historical fiction and psychological realism
Time of work: 1900-1930
Locale: Russia
Subjects: Love and romance, politics and law, and war
Recommended ages: 15-18

> *Yuri Zhivago finishes medical school at a tumultuous point in Russian history and learns that life and art cannot be subordinated to politics or other ideologies.*

> *Principal characters:*
> YURI ANDREEVICH ZHIVAGO, called Yura in childhood, a young man who lives a poetic life despite the impositions of war and revolution
> ANTONINA GROMEKO, called also Tonia, Zhivago's legal wife
> LARISA GUISHAR, called mostly Lara, a young woman seduced by Komarovsky, who later becomes the wife of the revolutionary Pavel Antipov and the lover of Zhivago
> VIKTOR KOMAROVSKY, the lawyer who drove Yuri Zhivago's father to his death, the seducer and eventual destroyer of Larisa Guishar
> EVGRAF ZHIVAGO, sometimes called Grania, Yuri Zhivago's half brother with "slanted eyes" from Siberia who, because of his ties to the land, remains as successful in the new world as he had been in the old
> PAVEL ANTIPOV, called Pasha or Pashenka, the revolutionary son of a railway worker, the legal husband of Lara

Form and Content

The main character, Yuri Zhivago, starts out as a young man in unremarkable times, the turn of the twentieth century in Russia. History has other plans, however, for both Zhivago and Russia. The plot of *Doctor Zhivago* concerns the disruption of civilization as a result of cataclysmic events in history. The first scenes take place during the period of peace preceding the first Russian revolution of 1905. Soon, however, the revolution insinuates itself into Zhivago's experience. By the time of World War I, he is a doctor and works on the front. During the civil war, he is kidnapped by the White Army and made to serve among them. He escapes, but fate calls him back to Moscow, where he dies in a streetcar, of a bursting—broken—heart.

Much of the plot revolves around fate. The young Yuri becomes a doctor as he had planned and marries his intended bride, showing that will can be successfully exerted; but war, revolution, famine, and the Russian Civil War first displace him from his home, then send his family beyond his reach, and eventually breaks his life apart. In the warp between will and fate, he begins to understand the difference between living in a role that is made for one in life and living itself. In Siberia, he joins another woman, Lara, while still married to his wife, Tonia; he learns that here, far from the strictures of the city's quotidian existence and polite society, he has at last a soul mate, someone, who like him, looks to life as an end in itself. Thus, he finds a means for justifying the human soul, but not as the bizarre straining to some materialistic or ideological goal that counts victories in abstract categories beyond individual personal experience; he knows that it is this focus on achievement that often throttles life and human thought.

This work incorporates a traditional, novelistic structure that starts at a given point, diverges from it, and eventually returns to it, with many interesting deviations as well. One of these is a third section, not labeled either chapter or part, devoted exclusively to the poems ostensibly written by Yuri Zhivago, primarily during his seclusion at Varykino. These poems are a kind of psychological or philosophical echo of the experiences of Zhivago, an internal resonance of the external chronicle of his life found in the novel. In Varykino, he has time for the introspection and philosophizing that were long lacking in his life, and it is here that he wrestles with the sense of his own being, the necessity of love, and fate.

The prose text is divided into two parts: Part 1 corresponds to the period before the physical upheaval of Zhivago, and part 2, before the conclusion and epilogue, are devoted to the Siberian experience. Into the narrative itself are inserted such text as poems, signs, and proclamations, which was very typical of Russian writing of the 1910's and 1920's, when the action of this novel takes place, further reconstructing the historical period of the novel.

Analysis

The famous film version of the novel seems to be an extravaganza of glorious landscape forming the background to a complex love relationship; however, this is a simplified reading of the novel. In Boris Pasternak's *Doctor Zhivago*, the focus is on life and fate, with the complexities that war, revolution, and civil war bring to it. "Zhivago," here a surname, means "of the living," and the novel to a slight degree could even be taken at the level of allegory in which Yuri Zhivago, a healer and a poet, nurtures the human body and spirit during these critical times.

The main character is not a typical hero. He is a weak man, the son of a profligate, and the nephew of a sentimental writer. His nature is not aggressive; he seems, therefore, a little passive, although he clearly plays the active role of the doctor and escapes his captors on his own. He is a poet, caught not only in the earthly humdrum of the poets of other generations but also in the cataclysm of a vastly sweeping change in the entire world that he inhabits.

The theme of love involves the philosophy that love is elemental in nature, not romantic, with the profanity of the seduction of Lara by Viktor Komarovsky clearly juxtaposed with the pure, fated, soulful union of Lara and Yuri Zhivago. His fascination begins with their first meeting, when she is still much under the control of Komarovsky, and he feels a natural curiosity and attraction to her. Later, when she is the nurse Antipova, he tries "not to love her," although he is trying at the same time to love everyone and he recognizes this disparity. Finally, in Siberia, the last obstacles fall aside and their love can be fulfilled. It is only now that Zhivago understands fully the difference between the union of souls and earthly love. Meanwhile, in some of the worst situations that typically arose during this historical period, Zhivago finds himself the victim of disease and famine, the captive of the White Army during the civil war, and the estranged husband and father of his family.

While *Doctor Zhivago* is about life and love, it is also an act of criticism against the Soviet regime. The novel earned for Pasternak the Nobel Prize in Literature, but it was never published in the Soviet Union before the period called *glasnost*, when the loosening of power by the decrepit Soviet regime allowed the rehabilitation of many past artistic accomplishments. Indeed, the novel's impact on the West had a commensurate, if converse, effect on the repression of Pasternak by the Soviet regime. He was forced to renounce his work and soon, like Zhivago, died of a heart attack, the medical term that Pasternak had used in his novel to describe a profoundly broken heart.

In the novel, Yuri serves to makes clear that this is no way to live; he even becomes so downhearted that he blames the revolutionaries for not being competent in life and thus ruining a great part of the country. He tells Lara, "It turns out that those who inspired the revolution aren't at home in anything except change and turmoil. . . . Man is born to live, not to prepare for life." Thus, the revolution betrayed the very people that it had claimed to support and, worse, limited the experience of life.

The novel should be seen to operate on two levels at once: seamlessly expressing the philosophy of life and art that Pasternak believed and recounting the historical period of between 1900 and 1930 in Russia in a vivid, visual manner. Zhivago lives in a time that all but destroys his life force, yet he manages to forestall the inevitable and create a beautiful life for himself.

Critical Context

Many novels are devoted to the Russian Revolution. Most of the Soviet-model ones, such as Maxim Gorky's *Mat* (1906; *The Mother*, 1906) or Fyodor Gladkov's *Tsement* (1925; *Cement*, 1929) stress the machinelike qualities of the "new man," the Darwinian/Marxian improvement over human nature that "naturally" evolves in a better, communist environment. In some ways, *Doctor Zhivago* is one of the best novels about the Russian civil war. The realism of the situation is unmistakable and follows in accordance with the actual facts: Many people sought to avoid death by starvation in the cities either by emigration or seclusion in the provinces. The portrayal of both sides of the struggle is also unusual in its realism; so many authors, partisan to the Red Army by their own personal dedication or by coercion, portray the White Army in an unfavorable, inhuman light. Pasternak's battle scenes rank on a par with those of Leo Tolstoy for psychological realism.

Pasternak wrote what amounts to ideological anathema: that people are bigger and better than revolutions because they are alive and sentient, capable of both great and small acts, comfortable with and without strong ideological foundation, blessed with their aesthetic sensitivities and expressions. Philosopher Karl Marx relegated art to the utilitarian: Art must inform. Pasternak, with Zhivago, negated this erroneous view: Art is a part of human nature, the height of human attainment, something with which the Greeks and Romans would concur. *Doctor Zhivago* remains a classic work of literature, usually reserved for the college classroom but accessible to anyone with either a poetic nature or genuine interest in life.

Christine D. Tomei

DOGSONG

Author: Gary Paulsen (1939-   )
First published: 1985
Type of work: Novel
Type of plot: Adventure tale, moral tale, and psychological realism
Time of work: The 1980's
Locale: Alaska
Subjects: Coming-of-age, nature, and race and ethnicity
Recommended ages: 13-18

Russel Susskit, a fourteen-year-old Inuit boy who shuns the modern ways of his village, sets out on a solitary 1,400-mile journey by dogsled to find himself and his past.

> *Principal characters:*
> RUSSEL SUSSKIT, an Inuit boy who goes on a spiritual and physical journey by dogsled
> RUSSEL'S FATHER, an Inuit who has accepted the new cultural and religious practices that have changed the traditional Inuit way of life
> OOGRUK, a blind Inuit elder who still follows the old ways and who becomes Russel's mentor
> NANCY, a pregnant teenage Inuit girl whom Russel finds in the wilderness

Form and Content

Gary Paulsen has divided his novel into three major sections: "The Trance," "The Dreamrun," and "Dogsong." As the novel begins, Russel Susskit, a fourteen-year-old Inuit boy, feels that something is missing from his life, but he lacks the words to express what he does not fully understand. Since he is unable to help him, Russel's father advises his son to seek out Oogruk, a blind old man who still follows the traditional style of Inuit life. Oogruk immediately recognizes Russel's dissatisfaction with the modern culture that has supplanted many Inuit ways. Although Oogruk claims some of his memory is "dead and gone," he agrees to teach Russel what he remembers of the old ways. "The Trance" recounts how Russel learns and practices the Inuit traditions, which he finds more fulfilling than his earlier lifestyle.

During Russel's training, Oogruk places particular emphasis on the importance of personal songs in Inuit culture. According to Oogruk, the Inuit lost their songs because the missionaries taught them that songs were bad, but Oogruk tells Russel "when we gave up our songs because we feared hell, we gave up our insides as well." When Russel asks Oogruk to teach him a song, Oogruk tells him that he cannot be taught a song, that he must become a song, an observation which Russel does not fully understand until much later in the story.

After the death of Oogruk, Russel heads north with the old man's dogsled in a journey in which he finds himself tested by the forces of nature in the same way that Inuit men were tested prior to the contact with white civilization. Nature forces Russel to draw on personal resources that he does not know he has until his own survival depends on them. By the time that Russel finds Nancy, an Inuit girl who has left her home village to die in shame because of her pregnancy, he is capable not only of taking care of himself and his dogs but also of taking on the additional responsibility of caring for Nancy.

Paulsen has interspersed the story of Russel's journey with a series of dreams that Russel experiences involving an Inuit man from a much earlier time period. At first, the man in the dreams is a shadow figure, but as Russel's competency grows, Russel and the man in the dreams become the same person. Paulsen concludes the book with Russel's "Dogsong," a celebration of his dogs and his accomplishments during the journey. During his long, solitary journey northward, Russel has found both himself and his past.

Analysis

Dogsong is a novel of survival that can be read on many levels and by a wide range of age groups. On one level, Paulsen presents an adventure story in which Russel confronts storms, severe cold, and near starvation, as well as a huge polar bear that he must kill for food to keep both himself and his dogs alive. Surviving under these difficult circumstances, Russel gains a sense of accomplishment and feeling of competency that he might not have been able to achieve if he had remained in his home settlement in the relative comfort provided by his father. By the time that his mentor dies, Russel is no longer in need of instruction; the old ways have become sufficiently ingrained in him that Russel is able to survive on his own.

During the course of the story, Paulsen presents Inuit customs and beliefs in a sympathetic fashion. He allows readers to grow in understanding and acceptance of these customs and beliefs at the same time that Russel does. At the beginning of the novel, Russel feels vaguely dissatisfied with the snowmobiles and television sets that have widely been adopted by the people of his settlement, although he cannot put into words what makes him uneasy about these components of his lifestyle. With Oogruk as his mentor, Russel learns as much as the old man can remember of the old ways.

At first, Russel feels uncomfortable and almost silly while practicing some of the Inuit customs, such as placing food in the mouth of the animals that he has killed in gratitude for the food that they will provide. At the same time, however, he feels a rightness in his actions unlike anything that he has experienced earlier in his life. Later, these customs become ingrained in his nature, and he even feels a sense of regret when he does not have food available to place in the mouth of the polar bear that he kills. Russel also hears but does not fully understand what Oogruk tells him about the interdependence and bonding between humans and dogs until he spends time with the dogs as his only companions during his solitary journey. By the end of the journey, Russel and his dogs have bonded in the way that Oogruk had predicted they would.

On a more complex level, Paulsen presents a vision quest in which Russel searches for himself and his past. During his extended period of isolation from other people, Russel dreams of a man from a much earlier time period who kills a mammoth with only a spear, suffers many of the same hardships of nature that Russel experiences, and ultimately loses his family when they starve before he can return with meat for them. At first, the man in the dreams is not clearly defined, but, as the dreams progress, the man becomes Russel and, in real time, Russel becomes as competent as the man in his dreams. Russel also achieves his own song because of his adventures and his experiences with his dogs. The song, which Paulsen uses as the concluding pages of the book, with its repeated line of "Come see my dogs," becomes a celebration of the interdependency of Russel and his dog team. The dream sequence may present problems for some younger readers, particularly when the dreams and reality begin to blend into one. Although Russel's vision quest, and particularly his dreams, may create some confusion for these readers, for older readers they will provide additional depth to what might otherwise be simply an adventure story.

The novel employs the lyrical language that has become the hallmark of Paulsen's writing style and that makes the novel ideal for reading aloud. In fact, the story has the sound of the stories that people from an earlier time, reared in an oral culture, might have shared around a campfire.

Critical Context

Gary Paulsen had written more than twenty-five books for both adult and young adult audiences beginning in the mid-1960's, before publishing *Dogsong* in 1985. The novel became his first Newbery Honor Book and started a succession of popular young adult novels that moved him into the forefront of young adult authors.

An avid outdoorsman and dog sledder, Paulsen drew upon his personal experiences in the Iditarod—a 1,049-mile Alaskan dogsled race from Anchorage to Nome—to add authenticity to his account of Russel's journey. In addition, Russel's respect and love for his dogs echoes Paulsen's own relationship with the dogs that he has owned. After *Dogsong*, Paulsen wrote two fascinating nonfiction accounts, *Woodsong* (1991) and *Winterdance: The Fine Madness of Running the Iditarod* (1994), about his personal relationship with sled dogs.

Russel is the first of Paulsen's many teenage characters who "come of age" confronting the forces of nature, sometimes alone and sometimes with mentors such as Oogruk. For example, *Hatchet* (1987), Paulsen's second Newbery Honor Book and unquestionably his most popular novel, uses the same testing-by-nature theme, although the primary character in *Hatchet* is a middle-class, white teenager. Paulsen used a similar theme in *The Voyage of the Frog* (1989); in this story, his teenage protagonist is tested by the ocean in a solitary voyage in a small sailboat.

Paulsen's sympathetic treatment of Inuit culture is not unique. Since the publication of *Dogsong*, Paulsen has earned a reputation for sympathetic portrayals of a wide range of ethnic groups, including American Indians in *Canyons* (1990) and Mexicans in *The Crossing* (1987).

Ronald Barron

A DOLL'S HOUSE

Author: Henrik Ibsen (1828-1906)
First presented: Et dukkehjem, 1879
First published: 1879 (English translation, 1880)
Type of work: Drama
Type of plot: Domestic realism and social realism
Time of work: The late nineteenth century
Locale: A comfortable room in the Helmer residence
Subjects: Family, gender roles, and social issues
Recommended ages: 13-18

Taught to accept without question the role of submissive wife, Nora learns that her first duty is to herself as a person.

Principal characters:
   NORA HELMER, a young wife and mother who is proud of her efforts to restore her husband's health
   TORVALD HELMER, a lawyer who is protective and paternal in his role as Nora's husband
   DR. RANK, a family friend
   KRISTINE LINDE, a widow, Nora's childhood friend and confidante
   NILS KROGSTAD, a fired bank clerk

Form and Content

   A Doll's House, a realistic three-act play, focuses on late nineteenth century life in a middle-class Scandinavian household, in which the wife is expected to be contentedly passive and the husband paternally protective. Nora Helmer, however, has subverted this model. At that time, a woman could not sign a legal contract alone; thus, when her beloved husband, Torvald, became ill, Nora secretly obtained a loan by forging her father's signature so that they could travel to a warmer climate. As the play opens, Torvald is about to become manager of the bank and Nora has almost repaid the loan through odd jobs and scrimping on the household expenses. Nora discloses her actions to her friend Kristine Linde and exults in her accomplishment.
   The structure of the play is linear; after the exposition, the action becomes complicated with the appearance of Nora's debtor, Nils Krogstad, a man disgraced by crimes that he committed to protect his family. Insecure in his position at the bank, he threatens to expose Nora's loan and forgery unless she pleads his case to Torvald. In her ignorance, Nora had not fully understood that forgery is a criminal act.
   The major conflict of the play, concerning honesty in marriage, arises from this situation. Nora cannot discuss the blackmail with her husband, since her role in their relationship is that of a charming child; thus, she must plead for Krogstad. Torvald,

however, refuses to hear her plea, labeling Krogstad morally lost for the crimes that he committed and not fit to bring up his children. The parallel is not lost on Nora, who sends her children away from her at the end of the first act.

Nora's fear increases when Torvald rejects her second plea and fires Krogstad. As Kristine helps with her costume for the Christmas party, Nora confesses that Krogstad has left a letter to Torvald in the mailbox revealing everything. She is convinced that now a wonderful thing will happen—that, when Torvald discovers her actions, he will assume the blame and that she then will commit suicide. As the second act ends, Nora dances a violent tarantella in an effort to distract Torvald from opening the mailbox.

The final act begins with Kristine and Krogstad resuming a relationship formerly hindered by their economic circumstances. Although Krogstad now regrets his blackmail, Kristine decides that the letter should remain in the mailbox and that Torvald must discover the truth. Torvald reads the letter and immediately denounces Nora as a liar and a criminal, the destroyer of his future. When another letter arrives containing the promissory note, however, Torvald realizes that he is "safe." He forgives Nora, promising to "be conscience and will" to her thereafter. In the classic scene that follows, Nora speaks openly with her husband, the first such occasion in their entire married life, and admits her ignorance of herself and the world beyond. Declaring that she must leave Torvald and the children to find herself, she leaves and slams the door behind her.

Analysis

When Henrik Ibsen wrote *A Doll's House*, the institution of marriage was sacrosanct; women did not leave their husbands, and marital roles were sharply defined. The play, which questions these traditional attitudes, was highly controversial and elicited sharp criticism. The character of Nora Helmer, a favorite with actresses seeking a role of strength and complexity, has dominated the play from its inception. She is the one who gains audience empathy, who grows through the course of the play. Some early critics viewed Nora as a prime example of the "new woman," a breed seeking independence and self-definition, and the play as a polemic advocating women's rights. Some insisted that although a woman might leave her husband, she would never leave her children. Later critics faulted Nora's sudden conversion from a sheltered child stroking her husband's ego to a mature woman seeking independence. Yet, others maintained that Ibsen skillfully foreshadows Nora's departure in her behavior throughout the play in her gaiety, generosity, and unselfishness. Further, Ibsen himself declared that he was not writing solely about women but instead about issues of his society and about the need for individuals, both men and women, to be true to themselves.

Thus *A Doll's House* can be viewed thematically not only as a picture of an innocent nineteenth century woman struggling to achieve self-definition but also as a devastating indictment of a routine marriage between two ordinary people who lack awareness of themselves and who have differing views of right and wrong. Torvald unquestioningly accepts society's dicta of the husband as the breadwinner and moral authority, but Nora's attempt to conform as the submissive wife forces her into lies and deception. Both care about what people think; neither consciously considers opposing society's mores.

The need for communication contributes to the thematic pattern of the play. Nora and Torvald communicate only on the most superficial level; he speaks from the conventions of society but neither sees nor hears her, while she can only play out the role that he has constructed for her. This inability or unwillingness to express themselves verbally leads to unhappiness and pain.

The theme is echoed in the subplot of Kristine and Krogstad, both of whom have struggled with the cruelties of society. Kristine endured a loveless marriage in order to support her elderly mother and young brothers; Krogstad was forced into crime in order to care for his ill wife and children. Although within the plot their union seems somewhat contrived, Ibsen characterizes them as aware of themselves and honest with each other.

One of Ibsen's masterful touches is the use of concealment as a motif; it permeates the play in several manifestations and reinforces the major theme of the need for openness in marriage. Nora's first word, "hide," initiates the motif. Thereafter, she hides the Christmas presents, lies about eating macaroons, continues to deceive Torvald into believing that she is a spendthrift and flighty female, and invents distractions to prevent him from opening the mailbox. Torvald too participates in concealment. Fearing exposure in the third act, he starts and orders "Hide, Nora! Say you're sick" when the doorbell rings.

The primary agent of empowerment in *A Doll's House* is money. Private and public rewards result from its presence. It enabled Nora and Torvald to travel to Italy for his health. Money from Torvald's new salary at the bank will provide prestige for the Helmers and allow Nora, in particular, to breathe more easily. Yet, all the major figures—Torvald, Nora, Kristine, and Krogstad—have been affected adversely by its absence: from the deception in the marriage of Torvald and Nora to the prior unhappy marriage of Kristine and the criminal acts of Krogstad.

In the complex pattern that Ibsen has created, lack of self-knowledge, inability to communicate, and unthinking conformity to convention affect the institution of marriage most adversely.

Critical Context

A Doll's House is an important play both for its subject matter and for its method. Frequently anthologized and often revived, its subject matter, the exploration of a marriage, carries universal interest. Along with Ibsen's *Hedda Gabler* (1890; English translation, 1891) and *Gengangere* (1881; *Ghosts*, 1885), the focus on the behavior of a specific woman helped to pave the way for plays in which women in major roles think and behave as complex human beings rather than as cardboard figures.

Ibsen's method is equally notable; he achieves his effects through plainness and economy. The dialogue in *A Doll's House* is spare and conversational and true to each character. There are no long bombastic or poetic speeches; each exchange carries the action forward. Much of the emotional progress is nonverbal; the slamming of the door in the final moment is truly eloquent.

Ibsen chose a three-act, linear, climactic structure, almost classic in its regard for the Aristotelian elements of time and place but also a model for the realistic movement, with its emphasis on everyday, domestic details. The time span is three days, specifically Christmas Eve through the day after Christmas. The setting, a room in the Helmer household, is carefully described, with furniture and objects that help to delineate the characters.

A watershed, *A Doll's House* marked the beginning of Ibsen's greatest period of creativity, as well as a new direction for theater itself.

Joyce E. Henry

DON QUIXOTE DE LA MANCHA

Author: Miguel de Cervantes (1547-1616)
First published: El ingenioso hidalgo Don Quixote de la Mancha, part 1, 1605;
part 2, 1615 (English translation, 1612-1620)
Type of work: Novel
Type of plot: Adventure tale and psychological realism
Time of work: The early seventeenth century
Locale: The region of La Mancha in rural Spain and Barcelona
Subjects: Friendship and love and romance
Recommended ages: 15-18

Alonso Quixano, a gentleman around fifty years of age, decides to call himself Don Quixote de la Mancha and to become a knight errant in imitation of the heroes of the novels of chivalry that he reads incessantly.

Principal characters:
ALONSO QUIXANO, who becomes Don Quixote
ANTONIA QUIXANA, his niece, who lives with him
SANCHO PANZA, Don Quixote's squire, companion, and friend
ROCINANTE, Don Quixote's horse
DULCINEA DEL TOBOSO, the imaginary lady whom Don Quixote loves
NICHOLAS, the barber in Don Quixote's village
SAMPSON CARRASCO, a student from Don Quixote's village who,
dressed as a knight errant, challenges and defeats Don Quixote

Form and Content

Alonso Quixano declares himself to be Don Quixote and, dressed in an old suit of armor and riding a feeble nag called Rocinante, secretly leaves the home that he shares with his niece and housekeeper. After riding all day, he stops at an inn, which he imagines to be a castle, and there has the innkeeper perform a ridiculous ceremony that, in Don Quixote's mind, makes him a knight. Now he will be able to begin the work of knight errantry, serving his state by redressing wrongs and by participating in fabulous adventures that will bring him honor and fame. All his exploits he will dedicate to the lady of his fancies, Dulcinea del Toboso, a person loosely identified with Aldonza Lorenzo, a farm girl whom Don Quixote had admired at one time.

In Don Quixote's first opportunity to perform a good deed, he interrupts the beating of a young boy, Andrew, by his master, Juan Haldudo. Proud of his accomplishment, Don Quixote departs without realizing that his intervention later causes Andrew to suffer even more severely at the hands of his master. Following another adventure, Don Quixote is discovered badly beaten by a neighbor, who brings him home. While Don Quixote is recuperating, his niece and housekeeper, along with his friends, the village priest and the barber, burn the books of chivalry that have produced Don Quixote's madness, hoping thus to effect a cure.

Don Quixote recovers and entices his friend Sancho Panza to join him on a second journey in search of adventure by promising to make Sancho governor of some island that Don Quixote expects to win in the practice of knight errantry. In their first adventure together, the two men hold boldly contrasting points of view. Don Quixote sees what he believes are a number of giants whom he must attack, while Sancho sees the objects for the windmills that they really are. Thus begins a series of encounters until finally Don Quixote is brought home again through the efforts of the priest and barber at the end of part 1.

In part 2, Don Quixote and Sancho depart once more after hearing that a book has been written about them. Now, because of their long association, there is a lesser contrast in the manner in which they view the numerous adventures that they experience on their second journey together. Meanwhile, Sampson Carrasco, a student from Don Quixote's village, believes that the only way to cure Don Quixote's madness and to keep him at home is to do so according to the laws of chivalry. Disguising himself as a knight errant, Sampson follows Don Quixote and challenges him to fight. Following an initial failure, Sampson finally defeats Don Quixote in Barcelona and makes him promise to return home and abandon knight errantry for a year. After returning home, Don Quixote falls asleep ill, awakens, calls himself cured of his madness, renounces his career as a knight errant, and calmly dies.

Analysis

The success of *Don Quixote de la Mancha* is all the more remarkable considering that it was spawned by Miguel de Cervantes' feelings of frustration and rejection. After returning wounded from military service and five years of captivity in North Africa, Cervantes found slight success as he began his literary career, especially in his attempt to write for the theater. His domestic life brought little happiness, and he was justly disappointed when the Spanish crown for which he had fought denied him the bureaucratic appointment he sought in Spain's American colonies. Having to settle for a position as tax collector in Seville, he was arrested and imprisoned for performing his job improperly. According to legend, Cervantes began writing *Don Quixote de la Mancha* in jail.

In addition to his personal misfortunes, he saw his Spanish navy, the Armada, suffer a complete reversal of fate between 1571, when Cervantes helped defeat the Turks at Lepanto, and 1588, when the Armada was destroyed by the English navy. *Don Quixote de la Mancha* has the wistful tone that could only be produced by an almost-sixty-year-old author, remembering what it was like to have been a young, heroic dreamer, who has seen his own personal plans and those of his country fall through. The only fault of Cervantes—and of Don Quixote—is having dared to dream in the first place.

When Don Quixote sees windmills and imagines them to be giants, or when he sees two flocks of sheep and imagines them to be two armies converging in battle, his delusions of grandeur are a metaphor for the Spanish government's refusal to face economic and political reality at the time that the novel was written. In Cervantes' day,

Spain was at the height of its imperial power. Nevertheless, all the gold that Spain garnered from its colonies in the Americas did not enrich the country. On the contrary, the gold passed through customs in Seville and continued on its way to finance Spain's wars fought to maintain its imperial territories in northern Europe. Like Don Quixote's knightly behavior and posturing, Spain's power was an illusion with no basis in reality. *Don Quixote de la Mancha* and other Spanish literature of the time is said to belong to the "Golden Age," a term that refers not only to the high quality of Spanish literature at the time but also to the misguided optimism inspired by the gold in Spanish America. It is ironic that this novel and other Spanish literary masterpieces were spawned by a period of economic depression and political decadence.

In addition to serving as a social and political commentary on Spain in the early seventeenth century, *Don Quixote de la Mancha* is considered modern because of the way in which Cervantes developed his characters. From the point of view of Freudian psychology, Don Quixote and Sancho Panza are two halves of the same personality, id and ego. Although the hopeless dreamer and the crude pragmatist appear to have little in common, they need each other. In part 2, their divergent points of view gradually become less polarized until the two characters almost change places.

With the help of Sancho Panza, Don Quixote gradually develops a sense of humor as the novel progresses. At the beginning of the novel, Don Quixote is severe and somber. By the beginning of part 2, however, he is able to laugh at Sancho's clumsy attempt to imitate Don Quixote's language of chivalry. Soon thereafter, Don Quixote will be able to recognize the absurdity of his own inflated stance.

Sancho Panza also helps the reader laugh at Don Quixote and thereby understand him. If the reader witnessed Don Quixote's adventures and illusions without also having the benefit of Sancho's reaction, Don Quixote might be dismissed as a lunatic. Because of Sancho's patience with Don Quixote, however, the reader is likewise sympathetic to the deluded knight.

Critical Context

Since Cervantes published part 1 of *Don Quixote de la Mancha* in 1605, the work has been immensely popular. The immediate critical reception of the book was so great that it inspired a spurious sequel by Alonso Fernández de Avellaneda in 1614. Cervantes reacted to this counterfeit sequel by rushing to finish and publish part 2 in 1615, which he concluded with the death of the protagonist so that no other author might ride Cervantes' coattails to fame. Part 2 begins with a dialogue between Don Quixote and Sancho Panza in which they recognize that they are literary characters in part 1. They talk about which of their adventures are the favorites of the readers of *Don Quixote de la Mancha*. They even discuss how many copies of the novel's first part have been published and the number of languages into which it has been translated.

The work's popularity has never waned, and the character of Don Quixote has transcended literature to become a cultural icon, not only in Spain but around the world as well. In La Mancha and other regions of Spain, apocryphal stories of Don

Quixote complement the published text. In addition to being the protagonist of the masterpiece of the Spanish literary canon, Don Quixote is the subject of and inspiration for much Spanish folklore.

Because of Cervantes' masterful combination of subtle characterization and straightforward adventure, *Don Quixote de la Mancha* appeals to a broad spectrum of audiences. The work continues to be the subject of the most scholarly research, while it also has been adapted to children's books, animated comics, feature films in several countries, and a Broadway musical.

Douglas Edward LaPrade

DONALD DUK

Author: Frank Chin (1940-   )
First published: 1991
Type of work: Novel
Type of plot: Psychological realism
Time of work: The 1980's
Locale: San Francisco's Chinatown
Subjects: Coming-of-age, education, and race and ethnicity
Recommended ages: 13-18

During a Chinese New Year in San Francisco, twelve-year-old Donald Duk learns from his elders about the cultural heritage of Chinese Americans and about his own racial identity.

> *Principal characters:*
> DONALD DUK, a fifth-generation Chinese American boy who over-
> comes the devastating effects of stereotypes and who resolves to
> be true to his racial identity
> KING DUK, Donald's father, who teaches his son how to be an
> American without losing his cultural heritage
> UNCLE DONALD DUK, who introduces Donald Duk to his family
> history and the cultural heritage of Chinese Americans
> KWAN KUNG, the god of warriors and writers worshiped by Chinese
> railroad builders, who appears in Donald's dreams as the foreman
> of a Chinese railroad gang

Form and Content

Donald Duk tells a thought-provoking story of a fifth-generation Chinese American boy, Donald Duk, who awakens from the trauma caused by a racial stereotype perpetuated by the majority culture and decides to challenge it. Set in San Francisco's Chinatown, the events in the novel are related from a perspective authentically Chinese American and in a language uniquely fast-paced, humorous, and witty. Skillfully incorporated into these events are history, surrealistic dreams, psychological probings, and social realism. As with any other literary work with racial issues as its subject matter, this novel will inevitably cause some interesting discussions among its readers on such topics as racial identity and stereotypes, acculturation and assimilation, uniformity and diversity.

Donald Duk is troubled by his name. People laugh at him, thinking that he is named after the Disney cartoon character. He soon learns to deal with them, taking them by surprise by joining them in laughing at his name. Yet, there is another problem that he cannot get rid of with laughter—his identity as a Chinese American. Repeatedly, he has heard people at school and in the media claim that Chinese Americans are traditionally timid and passive, introverted and unassertive; therefore, they lack the very qualities that are thought to constitute heroism and a pioneering spirit in the United States. Believing what he has been told, Donald lives in a state of self-contempt and self-rejection, with a bitter aversion to everything Chinese. As the Chinese New Year approaches, he becomes increasingly depressed, for his past experiences have convinced him that the Chinese New Year will give his schoolteachers a chance to say in class the "same thing" that everybody else does about his people.

Yet, the New Year during which Donald is completing the first twelve-year cycle of his life (there are twelve years in the Chinese Zodiac) provides his elders in his family and in the community with the right opportunity to tell him what "everybody" has never said about his people. With a deep understanding of the boy's feelings and a strong sense of their responsibility for him, these elders begin to reveal to him the most important chapters in the history of Chinese Americans, a history written and preserved by themselves. Donald Duk learns that Chinese Americans came from a country that has produced its own Robin Hoods and that one of his ancestors was a legendary warrior of indomitable courage and bravery. He also discovers how his great-great-grandfather and other Chinese railroad workers confronted harsh conditions with courage, tenacity, and a pioneering spirit. He becomes so fascinated with their heroic feats that he begins to dream of these railroad builders blasting their way through Nevada, living in tunnels carved in deep frozen snow for two winters, setting a world record by laying ten miles of track in one day, and going on strike for back pay and the right to have Chinese foremen for Chinese work gangs.

The difference between the image of his ancestors that he now sees and the stereotype that he used to accept is so astonishing that he begins to wonder whether it is only an illusion. Research in the library, however, assures him that his dreams are actually flashbacks to the real events in history, events that have been excluded in history books by the majority culture. With his newly gained understanding of the cultural heritage of his people, Donald Duk is no longer troubled by his racial identity; he has freed himself from the feelings of self-contempt and self-rejection. When he goes back to school, he is ready and able to tell, with dignity, his version of the story of Chinese Americans.

Analysis

Donald Duk is, among other things, a story of initiation in which a young boy overcomes the devastating racial stereotyping of his people and grows up to be a Chinese American true to his cultural heritage. In this respect, it is an intriguing novel for young Americans from different racial groups, for they all have to confront, in one way or another, the stereotyping of their own races. The book contains a number of subthemes, all related to racial issues: prejudice, exclusion, alienation, the preservation of one's racial identity, and what it means to be an American.

The structure of the novel as a story of initiation consists of three phases: trauma, dream, and wake-up. When Frank Chin's young protagonist first appears in the novel, he feels bitter and restless, suffering from low self-esteem. As a Chinese American, he resents everything Chinese and desperately tries to distance himself from his own people. As Frank Chin shows in the psychological portrait of his young protagonist, Donald is simply traumatized by the prevalent misconception of Chinese Americans in mainstream American culture. He has been told again and again at school and by the media that Chinese Americans are devoid of the very qualities that define American heroism and ambition, that they are traditionally passive, submissive, and effeminate.

What brings him out of his resulting sense of alienation are his dreams of his great-great-grandfather and other Chinese transcontinental railroad builders, with their undeniably heroic role in the conquest of the American West. Chin makes it unmistakably clear that what appears in his young protagonist's dreams is not a wild fantasy or wish fulfillment but a dramatization in his mind of some of the most important feats accomplished by his ancestors. His dreams come as a direct result of a history lesson that he receives from elders in his family and in the community. It is a lesson in the history of Chinese Americans kept alive in their collective consciousness.

Chin presents Donald Duk's elders as a group of caring, thoughtful people conscious of their role in preserving their heritage in an environment that tends to distort it. Although always aware of Donald's problems, they choose to wait until the Chinese New Year when he is to complete the first cycle of twelve years of his life. Among these people is Uncle Donald Duk, who, right before the New Year, introduces his young nephew to the legend of Chinese Robin Hoods and the history of Chinese Americans beginning with the railroad. Then, there is King Duk, who teaches his son that he can and should be an American without losing his cultural identity. Finally, there are the elders in the entire Chinese American community who maintain their heritage in various ways with dignity and confidence. Chin's characterization of these elders emphasizes that Donald's triumph over the distorting stereotype imposed on his people is also a triumph for his family and the entire community.

Critical Context

For many generations, Chinese Americans have been stereotyped in the majority culture as weak, submissive, passive, and effeminate alien sojourners incapable of American heroism. Frank Chin's *Donald Duk* is among a limited number of literary works that seriously attempt to challenge such a caricature and to restore this group's true cultural heritage. By showing his protagonist learn the authentic history of Chinese Americans, Chin intends to claim that Chinese Americans are as courageous, assertive, and competitive as any other groups of immigrants, that Chinese American history is a legitimate, valiant part of the history of the American West. These claims can be provocative and disconcerting to those who consciously or unconsciously view Chinese Americans not as Americans but as foreigners and associate Chinese American culture not with American culture but with an alien culture in Asia.

When compared with Chin's earlier works, *Donald Duk* indicates a change in his view concerning the future of Chinese Americans and their cultural heritage. In an essay entitled "Yellow Seattle" (1976), Chin expressed his conviction that Chinese America is historically doomed to extinction. This gloomy view can be easily discerned in some of Chin's plays of that time, such as *The Chickencoop Chinaman* (1972) and *The Year of the Dragon* (1974). These works are permeated with a sense of decay and doom, with young people renouncing their own racial identity and families falling apart. Such a feeling is nowhere to be found in *Donald Duk*; on the contrary, the novel has an atmosphere of renewal and jubilant celebration, with a whole family and a whole community proudly and successfully passing on their heritage from one generation to the next.

Chenliang Sheng

DON'T YOU TURN BACK

Author: Langston Hughes (1902-1967)
First published: 1969; illustrated
Type of work: Poetry
Subjects: Coming-of-age, education, family, race and ethnicity, and social issues
Recommended ages: 10-18

This beautifully illustrated collection of forty-five poems by the one of the premier African American poets of the twentieth century was selected posthumously from his works by Harlem fourth-graders.

Form and Content

Edited by Lee Bennett Hopkins and illustrated by Ann Grifalconi, *Don't You Turn Back* is a collection of most of the best-known poems by the best-known African American poet of the twentieth century. It contains a nostalgic introduction by Langston Hughes's good friend, the scholar Arna Bontemps, a note on the selections by the editor, thirteen woodcut illustrations by Grifalconi, and indexes of titles and first lines. The poems are arranged in four sections: "My People," "Prayers and Dreams," "Out to Sea," and "I Am a Negro." Hughes's earliest poem, "The Negro Speaks of Rivers" is included, as are his most famous pieces. The title, *Don't You Turn Back*, is a line from "Mother to Son":

> So, boy, don't you turn back.
> Don't you set down on the steps
> 'Cause you finds it kinder hard.
> Don't you fall now—
> For I'se still goin', honey,
> I'se still climbin',
> And life for me ain't been no crystal stair.

These lines capture well the range of themes and forms in the volume: love, hate, hope, despair, and family piety and devotion. The language is familiar, often collo-quial, always accessible.

"Aunt Sue's Stories" tells of a gentle woman who, like Hughes, weaves stories for her favorite children of times from slavery days to the present. "Sun Song" likewise joins the sunbaked roads of Africa to those of Georgia. "Troubled Woman" asks readers to honor the wisdom sometimes discovered through pain. A mother's gifts to her children are recounted in "April Rain Song," "Lullaby," and "Stars." Friendship and inspiration are the refrains of "Hope," "Alabama Earth," "Poem," "Youth," and "Walkers with the Dawn." The section "Prayers and Dreams" possesses the greatest concentration of poems with the characteristic Hughes touch—a distinctive blend of *joie de vivre* and clear-sighted realism. The conclusion of "Dream Variation" evokes "Rest at pale evening . . . / A tall, slim tree . . . / Night coming tenderly/ Black like me." "Dream Dust" and "Dreams" speak to what is most important in life, the latter opening "Hold fast to dreams/ For if dreams die/ Life is a broken-winged bird/ That cannot fly."

The section "Out to Sea" includes ten poems recalling Hughes's lifelong love of rivers and oceans, using the metaphor of the sea to suggest the danger and glory of all life. "Long Trip" casts life in the guise of a sea voyage, the traveler surrounded by a wilderness of waves and deserts of water. "Moonlight Night: Carmel" is an impressionistic glimpse of the California coast, while "Sea Calm" and "Suicide's Note" paint word pictures of a threatening stillness. That theme is carried into "Island," where, recalling John Donne, the poet says no one need be an island. "Seascape" carries images from as far as England and Ireland. In the final section, "I Am a Negro," all these themes and images are brought to bear upon growing up black in America, a land of "black and white black white black people."

The volume had its origin in a poetry memorial held in June, 1967, one month after Hughes's death. Lee Bennett Hopkins, who had served as consultant to the Bank Street College of Education's Harlem Center, asked fourth-graders to choose their favorites among the poet's works. Their choices were read at the service and became the basis of *Don't You Turn Back*. The book's layout and design are particularly effective. In almost all instances, a full page is devoted to each poem, with the title in a different and complementary size and color from the text. Grifalconi's evocative woodcuts heighten the effect of the verse. Most appear opposite a single poem—two complementary works of art facing each other in admiration.

Poems by Langston Hughes were read at the funerals of civil rights activist Martin Luther King, Jr., jazz great Duke Ellington, and Supreme Court Justice Thurgood Marshall. That height and range of celebrity suggest how deeply loved his verse has been—as one critic put it, "from kindergarten to the offices of Presidents." It is fitting that, although the arrangement of poems was by Hopkins, the selection was made by schoolchildren.

Analysis

The appeal of these poems is easily traced. For more than four decades, Langston Hughes was the most prominent literary figure in black America and one of the first to create a literary career. He was notable for the variety of his writing, which included essays, poetry, drama, fiction, histories, journalism, and compiled anthologies. Hughes also collaborated in dozens of translations of his works. A literary ambassador, he remained aware of what was important in the black world and was known across that world as its primary literary interpreter. Life in urban America, with Harlem as its poetic emblem, was his metier, captured in bold strokes and subtle nuances. Using Harlem as his imaginative base, he would wander far and wide to explore what interested him most—the people of black America in all of their infinite variety. No one caught so vividly their manners, their speech, their gestures, their spirit, their thoughts, and especially their dreams.

Most of the poems in this collection are short—eight lines or less. Several of the most effective—such as "Winter Moon," "Sea Calm," "Ennui," "Suicide's Note," and "Seascape"—are among the shortest. All read well aloud, having taken shape in Hughes's own public readings. All are conversational: most monologues, some dialogues, as "Brothers," which opens "We're related—you and I,/ You from the West Indies,/ I from Kentucky." Such easy flow of speech convinces many readers that the poems, even though written during the first half of the twentieth century, are contemporary, speaking directly to today. The final and culminating poem in the collection, "Daybreak in Alabama," opens "When I get to be a composer/ I'm gonna write me some music about/ Daybreak in Alabama . . . ." This conversational success clothes the anthology, punctuated often with such now-famous lines as "I, too, sing America" from the poem "I, Too."

The overarching effect is of poet as chameleon and ventriloquist. Hughes is able to enter the voice and personality of his characters—young and old, Northern and Southern, wise and learning, male and female—without force or falsity. This effect is clearest in the sections "My People" and "I Am a Negro," where the dialogue form dominates, yet it is implicit in the rest of the poems as well. Equally striking is the range of original occasion, from the Great Migration to the private tragedy within a family, each captured with proper dignity. As Hughes phrased the situation in "My People," the opening poem in the collection, "The stars are beautiful,/ So are the eyes of my people."

Critical Context

Before Hughes, few African American authors wrote for a juvenile or young adult audience. After his decisive influence, many did. A significant portion, perhaps as large as a quarter, of his many volumes of prose and poetry was written for young people. Walt Whitman, Charles Waddell Chesnutt, and Paul Laurence Dunbar were among his own distant influences, and all wished directly to address and teach a younger generation. Yet Hughes's most immediate influence was the milieu of the Harlem Renaissance, that period between the end of World War I and the onset of the Great Depression when black writers and artists called for aesthetic opportunities unknown to previous ages. Novelists, biographers, playwrights, and sculptors were among the figures seeking newer, larger audiences. Poets were their acknowledged leaders, and Hughes, although young, captured the heady mix of ancestral obligations and newfound privileges in his 1926 essay "The Negro and the Racial Mountain." He used his connections within the world of publishing to obtain contracts for a score of writers of young adult literature.

Hughes also provided an important example for handling content. He was as honestly straightforward as his famous character Jesse B. Semple, the Harlem philosopher from newspaper columns and short stories. Simple, as he is also known, is the soul of home-grown simplicity, common sense, and innocence. He calls fraud and propaganda for what it is. He does not court the painful, but he does not run from it either. Although at times indignant at racial injustice, he is guided not by fear or paranoia but by a wise tolerance. Just so, Hughes said, did young people need an introduction to the world that they shall inherit—-without cynicism or psychological inhibition. The lessons that he would teach were those most easily ignored: the strength of love, a salutary optimism, and the simple joy of being alive.

Don't You Turn Back is unusual among Hughes's works because its shape and structure were determined by people other than the poet himself, yet it is also a measure of his success. It represents the happy but uncommon circumstance of a work compiled posthumously by others fulfilling the poet's intentions. Few have been so lucky.

John Sekora

DRACULA

Author: Bram Stoker (1847-1912)
First published: 1897
Type of work: Novel
Type of plot: Fantasy and thriller
Time of work: The 1890's
Locale: A castle in Transylvania and Purfleet and Whitby, England
Subjects: Sexual issues and the supernatural
Recommended ages: 15-18

*After Jonathan Harker visits Count Dracula in Transylvania to arrange the lease
of a property in England, his fiancée and her friends suffer the count's vampiric
depredations.*

> *Principal characters:*
> COUNT DRACULA, a vampire
> JONATHAN HARKER, a solicitor's clerk
> MINA MURRAY, Harker's fiancée
> DR. JOHN SEWARD, the proprietor of a lunatic asylum in Purfleet
> ABRAHAM VAN HELSING, a philosopher and metaphysician
> LUCY WESTENRA, a close friend of Mina
> ARTHUR HOLMWOOD, Lucy's fiancé, heir to the title of Lord Godalming
> QUINCEY P. MORRIS, an American friend of Dr. Seward
> RENFIELD, a madman confined in Seward's asylum

Form and Content

Dracula takes the form of a series of documents, most of them extracted from
diaries and journals, the remainder being letters and a handful of press cuttings. The
early chapters, from Jonathan Harker's journal, record his journey to the Carpathian
mountain region of Transylvania and his meeting with Count Dracula, who wishes to
purchase the Carfax estate at Purfleet near London. Once the papers are signed,
Jonathan finds that he is a prisoner. He discovers that the count has supernatural
powers and nearly falls victim to three female vampires, but he manages to escape.

The next few chapters introduce Jonathan's fiancée, Mina Murray, who is becoming anxious for his safety, and her friend Lucy Westenra, who has received three
proposals of marriage: from Dr. John Seward, from his American friend Quincey P.
Morris, and from Arthur Holmwood. Seward is the proprietor of a lunatic asylum
situated at the edge of the Carfax estate; the earliest entries from his diary inserted into
the text concern the eccentric carnivorous activities of a patient named Renfield, who
is awaiting the advent of his "Master."

Mina collects some press cuttings dealing with the arrival of a sinister deserted ship
in Whitby, where she and Lucy are staying. Shortly thereafter, Lucy begins to act

strangely. She falls ill and must be returned to Dr. Seward's care. Mina is buoyed up, however, by news from Budapest that Jonathan is alive, although stricken with a "violent brain fever," and she sets off to bring him home.

Seward, baffled by Lucy's curious symptoms, asks Professor Abraham van Helsing for help. Van Helsing realizes that Lucy is the victim of a vampire, but he is unable to save her. Mina and Jonathan arrive back in England to find that she appears to be dead. Lucy has actually become a vampire, however, and soon begins a predatory career of her own. Her three suitors must go to her tomb with van Helsing to drive a stake through her heart.

Jonathan's testimony allows van Helsing to identify the enemy and make plans to thwart him, but they fail to locate all the boxes of earth that Dracula has brought with him to England to serve as his resting places. Dracula diverts his predatory attentions to Mina, while van Helsing uses every device that he can to protect her. Renfield is persuaded to help Seward's friends, and the search for the remaining boxes continues.

When the Count has only one secure resting place remaining, he takes flight and returns to Transylvania. He is pursued to his lair by van Helsing, Holmwood (now Lord Godalming), and Harker, who have the half-captivated Mina with them. Seward and Quincey Morris follow in their train, delayed by Gypsies who are the Count's loyal followers. In the end, their superior weapons prevail. Dracula is destroyed by the mortally wounded Quincey Morris, and Mina is saved.

Analysis

Although it contains much material that might once have been considered unsuitable for young readers—which, inevitably, makes it even more appealing to them—the subject matter of *Dracula* is particularly relevant to adolescents. If one looks beyond the intricately gaudy appearances that Bram Stoker's vampires present to their adversaries, to the actual effects that they have on their victims, one sees immediately that their principal function is to arouse fervent and problematic sexual desires. Jonathan Harker is utterly beguiled by Dracula's lovely "brides," while Lucy and Mina are changed by Dracula's attentions from chaste Victorian maidens into slaves of passion. The passage describing Jonathan's unconsummated seduction and the passage describing the appearance of the undead Lucy to the three men who love her are intensely erotic, displaying with remarkable intensity all the ambivalence and anxiety with which puritanical Victorians regarded matters of sexuality (especially female sexuality).

The follies of the Victorian era are far behind modern readers, who are supposed to have much more enlightened attitudes about the urgent and sometimes peculiar impulses that arise from sexual desire, but that does not mean that such feelings have been rendered unproblematic, especially to those encountering them for the first time. It is inevitable that many adolescents who feel the onset of such desire in themselves and witness its effects on their peers should feel direly apprehensive, and this apprehension provides the psychological link that makes the story of Dracula so uniquely appealing to the young.

Stoker's decision to present the events of *Dracula* as a series of journal entries recorded by the major characters has two overlapping effects. The method gives the story a vital immediacy, allowing the reader to share each shock of revelation as it occurs, accumulating the pieces of the puzzle one by one. It also gives the narrative an indispensable intimacy, allowing the reader to share the puzzlement, the incredulity, and the acute sense of personal violation felt by the dutiful recorders of the series of events.

A further advantage in using several different first-person narrators is that the innocent viewpoints of Jonathan Harker and Mina Murray are counterbalanced by the more mature and better-informed narrative voices of Seward and Professor van Helsing. Although Jonathan, Mina, and Lucy are the reader's eyes and ears for the first half of the story, Seward's scrupulously scientific observations become dominant in the second part. When Jonathan's journal is reintroduced into the text after a long absence, it has been transformed into the voice of a man forced by experience to become wise.

The result of this calculated tipping of the scales is that horror and incomprehension are gradually overtaken and overwhelmed by a methodical and steadfast approach to the solution of the problem. Much is made of van Helsing's credentials as a scientist, and his attempts to combat Dracula's depredations are defiantly pragmatic, involving blood transfusions (which were not yet established as a conventional medical treatment in 1897). Much is made, too, of the technology that the heroes can bring to bear as they pursue Dracula to his lair: The vampire's minions have no answer to their Winchester rifles, and the blow that finally puts an end to the count is struck with a Bowie knife.

The resulting implication is perfectly clear: The monsters of superstition may be more powerful than one would wish, but they will crumble nevertheless before the combination of scientific analysis, good equipment, and constructive action. In *Dracula*, the battle between the products of superstition and the forces of reason is one in which the latter are equipped to win a decisive victory, an attitude that marks the novel out as a genuinely modern work. There is a certain irony in the fact that although Stoker presumably set out to demonstrate that the bogeymen of folklore no longer had the power to confound or destroy people armed with the intellectual apparatus of science and the material rewards of technology, what he actually accomplished was to invest the vampire with a new glamour far more powerful than any it had previously possessed. It is, after all, the sharply delineated and casually authoritative figure of Dracula, not the calculatedly eccentric and almost parodic character of van Helsing, that is indelibly imprinted on the imagination of the reader.

Critical Context

Dracula is the most famous of all horror novels, and its central character is one of the few literary figures to have become a household name, known to people who have never read the book. Stoker's elaborate description of the "rules" according to which vampires operate and may be opposed—the boxes of native earth that provide their resting places, their sensitivity to garlic and fear of crucifixes, their inability to cast reflections, and, above all, the fact that they must be destroyed by driving stakes through their hearts—became definitive, providing the narrative apparatus of dozens of films and hundreds of novels.

In recent times, Anglo-American culture has made a concerted effort to set aside the hang-ups of the Victorian era, recommending understanding and acceptance of one's own sexuality and an attitude of respectful tolerance toward the sexuality of others. It is not surprising, in this intellectual climate, that charismatic vampires cast in the same mold as Dracula should have lost their force as icons of evil. It is, however, a remarkable testament to the power of Stoker's imagination that instead of disappearing, or becoming merely comic figures, Dracula's most conspicuous modern analogues have become overtly heroic figures in the work of such writers as Anne Rice and Chelsea Quinn Yarbro.

Brian Stableford

EARLY SORROW
Ten Stories of Youth

Editor: Charlotte Zolotow (1915-   )
First published: 1986
Type of work: Short fiction
Subjects: Coming-of-age, death, emotions, family, and friendship
Recommended ages: 13-18

Ten short stories by different authors sensitively address the emotions of children and young adults experiencing death, unrequited love, divorce, emerging sexuality, and loneliness.

Form and Content

In this companion volume to *An Overpraised Season* (1973), Charlotte Zolotow has collected ten short stories in which a child or young adult experiences what Zolotow calls "early sorrow," personal pain made more acute by youth, a "time of terrible intensity."

Reynolds Price's poignant "Michael Egerton" is representative of the collection's theme. Its eleven-year-old narrator, who seems unusually sensitive and observant, although insufficiently mature to act according to his own principles, tells the self-incriminating story of his summer camp friendship with Michael Egerton, whose simple, unguarded honesty and thoughtful way of listening attract the narrator. He is flattered that Michael, the star of his cabin baseball team—someone clearly more poised, experienced, and mature than he is—seems to value him above the other boys. They spend their summer together, growing closer through talk. On the afternoon of the camp baseball playoffs, however, Michael's abrupt discovery that he has a "new father" so deeply troubles him that he skips the game, causing his team to lose. Angry, thoughtless, and immature, his cabin-mates grow increasingly cruel to Michael, until, on the final night of camp, the narrator watches as they tie Michael up, spread-eagled, and leave him in the cabin while they march off to the awards banquet. By the time that the narrator sneaks back to set him free, Michael has locked himself in the bathroom. Although the narrator longs to talk to Michael, he cannot make himself do what may be difficult, and so he returns to the larger group and the banquet without a word. The unembellished and objective style of the story is all the more sorrowful because it suggests how deeply the narrator now needs to record accurately his own lapse of kindness and friendship, the things that he so valued in Michael, and perhaps to do penance for it.

Other stories in the collection address youthful disappointment and loss in different ways. In Carson McCullers' "Like That," a thirteen-year-old girl becomes bitter and angry when her eighteen-year-old sister, Sis, distances herself from her close family in favor of a tumultuous, newly sexual relationship. In H. E. Bates's "Nina," a seventeen-year-old girl experiences for the first time the confusing combination of love, loss, and jealousy when she grows attached to a handsome musician friend of her dead father, only to discover that he is in love with her beautiful mother. In E. L. Doctorow's "The Writer in the Family," a young man named Jonathan is bullied by an authoritative aunt into writing letters pretending that his never-successful, now-dead father is alive and prosperous, for the sake of his hospitalized grandmother, who does not know that the father is dead. Jonathan suffers family criticism but learns something relevant about his father and himself when he chooses to kill off his father in writing in order to get on with his own life. Other stories in the collection are Elizabeth Enright's "A Distant Bell," Harold Brodkey's "The State of Grace," James Purdy's "Short Papa," Elizabeth Bowen's "The Visitor," Stephen Vincent Benét's "Too Early Spring," and Katherine Mansfield's "The Garden Party." In all these stories, the juvenile protagonists are portrayed as intelligent and sensitive, although flawed.

Analysis

Because each story in this collection addresses familiar human emotion and experience with subtlety, precision, accuracy, and depth, the book does appeal to discerning adult readers. Nevertheless, the points of view, themes, and even prose styles in the collection are particularly well suited for the juvenile to young adult readership that Zolotow has in mind.

Seven of the ten stories are written in the first-person narrative style, which is particularly compelling for the juvenile reader because it more fully engages their empathy for the lead character. It may be no accident that the three stories written in third person—"Nina," "The Visitor," and "The Garden Party"—are the least viscerally affecting, the least accessible, to young readers. For example, in spite of the lovely, precise phrasing and visual imagery in Mansfield's "The Garden Party," its third-person narrative creates an ironic distance between what the main character, Laura, says that she feels and what the reader believes that she feels. It is a distance that an adult reader may enjoy more than a juvenile reader who longs to identify with the beautiful and charming teenage protagonist. The works that use the first-person narrative make their protagonists' stories more immediate, more personal, and more painful. When Brodkey's main character in "The State of Grace" suffers "the terrible desire to suddenly turn and run shouting back through the corridors of time, screaming at the boy I was, searching him out, and pounding on his chest: Love him, you damn fool, love him," readers cannot help but feel his sorrow because they know and trust him—he is their friend and confidant, their narrator.

In one way or another, each of the collection's stories explores a theme especially relevant to juvenile and young adult readers: the effect of loss, disappointment, failure, and sorrow on young and relatively inexperienced characters. In several of the stories, the experience of sorrow itself is what pushes the protagonist into adulthood. When the title character of "Nina" unexpectedly discovers the man she loves sitting close to her mother, looking at her with "tenderness and longing," Nina initially feels only grief. Then she seems literally to regain her senses, noticing for the first time all day that the thorny scratches on her hand sting and that the gooseberries she has been eating leave the sour aftertaste of unripe fruit. Although this disappointment, this loss, may have introduced her to jealousy and cynicism, through it, she has also gained the power of perception: The world will no longer be so vague and confusing as it was before. In "The Writer in the Family," Jonathan cannot really be a writer, or really be an adult, until he claims his pen as his own, until he shows his Aunt Frances that he will write his own story, not hers. That story must be about his father's death, which he must acknowledge and force the others in his family to acknowledge in order to proceed with his own adulthood.

Even when sorrow does not lead directly to adulthood for a main character, the painful experience will help shape the adult that the child will eventually become. In retelling as an adult his summer camp story, the narrator of "Michael Egerton" repents his childhood betrayal of Michael. He has become the sort of adult who cares about integrity and regrets his inability as a child to assert his principles in the face of peer pressure. The narrator of "The State of Grace" clearly describes adult remorse over his childhood unwillingness to love. The concept that an adult's character is created out of a series of childhood experiences likely comes as no surprise to adult readers, but it can be a revelation to juvenile readers that the sorrowful experiences they are currently living will stay with them, ultimately informing the adults that they will become.

Not surprisingly, the prose styles of the ten authors anthologized here vary widely, but all the stories are accessible to and appropriate for juvenile readers. While some have language and sentence structures more complex than those with which a juvenile reader may be familiar, none is so challenging as to be problematic. The more relevant question is whether juvenile readers are fully capable of understanding the complex ideas just below the surface of certain short stories whose prose is deceptively simple.

Critical Context

Charlotte Zolotow, the editor of *Early Sorrow*, is a widely respected author of more than sixty children's books, including the Caldecott Honor Books *The Storm Book* (1952) and *Mr. Rabbit and the Lovely Present* (1962); *The New York Times* outstanding book of the year and *School Library Journal* best book of the year *William's Doll* (1972); the Christopher Award winner *My Grandson Lew* (1974); and the Redbook Award winner, *I Know a Lady* (1984). In addition to her prodigious work as an author, Zolotow has led a distinguished career as an editor and publisher of children's books for Harper & Row, as well as for her own publishing imprint, the Charlotte Zolotow Books division. Zolotow's own writing is marked by her unerring sensitivity to the feelings, both ferocious and fragile, of the young children for whom she writes. She brings this concern for honest and accurate emotion to *Early Sorrow*, selecting only those works that treat juvenile experience and emotion with the depth and feeling that she senses in her readers.

Shelley Blanton-Stroud

EAST O' THE SUN AND WEST O' THE MOON

Authors: Peter Christen Asbjørnsen (1812-1885) and Jørgen Moe (1813-1882)

First published: Selections from *Norske folkeeventyr*, 1841-1844, 1852 (as *Popular Tales from the Norse*, 1859; as *East o' the Sun and West o' the Moon*, 1921); illustrated

Type of work: Short fiction

Subjects: Animals, coming-of-age, gender roles, love and romance, and social issues

Recommended ages: 10-18

> *Asbjørnsen and Moe collected Norwegian oral stories—magic tales, trickster tales, and fables—that give pertinent information as to what to expect from life, both good and bad.*

Form and Content

The stories found in this selection from *Norske folkeeventyr* (Norwegian folktales) are all oral-formulaic: They are passed from generation to generation orally, and they are easy to remember since they are built on formulae—of language, of characters, of plots—which results in a certain style that separates folktales from literature. Stock phrases occur, such as "once upon a time." Often, three brothers try their luck at winning a princess, and inevitably the younger one is successful. A cat may be a princess in disguise. The poor but clever person (possibly in the shape of an animal) outwits the rich but stupid person. These formulae—they are numerous—are easily transferable from one tale to the next at the storyteller's discretion.

East o' the Sun and West o' the Moon contains examples of three of the major types of folktales: the magic tale, the trickster story or anecdote, and the fable. The very title of the volume refers to the setting of the magic tale, for it takes place in a never-never land, east of the sun and west of the moon, where anything can happen and where the magical is natural. A primary example is the title story. The plot of such a tale takes a well-known course: Initially, something is wrong or goes wrong; the hero or heroine sets out on a quest to right matters; he or she encounters magical helpers and/or opponents; they are subjected to tests; and, when those tests are passed, they are rewarded with "happiness forever after." This structure is in itself a major formula. It can be varied, but as a rule two human beings who belong together find and help each other. As they pass through dramatic and thrilling events, they defeat evil and ensure that goodness will reign. The magic tale is jubilantly optimistic.

In the trickster stories, the plot usually demonstrates how a smart person, often poor, uses his or her wits to trick a person of higher social standing. The mood is bawdy, the emphasis is on low humor, and the magic of the "once-upon-a-time-tale" has given way to the critical and satirical depiction of society, in this case a Norwegian farming society.

The fables depict animals, often engaged in the same kind of trickery, and that are fallible human beings in disguise. In the fable, however, the moral lesson becomes more pronounced than in the trickster story.

In some of these fables, Peter Christen Asbjørnsen and Jørgen Moe come close to the type of folktale called legend—one underrepresented in this collection. Legends are often told in response to a question. In "The Fox as Herdsman," a woman tries to hire a herdsman; she wisely rejects the bear and the wolf, but she is taken in by the fox. When she discovers that the fox has eaten her sheep and goats—which he, trickster that he is, gleefully tells her—she flies into a fit of rage and throws a morsel of cream at the fox, and that is "why the fox has a white tip to his brush." Similarly, in "Why the Bear Is Stumpy-Tailed," the tricky fox tells the bruin how to fish: He must stick his tail into a hole in the ice and wait for the fish to bite. The bear does exactly that, and soon his tail freezes. When he wants to leave, the end of the tail snaps off, and "that is why Bruin goes about with a stumpy tail this very day."

Analysis

The stories told are plot-oriented, the characters are depicted without much depth, and rarely do twists of events take place that are unexpected. Yet, listening to the well known can be wonderfully gratifying, and the stories do send messages, some nicely consoling, some unsettling; those who listened to the stories received knowledge of the world. The magic tale strongly makes the point that young people must grow up. In some stories, one sees the consequences of tests not being passed successfully. In "The Seven Foals," three brothers seek to raise their dirt-poor family out of poverty, but the two older brothers fail by giving in to temptation. The third son, the ne'er-do-well, the underdog—a common formulaic character—rises to the occasion and wins the princess and half the kingdom. In "East o' the Sun and West o' the Moon," a young girl is offered by her family in marriage to a bear; she is unhappy with her matrimonial state. Corrupted by her mother's wishes, she fails a test and loses her husband to a distant witch. At that point, she realizes that the bear is an accursed prince, knows that she loves him, and overcomes all obstacles to regain him. A passive woman becomes an active, resilient heroine. The point at which a person must mature and go through a rite of passage is stressed through this trial-and-error pattern.

These seemingly sweet and harmonious stories can be used as a means for social criticism. One powerful story is "Mastermaid," in which a young man is assisted so well by his magical helper—his future spouse—that they manage to escape together with the treasures of a troll. One can see the troll as a repressive force in society and, consequently, claim that he deserves the treatment that he receives as a result of Mastermaid's trickery. The second part of "Mastermaid," however, is different. Even though the typical plot of the magic tale is detectable, the main purpose of the rest of the story is to spoof the authorities of the region—such civil servants as the sheriff, the attorney, and the constable—and thereby the text ventures into the genre of the trickster story. The emphasis is on humor, but a humor that has a social sting. "Mastermaid" and many other stories, such as "Tatterhood," demonstrate that resilient heroines are as common as courageous heroes.

Much further removed from the mood and tone of the magic tale and much coarser are "Gudbrand of the Hill-Side," "Goosey Grizzel," and "The Husband Who Was to

Mind the House." Humanity is viewed with considerable skepticism, and stupidity often seems to guide the characters. In "Big Peter and Little Peter," morality is left behind: As the younger brother tricks and cheats his older sibling, readers realize that success can be achieved by victimizing innocent people, and even by murder. The most grim of the trickster stories bluntly contradict the optimistic messages of the magic tales and reveal a world of mediocrity in which the smart, immoral person succeeds through dirty deeds.

Most of the fables in this collection tend to borrow the structure of the trickster stories or anecdotes. The characters are animals that fall in the categories of tricksters and victims. In the famous tale "The Three Billy Goats Gruff," the two younger goats persuade a troll not to eat them because they have a fatter brother behind them, and that gruff brother does in the troll. While justice seems to be served in some of these fables, others have more dubious outcomes. In "Well Done and Ill Paid," the fox helps a farmer chase away a bear by pretending to be a master marksman. Instead of rewarding the fox, however, the farmer—upon his wife's request—has his dogs chase the fox, which is why the fox utters the words of the story's title.

Critical Context

During the nineteenth century, Norwegian collectors and editors Peter Christen Asbjørnsen and Jørgen Moe traversed the countryside of their native land to listen to and record folktales. Those tales served a nation that was in the process of gaining its independence, for they demonstrated that Norwegian culture was saturated with splendid and comic stories that ordinary people had told for centuries. The example set by, among others, the Brothers Grimm led to a craving for folklore by the educated classes. Such tales continue to be immensely popular and are taught in many folklore courses throughout the world. In addition, these tales have had a strong impact on Norwegian literature, such as the dramas of Henrik Ibsen and the novels of Sigrid Undset.

These tales have been translated into English several times, but G. W. Dasent's selection from 1859 has proved to be a resilient publication. That translation is faithful to Asbjørnsen and Moe's oral tone; many nineteenth century collections of folktales are heavily edited, and the vernacular of the informants—those people who told them to the collectors the tales—was altered. Asbjørnsen and Moe, however, had a profound respect for their storytellers and preserved the oral quality in their recording of the tales and that, in part, may be why these stories continue to enthrall readers.

Niels Ingwersen

EAT A BOWL OF TEA

Author: Louis Chu (1915-1970)
First published: 1961
Type of work: Novel
Type of plot: Domestic realism, psychological realism, and social realism
Time of work: 1941-1949
Locale: New York City and San Francisco
Subjects: Family, love and romance, race and ethnicity, and sexual issues
Recommended ages: 15-18

Ben Loy Wang, a young Chinese American man, must contend with a domineering father, a cheating wife, and his own sexual impotence.

> *Principal characters:*
> WANG BEN LOY, a young Chinese American waiter
> LEE MEI OI, his bride
> WANG WAH GAY, Ben Loy's father

Form and Content

Eat a Bowl of Tea is a romantic comedy realistically depicting the "bachelor society" of American Chinatowns shortly after World War II. The novel opens on the protagonist Wang Ben Loy, a newlywed bridegroom awakened by the doorbell of his apartment in New York's Chinatown. At the door, he finds a prostitute soliciting an old client. Ben Loy convinces her of his marital state, then rejoins his bride, Mei Oi, in bed; meanwhile, Mei Oi's interior monologue reveals that Ben Loy has recently become impotent.

Flashbacks establish the characters of Ben Loy and his father and describe the events leading up to his marriage and impotence. Ben Loy is a Chinese American in his twenties, a filial son to his stern Confucian father, Wah Gay, owner of a gambling establishment in New York's Chinatown. Wah Gay, an émigré to America, had returned in 1923 to his native Sunwei in Kwangtung Province. He married, stayed until his wife bore a son, and then left her and their infant in China for twenty-five years while he established himself in the United States. Ben Loy grew up in China until 1941, when his father sent for him. After a year of schooling and another year waiting tables, Ben Loy joined the U.S. Army, then returned to restaurant work. In 1948, he traveled to China to fulfill his filial obligations by marrying Mei Oi, the daughter of Wah Gay's longtime friend Lee Gong. Although their match is arranged, Ben Loy and Mei Oi were attracted to each other, and their nuptial consummation in China was joyous and sexually fulfilling. Now that they have returned to New York to set up house, however, Ben Loy has become impotent.

The plot complication intensifies when Mei Oi's feelings of husbandly neglect drive her into the arms of a notorious Chinatown playboy and seducer, Ah Song. When

Mei Oi becomes pregnant, she initially passes off the expected child as Ben Loy's, much to the family's pleasure. Unfortunately, Ah Song is seen sneaking out of her apartment, and Chinatown soon buzzes with gossip of Mei Oi's infidelity. Eventually, Wang Chuck Ting, president of the Wang Family Association, hears of the affair and informs Wah Gay of this family disgrace. The novel's tragic climax occurs when Wah Gay ambushes Ah Song sneaking out of Mei Oi's apartment and slices off his left ear. Wah Gay is then forced to hide from the police in a friend's New Jersey home.

In the resolution, Chinatown's unofficial judicial system intervenes, and Ah Song is condemned to five years of ostracism. Having lost face, Wah Gay and Lee Gong exile themselves from New York. Ben Loy and Mei Oi leave New York for San Francisco, where Ben Loy is free from patriarchal control, and he accepts Mei Oi's baby as his child. Eventually, Ben Loy seeks a cure for impotence from a Chinese herbalist, who makes him "eat a bowl of tea" brewed with medicinal herbs. This bitter medicine miraculously allows Ben Loy to recover his virility, and he and Mei Oi renew their love and look forward to having another baby.

Analysis

Eat a Bowl of Tea is a comic, satirical novel that probes the way of life prevailing in the American Chinatown society of the 1940's. Its plot develops along classically comedic lines, and its central conflict is between a generation of elders and a generation of young people, between the tradition-bound first-generation Chinese sojourners who came to America primarily to make money (since racist laws excluded them from establishing families in America) and the new-generation Chinese Americans who were in America to make it their homeland (the laws having begun to change in the 1940's). Ideologically, this conflict is a clash between the Confucian Chinese ethic of family hierarchy on the one hand and the American Dream of the individual's right to pursue happiness and identity on the other. Wah Gay and Lee Gong represent the Confucian older generation, while Ben Loy and Mei Oi represent the younger generation of Chinese Americans. For example, Wah Gay treats his son as his property and his responsibility, allowing Ben Loy no opportunity to develop his individuality—Wah Gay makes all the decisions regarding Ben Loy's education, career, and marriage.

Louis Chu shows that this oppressive familial structure leads to disingenuousness and hypocrisy. Wah Gay's insistence of playing the role of the provident father creates an ironic tension between his ideal image of himself and his real circumstances: His livelihood—operating a gambling establishment—is hardly an exemplary one for a model Confucian father. Ben Loy, on the other hand, must keep up appearances in order to conform with his father's desired image of him as a good, hardworking boy. Behind this façade of ideal filial duty, however, Ben Loy surreptitiously finds release by frequenting prostitutes, which threatens the fruitfulness of his marriage and thus endangers the continuity of the family, ideal or otherwise.

After the novel's crisis, the obstructing representatives of the older generation, Wah Gay and Lee Gong, lose their authority and fade into voluntary exile. Chu shows the

Confucian system of family hierarchy in retreat. The action then focuses on the now-unobstructed actions of the younger generation, Ben Loy and Mei Oi, as they attempt to rebuild their marriage and their lives. They found this new sense of self and family not upon an authoritarian hierarchy but upon mutual love, understanding, and forgiveness. They also move from the old American East (New York) to the new American West (San Francisco). In so doing, Chu's youthful characters are following the archetypal American journey westward to find a second chance at happiness and self-realization on new frontiers.

Critical Context

First published in 1961, *Eat a Bowl of Tea* initially met with unappreciative reviews. It was neglected for almost two decades until a post-1960's generation of Asian American scholars, led by writers Frank Chin and Jeffrey Paul Chan, resuscitated it. The book was successfully filmed in 1988 by Wayne Wang and has been given a secure place in the canon of Asian American literature. Louis Chu's only published novel has earned for its author the accolade of Chinese America's first distinguished novelist.

The central conflicts of *Eat a Bowl of Tea*—the generational discord between traditional immigrant parent and assimilated American child and the clash between familial community and individual identity—have become frequently revisited sites of struggle by subsequent Chinese American writers. One thinks of Fred and Pa Eng in Frank Chin's play *Year of the Dragon* (1974), the author and her shamanistic mother in Maxine Hong Kingston's *The Woman Warrior: A Memoir of a Girlhood Among Ghosts* (1976), or the numerous mother-daughter duels in Amy Tan's novel *The Joy Luck Club* (1989). Chu's book is also prized because it is the first novel by a Chinese American insider depicting Chinatown life in a realistic, unexoticized way; more popular novels such as Lin Yutang's *Chinatown Family* (1948) and Chin Yang Lee's *Flower Drum Song* (1957) romanticized and stereotyped the subject. An especially notable difference is Chu's realistic mirroring of the conditions in the "bachelor society" of America's Chinatowns. This bachelor society originated because earlier racist American immigration laws excluded the wives of working-class Chinese men from entering the United States while equally racist miscegenation laws prevented Chinese men from marrying American women and establishing families. Thus, working men such as Wah Gay and Lee Gong returned home to marry and then left their wives in China while they sought employment in America, enjoying a conjugal visit perhaps once a decade (less frequently than most convicted felons in American prisons). In the Chinatowns of that period, then, the population was overwhelmingly male, mostly "married bachelors." Hence a woman such as Mei Oi, the war bride of a Chinese American soldier, was a precious rarity in her community.

Chu's realism is also evident in his dialogue. He renders the language of his working-class Chinatown characters with so fine an ear that one can hear the Cantonese cadences underlying the broken English and savor the authenticity of the speakers' colorful banter. Early book reviewers who expected Chu's ghetto characters to speak in standard English or Hollywood "Charlie Chan-ese" were bewildered, but the expressiveness and authenticity of Chu's rendered dialogue has since gained appreciation. Later Chinese American writers such as Chin and Tan have successfully followed Chu's lead in representing the real language of Chinese America.

C. L. Chua and Janet Fujimoto

THE EFFECT OF GAMMA RAYS ON MAN-IN-THE-MOON MARIGOLDS

Author: Paul Zindel (1936-   )
First produced: 1965
First published: 1971
Type of work: Drama
Type of plot: Domestic realism
Time of work: The early 1970's
Locale: The Hunsdorfer living room and a high school auditorium
Subjects: Drugs and addiction, education, emotions, and family
Recommended ages: 13-18

> *Tillie struggles to rise above her family's sordid existence and the negativism of her abusive mother, finally winning first prize in the school science fair and gaining self-respect.*

Principal characters:
> MATILDA (TILLIE) HUNSDORFER, a painfully shy high school student who is the victim of her mother's and older sister's abuses
> RUTH HUNSDORFER, her older sister, who is emotionally disturbed and who attends the same high school as Tillie
> BEATRICE HUNSDORFER, their mother, who is a disillusioned, embittered, and abusive alcoholic
> NANNY, an old woman deposited with Beatrice for nursing care
> JANICE VICKERY, Tillie's rival for the science fair prize and her complete antithesis
> PETER, the pet rabbit that represents love and security to Ruth and Tillie

Form and Content

The Effect of Gamma Rays on Man-in-the-Moon Marigolds is a pessimistic, slice-of-life picture of the "atomic age" family. This drama, written in two acts with five scenes each, centers on the Hunsdorfer family. Beatrice Hunsdorfer is divorced and attempting to support herself and her daughters by caring for terminally ill patients. She hates her life and blames everyone except herself for her misery. Beatrice takes out her frustrations on her daughters, as well as whichever patient happens to be boarding with her at the time. Lately, she has taken to harassing Mr. Goodman, the young science teacher who has befriended Tillie.

The first act of this short, quickly paced play belongs almost totally to Beatrice, who develops its exposition via three long monologues, two of them telephone conversations. Her monologue in scene 2 alternates between addressing Tillie and Nanny, disparaging and threatening them both while at the same time revealing Beatrice's shattered hopes and dreams. Yet, even though Beatrice carries the lion's share of lines and scenes, it is the character of Tillie who is the true focus of the play.

Tillie's real and uninhibited voice is most frequently presented to the audience in the form of recorded monologues that allow access to her most intimate thoughts. Tillie, through her science teacher, has become enamored with the concept of the atom—an infinitesimal, indestructible bit of matter that has always been and always will be. She worships the atom with a fervor approaching religious fanaticism. That worship occupies all of her waking thoughts, setting her apart from both Beatrice and Ruth, her pathetically histrionic older sister. Tillie is usually seen playing with or caring for Peter, the rabbit given to her by Mr. Goodman when the science class had finished with it.

Beatrice, sensing that Mr. Goodman and other teachers at the high school are taking an interest in her daughters and are attempting to help them, tries to alienate the teachers from the girls and the girls from their teachers. In an intimate scene with Ruth, Beatrice reveals her own fear of being left alone, but perhaps the most brutal scene in the first act is the final one, scene 5, after Ruth reveals that Tillie is a finalist in the science fair for her experiment in growing marigolds from seeds exposed to cobalt 60. When the principal calls the house to invite Beatrice to be present for the final science project evaluations, Beatrice's fear of exposure to the world causes her to revile and abuse Tillie verbally.

Act 2 begins on a more positive note. Beatrice has begun to regard Tillie's achievement as her own triumph. She is looking forward to appearing at the high school, not knowing that Ruth has confided to Tillie that all the teachers are waiting to see if Beatrice looks as crazy as she sounds on the telephone. Ruth also has learned that Beatrice's high school nickname was "Betty the Loon." She threatens to confront Beatrice with this information unless Tillie gives Peter to her, and Tillie agrees. When Beatrice tells Ruth that she cannot attend the school program, however, but must stay home with Nanny, the current boarder, Ruth vindictively tells Beatrice that everyone is waiting to laugh at "Betty the Loon." Beatrice sends Ruth to the school in her place.

The second brief scene is the project presentation of Janice Vickery, Tillie's major rival in the science fair. This scene demonstrates Janice's flippant attitude toward her project. The third brief scene is a return to Beatrice, now drunk, calling first the high school and then Nanny's daughter, telling her to make other arrangements for Nanny. The fourth very brief scene is Tillie's sincere and moving apostrophe to the atom, which stands in contrast to Janice's irreverent presentation. In scene 5, the sisters return in jubilation: Tillie has captured first prize. Beatrice, very drunk by now, has fatally chloroformed the rabbit and left its body in Ruth's room. When Ruth finds him, she goes into one of her convulsive fits. Beatrice refuses to call a doctor, and the play ends with one of Tillie's recorded monologues. This one, however, gives a hopeful note as Tillie says, "But most important, I suppose . . . my experiment has made me feel important. . . ."

Analysis

The Effect of Gamma Rays on Man-in-the-Moon Marigolds, a genuinely depressing play broken only by extremely black humor, is a societal reflection of the phenomenon of the dysfunctional single-parent family in the latter half of the twentieth century. In fact, the work is vaguely autobiographical. Beatrice (Betty) Frank was the maiden name of playwright Paul Zindel's mother. During his high school years, his mother, who was separated from Zindel's father, also boarded and cared for terminally ill patients. Zindel himself was a high school chemistry teacher, so it is no great stretch to equate the character of Tillie, with her love of science, to Zindel. He has admitted that he based the character of Beatrice, although with exaggeration, on his mother.

The most pervading image of the play is that of the mutations that derive from exposure to radiation. Tillie's science experiment is the literal representation of this theme. The extension of this image is how exposure to difficult issues in life has mutated Beatrice and how, in turn, her actions have mutated Tillie and Ruth. Tillie points out that seeds too close to the point of radiation die, seeds a moderate distance from the source mutate, and seeds farthest from the source are unchanged. Ruth, who is too close to Beatrice, is stunted—some part of her killed in the same way that some vital part of Beatrice was blighted—but Tillie has become the hybrid mutant, beautiful in her synthesis of the cruel and the creative.

The work explores the world of parent/child relationships and seems to reach the conclusion that children must create their own identities. Beatrice probably believes that her verbal and emotional abuse of her children toughens them, helping them face the real world. In actuality, this abuse simply isolates them from that world, so that, eventually, reality resolves itself into the sordid, removed environment in which they all exist.

Both Ruth and Tillie need to love Peter, the pet rabbit. The pet is central to their existence. Beatrice sees the rabbit as coming between herself and her children. The rabbit offers them the comfort and acceptance withheld by their mother. After many threats, Beatrice kills the rabbit in retaliation for Ruth's cruelty. The result destroys Ruth, who has lost her only source of love, but that same act strengthens Tillie, with her newly found senses of personal importance, acceptance, and self-worth and her love of science and the atom.

Critical Context

The Effect of Gamma Rays on Man-in-the-Moon Marigolds captured all the major drama awards in 1970: the Obie for best play, the New York Drama Critics' Award for the best play, the Vernon Rice Drama Desk Award for most promising playwright, and the 1971 Pulitzer Prize. The play hearkens back, in both tone and subject matter, to the earlier domestic dramas of Tennessee Williams and William Inge in the 1940's, and the character of Beatrice is reminiscent of Williams' older female characters.

This play was the first, and most successful, of three that Paul Zindel mounted in the early 1970's and prefigured a succession of novels for young readers that combined his hallmark traits of humor, pathos, poetry, and terror. In all cases, Zindel attempts to elevate everyday life into something more noble by giving some of his characters a form of personal realization and epiphany. As a result of their new understanding, his characters are able to cope with life, their parents, or their peers and still keep their self-respect. This message is a vital one for young people who need that example and encouragement.

H. Alan Pickrell

EGO-TRIPPING AND OTHER POEMS FOR YOUNG PEOPLE

Author: Nikki Giovanni (1943-   )
First published: 1973; illustrated
Type of work: Poetry
Subjects: Family, race and ethnicity, and social issues
Recommended ages: 13-18

> *Giovanni embraces the experiences of growing up black in America, focusing on the beauty, power, humor, and leaders, both political and artistic, that have shaped her world.*

Form and Content

Ego-Tripping and Other Poems for Young People is a creative, harmonious collection of twenty-two poems that are representative of some of Nikki Giovanni's best works. Included in the collection are several poems from previous publications. Speaking primarily in the first person, the poetic voice, or persona, is unmistakably the poet herself as exemplified in her most-often-anthologized poem, "nikki-rosa." In this poem, the poet chronicles a happy childhood in spite of the many hardships that she endured, including her father's drinking and poverty. Ultimately, as in every poem in this collection, the conclusion is hopeful, celebrating "Black love" and "Black wealth." George Ford's black-and-white illustrations depicting African heritage and sketches of black children in play help to clarify and dramatize the meanings of the poems. Ford creates a thematic canvas that artfully displays Giovanni's poetry.

Integrated into the collection is a playful sense of humor that involves readers, drawing them into the experiences at the onset. For example, the "kidnap poem" addresses the reader as "you," bringing the reader into the poem to be kidnapped by the poet. This simple yet provocative poem captures the essence or unifying element of the poetry. Giovanni, like Walt Whitman or Langston Hughes, asks for involvement from the reader—offering the opportunity to play, sing, to be a child again. In fact, when Giovanni was asked by President Jimmy Carter to join the President's Committee on the International Year of the Child in 1979, she replied: "As a former child, I accept." Giovanni reminds readers of the child in each of them who wants to come out and play.

Infused into each poem is a rhythmic style resonating with a jazz or blues musical tone. For example, in "ego-tripping," the title poem, the beat of a distant drum—an African drum—seems to play as one reads this poem about a woman who like a goddess can create and give birth to an ice age, the Nile, precious ores and jewels—and even children. The internal rhymes and simplistic beat blend to form a read-aloud poem designed for children to repeat to themselves as they, too, "fly like a bird in the sky."

With an instructional yet uplifting tone, many of the poems center on great African American leaders in music, art, and religion, including James Brown, Aretha Franklin, and Martin Luther King, Jr. Other poems capture the themes of restlessness and of revolution, as exemplified in "black power," "revolutionary dreams," and "revolutionary music." Unifying her personal struggles with those of the 1960's and 1970's, Giovanni gives voice to the African American experience, translating its uniqueness yet also accurately rendering the universality of growing up in a changing world.

Analysis

In *Ego-Tripping and Other Poems for Young People*, the poetic journey is both a personal and a universal one. The poems focus on childhood remembrances or those memories of the young adult trying to describe a chaotic world so that she can find her place in it. For example, "knoxville, tennessee" is told from the perspective of a young girl enjoying the freedom of summer in the South. For her, summer is to "go to the mountains with/ your grandmother/ and go barefooted/ and be warm/ all the time." Told through a child's point of view, these poems center on finding personal happiness, as illustrated in the poem "everytime it rains." The young girl of the poem struggles "to find/ the end of a rainbow," for she thinks that this will help her learn "how to laugh." In the end, she still does not laugh, but she at least recognizes when something is comical. Capturing the pensiveness of children, the poet pairs this poem with another on the opposite page. Entitled "alone," this poem also reiterates the self-absorption of children and shows that they can feel lonely even when they are with others: "i was lonely alone/ now i'm lonely/ with you."

Through "poem for black boys" and "poem for my nephew," the poet embraces the theme of black power and calls out to black children to do the same. "Where are your heroes, my little Black ones," the speaker asks in "poem for black boys." The answer at the conclusion of the poem is that they are their own heroes, who must invent their own games and teach the "old ones how to play." In the latter poem, the persona wishes to become "longer and taller and BLACKER." Both poems dramatize the importance of instilling black pride and a strong sense of self into its African American readers.

Having been an important voice in the Civil Rights movement of the 1960's, Giovanni includes poems that delineate the anger and frustration of a young black woman trying to make sense of it all. The theme of destroying a dream is articulated in both "word poem" and "the funeral of martin luther king, jr." In addition, they conclude with the image of a new world in which people are free and can become what they dream.

The dream imagery resonates in other poems as well. For example, in "dreams," the persona describes the differences between the innocent dreams of youth and the compelling dreams of adults. In her younger years, she dreams of becoming a sultry singer, but finally, as an adult, realizing that "black people aren't suppose to dream," she compromises and decides to become merely a "sweet inspiration," which is actually a meaningful understatement. Notably, this poem is paired with "revolutionary dreams," a poem that sketches the evolution of a young woman's dreams from militant to radical to natural in the process of becoming a woman who is capable of change, as symbolized in the image of a revolution.

Moreover, unifying the collection is the harmonious blending of a personal and universal perspective of the African American experience that is capable of translating a poet's and a nation's struggle for peace. In "communication," the need to find the perfect medium to transform the human spirit is music. If music is the "universal language," the poet argues, then let her be "one whole note." It is this desire to strike the right note, to be a part of change, that provides the melodious tone for the poetry. Although each of the poems may strike a different note in the reader, the poetry proves to be satisfying.

Critical Context

Following the birth of her son, Tommy, in 1969, Nikki Giovanni began writing children's poetry after having a successful, productive career as a poet and essayist. Her first such work was *Spin a Soft Black Song: Poems for Children* (1971), which like her adult collections of poetry focuses on African American pride and aestheticism. Directed at much younger readers than *Ego-Tripping and Other Poems for Young People*, this collection embraces the natural rhythm of language and its appeal to children in dance and song. Illustrating the bonding of mother and child, many of the poems center on the spoken and unspoken connections between the two. As in all her work, the sense of pride in the accomplishments of black leaders and the anger juxtaposed with humor that together seem to foster survival are blended into the poetry through dialogue. This is exemplified in "trips" in which a mother says, "GET UP FROM THERE YOU GONNA BE DIRTY," as her young child thinks to himself, "i want to tell her if you was/ my size the dirt would catch you up faster too."

Having been a significant voice during the Black Arts Movement of the 1960's Giovanni—"the Princess of Black Poetry," as she has often been called—captures the nature of the changes that have taken place in herself and in society. Often mirroring these conflicts and the consequences of misdirected anger, her poetry attempts to provide direction for young people through the building of self-esteem and black pride, both for the individual and for all African Americans. Her poetry chronicles the progress of African Americans, often including the names of prominent black leaders in the arts and the Civil Rights movement.

With each collection of children's poetry, the poet examines the complexities of growing up black in predominantly white America. For example, in *Cotton Candy on a Rainy Day* (1978), the tone is compromising and the spirit appears dampened. As in her other collections, the reader encounters the theme of loneliness; however, the poetry also focuses on disillusionment. Yet, inevitably in her work, disillusionment is merely another part of life, of living, that must be met honestly and realistically. Through her art, Giovanni gives her young readers the tools to confront and to combat an imperfect world, even during the most difficult of times, by emphasizing the universality of human experience as expressed through poetry.

Cynthia S. Becerra

THE EGYPT GAME

Author: Zilpha Keatley Snyder (1927-   )
First published: 1967; illustrated
Type of work: Novel
Type of plot: Mystery
Time of work: The mid-1960's
Locale: Orchard Avenue, in a large university town in California
Subjects: Family, friendship, and race and ethnicity
Recommended ages: 10-13

A group of children learn about Egypt and each other in their imaginative play of the Egypt Game, while the Professor, the proprietor of the nearby antique store, learns to become involved in the outside world once more.

> *Principal characters:*
> APRIL HALL, a thin, blond eleven-year-old girl
> MELANIE ROSS, a slender eleven-year-old African American girl
> MARSHALL ROSS, Melanie's four-year-old, sturdily built brother
> ELIZABETH CHUNG, a shy nine-year-old girl
> TOBY ALVILLAR, a popular sixth-grade boy who makes people laugh
> KEN KAMATA, Toby's best friend and a popular sixth-grader
> THE PROFESSOR, the mysterious proprietor of the A-Z Antique Store

Form and Content

The Egypt Game has short chapters with enticing titles that encourage its young audience to continue reading, especially if they are interested in ancient Egypt or become caught up in the mystery and excitement of the Egypt Game. The black-and-white illustrations by Alton Raible that accompany the text are effective. Most of them are of the children and depict what is occurring in the chapters.

The setting is a large university town in California with a diverse population that lives along Orchard Avenue, with the children attending the same elementary school. The neighborhood is composed of shops, small homes, and old apartment houses.

Eleven-year-old April Hall's glamorous, show business mother sends her to live with her paternal grandmother, whom April refers to as Caroline. April, who never knew her father because he was killed in the Korean War, resents having to live with Caroline and is anxiously awaiting a letter from her mother telling her to move back home. April looks upon the move to Caroline's apartment as temporary.

Caroline works at the university library and tells April that every noon until school starts, she is to go to the Rosses for lunch. They live in the same building, the Casa Rosada apartments, and have a four-year-old son and a daughter about April's age, who will come to get her. Melanie Ross knocks at the door and sees April with her blond hair piled on top of her head, wearing false eyelashes and her mother's old fur stole. After lunch, Melanie shows April her library.

As April is looking at Melanie's books, she pulls out an old, dull-looking geography book, and paper figures fall out. Melanie and April make up stories about the figures and come to enjoy each other's company and their imagining games. The Egypt Game begins when April finds a new book at the library about Egypt and a young pharaoh.

The mysterious Professor, the owner of an antique store, looks out a window of a storeroom at the back of his shop to see the two girls enter his property by moving a loose board in a fence. They are followed by Marshall, Melanie's four-year-old brother who is always accompanied by Security, a stuffed toy octopus; he is struggling to get through the fence. The girls find a lean-to shack containing a cracked and chipped plaster bust of the Egyptian queen Nefertiti, which they consider an omen. They call the shed "the Temple" and refer to the area as "Egypt." Soon, Elizabeth Chung, a nine-year-old who moves into the Casa Rosada apartments, and Toby Alvillar and Ken Kamata, sixth-grade classmates of April and Melanie, also become players in the Egypt Game.

One night, April is taking care of Marshall when she realizes that she has left her math book in the Temple, and she and Marshall go to retrieve it. April is nervous about going out at night and moves the board the wrong way. It makes a noise, and she is attacked by a stranger who attempts to strangle her. The Professor calls for help, and Marshall identifies the attacker, who confesses to have murdered a boy and a girl from the neighborhood.

Analysis

At the heart of this novel is the game itself. The Egypt Game requires both imagination and dedication of its players. April and Melanie complement each other very well in this regard. Elizabeth and Marshall repeat and follow directions for the rites. Toby, a jokester at school, is serious about the game. He and April have conflicts because each of them wants to be in charge. Elizabeth serves as peacemaker in allowing the boys to play and succeeding in persuading them to keep Egypt a secret. Ken seems to enjoy the game less than the others, becoming embarrassed at times; he would probably prefer to be playing basketball.

Zilpha Keatley Snyder also examines friendship and the awkwardness associated with fitting into a new crowd, issues to which most young readers can relate. April often wears false eyelashes, taking them off when she reads because she cannot see through them. Melanie, who makes friends easily and is understanding of other people's feelings, takes the eyelashes from April's room so that she cannot wear them the first day of school. Melanie knows that April does not relate well to people and that the children at school are not likely to accept her, especially if she were wearing false eyelashes. Eventually, the others do accept her, and Toby and Ken give her the nickname "February."

This process of establishing friendships continues when Caroline and Mrs. Ross suggest that April and Melanie walk to school with a new girl, Elizabeth Chung, who is nine years old and has just moved into the Casa Rosada apartments. Elizabeth is shy. April and Melanie decide that her profile looks very much like Nefertiti, and they name her "Neferbeth"; she becomes the fourth player in the Egypt Game. The four players make Egyptian costumes and wear them for Halloween. Two of the fathers of the students at Wilson School have volunteered to take the neighborhood children trick-or-treating. The four players hope to become separated from the others and meet to play the Egypt Game. They succeed, but Ken Kamata and Toby Alvillar follow them and are allowed to become the fifth and sixth players of the game.

In addition to the lighter topics of friendship and games, however, Snyder introduces a much more serious element into her novel. One day, a girl in the neighborhood is killed, and the children are no longer allowed to play outside. A boy from the neighborhood had been killed about a year before. April, for all her pretense of worldliness, is naïve and cannot imagine why someone would kill a child. Melanie explains that it is a sickness in a person.

An important theme of *The Egypt Game* is acceptance of others and the need to connect with society. All the children in the neighborhood except April and Marshall seem to be afraid of the Professor, perhaps because of his appearance—tall and bent over with deep-set, expressionless eyes. Marshall is the only one who knows that the Professor has been watching them at play. The Professor has lived within himself for twenty-five years ever since his wife was killed. He becomes a part of the real world again when he calls for help when April is attacked. The police think that the Professor is the attacker, but Marshall tells them that he was the one who said "Help." Marshall identifies the attacker as the spotted man with orange hair who carries things at the toy store (the red-haired man with freckles).

Critical Context

The Egypt Game was named a Newbery Honor Book in 1968. In 1967, it received the Lewis Carroll Shelf Award, the George G. Stone Recognition Award of Merit, and the first prize at the Spring Book Festival. It was on the American Library Association's List of Notable Books and the Horn Book Honor List for 1967.

The idea for *The Egypt Game* stemmed from what Zilpha Keatley Snyder refers to as the "Egyptian period" of her childhood, when she became totally absorbed in anything having to do with ancient Egypt. The setting and the characters of the six children came from her years as a teacher in Berkeley.

The diverse cast of ethnic characters was considered rare for the period in which Snyder was writing. The six children become friends, paying no attention to race or color: April and Toby are European American, Melanie and Marshall are African American, and Elizabeth and Ken are Asian American. The occupations of the African American parents, Mr. and Mrs. Ross, are not stereotypical: Mrs. Ross is an elementary teacher, and Mr. Ross is a graduate student at the university who is planning to teach poetry and literature. Mr. Ross calls April "the cruelest month."

Snyder used the public library as a child to help feed her imagination. Throughout *The Egypt Game*, the reader will note the importance that Snyder attaches to libraries and reading. Caroline works at the university library. April and Melanie go to the public library almost every day, where they are beginning to be called the Egypt Girls. Toby also uses the library; when playing the oracle in the game, Toby says he looked up the main words in a big book belonging to his father called *Somebody's Famous Quotations.*

Snyder had an active imagination when she was a child and has carried it into her career as an adult writing for children. *The Egypt Game* is often considered her best work.

Florence H. Maltby

EIGHT MULES FROM MONTEREY

Author: Patricia Beatty (1922-1991)
First published: 1982
Type of work: Novel
Type of plot: Historical fiction
Time of work: The summer of 1916
Locale: Monterey, California, and its surrounding area
Subjects: Family, gender roles, and travel
Recommended ages: 10-13

Fayette Ashmore and her younger brother learn about themselves and life as they accompany their widowed mother on a trip to set up library outposts in the mountains south of Monterey.

> *Principal characters:*
> FAYETTE ASHMORE, a thirteen-year-old who is seeking a way to impress her friends and help her mother get a job
> HERBERT (EUBIE) ASHMORE, Fayette's blond, blue-eyed, ten-year-old brother
> LETTIE ASHMORE, their widowed mother, who is training to be a librarian
> EDWARD HERBERT, the law partner of the late Mr. Ashmore, who has asked Mrs. Ashmore to marry him
> DENVER MURFREE, a temperamental mule driver hired to accompany the family on the trip
> GIL (POSSUM) TURLOCK, a reserved mountain man with a dark past, who prefers animals and nature to people

Form and Content

In the first sentence of *Eight Mules from Monterey*, Patricia Beatty promises mules, a wild mountain man, and gunslinging moonshiners. All three do provide problems for the Ashmores as they endeavor to take library books to Big Tree Junction, in the Santa Lucia Mountains, forty miles south of Monterey. In this historical adventure story, the young characters Fayette and Eubie emulate their late father's thirst for excitement (he was a Rough Rider with Teddy Roosevelt in the Spanish-American War). It is ironic that while visitors from all over the world flock to the Monterey peninsula to see the historic buildings and enjoy the beauty of the coast, Fayette and Eubie Ashmore find life there boring and ordinary. In addition, Fayette has another reason for wanting to go on the trip with her mother: She wants to impress the rich Hillman sisters, who brag about their grandmother on Nob Hill in San Francisco. This adolescent desire for acceptance is her main motivation, but Fayette is also concerned about the stability of her family's living situation. When her mother reveals that

Edward Herbert has proposed marriage, Fayette sees the trip as a way of possibly getting her mother a job and avoiding the acquisition of a stepfather.

The story is told from Fayette's perspective, and her initial impression of Denver Murfree and his mule team is negative. He thinks that she is a boy, and Fayette had imagined her arrival at Big Tree Junction on a pure white steed, not a scrawny black mule. In the last five chapters of this eight-chapter book, the travelers meet colorful mountain folk, isolated from world events such as World War I and the new invention of motion pictures, with its stars Charlie Chaplin, Theda Bara, and Mary Pickford. Murfree is injured, and Gil Turlock (also known as Possum) assumes his position. Lettie Ashmore learns of his criminal past but has no choice but to accept him if she wants to move forward. In addition to handling tempermental mules, they find themselves holding a funeral service for a typhoid victim and being shot at by moonshiners. Turlock protects the family by drinking with the men but is banished by Mrs. Ashmore, who abhors his behavior and does not understand his motives. The Ashmores attempt to travel without him, but only his return allows them to complete their mission, the establishment of a lending library at Big Tree Junction.

Eight Mules from Monterey concludes with an author's note in which Beatty outlines the factual content of the novel. The story is loosely based on a similar trip taken by Miss Anne Hadden in 1916. Except for the cover illustration by Ronald Himler, there are no illustrations or maps to help orient the reader.

Analysis

This novel may be characterized as "lighter" than some of Beatty's books, especially her later works about war. It repeats a theme used in such earlier books as *Lucy Makes a Match* (1979) and *That's One Ornery Orphan* (1980)—a heroine who breaks away from traditional female roles and tries to deal with the challenging life of the American West. In this case, the young protagonist shares center stage with her mother. In a time when women "in britches" are not considered natural and when social mores forced women to marry, the trip is a quest for self-actualization by Mrs. Ashmore. While Fayette's belief that they can survive without a male protector is not validated, both female characters become more self-reliant because of the experience.

Although Beatty's main purpose is to present an historically accurate story, *Eight Mules from Monterey* is also a tribute to her profession for she worked as a librarian at various sites before becoming a full-time writer. The power of reading and books and the great contributions that libraries and librarians make to society is a message interwoven in the story. Many plot problems are solved by conducting research in the books that the family is transporting. Ill-tempered and unfeeling figures in the novel are characterized as nonreaders. Mrs. Ashmore leaves a book of Bible stories "with uplifting pictures" for the moonshiners. Fayette, like Johanna Spyri's title character in *Heidi* (1884), a book that she has recently read, travels to the mountains and finds inner strength. Fayette is convinced that a copy of Edgar Allan Poe's story "The Fall of the House of Usher" (1839) is the catalyst for all the calamities that befall the family, and she tries to leave the copy at each stop; she is not successful until the end of the book, foreshadowing an easier trip back to Monterey for the "mulemobile." Ironically, an incident with her "hoodoo" book paved the way for their trip in the first place. Moral lessons are also described by literary allusions. Fayette judges Turlock by the way in which he looks and talks. Like his animal namesake, he appeared to be passive and cowardly. Fayette finally realizes that she has "judged a book by its cover." The fact that the ladies of Big Tree Junction wrote that they were "desperate" for books is the underlying premise for the entire story and is Beatty's ultimate compliment to literature.

A strong point of the novel is the incorporation of language of the period, both oral and written. While "nifty" and "classy" still retain their slang meaning, "gink" ("What a moth-eaten gink he was!") is no longer a part of everyday vocabulary. Beatty includes an excerpt from a poem written by Oliver Hereford and published in *Century* (1915) that proves that sonnets can be written about any topic, even a crocodile. Fayette sings the 1916 hit song "From the Land of Sky Blue Waters," which she learned by playing the record on a Victrola; a love of popular music by adolescents transcends time.

Beatty's main characters experience danger and injustice, but the final outcome is positive. No real harm occurs, and they have become wiser and more mature. This is an element found in all of Beatty's books and where she may deviate from reality: Her presentation of consistently unscathed main characters does not ring true. Nevertheless, *Eight Mules from Monterey* was selected as a National Council for the Social Studies Notable Children's Trade Book in the Field of Social Studies in 1983. This recognition reflects the depth of factual information that can be garnered from the narrative—a story that is enjoyable, but not memorable. A reflective reader who reads many of Beatty's books may question and tire of her consistent use of "happily ever after" endings.

Critical Context

From her first publication, *Indian Canoemaker* (1960), to her last book, *Who Comes with Cannons?*, published by her estate in 1992, Beatty combined more than fifty adventure stories with accurate historical detail. While some of Beatty's earlier works, written in collaboration with her first husband, were set in England, *Eight Mules from Monterey* demonstrates her interest in American historical themes and her love of her adopted state of California.

Beatty's greatest fascination was with the American Civil War, and her novels that explore life during that period are her most compelling. When the mountain people whom the Ashmores meet talk about war, they are referring to that conflict. In *I Want My Sunday, Stranger* (1977), a young Mormon boy looking for his horse follows a photographer from battle to battle. *Turn Homeward, Hannalee* (1984) and its sequel, *Be Ever Hopeful, Hannalee* (1988), look at life during and after the war from a Southern girl's perspective. *Charlie Skedaddle* (1987), which won the Scott O'Dell Award for Historical Fiction, chronicles the change of heart of a twelve-year-old Yankee drummer boy who could not wait to get into battle but deserts his regiment after the first enemy encounter. *Jayhawker* (1991) tells of a Kansas boy who carries on his abolitionist father's work.

Patricia Beatty truly puts the "story" in "history." Her books are always cited in major textbooks on children's literature as worthy examples of historical fiction, and they have won various awards. While her main characters are protected from the stark realism that is a growing trend in children's books, Beatty left a legacy of books that inform young people about the past in an entertaining manner.

Kay Moore

THE ELEPHANT MAN

Author: Bernard Pomerance (1940-   )
First presented: 1977
First published: 1979
Type of work: Drama
Type of plot: Psychological realism and social realism
Time of work: 1884-1890
Locale: London and Belgium
Subjects: Emotions, health and illness, and social issues
Recommended ages: 13-18

> *A horribly malformed young man is given haven in a London hospital, where he is medically studied, visited by fashionable society, and promised equality to others, which he discovers is an illusion.*

> *Principal characters:*
> JOHN MERRICK, a noted "freak" of Victorian England who becomes publicly admired when hospitalized and given the illusion that he is like other people
> FREDERICK TREVES, a surgeon responsible for securing a home for Merrick at London Hospital, Whitechapel
> ROSS, the manager of a sideshow exhibiting "The Elephant Man"
> MRS. KENDAL, a noted actress who befriends Merrick
> CARR GOMM, the administrator of the London Hospital

Form and Content

The Elephant Man is a biography drama whose title is the sideshow term that was applied to Joseph Merrick (1863-1890), who was so hideously malformed by an incurable and then-unknown disease (now diagnosed as neurofibromatosis) that he was cruelly exploited as a traveling show oddity. Merrick was rescued from such exhibition by the anatomist Dr. Frederick Treves, who arranged safe shelter for him in London Hospital, Whitechapel, which became Merrick's home for six years before his death in 1890. He became a curio studied by scientists and visited by members fashionable society, who found him both gracious and intelligent. Treves's published account of Merrick's life sparked Bernard Pomerance's interest in the life of this man, whom he calls "John Merrick" in this drama.

In twenty-two short scenes identified by title placard, The Elephant Man, in order to tell its story effectively, employs a presentational style identified as Epic Theater. This form, largely attributed to German dramatist Bertolt Brecht (1898-1956), presents a series of incidents without the restrictions of conventional theatrical construction, permitting a strong appeal to the spectators' reason. In the play's early scenes, Treves sees Merrick in a London sideshow and "borrows" him to be the subject of a medical lecture. (In this lecture scene, slides of the actual "Elephant Man" are shown, since the playwright stipulates that the actor portraying Merrick only suggest deformity by his posture and movement.) Later, Treves rescues Merrick from a London mob when the Elephant Man is fired and robbed by his manager, Ross. Treves takes Merrick to London Hospital, whose administrator, Carr Gomm, solicits sufficient public donations to provide lasting maintenance for Merrick. Treves determines with condescending compassion to create for his patient the illusion of normalcy. To this purpose, the physician enlists the actress Mrs. Kendal to befriend Merrick. As the play progresses, the focus shifts from physician to patient as the progress of Treves's social engineering is witnessed. The Elephant Man fits himself into the role of the correct Victorian gentleman, without fully questioning the rules that he is told to obey. Concomitant with his patient's social development, Treves comes to question his principles and those of his class, and he painfully begins to perceive Merrick's subtle exploitation by science and society.

As the metamorphosis of the former Elephant Man progresses, London society lionizes Merrick because he lets them see him not as an individual but as a mirror of the qualities that they like to claim. As their visits continue, Merrick's condition worsens, while at the same time he steadily builds a model of London's St. Phillip's Church. When he remarks to Mrs. Kendal that sexual loneliness continues to isolate him from other men and that he has never seen a naked woman, the actress kindly obliges by baring her breasts but is interrupted by a scandalized Treves, who orders her to leave for her impropriety. Interpreting the experience as defining his own limitations, Merrick realizes that his normality has been an illusion. Later, in a suicidal action, he lets his huge head drop unsupported, causing his suffocation.

Analysis

The subject matter of *The Elephant Man* and its implicit themes make it a drama with meaning for young people. The malformed young protagonist is a lonely out-sider encouraged to pursue social acceptance, a process that sacrifices his true self-development. Merrick realizes that the promise of equality is an illusion. The cruel lessons that he learns about the society outside himself have relevance to young persons who stand outside the adult world, with its conventional and contradictory standards.

One theme in the play concerns the false promise of imperialist Victorian England, arguably still extant today, that its subjects can win equality and acceptance by loyally conforming to its rules. Such elements as nationality, race, and class, however, work to erode this promise. In the play's context, John Merrick is instructed by Treves that he can be like other men if he follows the rules and appears gracious and grateful. Pursuing a path to promised normalcy, the Elephant Man pays a price for his conformity by becoming a mirror in which his narcissistic society visitors can see themselves. When Merrick questions the mercilessness of the hospital's decision to discharge a rule-violating orderly with children to feed, he is told by Treves that rules are for our own good. The realization that normalcy and equality with others is an illusion comes to Merrick when an outraged Treves forbids him to look at Mrs. Kendal's naked breasts and tells him that he must not forget what he is. Earlier, Treves has had a dream in which Merrick conducts a lecture about him just as he had lectured about his patient, pointing out the deformity of normalcy. Pomerance is concerned with the theme that society's conventional morality and the idea of normality are, at bottom, destructive illusions.

As the Elephant Man's social education increases, his physical condition degenerates, but concurrently he slowly builds a handsome model of London's St. Phillip's Church. This latter activity, Pomerance admits in his introductory remarks, constitutes a central metaphor for the action. Merrick describes the church as "an imitation of grace flying up and up from the mud." In progressively constructing the model (interpreted in the Christian tradition as God's building and Christ's body), which is finally completed just before his death, Merrick demonstrates that he is a sensitive artist striving toward grace. He builds a context that contains his body, no longer ugly or a mirror for others, which becomes an image of God. The model is truly Merrick's spiritual apotheosis.

Pomerance's play is theatrically effective and intellectually provocative in its ideas. More ideas are perhaps unleashed than are fully developed. Also the shift of focus from Treves to Merrick and then back to the former near the drama's conclusion somewhat obfuscates where the center of the play lies and suggests that the physician's loss of self-assurance should receive more preparation. Nevertheless, Merrick emerges as being superior to the narcissistic society that Treves provides for him, as well as to the medical community that uses him for its research and fund-raising. Merrick has learned that unquestioningly obeying questionable rules of the establishment leads neither to social equality nor to self-development. A passive sufferer aware of being exploited, Merrick rejects the world of false expectations and turns to a spiritual one, which he finds in his church model and in his death. The drama shows what happens to a lonely outsider who eventually rejects a patronizing world that will never be able to accept him as an equal and attains spiritual and moral superiority in the end by standing alone.

Critical Context

In his introductory remarks to the play, Pomerance acknowledges his debt to Sir Frederick Treves's *The Elephant Man and Other Reminiscences* (1923) and the reprinting of Treves's account in Ashley Montagu's *The Elephant Man: A Study of Human Dignity* (1973). Montagu's work awakened contemporary interest in Merrick's story and led to four confirmed produced dramatic treatments, the best known of which was Pomerance's award-winning play. It was first produced in London in 1977 and then on Broadway in 1979, where it became a critical and popular success. The play's several awards included a Tony, an Obie, and a New York Drama Critics' Circle Award. Critics generally approved of Pomerance's decision to have Merrick's deformity suggested through the actor's physical posture rather than through naturalistic makeup; the latter approach was used in David Lynch's film version of *The*

Elephant Man, which appeared in 1979 after the play's debut but was not based on it. Pomerance's subsequent plays have not been as successful, although his drama *Melons* (1985) also treats an outcast, an aging Apache leader exploited and oppressed by white civilization who dies in exacting revenge on an oil company intruding on Indian land.

Although not written precisely for young adults, *The Elephant Man* joins a distinguished group of plays that illuminate problems associated with disease and physical defects, such as Michael Cristofer's *The Shadow Box* (1977), in which terminal cancer patients deal with dying; Arthur Kopit's *Wings* (1978), which features a stroke victim; and Mark Medoff's *Children of a Lesser God* (1980), which portrays a young deaf woman's stormy relationship with her teacher. With *The Elephant Man*, Pomerance has written a compelling play on a biographical subject that will hold continued interest and value for a young adult audience.

Christian H. Moe

ELLEN GRAE

Authors: Bill Cleaver (1920-1981) and Vera Cleaver (1919-1992)
First published: 1967
Type of work: Novel
Type of plot: Social realism
Time of work: The early 1960's
Locale: Thicket, a small town in rural Florida
Subjects: Coming-of-age, family, friendship, and social issues
Recommended ages: 10-13

Honest, precocious, and given to storytelling, eleven-year-old Ellen Grae deals with a social and moral dilemma without resolution.

> *Principal characters:*
> ELLEN GRAE DERRYBERRY, an eleven-year-old who is sent to live with a surrogate family during the school year by her divorced parents
> GROVER, her best friend in Thicket, who is a few years older than Ellen Grae
> IRA, a middle-aged, mentally retarded man
> MRS. MCGRUDER, the well-meaning, kindly woman who cares for Ellen Grae during the school year
> ROSEMARY, Ellen Grae's stylish and "stuck up" roommate in Florida

Form and Content

Ellen Grae, the first book by Bill and Vera Cleaver, is distinguished by its characterization, plot, and style, aspects of writing that would become their hallmarks. The novel is told crisply, with short sentences and paragraphs, in solid but not patronizing prose, and from a first-person point of view. Almost novella-length and reading like a superbly crafted short story, the book itself is surprisingly brief considering the density of its material and its meaning.

The reader is introduced to Ellen Grae, who every year is sent to spend the school term with Mr. and Mrs. McGruder by her divorced (although loving) parents. The opening words reveal in a clipped, character-revealing dialogue an eleven-year-old who admits to being troublesome and independent in her thinking. The first-person narration is of great importance—although it has been a source of criticism in that Ellen Grae sees herself as well as others through a fairly sophisticated lens—because the lessons that are learned in the book are Ellen Grae's alone; she ends up sharing her values with no one else, save perhaps her fishing buddy, Grover. An omniscient point of view would not have allowed the reader to grow with the protagonist and come to some understanding of the moral dilemma in which she finds herself enmeshed.

The town "half wit," Ira, who speaks only to Ellen Grae and her friend, Grover, confides in her that he has, mistakenly and without premeditation, killed his parents (who had cruelly set out to kill him) and that he has buried them in a swamp. Ellen

Grae's personality traits, which are derived from her amicably divorced parents, are independence and a creative imagination, which sometimes predisposes her to preposterous, although humorous, exaggerations and stories. She is, however, quite capable of sorting truth from fantasy, and this is what causes the conflict. If she tells the truth about Ira, she believes that he may be sent to the "crazy house" or jail, and while she has no trouble ascribing guilt to Ira's parents (and not to him), she worries that they are not buried deep enough and that they have not had a proper burial.

Dealing silently with her moral quandary, Ellen Grae languishes. Soon her parents are sent for, and they succeed in prying the truth from her and forcing her to tell the story to the town sheriff, who accuses her of more excessive storytelling. In the end, when confronted with whether she had, indeed, fabricated this whole story, Ellen Grae finds it is easier to "admit" she had, thus angering and embarrassing her parents and making herself feel unsure and empty.

The ending of the novel is unresolved and ambiguous; Ellen Grae resumes her fishing trips with Grover, and her relationships with those who share her environment—her roommate, Rosemary, and Mrs. McGruder—are reinstated. Life will go on as before, as it always has in the quiet town of Thicket.

Analysis

When *Ellen Grae* first appeared in 1967, it was deemed too taxing for children of Ellen Grae's age because the moral dilemmas and conflicts with which she is faced were considered too difficult and/or inappropriate. Ellen Grae not only must decide whether to reveal a secret entrusted to her by a friend but also must deal with the adult issues of familial divorce, death, mental retardation, and poverty, balancing community values and personal values and independence in addition to the question of right and wrong.

The strength of *Ellen Grae*, however, is that the protagonist is shown to be capable of handling these quite difficult issues in an appropriate way because she can make decisions on her own, although she is not always comfortable with the outcome. The beauty and strength of the Cleavers' writing is that they make readers believe that Ellen Grae is capable of moral determinations. They do so by graciously moving readers slowly to the conflict and by using a first-person narrative.

The authors situate the story in a small, lazy Florida town where everyone is known to each other, foibles and all, as is Ellen Grae and her tendency to tell outrageously comic stories. Although Ira spills his story to Ellen Grae at the beginning of the book, the novel's first half is basically plot-free, even though the authors are skillfully heading toward a fast conflict and painful denouement. The plot moves as imperceptibly, quietly, and lazily as the overheated Florida town at Labor Day, when the conflict suddenly reemerges on a fateful treasure-hunting trip that Ellen Grae, Grover, and Ira take together to the swamp where Ira has allegedly buried his parents.

Humor also plays an important part in the first half of the book, as Ellen Grae's sophisticated comic stories provide both background for the conflict and relief when it comes. Ellen Grae's and Grover's humor stem from the authors' uncanny ear for children's speech and exaggeration; it is the natural humor of intelligent and imaginative children. By introducing humor sporadically into the text, the Cleavers elicit identification with and empathy for their protagonist, foreshadow elements of the plot, and imply the severity of Ellen Grae's plight by moving her humor to the background after she has become burdened with the responsibility of Ira's secret and its consequences.

The unconventional plot sequencing, along with the use of setting description and humor to establish character, is an aesthetic wonder considering the compactness of the book. Yet when the conflict comes, all these elements combine to draw the reader into the decision-making process that Ellen Grae faces. She is unable to decide whether to reveal her friend's secret, confused by what is morally right in her own mind and by her own sense of loss for herself as a result of her parents' rejection. Ellen Grae's feelings elicit strong emotional appeals to the reader to join her conflict and grow to maturity with her.

The ambiguous ending emphasizes the fact that the reader never knows for certain whether Ira's story is true, and the issue is, in fact, a moot point. Furthermore, it does not actually matter whether the reader agrees with what Ellen Grae did. What matters is that readers, like the carefully crafted protagonist, have been forced to scrutinize their own values about right and wrong for themselves. In the end, Ellen Grae learns the meaning of personal responsibility and loyalty to her friends, that responsibility is something that one must deal with alone, that it can be lonely being a morally committed person, and that doing what feels morally right does not always bring rewards. In short, Ellen Grae has learned that life is full of uncertainties and ambiguities and that some decisions are not comforting. That the reader is allowed to share the process of making value decisions with Ellen Grae is the strength of this eloquent book.

Critical Context

Ellen Grae, Bill and Vera Cleaver's first novel, was published in 1967, at a time when children's book fare was light, romantic, and episodic; mainly showcased intact families with young siblings; and often featured characters who romped around happily in the suburbs.

Ellen Grae signaled one of the earliest attempts to produce successfully a feisty, honest, thinking female character. (One thinks only of Louise Fitzhugh's title character in 1964's *Harriet, the Spy* as eclipsing her.) The Cleavers' book presented social values and norms not then seen in children's books; it was, for example, one of the first to present a protagonist of divorced parents, whose relationship is unstereotypically amicable and whom Ellen Grae calls by their first names. The themes of the book blatantly challenged and questioned prevailing norms and values by presenting a character who, at age eleven, was capable of coming to a state of self-awareness without the aid of adults.

From 1967 until 1981, when Bill Cleaver died, the couple produced seventeen books. The last, *Hazel Rye*, was finished by Vera Cleaver and published in 1983; she went on to write several novels until her death in 1992. Many of their books, two of which reintroduced Ellen Grae, include similarly strong female characters, notably *The Whys and Wherefores of Littabelle Lee* (1973) and the justly famous *Where the Lilies Bloom* (1969). The Cleavers never flinched from portraying social issues, often dealing with the difficult themes of mental retardation, death, alienation, poverty, and illness of the body and soul.

The Cleavers' books also set a high standard in excellent, well-researched regional writing for children, setting stories not only in the rural Deep South, but in the southern Appalachians and the Ozarks, as well as in metropolitan areas such as Chicago and Seattle.

The Cleavers were trailblazers of the realistic and seriocomic novel for young children, and it is a tribute to them that their works, beginning with *Ellen Grae*, still display dignity, grace, and honesty as they guide the reader eloquently toward personal growth.

Susan Steinfirst

EMMA

Author: Jane Austen (1775-1817)
First published: 1816
Type of work: Novel
Type of plot: Domestic realism
Time of work: The early nineteenth century
Locale: Highbury, a village in England not far from London
Subjects: Friendship, gender roles, love and romance, and social issues
Recommended ages: 15-18

A headstrong young woman learns that she cannot manipulate the lives of others and that she must appreciate the inner qualities rather than simply admiring the outward manners of her friends and neighbors.

Principal characters:
> EMMA WOODHOUSE, a young woman intent on scheming to help others marry but who is averse to marriage herself
> MR. WOODHOUSE, Emma's father, a likable recluse
> MR. GEORGE KNIGHTLEY, a neighbor of the Woodhouses
> MR. ELTON, a bachelor clergyman considered a prize catch by most women in Highbury
> HARRIET SMITH, a young woman whom Emma befriends
> FRANK CHURCHILL, the son of a local gentleman who lives with relatives away from Highbury
> JANE FAIRFAX, a young woman who visits relatives in Highbury and joins Emma's social circle

Form and Content

In *Emma*, Jane Austen tells the story of a young woman described by the narrator of the novel as "having rather too much her own way" and possessing "a disposition to think a little too well of herself." Although Austen claimed that her heroine was someone "whom no one would like but myself," Emma Woodhouse has captivated readers and critics, many of whom have acclaimed the novel as Austen's finest.

The second daughter of one of the ranking families in the village of Highbury, Emma is accustomed to directing the social lives of her reclusive father and other townspeople. Only her father's good friend Mr. Knightley, a bachelor nearly twice her age, speaks directly and forcefully to Emma about her meddlesome nature and about her misperceptions of others. The marriage of her governess Miss Taylor to local squire Mr. Weston, described in the opening paragraphs of the novel, convinces Emma that she has been a successful matchmaker. She immediately turns her attention to transforming Harriet Smith, a resident at a local boarding school, into a lady worthy of marrying the village's highly eligible cleric, Mr. Elton. After persuading Harriet that she is too good to marry a tradesman who genuinely loves her, Emma becomes distressed when she learns that Mr. Elton has no affection for Harriet; instead, he has fallen for Emma herself. With deftness and a touch of cruelty, she rebukes the minister, who departs Highbury for an extended vacation, during which he marries another woman.

Almost immediately thereafter, Emma becomes immersed in the social intrigue surrounding the impending arrival in Highbury of Frank Churchill; the son of Mr. Weston, Frank has been reared by an aunt from whom he has taken the family name. Emma seems almost too willing to flirt with Frank when he finally arrives. Concurrently, Highbury receives another visitor: Jane Fairfax, a polished but reclusive young woman who takes up residence with one of the families in Emma's social circle. Although Emma seems to have more in common with Jane than with Harriet, she is cool to her—perhaps from unacknowledged jealousy of Jane's talents.

In a series of social gatherings, Austen shows Emma scheming to make Frank fall in love with her, to marry off Harriet, and to demonstrate her superiority over the new Mrs. Elton. Her imagination and her schemings take her on various flights of fancy, until she is brought back to reality by the announcement that Frank has been secretly engaged to Jane before arriving in Highbury.

Throughout these escapades, Mr. Knightley remains a constant force of reserve and propriety. Considered by virtually everyone in Highbury as the epitome of a gentleman, he continually but gently rebukes Emma for her meddling and poor judgments. Only when she realizes that Harriet has fallen for Mr. Knightley and that he may be returning her attentions, however, does Emma become aware of her own love for him. The brief, matter-of-fact courtship between Emma and Mr. Knightley, her machinations to convince her father that her marriage is a good idea, and Harriet's reunion with her first love, Robert Martin, provide a comic and satisfying ending to the tale.

Analysis

Young readers will find in *Emma* a penetrating look at one of the most important issues that they face when growing up: the choice of a proper marriage partner. The novelist focuses on her title character, a young woman who seems to be able to ma-nipulate others to do her bidding. Financially secure and well placed socially, Emma may seem an attractive figure. Unfortunately, she is blinded by her self-centeredness and possesses an immature appreciation for adult social interactions. She is given to flights of imagination and invents motives for others in her social circle that fit her preconceptions about their attitudes and intentions. For her, matchmaking is a game, and while she appreciates the demands of married life, for most of the novel she is unwilling to acknowledge the serious nature of a commitment to that state.

Emma's actions are not simply self-defeating either; she causes pain to Harriet by building up the young woman's hopes for matches that cannot come to fruition, and she is on occasion callous in her behavior toward other young women toward whom she feels superior. Her treatment of Jane Fairfax, a genuinely nice woman who is in many ways more polished than she, is especially troublesome. As the story progresses,

Emma learns from her mistakes, although she is prone to repeat behavior that is detrimental both to herself and to others. Fortunately, she is finally able to come to understand how love and marriage are natural partners; with the good luck that characterizes most of Austen's heroines, she learns life's most important lessons from the man whom she eventually marries.

Austen's criticism is not confined to the young women in the novel. Frank Churchill's behavior, especially his flirtation with Emma at a time when he is engaged to Jane, is censored not only by Mr. Knightley but also by the narrator of the work. Austen provides readers with a counterpoint to Frank's improper behavior in the figure of Mr. Knightley, the quintessential English gentleman. Not given to excessive flattery, he is a keen judge of character, a practitioner of moderation in his social behavior, and a genuinely concerned neighbor and friend to members of both sexes.

The novelist also provides examples of good marriages that serve as models for those not yet married. Emma's sister Isabella, the wife of Mr. Knightley's younger brother John, is a happy mother of two young boys; the John Knightleys cheerfully accept their social roles, and they exhibit genuine love for each other and their sons. Similarly, Emma's former tutor Miss Taylor is happily married to Mr. Weston; although he already has a grown son, Frank, from his first marriage, Weston and his wife take special pride in their new daughter. Austen's description near the end of the novel of the beaming couple and their infant is a clear indication of the kind of domestic bliss that she considers the high point of married life.

In *Emma*, the heroine and other young people in the work learn how to judge character—their own and that of others. They also learn what is valuable in human relationships. Austen does not dismiss social class and status as important in forming a person's character; in fact, she is a strong supporter of the system that existed in England during her lifetime. Consequently, some readers may have difficulty accepting her assignment of characters within their social class. Nevertheless, in *Emma* Austen demonstrates that, no matter where a person falls within the social hierarchy, he or she must exhibit certain public graces and moral virtues to be considered truly admirable.

Critical Context

Although not as widely read as *Pride and Prejudice* (1813), *Emma* is frequently cited as Jane Austen's finest novel. Written at the height of her literary powers, the work manages to evoke a vivid picture of rural and village life in the late eighteenth and early nineteenth centuries while dealing with perennial questions about growing up and choosing a life partner; as a result, *Emma* is frequently included in surveys of English literature and in courses that stress domestic relationships or themes of maturation. Emma Woodhouse has been the subject of hundreds of critical studies; the author's ability to probe the psychological dimensions of her heroine and the supporting cast of characters has been cited as a special strength of the novel, and Austen is often classified as a precursor to the great novelists of psychological realism of the nineteenth and twentieth centuries: George Eliot, Henry James, and Virginia Woolf.

In recent decades, *Emma* has received significant attention from feminist critics, for whom Austen is a seminal figure in women's literature. Austen is one of those rare writers whose works appeal to audiences of all ages; accessible to young adults, her novels are ranked among the major works of English literature.

Laurence W. Mazzeno

EMPIRE OF THE SUN

Author: J. G. Ballard (1930-   )
First published: 1984
Type of work: Autobiography and novel
Type of plot: Adventure tale and historical fiction
Time of work: 1941-1945
Locale: Shanghai and a Japanese-controlled prison camp
Subjects: Coming-of-age, social issues, and war
Recommended ages: 15-18

Jim, a young boy living in Shanghai with his British parents, survives first in Japanese-occupied territory and then in a civilian POW camp through the end of World War II.

> Principal characters:
> JIM, a young boy born and being reared in Shanghai by his British parents
> DR. RANSOME, a fellow British expatriate
> BASIE, a raconteur and petty smuggler who alternately befriends and is befriended by Jim, depending upon who needs the other most
> MR. MAXTED, the father of Jim's best friend in Shanghai, later the man who runs the food cart in the Lunghua camp

Form and Content

J. G. Ballard declares this novel to be an account of his time in Shanghai and in the Lunghua prison camp during World War II. While this fascinating work may reveal much about its author, its scope and perceptions are universally applicable.

Jim has never known any life but that of an upper-class British expatriate in Shanghai. Ballard makes no pretense of nobility for the young Jim, who is rude to his servants and shows no comprehension of their lifestyle, as displayed by his surprise when one of his servants notes that her entire family lives in one room. From his sheltered perspective, Jim enjoys the fancy parties thrown by his father's fellow expatriates and others who are used to privilege.

All of this changes on December 8, 1941, when the Japanese military attacks an American ship, the *U.S.S. Wake*, and a British ship, the *H.M.S. Petrel*, in Shanghai harbor. Having declared war on the United States, Japan immediately begins a full occupation of Shanghai. Jim's father is injured while saving a British sailor from the *Petrel*, and he is taken to the hospital.

Jim, also taken to the hospital, manages to escape, while his parents are sent to be interred at the Woosung prison camp. Jim sees Shanghai transformed from a stratified but thriving metropolis into several bitter, prejudiced enclaves. He notes that "without its beggars," the city "seemed all the poorer." He spends some time trying to surrender, being stymied at each attempt. Ballard writes that "Jim had always despised anyone who surrendered, but surrendering to the enemy was more difficult than it seemed." It is observations such as these that make this novel's tone comparable to the works of Kurt Vonnegut or Joseph Heller.

As the Japanese troops tighten their control on the city, Jim meets Basie and Frank, itinerant Americans who are surviving by hustling, stealing, and salvaging goods. Basie, seeing Jim as an opportunity, helps him. Ultimately, Basie tries (and fails) to sell Jim into slavery. When Basie is about to throw him onto the street, Jim suggests they go to his parents' long-unoccupied house, which he describes as "luxuriant." Japanese troops have taken over the house, however, and they are captured and separated.

Jim is sent first to a detention center, where he meets several other expatriates, including Dr. Ransome, whom he helps in comforting the sick and injured. Jim rapidly realizes that the road to survival lies in taking care of himself, an impression solidified when Basie, ill, is brought to the detention center. When a group of prisoners (including Basie and Dr. Ransome) is being taken to the Woosung camp, Jim makes enough of a nuisance of himself that the Japanese include him in the group.

During the trip, through desiccated countryside, Jim develops a strained but friendly relationship with Dr. Ransome. The trip results in despair for Jim when the Woosung camp, where his parents are interred, refuses the prisoners. At the end of part 1, the prisoners reach the area that will be the Lunghua camp, with Jim separated, possibly permanently, from his parents.

Part 2 deals with Jim's life in the camp. Jim is lodged during this time with the Vincents, a dour British couple and their children, with whom he is neither friendly nor impressed. He works to survive, running errands for extra food and magazines, often provided by Basie. Eventually, he becomes the assistant to Mr. Maxted, the father of the boy who was his best friend in Shanghai. Mr. Maxted runs the prisoner's food cart in the camp, and this position helps Jim acquire the best of the rations.

As the war is ending, the prisoners are marched from the Lunghua camp toward Nantao. It is on that route that Mr. Maxted becomes fatally ill. Jim stays with him and others too sickly to continue their trip. Part 2 ends with the nearly simultaneous dropping of the atomic bomb on Nagasaki and the death of Mr. Maxted.

After the bombing, Jim, again traveling alone, wanders the country in search of his family. As with his initial attempt to surrender, nothing is easy. Along the way, he reencounters Basie, miraculously still alive after having escaped the Lunghua camp a day before the prisoners were freed for their march. Ultimately, Jim is reunited with his family, but his memories of Shanghai—and especially of his time in the Lunghua camp—will never be forgotten.

Analysis

The appeal of *Empire of the Sun* crossed many spectra. It echoes themes and images of Ballard's other works, and it is tempting to say that this autobiographical novel reveals the sources of many of those images. Although the general biographical facts of Ballard's life parallel Jim's, most of the time spent in the Lunghua camp is omitted from the narrative. (Some of that time is dealt with in this book's sequel, *The Kindness of Women*, published in 1991.) The narrative concentrates on Jim's perceptions more than his experiences, often giving events a surrealistic tone. The impression of surrealism is abetted by the detailed descriptions of Jim's environment, especially of people's physical appearances, uniforms, and aircraft.

Ballard's approach to women is reverential, even when Jim's dealings with them have been less than favorable. Principal among these women is Mrs. Vincent, with whose family Jim is quartered for the last two years of the war. Jim declares his fondness for Mrs. Vincent, although of no one else in her family, because she, like him, "appreciated the humor" of the Lunghua prison camp. Being able to appreciate humor in an absurd situation is a trait common to many of Ballard's characters and is essential to reading many of his other works, especially his "paste-up" novels such as *The Atrocity Exhibition* (1970) or *Vermilion Sands* (1971).

It is the British and their attitude—the same attitude Jim held at the beginning of the book—who are portrayed the worst. "All in all, Jim felt, the Americans were the best company . . . far superior to the morose and complicated British." Jim, already an expatriate who has never seen his homeland, feels a stranger among his own people. His transformation from a young boy who is incredulous that a family might all live in one room to the young man who survives by his wits and ingenuity has produced one of the great *Bildungsromans* of its time.

Many of Jim's actions are not noble—he steals and cheats in order to obtain extra rations—but he also gets water for the other prisoners on the way to the camp because he is brave enough to do what no one else will. He eats the maggots in the food, which other prisoners disdain, because he knows that they are a source of protein. He helps other prisoners but is always careful to make certain that he is in a position to benefit. He affiliates himself with whoever will treat him best.

All these actions reveal Jim's essential humanity. Most significant of all, perhaps, is that it is easy to forget that *Empire of the Sun* is a novel; its quality as a testament to history often overshadows Ballard's prose virtuosity. Yet, it is the virtuosity of the writing that enables Ballard to make Jim's keen observations revelatory of both the traumas of war and the human spirit, embodied in the character of Jim, that can survive such adversity.

Critical Context

J. G. Ballard's tale of survival is unique among World War II reminiscences, although there are several parallel tales. Jim is slightly younger than Anne Frank was during the war, witnessed a catastrophe as severe as the firebombing of Dresden, and takes actions similar to those found in the memoirs of Holocaust survivors. Perhaps the most apt parallel, however, is to Jerzy Kosinski's *The Painted Bird* (1965), a fictionalized tale with enough verisimilitude to seem autobiographical. If *Empire of the Sun* is regarded as a work of general literature, Ballard's perspective on war and wartime is perhaps most similar to Heller's in *Catch-22* (1961).

The brilliance of Ballard's work is that he filters young Jim's perspective through his adult sensibility without either talking down to the reader or losing Jim's attitude. As Jim's attitudes change—from his early realization "that kindness, which parents and teachers had always urged upon him, counted for nothing" to Dr. Ransome's telling him "you'll never believe the war is over"—his actions are consistent.

Additionally, this book may have revealed the origins of some of the recurring imagery in Ballard's works, such as low-flying planes and an empty swimming pool. As an aid to understanding Ballard and his works, this book is invaluable. It is not necessary to read Ballard's other works, however, to marvel at the depth and range of Jim's journey in a fictionalized wartime memoir that ranks with the most memorable of all time.

Kenneth L. Houghton

THE ENCHANTED CASTLE

Author: E. Nesbit (1858-1924)
First published: 1907; illustrated
Type of work: Novel
Type of plot: Fantasy
Time of work: The early twentieth century
Locale: A country village in western England
Subjects: Coming-of-age, family, friendship, and love and romance
Recommended ages: 10-13

Siblings Gerald, Kathleen, and Jimmy and their friend Mabel discover an enchanted ring that lands them in various predicaments but also illuminates for them the connection between magic and love.

> *Principal characters:*
> GERALD, the oldest of the children, who masterminds their summertime adventures
> KATHLEEN, a pupil at the school where she and her brothers are spending the holidays
> JIMMY, Gerald and Kathleen's younger brother
> MABEL, the niece of the housekeeper at Yalding Towers and the discoverer of the magic ring
> MADEMOISELLE, the French mistress at Kathleen's school, who is nominally in charge of Kathleen and her brothers
> LORD YALDING, the owner of Yalding Towers and Mademoiselle's long-lost lover

Form and Content

The Enchanted Castle shares its episodic structure with many of E. Nesbit's other fantasies; here, as is typical of this author's works, a group of children discovers a magic that leads them into a series of more or less self-contained adventures. These adventures are narrated with Nesbit's customary lighthearted charm, although occasionally a more serious tone takes over.

The story begins when an outbreak of measles prevents Gerald, Kathleen, and Jimmy from spending their summer holidays at home. Instead, they are marooned at Kathleen's school, supervised only by Mademoiselle, the French mistress—who, as Gerald observes, is unexpectedly young, pretty, and tolerant. Gerald, a well-spoken boy with a shrewd sense of what pleases adults, is able to win from her considerable freedom for himself and his brother and sister, so that the three may spend their days exploring the countryside. On their first hike, they discover the local showplace, Yalding Towers, which they decide to interpret (correctly, as readers shall see) as an "enchanted castle." At the center of a maze on the estate, they encounter the housekeeper's niece, Mabel, who is reenacting the story of Sleeping Beauty. Mabel attempts to persuade them that the magic in which they are pretending to believe really exists; she takes them to the castle's treasure room, declares that a ring displayed there is a ring of invisibility, and puts it on. Much to Mabel's astonishment, she does indeed disappear, and the stage is set for a summer of enchantment.

The children embark upon several adventures involving invisibility: They take the unseen Mabel to the fair so that Gerald can earn money as a "conjurer" with an invisible assistant; Gerald himself puts on the ring and becomes a detective to thwart a band of burglars; and the school housemaid, Eliza, nearly loses her fiancé when she unexpectedly participates in the magic. As the children gradually learn, however, the ring is not, strictly speaking, a ring of invisibility. The ring performs whatever function its wearer has claimed for it. Thus, readers next see it metamorphose into a wishing ring—whereupon it inconveniently gives life to some dummies that the children have constructed to augment the audience for their home theatricals and, still worse, turns Jimmy into a city magnate and Kathleen into a statue. It subsequently turns into a ring that makes the wearer twelve feet tall. By this point, the four children have befriended the castle's new owner, Lord Yalding, who turns out to be Mademoiselle's erstwhile beloved. He does not believe in magic and knows nothing about the castle's many secrets, from the treasure room to the living statues of gods and dinosaurs that gather every moonlit night. In attempting to end his skepticism, reunite the lovers, and restore Lord Yalding's fortunes, the children learn that the enchantment that makes childhood glorious is incompatible with adult romance: The magic must be sacrificed so that the love of Lord Yalding and Mademoiselle may come to fruition.

Analysis

Like Nesbit's other works, *The Enchanted Castle* first appeared as a serial in the *Strand*, a popular magazine aimed more at adults than at children, and some critics have complained that the story is inappropriate for sensitive young readers because of its focus on the panic that can accompany enchantment. Not only do the dummies ("Ugly-Wuglies") who come to life because of Mabel's careless wish launch a murderous attack on Lord Yalding before reverting to their inanimate state, but it also turns out that those who do not wear the ring are subject to a phobic terror at the conditions of some of the adventures. Moreover, adults are even more susceptible than children to this feeling: Eliza runs shrieking through the town after touching one of the animated statues, an American ghost hunter flees Yalding Towers after coming face to severed head with the object of his quest, and Lord Yalding himself experiences a "terror of madness" when the ring causes him to doubt his own sanity. While by modern standards the horror is tame, *The Enchanted Castle* is unique in the Nesbit canon for its emphasis on magic as not merely inconvenient or exciting (and it certainly possesses both qualities) but also fearful.

The novel suggests that this fear may be associated with loss of control over the self. Thus, those who wear the ring are often incapable of removing it when they would like to do so, just as those who encounter manifestations of the magic cannot face those manifestations with equanimity. The fantastic is larger than life and suspends the comfortable rules of reality, under which people age at a constant rate, grow only within limits, and can be sure that things constructed out of paper, old clothing, and walking-sticks will not suddenly become sentient and enraged. Impatient with rules and unused to having full control over themselves in any case, children can better tolerate the magic than can adults. Yet, if flexible childhood can—like Nesbit's prose—unite the mundane and the supernatural, the narrative makes clear that maturity demands a more prosaic form of wonder. The magic ring's final transformation makes it "normal": It becomes the wedding ring that binds Lord Yalding and Mademoiselle together.

Thus, if imagination is the source of one form of happiness, it is inimical to the happiness associated with adult control over the self and the emotions, and, insofar as the children learn any lesson in this narrative, they learn that reality is best. One may choose to read *The Enchanted Castle* as Nesbit's exploration of some of the pleasures and horrors of her own childhood; the antediluvian beasts and classical statues that populate the grounds of Yalding Towers recapitulate exhibits at the Crystal Palace that were favorites of the young Nesbit, while the Ugly-Wuglies recall the figures that she constructed in her adult years as part of an attempt to master the terror that overwhelmed her when, as a schoolgirl, she was taken to see the mummies of Bordeaux. The narrative, then, at once reanimates creatures of her memory of her fancy and deprives them of life at its conclusion, allowing both author and reader the pleasure of conjuring up creatures difficult to control and the still-greater pleasure of controlling them through the finality of a closed book. Arguably, the more humorous passages of *The Enchanted Castle* play with the same theme of achieving power over something more powerful than oneself, as the children not only learn the capacities of the ring but also engage in the more common childish endeavor to outfox adults in order to gain a freedom not normally vouchsafed to those of tender years. Despite the novel's episodic structure, this commonality of theme succeeds in unifying *The Enchanted Castle*, to the point that it becomes a quasi allegory about growing up.

Critical Context

Perhaps the preeminent Edwardian fantasist and also an important domestic novelist for children, Edith Nesbit was influenced by authors such as F. Anstey and became a major influence on such contemporary figures as Edward Eager; all three achieve comedy through juxtaposing the prosaic and the fantastic, and Nesbit's placement of ordinary characters in extraordinary circumstances contributes substantially to her continuing appeal.

The Enchanted Castle appeared toward the end of Nesbit's career, as she served an apprenticeship in hack work before producing *The Story of the Treasure Seekers* (1899) and after 1913 wrote, if at all, primarily for adults. Like its immediate predecessors, *The Story of the Amulet* and *The Railway Children*, both published in 1906, and like the fantasies that would follow, *The Enchanted Castle* hints at more serious issues than do certain other of Nesbit's works. Hence, it has elicited differing responses from her fans, some deeming it inferior to the more purely comic works, and others considering it as marking a maturity in her vision. Among those preferring Nesbit in her graver mode was C. S. Lewis, who favored *The Story of the Amulet*. *The Enchanted Castle* shares that work's concern with the seriousness of achieving one's heart's desire and the pleasure of mingling myth (here, the Greek gods) with modernity—tropes that resurface in Lewis' Narnia. That Nesbit continues to delight discerning readers testifies to the importance of her achievement.

Claudia Nelson

THE ENCYCLOPEDIA BROWN SERIES

Author: Donald J. Sobol (1924-   )
First published: 1963; illustrated
Type of work: Novels
Type of plot: Domestic realism and mystery
Time of work: The present
Locale: The fictional American town of Idaville
Subjects: Crime, family, friendship, gender roles, and jobs and work
Recommended ages: 10-13

Child detective Encyclopedia Brown solves neighborhood mysteries, as well as real crimes that stump his police chief father, through careful observation and practical knowledge of human behavior, history, and science in this popular series.

Principal characters:
LEROY "ENCYCLOPEDIA" BROWN, a fifth-grade detective with a photographic memory who solves mysteries for neighborhood children and for the Idaville Police Department
CHIEF BROWN, Encyclopedia's father and Idaville's chief of police, who trusts his son's attention to the details of his toughest cases
MRS. BROWN, Encyclopedia's mother, a former high school English teacher who serves up pie and grammatical advice while Encyclopedia solves his father's cases
SALLY KIMBALL, Encyclopedia's tough but pretty junior partner and bodyguard
BUGS MEANY, the wise-cracking town bully and leader of the Tigers, a group of older kids who often trick and steal from neighborhood children
WILFORD WIGGINS, a lazy high school dropout who concocts get-rich-quick schemes

Form and Content

In each of Donald Sobol's gently humorous Encyclopedia Brown juvenile detective books, readers can find all the clues necessary to solve ten mysteries along with Leroy "Encyclopedia" Brown, a bookish ten-year-old detective who lives in a fictional seaside town, Idaville, with his father, the police chief, and his mother, a full-time homemaker. Encyclopedia's solutions and problem-solving strategies are always printed like an answer key at the back of the book.

In the first chapter of each installment, Sobol reviews the central premise of the series. Although Idaville may seem like "the usual American town," at its heart is a notable anomaly: For nearly one year, no Idaville child or adult has succeeded in breaking the law. This record has less to do with Chief Brown's smart and able police department than with his smart and able son, who secretly solves the chief's toughest cases over dinner in the kitchen of the Browns' red brick house on Rover Avenue. Sobol suggests that Encyclopedia succeeds where others fail largely because he remembers everything that he reads, and he reads voluminously. In fact, a small portion of Encyclopedia's cases support this view, turning as they do on his knowledge of science or history. In "The Case of the Civil War Sword," in *Encyclopedia Brown, Boy Detective* (1963), Encyclopedia uncovers Bugs Meany's plot to trick a younger child into trading his bicycle for what Bugs claims is a sword once belonging to Civil War General Stonewall Jackson. Encyclopedia deduces that the sword is a fake because of two historical errors in its inscription, which reads "To Thomas J. Jackson, for standing like a stone wall at the First Battle of Bull Run on July 21, 1861. This sword is presented to him by his men on August 21, 1861." Encyclopedia knows that Jackson's men would not have used the North's term, Bull Run, but would have called it the Battle of Manassas. He also notes that on the inscription date of August 21, 1861, Jackson's soldiers would not have referred to the "first" battle, because they could not have known that there would be a second. This sort of solution, requiring specific historical knowledge not provided within the set of given facts, is uncommon in the series.

In most Encyclopedia Brown cases, readers need no prior historical or scientific knowledge to participate in solving the mystery. They must simply exercise their deductive reasoning skills: reviewing the facts, noting incongruities and unusual connections, and applying commonsense knowledge of human behavior to predict how a victim or a culprit might behave in a given situation. Using these methods in "The Cast of the Brain Game," in *Encyclopedia Brown and the Case of the Disgusting Sneakers* (1990), Encyclopedia discovers how Tyrone Taylor has helped Cindy Hayes cheat to win a party game, the object of which is to list nine three-letter body parts. When Cindy is accused of cheating, Encyclopedia reviews the facts. Tyrone was looking over his mother's shoulder as she read the contestants' lists. When his mother announced a run-off to break a tie between Cindy and another child, Tyrone left the room and promptly returned, conspicuously chewing a wad of gum. After staring for a moment at Tyrone, Cindy scratched out a ninth answer, winning the game. Encyclopedia notes Tyrone's irregular actions, which seem connected to what Encyclopedia knows of Tyrone's romantic personality. By checking the last word on Cindy's list, Encyclopedia confirms his suspicion that Tyrone, trying to please his new girlfriend, signaled the body part that she had not thought of yet: gum.

Analysis

Although some teachers, parents, and librarians worry that reading the many Encyclopedia Brown installments may keep children from reading more difficult work of greater literary value, young readers' interest in the series is quite reasonable, at least in part because the Encyclopedia Brown books' purpose, structure, and plots neatly fit the emotional and cognitive development of the average ten-year-old. Aware of and interested in personal relationships as well as the system of rules that govern them, ten-year-olds are fascinated by conflict resolution. Every Encyclopedia Brown case revolves around some pattern of legal or moral noncompliance, which either results in personal conflict or stems from it.

In "The Case of the Hidden Will," in *Encyclopedia Brown and the Case of the Dead Eagles* (1975), a dead Mr. King tricks and scolds his sons from the grave, hiding his final will in a place that they can only find by solving a riddle. He does this because three of them have been lazy and one has been disloyal. Sobol makes clear that this unhappy circumstance is a result of the grown sons' insufficient family feelings, which can only be resolved by punishing and excluding the son who embezzles from his father and challenging the sons who care so little for the family business, and their father, that they malinger. Although this exact scenario is unlikely to take place in the readers' personal lives, it does hint at more familiar family jealousies and betrayals, the stuff of many ten-year-olds' deepest anxieties.

Able to conceive of an event not only from beginning to end but also backward from end to beginning, typical Encyclopedia Brown readers love a logical puzzle, which the books provide because of both their general definition as mysteries and their specific, almost gamelike structures. Since mystery solving is a skill that readers can develop with practice, the more installments that they read, the better they become at the mystery game. This feature of the series especially motivates Sobol's readers, because young people typically long to believe in and demonstrate their achievement and competence in relation to others.

Even when Encyclopedia Brown readers cannot solve the mystery personally, they can at least project themselves onto their high-achieving, competent protagonist, Encyclopedia. Although he may look like a normal fifth-grader (not unlike his readers), he actually conceals special skills that no one but his parents fully apprehend (again, not unlike his readers). It is, after all, the fifth-grade detective, not his police chief father, who makes Idaville crime-free, whether the general population knows it or not. Female readers also have an appropriate protagonist with whom to identify in the competent Sally Kimball, Encyclopedia's junior partner and bodyguard. Generally characterized as prettier than any other girl in the fifth grade and tougher than any boy, Sally can only be beaten in a brainteaser by Encyclopedia. Perhaps because they are so closely matched, the two of them respect each other, Sally often focusing her lively talk on his intelligence and Encyclopedia often referring to her strength. Therefore, in addition to appealing to his readers' need for a competent, successful protagonist, Sobol also at least superficially models a healthy and respectful boy-girl friendship.

Because the Encyclopedia Brown books do not challenge their readers with especially complex characterization or subtle themes—providing instead, like most mysteries, the instant gratification of plot and puzzle—they are not likely to provoke great breadth of thought or depth of feeling. Nevertheless, they do satisfy a number of their readers' needs and consequently promote voracious reading.

Critical Context

Donald Sobol has achieved much popular success with the Encyclopedia Brown series, which began in 1963. He received the Pacific Northwest Readers' Choice Award for *Encyclopedia Brown Keeps the Peace* (1973) and established his work as a respectable part of a long and popular tradition of juvenile mystery series, including the Nancy Drew, Hardy Boys, and Boxcar Children books. Sobol has also been recognized for his overall contribution to the genre with a special Edgar Award from the Mystery Writers of America, which is significant because it recognizes the ties between juvenile mystery and adult mystery. It is no accident that the Encyclopedia Brown series mimics some of the conventions of the adult mystery, characterizing Bugs Meany as a wise-guy toughie and Sally Kimball as a quick-talking, street-smart girl-with-a-heart-of-gold. Juvenile readers cannot help being influenced by the voracious mystery-reading habits of their parents, and parents often enjoy reading aloud the junior version of their own escapist fiction.

Shelley Blanton-Stroud

ESCAPE TO FREEDOM
A Play About Young Frederick Douglass

Author: Ossie Davis (1917-   )
First presented: 1976
First published: 1976
Type of work: Drama
Type of plot: Historical fiction
Time of work: The 1830's
Locale: The Eastern Shore of Maryland and Baltimore
Subjects: Education, race and ethnicity, and social issues
Recommended ages: 10-15

> *By educating himself, the young Frederick Douglass is able to free himself from slavery and begin the work that will lead to the freedom of others.*

Principal character:
FRED BAILEY, an African American slave approximately thirteen years old

Form and Content

The play *Escape to Freedom* is a fictionalized biography of the early days of abolitionist, orator, and publisher Frederick Douglass told through a prologue and five scenes. Noted African American actor and playwright Ossie Davis employs direct narration, dramatizes situations, and intersperses the play with African American folk music. Utilizing a bare stage with set pieces, the play moves quickly from scene to scene and from place to place as the young Fred Bailey, who is later to become Frederick Douglass, plans and executes his escape from the horrors of slavery.

The story of *Escape to Freedom* is developed through flashbacks as the narrator, the adult Frederick Douglass, looks back on his childhood as a slave in various locations in Maryland. Other actors in the cast play a variety of characters, from slave owners to friends and confidants. They also function as a musical ensemble and as soloists, singing the folksongs that complement the action. Set changes are accomplished by the actors as they position the chairs, tables, and other items used to suggest the movement from one locale to another.

While the play deals directly with the harshness of American slavery, it is not a diatribe. Davis successfully presents the conflicting views of white people regarding the humanity of those who were enslaved and the morality of the institution itself. Just as young Fred is victimized and abused by those white people who support and benefit from the system, so too is he aided by those who question and challenge it.

The story begins as Jethro, an older slave, tells Fred of his visit to Baltimore in which he saw free black people. Fred is impressed by what he hears, and his interest is increased when he is told that he is being sent to Baltimore to assist his master's nephew and be a companion to their son. The nephew's wife, Sophia, proves to be a religious woman who believes that all people are equal under God. Seeing Fred as a curious and intelligent child, she begins teaching him to read. Her husband, Hugh, quickly and vehemently informs her that it is against the law to teach slaves to read and that to do so "spoils the slave." Fred believes that reading is the key to freedom and continues his education in secret. The result, however, is frustration as his mind is soon opened to worlds that are denied to him. A chance meeting with a sailor from the North further awakens him to the injustice of slavery and encourages him to add writing to his skills. He plans to escape by writing his own pass and free papers. The death of his owner, Colonel Lloyd, requires him to leave Baltimore and return to the farm at St. Michael's.

Once Fred is back on the farm, his master has a religious conversion that leads Fred to believe that he has changed his views regarding slavery. Unfortunately, this is not the case, and Fred is reprimanded when he is caught teaching other slaves to read biblical texts. He is sent to a man who is well known for his ability to "break" rebellious slaves.

The harshness of the new master has its effect on Fred, and he soon finds himself demoralized and depressed. The work of the new plantation does not suit the teenage slave, and he makes mistakes that lead him to a physical encounter with the slave breaker. Forced to fight back, he overpowers his master and is sent back to Baltimore where he is hired out to work in the shipyards.

While in Baltimore, Fred becomes involved with the community of free black people and meets Anna, the woman who will later become his wife. He also meets Mentor, a free black man who is a seaman. These associations further add to Fred's desire for freedom. With help from Mentor, he obtains seaman's papers and is able to escape to freedom in New York, where he becomes a leading spokesperson for the abolition of slavery, the publisher of *The North Star Journal*, an adviser to President Abraham Lincoln, and ambassador to Haiti.

Analysis

Escape to Freedom works on several important levels. As history, it challenges some assumptions about American slavery. Literature for young people often ignores the key questions of this period in U.S. history in an attempt to avoid villainizing Southern slaveholders. Davis' work, however, clearly demonstrates and states that the system dehumanized both the slave and the master. Moral issues arise in each scene as the various characters attempt to find comfortable explanations for the actions that they must take. Sophia has difficulty reconciling the contradictions between her Christian beliefs and her responsibility to her husband and community. The play suggests that, for many slaveholders and supporters of the system, the question of morality was overshadowed by the need for economic stability, and that stability was based on the continuation of slavery.

Escape to Freedom pulls no punches in its depiction of American racism, but it also tells the audience that, even during this harsh period in history, liberation was achieved through interracial cooperation. At every step of his journey to freedom, young Fred was helped by sympathetic individuals of both races.

The playwright presents young Fred Bailey as an avid student, learning from books but also taking his lessons from life. When he and Jethro are reprimanded by a female slave for stealing the master's fruit, Jethro tells her that the fruit is his to eat by right, since it is the work of slaves that produced the harvest. In the next scene, Fred overhears his master claiming that "the worst thing you can do for a slave . . . is to teach him to read." From this statement, Fred begins to unravel what he calls "the greatest puzzle," how white people are able to keep black people enslaved. He determines that as long as Africans are kept ignorant to the ways of the West, they will always be slaves.

In the fourth scene, Fred learns another important lesson in how slaves are controlled when, on holidays, they are encouraged to dance, sing, and get drunk. "The slave masters knew," he says, ". . . that if they could keep us singing and dancing and cutting the fool like a bunch of idiots we wouldn't be angry anymore—would lose our desire to fight back—to escape." From these and other situations, young Fred learns that to escape a bad situation, one must first understand it. Liberation is achieved only when the individual stays focused on freedom.

The underlying theme throughout the play is the importance of self-knowledge, knowing oneself no matter what others say. In order to obtain release from his bondage, Frederick Douglass first had to free his mind. He had to overcome his fear of his captors and learn to outthink them. Davis makes it clear that this is no easy task, and one sees the principal character wavering in his commitment when confronted with physical abuse and other setbacks over which he has no control.

Another important aspect of *Escape to Freedom* is that, as a play, it is extremely performable by young actors and adults. The characterizations are complex but clear, and the script gives useful information for the staging of the play. The inclusion of African American folk music as a theatrical device is an interesting method of creating cohesion while advancing the action. Although the script is written for seven performers, it is also possible to mount the work with a larger cast, therefore making it a viable project for schools and other groups.

Unlike many plays that come to life only in production, Davis' work also satisfies as desk reading. The dialogue is sharp, and the descriptions are clearly stated without the use of theatrical terminology.

Critical Context

Although many novels and plays deal with American slavery, few of these works are specifically directed to or written for young people. Fewer still are written from the standpoint of the slave. Notable exceptions are Alice Childress' plays on Harriet Tubman and Martin Luther King, Jr. Together with *Escape to Freedom*, the three plays constitute an important approach to the teaching of American history, both in the formality of the classroom and for general audiences as entertainment.

Don Evans

ESCAPE TO WITCH MOUNTAIN

Author: Alexander Key (1904-1979)
First published: 1968; illustrated
Type of work: Novel
Type of plot: Adventure tale and science fiction
Time of work: The late 1960's
Locale: A city in the Blue Ridge Mountains
Subjects: Family, social issues, and the supernatural
Recommended ages: 10-13

> *Tony and Tia, two children with amazing abilities, search for their people while being pursued by evil forces.*

Principal characters:
TONY MALONE (later CASTAWAY), a boy with psychic abilities who tries to take care of himself and his sister while finding out where they both came from
TIA, Tony's sister, who can open locks and communicate with animals
FATHER O'DAY, a kindly priest who befriends and helps the two siblings
WINKIE, Tia's unusual cat
LUCAS DERANIAN, an evil man who pretends to be the children's uncle and who wants to capture them because of their abilities
WERNER KARMAN, Deranian's henchman

Form and Content

Escape to Witch Mountain is a fast-paced science-fiction novel filled with adventure. Except for the final section of the final chapter, the story is told in the third person but through Tony's point of view. The reader sees the events through Tony's eyes and is privy to his thoughts. The short chapters are subdivided into sections, and each chapter ends with some type of cliffhanger statement to keep the reader moving through the book. By doing so, Alexander Key keeps up the pace and suspense through the story. The novel, as first published, is also accompanied by line drawings by Leon B. Wisdom, Jr.

The story begins with Tony and Tia being sent to Hackett House after the woman with whom they have been living, Granny Malone, dies after an accident. Hackett House is a home for problem children, and Tony and Tia must carve out their place there. Neither of them is happy, for both have strange abilities that keep them apart from other children: Tony has psychic powers, and Tia can unlock doors and contact animals with her mind. In addition, Tia can communicate only with Tony, which makes things even more difficult. The two children want to find out where they have come from, and their only clue is the Star Box, a box with twin stars on it that Tia has always had with her.

The two siblings receive a clue about the box from a nun, but she dies before sending them any information. Then, Lucas Deranian arrives at the orphanage, claiming that he is their uncle; he arranges to become their guardian. Tia remembers that this man took them to live with Granny and that he is evil. The two run away and seek help from Father O'Day, a priest they heard of while living with Granny Malone. They tell Father O'Day everything, demonstrate their unusual abilities for him, and show him a map that Tia found in the Star Box. He arranges transportation for them to Stony Ridge, the place listed on the map.

Deranian shows up again, and the children leave without Father O'Day, taking the bus to their destination, with Deranian in pursuit. They are caught by a greedy sheriff but escape using their powers. While on the run, they remember more about their past. They know that they are castaways, that they escaped from someplace with their uncle but that he died. Eventually, they remember that they came from another planet. Tony and Tia are reunited with Father O'Day. With his help, they first thwart Deranian's attempt to capture them and then find the rest of their people.

Analysis

For the most part, *Escape from Witch Mountain* is an exciting adventure story. Tony and Tia are sympathetic orphans, Father O'Day is a friendly helper, and Lucas Deranian is an evil villain. Alexander Key does more, however, than simply tell a good story. He also paints an unattractive portrait of human society and, in contrast, creates a sense of wonder and magic through Tony and Tia.

The novel follows a fairly conventional plot. The two main characters are orphans searching for their home and people. In order to find both, they must go on a journey filled with perils. Before they even begin their quest, they have to escape the orphanage and find their way to Father O'Day's mission. During the journey, they encounter several more obstacles to overcome: being arrested by a greedy sheriff, being hunted by superstitious townsfolk, and being chased by unscrupulous villains. After several near escapes and chases, and with the help of Father O'Day, they eventually find their way to Witch Mountain, where the rest of their people have settled.

Although Key provides a simple plot, his settings and the societies through which the two children move are slightly more complex. Tony and Tia have been living in a run-down neighborhood in a tenement building. It is an ugly world that they leave with the social worker, only to arrive at the more unpleasant world of Hackett House. The orphanage is ruled by the grim Mrs. Grindley, who locks them out of the library and is always inclined to believe the worst. Tia's Star Box is stolen soon after they arrive, and Tony has to fight a bully armed with a homemade blade in order to get it back. When the children are allowed a trip to Heron Lake, it is a run-down camp, obviously used for city kids. The only seeming bright spot in this environment is Father O'Day, who runs a mission down by the waterfront.

When Tony and Tia leave the city, they go to a small rural town and are immediately arrested by Chief Purdy. It becomes apparent that the chief is much more interested in the reward for their capture than he is in truth, justice, or compassion. He threatens to beat Tony with a belt so that he can get the truth, even though Tony has already told it to him. When Tony uses his powers to escape, Purdy labels him a witch and has the entire countryside hunting for them with guns. In fact, they are shot at as they approach one farm.

The world that Key depicts is one filled with greed and prejudice. Tony and Tia's Uncle Bene was killed as he tried to free them from the control of the Communist government in Hungary, which wanted to use the children's abilities for their own ends. The ship captain to whom Bene entrusted the children betrayed them for money. Mrs. Grindley tells them that she will keep their money so that it will not be stolen. Deranian wants the children for the power that they will bring him.

Key contrasts this portrait of human society with Tony's description of his people. On the planet from which the children come, people do not own property; they do not have the concept of money. When they came to Earth, these were the hardest lessons that they had to learn. They also had to cope with the prejudices and greed of humans. They concocted stories to make sure they stayed safe. The kindness and compassion of this people are shown through Tia in particular. Chief Purdy has kept a pair of bears locked up and underfed in order to benefit the tourist trade in town. Tia puts the bears before her own safety and releases them because she feels so sorry for them. Key criticizes human traits through these characters from another world.

The fact that Tony and Tia are from another planet is what gives the book its wonder and magic. Tony can make dolls dance when he plays the harmonica. While in the woods, rabbits and deer come to hear him play. When he escapes Chief Purdy, he makes the broom come alive. Through his writing, Key makes the scenes come alive for readers as well.

Critical Context

Escape to Witch Mountain probably became more famous, and more widely read, after it was made into a Walt Disney film in 1975. The motion picture *Return from Witch Mountain* (1978), once more featuring Tony and Tia, was more a sequel to this film version than to the original book. The written sequel was also based on the motion-picture sequel and not on the original book.

Escape to Witch Mountain is clearly science fiction, but it is also in some ways a work of social realism. The tenement situation and the dismal orphanage are real-world occurrences, even if many of the activities of Tony and Tia are not. The prejudice that the two children encounter is also part of the real world. This mixture of social realism, along with the contemporary setting, makes the book different from what is usually considered young adult science fiction, such as those works written by Andre Norton and Robert Heinlein. Placing the alien or the fantastic in the mundane world is Key's way of showing the dark side of human nature. It is a theme that he pursued in other works as well, such as *The Forgotten Door* (1965), a winner of the

Lewis Carroll Shelf Award. In other works, such as *The Magic Meadow* (1975) and *Flight to the Lonesome Place* (1971), his characters flee the hardships of society by escaping to magical places. This combination of the fantastic and the realistic makes Key's stories thought-provoking as well as entertaining.

P. Andrew Miller

EXPLORING CHEMISTRY

Author: Roy A. Gallant (1924-   )
First published: 1958; illustrated
Type of work: Science
Subjects: Jobs and work and science
Recommended ages: 13-15

The history of chemistry, the endeavors of great chemists, and the existing and future applications in this field are described for nonscientists.

Form and Content

Exploring Chemistry is a well-written description of the science of chemistry that is intended to introduce the field in an appealing fashion to nonscientists between the ages of thirteen and fifteen. Written mostly in the third person, the book is divided into four unnumbered chapters—"Why Did Chemistry Begin," "Matter and the Alchemists," "The New Chemistry," and "Frontiers of Chemistry"—each of which is a well-illustrated exploration of a facet of chemistry that prepares readers for the next chapter.

Roy A. Gallant starts his book by explaining why chemistry began. In antiquity, human beings first attempted to find ways to meet their many material needs by manipulating the world around them—for medicines, for fuels, for agricultural chemicals, and so forth. He also points out that the practice of modern chemistry provides an adequate supply of these things.

Among the first examples given in the book are the use of fire and the ability to turn clays and metals into needed implements and weapons. Gallant clearly shows that the development of these divergent yet cojoined endeavors led to science and then to chemistry. As he notes, "It is the way that man works, the method he uses, that makes him a scientist." The accidental discovery of fire is linked to later "accidents" that led to pottery, metal working, and glass making. Throughout, it is made explicit that accurate record-keeping and inquisitiveness led to the accumulation of more information. It was this information that set the stage for the development of science and of modern chemistry.

In "Matter and the Alchemists," Gallant explains how the protochemists of antiquity prepared recipes for making materials and used them for many generations without understanding them. He next identifies the Greek philosopher-scientists (or natural philosophers) after 600 B.C., who wished to identify why materials could be made and what matter really was. Men such as Empedocles (c. 490-430 B.C.) were severely limited by the lack of advanced technology and supposed that all things were made by the mingling of four basics, which were named elements: earth, air, fire, and water. Their teachings, after modification by Democritus (c. 460-c. 370 B.C.), who identified atoms as the smallest pieces of matter, stagnated for many centuries because physical experiments were not carried out.

Next on the scene were the alchemists, who sought to make gold from base metals and reigned until A.D. 1400. Their incorrect theories, Gallant notes, at least arose from carrying out physical experiments. In addition, they developed many techniques for making substances and pieces of laboratory equipment that proved useful to later chemists, and (in "The New Chemistry") Gallant describes how these individuals coined their own erroneous concept in the sixteenth century. Alchemists such as Paracelsus (1493-1541) proposed that matter was made of a fabulous material called "phlogiston." The disproof of the existence of phlogiston and its replacement with correct ideas, such as a valid explanation of the elements and a modern atomic theory, came next. These crucial scientific changes may be attributed to the work, over two centuries, of chemists such as Robert Boyle (1627-1691), Antoine-Laurent Lavoisier (1743-1794), Joseph-Louis Proust (1754-1826), and John Dalton (1766-1844).

Gallant points out that, after this stage in the development of chemistry had been reached, the rate of achievement in this science greatly accelerated. For example, between Dalton's time and the 1950's, chemistry developed so quickly and so extensively that it became necessary to divide it into five areas: analytical, biological, inorganic, organic, and physical chemistry. Further advances led to subdivisions of these specialty areas. Many exciting aspects of both theoretical and practical chemistry are described in *Exploring Chemistry*.

Finally, Gallant notes in "Frontiers of Chemistry" that the chemistry of his own time is essential to virtually every aspect of life: to making clothing, to producing and protecting crops in the fields, to protecting humans from and curing diseases, and to making rocket fuel, to name a few. He also points to many other events in chemistry, filling most areas of human needs, that were expected to occur after the 1950's; most of them did.

Analysis

The title *Exploring Chemistry* explains the goals of Gallant's book, and he explores chemistry in a quite enjoyable fashion. First, some of the values of this field to modern (1950's) society are closely scrutinized. Then, Gallant elaborates on the development of the science of chemistry over the centuries, in ever-accelerating fits and starts. Much is made of the need for both precise thinking and extensive physical experimentation by chemists. In that light, Gallant shows that the beginnings of modern chemistry were not possible until the seventeenth century, when technology reached a minimum state required for further progress. Nevertheless, the contributions of natural philosophers of antiquity, who were hampered by lack of technology, and of alchemists, who sought mostly to make gold, are also shown to be very important.

The description of the fascinating nature of chemistry is aided by the many illustrations that were conceived by Gallant's artist-collaborator, Lee Ames. Gallant identifies the known elements and describes the discovery of new ones, defines the subatomic particles that make up the atoms of the myriad different kinds of matter, and conceptualizes the needs of society for foods and for many other items. The profession of chemistry is thus shown to be being quite rewarding and very enticing.

Another exciting aspect of the book comes from its many predictions about the future of chemistry, from the perspective of the 1950's, including advances in the areas of fuel, agricultural, organic, biological, theoretical, and medicinal chemistry. These advances are, like the rest of the book, described simply and in an understandable manner. The hindsight available to readers who now live in the future that Gallant described will probably foster an interest in chemistry for several reasons. The science of chemistry seems to have a predictive quality, because many concepts suggested by the author were actualized. On the other hand, not everything that is conceptualized comes to pass, and a career in chemistry offers the excitement of challenge, potential, and risk. Furthermore, the science of chemistry is shown to have become increasingly essential to society.

Critical Context

Exploring Chemistry is an older book that still offers an excellent beginning for surveying the basis for, the development of, and some rewards of the practice of chemistry. It seems most suitable for history of science courses and courses that, in some elementary and middle schools, seek to delve into the foundations of science and into its many ramifications.

Roy A. Gallant clearly shows how natural philosophy, alchemy, and basic science were blended to create modern chemistry. It is also made explicit that chemists must be bright, intuitive, and willing to take risks to develop new things. The great rewards of conceptualizing and actualizing chemistry are implied, and the book would be a good primer to explain to young people what chemistry is, what it can become, and why they may wish to become chemists. The necessary intellectual requirements and the labor-intensive nature of the profession are identified by past examples, promoting realistic career choices.

Exploring Chemistry contains numerous good black-and-white and color illustrations that help to focus the interest of young readers. All these aspects make the book useful for young people as a means of evaluating chemistry and what it is like to be a chemist or a science historian.

Exploring Chemistry is one of many writings by Gallant, who has endeavored in such works as *Exploring the Universe* (1956) and *Exploring the Weather* (1957) to explain science. It is nicely written and is a useful preview or adjunct to the chemistry texts written for students in elementary and secondary school science courses. While the book only conceptualizes chemistry up to the 1950's, it does so well and lacks most of the dated and therefore erroneous information that makes many such books quite useless. Gallant's book is not as detailed as some others in the area, such as Elizabeth K. Cooper's *Discovering Chemistry* (1959), but it engages the reader in the wonder of chemistry.

Sanford S. Singer

THE FACE ON THE MILK CARTON

Author: Caroline B. Cooney (1947-   )
First published: 1990
Type of work: Novel
Type of plot: Domestic realism
Time of work: The present
Locale: Connecticut
Subjects: Family and love and romance
Recommended ages: 10-15

> *Janie Johnson thinks that she leads a very ordinary life until the day she sees her own picture on a milk carton in a notice about a missing child and is plunged into the mystery surrounding her identity.*

> Principal characters:
> JANIE JOHNSON, a high school sophomore
> MIRANDA JOHNSON, Janie's mother
> FRANK JOHNSON, Janie's father
> REEVE SHIELD, a high school senior who lives next door to the Johnsons
> LIZZIE SHIELD, Reeve's older sister, who is in law school

Form and Content

In *The Face on the Milk Carton*, Caroline B. Cooney tells Janie Johnson's story from the limited omniscient point of view. This straightforward approach allows Cooney to focus on Janie, to give the reader access to Janie's thoughts, and to provide glimpses of the flashbacks that occur in Janie's mind as she remembers her life before the age of three.

The protagonist is a high school sophomore who, thinking her life is dull, seeks to add "personality" by changing the spelling of her name from "Jane" to "Janie." Eating lunch in the school cafeteria with her friends, she looks at a milk carton and sees a photograph of herself when she was three years old. The name beneath the picture, however, is Jennie Spring, and the information states that she was reported missing by a family in New Jersey.

Although she loves the Johnsons, Janie begins to gather clues about her early life. Her mother acts strangely when Janie needs her birth certificate to get a driver's license and passport. There is also the absence of any baby pictures of Janie. Finally, in an attic trunk, she finds the polka-dot dress shown in the missing person photograph.

When Janie confronts the Johnsons, they tell her that rather than being their daughter, she is their granddaughter. Their daughter Hannah, who was brainwashed by a cult, came home one day with her own daughter, young Janie. When Hannah left to rejoin the cult, she left Janie behind. Fearing that the cult would come to take Janie away, the Johnsons changed their name and, with the help of an attorney, moved, leaving no forwarding address.

While wanting to believe the Johnsons, Janie cannot forget the information from the milk carton. Skipping school, she persuades her boyfriend Reeve to drive her to the New Jersey town where the Spring family lives. There she watches as the Spring children arrive home and are greeted by their mother. Janie and the Springs have the same red hair. Putting together the information from her flashbacks, Janie realizes that she was once part of this family.

As she learns more about the past, she realizes that the Johnsons did not kidnap her from the Springs; Hannah did. Torn between her love for the Johnsons and the pain that she knows the Spring family has suffered, Janie writes detailed notes about what she has found and sinks into despair. She even blames herself for the kidnapping. Her refusal to tell the Johnsons drives a wedge between her and Reeve, and they break up.

Events come to a head when Janie puts her notes in an envelope that she has addressed to the Springs. When she finds the clip in her notebook broken and the envelope missing, Janie realizes that someone may find the letter and mail it. She turns to Reeve, who contacts his sister Lizzie. Although it is Lizzie who, along with Reeve and Janie, tells the Johnsons the entire story, it is Janie who places the phone call to the Springs that ends the novel.

Analysis

On the surface, *The Face on the Milk Carton* is a good mystery story. Clues accumulate to keep the action moving as Janie Johnson tries to discover her true identity: the lack of baby pictures, the panic over a request to see her birth certificate, and information from the back issue of *The New York Times*. In addition, Janie's memories appear in the form of quick glimpses of the past, the incomplete recollections of a three-year-old child. Is she really the girl in the polka-dot dress on the milk carton? Everything builds to a climax as Janie tries to decide whether to contact the Springs and how to confront the Johnsons.

If there were nothing more in this novel, the dramatic plot would be enough to make it a suspenseful page-turner. Below the fast-paced mystery, however, is a book that explores teenage emotions and relationships as it focuses on the need for people to belong and to have a sense of identity and importance.

As Janie falls into a romantic relationship with Reeve, she constantly struggles with problems surrounding the deeper emotional love that comes from being a member of a family. Her normal teenage concern about making her name sound unique turns into a greater concern as she seeks to determine both who she really is and what kind of person she is. If she really loved the Springs, why did she go with Hannah? If she really loves the Johnsons, why is she obsessed with the Springs? If she contacts the Springs, does that mean she does not love the Johnsons? Such questions race through Janie's mind.

Reeve plays an important part in the novel, primarily as a foil for Janie. Fun-loving when she is serious, he remains stable as she becomes more upset. Yet, Reeve is not without his own problems of identity. The youngest in a family of overachievers, he is judged against the successes of his two older sisters and his older brother. He believes that his family thinks of him as the "dumb one." While Janie knows that Reeve is not stupid, her own problem is so great that she is not able to help him. Instead, it is Reeve who must become the strong individual.

As in many of her novels, Cooney does an excellent job of presenting her characters through dialogue. She shows the normal growing pains and frustrations of a teenager in the late twentieth century—the excitement of a football game, the thrill of getting a driver's license, and the rush of falling in love. These routine activities fade into the background, however, as Janie must confront the real dilemma of her kidnapping.

Cooney lets the reader share in the out-of-control feeling that slowly overtakes Janie. Tension builds as Janie unearths more clues, and she refuses to admit that the people whom she calls "Mommy" and "Daddy" may be criminals. Even when Janie realizes that Hannah, not the Johnsons, performed the kidnapping, her problems are far from over. Finally, she prepares the letter for the Springs. In this action, Janie seems almost detached from herself, looking on as if she were merely a puppet in a play. The conclusion provides a welcome relief for the reader and the characters.

The combination of the mystery of the kidnapping and the tension that builds within the main character creates the overall suspense in the novel. Unlike many of Cooney's other works, this novel does not arrive at a "happily ever after" ending. The reader is left to wonder what will happen after the phone call, when the Johnson and Spring families must deal with the realities of the situation.

Critical Context

Although not included on any "best books" lists when first published, *The Face on the Milk Carton* has become popular with young adults. In addition to receiving the Pacific States and Iowa Teen awards, the novel was an International Reading Association-Children's Book Council (IRA-CBC) Children's Choice Book. Its sequel, *Whatever Happened to Janie* (1993), was an American Library Association Best Book for Young Adults.

Throughout *The Face on the Milk Carton*, Cooney presents only one side of the story—that of Janie and the Johnsons. In the sequel, she presents the story of the Springs, including their life in the years without Janie (their Jennie) and the adjustments that have to be made when Janie rejoins the family.

The subject of kidnapping has been discussed in other young adult novels, although not in the same manner as in *The Face on the Milk Carton*. In *Taking Terri Mueller* (1981), by Norma Fox Mazer, a young girl is kidnapped by her noncustodial parent. In *The Twisted Window* (1987), by Lois Duncan, Brad kidnaps a young girl to replace the sister whom he accidentally killed. Jean Thesman's Rachel in *Rachel Chance* (1990) tries to find her young brother, who has been kidnapped by a religious group. In contrast, Cooney deals with the emotional problems of a kidnapped child who has been living with a wonderful family that knows nothing about her past.

Katherine T. Bucher

FAMOUS ASIAN AMERICANS

Authors: Janet Normura Morey (1951-   ) and Wendy Dunn (1949-   )
First published: 1992; illustrated
Type of work: Biography
Time of work: From the 1920's to the 1990's
Locale: The Philippines, New York, China, New Jersey, Minnesota, and California
Subjects: Actors, athletes, race and ethnicity, scientists, and writers
Recommended ages: 13-18

The fourteen Asian Americans profiled here succeeded in achieving prominence in various areas of human endeavor, making tremendous contributions to the country.

Principal personages:
    JOSE ARUEGO, an author-illustrator of children's books
    MICHAEL CHANG, a world champion tennis player
    CONNIE CHUNG, a broadcast journalist
    MYUNG-WHUN CHUNG, the director of Opéra de la Bastille in Paris
    WENDY LEE GRAMM, the chair of the Commodity Futures Trading
        Commission of the federal government
    DANIEL K. INOUYE, a U.S. senator
    MAXINE HONG KINGSTON, a writer
    JUNE KURAMOTO, a musician and songwriter
    HAING NGOR, a doctor and Oscar-winning actor for *The Killing Fields*
        (1984)
    DUSTIN NGUYEN, an actor
    ELLISON S. ONIZUKA, an astronaut who died on board the *Challenger*
    I. M. PEI, a world-renowned architect
    SAMUEL TING, a Nobel Prize-winning physicist
    AN WANG, an inventor and businessman

Form and Content
    This collective biography features Asian Americans who distinguished themselves in the fields of arts, music, literature, sports, media, science, architecture, government, business, and other professions. These brilliant individuals represent six different ethnic groups under the rubric of "Asian American": Chinese, Japanese, Korean, Vietnamese, Cambodian, and Filipino. Some of them are first-generation Asian Americans—Jose Aruego, Haing Ngor, Dustin Nguyen, June Kuramoto, Samuel Ting, and An Wang—while the others are of the second or third generation. They come from very different family backgrounds. For example, the father of the famous writer Maxine Hong Kingston was a scholar and schoolteacher in China but after immigrating to the United States went into the laundry business. As a child, Kingston helped with the work in her father's store. In contrast, the father of renowned architect

I. M. Pei was a wealthy banker in China who sent his son to be educated in the United States.

Despite their different backgrounds and professions, the figures in *Famous Asian Americans* share some characteristics: drive, talent, courage, diligence, persistence, and a belief in themselves. For many of them, success did not come easily. It is these remarkable qualities that enabled them to excel in their fields and realize the American Dream. For example, journalist Connie Chung was always ready to tackle new challenges and scale new heights in her career. She continues to work hard, sometimes seventeen hours a day, and is such an energetic person that her colleague Dan Rather once called her a "nuclear reactor of energy." The musician and songwriter June Kuramoto seems to speak for all of these individuals when she says that she would like to be remembered as a person who worked hard for what she believed in—someone who "did not give up, kept a positive attitude, and made things happen."

Rather than a voluminous biography of each individual, Janet Normura Morey and Wendy Dunn provide vignettes that each span slightly more than ten pages. Brief as they are, all fourteen vignettes have a consistent format made up of three components: the individual's family story, achievement, and remembrances. The family story delineates the subject's cultural heritage and shows the influence of his or her family. The authors also describe the individual's major achievements and their significance. The third element of the biography is the individual's own recollections of past experiences. These three components are not laid out in separate sections but are interwoven skillfully into a smoothly flowing story that captures each individual's background, personality, and achievements.

Black-and-white photographs from the personal collections of the subjects are interspersed throughout the book, between two and four for each entry. These images show the individuals by themselves, with their families, at work, or at an important moment of their lives and reinforce the reader's impression of the book's subjects.

The foreword by Harry H. L. Kitano, a noted scholar of sociology, helps the reader view the experiences of these individuals and value their contributions in the historical context of immigration and racial conflicts. A selected bibliography at the end of the book suggests further readings.

Analysis

It is a great challenge to present fourteen people's life stories within the limited space of less than two hundred pages: Important facts must be presented in a way that makes the account pleasant to read. In the hands of lesser authors, these biographies could be merely a collection of facts and dates, lifeless and dull. Morey and Dunn succeed in making these individuals come to life on the page by presenting the essence of their experiences and personalities in a lively manner.

In most cases, an entry is not simply a straightforward narrative from family roots to the height a subject's achievement. It often starts with a dramatic moment in the subject's life or the highlight of his or her career. For example, Michael Chang's story begins with the glorious moment of winning the French Open at the age of seventeen.

"Some kids go to Paris to study history, others go to make it," a newspaper comments on his success. Even when the biography starts with the family history, it is often immediately tied to the individual's achievement. The story of astronaut Ellison Onizuka starts: "When Kichiher and Wakano Onizuka voyaged to Hawaii from the Fukuoka prefecture in Japan, they never dreamed that one day their grandson would fly among the stars." An opening such as this instantly draws young readers into the story.

The extensive use of quotation from the subject also enlivens the narrative. At many points, the authors let the subjects speak for themselves. For example, when relating Wendy Lee Gramm's family values, they insert long quotations from her: "I like to be with the children. . . . We do have plenty of events we have to attend, but we do not accept many dinner invitations because we would rather be home with the children." The subjects' own voices lend credibility and a sense of intimacy to the story. The reader seems to converse with these famous people about their experiences and to share their insights into life.

From time to time, the matter-of-fact narration is enlivened by humorous anecdotes. Readers cannot help but chuckle over this incident in Connie Chung's story: On one live broadcast, as the cameras were about to roll, the chain of her watch became caught on her blouse microphone, with her hand near her throat. To disguise her awkward gesture, her co-anchor also held his hand to his chest. The reader cannot resist smiling at this episode in the life of Pei: The architect, who did not care for rock and roll, was selected to design the Rock and Roll Hall of Fame. Although he always told his children to lower the volume when they played rock music, he was now listening to tapes of the Beatles, Chuck Berry, and Bob Dylan as part of his research.

Intriguing anecdotes such as these were not invented by the authors to entertain the reader. This book is not a collection of fictionalized biographies but rather one of well-documented accounts of the fourteen individuals' lives. In the process of preparing the book, the authors interviewed some subjects and obtained information from most of their family members and assistants. As Morey and Dunn note in the preface, "All the subjects or their designated aides have approved the material in their own chapter."

In addition to adhering to an accurate presentation, the authors also maintain a remarkably unbiased tone. They portray these fourteen talented people with warmth and admiration, but instead of extolling them in adulatory terms, they characterize them objectively as life-and-blood human beings. These individuals are held up as role models for young readers to emulate, but the authors do not overdramatize their worthiness, placing them on pedestals as objects of worship. The life stories of these famous Asian Americans will certainly inspire young readers to strive for success in life and to learn more about cultural heritage in the United States.

Critical Context

Outstanding minority figures were once underrepresented in juvenile biographies, but, with the concept of multiculturalism, biographies of these figures began to enter the mainstream of juvenile literature. *Indian Chiefs* (1987), by Russell Freedman; *Sojourner Truth: Ain't I a Woman?* (1992), by Patricia C. and Fredrick McKissack; and *Malcolm X: By Any Means Necessary* (1993), by Walter Dean Myers, are excellent examples of such works, to name only a few. Morey and Dunn's *Famous Mexican Americans* (1989) and *Famous Asian Americans* are among the best collective biographies of prominent minority people to come out of this trend. The authors present the accomplishments and contributions of contemporary minority heroes to a young audience in a concise yet comprehensive manner. They are recommended as reading materials for multicultural literature courses at the college level and for multicultural education units at the primary and secondary levels.

Famous Asian Americans can be seen as a sequel to *Famous Mexican Americans*, featuring the same number of individuals and sharing the same format and style with its predecessor. Both books are characterized by a well-crafted treatment of the subjects' ethnic experiences and aspirations, but the latter is an improvement upon the former. *Famous Asian Americans* highlights its subjects' experiences in a vigorous, exciting narrative, unencumbered by facts and dates, animated and enriched by glimpses and insights from the subjects and their family members and assistants.

Mingshui Cai

FARMER GILES OF HAM

Author: J. R. R. Tolkien (1892-1973)
First published: 1949
Type of work: Novel
Type of plot: Fantasy and folktale
Time of work: The legendary past
Locale: Middle England
Subjects: The supernatural and war
Recommended ages: 10-13

> *Farmer Giles, having accidentally put a giant to flight, must then save the kingdom from a marauding dragon.*

Principal characters:
　　Aegidius de Hammo (Farmer Giles), a prosperous farmer in Middle
　　　England
　　Garm, his talking dog, who is both proud and frightened of his master
　　Chrysophylax Dives, an ancient Welsh dragon, the owner of a
　　　fabulous treasure
　　Augustus Boniface, the king of the Little Kingdom
　　The blacksmith, the village pessimist
　　The miller, a rival of Farmer Giles

Form and Content

　　Farmer Giles of Ham is a mock folktale, supposedly translated from a medieval Latin original. It purports, among other things, to reveal the origins of certain place names in Oxfordshire, which is more or less the locale of "The Little Kingdom." It is certainly located, at some unspecified time in the past, in the Midland counties of England, with the mountains of Wales to the west.

　　From these mountains comes the first event to disturb the pleasant routine of Farmer Giles's rural life. A deaf and nearsighted giant gets lost and stumbles through the English marches, trampling everything in his path. Giles's talking dog, Garm, hears and sees this giant as he approaches their part of the world and, panic-stricken, wakes Giles and his wife in the middle of the night. Farmer Giles loads an ancient blunderbuss, never before fired in anger, and hits the giant in the face as he appears over a hill. The giant, thinking that he has been stung by a fierce insect, decides that the place is unhealthy, turns around, and stumbles back home. Garm boasts to the whole village that his master has fought off the giant. The king in his palace some miles away hears of this and, as a token of gratitude, sends Giles an old sword from his treasury for which he has no further use.

　　Giles enjoys his newfound reputation, that is until a Welsh dragon, hearing from the giant how pleasant Middle England is and being extremely hungry, sets out to find himself a feast. Chrysophylax soon reaches the Little Kingdom and eats his fill of animals and people. The king summons his knights, but in vain. As the dragon approaches Ham, Giles is expected by all the villagers to be their champion. More by luck than judgment, Giles outfaces the dragon, thanks to the fact that the old sword is the famous Tailbiter, weapon of former dragonslayers. The dragon departs, having promised to return with money to serve as reparation for the damage caused.

He does no such thing, however, and the king, whose treasury needs replenishing, summons Giles to lead a party of knights to retrieve the promised compensation. Again, somewhat more by luck than by skill, although with some courage (especially by Giles's horse) the farmer bargains with Chrysophylax, using the threat of Tailbiter, not only to render up much of his wealth but also to carry it back for him. Giles decides to keep the money for himself. The king is powerless to prevent this action, his knights having been routed by the dragon. The king confronts Giles but, with the dragon firmly on Giles's side, must retreat. Giles advances in power and prestige, and he eventually takes over the title of king. The dragon departs, and Giles prospers happily ever after.

Analysis

The basic genre of *Farmer Giles of Ham* is the mock epic or mock heroic. J. R. R. Tolkien uses his scholarly knowledge of medieval heroic legends to parody them, to compare small with great as if both were equal, and to render farcical the typical episodic motif of such stories. There are even hints of the great Old English epic poem *Beowulf* (c. 1000), as Giles battles both giant and monster. The mock genre is also heightened by Tolkien's apparently scholarly introduction to the story, with its claim that the story has been translated from Latin.

The humor of the book arises directly from this approach. Everything is miniaturized, in the way that Jonathan Swift does in *Gulliver's Travels* (1726-1727), to create irony. The kingdom is very small, no bigger than a county. The king's power is just as small in the beginning, with an idle lot of courtiers and officials, and even smaller when challenged by anything—be it giant, dragon, or Farmer Giles himself. The damage done by the giant and the dragon amounts to no more than a few squashed cows and knocked-down houses, with only one priest eaten. As with Swift, the insignificance of the aristocracy exposes their petty weaknesses and vainglory, rendering them laughable rather than perilously incompetent. No danger is ever really posed.

This vainglory is humorously reproduced in Giles's own behavior after his presentation with Tailbiter. While there is peace, he proudly displays the sword and rehearses his so-called act of bravery, an act that has as much to do with defending property against a trespasser as anything. When renewed danger threatens, however, Giles hides it away in a cupboard. He is given a rival, too—the miller—just as the knights quarrel among themselves over precedence. The low-life comedy of the miller's jealousy and the blacksmith's pessimism (never so happy as when his gloomy predictions are coming to pass) works well, as do Giles's down-to-earth comments, especially to Garm.

The talking animals provide humor also, especially Giles's boastful and cowardly dog and Chrysophylax, who in his way is as reluctant to fight as Giles. Their battles are only quite accidentally feats of arms; they are mainly verbal duels, trying to outwit each other. The possession of Tailbiter reveals the dragon to be as cowardly as Giles would be if he did not have the sword. Giles's horse turns out to be the bravest creature around; she does not talk. The humor of these encounters is found in the very ordinary meeting the very extraordinary, both sides behaving as if it were all quite normal. The anachronisms—for example, of gunpowder in an age of knights and giants—are a more subdued source of humor.

Out of the farce, however, several serious themes typical of Tolkien emerge. Despite the trappings of hierarchy, these themes are strongly democratic. The main theme is that even ordinary people can have something of the heroic in them, if they are the right people for the right time. Without his being aware of it, Giles's resourcefulness and ability to drive a bargain are actually forms of bravery. When pushed, he is willing to operate against unknown dangers. Ignorance is bliss, but what he has unknowingly done is return his people and himself to a more ancient, less "civilized" heroism.

The converse theme centers on the degeneracy of kings and knights. They have reached positions of power through inheritance from forebears who in their time were brave, but peace has made them soft, their gentility mere pettiness. They deserve to be swept away and the cycle of knighthood by merit begun again.

The book is illustrated charmingly by Pauline Baynes, who was to go on to illustrate the Narnia stories of Tolkien's colleague and friend, C. S. Lewis.

Critical Context

Farmer Giles of Ham is one of a small number of humorous stories told by John Ronald Reuel Tolkien for his young family of four children; *Smith of Wootton Major* (1967) is another. They differ from the more famous *The Hobbit* (1937) by being unconnected with the history of Tolkien's Middle Earth. Nevertheless, strong similarities exist between *Farmer Giles* and *The Hobbit*: The Shire is based on the same stretch of English countryside as the Little Kingdom. In addition, both heroes are ordinary, small people who are thrust into greatness by accident. In being so thrust, however, they find resources within themselves to accomplish what is a heroic task. Dragons and giants also feature widely.

Farmer Giles of Ham reflects Tolkien's own scholarly interests. He had been working on a new edition of the medieval poem *Sir Gawain and the Green Knight* from the Arthurian tradition; perhaps the story represented some light relief for Tolkien as he ground his way through the necessary scholarship for the poem.

The mock heroic tone had appeared in some of the earlier Victorian fairy stories, especially those by Charles Dickens and William Makepeace Thackeray, and in fantasies, as in the Alice books by another Oxford don, Charles Dodgson (who wrote under the name Lewis Carroll). Tolkien's parody form was in some ways renewing this older tradition within children's literature. In more recent years, many such parody fairy stories or fantasies have appeared, often with feminist or politically subversive messages, such as C. McNaughton's *King None the Wiser* (1981) and I. Williams' *The Practical Princess and Other Liberating Fairy Tales* (1978).

David Barratt

A FIRE IN MY HANDS
A Book of Poems

Author: Gary Soto (1952-   )
First published: 1990; illustrated
Type of work: Poetry
Subjects: Coming-of-age, emotions, family, friendship, and race and ethnicity
Recommended ages: 13-18

Soto provides twenty-three autobiographical lyrics about his growth, as a Mexican American, through boyhood and adolescence in the San Joaquin Valley and into young fatherhood in Berkeley, California.

Form and Content

This collection of free-verse lyrics is spoken by the author. In a brief preface, Gary Soto discusses his unexpected passage into the world of poetry and reminds young people to trust their own experiences to be ripe for poetic exploration. *A Fire in My Hands* concludes with four pages of questions and answers concerning Soto's creative strategies. Throughout the body of the work, each poem is preceded by a two-or three-sentence anecdote characterizing the experience or event that generated the poem, certifying that the lyric voice here is Soto's own. Twelve poems are complemented by ink drawings that capture some salient part of the topic under investigation.

Free verse suits the casual and straightforward tone of these poems. The voice is, by and large, that of a storyteller conveying bittersweet vignettes through lively imagery. Descriptions are vivid and, regardless of the pain that haunts some of the experiences recounted, have a luminous quality, which is especially manifest in the climactic images of the poems. The tiny narratives that house these lyrics are ultimately vehicles for quiet and enlightening revelations. Soto manages to create this tone without turning the poems into fables or lectures and without letting the narrative become overwhelmed by lyric utterances. These revelations emerged via lucidly portrayed objects, acts, or thoughts. His candid voice also makes narrative details stand out at once realistically and ironically. For example, in "Pepper Tree," a poem about nurturing growth in a hard setting, a store's name, Lucky Day, is both banally realistic and spiritually pointed. Such subtlety constantly informs the natural speech of this believable and empathic adult as he talks to young people.

Analysis

While these lyrics stand on their own and do not rely directly on one another, they are nevertheless governed by a gently encompassing order. The first thirteen are recollective of a more distant personal past than the final ten. They move from Soto's eighth through his nineteenth year. Even when the present tense is used, it immerses readers more directly in the past. The fourteenth poem, "Morning on This Street," begins with the poet listening to a brother talking about love's ephemeral nature. Soto then walks into the street and witnesses an old homeless couple, the wife in a cart and the husband pulling it. He conceives of the cardboard with which "Earl the Cartman" has surrounded his wife as a "rough Temple." He concludes that, "It's for his wife/ That he lives and pulls a rope/ To its frayed end." He believes that "This is marriage." From this poem through the twenty-third, Soto writes about his immediate family, about living as gracefully as possible with his wife and daughter in a trying world. The daughter becomes the focus, allowing Soto to remain in touch with childhood and link his past to his daughter's present.

In "Black Hair," the first poem, Soto recollects being a scrawny eight-year-old living vicariously through an older boy. The sanctity of baseball is subsumed by the speaker's regard for Hector Moreno, who "lined balls into deep/ Center."

The poem shows how Soto's earliest feelings of inadequacy yielded to self-esteem, even "in the presence of white shirts," clothing set against the boy, described as a "brown stick/ of light." Living Moreno's home run, Soto imaginatively joins the older Mexican boy rounding third and "coming home/ to the arms of brown people." The poems that are specifically about ethnicity—this one and "Kearney Park"—are celebratory, despite the difficulties presented by the "white shirts." More often, however, it is the hardships of Soto's community, only indirectly caused by his being Mexican, that stand as obstacles in the poems about his youth.

These pieces are noteworthy for Soto's ability to capture, simultaneously, both the problems of Mexican Americans and the general problems of youth. "Brown Girl, Blond Okie" is a case in point. The speaker and his crony, Jackie, each with a different ethnic ideal of the beloved, sit together trying to imagine whom they shall be able to love enough "to open up to," so that they may express the awfulness of their crooked teeth and dirty hair. They are poor, ungainly kids who are stuck, in puberty, with the feeling that they are irredeemable. Yet, their sense of being "in trouble" is comic in its preadolescent hyperbole and suggests their human bond more than a psychological crisis. The Soto that readers meet in "That Girl" is still overwhelmed by this feckless yearning and the appropriately exaggerated notion of a girl not being like himself. (Nevertheless, the twelve-year-old Soto of "Oranges" skillfully wins a girl, and the Soto of "Kearney Street" is well established with a girlfriend.)

"How to Sell Things" is a lesson in salesmanship. Readers must respect the innocent connivance of a boy with nothing but a bag of oranges for his fashioning of a successful social life. His knowledge of how to break down any "Grandma," even the hard ones, with the help of a compatriot dog's tricks is winning. So is his understanding that Sunday is the best day, because that is when "God is looking around/ For something to do." Readers see that he has "made it" and have been amusingly and sanely coached in how to do the same. This poem precedes "Oranges," whose line of epiphany provides the volume's title. The speaker gets a lovely ten-cent chocolate for his girl from a saleslady by offering her all his money—a nickel—and an orange and by gazing straight into her eyes, which the woman understands precisely. Holding the beautifully wrapped gift, his date is transformed from "a girl" to "my girl." Recurrently, such moments of intimacy and understanding in the poems redeem the world's coldness.

"Pepper Tree" follows the poem about the homeless couple. It is pivotal, representing the best that Soto has learned from his past and what he would wish on the future, a future made cogent and meaningful through the presence of his daughter. This knowledge is affective and passionate, not academic. He remembers coming to "a rough area" of Berkeley, California, and planting a pepper tree by staking it to a piece of lumber that was once a part of a house, aided both by literal rain and by the "rain" of his little girl's steady utterance to the tree, "Get Big." He wants the tree "Heavy with sparrows." In an even more telling image, because it mixes Soto's senses of hardship and grace so economically, he wants the tree's branches, "if a gull has an off day," to "bear its screams" and, under such "weight," to "be here tomorrow."

Through the remaining poems, Soto communes with his daughter, giving her good advice and knowing that at times she is and must be deaf to the tenor of his counsel and the re-creation of his past for her benefit. Readers relate to someone whose parental shortcomings are common, which he accepts with amusement and survives with love and good sense.

Critical Context

Nothing special contextualizes this skillful verse; in form, nothing is experimental. Yet, what is attempted in *A Fire in My Hands* is mastered. Gary Soto's strategy of attaching anecdotes to the poems is a good one, both because it suggests to the reader how ordinary experiences, not extraordinary adventures, give rise to poetry and because it impresses the reality of Soto himself into the poems, which are narrative in form but not confessional. The speaker may interest readers in the United States because he is Mexican American and has life experiences common to a large minority group. It is more significant, however, that readers hear an exquisitely humane voice speaking for and about all people. His is a very American voice, a voice made universal by its command of native idiom. Soto has neither sugar-coated the facts of youthful life in the United States nor betrayed its positive features with a predictably ugly realism. Life in these poems is whole. Readers will not find them significantly different from the rest of Soto's poetry even though they touch so much upon youth. His is always a down-to-earth way of speaking, of exploring ordinary ground with an eye, and an ear, for rarity.

David M. Heaton

THE FIRST BOOK OF JAZZ

Author: Langston Hughes (1902-1967)
First published: 1955; illustrated
Type of work: Art, biography, and history
Subjects: Composers, musicians, and singers
Recommended ages: 10-13

> *Hughes traces the history of the development of jazz as a unique American musical form and provides autobiographical information about some American jazz greats.*

Principal personages:
W. C. HANDY, the "father of the blues," who put blues down on paper
LOUIS "SATCHMO" ARMSTRONG, a legendary jazz trumpeter
BESSIE SMITH, a famous blues singer
JELLY ROLL MORTON, a ragtime and blues pianist
DUKE ELLINGTON, a keyboardist and one of America's greatest jazz composers
JOHN COLTRANE, a jazz saxophonist
CHARLIE PARKER, a saxophonist who played bebop
MILES DAVIS, a "cool" jazz trumpeter
ORNETTE COLEMAN, a musician associated with "free-form" jazz, which broke previous musical rules

Form and Content

The 1955 edition of *The First Book of Jazz* was updated in 1976 by publishing company Franklin Watts, well after Langston Hughes's death in 1967. Both editions present the history of the development of jazz, discuss seminal figures in that history, and identify key elements of the form itself. The earlier edition incorporates lively drawings by Cliff Roberts, one double-page spread of head shots of jazz greats, and lists of famous jazz musicians and recordings. The 1976 edition eliminates the drawings and the lists, substituting black-and-white photographs of musicians in action and of posters advertising musical events, liberally distributed throughout the book.

Both editions incorporate lyrics of worksongs, spirituals, and jubilees associated with the development of jazz and selected lines of music itself. Those readers able to read music could actually play a few bars, for example, of boogie-woogie and get a sense of the sound. They could play a line of the "straight" version of "Loch Lomand" and then play a line of the "swing" version to hear the impact of the introduction of the elements of jazz on a traditional Scottish song. For those unfamiliar with musical terminology, a glossary appears at the end of the later edition of the book. Both editions have an index for handy reference to the wealth of information presented.

Hughes's organizational pattern for the book is loosely chronological. He begins the presentation of historical information with a discussion of the rhythms of African drums and the cultural significance of drumming, explaining how drumming came to Congo Square in New Orleans from West Africa. Hughes then takes readers to the worksongs, field hollers, jubilees, and spirituals that form the bedrock of the blues. He includes minstrel shows in his history, focusing on the musical aspects of these productions. The jazz forms of blues, ragtime, and boogie-woogie are explained, and a whole section is devoted to the role of the trumpet in the development of jazz, with expansive reference to Louis Armstrong. The uncertainty of the origin of the term "jazz" and various speculations are discussed.

Several central elements of jazz—such as improvisation and syncopation—are identified, with emphasis on the fact that jazz musicians may not read music and that jazz improvisation allows for a basic melody to be played differently each time that it is performed. Hughes also addresses the introduction of different musical instruments to jazz playing and the changes in the size and makeup of the jazz band.

The author discusses the swing music of the late 1920's and 1930's, with Duke Ellington, Benny Goodman, Glenn Miller, Cab Calloway, Tommy Dorsey, Count Basie, and others featured during this era in which black and white musicians began to play together in the same bands. The 1940's brought bebop, with revolutionaries Thelonious Monk, Charlie Parker, and Lester Young. The 1955 edition of *The First Book of Jazz* concludes with Hughes's treatment of bebop, while the 1976 edition continues with the "cool," or progressive jazz of the 1950's, as played by Miles Davis, the Modern Jazz Quartet, and Stan Kenton. It then moves into the jazz rock of the 1960's, with Davis shifting gears and leading the way into this new blend, which used electrical instruments.

The 1976 edition concludes with a description of the free-form jazz movement of the 1960's, led by Ornette Coleman. In free-form jazz, musicians seem to break all the musical rules. Several players improvise simultaneously, laws of harmony are abandoned, and there is no set rhythm or key to follow. The rejection that this movement experienced is addressed, as is Coleman's profound influence on the development of jazz.

Analysis

A feature that is likely to contribute strongly to a successful literary experience for the young readers of either edition of *The First Book of Jazz* is that Hughes relates musical history in terms of the people involved. Using his considerable insight into the workings of the human mind, he fleshes out facts in incidents in which musicians appear as accessible, real people. Young readers are especially likely to be personally engaged by stories of the musicians as children, compelled by some inner longing to make music. The book begins with seven-year-old Louis Armstrong "singing for pennies on the streets of New Orleans." In a sentence, Hughes pinpoints the city most closely associated with the birth of jazz, identifies one of the most influential jazz greats, and entices young readers to identify with that individual through vividly setting a scene depicting Armstrong as a child.

Hughes uses the great Louis Armstrong, nicknamed "Satchmo," as a throughline for his exploration of jazz history. After appearing first as that seven-year-old on page 1, he reappears regularly throughout the text, often to introduce a chapter. The choice of Armstrong to perform this role for the text is especially appropriate, since his career stretched almost from the beginnings of jazz itself until the late twentieth century.

The author's depiction of the development of jazz seems somewhat romanticized. Repeatedly, the people who make music are referred to as doing it "just for fun," implying a triviality that workers in the fields, worshipers singing spirituals that implore release from the trials of everyday life, and jazz artists struggling to survive might find at odds with their own motivations for making jazz music. Although this book is intended for young people, a heavier dose of reality would be appropriate for today's readers. Even its updating in 1976 could not bring the text in line with the sensibilities of the 1990's. That drawback, along with the fact that the chronology of even the later edition ends with the late 1960's, dates this book.

On the other hand, this volume provides a wealth of information that is accessible, easy-to-read, and presented in an engaging style for young readers. The various roots of jazz are identified clearly and accurately, and the elements that distinguish jazz from other music are presented in an understandable manner. The different forms that jazz has taken from its beginnings in the polyrhythms of African drumming through the field calls of enslaved Africans on Southern plantations to their spirituals, through blues, ragtime, swing, bebop, progressive, rock, and free-form jazz, are drawn in a way that clearly distinguishes one from the other, while acknowledging common characteristics that the forms share.

The author's presentation of material in the context of the people who created jazz music breathes life into the topic. Ideally, readers could listen to examples of the music while reading information from the text. Indeed, the early edition suggests specific 33 1/3 rpm records, now seen as collectors' items, which are recommended for listening. The combination of music and text would bring both engagement and enlightenment. Yet, even without an experience of the music itself, Hughes's special sensitivity and respect for language and for how human beings function bring the story of the development of jazz alive for readers.

In regard to the use of visual elements, the updated 1976 edition seems to have sought to improve the work by using photographs. While it is certainly interesting to see the musicians themselves, the formatting of the photographs is uninspired and lifeless. For the most part, one framed photograph is offered per page. The black-and-white drawings of the earlier edition, by contrast, provide a sense of movement and excitement that seems more appropriate to the music of jazz.

Critical Context

Historical works on the development of jazz are often suited for older readers and frequently tie the music to sociopolitical conditions; Amiri Baraka's *Blues People: Negro Music in White America* (1963) and *Black Music* (1967) are examples. Langston Hughes's treatment, however, is clearly suited for younger readers and is strikingly free of rationales embedded in a sociopolitical context. While this stance strips jazz of important aspects of its roots, it does put the music itself center stage. Inevitably, sociopolitical factors hover just beneath the surface, such as the fact that virtually all the African American originators of this distinctly American art form were poverty stricken in their youth, but the music and its creators are what this book is about. That Hughes—a keen observer and re-creator of human language and foibles, a short-story writer, a poet who frequently used a blues structure for his poetry, and a stellar light of the Harlem Renaissance—should extend his writing about "his people" to write specifically about jazz musicians was both natural and fortunate. What is less fortunate is the occasional oversimplification that creates a feel of superficiality. The author's repeated insistence, for example, that "jazz is fun" ultimately grows tedious. The implication, uncharacteristic for Hughes, is that these talented, passionate jazz musicians who battled poverty and racism throughout their lives were happy-go-lucky party lovers, out for a good time.

Michele McNichols

THE FLEDGLING

Author: Jane Langton (1922-   )
First published: 1980
Type of work: Novel
Type of plot: Fantasy
Time of work: The 1970's
Locale: Concord, Massachusetts
Subjects: Coming-of-age, friendship, and nature
Recommended ages: 10-13

From her friend, an old Canada goose, eight-year-old Georgie learns two important lessons: how to fly (the gratification of her deepest wish) and her responsibility to protect the earth.

Principal characters:
 GEORGINA (GEORGIE) DORIAN, a quiet, observant, reflective
  eight-year-old, small for her age, who believes that she can fly
 THE GOOSE PRINCE, a Canada goose, an aging widower who befriends
  Georgie and teaches her to fly
 ELEANOR HALL, Georgie's orphaned fourteen-year-old stepcousin, who
  is caught in the turmoil of adolescence
 EDWARD (EDDY) HALL, Eleanor's twelve-year-old brother, whose
  current passion is model rockets
 FREDERICK HALL (UNCLE FREDDY), Georgie's stepfather, an exuberant
  professor of Transcendentalism and the guardian of Eleanor and Eddy
 ALEXANDRA DORIAN HALL (AUNT ALEX), Georgie's mother and Uncle
  Freddy's colleague and wife
 MR. RALPH ALONZO PREEK, the insensitive and misguided local bank
  president
 MISS MADELINE PRAWN, the Hall family's nosy neighbor

Form and Content
 From its opening scene, *The Fledgling* conveys a sense of the cycles of life. An old goose on his last migration through Concord, Massachusetts, spots in Walden Pond a special present that he will pass on to the novel's protagonist, who will find both wonder and comfort in this gift. Georgie first appears in the novel trying once again, under the gaze of a bust of Henry David Thoreau, painfully, unsuccessfully, to fly down the dark front hall steps. Eleanor and Eddy rush in to gather up their undersized, crazy cousin, whom they fear will never turn out normal. Georgie's mother worries about Georgie as well, but she allows her daughter her own choices: a beloved corncob doll, a favorite pair of red overalls, and, most important, the realization of a

dream, leaving nightly to fly with the Goose Prince.

In a reversed hunting scene that illustrates the varying third-person point of view in the text, Georgie's red overalls catch the eye of the old goose as he flies overhead, looking for someone to whom he might give his present. When the goose first approaches Georgie, he is frightened away by interfering Ralph Preek, who will become obsessed, Ahab-like, with hunting down the animal. Georgie has understood what Mr. Preek has not: that the Goose Prince is trying to be her friend and that he wants to teach her to fly. Mr. Preek resolves to destroy the "large duck" that he believes holds Georgie in its power, and, in one of the many instances of parallelism in the text, he practices aiming his new shotgun—at a photograph of Thoreau on the living room wall.

Despite the intrusion of Mr. Preek, the old goose comes to Georgie's window to begin a series of enchanted nights in which he teaches her to fly. The phases of the moon—signs of the cycles of nature—mark Georgie's advancing aeronautic skill and the growth of a friendship of quiet understanding with the Goose Prince, who tells Georgie that he has a present for her. The circle begins to close on the first night of the hunting season, when Ralph Preek, aiming at the two big ducks that he has been stalking, is disappointed to have brought down only the smaller of the two—Georgie. Georgie's family intensifies its efforts to protect their fledgling, but Georgie summons her Goose Prince a final time, after what she believes is the last hour of the hunting season. Georgie recognizes that she has become too big to fly—her red overalls are now halfway up her shins—but wants to say goodbye. Because the night has come to set back the clocks, midnight strikes twice, and Georgie suffers the closing of the circle: the murder of her prince by the vigilant Mr. Preek, who has been alerted by meddlesome Miss Prawn. The Goose Prince's gift has been lost, and Georgie enters into a cycle of mourning. She is healed by finding the goose's present: a small, blue-and-white-streaked ball. Having already promised the prince to "take good care of it," Georgie witnesses in the darkness of the front hall closet the transformation of the ball into a great gleaming globe that is "the whole world."

Analysis

In a novel that illustrates that there may be many definitions to the word "family"— Georgie lives with her mother (who is consistently called "Aunt Alex" in the text), her stepfather, two orphaned stepcousins, six cats, and the busts of various Transcendentalist philosophers (which are considered part of the family)—the theme of protection is prominent. Eleanor and Eddy's Georgie Protection Society widens out to the environmental message conveyed in the metamorphosis of the blue-and-white ball. It is the responsibility of Georgie's generation to meet the threats that endanger the earth, which range in *The Fledgling* from the beer cans floating in Walden Pond to hunters who justify their killing with assertions that they are maintaining the balance of nature. Georgie shows that she will be an able protector, having already saved a housefly from her uncle's fly swatter and flown in the path of Ralph Preek's buckshot to shield the Goose Prince.

In *The Fledgling*, Jane Langton weaves together the cycles of the natural world and those of the human. As the circle of the old goose's life is brought to a close, the increasing shortness of Georgie's red overalls, like pencil marks on a wall, records Georgie's physical and emotional growth. Just as Georgie's dream of wanting to fly is a fantasy shared by many children, Georgie provides young readers with a model for making one's way through the later stages of childhood. Georgie is a "fledgling," who exhibits the independence (she equips herself for her journey and sets off for Walden Pond alone) and belief in herself (she knows she can fly) that lay the foundation for the work ahead in adolescence, the finding of identity. Her development is helped by parents who sufficiently resist their own protective impulses so that their daughter can grow. Georgie's mother waits anxiously for her daughter to return home every night from flying lessons with the Goose Prince, but she stands quietly at the window, allowing Georgie to leave. For the child, belief in oneself comes at first from significant others—the Goose Prince helps Georgie's parents fill that role—and from one's own sense of accomplishment. Midway through the novel, in the chapter "Fledgling No Longer," Georgie not only has mastered flying but also can perform acrobatic tricks in the air that are even beyond the ability of the Goose Prince. Young readers, able to fly with Georgie in their imaginations, share in her success and, believing that anything is possible, are given the whole world.

The setting of Concord, Massachusetts, home of Henry David Thoreau and the Transcendental movement of the mid-nineteenth century, signals another significant theme in *The Fledgling*. Not only is Thoreau invoked at the novel's opening, but Georgie lives in the fantastic turreted house, the dark spaces of which are rich with imaginative possibilities, that provides a home for the Concord College of Transcendental Knowledge, founded by her stepfather. Uncle Freddy recognizes that Georgie knows "something too young and wild for him to remember." Georgie embodies the Transcendental qualities of youth lauded by Thoreau in the novel's epigraph. Before beginning her tea party—the simplicity of which Thoreau would approve, with its acorn cups and maple seed crackers—Georgie sits in her bush house and listens to the bird sounds, the hum of an airplane, and even to the bugs inside an egg case on a twig. When the Goose Prince comes for her, she is "instantly alert, her body tense with listening." Because she is so in touch with that which is beyond her self, in contrast to her older cousin Eleanor, Georgie is ready for the contact with nature that will lead her to an experience outside the limits of physical laws, a truly transcendental experience. She meets the Goose Prince, and she flies. Significantly, at the end of the novel, Georgie sleeps soundly, not hearing the noise of a late flock of geese migrating through Concord. The soundness of Georgie's sleep represents the peace that she has found in recovering the Goose Prince's gift, but it also shows that she is moving out of the cycle of her childhood. Georgie has gained a strengthened belief in herself, but she will, like Eleanor, inevitably lose some of what Thoreau calls "wildness," that susceptibility to transcendental possibility to which she has been open in her ninth year.

Critical Context

Considered Jane Langton's highest literary achievement, *The Fledgling* was a Newbery Honor Book for 1981 and a nominee for an American Book Award in 1982. This work is the fourth in a five-book fantasy series (Langton's favorites among her works) about the Hall family, consisting of *The Diamond in the Window* (1962), *The Swing in the Summerhouse* (1967), *The Astonishing Stereoscope* (1971), *The Fledgling*, and *The Fragile Flag* (1984). Georgie Dorian makes her first appearance in *The Swing in the Summerhouse* as a four-year-old with a passionate desire to read so that she can decode the messages in the world around her. In *The Fledgling*, Georgie takes center stage to receive the message in the gift that the Goose Prince has given her. In *The Fragile Flag*, Georgie fulfills her responsibility to protect the earth by leading a children's march to Washington, D.C., where she persuades the president to cancel a nuclear missile program. Langton's political activism, born of the Vietnam War era, underpins this last of the Hall family novels. Important to all five of the novels is Langton's residence near historically rich Concord, Massachusetts. That Langton would choose for the epigraph of *The Fledgling* a quotation not from Thoreau's familiar *Walden* (1854) but from his posthumously published essay "Walking" (1862) shows the depth of her immersion in the Transcendental tradition.

Laura Davis-Clapper

FLOWERS FOR ALGERNON

Author: Daniel Keyes (1927-   )
First published: 1966 (expanded from a 1959 novelette)
Type of work: Novel
Type of plot: Science fiction
Time of work: March 3 through November 21 of an unstated year in the near future
Locale: New York City and Chicago
Subjects: Coming-of-age, emotions, love and romance, and science
Recommended ages: 13-18

As the result of an experiment, Charlie Gordon, a mentally handicapped adult, becomes a genius and then regresses, learning that intelligence is not enough without emotional understanding and human love.

> *Principal characters:*
> CHARLIE GORDON, a thirty-two-year-old with an IQ of 68 when the experiment begins
> ALICE KINNIAN, a teacher of mentally retarded adults, later Charlie's friend and then his lover
> DR. STRAUSS, a psychiatrist, neurosurgeon, and director of the experiment
> PROFESSOR HAROLD NEMUR, a psychologist and director of the experiment
> GIMPY, the head baker at Donner's bakery, where Charlie works as a janitor
> MATT GORDON, Charlie's father
> NORMA GORDON, Charlie's sister
> ROSE GORDON, Charlie's mother
> ALGERNON, a laboratory mouse, the subject of the experiments before Charlie
> FAY LILLMAN, a messy artist who loves life, Charlie's neighbor and his lover after the intelligence increase

Form and Content

In the form of diary entries by Charlie Gordon, *Flowers for Algernon* tells an emotionally wrenching story and implies much about human nature, psychology, and values. Charlie, a thirty-two-year-old with an intelligence quotient (IQ) of 68, is the first human subject of an experimental procedure to increase intelligence, funded by the Welberg Foundation and conducted at Beekman University (somewhere in New York City) by Professor Harold Nemur, psychiatrist and neurosurgeon Dr. Strauss, and Burt Selden, a graduate student in psychology. Charlie is suggested as a candidate by Alice Kinnian, his teacher at the Center for Retarded Adults at Beekman, because of his kind temperament and desire to learn.

At the laboratory, Charlie meets Algernon, a white mouse that has undergone the procedure and that can beat Charlie at running mazes. At Dr. Strauss's suggestion, Charlie begins keeping what he calls "progris riports"; their bad spelling and misunderstandings show Charlie's mentally handicapped state. After the surgery, Charlie's intelligence and memory both increase, which is conveyed by his writing: in better spelling, more elaborate sentences, expanded vocabulary, and intellectual references.

The changes, however, bring problems and unhappiness as well as abilities and enjoyment. Charlie loves learning, and he happily reads (at greater and greater speeds) and discusses abstract ideas with Beekman students. He also realizes that the people around him make fun of him—including Gimpy, Joe Carp, and Frank Reilly, his "best friends" at the bakery where he works—and he begins to remember childhood traumas. Charlie catches Gimpy cheating the bakery; the men at the bakery protest the presence of the new Charlie, and he is fired. Even Fannie Birden, a kind coworker, declares that Charlie's change is against God's will.

Charlie's intelligence soon reaches genius level (an IQ of 185), causing problems with Strauss, Nemur, and Kinnian. Charlie falls in love with Alice, but she knows that he will soon be too intelligent for her. Charlie thinks that Nemur treats him like a laboratory animal, and, when he surpasses Nemur in intelligence, both behave badly. Nemur is condescending, and Charlie has grown arrogant and unforgiving.

When Charlie is taken to a psychological conference in Chicago, he flees with Algernon, returning to New York City but not to Beekman. There he begins a casual affair with his neighbor Fay Lillman, a painter whose trust and openness to life are needed by the now-cynical Charlie. Charlie remembers more about his childhood, including his mother's desire to make him "normal" and his parents' arguments. He goes to the Bronx to see his father but leaves without identifying himself. When drinking with Fay, Charlie regresses to his preexperiment self.

Increasing evidence indicates that the procedure is temporary, leaving its subjects worse than before. Algernon grows irritable and forgetful, then alternately lethargic and violent. Charlie persuades the Welberg Foundation to put him on the project as a scientist, and his genius reveals a central error by Strauss and Nemur. In "The Algernon-Gordon Effect: A Study of Structure and Function of Increased Intelligence," Charlie proves that he too will regress. He visits the Warren State Home in Long Island, where he may have to be placed.

Furiously working in his remaining time, Charlie moves into the laboratory; Fay resents this abandonment but soon finds a new boyfriend. Charlie is almost haunted by his old self, and he realizes that "intelligence without the ability to give and receive affection" cannot succeed. Algernon dies, and Charlie buries him.

The last three months of entries document Charlie's regression, worsening in spelling and grammar. Charlie visits his mother and sister Norma while he can, shocked to find his mother senile and Norma a kind person, proud of Charlie. Alice returns to Charlie, stating that they are now again on the same level; they make love—"a mystery," "more than sex"—and she stays until Charlie drives her away.

In the end, Charlie is back working at the bakery, sexually adolescent again, barely able to read and write; he even shows up for his old adult reading class, to Alice Kinnian's distress. He seems to have regained his old sweetness while having learned some things about human nature.

Analysis

Although protagonist Charlie Gordon is an adult, *Flowers for Algernon* is a coming-of-age story with which both children and adults readily identify. As his intelligence increases, he must confront emotional, social, and ethical issues previously beyond his understanding. As he regresses, he faces loss with dignity and determination.

As critic Robert Small, Jr., points out, the question "What if I were smarter?" occurs to all children and adolescents, especially in the competitive school environment. Daniel Keyes answers that question well, in a complicated but not a confusing manner, showing the benefits and pitfalls of genius.

Many critics have praised the novel for its treatment of the mentally handicapped. Keyes's depiction is emotionally powerful but flawed; for example, Charlie's sexual desire fully awakens only after the operation (he is surprised by his first nocturnal emission), although in reality mental retardation does not prevent sexual maturity. Nevertheless, that awakening may contribute to Charlie's appeal among young adult readers, and the novel's plea for empathy is obvious and convincing. The most accurate depiction of mental illness can be found when Charlie visits the Warren State Home, a scene that seems to be based on an actual visit to the institution.

Although the reader identifies with Charlie emotionally, other characters present conflicting views, enriching the novel. When Charlie and Alice debate human nature, both make good points; the bakery coworkers are shown both harassing Charlie and befriending him, a realistically paradoxical mix.

Some critics argue that, for science fiction, *Flowers for Algernon* contains little fictional science. Actually, the process is described in some detail, including surgery, enzyme treatments, and subliminal teaching during sleep, although the emphasis is on the resulting changes in Charlie. Much speculation in the novel concerns Freudian psychology, with Keyes examining such issues as the importance of the unconscious, the remembrance of past traumas to cure current problems, and the dangers of a sexually repressive upbringing.

Critic Paul Williams sees stories about increased intelligence, such as *Flowers for Algernon* and Poul Anderson's *Brain Wave* (1954), as a modern myth, perhaps condensing the past centuries of human scientific development to an individual scale. If so, he points out, Charlie's return to his prior state, or worse, may show modern society's insecurity about technology and anxiety about the state that would result should it be lost.

Critical Context

Flowers for Algernon has won recognition both inside the science-fiction community and among mainstream readers. The 1959 novelette, published in *The Magazine of Fantasy and Science Fiction*, won the World Science Fiction Society's Hugo Award for Best Novelette in 1960; it is frequently anthologized, including in the *Science Fiction Hall of Fame*, edited by Robert Silverberg, and in literary anthologies for middle schools and high schools.

The novel is included on many educational reading lists, including those by the National Council of Teachers of English and the American Library Association, and it is taught in colleges. The story has been filmed twice: as the television play *The Two Worlds of Charlie Gordon* in the 1960's and as the film *Charly* (1968), for which star Cliff Robertson won an Oscar.

For all its general popularity and special appeal to adolescents and young adults, *Flowers for Algernon* is highly controversial. The primary complaint by parents concerns its sexual content. The scenes are tame and inexplicit, but they both show Charlie's sexuality and approve of it. Some parents are also bothered by the depiction of religion, as Charlie's growing intelligence makes him question the existence of God, and two religious characters (Fannie Birden and Charlie's postoperative nurse) are portrayed as bigoted.

Nevertheless, the story, in both forms, will endure, because its complex treatment of a simple "what if?" question appeals to readers of all ages. It is easier for most readers than other science-fiction stories of increased intelligence—from Olaf Stapledon's *Odd John* (1935), through Stanley G. Weinbaum's *The New Adam* (1939) and Wilmar H. Shiras' *Children of the Atom* (1953), to Thomas M. Disch's *Camp Concentration* (1968) and Frederik Pohl's "The Gold at Starbow's End" (1971), which was expanded to the novel *Starburst* (1982)—yet raises the same important questions. Keyes brings to *Flowers for Algernon* the keen psychological insight also seen in his nonfiction case history of multiple personality disorder, *The Minds of Billy Milligan* (1981).

Bernadette Lynn Bosky

FLOWERS IN THE ATTIC

Author: V. C. Andrews (c. 1936-1986)
First published: 1979
Type of work: Novel
Type of plot: Psychological realism and thriller
Time of work: The 1950's
Locale: The foothills of Virginia
Subjects: Emotions, family, and sexual issues
Recommended ages: 15-18

After the untimely death of their father, Cathy Dollanganger and her three siblings struggle to grow up in the midst of a family that wishes to deny their existence and to learn the terrible secrets that are hidden in the secret rooms of Foxworth Hall.

> *Principal characters:*
> CATHY DOLLANGANGER, a twelve-year-old girl who dreams of becoming a beautiful ballerina
> CHRISTOPHER DOLLANGANGER, JR., her fourteen-year-old, scholarly brother
> CARRIE DOLLANGANGER, their four-year-old sister
> CORY DOLLANGANGER, Carrie's twin brother
> CORRINE FOXWORTH DOLLANGANGER, the children's beautiful but weak-willed mother
> THE GRANDMOTHER, the woman who keeps the children imprisoned in the attic of Foxworth Hall
> MALCOLM NEAL FOXWORTH, the children's grandfather, a sickly man who uses his wealth to control the people around him

Form and Content

V. C. Andrews' *Flowers in the Attic* is a painful account of four children's attempt to survive in a family that despises their existence. Although the author stated numerous times that the novel is fiction, the rumor persists that it is based on a true story—a comment noted in the British edition of *Flowers in the Attic* published by Fontana. Perhaps the rumor persists because, written in the first person, this novel presents itself as a fictionalized rewriting of journal entries kept by the protagonist and published under an assumed name, Cathy Dollanganger, in order to shame the family that humiliated and imprisoned her and her siblings Christopher, Carrie, and Cory.

Their parents, Corrine and the elder Christopher, were half uncle and half niece, and they defied their wealthy family's wishes in order to marry and have a family. Although they were initially successful at maintaining a life distant from their past troubles, Corrine convinced her husband to live beyond their means—that having luxuries was a necessity. After the elder Christopher is killed in a car accident, Corrine is left with many debts and no means to pay. She turns to her parents for help, assuming that she will be able to win them over in spite of her earlier defiance. Unfortunately, accepting her parents' help means that she must deny the children she had during her marriage. Her father, a highly hypocritical man, will cut Corrine off from a considerable inheritance if he ever learns that she had children—to him, they are "devil's spawn" and inherently evil. Corrine's mother, who knows of the children's existence, is no different and decides to torture them as punishment for their mother's sins.

Unaware of what is to happen to them, Cathy and her siblings are told that they will only have to live in the attic of Foxworth Hall for a short time while their mother uses her persuasive wiles on their sickly grandfather. Weeks stretch into months, however, and they end up spending nearly four years of their childhood trapped in a dusty attic. They struggle to make their lives as happy as possible, cleaning the attic and decorating it with paper cut-outs to mimic the passing seasons in the outside world. They learn to lean on one another; Cathy and Chris become like parents to their younger siblings, and their devotion to each other develops into a romantic, sexual relationship.

After much time has passed, Cathy realizes that her pessimistic feelings concerning her mother are true. Corrine does not acknowledge her children even after their hateful grandfather has died, since to do so would cause her to lose her inheritance. She remarries, convinced that she can keep her children as hidden as her secret past. Only after the tragic death of Cory from poisoning—all the children have been fed small doses of arsenic over a period of time—do Cathy and Chris decide that they cannot rely on their mother. Using their ingenuity, they devise their own means of escape and leave Foxworth Hall.

Analysis

Flowers in the Attic, its three sequels—*Petals on the Wind* (1980), *If There Be Thorns* (1981), and *Seeds of Yesterday* (1983)—and its "prequel," *Garden of Shadows* (1987), are a series of books that present how evil is born out of a desire for money and power. Malcolm Neal Foxworth, jealous of his father, makes wealth the primary focus of his life, suppressing all the good that is within him. He marries a woman whom he does not love because she is a good secretary, alienates his children when he finds that he cannot force them to become what he wants, isolates his daughter from friends and neighbors so that she will be completely dependant on him for affection and support, and forces his grandchildren to live a suffocating existence in his attic in order to punish Corrine.

Because Malcolm is a Foxworth, the patriarch of the wealthiest and most powerful family in his town, he feels superior to other people and thinks that he can do whatever he wants to whomever he wants. He encourages dependency within his family that inevitably leads to incestuous relationships; his lonely fourteen-year-old daughter falls in love with her half uncle because the elder Christopher Dollanganger is the one man whom she is allowed to see. Because Corrine's children, Cathy and Chris, are confined to live together without any semblance of privacy as they become adults, they form an inappropriate attachment and, unavoidably, become sexually dependant on each other. All the secrets in the family could have been avoided by understanding and openness. Malcolm Foxworth's legacy of greed continues through the family, passing from father to daughter. Corrine, Malcolm's daughter, learns her father's values and applies them well when she chooses money and the good life over the happiness and health of her four children.

For the late adolescent reader, *Flowers in the Attic* and its sequels are books that teach self-reliance and compassion. Anyone who has grown up feeling confined by the restrictions of childhood and the reluctance of parents to acknowledge their growing independence will sympathize deeply with Andrews' vivid portrayal of Cathy's turbulent emotions; in a way, all children are "flowers in the attic" as they shed the restrictions of youth and accept the responsibilities of adulthood. Furthermore, the kindness and self-sacrifice that the children demonstrate for their weak mother and unfeeling grandparents contrasts starkly with their family's ancestral greed. When the children are denied food for weeks after they protest their unjust imprisonment, Chris gives the two younger children his blood to drink; the elder children's dedication to protect and care for their younger brother and sister, whatever the cost, will inspire adolescent readers even as it shocks them.

Critical Context

When V. C. Andrews' book appeared in 1979, it proved to be a remarkable success, although a hard-to-categorize one. *Flowers in the Attic* was only released for two weeks before it made the best-seller lists and remained there for fourteen weeks. The first three Dollanganger novels were recordbreakers for Pocket Books, the first two alone selling more than seven million copies within two years. Other books by Andrews, drawing on the same themes, would follow: *My Sweet Audrina* (1982) and the Casteel series, including *Heaven* (1985) and *Dark Angel* (1986), among others. The popularity of her themes has continued beyond their creator's death. After Andrews' death in 1986, her family selected a ghost writer not only to finish Andrews' Casteel series for publication but also to continue writing novels in her name, such as *Dawn* (1990).

Although she is frequently depicted as a writer of mainstream horror and a contemporary of Steven King and Richard Matheson, Andrews saw herself as a writer of adult fairy tales, situations where individuals face enormous odds in life and are strengthened by their trials. *Flowers in the Attic* does what no previous book had done—present a terrifying but believable account of family cruelty and incest to young adults. Because of its strong content, the book was called pornographic and banned from library bookshelves in some places. Andrews' own secrecy about her birth year and her general reclusiveness did little to dispel the rumors that swirled around her. Instead, before her death from cancer in December, 1986, Andrews chose to write in spite of the moral qualms of those who would be offended by what she had to say. Her stubbornness, like that of her character Cathy, allowed her to write memorably about developing strength of character.

Julia M. Meyers

F.O.B.

Author: David Henry Hwang (1957-   )
First presented: 1978
First published: 1983
Type of work: Drama
Type of plot: Psychological realism
Time of work: The 1980's
Locale: A Chinese restaurant in Torrance, California
Subjects: Gender roles, race and ethnicity, and social issues
Recommended ages: 15-18

This play focuses on an encounter between Dale, an American-born Chinese, and Steve, a wealthy Chinese immigrant desiring acceptance by both Chinese Americans and mainstream America who must overcome the prejudice of Dale and his cousin Grace before he confronts society at large.

   Principal characters:
      DALE, a second-generation Chinese American
      GRACE, Dale's cousin, a first-generation Chinese American
      STEVE, a newly arrived Chinese immigrant

Form and Content
   F.O.B. opens with a prologue: Thoroughly Americanized Dale defines "F.O.B." as "Fresh Off the Boat"—a derogatory label for Chinese immigrants who are unfamiliar with the American way of life. Desiring inclusion in American society, these immigrants fail to achieve seamless integration into mainstream culture because of their incomplete understanding of cultural patterns. F.O.B.'s also fall short of total Americanization through their inability to relinquish their dependence on the Chinese American community.
   Act 1 opens in Grace's family restaurant; Grace is struggling to wrap a box in tape. Steve enters, rich and confident that he is desirable to any Chinese woman. Grandly identifying himself as the warrior god Gwan Gung, Steve orders Grace to serve him. Grace refuses, announcing that she is Fa Mu Lan, the mythical woman warrior. As events fail to comply with his carefully formulated plans, Steve grows confused. He tries—and fails—to gain possession of Grace's mysterious box.
   Dale arrives to join Grace and Steve for dinner; Dale and Steve soon begin a series of competitions and verbal skirmishes. When Steve invites Grace to go dancing after dinner, Dale immediately takes offence at what he interprets as presumptuous behavior from an upstart immigrant. The situation worsens when Steve dumps hot sauce on Dale's food. Dale retaliates by emptying the bottle of hot sauce onto Steve's plate. They begin an eating contest, each man trying to prove that he can gulp down overspiced food without flinching.

In act 2, Dale intensifies his attacks, referring frequently and derisively to Steve's F.O.B. status, while Steve fights back by reidentifying himself with Gwan Gung. To create a diversion, Grace announces a game of "Group Story." Almost immediately, the group narrative becomes a mythologized account of the Chinese experience in the United States dramatized through the conflicts between Steve, once again in his Gwan Gung persona; Grace, fully empowered (in her mind) as Fa Mu Lan; and Dale, the assimilated American Chinese. The storytelling escalates into a mock sword fight with traditional weapons, symbolically reducing Steve to an impoverished F.O.B. and allowing Grace to bestow on him the gift of a pancake from her box. Steve and Grace draw together—warrior god bonding with warrior woman—and later, when Steve again asks Grace to go dancing, she assents.

F.O.B. ends with a brief coda. Dale is alone, examining the box and swords that have figured prominently in the evening's events. As the lights dim, Dale repeats his definition of F.O.B.: "Clumsy, ugly, greasy . . . Loud, stupid. . . ." The encounter with Steve has not altered Dale's prejudice against new Chinese immigrants.

Analysis

Skillfully integrating traditional Chinese icons into a realistic portrayal of contemporary Chinese Americans, David Henry Hwang dramatizes issues that are crucial to definitions of American life. *F.O.B.* focuses on the themes of assimilation and acculturation as they relate to personal, cultural, and ethnic identity. Through three characters representing distinct stages in the Chinese American experience, Hwang asks important questions, but—because Chinese American history is still being written—provides no definitive answers. Through Grace, Steve, and Dale, Hwang shows that minority Americans face barriers within their own communities as well as in the wider context of American society.

Representing American-born Chinese, Dale scorns F.O.B.'s, whom he describes as "Like Lenny in *Of Mice and Men*." The comparison reveals his utter Americanization. His allusions come from American literature, his friends from the Hollywood Hills, his ambitions—a Porsche Carrera, a show at the Roxy, dinner at Scandia's—from the American Dream. As he points out, "I've had to work real hard . . . to not be a Chinese, a yellow, a slant, a gook." Dale despises his parents—once F.O.B.'s themselves—whom he calls "yellow ghosts," who have "tried to cage me up with Chinese-ness when all the time we were in America." He feels threatened by F.O.B.'s such as Steve, who is rich enough to pay for his Americanization. Confronted with an F.O.B. able to buy at least a semblance of assimilation, Dale is forced to realize how tenuous his own American persona is, how dependent on externals—clothing, automobiles, cultural tastes—that Steve already possesses.

Caught between Dale and Steve, Grace is a first-generation Chinese American. Ten years old when she first arrived in the United States, Grace has experienced the prejudice of ABCs (American-born Chinese) against new arrivals. She remembers bleaching her hair in a desperate bid at "getting in with the white kids" when her Chinese peers ignored her. Now a university student, she accepts an identity that is equal parts Chinese and American. She can never be like Dale, but, unlike Steve, she does not assume that a public display of wealth will suffice.

Steve represents everything that Dale has worked to eradicate from his own identity. Although Steve is expensively dressed, his behavior and language subtly mark him as an F.O.B. He fails to recognize that Grace is not a traditional submissive Chinese woman. He is baffled by idiomatic English. Worse, he believes that ostentatious spending—on a chauffeured limousine—will pay his way to assimilation into American society.

At the heart of *F.O.B.*, and central to Hwang's intentions, are the narrative monologues that provide clues to the play's meaning and direction by highlighting essential components of a speaker's identity while simultaneously revealing a chapter in the history of Chinese immigration to the United States.

Dale's prologue and coda define the play's title, hinting at conflicts between characters and outlining the play's themes. Dale clearly has no affection for F.O.B.'s; his animosity is the first barrier that Steve encounters. Because Dale represents Chinese American society, Steve must overcome Dale's enmity before attempting assimilation into mainstream America. Dale's two monologues within the play underscore his prejudice against immigrants. In the first, Dale ridicules thousands of Chinese who have come to the United States looking for success. The second monologue reveals Dale's pride in his complete assimilation as well as his scorn for his parents, who consider themselves Chinese despite their many years as American citizens.

Grace's monologues articulate her growing awareness of herself as an American, her gradual development of a distinct identity that borrows from her Chinese heritage the bold woman warrior rather than the shy maiden. Fa Mu Lan is central to Grace's monologues. Through this warrior, Grace articulates the pain of otherness and her fear that assimilation will destroy her ethnic identity.

The full story of the Chinese experience in the United States is shaped through Steve's monologues, each spoken in the persona of a Chinese immigrant. When the play opens, Steve speaks as the mythical warrior Gwan Gung. He is brash and overbearing, confident that his money will buy him acceptance. As the evening progresses, Steve begins to realize that he cannot push his way into the Chinese American community. His immediate entrée into mainstream American culture is impossible. His next monologue, spoken as an immigrant in 1914, recounts the struggles of the earliest Chinese immigrants, concluding with the frustrated query "This is the fifth time I come here. . . . Why will you not let me enter?" Clearly, the situation has not improved. The third monologue is the bitter reminiscence of an immigrant tricked by the "white ghosts" into coming to the United States only to discover that the Gold Mountain is a myth. By now, Steve understands that America sees him only as an immigrant; despite his ostentatious display of wealth, he is just another F.O.B. At the end of the play, broken by the bleak history of half a dozen waves of Chinese immigrants, Steve is reduced to acting the role of the unsuccessful immigrant who must beg for any form of labor that will earn him food.

Critical Context

David Henry Hwang catapulted Asian American drama into the theatrical mainstream with *F.O.B.*, which was produced by the O'Neill International Playwrights Conference and by the Public Theatre before winning an Obie Award. Two plays, *The Dance and the Railroad* (1981) and *Family Devotions* (1981), completed his Chinese American trilogy. For his next four plays—*The House of Sleeping Beauties* (1983), *The Sound of a Voice* (1983), *Rich Relations* (1986), and *As the Crow Flies* (1986)— Hwang went beyond his own community, attempting to universalize his work. In 1988, he won the Tony Award and the Outer Critics Circle Award for *M. Butterfly*, which explores several major issues: the "angst about being Asian in a . . . Caucasian world," gender bending, Asian stereotypes, race and culture, and identity and otherness. Hwang revisited most of those issues in *Bondage* (1991) and *Face Value* (1992).

As an acclaimed playwright, David Henry Hwang has given Asian Americans visibility in mainstream American theater. Additionally, he has brought to the stage serious treatments of issues and ideas that resonate for America's ethnic and minority communities.

E. D. Huntley

FOR COLORED GIRLS WHO HAVE CONSIDERED SUICIDE/ WHEN THE RAINBOW IS ENUF

Author: Ntozake Shange (Paulette Williams, 1948-   )
First presented: 1976
First published: 1976
Type of work: Drama
Type of plot: Social realism
Time of work: Mostly the 1970's, with some parts set in the 1950's and 1960's
Locale: Various cities in the United States
Subjects: Coming-of-age, gender roles, race and ethnicity, sexual issues, and social issues
Recommended ages: 15-18

This series of poems with dance accompaniment explores important issues in the lives of African American girls and women.

> *Principal characters:*
> LADY IN BROWN
> LADY IN YELLOW
> LADY IN PURPLE
> LADY IN RED
> LADY IN GREEN
> LADY IN BLUE
> LADY IN ORANGE

Form and Content

While certainly a dramatic work, meant primarily to be performed, *for colored girls who have considered suicide/ when the rainbow is enuf* is not a play in the traditional sense. Rather, it is a series of twenty loosely related poems intended to be recited by seven actresses, with dance integrated into the performance. Ntozake Shange (pronounced "en-toh-ZAH-kee SHAHN-gay"), in fact, calls the work not a play but a "choreopoem." The cast consists of seven unnamed actresses/dancers, designated simply as lady in brown, lady in yellow, lady in purple, lady in red, lady in green, lady in blue, and lady in orange. In a performance, the seven actresses trade off the leading role, change characters, interrupt one another, dance to accompany one another's recitations, and create a unified whole out of the disparate material of the poems.

Among the important themes in the work are issues related to growing up, especially growing up as an African American girl. One poem, "toussaint," concerns an eight-year-old girl in St. Louis in 1955 who wins the library's summer reading contest after discovering a biography of Haitian slave revolt leader Toussaint L'Ouverture. When it is discovered that she read books from the adult reading room, however, she is disqualified from the contest. She decides in her dejection to run away to Haiti and meet her hero Toussaint. After leaving home, she meets and befriends a little boy (whose name turns out to be Toussaint Jones) and finally realizes that she must stay in St. Louis and face the world into which she has been born. Another poem, "graduation nite," is the triumphant story of a high school graduate in the 1960's who retells, with breathless exuberance, how she danced and won over the crowds of teenagers at a graduation party. It is a coming-of-age celebration that ends with the young woman losing her virginity in the back of her boyfriend's Buick and asserting, "we waz finally grown."

A second important theme is that of male-female relationships and the problems to be found within them. Poems with titles including "no assistance," "sorry," and "no more love poems" suggest the pain and difficulty of negotiating gender roles and finding happiness with men, who often do not understand women's emotional needs. These poems range from self-pitying to confident to angry. In them, the women call upon their inner resources and on one another to help deal with the emotional turmoil caused by romantic and sexual relationships. The cumulative effect of these works is to suggest the strength and resilience of the characters.

In other poems, however, Shange goes on to consider the most troubling sorts of personal relationships—those involving abuse. The poem "latent rapists" reveals the terror that many women feel as they begin to realize that their friends and coworkers may not be trustworthy and are statistically as likely to rape them as "the stranger/ we always thot waz comin." In "a nite with beau willie brown," a troubled Vietnam War veteran physically and emotionally abuses his girlfriend, Crystal, and their two children. In a shocking scene at the end, Beau Willie drops the children from a fifth-story window after Crystal has refused to marry him.

Analysis

For colored girls . . . was not originally intended for a juvenile or young adult audience. Its themes include abortion, rape, and domestic violence, and several of the poems also include adult language. Nevertheless, the work has much to offer young adults, particularly in helping them to think through some of the important issues that African American women and girls confront in their daily lives. In addition to showing how these characters are separated from mainstream America, however, Shange also makes clear how the problems encountered by her characters are similar to those faced by persons from all backgrounds.

The choreopoem was not written all at once with its present structure and production strategy in mind. Rather, it grew out of a series of poetry readings and dance performances that Shange and another dancer, Paula Moss, gave in the San Francisco area in the early 1970's. The performances originally took place in bars, coffee shops, and small college venues, and the poems and choreography developed and changed considerably over time. When local success led Shange to take the show to New York in 1975, she settled on which poems were to be included and in what order, enlisted the services of a director, and hired additional actress/dancers, bringing the total to seven. This rather unusual evolution of the work leads to some interpretive difficulties for readers of the work.

Perhaps the first difficulty to be overcome, one that would not pose a problem for a theatrical audience, is Shange's idiosyncratic spelling, capitalization, and grammar. The author has explained that her refusal to follow the traditional rules of English—and her choice instead to write in a manner that approximates the dialect spoken by her African American characters—is the result of a conscious political decision. She does not simply ignore the rules, but she chooses with care where to follow them and where to break them in order to produce for her readers an experience most like the oral reading (in dialect) that was the form originally intended for the poems. In doing so, she hopes to make her readers aware that traditional English is not a "neutral" language but in fact reflects the history and dialect of the dominant classes. (It was this same awareness of the political nature of language that led the playwright to change her name officially from "Paulette Williams" to the African "Ntozake Shange.")

A second problem posed for readers is a familiar one for dramatic works: how to read a piece not originally meant to be read, but rather intended to be seen and heard. While this is often a difficulty for readers of plays, the problem is intensified with Shange's choreopoem because so many of the literary elements of traditional plays— plot, character, and obvious chronology, for example—are absent in the work. In addition, dance is a crucial part of the performance of *for colored girls . . .* , and there is no adequate way to convey this element on the page of a script. It is especially important for readers of this piece, therefore, to keep in mind the original intent of the author. They should try to imagine a performance of the work and the sort of power that would be added to the poetry with the inclusion of dance and other choreographed movement.

Despite these difficulties, however, *for colored girls . . .* repays the effort of reading it. It is a powerful work, demonstrating a wide emotional range and addressing a variety of issues and tastes. It shows characters navigating some of life's difficult moments, learning from them, and coming out stronger than they were. Clearly, interest in such an approach is not limited to African Americans, and for this reason the work appeals to a broad audience.

Critical Context

One thing that set *for colored girls . . .* apart from the mainstream of African American literature from the time period in which it was first produced is that the work was not within the protest tradition. This tradition gave a voice to the fears and frustrations of African Americans as they reacted against the effects of white racism in the United States. Shange did not choose in this case to use racial oppression as a lens through which one could see all African American experience. This work is not about oppression of black people by white people. In fact, there are no white characters and few references to white people in any of the poems. Rather than participate in the main thread in African American literature of the 1960's and 1970's, Shange chose to portray African American women simply as people, rather than viewing them first and foremost as members of an oppressed class.

After receiving good reviews and strong popular support in its New York theatrical run, *for colored girls . . .* rather quickly reached the status of a modern classic. It receives regular revivals and performances throughout the United States and has begun to be taught in high school and college classes as well. It remains Shange's best-known work, although she continues to publish poetry, give readings, and write dramas, including the critically successful *Spell #7* (1979), which examines the degrading stereotypes faced by African American performers.

Janet E. Gardner

FOUNDING MOTHERS
Women of America in the Revolutionary Era

Author: Linda Grant DePauw (1940-   )
First published: 1975; illustrated
Type of work: History
Time of work: 1776-1787
Locale: Colonial America (later the United States)
Subjects: Gender roles, jobs and work, social issues, and war
Recommended ages: 15-18

While history generally remembers the men of the revolutionary war era, DePauw provides an overview of women's contributions to the economic, political, and social well-being of the new country.

Principal personages:

ABIGAIL ADAMS, the wife of Patriot leader John Adams and an advocate for women's rights

MARTHA WASHINGTON, George Washington's wife, who helped coordinate the "Association" that raised money for soldier's needs

DAUGHTERS OF LIBERTY, a group of women who organized to support the Patriot cause

MARY HAYS, a woman who fought with the Continental soldiers after her husband was wounded at the Battle of Monmouth and became known as "Molly Pitcher"

DEBORAH SAMPSON, a soldier in the Continental Army disguised as "Robert Shurtluff"

PHILLIS WHEATLEY, a slave who became the first published black female poet

SYBIL LUDINGTON, a sixteen-year-old girl who rounded up her father's militia to fight the British in Danbury, Connecticut

MERCY OTIS WARREN, a playwright and historian who became an active Patriot propagandist

Form and Content

Since half of the American population in the revolutionary era were women, it is fitting to study the roles that they played and how they influenced the formation of the country. In *Founding Mothers: Women of America in the Revolutionary Era*, Linda Grant DePauw has supplemented extensive historical research with excerpts from primary source material, such as diaries, newspapers, and books. Working from the premise that women of this tumultuous era had more opportunity to participate in various occupations and roles than those who followed in the nineteenth century, DePauw dispels the notion of women in the revolutionary era as "the weaker sex."

Founding Mothers presents the stories and words of women of different lifestyles, ethnic backgrounds, social classes, and political affiliations. It is a major step in looking at the past without gender biases.

The first three chapters of the book look at women's world in general: marriage and the responsibilities of caring for the domestic triad of home, husband, and children. This examination includes women's financial contributions, as they stemmed primarily from household industry. Women's legal rights, especially pertaining to marriage and property, are also outlined. Chapters 4 and 5 show some of the ethnic diversity of the population in the revolutionary era. Black women (mainly slaves) and American Indian women (a vital element to their societies) were a part of this era, but they are usually discussed collectively with their white sisters. Political beliefs underscore the lives of Loyalist women and Daughters of Liberty in the next two chapters. The book concludes with the impact of the war itself on women and their rights, which ironically seemed to fade following the American victory. A detailed index and table of contents help the reader locate specific data. A supplemental reading list of books and articles, divided by chapter topics and fairly contemporary to DePauw's work, is included. No references are provided for the material cited in the text itself. Wood engravings, skillfully crafted by Michael McCurdy, introduce each chapter. This artistic medium was common in the revolutionary period and visually supports the content of the text. There are no drawings, paintings, or engravings of the women themselves.

Analysis

If mentioned at all in history textbooks, women's history is often relegated to a discussion of upper-class white women or stereotypically atypical women. DePauw's attempt to describe and differentiate between women's roles according to ethnicity, political beliefs, and social class in a nonfiction book is a deviation from the typical format of presentation. Women's history has often been viewed through biographies of women known because of their association with famous men (Abigail Adams, Martha Washington) or white women who broke the feminine boundaries of their era (Mary Hays, Deborah Sampson). The only other ethnic group prominent in juvenile literature consists of those African American women who were involved in the abolitionist movement in the nineteenth century (Harriet Tubman, Sojourner Truth). Writings about Loyalists, men and women who sided with the British during the revolutionary war, have always been scarce. The inclusion in *Founding Mothers* of American Indian women, Loyalist women, women from the working class, and women from all walks of life who were Daughters of Liberty presents a more realistic overview of revolutionary America.

When DePauw discusses well-known women, she expands on common knowledge. Abigail Adams is famous for advising her husband to "remember the ladies" when he was writing the Declaration of Independence, but her advocacy for improved education for women is often overlooked. This was also an interest of Mercy Otis Warren, whose plays mocked the British during the revolutionary war. Martha Washington is usually remembered positively for her support of her husband's wartime efforts, but her own active role in the largest wartime organization of women to raise money for the patriot soldiers is seldom mentioned. *Founding Mothers* establishes a firm knowledge base for those who have little background in women's history and expands the awareness of the well-versed.

DePauw also demonstrates that the stories of all women, including common, unknown individuals, have historical value. While the story of Phillis Wheatley, the first published black female poet, forms the basis for several books, another female slave poet, Lucy Terry, is virtually unknown. Sybil Ludington, a sixteen-year-old girl who alerted her town to the presence of British soldiers, did not have her accomplishment publicized, as the poet Walt Whitman did for Paul Revere. Historians have primarily viewed the revolutionary era from the accounts of the war or the constitutional conventions—venues from which women were absent. Women's stories were often considered trivial and were not passed on. If papers existed, they were often saved under the family or husband's name, making later discovery difficult. DePauw is a consultant to the National Archives, and it is evident in *Founding Mothers* that she has done extensive research in that collection.

Yet, even DePauw's picture is incomplete. She gives only cursory attention to women in three areas: religion, immigration, and education. The impact of women such as Mother Ann Lee, the founder and spiritual leader of the Shakers; Jemimah Wilkinson, who called herself the Publick Universal Friend; and Barbara Heck, known as the mother of American Methodism, should be examined. Religion held a prominent place in everyday life in the eighteenth century, and the Great Awakening early in the century paved the way for greater acceptance of female religious leaders. Another area that could have received greater attention was women who came from other countries. Immigrants arrived daily, and life for recent arrivals, especially women, was tenuous. Finally, since teaching was an accepted profession for women in the eighteenth century and participants had some type of literacy training, teachers were likely candidates to record their thoughts about their profession and lives in daybooks, journals, letters, or reports. Yet, DePauw included little about women in education. These omissions detract from the otherwise informative text.

Additionally, much more could be learned about the customs, dress, and physical appearances of eighteenth century women if illustrations had been included. These drawings are readily obtainable from historical societies and the Library of Congress, and their omission is a significant oversight.

Critical Context

Linda Grant DePauw is a professor of history at George Washington University in Washington, D.C., and most of her writing is scholarly, but she has written several books for juvenile readers. *Founding Mothers*, her first book, was written especially for the American bicentennial celebration in 1976 and was named an American Library Association Notable Book and a *School Library Journal* Best Book of the Year. These awards surprised DePauw because she did not consider herself a juvenile author.

Founding Mothers is included in sales materials of the National Women's History Project, headquartered in Windsor, California, and is often cited in books about women's history written for adults.

Building on a theme she introduced in that book, DePauw wrote *Seafaring Women* (1982), which chronicles the stories of women who went to sea—some in traditional roles (the wives of whalers and traders) and some mastering the sea as pirates and sailors. The author again punctuated her research with excerpts from letters and journals, and her chapter on seagoing careers should entice would-be sailors among young women.

Although DePauw has not been a prolific writer for adolescents, she has made a significant contribution to their literature. By raising awareness of women's roles in America's past, she made evident the parallels to current views of women's rights and roles. Moreover, her differentiation of women's roles according to ethnicity and social class provides a more realistic overview of women's contributions to society. Finally, because students generally prefer reading stories rather than factual data, nonfiction is often viewed as the stepchild of fiction, an opinion also precipitated by the lack of quality nonfiction. While DePauw's style of writing reflects her scholarly background, the fascinating information and anecdotes that she includes will entertain and act as a springboard for additional reading.

Kay Moore

FRANKENSTEIN

Author: Mary Wollstonecraft Shelley (1797-1851)
First published: 1818
Type of work: Novel
Type of plot: Moral tale, science fiction, and thriller
Time of work: The eighteenth century
Locale: The Arctic, Switzerland, Germany, and Great Britain
Subjects: Death, family, and science
Recommended ages: 15-18

> *Victor Frankenstein, a scientist eager to create life, conveys to an ambitious arctic explorer his reason for appearing so suddenly on the desolate, icy wastes by telling him of his manufacture of a creature and the disastrous consequences.*

Principal characters:
> VICTOR FRANKENSTEIN, a young man whose studies enable him to put together a creature from various human body parts and invest it with life
> THE MONSTER, created and rejected by Victor, who swears revenge upon him and his family and friends
> WILLIAM FRANKENSTEIN, the young brother of Victor, the monster's first victim
> JUSTINE MORITZ, a young servant of the Frankenstein family, who is accused of and executed for the murder of William
> ELIZABETH LAVENZA, a young woman adopted by the Frankenstein family who later marries Victor
> HENRY CLERVAL, Victor's friend, who serves as a foil for his character
> THE DELACEY FAMILY, who unknowingly provide the monster with the means of learning language and who demonstrate that love and affection can exist—but not for him
> ROBERT WALTON, the Arctic explorer who, like Victor, puts the pursuit of knowledge above family and friends and who becomes Victor's confidant
> MRS. MARGARET SAVILLE, Walton's sister, to whom he writes the tale that Victor confides to him

Form and Content

The structure of *Frankenstein* is epistolary, a popular novel framework in the nineteenth century that might be unfamiliar to contemporary readers. The story consists of letters from Robert Walton to his sister, Margaret Saville. At first, they contain incidents of his own Arctic exploration and reveal him as a man obsessed with a "love for the marvellous" that lures him from mundane pursuits that would anchor him to humanity. When he encounters Victor Frankenstein, the epistolary framework dissolves, and Victor tells his tale in the first person.

Growing up in a wealthy Geneva household, Victor passes a happy childhood in the company of Elizabeth Lavenza and Henry Clerval. At seventeen, he enters the University of Ingolstadt in Germany, where he is determined to discover the origin of life. He succeeds in animating a piecework human body, but he is horrified and flees from the creature that he has fashioned. Two years later, after he receives news that his brother William has been murdered, Victor sees the monster and intuitively knows him to be the murderer. Victor remains silent even though Justine Moritz is convicted of the crime and executed. Later, he meets the monster on Mt. Montanvert and listens to his story.

Having found shelter in a hovel attached to a cottage inhabited by the DeLacey family, the monster learned to speak. When the DeLaceys took in Safie, an Arab woman whom they had known in wealthier and happier days in Paris, they taught her to read, and the monster followed the lessons along with her. He had Victor Frankenstein's journal and so learned of his creator. He also read John Milton's *Paradise Lost* (1667, 1674) and identified with Satan, who was rejected by his creator and who seeks revenge by making war on humanity. Rejected by the DeLaceys when he revealed himself to them, the monster decided to travel to Geneva to find his creator. He murdered William when the latter feared and rejected him.

The monster explains to Victor that he is malicious only because he is isolated and miserable, and he persuades Victor to make him a mate. Victor goes to Scotland with Henry Clerval with this purpose in mind, only to destroy his half-finished female as the monster looks on. The monster retaliates by killing Clerval and by strangling Victor's wife, Elizabeth, on their wedding night. Victor vows to pursue the creature relentlessly, as obsessed about killing him as he was about creating him. As his tale ends, the novel resumes its epistolary framework.

Walton relates the death of Victor Frankenstein. When he himself encounters the monster, he does not kill him as Victor requested but listens to the story from his perspective. The monster depicts himself as loving Victor and suffering deeply from remorse. He claims that he was created to be susceptible to love and sympathy and was wrenched apart when offered only misunderstanding, rejection, and violence. Promising to end his own life, the monster leaves Walton to ponder the meaning of the events that he has heard.

Analysis

Because many young readers come to *Frankenstein* with preconceived ideas of the content, derived from a plethora of television and film renditions, the complexity and ambivalence of the actual text may present a challenge. The epistolary structure of the novel is important, as readers never hear the monster's tale directly. It is always filtered through Frankenstein's narration, Walton's writings, or both.

Resonating through the novel is Samuel Taylor Coleridge's *The Rime of the Ancient Mariner* (1798), a poem that Mary Shelley knew well and quotes in the text. Like the

Mariner, Frankenstein is compelled to tell his tale to one who might profit from it. Unlike the Mariner, however, there is no evidence that Frankenstein has gained clear insight into himself and repented. When he, near death from cold and exhaustion, first accosts Walton, he verifies that their direction is north before accepting help. Later, he eloquently pleads with Walton's men to remain steadfast in their exploration no matter what the danger or the cost. He tells Walton that he finds nothing blameable in his past conduct. Dying, he urges Walton to seek happiness in tranquillity and avoid ambition. His final words throw this self-awareness into doubt, however, for he admits that while his own hopes were blasted, someone else might succeed.

In Coleridge's tale, the listener goes away a sadder and a wiser man. Walton, who has listened to both Frankenstein and the monster, does likewise, his idealism tempered by an acknowledgement of human frailty and balanced with a more wholesome realization of the need for close human ties. He turns the ship south, putting commitment to the needs of his men ahead of his desire for renown and glory. Frankenstein and the monster remain ambivalent characters. There is much to applaud and appreciate in Frankenstein's driving ambition and much to pity in his gradual abandonment of all human affection and his obsession first with the pursuit of knowledge and then of revenge. In the monster, there is much with which to sympathize and much to condemn. One reason that Shelley's book has remained popular is that it captures modern humanity's paradoxical fascination with gaining control of nature through scientific discoveries and fear of what those discoveries can unleash.

The novel can be interpreted in several ways. Because the original edition bears a quotation from *Paradise Lost* and because the monster derives all of his theology from that work, it is easy to see in *Frankenstein* an analogy for God's creation of human beings and their exile to a world of pain and loss after the Fall, which might be taken as God's rejection. In addition, what psychologist Sigmund Freud would later define as the id often takes the shape of a double. It is possible to see the monster as Frankenstein's double and to find deeply repressed reasons for why Frankenstein would wish the death of the people whom the monster murders. One can also see Frankenstein as a symbol of reason and the monster as the emotion that he must suppress in order to achieve his ambitions; such feelings can be suppressed only temporarily, with disastrous consequences. Henry Clerval is in many ways a foil for Frankenstein and Walton. Like them, he is idealistic. Unlike them, he puts filial duty above ambition. While he achieves his goals, he does not do so at the expense of relationships, which always remain his major priority.

Critical Context

Mary Shelley was only eighteen when she wrote *Frankenstein* in response to a proposal by the poet Lord Byron, whom she and her husband, the poet Percy Bysshe Shelley, were visiting in Switzerland, that they each create a ghost story. Out of that evening's entertainment, *Frankenstein* was born. Shelley discusses the inspiration for the novel in a preface that is included in most editions.

Widowed at the age of twenty-four, Shelley supported herself and her son through her writing. In addition to critical editions of her husband's works, she wrote six other novels. None of them attained the popularity of *Frankenstein*, which she revised and republished in 1831. The novel spawned numerous stage adaptations, beginning as early as 1823. With the invention of film, the story saw new life in even greater variety. Of note among literary spinoffs of the basic tale is Brian Aldiss' *Frankenstein Unbound* (1975), which features a time warp in which a contemporary American meets Mary Shelley and the monster. The original text of *Frankenstein* remains a complex and richly rewarding novel that invites readers to ponder their personal goals and ambitions as well as the direction toward which modern life is moving.

Christine R. Catron

FREAKY FRIDAY

Author: Mary Rodgers (1931-   )
First published: 1972
Type of work: Novel
Type of plot: Fantasy
Time of work: The early 1970's
Locale: New York City
Subjects: Family and the supernatural
Recommended ages: 10-15

Thirteen-year-old Annabel wakes up one morning in her thirty-five-year-old mother's body, spends a day dealing with life from an entirely different vantage point, and finds a new appreciation for her family, friends, and teachers.

Principal characters:
ANNABEL ANDREWS, a thirteen-year-old girl who spends a day in her mother's body
BEN ANDREWS ("APE FACE"), Annabel's despised younger brother
ELLEN ANDREWS, Annabel's mother, who spends the day in Annabel's body
BILL ANDREWS, Annabel's father, an account executive for an advertising agency
BORIS HARRIS, the son of the upstairs neighbor, the object of Annabel's teenage crush
MRS. SCHMAUSS, the Andrews' housekeeper and baby-sitter
MR. DILK, the school principal
DR. ARTUNIAN, the school psychologist
MISS McGUIRK, Annabel's homeroom teacher
MR. and MRS. FRAMPTON, clients of Annabel's father

Form and Content
Freaky Friday is told as the first-person narrative of thirteen-year-old Annabel Andrews. The story opens as Annabel suddenly wakes to find that she inhabits the body of her thirty-five-year-old mother, Ellen. After Annabel's father (Ellen's husband) and her little brother (Ellen's son) leave for work and school, Annabel can freely explore the possibilities of her strange situation. She is delighted with her mother's body, especially with her teeth, which are white and straight—and without Annabel's braces. She is also delighted that she does not have to go to school, since she has not even begun her overdue English assignment.

Because she now lives in her mother's body, Annabel decides to do "motherly" chores. First, she tries laundry, overfills the machine, and puts in too much detergent; the washing machine promptly overflows and stops. After the repairman whom she calls promises to be there next week, Mrs. Schmauss, the housekeeper, arrives. Because Annabel has disliked Mrs. Schmauss for years, she and Annabel "have words," and Annabel fires her. Annabel then brushes her mother's beautiful straight teeth, dresses in one of her mother's slinky black outfits better suited to evening wear, experiments at her mother's makeup table, and generally has a good time playing grownup.

After lunch, Annabel goes to the liquor store to restock the liquor cabinet. On her way home, still wearing the slinky black outfit, she encounters a police officer and a crowd of onlookers gathered around a wailing child. The little boy is her brother, Ben—Annabel has forgotten to meet the school bus. Noting Annabel's outfit and the shopping bag full of liquor, the officer draws the obvious conclusion, but Ben defends Annabel, whom he believes to be his mother. The crowd disperses, the police officer leaves, and Annabel and Ben go home.

Later, Annabel's father calls to remind his wife of her parent-teacher conference about Annabel that afternoon. Since Annabel has fired Mrs. Schmauss, who usually does the baby-sitting, no one is available to watch Ben while Annabel goes to the conference. She calls Boris, the son of their upstairs neighbor and the object of Annabel's crush, to ask him to baby-sit Ben.

As her mother, Annabel attends the parent-teacher conference, during which she alternately defends and criticizes herself as a student. After the meeting, Annabel returns home to find Ben missing. When she asks Boris what happened, he says that a beautiful young girl came to the door and took Ben out for ice cream. Annabel immediately assumes that the girl has kidnapped Ben, and she calls the police.

Totally overwhelmed by the stresses of living in an adult body and meeting adult expectations, Annabel collapses on her bed, crying and calling for her mother. Suddenly, Annabel's mind transfers to her own body and Annabel's mother, in mind and body, appears there beside her. Ellen explains that Ben is not missing: He has been out with Annabel, the beautiful young girl whom Boris described. Annabel is disbelieving and claims that Boris considers her an ugly girl with a mouth full of metal. Ellen explains that she has spent the day in Annabel's body and that she went to the orthodontist to have Annabel's braces removed. Looking in the mirror, Annabel sees herself as a lovely girl with beautiful, white, straight teeth.

After Annabel and her mother recount the day's events to each other, Boris comes downstairs to see what has happened. He and Annabel, minus her mouth full of metal, get reacquainted.

Analysis

In *Freaky Friday*, Mary Rodgers creates a scenario featuring a young, upscale, two-parent, two-child, one-income household in a city apartment, complete with dog, housekeeper, and upstairs neighbors. This "perfect family" does not match many teenager's home situations and instead portrays an ideal situation.

Rodgers displays an uncanny ability to create believable teenage dialogue that does not sound as if it has been filtered through an adult mind. Her writing style—unstilted, natural, and gently humorous—appeals to her readers' sense of the ridiculous without ridiculing her young protagonist. The plot plays to her young readers' sense of the fantastic, yet it seems strangely realistic and reasonable. Although the reader never knows by what magic the exchange of mother and daughter occurs, the story as it unfolds needs no explanation. The final plot twist reveals that *Freaky Friday* is the English term paper that Annabel had not finished.

Freaky Friday quietly sketches some of the real concerns of parents and teachers, such as untapped potential, adolescent misconceptions about adult roles, and the necessity of challenging minds such as Annabel's. At the same time, the novel provides a fascinating glimpse into the thirteen-year-old female mind. Almost any budding teenage girl could be Annabel, complete with crush, braces, a pesky sibling, and self-doubt.

Freaky Friday percolates with wishful thinking, the kind in which almost every thirteen-year-old indulges. It is the ultimate daydream. The novel carries with it, however, something that a daydream usually does not—a dose of reality. Rodgers, in an unobtrusive manner, shows her young readers the points of view of a parent and a teacher; she also affords a peek into a younger sibling's mind. Learning her mother's perspective, Annabel discovers that Ellen's adult life is not without its responsibilities and limitations. After she has a chance to see herself from her teacher's points of view, Annabel realizes that teachers are not monsters out to spoil her fun. Finally, she discovers that her little brother is not the completely worthless creature that she has always considered him to be; in fact, he idolizes her.

In a way, *Freaky Friday* becomes the object lesson every parent wants to find a way to teach. Without being preachy, Rodgers takes a middle-of-the-road position in the eternal tug-of-war between the precocious teenager and the exasperated parent; between the exceptional, but unchallenged student, and the frustrated, but caring teacher. Using dialogue as her vehicle, Rodgers illustrates Annabel's shortcomings and strengths, as well as those of her parents. She portrays as saints neither Annabel as a student nor Annabel's teachers, but provides believable portraits of all her characters.

Annabel's appreciation for her mother's role in the family, and her mother's increased understanding of Annabel, develops clearly as the novel's predominant theme. Annabel's discovery of Ben's real feelings about his big sister and her budding romantic feelings for her neighbor Boris are treated with the author's ever-present gentle humor. Rodgers' realistic and often poignant description of the parent-teacher conference rings true for every parent who has ever attended one and to every adolescent who has ever been the subject of one.

Critical Context

Although not usually taught as part of the educational curriculum, *Freaky Friday* appears frequently on summer reading lists and lists of extra-credit book review choices. Critics find that beneath what seems to be fanciful fluff is a sturdy foundation of good behavior modeling for young adolescent girls. In the novel, every problem has a solution; every conflict, a resolution. Annabel's newly acquired genuine appreciation for her parents, her little brother, her teachers, and her schoolwork strains credibility only if the reader expects literal truth.

Mary Rodgers is the daughter of Richard Rodgers, the renowned composer of Broadway musicals, and is a well-known screenwriter, composer, and lyricist in her own right. Outside of the field of children's literature, she is probably best known for having written the score for the Broadway musical *Once upon a Mattress* (1959). Her other children's books include *The Rotten Book* (1969), about a naughty little boy named Simon. In addition, she has written two sequels to *Freaky Friday*: *A Billion for Boris* (1974), describing Boris' acquisition of a television set that broadcasts tomorrow's programs, and *Summer Switch* (1982), which describes a switch between Annabel's brother, Ben, and their father, Bill. In 1977, Rodgers wrote the screenplay for the Walt Disney Studios film version of *Freaky Friday*.

Mary Rodgers' books for both children and young adults fall into the entertainment category: While providing a pleasurable reading experience, they also offer to the thoughtful reader the opportunity to "walk a mile in another's shoes."

Barbara C. Stanley

FRENCH LEGENDS, TALES, AND FAIRY STORIES

Author: Barbara Leonie Picard (1917-   )
First published: 1955
Type of work: Short fiction
Subjects: Friendship, love and romance, religion, the supernatural, and war
Recommended ages: 10-15

Picard presents several legends and tales important to French culture and also offers a selection of folktales not often encountered outside France itself.

Form and Content

French Legends, Tales, and Fairy Stories is a collection of twenty-three traditional French narratives, grouped under four categories: "Tales of the French Epic Heroes," "French Courtly Tales of the Middle Ages," "Legends from the French Provinces," and "French Fairy Stories." The first two categories consist of tales retold from written sources in medieval France; the latter two are derived from oral traditions that are still current. Several of the stories in the first three groups prove useful in understanding French literature and culture, among them "Roland and Oliver" and "The Battle of Roncevalles," both stemming from the Old French *La Chanson de Roland* (*The Song of Roland*); and such tales as "Aucassin and Nicolette," a widely read love story, and the legend of "Mélusine," whose title character is credited, in folklore, with many landmarks in the neighborhood of Poitou, including the castle of Lusignan. The final section of the book presents several French fairy tales that are interesting partially because of their resemblance to (and differences from) other familiar tales, such as "Ripopet-Barabas," whose plot and central characters recall those of "Rumpelstilt-skin."

The tales are short enough to be read in one sitting by young readers, averaging approximately ten pages. (The longest is "The Miller and the Ogre," at fifteen pages.) The tales in the first section all come from the "Matter of France," the cycle of legends and tales concerning Charlemagne and his immediate successors, once important in helping to form a distinct French national consciousness. For example, "Roland and Oliver" and "The Battle of Roncevalles," both suggest that later generations perceived the age of Charlemagne as a golden age of passion, pride, and derring-do, a heritage that helped define what it meant to be French. The section devoted to courtly tales presents some of the best-known stories of love and chivalry from the Middle Ages. The final two sections deal more properly with folklore than with a literary heritage. They contain tales that are still told both to children and to adults as part of social gatherings in French villages, particularly on long winter evenings.

Analysis

Barbara Leonie Picard renders her tales into highly readable language and yet avoids any semblance of writing down to unsophisticated minds; indeed, although she intended the stories for youthful audiences, any reader interested in traditional tales may enjoy her versions. Without altering the plots or characterizations, Picard has abridged some of the old tales considerably; she also manages to make the sometimes inscrutable medieval characters accessible to modern readers. For example, Roland's decision not to summon help at the battle of Roncevalles puzzles many students, but Picard, developing the quarrel between Oliver and Roland in *The Song of Roland*, brings to life Roland's combination of foolhardy resolve in facing his enemies and despair over the unlikelihood of aid arriving in time. Picard's text portrays Roland as strong and proud, if gravely erring in judgment. Her retelling similarly preserves the ferocity of the battle with the numbers and names of the slain, while sparing the readers the surrealism of boiling blood, oozing brains, and ever-flowing tears that engaged the medieval poet.

Picard generally avoids the exaggerations of the original tales when they would weaken credibility for modern readers. For example, Charlemagne is described as being very old, but not as being well into his second century, as he is in *The Song of Roland*. When explanation is needed, as in some of the fairy legends of northern France, Picard provides it briefly and gracefully. For example, in order to explain the hostility of korrigans, a type of dangerous fairy, for Christian priests, Picard mentions that the korrigans seem to be omitted from the salvation and redemption offered to mortals in Christian belief and therefore detest Christian clerics. Such a religious idea is part of a French villager's received culture and so might go unexplained in the original; Picard includes only enough to illustrate and exemplify, without weighing down her tale.

Writing down oral tales, such as those in the latter two sections of the book, also requires other choices, not the least of which involves choosing which versions of the tales to utilize. In "The Peasant and the Wolf," a werewolf repays a poor man's kindness with a fine cow. In some variants, he rewards the peasant with a noble stallion instead. Some accounts also omit the werewolf's attempt to punish the peasant's wife for her scolding by giving the peasant a box to be opened only by his wife when she is alone. When the peasant becomes curious and opens the box, a magic flame shoots out and consumes the forest instead of his wife, as the werewolf intended. This detail of the Savoyard variant chosen by Picard explains why Bessans is primarily a grassland.

An other issue for the author is to what extent one should describe locales and other things familiar to the original audience. In addition to the plain of Bessans, there are stone rings found in Brittany (featured in "The Stones of Plouhinec"), the chalk cliff in Normandy known as *La Côté des Deux Amants* ("The Cliff of the Two Lovers"), and the historical union of the kingdoms of Provence and Naples ("Pierre of Provence"). Picard chose effectively; her texts state the major facts briefly, while omitting less important ones, such as the appearance of Lusignan in "Mélusine."

Picard's choice of tales is useful for young readers who desire to strengthen their understanding of French culture. In addition to the importance of the written works and legends that she included, her selection of fairy stories introduces many elements common to French fairy tales generally. For example, the curse placed on fairy women in "Mélusine," that they become partial serpents every Saturday, is related to many similar motifs in other French tales, such as those of Marie-Catherine d'Aulnoy, author of *Contes de Fées* (1697; *Fairy Tales by the Countess d'Aulnoy*, 1856). In Aulnoy's "Le Prince lutin" ("Prince Sprite" or "The Invisible Prince"), a fairy turns into a snake once in each century. The playful little people, *lutins*, whom Picard calls "imps" and "hobgoblins," appear in "Ripopet-Barabas" dancing beneath a tree and in "The Hobgoblin and the Washergirl" as sympathetic but timid phantoms. Also appearing in "Ripopet-Barabas" is one of the grotesque and often-hostile dwarves who sometimes seek to trap young women into marriage in return for some favor. The most widely known of these is again from Aulnoy's tales, "La Nain jaune" ("The Yellow Dwarf"). Another common motif, that of a human transformed into an animal and ultimately restored by someone else's faithful love, is central to "The Mouse-Princess." This device is familiar to many readers from Aulnoy's "La Chatte blanche" ("The White Cat") and Jeanne-Marie Leprince de Beaumont's "La Belle et la Bête" ("Beauty and the Beast," 1756, 1765; retold from a 1737 novella of the same title by Suzanne-Gabrielle de Villeneuve).

In addition to introducing English-speaking readers to typical French tales, Picard conveys the excitement, fancy, and humor of the originals, via the contests between brothers in "The Mouse-Princess" and "The Three Oranges," such exotic paraphernalia as the magic ship in "The Ship That Sailed on Land," and the accumulation of unlikely details in "The Miller and the Ogre." Readers get a clear sense of what entertains the French children who listen to these tales.

Critical Context

Barbara Leonie Picard is well known and respected for her adaptations of the literature and folktales of many cultures, including works from Celtic, British, German, and Persian sources. Although the writing of such tales necessitates many editorial decisions, Picard does not take the liberties in which recounters of traditional material sometimes indulged; she maintains the plots of the originals so that a reader of her versions knows the story line and understands something of its social context. In addition to the religious, historical, and geographical allusions in her stories, Picard also mentions relevant details of daily life, such as washing laundry in a stream in "The Hobgoblin and the Washergirl." Even the names remain French, with one exception: "Olivier" has become the more familiar "Oliver." Generally, Picard's accuracy with details matches her ability to make the tales interesting, as is the case with other examples of her work. For example, in the preface to *Tales of Ancient Persia, Retold from the "Shah-Nama" of Firdausi* (1972), Picard discusses the identity of the Turanians (*Turani*), the traditional enemies of the ancient Persians, the Zoroastrian religion, and the traditions concerning the life and death of the poet who composed the *Shah-Nama*.

Such careful accuracy is not always found in adaptations of foreign literature and folklore; the attempt to be precise often hinders the effort to present a readable, enjoyable narrative. This is especially true in works for younger readers, for whom adapters wish overwhelmingly to write a good story, rather than to fret over details of background. Picard's success at doing both is noteworthy.

Paul James Buczkowski

FRIDA KAHLO
Torment and Triumph in Her Life and Art

Author: Malka Drucker (1945-   )
First published: 1991; illustrated
Type of work: Biography
Time of work: 1907-1954
Locale: Coyoacán and Mexico City, Mexico; Detroit; New York; San
    Francisco; and Paris
Subjects: Artists and revolutionary leaders
Recommended ages: 15-18

*Mexico's best-known female painter and a rebel whose life was shaped by an
accident, art, and marriage to a difficult genius, Kahlo tried to assert her feminism, artistry, and revolutionary sentiments over a lifetime of physical and emotional
pain.*

Principal personages:
  Magdalena Carmen Frida Kahlo y Calderón, a celebrated
    Mexican painter of mixed parentage
  Guillermo Kahlo (originally Wilhelm Kahl), the
    German-Hungarian Jewish father of Frida, who was influential in her
    life
  Matilde Calderón Kahlo, the Spanish-Indian second wife of
    Guillermo Kahlo and mother of four daughters, including Frida, who
    called her "The Chief"
  Diego Rivera, Frida's husband, an illustrious muralist who painted
    frescoes in Mexico and the United States
  Alejandro Gomez Arias, Frida's schoolmate and first boyfriend, who
    became vice president of Mexico's Popular Party and held high
    public office
  José Vasconcelos, a well-known Mexican educator, writer, onetime
    minister of education, and presidential candidate who was supportive
    of Frida
  André Breton, a French writer and founder of the surrealist
    movement who invited Frida to exhibit in Paris
  Isamu Noguchi, a famous Japanese American sculptor who was
    Frida's onetime lover
  Leon Trotsky (originally Lev Davidovich Bronstein), an exiled
    Russian revolutionary leader who helped found the Soviet Union,
    resided in the home of the Riveras, and became Frida's lover,
    assassinated by a presumed Stalinist agent in 1940

Form and Content

This biography examines the life of an artist who was the daughter of a German-Hungarian Jewish father and a Spanish-Indian mother, was brought up as a Catholic, withstood a childhood bout with polio, was twice married to the same philandering genius, had affairs with an exiled Communist revolutionary leader and a famous Japanese American sculptor, became a dedicated Communist, and suffered for the rest of her life of forty-seven years from a serious bus and streetcar accident that she experienced at eighteen.

Magdalena Carmen Frida Kahlo y Calderón, better known as Frida Kahlo, was a five-foot, one-hundred-pound, diminutive woman with joined eyebrows and a suspicion of hair above her upper lip who constantly enchanted and confused people with her dualities and contradictions: her intellect and sensuality, her daintiness and toughness, her pain and joy.

Malka Drucker's *Frida Kahlo* was written for the Barnard Biography Series, the purpose of which is to profile heroic women, providing girls with role models for creativity and other desirable qualities. Kahlo was selected as such an individual, despite her status as a self-styled martyr and lifelong invalid whose leg was finally amputated a year before her death from pneumonia. She was a high-spirited flirt and a rebellious "bad girl" who would often misstate her birth date to make it coincide with the beginning of the Mexican Revolution of 1910.

Analysis

Her life full of pain and emotional drama but also triumph was expressed in Frida Kahlo's mostly autobiographical paintings. Her work, often done flat on her back in bed, had a directness that many have found shocking but that others, including her husband and inspiration, Diego Rivera, have found mesmerizing. Kahlo's symbolic representation of herself as a saint, or a goddess, or a man, or a deer puzzled still others. Yet, this reaction was in keeping with the unpredictable character whose final diary entry in 1954, in keeping with her melancholic life, read (in translation): "I hope for a happy exit and I hope never to come back."

While most of Kahlo's artistic themes are autobiographical (55 paintings out of 143), her style has a surrealist twist free of reason's control and convention, even though she objected to being categorized in any particular style. As she insisted, "I never painted dreams. I painted my own reality." For example, in *My Grandparents, My Parents, and I (Family Tree)*, painted in 1936, she represents herself as a young, naked girl standing in the courtyard of a building. She is holding a red ribbon that streams upward, bifurcated to link herself and her parents, then forking off to form puffs of clouds where her two sets of grandparents are cradled. Attached to the bow of her mother's wedding gown belt is an umbilical cord running to an embryo outside her body like a purse of flesh. In *The Two Fridas* (1939), the saint and the tropical native goddess hold hands, joined by a thin artery that connects their hearts, which are exposed and float in front of the fully clothed Fridas. In *The Wounded Deer* (1946), a small animal with Kahlo's head, its body pierced with arrows, wobbles unsteadily through the woods. Several of her paintings were found to be too shocking to be exhibited at a 1939 French surrealist show in Paris arranged by André Breton, the founder of the movement. Although Kahlo returned from France greatly disappointed, the Louvre, the country's most prestigious national art museum, bought *The Frame*, Kahlo's self-portrait painted on glass.

Her occasional still-life paintings—such as *Long Live Life* (1954), featured in Drucker's book, or *What the Water Gave Me* (1938), which is not included—suggest a sensuous and surrealist effect and an intuitive relationship with nature. Political messages also find room in her depictions. For example, in 1950 she painted a hammer-and-sickle, the Communist Party insignia, on the metal corset that she had to wear to support her spine; this image is depicted in Drucker's biography. Kahlo's preferred format, however, was clearly the self-portrait.

The holding up of artists as role models likely to interest young readers is a relatively new phenomenon. Until recently, people of action (political and military leaders, explorers, inventors, and sports figures), not of culture, were popular biographical subjects. In the 1980's, however, the lives and works of artists came increasingly into favor among readers, not only adults but adolescents as well. Drucker's *Frida Kahlo* is in keeping with this trend, but it provides even more. The author gives her subject the distinctly heroic presentation of a skilled artist who epitomizes feminism, who emphasizes Mexican nativism, and who can generate sympathy because of the tribulations associated with her physical condition. Young readers can also relate to Kahlo's childhood, when the girl felt her mother's disapproval of her ways. Along the way, Drucker does not allow her readers to forget that in addition to pain and being a woman in a man's world, Frida Kahlo's torment included her marriage to the trying Rivera, known as "El Maestro" (the master), twenty-one years her senior, whom she seemed to have loved and admired as a great artist. Yet, as Kahlo herself once wrote, "I have suffered two accidents in my life, . . . one in which a streetcar ran over me. The other is Diego."

Those intrigued with the tragic lives of poets Anne Sexton and Sylvia Plath may recognize echoes of their stories in the life of Frida Kahlo. For others interested in the downtrodden and minority groups, the homespun, confessional, and bluntly expressive qualities of Kahlo's paintings that deal with the circumstances of her life, reflecting her belief that art is the product of suffering and no one suffers more than a woman, should play well. After Kahlo's death in 1954, her art was elevated to new heights of adulation in Mexico and later in the United States.

Critical Context

The 1990's brought multiculturalism, a renewed feminism, and a post-Cold War reevaluation of communism to the United States. Malka Drucker capitalizes on this trend to tell the story of a physically handicapped Mexican woman of diverse ethnicity and religious background and communist affiliation, who stood up for her country's Indian minority and native art and its revolutionary regime while despising those who sat in cafés discussing culture and art. Drucker's biography is a groundbreaking work, but she has spirited competition, not only in the form of such books as Hayden Herrera's *Frida Kahlo: The Paintings* (1991) or the abridged and translated version of Martha Zamora's *Frida Kahlo: The Brush of Anguish* (1990) but also from Kahlo herself. Any verbal recounting of the artist's tortures pale beside Kahlo's dramatic pictorial representation of her own bloody miscarriage, the operation on her spine, the amputation of her leg, or the morose longing for her absent and unfaithful husband.

The relatively few color plates and black-and-white photographs in Drucker's book—such as of the gigantic Rivera holding his wife's hand in her 1931 painting *Frida and Diego Rivera*—are well selected, but, given Kahlo's social and political activism, at least one relevant illustration would have been appropriate for inclusion: for example, *Marxism Will Give Health to the Sick* (1954). Indeed, a few days before her death in July, 1954, Kahlo got out of bed to appear at a public rally protesting the U.S. involvement in the toppling of the leftist government of Jacobo Arbenz Guzmán in Guatemala.

The bibliography and, especially, the chronology of the major events in Kahlo's life are very helpful. Art historian Laurie Anderson's introduction places things in context and raises many questions about Kahlo's enigmatic persona.

Peter B. Heller

FRONTIER LIVING

Author: Edwin Tunis (1897-1973)
First published: 1961; illustrated
Type of work: History
Time of work: 1710-1889
Locale: The United States
Subjects: Arts, education, family, jobs and work, travel, and war
Recommended ages: 13-18

>   *Describes and illustrates the conditions of daily living on the American frontier as settlement progressed westward from the Atlantic coast across the continent to California.*

Form and Content

Frontier Living, like author-illustrator Edwin Tunis' earlier work *Colonial Living* (1957), describes the artifacts and conditions of daily living in the United States during an earlier era. Tunis sets the stage for *Frontier Living* with a brief introductory chapter on the earliest settlements along the eastern seaboard. From there, he moves generally west, sometimes swinging south or north, sometimes pausing to give more thoughtful consideration to a broader topic such as road and river travel. The chapter headings include "The Deepwater Frontier," "The Piedmont," "The Southern Valleys," "The Great Salient," "Road and River," "The Old Northwest," "The Cotton Frontier," "Shrinking Distances," "Beyond the Mississippi," "Caravans to Santa Fe," "The Fur Trade and the Mountain Men," "The Bitter Road to Oregon," "The Harried Saints," "Alta California," "El Dorado," "Two Thousand Miles," "The Cow Hunt and the Cowhand," "The Sodbusters and the Cattle Drives," and "The Run." Each chapter is further divided into sections of varying length on topics such as food, hunting, and housekeeping. Some chapters also include an essay that establishes the historical framework for the surrounding material. All include meticulously rendered black-and-white illustrations, one or two to a page, most with captions. Some of the illustrations are maps.

In his foreword, Tunis suggests that he is working against a common assumption that the word "frontier" refers primarily to the settlement of the American West, and he states his intention of restoring a proper sense of proportion by "presenting conditions east of the Mississippi River in rather more detail than those west of it." Some of the information about the physical details of living, such as houses and housekeeping, apply to the entire pioneer experience, so that the later chapters can focus more narrowly on what was unique about traveling the Oregon Trail or living in a Nebraska sod house. Although *Frontier Living* contains more straightforward history than *Colonial Living*, like its predecessor it includes many fine explanations of mechanical devices and craft processes.

Frontier Living provides a complete table of contents and an index. The index covers many of the illustrations as well as the text and distinguishes between the two with an asterisk after the page number for illustrations.

Analysis

Tunis' tone and style is more appropriate for the adult reader than young people at the lower end of the recommended age range. His diction often has a formal tone that may not appeal to young readers, as in this example: "A decoction of white walnut bark was believed to act as a purgative if the bark were peeled downward from the tree; upward peeling of the same bark produced an emetic!" The text is full of descriptions of tools and household items and all of the physical details of daily life on the frontier. Many of the terms used, such as "staves" (as in barrels), if not technical, are at least uncommon and may be unfamiliar to some adult readers and almost all young people. Most, however, are defined in context or clarified by an accompanying illustration.

Tunis' use of unfamiliar words and phrases is in part attributable to his choice of subject matter, but his style is rendered even more dense by his preference for long, compound sentences and paragraphs packed with detailed information. The print size is small, and while the frequent illustrations help create white space, the total effect may be overwhelming to younger readers.

On the other hand, Tunis draws his readers in with the effective use of fictional techniques and humor. For example, he begins a sketch on childhood and sports by pointing out: "A boy growing up in the woods was quite untroubled by any thought of the three R's, but he learned from babyhood the things he had to know for coping with a forest life." Illustrations such as the picture of a team of oxen running away with a sled in the chapter "Beyond the Mississippi" often have a humorous touch. The illustrations are uniformly excellent; it is not surprising that they have been widely praised. As in *Colonial Living*, many of them play an important role in amplifying and clarifying the narrative. Others break up otherwise closely typeset pages into visually manageable bites, and some—for example, the picture of the runaway oxen or of a black cat accompanying an essay on witchcraft—are simply charming addenda.

Tunis is candid and evenhanded in his portrayal of frontier people, both American Indians and white settlers. He acknowledges the element of truth in the romantic ideal of the strong, fearless, self-reliant frontiersman, but he also points out that these men had other less admirable qualities:

> More than a third of them couldn't write their names. They were unwashed and infested with fleas, bedbugs, and body lice. In justice it must be said that no one who slept under a bearskin on a cold night could very well avoid these companions. But bearskins didn't make people superstitious, foulmouthed, and belligerent, as the majority of these were.

Tunis does not attempt to gloss over the racist attitudes of the white settlers toward American Indians. "They hated the sight and thought of an Indian." Although the text is written from the point of view of the white frontiersmen and women, the author portrays American Indians relatively sympathetically, as in this comment: "They were fighting for survival, using the tactics of frightfulness and stealth. Stealth was natural to them; frightfulness seemed justified by desperation."

Tunis has somewhat less to say about women as a segment of the frontier population. Some of the lack of attention may be attributable to the fact that women were fewer in number than men, particularly in the early years. For example, he describes only a boy's activities in "Childhood and Sports" and other essays that might well have included girls or women. He does picture them as participants or spectators in at least some of the drawings. He places girls in his illustration of a one-room school, for example, and girls are included in a group of children watching a tinker repair a pot. Tunis takes time to note that although frontiersmen often died violent deaths, women were more likely to be worn out by unrelieved drudgery and high rates of childbirth.

Because of the chronological overlap, some of the material in the early chapters of *Frontier Living* duplicates text in *Colonial Living*, for example house building and the process of making flax into linen. *Frontier Living* includes an index to both text and some illustrations, which increases its value as a reference tool. It would have been even more helpful had the author provided a bibliography.

Critical Context

Frontier Living, Tunis' sixth book, was published as a companion to *Colonial Living*. It was favorably reviewed at the time of publication by the *Bulletin of the Center for Children's Books* and *The Horn Book Magazine*, and it was cited by May Hill Arbuthnot and Zena Sutherland in early editions of their textbook *Children and Books* (1964, 1972). It was named a Newbery Honor Book in 1962.

Frontier Living is no longer cited in major textbooks on children's literature, except for the expected listing as a Newbery Honor Book. It is, however, listed in the sixteenth edition of *Children's Catalog* (1991). As a Newbery Honor Book, it is likely to be found in many public and school libraries for years to come. Yet, even without that award, Tunis' illustrations would ensure the book's place as an early example of excellence in nonfiction for children. His meticulous use of pen and ink to reveal the secrets of early American technology are a precursor of David Macaulay's books *Castle* (1977), *Cathedral* (1973), *Mill* (1983), and others. Although the publishers of many newer nonfiction books seem to prefer photographs as illustrations, it is hard to imagine any photograph that could improve upon the accuracy and clarity of Tunis' drawings.

Another critical factor in evaluating nonfiction for young people is the extent to which the contributions of women and minorities are addressed. Tunis' treatment of American Indians was so notable for his time as to be mentioned in contemporary reviews, although he scarcely mentions other minorities.

Frontier Living has more utility as a reference tool than its companion volume, *Colonial Living*, because of its index. The inclusion of illustrations in the index add considerably to its reference value.

Kathleen M. Hays

FUTURE SHOCK

Author: Alvin Toffler (1928-   )
First published: 1970
Type of work: Social science
Subjects: Science and social issues
Recommended ages: 15-18

> *Toffler argues that the increasing pace and scope of change in modern technological civilization is creating a dangerous condition of "future shock" which must be understood and addressed.*

Form and Content

Based on extensive research and years of preparation, Alvin Toffler's massive *Future Shock* argues that the world is undergoing a fundamental transformation from agricultural and industrial societies to a new, "superindustrial" society driven by high technology, service industries, and rapid change in all areas of life, with potentially ruinous effects on its citizens. Toffler conveys his information and conclusions in an accessible writing style for general readers, while lengthy notes and a bibliography at the end of the book identify his numerous sources and list resources for further research. The book is carefully organized, with a short introduction preceding twenty chapters grouped into six parts; each chapter is further divided into sections, all listed in the table of contents. A typical section will begin with an interesting anecdote; then provide some general observations, results of scientific research, or statistics; briefly quote one or more experts in the field; and offer a few speculations about future developments before moving on to the next subject.

According to the three chapters of part 1, "The Death of Permanence," earlier human societies were characterized by a sense of stability in all aspects of life, including place of residence, work, family, and social norms. Such permanence is now impossible in a technologically advanced society of ever-increasing and ever-accelerating change. Modern human life will instead be distinguished by three characteristics, separately discussed in parts 2, 3, and 4: "Transience"—people will constantly change their possessions, homes, social lives, jobs, and personal interests; "Novelty"—people will regularly be confronted by new and unfamiliar technologies, types of experiences, and family structures; and "Diversity"—people will face a bewildering variety of choices in their purchasing decisions, social groups, and lifestyles. Each aspect of these characteristics is discussed in a separate chapter. In the two chapters of part 5, "The Limits of Adaptability," Toffler points out that overstimulation and radical changes in life, according to clinical studies, can inflict physical and mental damage on individuals, and he argues that protean modern society may increasingly induce a debilitating physiological and psychological condition he calls "future shock." This reaction is related to the "culture shock" of moving into a new culture but is more severe, as its victims will lack the option of moving back into their old, familiar culture. If left unacknowledged and untreated, this condition might even lead to widespread nervous breakdowns and dysfunctional behavior in a "future-shocked society." Accordingly, in the four chapters of part 6, "Strategies for Survival," Toffler outlines the ways in which governments and private organizations might respond to this imminent threat: developing or improving counseling and support programs for troubled individuals, restructuring education to emphasize an orientation to the future, anticipating the effects of new technology and possibly intervening to slow or stop its introduction, and bringing together all members of society to think about, discuss, and decide on their future goals.

Analysis

As people move further into the future world that Toffler envisioned in 1970, some aspects of *Future Shock* will inevitably seem outdated to modern readers. Certainly, a few of his specific predictions—widespread use of paper dresses, completely modular buildings, and the disappearance of street gangs—have not been, and apparently will not be, fulfilled. Nevertheless, Toffler's overall analysis of modern society in the first four parts of *Future Shock* remains relevant and valuable. Many readers will readily relate to the notion that transience, novelty, and diversity increasingly characterize their lives, and they will find that a number of contemporary concerns—the obsolete model of lifelong employment in one company, new and less hierarchal forms of business organizations, the splintering of society into small interest groups, a diminished feeling of commitment to a larger "community," the deterioration of the traditional family structure, and the overwhelming number of available choices in entertainment and consumer products—are anticipated and described in *Future Shock*. Toffler manages to hold his readers' attention with a brisk, variegated approach; most chapter sections are only about a thousand words long, and each topic is developed clearly but not excessively. Younger readers who would like to find a unified explanation for any number of seemingly unrelated modern phenomena may find that *Future Shock* offers an intriguing and stimulating solution, and they will find it educational and enjoyable to connect Toffler's concepts to the special concerns of their own situations.

While Toffler's examination of modern technological civilization retains much of its power, his diagnosis and recommended treatment of its problems, outlined in parts 5 and 6 of *Future Shock*, have not aged well. Psychologists have not embraced "future shock" as a valid or useful label for a mental condition, and, although many citizens of advanced societies display aberrational personalities and behavior, there are no signs of the general mental collapse that Toffler feared. In 1970, he may have underestimated the ability of most people to adapt to the rapid pace and constant changes in their lives; one modern practice that Toffler obliquely anticipates, "cocooning"—spending most of one's time in the familiar environments of home and the company of close friends—may represent one successful strategy for coping with an otherwise overstimulating and transitory existence. Toffler's various suggestions for action in part 6 seem alternately paternalistic, such as setting up special counseling services to help people adjust to new jobs and homes or carefully controlling the pace of technological innovation, or overly idealistic, such as solving deep conflicts over the future directions of society simply by bringing people together in community meetings to discuss goals and achieve a consensus. Significantly, in later writings, Toffler largely focused on developing and expanding the social analysis of the first four parts of *Future Shock*, downplaying the concept of "future shock" and specific programs to alleviate it, and expressing greater optimism—most forcefully in *The Third Wave* (1980)—about coming social changes and their beneficial effects.

Overall, Toffler's arguments can be, and have been, criticized in several ways. At times, he may be overly enthusiastic about technological innovations and too inclined to dismiss their opponents as ineffectual reactionaries or compulsive naysayers. In addition, focusing on the wealthy citizens of superindustrial civilization, he sometimes seems relatively indifferent to the ongoing problems of underdeveloped Third World countries and the less affluent members of Western societies. Some will be inspired by Toffler's general optimism about the future, while others will believe that he is naïve about advanced science and its consequences. In sum, the coming society that Toffler predicts may be neither as ubiquitous nor as desirable as he sometimes wishes to claim. Nevertheless, even those who reject many of its conclusions will agree that *Future Shock* is an informative and provocative examination of its subject, and Toffler himself stated in the introduction that his major purpose was to get his readers to think more about the future, not necessarily to offer definitive judgments about the future.

Critical Context

The publication and remarkable popularity of *Future Shock* was a significant event in its time. The public gained a new awareness of "futurism"—the discipline that systematically and scientifically studies the future—and Toffler earned a reputation as a major "futurist." *Future Shock* received the McKinsey Foundation Book Award in 1970 and the Prix du Meilleur Livre Étranger from France in 1972, was repeatedly cited in popular and scientific articles, and even inspired fictional responses, such as John Brunner's *The Shock Wave Rider* (1975). Toffler frequently appeared on television and later met with such world leaders as Ronald Reagan and Mikhail Gorbachev. The ideas in *Future Shock* have had a discernable impact on modern society, making the book not only valuable but historically important as well. A bibliography of forty-five books on "future studies" in Toffler's *The Third Wave*, all but seven published after *Future Shock*, provides one measure of the book's broad influence.

While Toffler wrote several other books, the most important of these were the direct successors to *Future Shock*: *The Third Wave* and *Powershift* (1990). Introducing the latter volume, he describes these books as his "trilogy": *Future Shock* focusing on the "process" of change, *The Third Wave* anticipating its outcomes or "direction," and *Powershift* analyzing the "control" of change. While very readable, *Future Shock* is a long book—five hundred pages in paperback—so it has rarely served as a classroom text. Yet, because Toffler organized the book as a series of brief discussions of discrete topics in separate sections, many parts of *Future Shock* can be excerpted and read separately. Selections have often appeared in anthologies of readings for high school and college composition classes, and portions of the book might contribute to class discussions of current social problems. A 1972 documentary based on the book, made with Toffler's participation and available on videotape, has also been employed in the classroom.

Gary Westfahl

GENTLEHANDS

Author: M. E. Kerr (Marijane Meaker, 1927-　　)
First published: 1978
Type of work: Novel
Type of plot: Social realism
Time of work: The mid-1970's
Locale: The small, bayside tourist town of Seaville in Upstate New York
Subjects: Coming-of-age, family, love and romance, race and ethnicity, and social
　issues
Recommended ages: 13-15

During the summer of his sixteenth year, Buddy Boyle inadvertently unearths an old family secret while experiencing first love with a girl from a higher social class.

　　Principal characters:
　　　　BUDDY BOYLE, a sixteen-year-old who is attempting to discover his
　　　　　identity by rebelling against his middle-class upbringing and
　　　　　searching for the truth about the grandfather he never knew
　　　　SKYE PENNINGTON, Buddy's summer girlfriend, an eighteen-year-old
　　　　　socialite
　　　　FRANK TRENKER, Buddy's grandfather, a former warden of a Nazi
　　　　　concentration camp
　　　　NICHOLAS DELUCCA, the cousin of one of Trenker's victims who
　　　　　eventually exposes Trenker as a war criminal

Form and Content

Gentlehands is the mild yet effective tale of a teenager's first experience with love that leads him to a disturbing discovery about his maternal grandfather's involvement in Nazi war crimes. Set in the mid-1970's in Seaville, New York, the story is a timeless one in that people have always allowed themselves to be isolated from one another by such self-imposed barriers as money and race. While M. E. Kerr offers readers a frank portrayal of human intolerance and prejudice, few would find the tone of the book to be sermonizing.

The story itself is quickly read and easily followed. The protagonist, Buddy Boyle, is first encountered in the middle of a summer romance with Skye Pennington, a vacationing socialite two years his senior. His middle-class family strongly opposes the attraction, claiming that Skye will make Buddy forget where he comes from but obviously fearing that Buddy will be hurt. Buddy continues to pursue the relationship, often covertly, ignoring his obligations to his own family and to his job at the Sweet Mouth Soda Shop.

Eventually, Buddy does begin to feel the need to impress Skye, and he takes her to meet Frank Trenker, the grandfather with whom he himself has had no contact throughout his life. Buddy is easily charmed by his wealthy, sophisticated grandfather, who is kind to Buddy and Skye and to the stray animals that he often takes into his home. After briefly living with his grandfather, however, Buddy learns that Nicholas DeLucca, a man whom Buddy met at a party and who inadvertently led him to his grandfather, is seeking Trenker as the murderer of his cousin in a Nazi concentration camp.

Ultimately, the truth that Buddy's grandfather, known as Gentlehands in Germany, was indeed a cruel concentration camp warden is revealed in the town newspaper. Buddy, with mixed feelings, seeks out his grandfather but finds that he has fled to safety. Although Buddy is disappointed in his grandfather, he has learned from him to be true to oneself and to value family closeness. This revelation, along with Buddy's newfound appreciation of his family and Skye's eminent departure for college, brings their dwindling romance to its conclusion.

Analysis

Although dominated by two story lines loosely tied together, *Gentlehands* has one major theme—intolerance. The intolerance of Frank Trenker led him to murder Jewish concentration camp inmates, and the misunderstanding of both Skye and Buddy's family for members of a different social class lead only to insensitive comments and bickering. Both issues make the book an important one. It teaches a vital lesson to be learned in youth: Without knowledge and a sense of equality, communication is lost and ill-will is bred.

Out of this need for tolerance also springs an awareness of the need for respect and honesty. Buddy feels deceived by his grandfather, but, at the same time, he is deceiving and neglectful of his family. His awareness of this hypocrisy, as well as his newfound desire for familial closeness, leads him to the maturity that he lacks at the beginning of the book, when his only concerns seem to be spending time with Skye and his great awe of the differences in wealth that he encounters at both her home and the home of his grandfather.

Perhaps the greatest lesson of the novel, however, is an unexpected one. Early adolescence is often a time of seeing the world in either black or white, without an acceptance of the shades of gray that color the majority of life experiences and encounters. When Buddy sees his grandfather as both Gentlehands and the gentle man with whom he has spent time, Buddy begins to come of age. Evidence is shown that Buddy has indeed recognized some of the subtleties of this transformation when he says to Skye, as she is finally about to meet Buddy's true family and is concerned with her appearance, "You look fine. No one else will be all in blue." Further, he arrives at the costume party in the final scene wearing a question mark, as if he has accepted himself for what he is—a young man still in search of himself.

Critical Context

Although published after Robert Cormier's *The Chocolate War* (1974), a book which began a trend in young adult fiction toward more harshly realistic stories,

Gentlehands is milder in tone and less shocking in nature while still facing some of the difficult problems involving maturity, self-identity, racial relations, and social issues. Along with other works by M. E. Kerr such as *Dinky Hocker Shoots Smack!* (1972), the story of a young girl desperate for her mother's attention, and *The Son of Someone Famous* (1974), a boy's search for self-identity in the face of his parent's success, *Gentlehands* compassionately addresses the problems of adolescence. All of Kerr's books are immensely popular with teenage readers and with educators.

Emma Cox-Harris

GERMAN HERO-SAGAS AND FOLK-TALES

Author: Barbara Leonie Picard (1917-   )
First published: 1958; illustrated
Type of work: Short fiction
Subjects: Love and romance, social issues, and war
Recommended ages: 13-18

A collection of the great medieval Germanic epics as well as fourteen well-known German folk and fairy tales are made accessible to young readers through Picard's adept retelling.

Form and Content

As the title suggests, *German Hero-Sagas and Folk-Tales* is divided into two parts. In the first section, Barbara Leonie Picard retells in condensed, third-person prose four celebrated medieval Germanic epic narratives: *Gudrun, Dietrich of Bern, Walther of Aquitaine,* and the *Nibelungenlied.* Originally employing elaborate medieval strophic forms and composed variously in Middle High German or Old Norse, Picard's modern adaptations masterfully capture much of the authentic atmosphere associated with the epic milieu. While the shortening of the narratives necessarily results in the loss of some detail, Picard nevertheless is able to retain the central features of the respective plots as well as their salient thematic characteristics.

These sagas offer insights into the often grim and fatalistic, yet always fascinating medieval European heroic world. Such components as ill-fated marriages, knightly sport and warfare, fierce liege and kinship loyalty, and still fiercer vengeance are common to the epics presented in this collection. The *Nibelungenlied* (song of the Nibelungs), the story of Siegfried and Kriemhild, is at once representative and also perhaps the most striking of the heroic epics. Famous for slaying a dragon, bathing in its blood, and wresting a cache of gold from the Nibelung dwarfs, young prince Siegfried hears of the lovely maiden Kriemhild of Burgundy, who lives in Worms at the court of her three royal brothers: Gunther, Gernot, and Giselher. A visit to the Burgundian court strengthens Siegfried's determination to marry Kriemhild. In return for her hand, Siegfried offers to help King Gunther woo Brunhilde, the queen of Eisenland (Iceland).

Gunther and Siegfried are successful, but only by means of deceit and with the help of Siegfried's "Tarnkappe," his magical cloak of invisibility. After both couples are wed, Brunhilde discovers that she has been tricked and considers her honor impeached. She calls for vengeance, and Gunther's vassal Hagen (with only reluctant support from Gunther) undertakes the deed by thrusting Siegfried's own sword through his back while Siegfried is drinking from a spring. Hagen also steals Siegfried's gold from Kriemhild and hides it deep in the Rhine in order to deprive her of the means to attract vassals who could carry out her inevitable retaliation.

The remainder of the saga tells the story of Kriemhild's lengthy and bitter revenge.

She waits in mourning for years until she receives a marriage proposal from the recently widowed King Etzel (Attila) of Hunland. Out of loyalty to Siegfried and because Etzel is a heathen, she is initially reluctant to marry, but she ultimately accepts the proposal because she sees in it the opportunity for vengeance. Another period of years lapses and Kriemhild, now a queen in Hunland, urges Etzel to invite her brothers together with Hagen to the court for feasting and games. Hagen advises his lords to decline the invitation, but the royal brothers believe that after such a long time Kriemhild will certainly have forgotten her ill will. Etzel suspects nothing and receives the Burgundians magnificently, but Kriemhild soon invokes the allegiance of her vassals to initiate the bloody act of revenge, and the Huns and Burgundians begin to slaughter one another. The battle continues for several days and nights until only Gunther and Hagen are left alive of all the Burgundians. Kriemhild has her own brother decapitated and then herself shows Gunther's head to Hagen, demanding that Hagen reveal where he has hidden Siegfried's gold. Hagen refuses to concede, and the enraged Kriemhild cuts off his head. Aghast at the atrocity, the venerable Hildebrand—a friend of Etzel and with Etzel's consent—slays Kriemhild with his sword.

The second section of *German Hero-Sagas and Folk-Tales* is devoted to fourteen of the most popular German folktales and fairy tales. These stories include the gruesome "Mousetower," in which the evil Bishop Hatto is eaten alive by mice after he burns to death the poor of his city in order to ease a famine; "Till Eulenspiegel," whose merry pranks inspired a tone poem by Richard Strauss; and the tale of "The Heinzelmännchen," the kindly elves who take delight in helping servants, housewives, and craftsmen with their chores. Also found here are "Karl the Great and the Robber," "The Water-Sprite and the Bear," "The Seven Proud Sisters," "The Ratcatcher of Hamelin," "Richmuth of Cologne," "The Werewolf," "The Knight of Staufenberg," "The Seven Mice," "Reineke Fox," "Eppelin of Gailingen," and "Big Hermel." Whereas the sagas are set in the society of the medieval heroic court and have their origins in the oral traditions of the distant past, the German folktales in this second section, by contrast, stem typically from the fifteenth and sixteenth centuries and find their settings in the workaday life of the poor and the peasantry.

German Hero-Sagas and Folk-Tales is furnished liberally with simple, if somewhat romanticized, illustrations by Joan Kiddell-Monroe.

Analysis

Almost nothing is known about the poets who wrote the hero-sagas included in this collection. In the case of the *Nibelungenlied*, there is a likelihood that the author had some connection to the bishop of Passau (1194-1204), but whether the poet was a courtier, a commoner, or a monk, for example, must regrettably remain a matter of conjecture. Since certain strands of the story circulated in various forms in other medieval sagas as well, there is no doubt that the poet drew on earlier sources. The formulaic features characteristic of the epics point to their origins in the oral traditions of the remote past, although the precise point at which the oral forms were transformed into written documents cannot be determined. Because the ancients did not draw clear distinctions between factual history on the one hand and poetic genres on the other, it is difficult to determine exactly where in each saga history gives way to literary fantasy. The second part of the *Nibelungenlied* has its basis in verifiable historical fact—the annihilation of the Burgundians by the Huns in the year 435. Yet, the core of the story centers on the revenge motif, which is acutely personal.

To a certain extent, then, these verse epics may be viewed as forerunners of the modern historical novel: While the conversations and many of the events in the lives of the leading personages are largely fictionalized, the epics nevertheless portray accurately the ethics, customs, and social norms of a society. Even in Picard's modern rendering, readers can gain a sense of how such highly prized values as honor, loyalty, and lavish magnanimity combine with jealousy and vengeance to bring about the demise of heroes and their peoples. The sagas place in the foreground above all heroism and grandeur in the face of tragedy, and the intensely tragic dilemma invariably results from a conflict of cherished values. Thus, Kriemhild's predicament arises when she is forced to choose between her strong loyalty toward her brothers and the rigidly formalized requirements compelling her to avenge Siegfried's death.

Critical Context

The value of *German Hero-Sagas and Folk-Tales* lies in how it makes accessible to young audiences a culture far removed from their own. Heroic society with all its accoutrements comes alive in Barbara Leonie Picard's retelling—the food and cloth- ing, the journeys and festive diversions, the sordid and bloody feuding, the terrible and exacting oaths, the foundation and collapse of vast empires. Because she has had to reduce massive amounts of material to a manageable size (the *Nibelungenlied* in the original Middle High German consists of more than 2,300 stanzas), one could quibble over the criteria that have determined Picard's choice of abridgments. It is odd, for example, that she has given her rendering of the *Nibelungenlied* the title "Siegfried," when this figure is not present for the entire second half of the story (neither in the original nor in Picard's version) and Kriemhild is patently the focus of attention for most of the work. Other modifications indicate most likely, and perhaps justifiably, Picard's attempt to adapt her versions specifically to a young readership: At the end of Picard's retelling, Hildebrand cuts off Kriemhild's head, while in the original poem Kriemhild is hewn to pieces. Nevertheless, Picard's adaptations of sagas and folktales should be considered among the most informed and proficient attempts to acquaint juvenile and young adult audiences with these standard works of Germanic culture.

Steven R. Huff

GET ON BOARD
The Story of the Underground Railroad

Author: Jim Haskins (1941-   )
First published: 1993; illustrated
Type of work: History
Time of work: From America's colonial period until 1865
Locale: Free and slave states in the United States
Subjects: Race and ethnicity and social issues
Recommended ages: 10-15

From American colonial times until the Civil War, many slaves escaped to freedom via an organized network of contacts called the Underground Railroad; the narratives written by these fugitive slaves represent the origins of African American history and literature.

Principal personages:
HARRIET TUBMAN, the "Moses of the Underground Railroad"
JOSIAH HENSON, the inspiration for Harriet Beecher Stowe's novel
    Uncle Tom's Cabin (1852)
CRISPUS ATTUCKS, a fugitive slave and first American to die in the
    revolutionary cause
THE REVEREND J. W. LOGUEN, the "King of the Underground Railroad"
LEVI COFFIN, the "President of the Underground Railroad"
FREDERICK DOUGLASS, the author of a famous slave narrative

Form and Content

Get on Board: The Story of the Underground Railroad is divided into twelve chapters and is illustrated with reproductions of photographs, paintings, sketches, and documents. Facing the first page of the text is a map of the United States in 1860 depicting the routes that fugitive slaves took from the slave states in the South to the free states and to Canada in the North. Collectively, these routes became known as the Underground Railroad, replete with station masters, conductors, and passengers. Following the text is a time line that offers a chronology of highlights in the Underground Railroad's history, beginning in 1518 with the arrival of the first African slaves in the West Indies and concluding in 1865 with the end of slavery with the victory of the Union troops in the Civil War and the ratification of the Thirteenth Amendment to the U.S. Constitution. A bibliography and index follow this chronology.

The book offers a summary of social movements and legislative actions, from America's colonial period until the Civil War, which led to the end of slavery. Jim Haskins intersperses this general history with accounts of individuals who escaped slavery, often quoting from their letters or diaries. The first organized attempts to help slaves escape to free territory were mounted about the time of the American Revolution. The first abolition society was formed in 1775 in Philadelphia. It follows that some of the earliest legislation passed in the newly formed United States concerned the prosecution of escaped slaves. In fact, the Constitution included a statement that became known as the "fugitive slave and felon clause" because it provided for the return of escaped slaves to their owners. Because many people in free states ignored this clause and helped fugitive slaves, Congress passed the Fugitive Slave Act in 1793 in order to make it a criminal offense to help slaves escape. The Fugitive Slave Law of 1850 reinforced previous laws providing for the return of escaped slaves. During the first half of the nineteenth century, the debate over slavery gradually divided the country and eventually resulted in the Civil War.

The most distinctive feature of Haskins' book is its inclusion of accounts of individuals who escaped slavery, assisted fugitive slaves, or both. He devotes one entire chapter to the story of Harriet Tubman because her life is emblematic of the Underground Railroad. Tubman was born into slavery on a Maryland plantation, and she fled north in 1849. She lived for a while in Philadelphia, where she became familiar with the Underground Railroad and with the Philadelphia Vigilance Committee, another organization that helped fugitive slaves reach freedom. Tubman began making trips back to Maryland to help other slaves escape, and she made so many such trips that she became known as Moses. In the course of her many rescue missions, Tubman collaborated with the Reverend J. W. Loguen, called the "King of the Underground Railroad"; with John Brown, who would lead the doomed antislavery uprising in Harpers Ferry, Virginia, in 1859; and perhaps with Frederick Douglass, the escaped slave who eventually became a respected orator and the U.S. minister to Haiti.

Analysis

One of Haskins' intentions in his book is to recognize the active role of African Americans in the history of the United States. On a couple of occasions, he states directly that most historical accounts have been written from a white point of view, and he wants to remedy this situation. One could say that Haskins wants to rewrite American history from a black perspective, and the story of fugitive slaves is a logical point of departure for such an enterprise. For example, Haskins observes that the first person to die in the events leading up to the revolutionary war was Crispus Attucks, an escaped slave who was killed in 1770 in the Boston Massacre. Haskins relates this anecdote in order to compel the reader to think of the American Revolution as something other than a rebellion by white colonists of European descent. The revolutionary war was also the beginning of organized abolition movements. Haskins further forces the reader to question the generally accepted version of American history by calling to attention the racist attitudes of a famous white American who is usually considered to be the hero of the revolutionary war: He notes that George Washington complained in 1786 about the Quakers, who had helped one of his slaves escape to freedom.

Haskins mentions numerous forgotten books, many of them narratives written by escaped slaves who participated in the Underground Railroad. He cites so many such books that *Get on Board* becomes something of a history about the writing of the history of the Underground Railroad. Haskins tries to re-create the dramatic circumstances that led certain escaped slaves to write their memoirs, thereby encouraging his reader to read these primary historical texts. For example, he cites Wilbur H. Siebert's *The Underground Railroad from Slavery to Freedom* (1898) as a source of maps of the Underground Railroad. Haskins also tells how the publication of the autobiographical *The Rev. J. W. Loguen as a Slave and as a Freeman* (1859) led to Loguen's being located by his former owner. Haskins then reproduces long excerpts from letters between Loguen and the owner, each accusing the other of Christian hypocrisy. Haskins quotes a long passage from *Reminiscence* (1876), by Levi Coffin, the "President of the Underground Railroad," which offers a realistic account of how the author was occasionally awakened by fugitive slaves, to whom he would offer food and lodging.

Haskins acknowledges that his own book is really an effort to revitalize interest in contemporary accounts of his subject matter when he recognizes William Still's *Underground Railroad Records* (1872) as the first history of the Underground Railroad. Still was one of the leaders of the Philadelphia Vigilance Committee and kept its records. It is clear that the first step in Haskins' attempt to rewrite American history from a black perspective is simply to recognize the already existing tradition of African American writers, dating back to America's colonial era and proceeding through the times of slavery. Ironically, the immediate popularity of these slave narratives resulted in increased danger to the remaining slaves who were contemplating escape. Frederick Douglass complained in his autobiography *My Bondage and My Freedom* (1855) that many abolitionists had unwittingly compromised slaves by alerting slaveholders to the imminent danger of the slaves' flight.

Get on Board also suggests that the Underground Railroad made a lasting impression on African American culture. Many Negro spirituals acquired double meanings, not only expressing religious devotion but also offering slaves directions to free territory. The slaves also played traditional African drums to send messages until their masters outlawed their use, whereupon the slaves devised dances by which to send messages with their feet against the floor. Another result of the Underground Railroad was the hush puppy, a corn stick laced with strychnine that fugitive slaves set out for the slave catchers' hunting dogs.

Critical Context

A paragraph entitled "About the Author" at the end of *Get on Board* observes that this is one of more than eighty books of nonfiction that Jim Haskins has written for juveniles and young adults. Among his other books are biographies of Martin Luther King, Jr., the civil rights leader of the 1950's and 1960's; Scott Joplin, the ragtime musician; and Rosa Parks, the woman who called attention to discrimination against African Americans by refusing to sit at the back of the bus in Montgomery, Alabama, in 1955. Other books by Haskins are about African American music and dance. His career represents a concerted effort to introduce students to African American history and culture, thereby complementing the Eurocentric versions of American history.

In *Get on Board*, Haskins' ultimate testament to the power of history and the written word is the discussion of Harriet Beecher Stowe's *Uncle Tom's Cabin* in which he identifies the historical personages that Stowe fictionalized in her novel; for example, Josiah Henson is usually considered to be the inspiration for the character of Uncle Tom. Perhaps because of its historical verisimilitude, *Uncle Tom's Cabin* was considered such a threat to slavery that possessing the book could be a criminal offense. Just as Stowe's book condemning slavery was censored in the 1850's, Haskins is suggesting that all African Americans continue to be censored to some degree because the white perspective still dominates American historical accounts. *Get on Board* is part of Haskins' attempt to call attention to African American history and historians.

Douglas Edward LaPrade

THE GHOST BELONGED TO ME

Author: Richard Wayne Peck (1934-   )
First published: 1975
Type of work: Novel
Type of plot: Fantasy and mystery
Time of work: 1913
Locale: The small town of Bluff City
Subjects: Family, friendship, and the supernatural
Recommended ages: 10-15

When Alexander Armsworth, his great-uncle Miles, and his would-be girlfriend Blossom discover a mysterious ghost residing in Alexander's barn, a series of adventures begins, culminating in a journey to the ghost's ancestral home and her family graveyard.

Principal characters:
　　ALEXANDER ARMSWORTH, a thirteen-year-old boy who sees the ghost first and becomes her friend
　　BLOSSOM CULP, a poor but clever girl who helps Alexander
　　MILES ARMSWORTH, Alexander's eighty-five-year-old great-uncle, an explorer
　　INEZ DUMAINE, the ghost who appears to Alexander
　　LUCILLE ARMSWORTH SEAFORTH, Alexander's older sister, a debutante
　　JOE ARMSWORTH, Alexander's father
　　LUELLA ARMSWORTH, Alexander's high-society, loving mother
　　TOM HACKETT, Lucille's amorous boyfriend, the son of a wealthy family
　　JAKE MCCULLOCH, an unscrupulous undertaker
　　MORTIMER BRULATOUR, a reporter for the New Orleans *Delta Daily*

Form and Content

The Ghost Belonged to Me is a first-person narrative relating the supernatural experiences of a young boy, Alexander Armsworth, and his quest to allow a sad ghost finally to lie with the rest of her family's remains. The novel consists of twenty-two chapters that present an engaging story of life in a small town.

Alexander is initially informed of the ghost's existence by his would-be girlfriend, Blossom Culp; her mother sees a halo of pink light around the Armsworth's barn and tells her daughter that it signified the death of a young girl. Although tempted not to believe this incredible story, Alexander is persuaded to enter the loft where, instead of a ghostly girl, he finds Trixie, a half-drowned puppy with an injured leg. He provides it with food, water, and a place to sleep, and he plans to adopt it. The physical presence of the puppy at first seems to discredit Blossom's story, but when Alexander later is unable to find Trixie anywhere, he accepts Blossom's words as the truth. He soon discovers that Trixie is the spectral companion of the ghost of Inez Dumaine, a young woman who died in a steamboat accident and was laid to rest underneath a hitching post next to the Armsworth house.

As if dealing with ghosts were not enough, Alexander's older sister, Lucille, is in the process of "coming out" into society as a debutante and is hoping to snare Tom Hackett, the scion of a wealthy pharmaceuticals magnate, for a husband. She and her mother organize a coming out party that they hope will announce their rising status in the community. This plan creates no end of trouble: Alexander's great-uncle Miles gets on Luella's already-strained nerves, and Tom Hackett has been pressuring Lucille to go further with him sexually than she would like to without formally becoming engaged. Alexander is dragged into the middle of preparations for the party, an affair that disgusts him only slightly less than his sister's amorous interludes.

He finds some comfort, however, in helping his great-uncle Miles construct a pavilion for Lucille's party. He confides the story of his ghostly friend to his great-uncle and is gratified when the old man believes him. Miles, a man who has strong connections with the past, not only believes the story but also vows to help Alexander comfort Inez. Getting the permission of the county coroner to excavate Inez's make-shift grave, they find the poor girl's bones and decide to return her to her hometown, New Orleans, for a proper burial. These plans are nearly halted when an unscrupulous reporter, Mortimer Brulatour, attempts to take the body away from them during the passage south.

Not to be left behind, Blossom Culp stows away on the train that Alexander and Miles take to New Orleans. She watches over the precious cargo, making sure that it reaches its destination safely. It is through her ingenuity (and her good spelling) that Brulatour is finally outwitted. Once in New Orleans, Miles presents his problem to a close female friend, the owner of a boarding house, and she agrees to help them sneak Inez's body into her family graveyard. In addition, seeing poor Blossom's patched dress and snagged black stockings, she takes the young girl under her wing and makes her up into a beauty that even a thirteen-year-old boy such as Alexander can appreci-ate. Blossom and Alexander are nearly in love themselves when they realize that Miles is seeing his girlfriend for personal reasons that match their own.

With the local help, Alexander, Miles, and Blossom are able to place Inez to rest among her ancestors and return home safely. Alexander has gotten to know his great-uncle only just in time: A few weeks after their triumphant return from New Orleans, the old man dies, leaving Alexander and Blossom to continue growing up alone.

Analysis

Thematically, greed and dishonesty seem to play a strong part in the motivations of most of the characters in *The Ghost Belonged to Me*. Although Inez Dumaine died in an accident, the steamboat captain who had promised to keep her safe robbed her dead body and used her money to build a grand house for himself. Alexander's mother and Lucille long to be members of high society in Bluff City and will let nothing stand in their way. Tom Hackett pushes Lucille into greater sexual involvement without promising her what she wants, and Lucille wants to possess Tom Hackett's name more than she wants to possess him.

This greed does not stop with Alexander's family. After Inez Dumaine's remains are discovered, Brulatour and Jake McCulloch, the local undertaker, squabble over who will be able to use the body first; the undertaker wants to show off the bones as an advertisement for his services, while the reporter wants Inez's bones for a story he intends to write concerning her return home.

Only Alexander and his closest friends seem unaffected by the displays of greed around them. Although Alexander comments initially in the novel that "the ghost belonged to me," he never keeps her a secret, nor does he attempt to use her for his own advantage. Alexander is likened by his father to his great-uncle Miles, who is reputed to be the most honest man in Bluff City (a reputation that does not please Alexander's mother), and Alexander shares Miles' concern for maintaining respect for the dead. Blossom Culp, who initially alerts Alexander to the ghost's presence, never exaggerates her role in the mystery; she claims not to be able to see or speak to the Unseen.

Young people will find much to enjoy in this ghost story. Richard Peck's writing style is light and effervescent, and he never quite takes his tale seriously; the book ends up as half a tribute to and half a spoof of the traditional ghost story. The novel moves along at a brisk pace that will keep younger readers entertained. For the older readers, the novel presents a deftly handled budding love affair between the protagonist and his friend. Although Alexander is tempted at the beginning of the book to think of Blossom as a poor, "spidery-legged spook" (Lucille calls her an arachnid because of her thin legs and her black wool stockings), she is allowed, appropriately, to "blossom" in New Orleans with the help of some new clothes and a becoming hairstyle. Alexander learns from Blossom the value of seeing beyond the surface of people—something that his sister Lucille and his mother Luella must learn the hard way.

Critical Context

The Ghost Belonged to Me, an American Library Association Notable Book, and its sequels *Ghosts I Have Been* (1977), *The Dreadful Future of Blossom Culp* (1983), and *Blossom Culp and the Sleep of Death* (1986) are a bit different from Richard Peck's usual writings. Peck has most often written books that deal with the problems faced by young adults, rather than children. Thirteen-year-old Alexander is younger than, for example, the fifteen-year-old protagonist of *Don't Look and It Won't Hurt* (1972) and the three friends in *Remembering the Good Times* (1985). Peck's most famous work, *Are You in the House Alone?* (1976), deals seriously with the aftereffects of rape and never departs from its somber tone. *The Ghost Belonged to Me* is a book intended to entice young people into reading; its endearing characters have lives with a touch of mystery to them and that confirm the presence of the supernatural without being frightening.

Julia M. Meyers